DECKER'S

PATTERNS OF

EXPOSITION 14

Randall E. Decker

Robert A. Schwegler
University of Rhode Island

HarperCollins *CollegePublishers*

Senior Acquisitions Editor/Executive Editor: Patricia Rossi
Developmental Editor: Marisa L'Heureux
Cover Illustratrion/Photograph: KLEE, Paul.
Fire at Evening [Feuer Abends]. 1929.
Oil on cardboard, 13³/₈ × 13¹/₄".
The Museum of Modern Art, New York.
Mr. and Mrs. Joachim Jean Aberbach Fund.
Photograph © 1995 The Museum of Modern Art, New York.
Photo Researcher: Scott Foresman
Electronic Production Manager: Angel Gonzalez, Jr.
Publishing Services: Ruttle Graphics, Inc.
Electronic Page Makeup: Ruttle Graphics, Inc.
Printer and Binder: R. R. Donnelley & Sons Company
Cover Printer: Coral Graphics Services, Inc.

Decker's Patterns of Exposition, 14th Edition

Copyright © 1995 by HarperCollins College Publishers

Library of Congress Cataloging-in-Publication Data

Decker's patterns of exposition 14 / [edited by] Randall E. Decker,
  Robert A. Schwegler. — 14th ed.
    p. cm.
  Includes bibliographical references (p.).
  ISBN 0-673-52338-1 (SE : PB). — ISBN 0-673-52339-X (IE : PB)
  1. College readers.   2. Exposition (Rhetoric)   3. English language—Rhetoric.
I. Decker, Randall E.   II. Schwegler, Robert A.   III. Title: Patterns of exposition.
PE1417.P386 1995
808'.0427—dc20   94-29863
                                                              CIP

94 95 96 97 9 8 7 6 5 4 3 2 1

Contents

Thematic Contents / xvii

Essay Pairs / xxiii

To the Instructor / xxvii

Introduction: Writing and Reading / 1

BRENT STAPLES,
Just Walk on By / 8

1 Illustrating Ideas by Use of *Example* / 51

LEE RASPET,
It's Always Awful (Student Writing) / 55

ANDY ROONEY,
In and of Ourselves We Trust / 57

This columnist decides that stopping for red lights is part of a contract Americans have with each other. And we trust each other to honor the contract.

ELLEN GOODMAN,
Children on Their Own   /   61

> Being "home alone" is more than a child's fantasy about independence. It is a threatening reality faced by many children (and their parents).

ALAN BUCZYNSKI,
Iron Bonding   /   65

> Do men share feelings? Of course, says this ironworker, but they do it through stories and other indirect tactics.

WILLIAM F. BUCKLEY, JR.,
Why Don't We Complain?   /   70

> The dean of conservative writers believes that we've become so numb to mistakes and injustices that we no longer have the spunk to complain about anything. And this apathy could have grave consequences.

BARBARA EHRENREICH,
What I've Learned from Men   /   78

> Acting like a man means speaking up for your rights, says this feminist, and it is a way of behaving that women can learn from men. As an example, she tells of a time when she acted in a manner that was too ladylike.

2   Analyzing a Subject by *Classification*   /   87

HEATHER FARNUM,
Piano Recitals (Student Writing)   /   92

JUDITH VIORST,
What, Me? Showing Off?   /   94

> Though we may be reluctant to admit it, we all show off, and we do it in many different ways.

RENEE TAJIMA,
Lotus Blossoms Don't Bleed:
Images of Asian American Women   /   102

> The Asian American women in Hollywood movies do not bear much
> resemblance to real people. And the roles they play are sometimes
> absurd and sometimes insulting.

JUDITH STONE,
Personal Beast   /   112

> Looking for a pet? Why settle for a dog or cat when you can have a
> pot-bellied pig, a llama, or a ferret?

BRENDA PETERSON,
Life Is a Musical   /   120

> Feeling down? You might want to follow this writer's lead by creat-
> ing tapes of music that help shut out "the noisy yak and call of the
> outside world."

DON KUNZ,
Nutty Professors   /   128

> On television, in the movies, and in cartoons, professors are strange
> creatures says this college professor whose father warned him that
> college teaching might lead to madness.

3   Explaining by Means of *Comparison*
and *Contrast*   /   141

SUSAN HAEBERLE,
The Day Care Choice (Student Writing)   /   146

MARK TWAIN,
Two Ways of Seeing a River   /   149

> What happens when you start looking at a thing of beauty in terms
> of its use?

BRUCE CATTON,
Grant and Lee: A Study in Contrasts / 153

> A famous historian identifies these two great Civil War generals as
> the embodiments of the passing and rising orders.

ANNA QUINDLEN,
Men at Work / 159

> The five o'clock dads of years ago, home for dinner with their fami-
> lies, are being replaced by eight- and nine-o'clock dads who miss
> out on much of family life.

PHILLIP LOPATE,
A Nonsmoker with a Smoker / 164

> Many things pass through the mind of the nonsmoking member
> of a couple: anger, regrets, concern, and even some surprising
> fantasies.

ALICE WALKER,
Am I Blue? / 170

> This well-known author entertains the possibility that we are not as
> different from animals as we think, and she looks at the way a horse
> named Blue displayed feelings we are accustomed to thinking of as
> particularly "human."

4 Using *Analogy* as an Expository Device / 179

KEVIN NOMURA,
Life Isn't Like Baseball (Student Writing) / 183

BILL BRADLEY,
How to Get the Big Picture / 185

> A U.S. Senator tells how learning to look out of the corners of your
> eyes can help you develop an understanding of events and predict
> the consequences of your actions.

LOREN C. EISELEY,
The Brown Wasps / 188

In a reflective mood, this distinguished anthropologist-philosopher-author makes an analogical comparison between homeless old men in a railroad station and brown wasps waiting to die, still clinging to the old abandoned nest in a thicket.

BILL McKIBBEN,
Sometimes You Just Have to Turn It Off / 198

All day long the sounds of television and radio echo in our heads. Sometimes, suggests this writer, we need to get away from these sounds in order to be able to understand both nature and ourselves.

TOM WOLFE,
O Rotten Gotham—Sliding Down
into the Behavioral Sink / 203

Our leading New Journalist says that New York City drives people crazy—and you can observe the same effects of overcrowding in a jammed cage of rats.

PATRICIA RAYBON,
Letting in Light / 213

Washing windows may seem an unusual task for an educated person, but this journalist argues that the work helps us understand ourselves and lets light into our spirits.

5 Explaining Through *Process Analysis* / 219

KARIN GAFFNEY,
Losing Weight (Student Writing) / 223

DONALD M. MURRAY,
The Maker's Eye: Revising Your Own Manuscripts / 227

A professional writer and former journalist, speaking from his own experience and quoting numerous other successful authors, emphasizes the importance of revision and suggests procedures that have proven effective.

ANN FARADAY,
Unmasking Your Dream Images   /   234

> Many of us would like to know what our dreams mean. This author
> describes one way to interpret them and says that we are the people
> who are best equipped to understand our own dreams.

L. RUST HILLS,
How to Eat an Ice-Cream Cone   /   241

> Eating an ice-cream cone can be hard work requiring lots of plan-
> ning. The job gets even trickier when you do it with your family
> around.

LAURA MANSNERUS,
Count to 10 and Pet the Dog   /   251

> Some researchers believe that excessive anger can ruin your health
> and even kill you. Even if the case against anger hasn't been proven,
> taking steps to control your temper is probably a good idea, sug-
> gests this writer.

JESSICA MITFORD,
To Dispel Fears of Live Burial   /   259

> A contemporary muckraker parts "the formaldehyde curtain" for a
> hair-raising look into an undertaker's parlor.

6 Analyzing *Cause-and-Effect* Relationships   /   269

TIMOTHY DUNBAR,
Students Who Cheat (Student Writing)   /   274

BOB GREENE,
Thirty Seconds   /   277

> A television commercial can turn a person into a celebrity overnight.
> How this happened and how it affected the person is the subject of
> this essay.

SUSAN PERRY and JIM DAWSON,
What's Your Best Time of Day? / 284

> When is the best time to study for an exam? To relax with friends? This intriguing essay talks about the when and the why of the cycles that govern our lives and behavior.

LINDA HASSELSTROM,
A Peaceful Woman Explains Why She Carries a Gun / 289

> This writer and rancher explains that for a woman in an often hostile world, carrying a gun may be a good way to even the odds and prevent violence.

PAUL THEROUX,
Self-Propelled / 296

> The author asks why anyone would try rowing across the ocean solo and gets an answer of sorts from someone who completed the seemingly foolhardy journey.

WILLIAM SEVERINI KOWINSKI,
Kids in the Mall: Growing Up Controlled / 301

> What do the malls teach teenagers? All sorts of lessons, few of them very useful and some of them perhaps even harmful.

7 Using *Definition* to Help Explain / 311

LORI L'HEUREUX,
Stars (Student Writing) / 315

MARIE WINN,
Television Addiction / 320

> There are several ways in which uncontrolled television viewing fits the definition of addiction, and this author spells them out.

ROGER WELSCH,
Gypsies   /   325

> What is there to admire in a group of people who have made thievery into a fine art? Plenty, or at least that is what this writer and anthropologist believes, and he offers some reasons.

RICHARD BEN CRAMER,
Know Your Way Home   /   333

> No matter how independent or footloose you imagine yourself to be, sooner or later you have to find someplace to call "home" says this award-winning reporter and writer who finally settled down after spending many years in temporary lodgings in exotic locales.

KESAYA NODA,
Growing Up Asian in America   /   340

> Finding an identity as an Asian, an Asian American, and an Asian American woman was a difficult but essential task of self-definition for this author.

CECIL HELMAN,
Half Green, Half Black   /   350

> This physician and researcher looks through the history of medicine for startling confirmation of the power of our minds to make us sick or well.

8   Explaining with the Help of *Description*   /   361

CAREY BRAUN,
Bright Light (Student Writing)   /   366

SHARON CURTIN,
Aging in the Land of the Young   /   368

> All of us, says a former nurse, are so afraid of aging that we treat old people as personal insults and threats to our society.

JOYCE MAYNARD,
The Yellow Door House / 373

> Visits to the house where she grew up give this writer a chance to
> reflect on her parents' lives, her own, and those of her children.

GEORGE SIMPSON,
The War Room at Bellevue / 379

> The author takes us through one unforgettable evening in the emer-
> gency room of a huge city hospital. But, says the head nurse, the
> succession of crises was "about normal . . . no big deal."

LUIS J. RODRIGUEZ,
The Ice Cream Truck / 387

> What does life in an impoverished barrio look like from the inside?
> This writer, a former gang member, provides a glimpse.

E. B. WHITE,
Once More to the Lake / 393

> A visit with his son to the lake where he used to spend summer
> vacations gives this famous essayist a kind of double vision that
> mingles memories of the past with scenes from the present.

9 Using *Narration* as an Expository Technique / 405

DENNIS SANTOS,
Fighting Fat (Student Writing) / 409

MARTIN GANSBERG,
38 Who Saw Murder Didn't Call the Police / 411

> Years after the fact, the murder of Kitty Genovese is still a harrow-
> ing tale of urban apathy.

RITA WILLIAMS,
The Quality of Mercy   /   417

> Crime is not a black and white issue for the African-American writer
> who shares her first-hand experience as a victim facing young and
> potentially violent criminals.

SANDRA CISNEROS,
Only Daughter   /   424

> While she was growing up, this author's father had a hard time see-
> ing her as anything other than a potential wife and mother. But one
> day he came to acknowledge his only female child as the writer she
> had become.

GEORGE ORWELL,
A Hanging   /   429

> The well-known essayist and author of *1984* writes of an experience
> in Burma and makes a subtle but biting commentary on both colo-
> nialism and capital punishment.

DONALD HALL,
The Embrace of Old Age   /   436

> A seventy-fifth wedding anniversary and a hundredth birthday
> coming at the same time mean little to a young boy, unless, of
> course, they are accompanied by a party. Yet a party like this is
> likely to be filled with old people.

10 Reasoning by Use of *Induction*
and *Deduction*   /   443

SHEILAGH BRADY,
Mad About MADD (Student Writing)   /   449

BARBARA EHRENREICH,
Star Dreck   /   453

> What is really important for this country is the serious study of
> stars—the kind that appear on the covers of magazines, on televi-
> sion, and on movie screens.

JO COUDERT,
Don't Come as You Are / 458

> You owe it to yourself to spend time caring for your appearance. Your friends and colleagues are also likely to appreciate your efforts.

PETE HAMILL,
The Neverglades / 462

> The Everglades used to be one of the wonders of the world, filled with so many birds that the sky would turn black when they took to the air in the morning. Now, the "river of grass" is dying and Florida may become the world's newest desert.

PATRICIA KEAN,
Blowing Up the Tracks / 470

> Our school systems have long taken for granted that students learn best when they are segregated by ability. Yet as this writer points out, those teachers and schools who have been willing to break the mold find that mixed classrooms are often the most successful.

11 Using Patterns for *Argument* / 481

STANIS TERENZI,
Rain Forest Destruction (Student Writing) / 489

BRIAN JARVIS,
Against the Great Divide / 492
Argument Through Example

> If black and white high school students form separate social groups, we may all suffer, says this student, and he calls on schools to foster shared activities and build understanding.

MICHAEL PERRY,
The Dilemma of a Good Samaritan / 497
Argument Through Example

> Caring for accident victims is a demanding and potentially dangerous job. Having to worry about AIDS places an even greater burden on the helpers.

BARBARA KELLER,
Frontiersmen Are History / 502
Argument Through Cause and Effect

> Unrestricted gun ownership was fine when most of us were farmers and many of us lived on a dangerous frontier, says this lawyer who believes that our traditional love affair with guns now causes our society great harm.

JOANNE JACOBS,
Producing Multiple-Choice Students / 507
Argument Through Cause and Effect

> Alternatives to letter grades may seem like kinder and more effective alternatives, but this newspaper columnist argues that the new strategies confuse both students and parents while failing to set goals to which students can aspire.

RICHARD LYNN,
Why Johnny Can't Read, but Yoshio Can / 512
Argument Through Comparison and Contrast

> How good are our schools compared to those of Japan? Not very good, says this writer, and he proposes ways to improve them, including solutions that may raise the hackles of some readers.

BARBARA LAWRENCE,
Four-Letter Words Can Hurt You / 521
Argument Through Definition

> Dirty words have a history of violent meanings. This history, not narrow-minded sexual hangups, is what makes the words harmful and offensive.

MARTIN LUTHER KING, JR.,
Letter from Birmingham Jail / 526
Complex Argument

> The martyred civil rights leader explains in this now-classic letter just why he is in Birmingham, and justifies the activities that led to his jailing.

Further Readings / 547

ANDREW HOLLERAN,
Bedside Manners / 548

> The tragedy of AIDS calls on our deepest resources as human beings in caring for each other and in understanding ourselves.

MARGARET ATWOOD,
Pornography / 553

> We are naive if we think that all pornography appeals to sexual fantasies, points out this well-known novelist. Some of it contains scenes of cruelty even those people rightly concerned about freedom of expression are likely to find repulsive and dangerous.

JOHN McPHEE,
Earthquake / 560

> McPhee traces an earthquake through Northern California from its beginnings through each stage of destruction, looking at what happens and why.

GLORIA ANZALDÚA,
Tlilli, Tlapalli: The Path of the Red and Black Ink / 572

> Writing is a magical and sacrificial act, claims this author, and she takes readers on a journey through Mexican culture and a writer's mind.

A Guide to Terms / 583

Thematic Contents

Men and Women

Alan Buczynski, Iron Bonding, 65

Barbara Ehrenreich, What I've Learned from Men, 78

Anna Quindlen, Men at Work, 159

Linda Hasselstrom, A Peaceful Woman Explains Why She Carries a
Gun, 289

Kesaya Noda, Growing Up Asian in America, 340

Sandra Cisneros, Only Daughter, 424

Barbara Lawrence, Four-Letter Words Can Hurt You, 521

Margaret Atwood, Pornography, 553

Work

Alan Buczynski, Iron Bonding, 65

Don Kunz, Nutty Professors, 128

Mark Twain, Two Ways of Seeing a River, 149

Anna Quindlen, Men at Work, 159

Bill McKibben, Sometimes You Just Have to Turn It Off, 198

Tom Wolfe, O Rotten Gotham—Sliding Down into the Behavioral
Sink, 203

Patricia Raybon, Letting in Light, 213

Jessica Mitford, To Dispel Fears of Live Burial, 259

Richard Ben Cramer, Know Your Way Home, 333

Sharon Curtin, Aging in the Land of the Young, 368

Luis J. Rodriguez, The Ice Cream Truck, 387

Barbara Ehrenreich, Star Dreck, 453

Michael Perry, The Dilemma of a Good Samaritan, 497

Barbara L. Keller, Frontiersmen Are History, 502

Culture and Customs

Andy Rooney, In and of Ourselves We Trust, 57

Renee Tajima, Lotus Blossoms Don't Bleed: Images of Asian American
     Women, 102

Judith Stone, Personal Beast, 112

Brenda Peterson, Life Is a Musical, 120

Don Kunz, Nutty Professors, 128

Roger Welsch, Gypsies, 325

Richard Ben Cramer, Know Your Way Home, 333

Kesaya Noda, Growing Up Asian in America, 340

Cecil Helman, Half Green, Half Black, 350

Sandra Cisneros, Only Daughter, 424

Joanne Jacobs, Producing Multiple-Choice Students, 507

Richard Lynn, Why Johnny Can't Read, but Yoshio Can, 512

Politics and Leaders

Brenda Peterson, Life Is a Musical, 120

Bruce Catton, Grant and Lee: A Study in Contrasts, 153

Bill Bradley, How to Get the Big Picture, 185

George Orwell, A Hanging, 429

Martin Luther King, Jr., Letter from Birmingham Jail, 526

Personality and Behavior

Brent Staples, Just Walk on By, 8

Judith Viorst, What, Me? Showing Off?, 94

Judith Stone, Personal Beast, 112

Brenda Peterson, Life Is a Musical, 120

Don Kunz, Nutty Professors, 128

Phillip Lopate, A Nonsmoker with a Smoker, 164

Alice Walker, Am I Blue?, 170

Bill Bradley, How to Get the Big Picture, 185

Loren C. Eiseley, The Brown Wasps, 188

Tom Wolfe, O Rotten Gotham—Sliding Down into the Behavioral
     Sink, 203

Patricia Raybon, Letting in Light, 213
Ann Faraday, Unmasking Your Dream Images, 234
L. Rust Hills, How to Eat an Ice-Cream Cone, 241
Laura Mansnerus, Count to 10 and Pet the Dog, 251
Bob Greene, Thirty Seconds, 277
Susan Perry and Jim Dawson, What's Your Best Time of Day, 284
Paul Theroux, Self-Propelled, 296
Marie Winn, Television Addiction, 320
Kesaya Noda, Growing Up Asian in America, 340
Cecil Helman, Half Green, Half Black, 350
Jo Coudert, Don't Come as You Are, 458

Nature and the Environment

Mark Twain, Two Ways of Seeing a River, 149
Alice Walker, Am I Blue?, 170
Bill McKibben, Sometimes You Just Have to Turn It Off, 198
Pete Hamill, The Neverglades, 462
John McPhee, Earthquake, 560

Morals, Crime, and Punishment

Judith Viorst, What, Me? Showing Off?, 94
Alice Walker, Am I Blue?, 170
Sharon Curtin, Aging in the Land of the Young, 368
Luis J. Rodriguez, The Ice Cream Truck, 387
Martin Gansberg, 38 Who Saw Murder Didn't Call the Police, 411
Rita Williams, The Quality of Mercy, 417
Martin Luther King, Jr., Letter from Birmingham Jail, 526
Andrew Holleran, Bedside Manners, 548
Margaret Atwood, Pornography, 553

Growing Up/Getting Old

Ellen Goodman, Children on Their Own, 61
Loren C. Eiseley, The Brown Wasps, 188
William Severini Kowinski, Kids in the Mall: Growing Up
    Controlled, 301
Richard Ben Cramer, Know Your Way Home, 333
Kesaya Noda, Growing Up Asian in America, 340

Sharon Curtin, Aging in the Land of the Young, 368
Joyce Maynard, The Yellow Door House, 373
E. B. White, Once More to the Lake, 393
Donald Hall, The Embrace of Old Age, 436

Differences

Brent Staples, Just Walk on By, 8
William Severini Kowinski, Kids in the Mall: Growing Up
    Controlled, 301
Roger Welsch, Gypsies, 325
Richard Ben Cramer, Know Your Way Home, 333
George Simpson, The War Room at Bellevue, 379

Families and Children

Ellen Goodman, Children on Their Own, 61
Judith Viorst, What, Me? Showing Off?, 94
Anna Quindlen, Men at Work, 159
Patricia Raybon, Letting in Light, 213
L. Rust Hills, How to Eat an Ice-Cream Cone, 241
William Severini Kowinski, Kids in the Mall: Growing Up
    Controlled, 301
Joyce Maynard, The Yellow Door House, 373
Sandra Cisneros, Only Daughter, 424
Donald Hall, The Embrace of Old Age, 436

Society and Social Change

Andy Rooney, In and of Ourselves We Trust, 57
Ellen Goodman, Children on Their Own, 61
William F. Buckley, Jr., Why Don't We Complain?, 70
Barbara Ehrenreich, What I've Learned from Men, 78
Phillip Lopate, A Nonsmoker with a Smoker, 164
Linda Hasselstrom, A Peaceful Woman Explains Why She Carries a
    Gun, 289
Rita Williams, The Quality of Mercy, 417
Patricia Kean, Blowing Up the Tracks, 470
Michael Jarvis, Against the Great Divide, 492
Richard Lynn, Why Johnny Can't Read, but Yoshio Can, 512

Andrew Holleran, Bedside Manners, 548
Margaret Atwood, Pornography, 553
Gloria Anzaldua, Tlilli, Tlapalli: The Path of the Red and Black
  Ink, 572

Essay Pairs

Among the selections in *Patterns of Exposition 14* are a number of essay pairs whose similarities in topic or theme and contrasts in perspective or style offer interesting insights. These relationships show that the strategies a writer chooses can affect the way readers come to view the subject matter of an essay. The following list identifies some sets of essays that are particularly well suited for study and discussion; there are, of course, many other interesting and revealing ways of pairing the selections in the text.

A few of the pairs illustrate different ways of using the same pattern, such as example or definition. In other sets, the patterns offer contrasting strategies for expression or alternate ways of viewing a subject.

Andy Rooney, In and of Ourselves We Trust, 57
Paul Theroux, Self-Propelled, 296

Ellen Goodman, Children on Their Own, 61
Anna Quindlen, Men at Work, 159

Alan Buczynski, Iron Bonding, 65
Brenda Peterson, Life Is a Musical, 120

William F. Buckley, Jr., Why Don't We Complain?, 70
Barbara Ehrenreich, What I've Learned from Men, 78

Renee Tajima, Lotus Blossoms Don't Bleed: Images of Asian American
    Women, 102
Don Kunz, Nutty Professors, 128

Judith Stone, Personal Beast, 112
Alice Walker, Am I Blue?, 170

Mark Twain, Two Ways of Looking at a River, 149
E. B. White, Once More to the Lake, 393

Bruce Catton, Grant and Lee: A Study in Contrasts, 153
Barbara Ehrenreich, Star Dreck, 453

Phillip Lopate, A Nonsmoker with a Smoker, 164
Laura Mansnerus, Count to 10 and Pet the Dog, 251

Loren C. Eiseley, The Brown Wasps, 188
Sharon Curtin, Aging in the Land of the Young, 368

Bill McKibben, Sometimes You Just Have to Turn It Off, 198
Marie Winn, Television Addiction, 320

Tom Wolfe, O Rotten Gotham—Sliding Down into the Behavioral Sink, 203
Pete Hamill, The Neverglades, 462

Patricia Raybon, Letting in Light, 213
William Severini Kowinski, Kids in the Mall: Growing Up Controlled, 301

Donald M. Murray, The Maker's Eye, 227
Gloria Anzaldua, Tlilli, Tlapalli: The Path of the Red and Black Ink, 572

Ann Faraday, Unmasking Your Dream Images, 234
Cecil Helman, Half Green, Half Black, 350

Jessica Mitford, To Dispel Fears of Live Burial, 259
Jo Coudert, Don't Come as You Are, 458

Linda Hasselstrom, A Peaceful Woman Explains Why She Carries a
      Gun, 289
Barbara Keller, Frontiersmen Are History, 502

Richard Ben Cramer, Know Your Way Home, 333
Joyce Maynard, The Yellow Door House, 373

Kesaya Noda, Growing Up Asian in America, 340
Sandra Cisneros, Only Daughter, 424

George Simpson, The War Room at Bellevue, 379
Luis J. Rodriguez, The Ice Cream Truck, 387

Martin Gansberg, 38 Who Saw Murder Didn't Call the Police, 411
Rita Williams, The Quality of Mercy, 417

Sharon Curtin, Aging in the Land of the Young, 368
Donald Hall, The Embrace of Old Age, 436

Patricia Kean, Blowing Up the Tracks, 470
Richard Lynn, Why Johnny Can't Read, but Yoshio Can, 512

Michael Perry, The Dilemma of a Good Samaritan, 497
Andrew Holleran, Bedside Manners, 548

Brian Jarvis, Against the Great Divide, 492
Martin Luther King, Jr., Letter from Birmingham Jail, 526

Barbara Lawrence, Four-Letter Words Can Hurt You, 521
Margaret Atwood, Pornography, 553

To the Instructor

Patterns of Exposition 14 retains the basic principles and the general format of previous editions. Use of the book remains high, and we continue to poll instructor-users for evaluations of the selections and about the need for basic changes in the framework. We also reviewed the responses of students who returned questionnaires like the one at the back of this book. Although obviously we are unable to comply with all requests, we have seriously considered and fully appreciated all of them, and we have incorporated many suggestions into this new edition. We have responded, as well, to requests for added essays in some of the most heavily used sections of the book.

The annotated demonstration paragraphs located at the end of introductory sections are followed by sample paragraphs drawn from a variety of publications. These paragraphs illustrate some of the structural and stylistic variations professional writers often add while employing the basic patterns. Some of these authors are well known for their work; others less so, though the sample paragraphs may call attention to the quality of their writing. New to this edition are student essays illustrating some of the many ways each pattern can be adapted to expository (or argumentative) purposes. Though one pattern clearly predominates in each sample essay, the writers draw on the other patterns as their goals for writing require. The essays are by no means polished, professional efforts, yet they are good starting points for discussion, and they illustrate effective and occasionally imaginative writing techniques.

A considerably revised "Introduction: Reading and Writing" incorporates current theory as a basis for practical advice about the process of writing and about the ways reading can lead to and support writing. The discussion also provides practical advice about reading the selections in the text for both comprehension and aware-ness of technique. Included in the section is Brent Staples's well-known essay "Just Walk on By," accompanied by commentary that illustrates the activities involved in comprehension and response to reading. The discussion also outlines specific reading and writing activities that instructors may wish to assign or that students may decide to employ on their own.

Because so many instructors find it useful, we continue to retain the table of contents listing pairs of essays. Each pair provides con-trasts (or similarities) in theme, approach, and style that are worth study. The essay pairs can form the focus of class discussion or writ-ing assignments.

Although the focus of the text as a whole is on exposition and the rhetorical patterns it employs, we recognize that many instruc-tors like to include a section on argument in their courses, and that argument often uses the same rhetorical patterns as exposition. Selections from the argument chapter may be added to those in the expository chapters to further illustrate the usefulness of the pat-terns. The argument chapter is similar in arrangement and approach to the other sections of the text.

The "Further Readings" section provides four contemporary selections provoke discussion of ideas and strategies. The pieces also suggest some intriguing forms and goals essays can pursue in the hands of skilled and daring writers. The essays in this section can be used on their own or with the other sections of the book. They pro-vide stimulus for writing and discussion as well as illustrations of strategies for students to use in their own writing.

But throughout *Patterns of Exposition 14* we have tried, as always, to make possible the convenient use of all materials in what-ever ways instructors think best for their own classes. With a few exceptions, only complete essays or freestanding units of larger works have been included. With their inevitable overlap of patterns, they are more complicated than excerpts illustrating single princi-ples, but they are also more realistic examples of exposition and more useful for other classroom purposes. Versatility has been an important criterion in choosing materials.

Thirty-five of the selections best liked in previous editions have been retained. Twenty-seven selections are new, and all but a few of these are anthologized for the first time.

Their arrangement is but one of many workable orders; instructors can easily develop another if they so desire. The Thematic Contents and the table of Essay Pairs also suggest a variety of arrangements.

We have tried to vary the study questions—and undoubtedly have included far more than any one teacher will want—from the purely objective to those calling for some serious self-examination by students. (The Instructor's Manual supplements these materials.)

Suggestions for writing assignments to be developed from ideas in the essays are located immediately after each selection. But for classes in which the instructor prefers writing to be done according to the expository pattern under study at the time, regardless of subject matter, topic suggestions are located at the end of each section.

"A Guide to Terms," where matters from *Abstract* to *Unity* are briefly discussed, refers whenever possible to the essays themselves for illustrations. To permit unity and easy access, it is located at the back of the book, but there are cross-references to it in the study questions.

In all respects—size, content, arrangement, format—we have tried to keep *Patterns of Exposition 14* uncluttered and easy to use.

Acknowledgments

For their help and support, the editors would like to thank the following staff of HarperCollins College Division: Patricia Rossi and Marisa L. L'Heureux.

The second editor wishes to thank Brian Schwegler for his ideas and responses; Christopher Schwegler for his smiles; and Nancy Newman Schwegler for her love, insight, and support.

The continued success of *Patterns of Exposition* is due to a great extent to the many students and instructors who respond to questionnaires and offer helpful suggestions, making the job of revision easier. Special thanks go to the following reviewers: Homai Behram, Montgomery College; Judith M. Boschult, Phoenix College; Charles Cochran, Marshalltown Community College; Huey Guagliardo, Louisiana State University-Eunice; Steven Hind, Hutchinson Community College; Muriel E. J. Klafehn, University of Akron; Kathleen Hudson, Schreiner College; Charlene Roesner, Kansas Wesleyan University; Lucy Sheehey, Portland Community College; Richard

Tracz, Oakton Community College; Pamela T. Pittman, University of Central Oklahoma; Peter Sherer, Harper College; Michael B. Herzog, Gonzaga University; Gwendolyn S. Jones, Tuskegee University; Marci Sellers, Erie Community College.

Randall E. Decker
Robert A. Schwegler

Introduction: Writing and Reading

You encounter **expository writing** every day in one of its many forms, including essays, magazine articles, reports, memos, newspaper reports, and nonfiction books. Readers look to expository writing for facts and insights—for the sharing of experiences and concepts.

Yet good expository writing can do more than present detailed, reliable information. It can take you inside ideas and give you reasons for accepting (or rejecting) them. It can transport you to unfamiliar places and enable you to share someone else's experiences. Exposition can stick to the facts, simply and objectively, or it can recreate an author's voice and feelings in rich, evocative detail. Often it surprises, helping alter the way we see and understand, as in the following passage from Pete Hamill's "The Neverglades."

> Then, before dawn, at Naples, she turned onto the Tamiami Trail. And stopped talking.
>
> In memory, a lavender wash covered the world. We parked and stepped out of the car. I looked out at a flat, empty prairie, its monotony relieved by the occasional silhouettes of nameless trees against the blank early-morning sky. "What is this?" I asked. "Where are we?"
>
> "Listen," she whispered.
>
> And I heard them, far off, almost imperceptible at first: thin, high, and then like the sound of a million whips cutting the air. They came over the edge of the horizon and then the sky was black with them. Birds. Thousands of them. Tens of thousands. Maybe a million. I shivered in fear and awe. The woman held my city-boy's hand. And then the vast dense flock was gone. The great molten ball of the sun oozed over the horizon.
>
> "We're in The Everglades," she said.

At this point, you are probably wondering if, as a student writer, you can reasonably expect to create expository prose that would fulfill your own high expectations (and those of other readers). Our answer is "Yes," because we believe that with attention and effort you can write expository (and argumentative) essays that are clear, informative, convincing, and well worth reading. But we also know that effective writing requires attending to your skills, not just as a writer but also as a reader, for reading and writing work closely together in important ways, some of which become apparent only when you pay conscious attention to the many activities that make up the reading process and the writing process.

Attending to Reading

Could you describe something you have never seen? Something you have never heard, touched, smelled, or tasted? Probably not—or only by visualizing familiar objects and scenes and building imaginatively on them for your description.

In a similar fashion, to create an effective essay, you need to be able to visualize where you (and it) are going. You need to be familiar enough with the kind of writing you are doing so that you can envision the different parts your essay will contain and how they will fit together. And you need to be aware of ways you can introduce topics, details, and ideas and of how you can link them to convey an essay's central idea or **theme** in order to inform or persuade your readers (See "Guide to Terms": *Unity.*) If you can't envision or create a plan that ties together an essay's parts, then don't be surprised if your readers get lost along the way or end up at a different destination than the one you intend.

How can you choose an appropriate design for your writing— a pattern that grows from your subject and your ideas as well as one that readers can readily recognize? You should, of course, be alert for patterns that emerge as you explore a subject, plan an essay, or draft and revise. Yet patterns seldom step forward on their own; you need to be aware of different shapes writing can take in order to be able to recognize possible patterns and to develop them as you write. One particular good way to develop this necessary awareness is to pay attention to strategies other writers use effectively and creatively.

Becoming Aware of Patterns

If patterns of expression came easily and naturally to mind, then recognizing them as we read or using them as we write would be simple tasks, requiring, at most, a bit of practice. Admittedly, some writing strategies are akin to basic ways of thinking. Classification, narration, cause-effect, and the other patterns of exposition and argument around which this text is built reflect some of the most common and useful modes of critical thinking. In our everyday lives, for example, we frequently make comparisons and contrasts, and they are common in reading and writing, as the following example demonstrates.

> Located on the west coast, our pueblo is a place of contrasts: the original town remains as a tiny core of ancient houses circling the church, which sits on a hill, the very same where the woodcutter claimed to have been saved from a charging bull by a lovely dark Lady who appeared floating over a treetop. There my mother lives, at the foot of this hill; but surrounding this postcard scene there are shopping malls, a Burger King, a cinema. And where the sugar cane fields once extended like a green sea as far as the eye could see: condominiums, cement blocks in rows, all the same shape and color. My mother tries not to see this part of her world. The church bells drown the noise of traffic, and when she sits on her back porch and looks up at the old church built by the hands of generations of men whose last names she would not recognize, she feels safe—under the shelter of the past.
>
> Judith Ortiz Cofer, *Silent Dancing: A Partial Remembrance of a Puerto Rican Childhood*

Yet the forms that patterns of expression can take are varied and complex, and important though these patterns are, they can easily slip out of the foreground of your attention as you read or write. This is especially true when you are concentrating on an essay's details and meaning.

Strategy   To recognize patterns of exposition and argument as you read and to keep them in mind as you write, view each pattern as a way of asking or answering questions about a subject.

Example: What are some typical instances or illustrations? What generality is illustrated by these examples?

Classification: What are the different categories? Why are the differences among the categories important?

Comparison and Contrast: What are the similarities and differences? What can we learn from the similarities and differences?

Analogy: What key points do these unlike subjects have in common? How do the similarities help us to understand either one?

Process Analysis: How does it work? How can we do it? What might I gain from understanding the operations?

Cause and Effect: What are the likely causes? Effects? How can an awareness of the possible causes and effects contribute to our understanding of people and events?

Definition: How might it be defined? In what ways does a definition aid us in understanding the importance or consequences of an idea, object, person, or event?

Description: What is its appearance and what are its characteristics? In describing the subject, what can we learn about its meaning, character, or influence?

Narration: What happened? What do the events reveal about the participants or about other events we are likely to experience?

Induction and Deduction: What generalization does the evidence suggest? What further conclusions can we draw from a generalization? How do these processes of reasoning help us understand events or social phenomena?

Reading for Thesis and Theme

An effective essay does not drift from idea to idea but instead links its various elements—idea to idea, detail to detail—in order to develop a central **theme** or perspective. (See "Guide to Terms": *Unity*.) In many expository essays, the unifying theme takes the form of a key idea, interpretation, or observation that can be summed up for readers in a **thesis statement** (See Guide: *Thesis*.) and then developed or supported through details and discussion. In argument essays, the thesis statement generally conveys a **proposition** (See Guide: *Proposition*), an opinion or proposed course of action with which a writer hopes to convince readers to agree.

Even when an author makes an essay's theme abundantly clear, readers may lose sight of it. Individual ideas, details, and examples in an essay can be so intriguing or significant in themselves that they compete for your attention, drawing it away from the theme that serves as a focal point for the whole. As you write, moreover, you can easily become so involved in constructing the parts of an essay that you lose sight of their relationship to your central idea.

Yet if thesis and theme are so important, why do we need to develop the habit of paying special attention to them as we read and write? One reason people often need to pay attention to thesis and theme is that this is a skill we practice only occasionally in informal speaking and writing. In conversation, for example, we often state an opinion or idea and develop it for only a few sentences, then move on to another topic, frequently in response to what our conversational partners have said, as in the following example.

I think one reason people give up trying to learn a musical instrument after a week or two is that they aren't learning as quickly as they thought they would.

That's right. Sports are like that. Some of my friends took up tennis, bought expensive rackets, tennis shoes, then quit after two lessons.

Speaking of sneakers, have you heard about the ones that have lights and play a song?

In contrast, writing is an extended monologue, and your readers will expect you to stick to a topic, to develop your central theme from paragraph to paragraph, and to keep from rambling. As anyone who has spoken before an audience can attest, sticking to a point and developing it does not come naturally. Resisting the temptation to drift, and making sure your ideas and information are clearly related to each other and to your central theme takes hard work.

Strategy To read with an awareness of thesis and theme, pay attention to the ways skillful writers state a thesis, highlight key ideas, link sentence to sentence, paragraph to paragraph, and idea to central theme or thesis statement. To hold these techniques in memory for use in your own work, try making notes in an essay's margin to call attention to them.

Focuses on topic, uses repetition to link

I read an astounding obituary in *The New York Times* not too long ago. It concerned the death of one Jack Ryan. A former husband of Zsa Zsa Gabor, it said, Mr. Ryan had been an inventor and designer during his lifetime. A man of eclectic creativity, he designed Sparrow and Hawk missiles when he worked for the Raytheon Company, and, the notice said, when he consulted for Mattel he designed Barbie.

States theme
is opening
paragraph

If (Barbie) was designed by a man, suddenly a lot of things made sense to me,
things I'd wondered about for years. I
used to look at Barbie and wonder, What's
wrong with this picture? What kind of
woman designed this doll? Let's be honest:
Barbie looks like someone who got her
start at the Playboy Mansion. She should
be a regular guest on *The Howard Stern
Show*. It is a fact of Barbie's design that
her breasts are so out of proportion to
the rest of her body that if she were a
human woman, she'd fall flat on her face.

Echoes theme
and uses
contrast to
make a key
point

If it's true that a woman didn't design
Barbie, you don't know how much saner that
makes me feel. Of course, that doesn't
ameliorate the damage. There are millions
of women who are subliminally sure that a
thirty-nine-inch bust and a twenty-three-
inch waist are the epitome of lovability.
Could this account for the popularity of
breast implant surgery?

Emily Prager, "Our Barbies, Ourselves"

Active Comprehension

To say that you ought to pay attention to an essay's content and
meaning as you read might seem to state the obvious. Aren't these,
after all, the main reasons people read? In practice, however, readers often pay selective attention. Too often, they read for only part of
the meaning (the part they understand right away) or for only part
of the content (the part that interests them most). Or, worse yet, they
pay so little attention to an important section of an essay that they
misunderstand or misinterpret the rest.

Strategy   To read for thorough, overall understanding of an essay,
practice active comprehension. Make note of important
ideas and information as you move through an essay,
perhaps by making notes in the margins of the text or by
writing down important points in a reading journal. (See

pp. 16–18.) Stop frequently at the ends of paragraphs or other sections in an essay to ask and answer questions like the following:

- What is the topic of this paragraph or passage? What does the author have to say about the topic?
- How are the ideas and details in this passage related to those in the prior section? The following section?
- What point of view or opinion is the writer offering in this passage? How is it related to the central theme?

Questions that Lead to Critical Reading

The questions following the selections in this text emphasize critical reading by calling attention to an essay's purpose and ideas ("Meanings and Values"), its various strategies ("Expository [or Argumentative] Techniques"), and its use of language ("Diction and Vocabulary"). You can also treat the questions as models of ways to view your own writing critically or to examine and analyze expository and argumentative writing you encounter elsewhere.

Strategy   To develop critical skills for reading and revising draft essays and to explore ways to analyze and evaluate another writer's work, answer the questions following the selections in this text. Remember that in reading critically you often develop responses to an author's ideas and values that are worth developing in your own writing.

To observe the process of critical reading in action, read the essay below and the questions that follow. After each question we offer a sample response, but not with the intention of excluding other, equally valid ways of responding. As you read, make marginal notes reflecting any responses you have to the ideas and values expressed in the essay or to the techniques the writer employs. Make notes, too, about ways you think other writers might respond to the essay. (See pp. 16–18 for advice on responding and making notes.) Pay attention as well to the biographical information and introductory comments at the beginning of the essay. As is the case with the other selections in the text, this material points out significant features of the essay and provides background information that can provide an appropriate context for understanding and analyzing the piece.

(You may wish to follow "A Process for Reading" described on pp. 15–16.)

BRENT STAPLES

BRENT STAPLES was born in 1951 in Chester, Pennsylvania. He received his B.A. in 1973 from Widener University and his Ph.D. (in psychology) in 1982 from the University of Chicago. He is a member of *The New York Times* editorial board, writing on matters of culture and society. He was formerly a reporter for the *Chicago Sun-Times* and an editor of *The New York Times Book Review*. Staples is the author of *Parallel Time* (1994), a memoir.

Just Walk on By

The power of examples to enable a reader to see through someone else's eyes is evident in this selection. Though many of the examples in the essay draw on a reader's sympathy, their main purpose appears to be explanatory; hence, the author accompanies them with detailed discussions. The result is a piece that is both enlightening and moving.

My first victim was a woman—white, well dressed, probably in her early twenties. I came upon her late one evening on a deserted street in Hyde Park, a relatively affluent neighborhood in an otherwise mean, impoverished section of Chicago. As I swung onto the avenue behind her, there seemed to be a discreet, uninflammatory distance between us. Not so. She cast back a worried glance. To her, the youngish black man—a broad six feet two inches with a beard and billowing hair, both hands shoved into the pockets of a bulky military jacket—seemed menacingly close. After a few more quick glimpses, she picked up her pace and was soon running in earnest. Within seconds she disappeared into a cross street.

That was more than a decade ago. I was 22 years old, a graduate student newly arrived at the University of Chicago. It was in the echo of that terrified woman's footfalls that I first began to know the unwieldy inheritance I'd come into—the ability to alter public space in ugly ways. It was clear that she thought herself the quarry of a mugger, a rapist, or worse. Suffering a bout of insomnia, however, I was stalking sleep, not defenseless wayfarers. As a softy who is scarcely able to take a knife to a raw chicken—let alone hold it to a person's throat—I was surprised, embarrassed, and dismayed all at once. Her flight made me feel like an accomplice in tyranny. It also made it clear that I was indistinguishable from the muggers who occasionally seeped into the area from the surrounding ghetto. That first encounter, and those that followed, signified that a vast, unnerving gulf lay between nighttime pedestrians—particularly women—and me. And I soon gathered that being perceived as dangerous is a hazard in itself. I only needed to turn a corner into a dicey situation, or crowd some frightened, armed person in a foyer somewhere, or make an errant move after being pulled over by a policeman. Where fear and weapons meet—and they often do in urban America—there is always the possibility of death.

In the first year, my first away from my hometown, I was to   3
become thoroughly familiar with the language of fear. At dark, shadowy intersections in Chicago, I could cross in front of a car stopped at a traffic light and elicit the *thunk, thunk, thunk, thunk* of the driver—black, white, male, or female—hammering down the door locks. On less traveled streets after dark, I grew accustomed to but never comfortable with people who crossed to the other side of the street rather than pass me. Then there were the standard unpleasantries with police, doormen, bouncers, cab drivers, and others whose business it is to screen out troublesome individuals *before* there is any nastiness.

I moved to New York nearly two years ago and I have remained   4
an avid night walker. In central Manhattan, the near-constant crowd cover minimized tense one-on-one street encounters. Elsewhere— visiting friends in SoHo, where sidewalks are narrow and tightly spaced buildings shut out the sky—things can get very taut indeed.

Black men have a firm place in New York mugging literature.   5
Norman Podhoretz in his famed (or infamous) 1963 essay, "My Negro Problem—And Ours," recalls growing up in terror of black males; they "were tougher than we were, more ruthless," he writes—and as an adult on the Upper West Side of Manhattan, he continues, he cannot constrain his nervousness when he meets black men on certain streets. Similarly, a decade later, the essayist and novelist Edward Hoagland extols a New York where once "Negro bitterness bore down mainly on other Negroes." Where some see

mere panhandlers, Hoagland sees "a mugger who is clearly screwing up his nerve to do more than just *ask* for money." But Hoagland has "the New Yorker's quick-hunch posture for broken-field maneuvering," and the bad guy swerves away.

I often witness that "hunch posture," from women after dark on 6 the warrenlike streets of Brooklyn where I live. They seem to set their faces on neutral and, with their purse straps strung across their chests bandolier style, they forge ahead as though bracing themselves against being tackled. I understand, of course, that the danger they perceive is not a hallucination. Women are particularly vulnerable to street violence, and young black males are drastically over-represented among the perpetrators of that violence. Yet these truths are no solace against the kind of alienation that comes of being ever the suspect, against being set apart, a fearsome entity with whom pedestrians avoid making eye contact.

It is not altogether clear to me how I reached the ripe old age of 7 22 without being conscious of the lethality nighttime pedestrians attributed to me. Perhaps it was because in Chester, Pennsylvania, the small, angry industrial town where I came of age in the 1960s, I was scarcely noticeable against a backdrop of gang warfare, street knifings, and murders. I grew up one of the good boys, had perhaps a half-dozen fist fights. In retrospect, my shyness of combat has clear sources.

Many things go into the making of a young thug. One of those 8 things is the consummation of the male romance with the power to intimidate. An infant discovers that random flailings send the baby bottle flying out of the crib and crashing to the floor. Delighted, the joyful babe repeats those motions again and again, seeking to duplicate the feat. Just so, I recall the points at which some of my boyhood friends were finally seduced by the perception of themselves as tough guys. When a mark cowered and surrendered his money without resistance, myth and reality merged—and paid off. It is, after all, only manly to embrace the power to frighten and intimidate. We, as men, are not supposed to give an inch of our lane on the highway; we are to seize the fighter's edge in work and in play and even in love; we are to be valiant in the face of hostile forces.

Unfortunately, poor and powerless young men seem to take all 9 this nonsense literally. As a boy, I saw countless tough guys locked away; I have since buried several. They were babies, really—a teenage cousin, a brother of 22, a childhood friend in his mid-twenties—

all gone down in episodes of bravado played out in the streets. I came to doubt the virtues of intimidation early on. I chose, perhaps even unconsciously, to remain a shadow—timid, but a survivor.

The fearsomeness mistakenly attributed to me in public places often has a perilous flavor. The most frightening of these confusions occurred in the late 1970s and early 1980s when I worked as a journalist in Chicago. One day, rushing into the office of a magazine I was writing for with a deadline story in hand, I was mistaken for a burglar. The office manager called security and, with an ad hoc posse, pursued me through the labyrinthine halls, nearly to my editor's door. I had no way of proving who I was. I could only move briskly toward the company of someone who knew me.

Another time I was on assignment for a local paper and killing time before an interview. I entered a jewelry store on the city's affluent Near North Side. The proprietor excused herself and returned with an enormous red Doberman pinscher straining at the end of a leash. She stood, the dog extended toward me, silent to my questions, her eyes bulging nearly out of her head. I took a cursory look around, nodded, and bade her good night. Relatively speaking, however, I never fared as badly as another black male journalist. He went to nearby Waukegan, Illinois, a couple of summers ago to work on a story about a murderer who was born there. Mistaking the reporter for the killer, police hauled him from his car at gunpoint and but for his press credentials would probably have tried to book him. Such episodes are not uncommon. Black men trade tales like this all the time.

In "My Negro Problem—And Ours," Podhoretz writes that the hatred he feels for blacks makes itself known to him through a variety of avenues—one being his discomfort with that "special brand of paranoid touchiness" to which he says blacks are prone. No doubt he is speaking here of black men. In time, I learned to smother the rage I felt at so often being taken for a criminal. Not to do so would surely have led to madness—via that special "paranoid touchiness" that so annoyed Podhoretz at the time he wrote the essay.

I began to take precautions to make myself less threatening. I move about with care, particularly late in the evening. I give a wide berth to nervous people on subway platforms during the wee hours, particularly when I have exchanged business clothes for jeans. If I happen to be entering a building behind some people who appear

10

11

12

13

skittish, I may walk by, letting them clear the lobby before I return, so as not to seem to be following them. I have been calm and extremely congenial on those rare occasions when I've been pulled over by the police.

And on late-evening constitutionals along streets less traveled   14
by, I employ what has proved to be an excellent tension-reducing measure: I whistle melodies from Beethoven and Vivaldi and the more popular classical composers. Even steely New Yorkers hunching toward nighttime destinations seem to relax, and occasionally they even join in the tune. Virtually everybody seems to sense that a mugger wouldn't be warbling bright, sunny selections from Vivaldi's *Four Seasons*. It is my equivalent of the cowbell that hikers wear when they know they are in bear country.

Meanings and Values

1. How is it likely that the author's "victim" (par. 1) viewed him?
    She probably regarded him as an unknown and menacing figure, potentially a rapist or mugger, a source of threat and violence.

2. What does the author have to say about his personality and values in paragraphs 2, 7, and 9?
    These paragraphs focus on the author at age twenty-two. He was relatively young and innocent of the racial tensions of a major urban area, particular of the way whites would view him. He is surprised that other people might regard him as a threat, having survived the violent neighborhood in which he grew up by avoiding the violence and by refusing to follow "tough guy" patterns of behavior. Indeed, he describes himself as one who continues to try to avoid violent behavior.

3. Identify the statement of the essay's central theme that the author offers in paragraph 2, and then state it in your own words.
    The second sentence of paragraph 2 speaks of "the ability to alter public space in ugly ways" as an "unwieldy inheritance" passed on to African-American males. Here is a possible statement of the theme: One of the consequences of racism is that it causes young black males in general to be viewed as hostile and dangerous, and this inaccurate judgment distorts social relationships by creating unnecessary fear and hostility.

4. In what ways are the contrasting perspectives on the author given in the opening (par. 1) and in paragraphs 2, 7, and 9 related to the central theme?

    The different perspectives help readers understand how the stereotyped view of young black males as victimizers can itself serve to victimize the many men who do not deserve to be viewed in this way. This contrast helps convey the central theme by highlighting the injustice of the stereotype and its negative consequences.

5. Does the author's presence (or the presence of other young black males) affect only women? If not, who else does it affect?

    It also affects automobile drivers of all kinds ("black, white, male, or female," par. 3); white men (par. 5); and perhaps even police (par. 11).

Expository Techniques

1. What expectations about the subject of the selection are most readers likely to hold after reading the opening sentences? Are these expectations fulfilled by the essay?

    They are likely to believe the essay will be about rape, mugging, or other violent crimes. The essay deals with these matters, but not in the way many readers are likely to expect. Reversal is the key. In the course of the essay, the author's personality is shown to be the opposite of what might be expected. The essay shows how he (and other black men) can reasonably be viewed as being victimized by stereotypes that reflect a kind of racism that is still part of our culture.

2. The quotations in paragraph 5 contribute to the essay in what ways?

    They give an "outsider's" point of view to contrast with the author's "inside" point of view, broadening and deepening the quality of the explanation and suggesting some reasons people react as they do to the author and to other young men in similar positions.

3. Discuss the strategies the author employs to explain why he and other black males can be considered victims of stereotyping and of the surroundings in which they grew up.

    He gives examples of typically dangerous or humiliating responses the men encounter. He describes the feelings of

> *alienation and dismay that are the result of having one's*
> *values and motives viewed as hostile. He also tells of the spe-*
> *cial steps he has had to take to defuse trouble in ordinary sit-*
> *uations. In addition, he points out that many young black*
> *men are themselves victims of violence.*

5. Characterize the author's response to Podhoretz's comment
   about the "special brand of paranoid touchiness" (par. 12) of
   blacks. Tell why it is appropriate that the paragraph quoting
   Podhoretz on "paranoid touchiness" comes after the two examples presented in paragraphs 10 and 11.

   > *He probably thinks it amounts to blaming the victim; he*
   > *shows in the essay that the "touchiness" has clear causes*
   > *and is by no means paranoid. The placement is appropriate*
   > *because the preceding paragraphs help show that touchiness*
   > *is often justified, not a product of paranoia. The placement*
   > *also helps suggest that Podhoretz's view is another example*
   > *of the racism that victimizes black men.*

Diction and Vocabulary

1. The diction of this essay is often quite formal: for example, "The
   fearsomeness mistakenly attributed to men in public places
   often has a perilous flavor" (par. 10). Discuss the likely effect of
   such diction on the way readers view the author's character and
   values. (See "Guide to Terms": *Diction*.)

   > *The diction makes the author seem educated, upper class,*
   > *and restrained—not the kind of person likely to commit*
   > *street crimes.*

2. Tell why the following sentence from the end of the essay can
   be considered a summary of some of its important ideas: "It is
   my equivalent of the cowbell that hikers wear when they know
   they are in bear country" (par. 14).

   > *The danger an innocent hiker faces from bears is similar to*
   > *the danger Staples faces from people who misjudge his*
   > *motives when he is out walking. The sentence sums up*
   > *the essay's points about misunderstanding, threat, and*
   > *victimization.*

3. If you find any of the following words puzzling, look them up
   in a dictionary: quarry, unnerving, dicey (par. 2); taut (4); warrenlike, bandolier (6); lethality (7); consummation (8); perilous,
   ad hoc (10); cursory (11); constitutionals (14).

quarry = something that is hunted; *unnerving* = unsettling; *dicey* = tense; *taut* = tense; *warrenlike* = similar to a mass of tunnels made by rabbits; *bandolier* = a belt containing cartridges and worn across the chest; *lethality* = capability to cause death; *consummation* = coming together or fulfillment; *perilous* = filled with danger; ad hoc = for a specific purpose; *cursory* = hasty and superficial; *constitutionals* = walks taken for one's health

A Process for Reading

No single way of reading is best, yet some approaches are certainly more effective than others as ways of comprehending an author's ideas or of producing creative responses that can eventually take written form themselves. Instead of a lock-step system for reading, therefore, we offer the following suggestions you can employ according to the reading situation. In choosing among the suggestions, take into account your needs for information, ideas, or even entertainment as well as the nature of the text you are examining.

For the First Reading:
   1. As you read for the first time, relax. Read the selection casually, as you would a magazine article, for whatever enjoyment or new ideas you get without straining. Do not stop to look up new words unless the sentences in which they are used are meaningless until you do. Have a pen or pencil in hand and mark all words or passages you are doubtful about, and then go on.
   Jot down spontaneous reactions to the essay: disagreements and agreements as well as experiences and speculations of your own that the reading prompts. Do not allow yourself to be drawn too far away from the reading by your jottings, but do capture the fleeting thoughts so you can later call them to mind.
   2. After the first reading, put the book down. For a few minutes think over what you have read. Don't spend too much time at this point figuring out exactly what the writer has to say. The memories, feelings, and opinions that come to mind at this stage are an important part of the reading process. They can be the basis for detailed comprehension or for your own writing. If you keep a reading journal (See "Reading Journal" p. 18.), this is a time for entries exploring the text and your responses to it.

3. Use the dictionary to help you understand words you have marked. Do not make the mistake of finding and trying to memorize the first or the shortest definition of a word. Instead, examine the various meanings and look for the word's uses as a noun, verb, and modifier. *Think* about them. Pronounce the word. Use it in a few sentences. Identify it with similar words you already know. Then see how the author has used it.

4. Read and think briefly about the assigned questions and remarks following the selection. (The paragraphs in each selection are numbered for easy reference.)

For the Second Reading:

5. Reread the essay, pausing at times to think and *question.* Underline important ideas; mark sentences or phrases that seem especially interesting, misleading, amusing, or well expressed. Pursue your own ideas, responses, objections, and speculations in marginal notes or in a writing journal.

6. Return to the questions at the end. You will probably find you have already provided most of the answers. If not, give the questions further thought, referring again to the essay and to "A Guide to Terms" (at the end of the book) or to earlier explanations wherever necessary for thorough understanding.

7. Reread the essay in whole or part as many times as necessary to understand any passages you find especially challenging and to observe in detail any writing strategies you might wish to employ in your own essays.

After Reading:

8. *Evaluate* the selection. What was the author trying to explain? Was the author successful in explaining? Was the endeavor worthwhile? For what point of view was the author arguing? Was the argument convincing? What lessons for writers can be drawn from the selection?

Responding As You Read

As we read an essay for comprehension, we often have a second stream of thoughts in our minds as well—one in which we carry on a dialogue with the author, commenting on or arguing with ideas, admiring passages, or raising questions about the topic. Whether this dialogue takes place in the foreground of our attention or remains a quiet rumbling in the background depends on the content and challenges posed by the essay as well as our own attitudes. An essay that presents disquieting ideas or information is likely to bring our responses, feelings, and questions into the foreground. On the other hand, an essay that is difficult to understand may lead us to keep our judgments and ideas in the background as we work on comprehension.

Capturing this fleeting dialogue gives you a rich source of ideas and purposes for your writing as well as a way to become acquainted with writing techniques you especially admire. Here are some suggestions for writing activities that can help you capture and explore your responses to an essay.

Strategy ## Marginal Notes

Use the margins of the text to record disagreements and agreements with what the author has to say or to hold shorthand references to memories and ideas that might be developed in essays of your own.

As we read, many ideas for our own compositions come to mind, but unless they are recorded, even in brief form, they are likely to disappear by the time we get down to writing. Admittedly, making extensive marginal notes can sometimes interfere with the pleasure we take in reading an essay and learning about an intriguing topic. Keep your notes short and perhaps even develop a set of abbreviations to use in them. On the other hand, an essay may be so interesting that you fail to make notes and thus miss recording ideas for later use. Try to develop a habit of stopping every page or two to see if there are any notes you wish to make.

Strategy ## Three Questions

In the margins of an essay or in a notebook that you keep to record your responses to reading, jot down brief answers to these questions, identifying each kind of answer by a letter corresponding to the type of question.

W (= *Why Interesting?*) Why do I find this topic, passage, or example interesting?

D (= *Detail?*) Do the concrete details and the detailed explanations and arguments this author provides seem especially convincing?

M (= *More Information?*) What more would I like to know about this topic? Are other readers likely to be interested in it as well?

Strategy   **Reading Journal**

> Keep a notebook of ideas, feelings, and experiences that come to mind either as you read or later as you reflect on your reading.

Your reading journal can be a source of ideas for essays or parts of essays in the future. Try to label the entries according to the name of the essay. If possible, label the kinds of entries as well. Use headings that will be useful to you later; for example, "Ideas," "My Opinions," or "Possible Topics."

Strategy   **Double-Entry Notebook**

> Draw a vertical line down the middle of the pages of your reading journal. (See above.) On the left side of the page, make brief notes summarizing the content of what you read. On the right side, record questions that occur to you as you read. The questions can be trivial or serious. They may be about the author, about what is coming next in the selection, or about a subject related to the one under discussion.

The summaries in a double-entry journal aid your understanding of what the author has to say and can be a source of information for your writing. The questions tell you about your reading process, provide insight into the ideas and problems that concern you, and can be springboards for essays of your own.

Attending to Writing

When you jot down a grocery list or leave a note for a friend, you do not need to pay too much attention to the choices you make as you write. For anything but the most routine and predictable kinds of writing, however, a lack of attention can be a recipe for disaster. To write successfully, you need to attend consciously to your writing, both to the process itself—planning, drafting, and revising—and to the likely responses of your readers. This is certainly true for an essay in which you want to present complicated information or ideas in a clear and convincing manner. It also holds true for a seemingly routine memo or report whose presentation may nonetheless shape the positive (or negative) reactions of the people to whom it is addressed.

Attending to writing means first of all being aware of the different tasks involved in composing: planning, drafting, and revising. It also means being aware of strategies for accomplishing these tasks and of the need to vary strategies according to subject and situation. Knowing when to shift from one strategy to the next and having a second or third strategy to fall back on are crucial skills for a conscientious writer.

Knowing How (and When) to Plan

Experienced writers use all sorts of planning techniques, some of which may seem quite formal and others, like *freewriting*, (See pp. 24–26.) which at first may not even seem like planning activities. But experienced writers always plan. They know that unless you can envision what you want to say and how you want people to read your work, your writing will almost always be aimless, disjointed, and confusing.

You should be ready to start planning whenever you get an assignment that calls for writing or whenever you begin thinking about a subject you wish to explore in writing. Even when you are drafting or revising an essay, you should keep on planning in the sense of paying attention to your goals and to the ways you want readers to react. Planning means *focusing:* on a subject and a topic, on a purpose and an overall design, and on the arrangement of specific parts in an essay.

Focusing on a Subject and a Topic.
Subject and topic sound similar but they differ in some important and practical ways. A *subject* is a loose body of information, ideas, and experiences on which you can draw as you write. A topic consists of details and ideas that are already selected and shaped in some ways; this shaping allows you to recognize a topic as something people might like to read about and something you can imagine yourself writing about. For example, if in trying to come up with content and focus for your writing you begin thinking about your childhood, you have started exploring a possible subject: a mass of events, feelings, details, people, seasons, colors, and so on. In contrast, if you focus your recollections of childhood on the time you almost drowned, you have found a potential topic: a cluster of information and ideas that

already has at least a rough shape and a hint of purpose or theme. Your focusing on a particular incident (topic) enables you to begin thinking about ways to present the event and about how your choices might shape the way readers react.

Exploring a subject is a good way to come up with possible topics; *deciding on a topic* is a first step in focusing and planning your writing. Starting with a subject and narrowing it to a topic is a perfectly good way to begin writing, but it is not the only way. Sometimes, for example, you may start with a particular topic in mind or often, an assignment will specify a topic (and maybe even a purpose and a general plan).

Nonetheless, thinking about possible subjects is generally a good place to begin because you move beyond the familiar to explore fresh and potentially intriguing ideas. (Even if you have been assigned a subject, you can still explore the many perspectives you can take in writing about it.) Though you can explore possible subjects simply by letting your mind range freely, you risk losing track of the many subjects and ideas you encounter in your mental travels. For this reason, most writers like to think about possible subjects with pen in hand or at a computer keyboard.

Strategy   **Brainstorm** possible subjects by letting your mind run freely, leaping from one cluster of ideas, information, and experiences to another. Every time you recognize such a cluster, give it a name and put it on a list of possible subjects.

You can also brainstorm and list while you are reading, talking with others, listening to a speaker, or watching a program. (For freewriting as a way to explore subjects, see pp. 24–26.)

When your list is finished, you may wish to circle the subjects you find most promising or think your readers would find most interesting.

When he was asked to prepare an essay offering a generality and explaining it through examples, Bernie Stevens made the following list of possible subjects.

```
I could write about . . .

High School--pretty dull

College?
```

```
Sports--College sports
Typical College sports--football etc.
Less familiar college sports
Lacrosse
Field Hockey  (high school too)
Golf
Hockey (good to watch)
Figure skating (a college sport?)
Swimming
What it's like to be on a college team
```

Strategy **Extend Brainstorming** by picking one or more subjects from your original list and generating a further list of associated subjects. When you have finished creating the extended list, circle the subjects you consider the most promising.

Bernie Stevens presented his initial brainstorming list (see above) to his peer group in writing class, and the discussion that followed helped him extend the list.

```
POSSIBLE SUBJECTS     EXTENDED

Less familiar         Field Events--hammer, javelin,
college sports        triple jump
                      Woodsman (axes, sawing)--for
                      women too
                      Volleyball
                      Sailing

Golf                  Competitive team golfing
                      Golf as a sport rather
                      than recreation
                      Division I competition
                      Physical and mental sides
                      Golfers (college golfers)
```

What's it like to be on a college team?	Athletic teams--social and psychological Athletes in college College athletes in big-time sports College athletes in lesser-known sports Time and energy demands of college sports Personal experience as student athlete

Focusing on a Topic.

When you have a subject in mind you can begin envisioning how that subject might develop into a topic for an essay. Many writers identify potential topics by keeping certain questions in mind as they think about a subject. They use such questions to help identify their goals and interests in writing, to recognize aspects of a subject likely to interest readers, or develop perspectives worth exploring in writing.

Strategy   Use **focusing questions** to guide your thinking about a subject and to identify potential topics and goals for writing. Create a list of potential topics, making notes of possible purposes for writing or patterns for arranging and developing an essay. If you wish, repeat the process by focusing on one of the topics and extending your thinking to identify additional, related topics that may be fresher or more intriguing than your original ones.

Possible Questions

What parts of this subject or ways of looking at it interest me the most? Is the subject as a whole interesting or does some part of it or specific way of looking at it seem more intriguing?

What aspect or perspective of the subject is most likely to interest readers?

What would I most like to learn about this subject? Would readers like to learn the same thing?

What feelings about the subject do I want to share with readers? What knowledge, opinions, or insights do I want to share?

What topics and arrangements are suggested by the patterns of exposition and argument illustrated in this text?

What examples come to mind as I think about the subject, and why might they be worth talking about? (See Chapter 1, "Illustrating Ideas by Use of *Example*.")

What groups or categories does the subject form and what do they reveal? (See Chapter 2, "Analyzing a Subject by *Classification*.")

What parts of the subject suggest interesting similarities or differences? (See Chapter 3, "Explaining by means of *Comparison* and *Contrast*.")

Does the subject suggest any analogies? Would one of the analogies be worth exploring as the topic of an essay? (See Chapter 4, "Using *Analogy* as an Expository Device.")

Is there some part of this subject that readers might want to know how to do or whose workings are interesting enough to deserve explanation? (See Chapter 5, "Explaining through *Process Analysis*.")

Are there some events or phenomena whose causes might surprise or interest readers or whose likely effects are worth considering? (See Chapter 6, "Analyzing *Cause-and-Effect Relationships*.")

What key terms or concepts are important enough to deserve clearer understanding or puzzling enough to require clarification? (See Chapter 7, "Using *Definition* to Help Explain.")

Does the subject include any scenes or people whose meaning or significance might be revealed through a detailed portrait? (See Chapter 8, "Explaining with the Help of *Description*.")

Are there any meaningful stories that the subject brings to mind? (See Chapter 9, "Using *Narration* as an Expository Technique.")

What aspects of the subject suggest specific conclusions? Do these conclusions suggest ways of viewing other parts of the subject? (See Chapter 10, "Reasoning by the Use of *Induction*.")

What specific issues, opinions, disagreements, and possible actions are involved? (See Chapter 11, "Using Patterns for *Argument*.")

Here is the topic list generated by Mary McCloskey as she worked on a writing assignment that asked her to discuss a topic in the area of sports and fitness.

SUBJECT   POSSIBLE TOPICS

Women in Sports   People are trying to make
                           women's sports more popular.
                           More people watch men's sports.
                           Are some kinds of sports
                           traditionally for women or
                           are there some in which women
                           are more likely to excel?
                           More professional men's sports.
                           What are the possible
                           consequences of Title IX for
                           college sports?
                           (What exactly is Title IX?)
                           Men's sports are more
                           popular. Why? How can this
                           be changed?
                           Women's sports are often more
                           exciting? Is this true?
                           How do people benefit from
                           watching women's sports and
                           may they feel that the sport
                           is less challenging and that
                           they can get involved?
                           Male spectators enjoy
                           watching women's tennis
                           because they learn things to
                           use when they play.

   Clustering and **freewriting** are two other techniques for focusing on a topic. They have the additional advantage of helping you get started with plans for an essay's content and arrangement.

Strategy   Jot down your ideas about a subject and create **clusters** by circling related thoughts and drawing lines among them.

The clusters you create should highlight one or more topics and may also suggest purposes and designs for your writing.

Here is how Sevon Robertson used clustering as a way to begin working on an assignment that asked her to draw conclusions about her first two months as a college student.

What I've learned as a college student--boring classes.

Professor W--incredibly boring

Idea for the paper: seems like a waste of time to attend some classes.

Doesn't take daily attendance

8am class

Outlines the book in the lecture

Monotone

Syllabus tells you everything you need to know--why attend?

Professor C like Professor W but not quite as bad

Professor M much better adds new material in lecture

Strategy **Freewrite** to discover and explore a topic. Jot down all the thoughts that come to mind until a topic begins to emerge along with the beginnings of a plan for writing. Don't worry about spelling, grammar, or complete sentences, but do focus on exploring ideas and details.

After clustering her ideas, Sevon Robertson decided that while many of them fit together under the topic "Boring Classes," some of them suggested a contrast—interesting and worthwhile classes. She decided to freewrite to see how all these ideas might fit together, and in doing so she realized that she was interested in contrasting the different kinds of classes she had experienced, boring ones and worthwhile ones.

I have been attending classes for about five weeks now and I have already come to the conclusion that some classes are a waste of time to attend. I have also discovered that some are really worthwhile.

Professor C and Professor W (names changed to protect the guilty) are both guilty of being boring. Not only do they speak in monotone, they never, never ever stray from the textbook. In other words they give you an exact outline of each chapter and they don't say anything that isn't already in the text. That fact is especially irritating to me because Professor C teaches an 8am class (drop this cause it sounds like I'm spoiled).

Professor C's syllabus tells his students their homework assignments which is to answer the questions at the end of each chapter so it is possible not to attend any of Professor C's classes, not even for examples, because his examples are not during class time (confusing, work on it)!

Professor C also doesn't take attendance at all, so the student has no incentive to attend his class. I won't be totally one sided, perhaps Professor C doesn't take any form of attendance because it would waste time since it's a big class. Professor W is a little less boring than Professor C, but she speaks in an even worse monotone, so it doesn't matter that what she has to say is occasionally worth listening to.

On the other hand, Professor M teaches a really worthwhile class. He takes attendance regularly but he doesn't need to because very few people ever miss class. It is at 11am so most people (except for the really late sleepers) can't claim they slept in. But there isn't any reason to fall asleep in class either. Professor M gives lectures that cover all sorts of things that aren't in the textbook and a lot of time we leave class thinking about some of the incredibly interesting ideas about people he has presented (it is an anthropology course). He uses slides and movies to illustrate his points, but never too long. And he gets people to ask questions (even in a big class) and answers them in a way that tells you he is listening and he cares what you think. (O.K. Got to arrange this so won't be really confusing).

Choosing an Arrangement.

When you can state to yourself what you want to write about and why, then you have decided on a tentative topic for your writing. When you can envision where you want your writing to go, in a general sense at least, you should begin planning how to get there.

Being absolutely committed to a topic at this point is unnecessary and probably unwise. Experienced writers know the importance of remaining open to new ideas and being able to leave behind a topic that does not work out as well as they thought it would.

Strategy   Write yourself a note stating your potential topic along with possible goals for your writing (and, perhaps, anticipated reactions from readers). To remain flexible and open to new ideas, you might begin your statement with a phrase like "I'd like to . . ." or "I'm planning to . . ."

> I'm planning to explain the reasons why many college students lose their motivation to work hard at their studies.
>
> Bippin Kumar

> I'd like to tell what it felt like to be forced to leave my homeland, Haiti, so that my readers can understand why to leave something you love is to die a little.
>
> Fredza Légér

In focusing on a topic, you have already begun your planning, at least to the extent that you have begun thinking about what an essay might do and what material it might cover. But envisioning an essay's goal and some of its major points is seldom enough. People who try to draft an essay at this stage often find themselves stymied (unless they are using writing as a planning technique, see p. 28). With little idea of what order to follow in discussion or argument, and with only the roughest notion of what details, examples, and reasoning to include, they find writing going forward slowly, if at all.

To avoid this problem, spend time planning what information and ideas you wish to explore, how you wish to arrange the presentation, and what perspective you will offer. You can easily adapt techniques, such as brainstorming and clustering, to planning an essay and developing its content.

Strategy   **Brainstorm** by writing down the ideas, details, examples, subtopics, and arguments you think you may develop in an essay. Then **cluster** related items by circling them and using lines to link them. Begin arranging your essay by naming or numbering the clusters and putting them in a tentative sequence.

The patterns of exposition (and argument) illustrated in this book suggest questions you can use to explore your topic and develop ideas, examples, and details for your writing. In addition, they suggest ways to arrange your explanations and arguments.

Strategy   Turn the patterns of exposition (and argument) into questions that highlight ways to develop a topic and arrange an essay.

Example	What are some illustrations or examples? How can they be arranged to illustrate a particular generality?
Classification	Into what categories does the subject fall, and what are the characteristics of each? What is their order of importance or interest?
Comparison	In what ways do these items differ, and in what ways are they the same? Which similarities or differences are worth special attention and in what order?
Analysis Process	How does it work, or how can it be done? What arrangement will best clarify the steps, stages, or elements for readers?
Effect and Cause	Why did it happen, and what is likely to happen in the future? How can the discussion of causes or effects be best organized in order to clarify their relationship?
Definition	What is being defined, and what features characterize it and set it off from other things? What order of presentation will make the definition clear to readers?

Description	What are its features (physical, emotional, etc.); how are these elements related in time and space? What order of presentation will best enable readers to understand the whole and the relationship of its parts?
Narration	What happened? To whom? When? Where? What is the best way to arrange the story to make a point?
Induction and Deduction	What generalization do the facts or events support? What further facts or events does the generalization help explain? In what order should the facts, events, and generalizations be presented in order to best illustrate the process of reasoning?
Argument	What is the proposition, and what is the supporting evidence? Which pattern of argument (or combination of patterns) will present the supporting evidence in the most convincing fashion?

For some writers, writing itself can be a way of discovering ideas, details, and possible arrangements. This strategy can be successful if it involves creation of a *zero draft* or *discovery draft*, but not if it means the painfully slow process of trying to create a detailed, well-organized first draft without adequate planning. Written at top speed and filled with partly developed thoughts and expressions, like freewriting (See pp. 24–25.), a discovery draft gives a writer a chance to try out ideas and arrangements and to see a plan for a paper emerge as the writing goes along. Though it can take more time than other planning methods, a discovery draft can be useful. Often writers stop partway into a discovery draft as soon as they have a clear idea of where the paper is going. Then they move on to some other planning techniques or to creating a full first draft.

Few writers can envision a paper's content and its arrangement in the kind of detail necessary to create a formal outline with numerous sections and levels of subheadings (see pp. 33–34). And even writers who can envision an essay in such detail may find themselves altering their plans during drafting and revision as they recognize new and better directions for their work. On the other hand, many writers use *informal outlines* and *purpose outlines* to test various possible plans for an essay.

Strategy When you have in mind the various ideas and details you wish to present in an essay, create an *informal outline* by arranging the ideas and details in groups (perhaps by clustering) and summarizing each group in a heading. Then write down the headings in the order you wish to present them, putting the most important ideas and details under each.

Alternative: Create a *purpose outline* by stating the purpose or role each group of ideas and details will play in the essay. Then arrange the groups in the order that you think will best accomplish your overall purpose.

Here is Bippin Kumar's purpose outline for a paper exploring the reasons why college students may lose the motivation necessary to succeed at their studies.

```
1. Get readers' attention by mentioning the bad
habits most of us have and that we may be able
to correct on our own. (minor causes of the
problem)
      lack of sleep
      disorganization
      distractions (television, etc.)
      roommates
2. Show how we are often responsible because of
the choices we make and explain that we need to
make wiser choices. (more serious causes)
      sports and other extracurricular activities
      friends and socializing
      Greek life
      letting ourselves get frustrated and angry
      over daily hassles (bookstores, commuting)
3. Conclude with problems that we can't avoid and
that may require special planning or counseling
to overcome. (most serious causes)
```

```
work
financial stresses
family demands or problems
lack of necessary skills
```

Arriving at a Thesis.
A successful essay has a central theme or perspective that it conveys to readers and that ties together its parts (See pp. 4–6.). Such a theme should begin to emerge during the planning process. If not, your attempts to complete a full draft of your essay are likely to be marked with confusion, misdirections, and restarts.

Most likely, you will alter, revise, or change your theme and perspective as you write, and such changes often make for a better essay. By the time your essay is complete, you will also have to decide whether to announce your theme directly to readers in a concise thesis statement (see 4–5), to present it less directly in a series of statements in the body of the essay, or to imply it through the details, arrangement, and discussion. No matter what choice you make for the final paper, you need to have a relatively clear idea of your theme and thesis before you begin drafting. Here are some helpful strategies.

Strategy **State your theme to yourself.** You can do this in several ways.

1. Start with a phrase like "I want my readers to understand . . ." or "The point of the whole essay is . . ."
2. Make up a title that embodies your main idea.
3. Send a note to your readers: "by the time you are finished with this essay, I hope you will see (or agree with me) that . . ."

If you want to share your knowledge of bicycling as a sport, for example, you might try one or more of these strategies, as in the following examples.

1. The point of the whole essay is that people can choose what kind of bicycle riders they want to be—recreational, competitive, or cross-country.
2. What Kind of Bicycle Rider Do You Want to Be?

3. By the time you are finished with this essay, I hope you will be able to choose the kind of bicycle riding recreational, competitive, or cross-country—that is best for you.

Strategy   **Create a tentative thesis statement.** In a sentence or two sum up your main point about the subject, the conclusion you plan to draw from the information and ideas you present, or the proposition for which you plan to argue. (You may eventually use a revised form of the tentative thesis in your completed essay.)

For example, when Ken Chin was preparing a paper on different meanings "recent immigrant," he used the following tentative thesis statement: "For some people, *recent immigrant* means a threat to their jobs or more strain on the resources of schools and social service agencies. For others it means fresh ideas and a broadening of our culture and outlook." In his final paper he used this thesis statement: "For some, *recent immigrant* means *cheap labor* or *higher taxes;* for others, it means *fresh ideas* and *a richer, more diverse culture.*"

Focusing on Drafting

Drafting involves a good deal more than setting pen to paper or fingers to keyboard and letting the words flow according to your plan. It means paying attention to the way each section of an essay relates to the other sections and to the central theme. It means making sure you begin and end the essay in ways that are clear, helpful, and interesting to readers. And it means making sure each section and each paragraph present sufficient, detailed information so that readers can understand your subject and have reasons to agree with your explanations and conclusions.

Drafting does not mean getting everything right the first time. Such a goal is likely to prove both exhausting and impossible to achieve. A much better goal is to draft with the most important features of an essay in mind and to work quickly enough so that you have sufficient time to revise later and then pay attention to details.

As you draft, therefore, make sure that you introduce readers to your topic, indicate its importance, generate interest in it, and suggest the direction your essay will take. The essays in this collection can provide you with models of successful strategies for beginning essays and the Guide to Terms: Introductions offers a detailed list of opening strategies. The Guide also provides advice about another important feature that should be a focus during drafting—your essay's conclusion.

Keep in mind the various sections you have planned for your essay, and, as you write, include statements that alert readers to their presence, along with transitions that mark the movement from one section to the next (or from paragraph to paragraph). Make sure, too, that in making shifts in time and place you do not confuse readers, but instead give them adequate indication of the shifts. Remember to provide readers with concrete, specific details and evidence that will give them the information they need about your topic, or the support necessary to make your explanations and arguments convincing.

Pay attention to the arrangement of your essay, especially to the patterns of exposition or argument you are employing. In an essay that classifies, for example, don't provide a detailed treatment of one category in the classification but skimpy treatment of the others—unless you have a special reason for doing so. Let your readers know, directly or indirectly, whatever pattern(s) you are employing. This will make them aware of your essay's design and will help to guide their attention to the key points you cover. Make every effort to stick to your central theme and to see that the parts of the essay are clearly related to it. If you have trouble developing a section because you need more information, or because you can't express ideas as clearly as you want, make a note of the things that need to be done and then move on.

When you are finished drafting, you may wish to create a formal outline to help you understand what you have included (or failed to include) in your draft and to check whether the arrangement of your essay is clear and reasonable. A formal outline can also help you identify those elements of your work that need attention during revision.

In a formal outline, you group the elements of an essay into different levels (I, II, III; A, B, C; 1, 2, 3; a, b, c, and so on) according to their level of generality. You should develop your outline logically, so that, for example, each level of an outline has at least two elements.

In outlining her paper on contrasting images of cigarette smoking, for instance, Rachel Ritchie was able to check whether she was providing a balanced and detailed treatment of the different portrayals of smokers and smoking.

   I. Cigarette smoking used to be regarded as socially acceptable and fashionable behavior.

     A. Movie heroes used smoking to display their confidence and sophistication.

       1. Handsome, virile men like Humphrey Bogart made cigarettes a part of their image.

       2. Glamorous leading ladies used cigarettes as elegant fashion accessories.

     B. Smoking was associated with social status and general well-being.

       1. . . .

  II. Today, experience and research have given smoking a deadly image.

     A. Many Americans die from cigarette smoking.

       1. In 1980, 485,000 Americans died from cigarette-related diseases.

       2. Recently, around 500,000 die each year (more than one-quarter of the deaths from all causes).

     B. . . .

Focusing on Revision

When you shift your focus to revising, you pay special attention to the success with which your draft essay embodies your intentions and meets your readers' likely expectations. You examine the draft to see if it does a good job presenting insights, reasoning, and details. You look at the draft from a reader's perspective to see if the discussions are clear and informative, the reasoning is logical, and the examples and supporting details are related to the central theme.

Revision starts with rereading—looking over your draft with the dual perspective of an author and a member of your potential audience. As you read for revision, keep track of the places that need more work and make note of the direction(s) your rewriting might take. You may be tempted to revise as you read, and for sentences or paragraphs that need a quick fixup, this approach is often adequate. In most cases, however, your revisions need to go beyond tinkering with words and sentences if they are to lead to real improvement. You will need to pay attention to the overall focus, to the need for additional paragraphs presenting detailed evidence, and to the arrangement of the steps in an explanation or argument. To see the need for such large-scale changes you need to read a draft paying attention to the essay as a whole, something you cannot do if you stop frequently to rework the parts. In addition, it makes little sense to correct the flaws in a sentence if you realize a bit later on that the entire paragraph ought to be dropped.

One good way to read for revision is to prepare questions that will focus your attention as you read—questions appropriate for your topic, your purposes, your pattern(s) of exposition or argument, and your intended readers.

Strategy　**Questioning Reading.** Develop a set of questions to focus your attention as you read a draft essay to decide how to revise. You may wish to direct attention to those features you worked on while drafting (introductions, for example, or transitions). You may wish to use questions that reflect the specific topic or purposes of your essay or that reflect the probable outlook of your intended readers. Make notes in the margins of your draft or on a separate sheet of paper (or computer file). Don't keep too many questions in mind as you read; instead, re-read as many times as necessary, each time with a different set of questions.

Possible Questions for Revision

General

　Does my essay have a clear topic and focus?
　Does it stick to the topic and focus throughout?
　How have I signaled the topic and focus to readers?
　Is the essay divided into parts? What are they?
　Are the parts clearly identified for readers?

Thesis and Theme

　Does the essay have a thesis statement? Is it clearly stated?
　Is the thesis statement in the best possible location?
　Should the thesis statement be more (or less) specific?
　Are all the different parts of the essay clearly related to the thesis statement or the central theme?
　In what ways have I reminded readers of the thesis or theme in the course of the essay? Do I need to remind them more often or in other ways?

Introductions and Conclusions

Does my introduction make the topic clear? Does it interest readers in what I will have to say?

Does my introduction give readers some indication of the arrangement of the essay and its purpose(s)?

Does the conclusion help tie together the main points of the essay or remind readers of the significance of the information and ideas I have presented?

Does my conclusion have a clear purpose or have I ended the essay without any clear strategy?

Information and Ideas

Have I presented enough information and enough details so that readers will feel they have learned something worthwhile about the topic?

At what specific places would the essay be improved if I added more information?

What information can be cut because it is repetitive, uninteresting, or unrelated to the topic or the theme of the essay?

Is my information fresh and worth sharing? Do I need to do more thinking or research so that the content of my essay is worth sharing?

Do the examples and details I present support my conclusions in a convincing way? Do I need to explain them more fully? Would more research or thinking enable me to offer better support?

Have I learned something new or worthwhile about my topic and communicated it to readers?

Sentences and Paragraphs

Have I divided the essay into paragraphs that help readers identify shifts in topic, stages in an explanation, steps in a line of reasoning, key ideas, or important segments of information?

Does each paragraph make its topic or purpose clear to readers?

Which short paragraphs need greater development through the addition of details or explanations?

Which long paragraphs could be trimmed or divided?

Do the sentences reflect what I want to say? Which could be clearer?

Are the sentences varied in length? Do they provide appropriate emphasis to key ideas?

Can I word the explanations or arguments more clearly?

Can I use more vivid and concrete language?

Would the paper benefit from more complicated or imaginative language? From simpler, more direct wording?

Reader's Perspective

In what ways are my readers likely to view this topic or argument? Have I taken their perspectives into account?

What do I want my readers to learn from this essay? What opinion do I want them to share? What do I want them to do?

Have I considered what my readers are likely to know or believe and how this will shape their response to my purpose(s) for writing?

(The essays presented in this text and the questions that follow them also suggest things you can ask yourself as you revise.)

As she read the following draft of an essay drawn from her experience as an immigrant from Haiti, Fredza Légér made marginal notes to guide her revisions. Because English is her second language, Fredza was particularly concerned about sentence structure and wording, yet she left most such questions for a later reading of her draft. For this reading she concentrated on ways to give her essay a clear focus, to make her theme evident to readers, and to provide examples and details that would help readers understand the relevance to their own lives of her belief that "to leave is to die a little."

```
        TO LEAVE IS TO DIE A LITTLE.


        Have you ever been away from home

   for a long period of time, like moving

   from one neighborhood to another, or
```

leaving home for the very first time
to go to college, or traveling to
somewhere where the rules, the culture,
and the foods are quite different from
what you have been used to since you
were born? You'd then realize, maybe
for the first time, how much your
family and friends meant to you, and

Is my main idea clear?

you'd start saying that "there is no
place like home."

Well my topic here is a
generality that you would really

Are these the right English spellings?

approve once you'd (esperienced) some
kind of departure or (escile) in your
life. Like me, for example, I used to
sing that sentence in a French song,
"Partir c'est mourir un peu"
(translated, "To leave is to die a
little") just because I loved to sing.
But these words began to have a
particular meaning to me when I left my
house and traveled to another country.

How do you say this in English?

I was born in Haiti--a Third
world country located in the (Carribeans)--
and I spent the first seventeen years
of my life there living with my large
family and friends. I'd always heard

people saying that Haiti is a beautiful country, that we were lucky to (life) in this island which used to be rich and could become rich if its people could manage it better, some would even say that they would die for their country, and i have indeed seen some doing it. But I was never a real patriot and never thought I would be until I got away and came here to the USA in August 1992. Every thing was so different when I came here. First of all, I had to deal with the language. English was always my favorite language back then in high school, but speaking it every day, and practicing it for three to four hours a week in a classroom weren't the same thing. There was also the weather. Haiti is a tropical island where it is always hot. In the USA it is cold with snow falling much of the time. There were a lot of other changes in my new life, but the great surprise was that, as (escited) as I was about living a brand new life, I never thought that I would miss my country--mainly because of the

I think I am repeating myself too much.

I should organize this better. I want to show how different it is to live in each country.

Are the circled words correct?

unsafety caused by political problems
we are still suffering there. I began
to say to myself things like "Home,
sweet home" and "There's not place
like home, no matter what others may
think of you."

> I want to talk about the lives other people have. This paper is too much about me. I do not know what examples to use.

It is hard sometimes to tell that
something is important to you when you
have it whenever you need it. Let's
take water, for example, nobody who
has water flowing twenty four hours a
day can really tell that it is
something indispensible to human kind.
But, if for some reason you run out of
water, your realize how much it means
to you. Likewise, one may never take
the time to analyze what his or her
culture is about or what it means to
belong to a particular ethnic group.
In Haiti I never gave a thought to my
ethnicity. But when I went to high
school in the US, I realized for the
first time that I had my own culture
that made me different from the other
students, and I that I belonged
somewhere else.

To leave is to die a little--this

has been my experience in leaving my native land. It is really like dying a little. For example, back in Haiti I was a very active person. I used to be friendly, and I enjoyed helping people around me, especially at school. I was glad to help my friends with math, English, or Chemistry homework, because those were my favorite courses. Also I enjoyed participating in different activities such as volleyball, chorus, and church activities. Everytime the class needed a representative outside the school, I was always there. But when I went to my American high school, everything changed. I had to pay special attention to everything happening around me so that I could learn what was expected of me. I felt like I was paralyzed because I couldn't go and talk to the other students, they wouldn't understand my accent. I felt bad also when I understood a math exercise and couldn't explain it to someone who was having trouble with it. "I wish everybody here could speak French or Creole," I've said many times to myself.

Do I need to separate this into two paragraphs?

How can I make the differences clearer?

This part is long. I think it might bore readers.

It was like dying to feel that you're
not being helpful. I'd lost my smile,
and I felt bad most of the time, always
blaming myself for everything that went
wrong. I was no longer an optimistic

I make myself sound so sad, but it's not really true. I don't want this just to be about me. How else can I conclude?

person, and most of the time I sat in
a corner trying not to disturb anyone.
I lost that feeling of belonging to a
group, and it really made me die a
little to feel lonely all the time even
when surrounded with people.

Before you revise (or in between successive drafts), looking at
your work through a reader's eyes can help you spot its strengths
and weaknesses and identify steps you can take to improve it.

Strategy   Ask a person or a group of people to read and comment
on the strengths and weaknesses of your draft essay. Ask
them, too, to suggest ways the writing might be
improved. Their comments are most likely to be useful if
you ask them to respond to specific questions and to make
concrete suggestions for improvement.

Here are some comments Chris Forbrich and Susan Haeberle
made on Fredza Légér's essay.

Does this essay have a clear and interesting thesis statement or generalization?

Your generalization was interesting, but we thought you might
have started it more effectively. You don't have to say
something like "my generality is," but you should have a clear
statement that indicates what your thesis is. You repeated
the generality in other parts of the essay, but you didn't make
it seem that this was the main idea you were trying to focus

our attention on. Sometimes it seemed that the examples were more important than the generality.

Does this essay provide detailed examples that support or explain the essay's thesis statement or generalization?

We enjoyed your examples about Haiti. They were well thought out. But you should break up the huge paragraph on the last page and expand on the examples. Maybe you could also include examples that remind us of things that we have left behind so that we could understand how your thesis applies to us and not just to your experience.

Are the sentences clear and effective? How might they be improved?

This part of your essay needs work. Some of the sentences go on and on, and there are some phrases that need to sound a bit more like regular English. Some of your sentences don't flow very well. Some of them are hard to follow and understand. We have made some suggestions on the paper and have indicated which sentences are confusing. We also think the people in the Writing Center might give you some help. Please consider making some of the paragraphs shorter and giving them a tighter focus.

Are there any places the grammar and spelling might be improved?

There are a lot of spelling errors (use a dictionary or spell checker). There are also some comma splices. You use a lot of contractions, so the essay seems a bit too informal.

Editing and Final Revision

After you have carefully rewritten your essay at least one time and perhaps several, you can focus on editing and final revision. In creating your finished paper, pay special attention to matters such as the style and clarity of sentences and paragraphs as well as correctness in grammar and usage. Before you hand in your final draft, carefully correct any typographical errors along with any mistakes in spelling or expression that remain.

Here is the final version of Fredza Légér's paper, including some revisions that she made during a last reading and editing before she typed the final copy. The comments in the margin have been added to highlight features of the essay.

TO LEAVE IS TO DIE A LITTLE

Title: attracts attention and states theme that is conveyed throughout the essay.

Can you recall a sad period in your life when you had to say goodby to a loved one or leave a safe and familiar place you called home? Have you ever had

Introduction: Presents the subject (separation and loss) and relates it to readers' experiences.

to move from one neighborhood where all your good friends and favorite memories happened to be? As a college student, can you remember what it was like during the first weeks on campus⟨?⟩ You moved from a comfortable place with caring people and
tasty food to a crowded (and possibly
~~dangerous) place~~ *and busy environment* where you had to rely on yourself all the time and were surrounded by unfamiliar faces. Many of us have had such experiences and have come to realize how fortunate we were when we were

Quotation helps highlight thesis statement. Thesis: the generalization is illustrated

surrounded by caring friends and family. That is why people have come up with familiar phrases like, "There's no place like home." Some people even describe and explored in the rest of the essay.

Remainder of paragraph introduces the examples from the writer's experience that illustrates the generalization.

Paragraph presents contrasts.

leaving a familiar place as a kind of dying. What do they mean by that?

The saying "To leave is to die a little" is something you can understand once you suffer a departure ∧of some kind *or loss* in your life. For example, I used to sing the chorus in a French song, "Partir c'est mourir un peu" ("To leave is to die a little"). I did this because I loved to sing and I liked the song. But these words developed a special meaning for me when I had to leave my home and travel to another country.

I was born in the country of Haiti, on an island in the Caribbean, and I spent the first seventeen years of my life living there with my large family and many friends. **Even though I enjoyed my life** ~~The Haitian people are~~ **in Haiti, the political problems the country was facing** ~~very patriotic, and have shown that they~~ **made leaving necessary. When I arrived in the United** ~~are willing to sacrifice their lives to~~ **States, I was at first relieved and excited, yet soon** ~~keep the nation independent. I never~~ **the difficulties of living in an unfamiliar country with a** ~~thought I would feel this kind of~~ **very different culture made me long for home.** ~~patriotism myself until I got away from~~ ~~Haiti and came to the United States in~~ ~~August 1992. everything was so different~~ **Haitians speak French** ~~when I came here.~~ First of all, I had to **or Creole, and I couldn't expect Americans to understand these languages.** deal with the language.√English was always my favorite subject in my Haitian

high school, but practicing it for three

                              is very different from
or four hours a week in a classroom ∨ and

having to speak it every day, wasn't quite
                                    ∧
                      Next
the same thing. There was also the

weather: Haiti is a tropical island where

it is always hot; in the United States it

can get quite cold and even snowy. There

were many other changes in my life, too.
                              I
As excited as a was about having a brand
              ∧
new life, I still began to miss my native

land badly. I even surprised myself by

feeling patriotic.

Theme echoed   It is hard sometimes to tell how
again.
                    important someone or something is to you

                    if you have not been separated from it or

                    from him or her at least once. Likewise,
                    people
Thesis   one may never take the time to analyze
(generalization)   their own   to understand
extended and   what his or her culture is or what it
refined.   makes them part of a specific group.
                    means to belong somewhere. For example,
          in Haiti, because I belonged to the majority group,   t.
                    I never gave my ethnicity a though ∧ when I
                    ∧   started living in a different society and
                    lived in Haiti. But when I ∨ began

Introduces next attending my American high school, I
set of examples
that illustrate realized that I had my own culture that
the extended
thesis.   made me different from the other

                    students.

Paragraph offers contrasting examples.

Back in Haiti, I used to be an active and social person. I really enjoyed being with my friends, and I liked to help them with their math, English, or chemistry homework because those were my favorite subjects. I played volleyball and participated in chorus and church activities for little kids. I was always ready to listen and I loved to talk. When I started attending high school in the U.S., the friendly and outgoing part of me died. I had to pay attention to every tiny event happening around me so that I would understand what was going on. I had to watch all the other students carefully so I would know how to behave myself. I felt like I was paralyzed because I could no longer talk to my friends to make them feel better. I got really upset when I understood a math homework assignment, yet could not manage to explain it to another student who was having trouble. "I wish everyone could speak French or Creole," I said to myself many times, but of course that was impossible because I had left that part of myself behind. I worried so much that

Transition between contrasting examples echoes the thesis.

I lost my smile without even being aware
of my loss at first. My optimism was
dead, and I used to sit in a corner
trying not to disturb the other kids.

Thesis restated as a way of introducing examples that draw on readers' experience.

"To leave is to die a little"--
however, one does not necessarily have to
travel far or become an immigrant to have
this experience. Loss can take many other
forms. People lose a trusted friend or a
close relative. No matter how often death
occurs around us, we never get used to
the way it separates us forever from
people we love. Their passing causes our
spirits to die a little, as well. Divorce
not only separates two parents but also
separates parents from children. The loss
of closeness between a parent and a child
can be like a death for both, especially
for the child.

Further supporting examples.

Losing a job can be a kind of
death, too. We share many hours of the
day with our fellow workers and often
come to trust them and rely on them. Even
when we change jobs for higher pay or
better prospects, we often destroy
important relationships and leave part of
ourselves behind. When a plant closes or

a company lets thousands of workers go, the loss is even greater. Not only does a part of each person die but also part of the community. We can recover from these losses and separations, of course, yet even in recovering, we know that each one is a little death.

"Partir c'est mourir un peu."

Closing echoes the thesis and sums up the overall theme while stating its significance for readers.

Perhaps this line from the song can help you understand the sadness you feel when you leave someone or something you love. New relationships can grow, and you can feel happy again, but you will always miss what you left behind.

1

Illustrating Ideas by Use of *Example*

The use of examples to illustrate an idea under discussion is the most common, and frequently the most efficient, pattern of exposition. It is a method we use almost instinctively; for instance, instead of talking in generalities about the qualities of a good city manager, we cite Harry Hibbons as an example. We may go further and illustrate Harry's virtues by a specific account of his handling of a crucial situation during the last power shortage or hurricane. In this way we put our abstract ideas into concrete form—a process that is always an aid to clarity. (As a matter of fact, with the "for instance" in this very paragraph, examples are employed to illustrate even the *use* of example.)

Lack of clear illustrations may leave readers with only a hazy conception of the points the writer has tried to make. Even worse, readers may try to supply examples from their own knowledge or experience, and these might do the job poorly or even lead them to an impression different from that intended by the author. Since writers are the ones trying to communicate, clarity is primarily their responsibility.

Not only do good examples put into clear form what otherwise might remain vague and abstract, but the writing also becomes more interesting, with a better chance of holding the reader's attention. With something specific to be visualized, a statement also becomes more convincing—but convincing within certain limitations. If we use the Volvo as an example of Swedish workmanship, the reader is probably aware that this car may not be entirely typical. Although isolated examples will not hold up well in logical argument, for ordinary purposes of explanation the Volvo example could make its point convincingly enough. In supporting an argument, however, we need either to choose an example that is clearly typical or to present several examples to show we have represented the situation fairly.

As in the selection and use of all materials for composition, of course, successful writers select and use examples cautiously, always keeping in mind the nature of their reader-audience and their own specific purpose for communicating. To be effective, each example must be pertinent, respecting the chief qualities of the generality it illustrates. Its function as an example must be either instantly obvious to the readers or fully enough developed so that they learn exactly what it illustrates, and how. Sometimes, however, illustration may be provided best by something other than a real-life example—a fictional anecdote, an analogy, or perhaps a parable that demonstrates the general idea. Here even greater care is needed to be sure these examples are both precise and clear.

Illustration is sometimes used alone as the basic means of development, but it also frequently assists other basic techniques, such as comparison and contrast. In either of its functions, authors may find their purpose best served by one well-developed example, possibly with full background information and descriptive details. But sometimes citing several shorter examples is best, particularly if the authors are attempting to show a trend or a prevalence. In more difficult explanations, of course, a careful combination of the two techniques—using both one well-developed example and several shorter examples—may be worth the extra time and effort required.

Whichever method is used, the writers are following at least one sound principle of writing: they are trying to make the general more specific, the abstract more concrete.

Sample Paragraph (Annotated)

The topic sentence—what the paragraph is about. Also the *generality* in need of specific examples.

Valley City and its suburbs have become so congested that people have begun moving to small towns two or more hours' drive away from the city center. In turn, these rapidly growing towns have begun experiencing growing pains and some strange contrasts. For instance, Palmville used to be a rural town with a dozen farms

Developed example.

inside the city limits and its own Department of Agriculture. Gradually the farms were sold and turned into tracts of one-family homes, shopping malls, and movie theaters. Now the head of the Department of Agriculture is responsible for two new pools, three golf courses (one under construction), and a physical fitness and nature trail— along with the three remaining farms.

Minor examples.

The McKetchie Family still operates its fresh fruit, vegetable, and egg stand on Route 20, only now the stand has a pizza restaurant on one side and the parking lot for the Palmville Mall on the other two sides. School enrollment has quadrupled over the past five years, and the Palmville Senior High (built in 1978) has temporary classrooms in trailers on the lawn in front of the main building.

Some *undeveloped examples* to show prevalence.

An old feed store, Abando's Groceteria, and Isaakson's Pharmacy are all that remain of the old downtown except for the City Hall.

Concluding example.

Figurative language. The simile emphasizes the "growing pains and strange contrasts" mentioned in the topic sentence.

The elegant Victorian City Hall now has a towering steel and glass Civic Center on one side and the sprawling new headquarters for the Nedco Corporation on the other side. The beautiful old building looks as out of place as a person who dressed for a formal dinner party and arrived to find a barbecue in progress around the backyard pool.

Sample Paragraph (Example)

Something strange is happening to our weather. And it didn't just begin last summer. During the past decade, the United States has seen three of the coldest winters and four of the warmest average years ever recorded, a string of weather extremes that would occur by chance less than once in 1000 years. Elsewhere, weather has also run to extremes—with the Soviet Union and India experiencing their highest temperatures. Last winter, snow fell on the gondolas of Venice, the usually sunny beaches of the French Riviera, arid South Africa and even subtropical Brazil.

It's Always Awful

Lee Raspet

No matter how beautiful the day is, how good I feel, or how well my life is going, I always seem to run into someone who wants to show me the thundercloud about to spread over the clear blue sky or the accident that just might happen. I am sure that not all these people are congenitally mean-spirited or dyspeptic (my grandfather's favorite word). As I have thought over their behavior, I have decided that their outlook is a matter of perception and position. They always look for trouble and put themselves in its way.

The weather always seems to draw out the pessimistic observer. One day last summer I was talking with a customer at the pharmacy where I work when I mentioned how beautiful it was outside. Without hesitation, the man let me know that it was going to rain the next day. He did not stop there, however, but went on to expand on his prediction by talking about a torrential downpour that might cause flash flooding and was sure to leave the air hot, humid, and unbearable. Having gotten into the topic, he offered me an advance forecast for winter—a prediction of extreme cold along with several feet of snow on the ground all winter long. He could not see the beautiful day outside because his attention was focused on all the terrible things that *might* happen.

Several weeks later I was out hiking when, after a brief shower, I witnessed one of the most beautiful rainbows I have ever seen. While I was looking up, I wandered into a group of other hikers complaining about how muddy the ground had become with the rain. They were staring at their boots and missing the gorgeous scene overhead. I felt it was my civic duty to point out what they were missing, but when I was done, they stared at me in disgust and went back to looking down at the ground. They could look in either of two directions, and they chose discomfort rather than beauty.

Some people not only look for trouble but also get right in its way, taking friends and family with them. One of my neighbors believes that life and everyone in it are on a mission to rob him. Last year he had three herniated discs removed from his back and two from his neck. He certainly had enough trouble already, but he managed to create more. Right after a heavy snow storm, I asked him if he needed help shoveling his driveway, but he refused my offer with a look that said he was sure I was just trying to get money from him. He let the eight inches of snow lie on his driveway until the next morning when it was thick and heavy with the rain that fell overnight. Neither he nor his spouse could get to work, and they both lost a day's pay, certainly more than it would have cost to hire someone to shovel the driveway. When three of us from the neighborhood finally persuaded him to let us shovel his driveway, he was surprised when we told him we did not expect money for the work. He was looking out for the other people's greed; we were looking to help someone in need.

ANDY ROONEY

ANDREW A. ROONEY was born in 1920 in Albany, New York. Drafted into the army while still a student at Colgate University, he served in the European theater of operations as a *Stars and Stripes* reporter. After the war Rooney began what has been a prolific and illustrious career as a writer-producer for various television networks—chiefly for CBS—and has won numerous awards, including the Writers Guild Award for Best Script of the Year (six times—more than any other writer in the history of the medium) and three National Academy Emmy awards. In 1965 Rooney wrote the script for the first Telstar transatlantic satellite broadcast, which was carried by all three networks and translated into eleven other languages. As well as being the author of seven books, Rooney has contributed to *Esquire, Harper's, Playboy, Saturday Review*, and several other magazines. He is probably most familiar for his regular appearances as a commentator on the television program "60 Minutes." Rooney also writes a syndicated column, which appears in more than 250 newspapers, and has lectured on documentary writing at various universities. His most recent books are *A Few Minutes with Andy Rooney* (1981), *And More by Andy Rooney* (1982), *Pieces of My Mind* (1984), *Word for Word* (1986), and *Not That You Asked . . .* (1989). He now lives in Rowayton, Connecticut.

In and of Ourselves We Trust

"In and of Ourselves We Trust" was one of Rooney's syndicated columns. Rooney's piece uses one simple example to illustrate a generality. He draws from it a far-reaching set of conclusions: that we have a "contract" with each other to stop for red lights—and further, that our whole system of trust depends on everyone doing the right thing.

Last night I was driving from Harrisburg to Lewisburg, Pa., a dis-   1
tance of about 80 miles. It was late, I was late, and if anyone asked
me how fast I was driving, I'd have to plead the Fifth Amendment
to avoid self-incrimination.

At one point along an open highway, I came to a crossroads   2
with a traffic light. I was alone on the road by now, but as I
approached the light, it turned red, and I braked to a halt. I looked
left, right, and behind me. Nothing. Not a car, no suggestion of headlights, but there I sat, waiting for the light to change, the only human
being, for at least a mile in any direction.

I started wondering why I refused to run the light. I was not   3
afraid of being arrested, because there was obviously no cop anywhere around and there certainly would have been no danger in
going through it.

Much later that night, after I'd met with a group in Lewisburg   4
and had climbed into bed near midnight, the question of why I'd
stopped for that light came back to me. I think I stopped because it's
part of a contract we all have with each other. It's not only the law,
but it's an agreement we have, and we trust each other to honor it:
We don't go through red lights. Like most of us, I'm more apt to be
restrained from doing something bad by the social convention that
disapproves of it than by any law against it.

It's amazing that we ever trust each other to do the right thing,   5
isn't it? And we do, too. Trust is our first inclination. We have to
make a deliberate decision to mistrust someone or to be suspicious
or skeptical.

It's a darn good thing, too, because the whole structure of our   6
society depends on mutual trust, not distrust. This whole thing we
have going for us would fall apart if we didn't trust each other most
of the time. In Italy they have an awful time getting any money for
the government because many people just plain don't pay their
income tax. Here, the Internal Revenue Service makes some gestures
toward enforcing the law, but mostly they just have to trust that
we'll pay what we owe. There has often been talk of a tax revolt in
this country, most recently among unemployed auto workers in
Michigan, and our government pretty much admits that if there
were a widespread tax revolt here, they wouldn't be able to do anything about it.

We do what we say we'll do. We show up when we say we'll   7
show up.

I was so proud of myself for stopping for that red light. And 8
inasmuch as no one would ever have known what a good person
I was on the road from Harrisburg to Lewisburg, I had to tell
someone.

Meanings and Values

1a. Explain the concept of a "contract we all have with each other"
(par. 4).

b. How is the "agreement" achieved (par. 4)?

2. Why do you suppose exceeding the speed limit (par. 1) would not
also be included in the "contract"? Or is there some other reason for
Rooney's apparent inconsistency?

3. Explain the significance of the title of this selection.

Expository Techniques

1a. What generality is exemplified by the solution to Rooney's red-light
enigma?

b. In this instance, what does the generality have to do with the central
theme? (See "Guide to Terms": *Unity.*)

c. Is there any disadvantage in this generality's location? Explain.

d. Does the example prove anything?

e. Do you think it is a good example of what it illustrates? Is it typical?

2. What other uses of example do you find in the selection?

3. How effective do you consider Rooney's closing? Why? (Guide:
Closings.)

4. What, if anything, do the brief examples in paragraph 6 add to this
piece? (Guide: *Evaluation.*)

Diction and Vocabulary

1. Does it seem to you that the diction and vocabulary levels of this selection are appropriate for the purpose intended? Why, or why not?
(Guide: *Diction.*)

2. Could this be classified as a formal essay? Why, or why not? (Guide:
Essay.)

Suggestions for Writing and Discussion

Choose one of the following passages from this selection to develop for further discussion. You may agree or disagree, or both, but organize your ideas for most effective presentation:

1. "[Most of us are] more apt to be restrained from doing something bad by the social convention that disapproves of it than by any law against it."

2. "Trust is our first inclination."

3. ". . . the whole social structure of our society depends on mutual trust, not distrust."

(NOTE: Suggestions for topics requiring development by use of EXAMPLE are on page 85, at the end of this section.)

ELLEN GOODMAN

ELLEN GOODMAN was born in 1941 in Boston, where she now lives. She was graduated cum laude from Radcliffe College and then spent a year at Harvard on a Nieman Fellowship. Goodman has been with the *Boston Globe* as a reporter since 1967 and, since 1974, has been a full-time columnist. Her "At Large" columns are now published in over two hundred newspapers across the country, and her commentaries have been broadcast on both television and radio. Goodman's work has also appeared in *McCall's*, the *Village Voice*, *Family Circle*, *Harper's Bazaar*, and many other publications. She has been the recipient of various journalistic honors and awards, including the 1980 Pulitizer Prize for distinguished commentary. Her columns have been collected in *Close to Home* (1979), *Turning Points* (1979), *At Large* (1981), *Keeping in Touch* (1986), *Making Sense* (1990), and *Value Judgments* (1993).

Children on Their Own

In this essay, first published as a newspaper column, Goodman draws examples from the lives of children depicted in popular movies and books and uses them to reflect on the lives of real children. In doing this, she offers insights into the fears and challenges that all children must face, as well as some that are the characteristic and troublesome products of our time.

There is a scene in *Home Alone* when Kevin McCallister stands before the mirror in his parents' bathroom, slaps some after-shave lotion on his tender eight-year-old skin, and lets out a howl. It comes just in time. One bracing shock of reality to remind us that Kevin is not quite yet the man of the house.

For the rest of this delicious movie, the son of the suburbs, the youngest child accidentally left behind in his family's frantic vacation exit, is nothing if not self-sufficient. He protects himself. He protects his home. And in the process, it seemed to this contented viewer that Kevin McCallister protects parents from the worst of their anxieties.

Home Alone is the surprise hit of this season. The smart money   3
in Hollywood never figured it would reach the top. They didn't count on the longing for a family movie in which the hero is a delight, the criminals are comic, and you don't have to put your hands over the kids' eyes.

But it's also a hit because *Home Alone* taps the most primal plot: 4
the fears that kids have about being abandoned and the fantasies they have of being on their own.

Kevin is the latest in a long line of deserted children. Before the   5
McCallisters took off for Paris without their youngest son, an entire anthology of children had learned to survive without parents: The lost boys of *Peter Pan* who had fallen from their prams never to be found again. The children of Disney, Dumbo and Bambi, left motherless in the world.

For a generation, Pippi Longstocking personified a child's fan-   6
tasy of independence. Even Dorothy, mysteriously orphaned into her Aunt Em's home and then wrenched away by another natural disaster, fended for herself in Oz.

There was never any need for a psychiatrist to analyze this   7
theme. At some point, children become aware of their dependency on adults who aren't always reliable. Parents can be anything from absentminded to abusive, from benignly neglectful to untrustwor-thy. Even the best of us can be busy or distracted. Even the most secure childhood can be shattered by death or divorce. This recogni-tion stirs a child's longing to be strong.

The theme has taken a harder twist lately as we fear that family   8
life is coming loose at the seams. Steven Spielberg's fractured fami-lies had parents too distracted to see even an E.T. in their midst. In *Honey, I Shrunk the Kids*, a harried father absentmindedly put his children in lethal danger in their own back yard. There was obvious symbolism in the dialogue of the quarter-inch children lost in the suburban grass: "We're too small. He can't hear us."

But *Home Alone* does more than appeal to the child's need to   9
believe in his survival. Nowadays parents need to believe it as well. And that's what has changed.

At the risk of turning comedy into sociology, Kevin is a poster   10
child for worries about "self-care," that euphemism for no care. Well

over two million kids between five and thirteen are "home alone" every weekday afternoon.

Kevin's parents left on vacation, but most have gone off to 11 work. Kevin's neighborhood was emptied for Christmas, but usually it's empty by 9 a.m. Today's working parents, anxious in their absenteeism, set up hot lines and rules . . . over the phone. We talk about childhood "resilience" and the value of their "independence"—and keep our fingers crossed.

The movie's upper-class family setting, a houseful of expensive 12 electronic gadgets, stands in as a visual accusation often launched against working families: that we are neglecting children for luxuries. Kevin's mother is not the only one who asks herself in crisis, "What kind of a mother am I?"

Onto this sociological backdrop steps an eight-year-old boy saying, "Hey, I'm not afraid anymore." Kevin on the big screen conquering his fear of the furnace. Kevin taking care of himself. Kevin protecting himself, his home and hearth from criminals who are less threatening than comic.

If *Home Alone* is every child's fantasy, it is also every parent's 14 fantasy. It's all there: the universal and anxious wish that, in this uncertain time, the kids will be all right. And the hope for a happy ending.

Meanings and Values

1. What generality or generalities does Goodman believe the movie *Home Alone* illustrates?

2. In what ways do the other movies and stories used by Goodman illustrate the same generality or modify and extend it?

3. What new phenomenon does the essay explore in paragraphs 10–14? Is the example from *Home Alone* an effective illustration of this phenomenon? Why, or why not? (See "Guide to Terms": *Evaluation*.)

Expository Techniques

1. Which of the examples Goodman presents are developed in detail? Which are relatively brief?

2. Would the essay have been more effective if more of the essays had been developed in detail? Be ready to explain your response. (Guide: *Evaluation*.)

3. What strategy does Goodman use to conclude the essay? (Guide: *Closings.*)

Diction and Vocabulary

1. Discuss how the writer varies sentence length to create emphasis in the following paragraphs: 1, 5, 9, and 13. (Guide: *Emphasis.*)

2. Identify the parallel sentence structures in paragraphs 2, 5, 13, and 14, and tell what the parallel structures help the writer accomplish. (Guide: *Parallel Structure, Syntax.*)

3. If you do not know the meaning of some of the following words, look them up in a dictionary: bracing (par. 1); primal (4); personified (6); benignly (7).

Suggestions for Writing and Discussion

1. Discuss whether Goodman's warnings about the way we are raising our children are justified or not. Draw on your own experiences and those of other people you know.

2. What kind of adults might children grow up to be if they are raised under the kind of conditions Goodman describes?

3. As a society, should we develop new ways of raising and nurturing children? What steps might we take?

(NOTE: Suggestions for topics requiring development by use of EXAMPLE are on page 85, at the end of this section.)

ALAN BUCZYNSKI

ALAN BUCZYNSKI is a construction worker and a writer who lives in the Detroit area.

Iron Bonding

Newspaper columns, magazine articles, and everyday conversations are often filled with generalities about the different ways men and women behave. This essay looks at the emotional life of men, offering a working person's perspective rather than that of the intellectuals and professional people often associated with the "men's movement." The essay first appeared in *The New York Times Magazine*.

"I just don't get it." We were up on the iron, about 120 feet, waiting for the gang below to swing up another beam. Sweat from under Ron's hard hat dripped on the beam we were sitting on and evaporated immediately, like water thrown on a sauna stove. We were talking about the "men's movement" and "wildman weekends." 1

"I mean," he continued, "if they want to get dirty and sweat and cuss and pound on things, why don't they just get *real* jobs and get paid for it?" Below, the crane growled, the next piece lifting skyward. 2

I replied: "Nah, Ron, that isn't the point. They don't want to sweat every day, just sometimes." 3

He said: "Man, if you only sweat when you want to, I don't call that real sweatin'." 4

Although my degree is in English, I am an ironworker by trade; my girlfriend, Patti, is a graduate student in English literature. Like a tennis ball volleyed by two players with distinctly different styles, 5

I am bounced between blue-collar maulers and precise academi-
cians. My conversations range from fishing to Foucault, derricks to
deconstruction. There is very little overlap, but when it does occur it
is generally the academics who are curious about the working life.

Patti and I were at a dinner party. The question of communica-   6
tion between men had arisen. Becky, the host, is a persistent interrogator: "What do you and Ron talk about?"

I said, "Well, we talk about work, drinking, ah, women."   7

Becky asked, "Do you guys ever say, 'I love you' to each other?"   8
This smelled mightily of Robert Bly and the men's movement.

I replied: "Certainly. All the time."   9

I am still dissatisfied with this answer. Not because it was a lie,   10
but because it was perceived as one.

The notion prevails that men's emotional communication skills   11
are less advanced than that of chimpanzees, that we can no more
communicate with one another than can earthworms.

Ironworkers as a group may well validate this theory. We are   12
not a very articulate bunch. Most of us have only a basic education.
Construction sites are extremely noisy, and much of our communication takes place via hand signals. There is little premium placed on
words that don't stem from our own jargon. Conversations can be
blunt.

Bly's approach, of adapting a fable for instruction, may instinc- 13
tively mimic the way men communicate. Ironworkers are otherwise
very direct, yet when emotional issues arise we speak to one another
in allegory and parable. One of my co-workers, Cliff, is a good storyteller, with an understated delivery: "The old man got home one
night, drunk, real messed up and got to roughhousing with the cat.
Old Smoke, well she laid into him, scratched him good. Out comes
the shotgun. The old man loads up, chases Smoke into the front yard
and blam! Off goes the gun. My Mom and my sisters and me we're
all screamin'. Smoke comes walkin' in the side door. Seems the old
man blew away the wrong cat, the neighbor's Siamese. Red lights
were flashin' against the house, fur was splattered all over the lawn,
the cops cuffed my old man and he's hollerin' and man, I'll tell you,
I was cryin'."

Now, we didn't all get up from our beers and go over and hug   14
him. This was a story, not therapy. Cliff is amiable, but tough, more
inclined to solving any perceived injustices with his fists than verbal
banter, but I don't need to see him cry to know that he can. He has

before, and he can tell a story about it without shame, without any disclaimers about being "just a kid," and that's enough for me.

Ron and I have worked together for nine years and are as close   15
as 29 is to 30. We have worked through heat and cold and seen each other injured in the stupidest of accidents. One February we were working inside a plant, erecting steel with a little crane; it was near the end of the day, and I was tired. I hooked onto a piece and, while still holding the load cable, signaled the operator "up." My thumb was promptly sucked into the sheave of the crane. I screamed, and the operator came down on the load, releasing my thumb. It hurt. A lot. Water started leaking from my eyes. The gang gathered around while Ron tugged gently at my work glove, everyone curious whether my thumb would come off with the glove or stay on my hand.

"O.K., man, relax, just relax," Ron said. "See if you can move it."   16
Ron held my hand. The thumb had a neat crease right down the center, lengthwise. All the capillaries on one side had burst and were turning remarkable colors. My new thumbnail was on back order and would arrive in about five months. I wiggled the thumb, an eighth of an inch, a quarter, a half.

"You're O.K., man, it's still yours and it ain't broke. Let's go   17
back to work."

Afterwards, in the bar, while I wrapped my hand around a cold   18
beer to keep the swelling and pain down, Ron hoisted his bottle in a toast: "That," he said, "was the best scream I ever heard, real authentic, like you were in actual pain, like you were really *scared*."

If this wasn't exactly Wind in His Hair howling eternal friend-   19
ship for Dances With Wolves, I still understood what Ron was saying. It's more like a 7-year-old boy putting a frog down the back of a little girl's dress because he has a crush on her. It's a backward way of showing affection, of saying "I love you," but it's the only way we know. We should have outgrown it, and hordes of men are now paying thousands of dollars to sweat and stink and pound and grieve together to try and do just that. Maybe it works, maybe it doesn't. But no matter how cryptic, how Byzantine, how weird and weary the way it travels, the message still manages to get through.

Meanings and Values

1. According to the writer, how do men communicate with each other on emotional matters?

2. In what ways are Buczynski and his fellow ironworkers similar in outlook and behavior to Robert Bly and others associated with the men's movement? In what ways are they different?

3. Buczynski concludes that "no matter how cryptic, how Byzantine, how weird and weary the way it travels, the message still manages to get through" (par. 19). Does he manage to convince you that men are able to communicate effectively on an emotional level? Why, or why not?

Expository Techniques

1. Identify those places in the essay where the generality being illustrated is stated more or less directly.

2. Would this essay be more effective if the opening paragraphs presented the generality in a thesis statement? (See "Guide to Terms": *Thesis*.)

3. What strategy does the writer employ in paragraphs 1–10 to open the essay? (Guide: *Introductions*.)

4. Identify the main examples Buczynski uses in this essay and discuss their effectiveness. (Guide: *Evaluation*.)

Diction and Vocabulary

1. Discuss how the simile in the third sentence of the opening paragraph, "like water thrown on a sauna stove," heightens the contrast between iron workers and people involved in the "men's movement." (Guide: *Figures of Speech*.)

2. Explain how the word choice in paragraph 5 emphasizes contrasts between academics and blue-collar workers. (Guide: *Diction, Emphasis*.)

3. How does the writer use sentence structure and word choice in paragraphs 15–17 to convey both the pain and drama of the incident as well as the participants' emotional reactions (or lack of them)?

4. If you do not know the meaning of any of the following words, look them up in a dictionary: maulers (par. 5); interrogator (6); articulate (12); allegory, parable (13); disclaimers (14).

Suggestions for Writing and Discussion

1. Discuss the role of stories, especially allegories or parables, in communicating emotion within your family or within some other community to which you belong.

2. In what ways other than stories do people share feelings and values? Do most people rely on one strategy to the exclusion of other ways of communicating?

3. To what extent are the communication strategies Buczynski describes characteristic of a particular group rather than of men in general?

(NOTE: Suggestions for topics requiring development by use of EXAMPLE are on page 85, at the end of this section.)

WILLIAM F. BUCKLEY, JR.

WILLIAM F. BUCKLEY, JR., was born in 1925 in New York, where he
now lives with his wife and son. He graduated from Yale University and holds honorary degrees from a number of universities,
including Seton Hall, Syracuse University, Notre Dame, and
Lafayette College. He was editor in chief of *National Review* from
1955 to 1990. In addition, he has been a syndicated columnist since
1962, and host of public television's "Firing Line" since 1966. Generally considered one of the most articulate conservative writers,
Buckley has published in various general circulation magazines
and has received numerous honors and awards. He lectures
widely and is the author of many novels and nonfiction books,
among them *God and Man at Yale: The Superstitions of "Academic
Freedom"* (1951), *Saving the Queen* (1976), *Stained Glass* (1978), *Who's
on First* (1980), *Marco Polo, If You Can* (1982) *Atlantic High* (1982)
Overdrive: A Personal Documentary (1983), *The Story of Henri Tod*
(1984), *The Tall Ships* (1986), *See You Later, Alligator* (1985), *High Jinx*
(1986), *Racing Through Paradise: A Pacific Passage* (1987), *Mongoose
R.I.P.* (1988), *On the Firing Line: The Public Life of Our Public Figures*
(1989), and *Tucker's Last Stand* (1990).

Why Don't We Complain?

First published in *Esquire*, "Why Don't We Complain?" is a good
illustration of the grace and wit that characterize most of Buckley's
writing. For students of composition, it can also provide another
demonstration of the use of varied examples—some well developed, others scarcely at all—to make a single generality more specific. And the generality itself, as we can see toward the end, is of
considerably broader significance than it appears at first.

It was the very last coach and the only empty seat on the entire train, 1
so there was no turning back. The problem was to breathe. Outside,

the temperature was below freezing. Inside the railroad car the temperature must have been about 85 degrees. I took off my overcoat, and a few minutes later my jacket, and noticed that the car was flecked with the white shirts of the passengers. I soon found my hand moving to loosen my tie. From one end of the car to the other, as we rattled through Westchester County, we sweated; but we did not moan.

I watched the train conductor appear at the head of the car. 2 "Tickets, all tickets, please!" In a more virile age, I thought, the passengers would seize the conductor and strap him down on a seat over the radiator to share the fate of his patrons. He shuffled down the aisle, picking up tickets, punching commutation cards. *No one addressed a word to him.* He approached my seat, and I drew a deep breath of resolution. "Conductor," I began with a considerable edge to my voice. . . . Instantly the doleful eyes of my seatmate turned tiredly from his newspaper to fix me with a resentful stare: what question could be so important as to justify my sibilant intrusion into his stupor? I was shaken by those eyes. I am incapable of making a discreet fuss, so I mumbled a question about what time were we due in Stamford (I didn't even ask whether it would be before or after dehydration could be expected to set in), got my reply, and went back to my newspaper and to wiping my brow.

The conductor had nonchalantly walked down the gauntlet of 3 eighty sweating American freemen, and not one of them had asked him to explain why the passengers in that car had been consigned to suffer. There is nothing to be done when the temperature *outdoors* is 85 degrees, and indoors the air conditioner has broken down; obviously when that happens there is nothing to do, except perhaps curse the day that one was born. But when the temperature outdoors is below freezing, it takes a positive act of will on somebody's part to set the temperature *indoors* at 85. Somewhere a valve was turned too far, a furnace overstocked, a thermostat maladjusted: something that could easily be remedied by turning off the heat and allowing the great outdoors to come indoors. All this is so obvious. What is not obvious is what has happened to the American people.

It isn't just the commuters, whom we have come to visualize 4 as a supine breed who have got on to the trick of suspending their sensory faculties twice a day while they submit to the creeping dissolution of the railroad industry. It isn't just they who have given up trying to rectify irrational vexations. It is the American people everywhere.

A few weeks ago at a large movie theater I turned to my wife 5 and said, "The picture is out of focus." "Be quiet," she answered. I obeyed. But a few minutes later I raised the point again, with mounting impatience. "It will be all right in a minute," she said apprehensively. (She would rather lose her eyesight than be around when I make one of my infrequent scenes.) I waited. It was *just* out of focus—not glaringly out, but out. My vision is 20–20, and I assume that is the vision, adjusted, of most people in the movie house. So, after hectoring my wife throughout the first reel, I finally prevailed upon her to admit that it *was* off, and very annoying. We then settled down, coming to rest on the presumption that: (a) someone connected with the management of the theater must soon notice the blur and make the correction; or (b) that someone seated near the rear of the house would make the complaint in behalf of those of us up front; or (c) that—any minute now—the entire house would explode into catcalls and foot stamping, calling dramatic attention to the irksome distortion.

What happened was nothing. The movie ended, as it had 6 begun, *just* out of focus, and as we trooped out, we stretched our faces in a variety of contortions to accustom the eye to the shock of normal focus.

I think it is safe to say that everybody suffered on that occasion. 7 And I think it is safe to assume that everyone was expecting someone else to take the initiative in going back to speak to the manager. And it is probably true even that if we had supposed the movie would run right through the blurred image, someone surely would have summoned up the purposive indignation to get up out of his seat and file his complaint.

But notice that no one did. And the reason no one did is because 8 we are all increasingly anxious in America to be unobtrusive, we are reluctant to make our voices heard, hesitant about claiming our rights; we are afraid that our cause is unjust, or that if it is not unjust, that it is ambiguous; or if not even that, that it is too trivial to justify the horrors of a confrontation with Authority; we still sit in an oven or endure a racking headache before undertaking a head-on, I'm-here-to-tell-you complaint. That tendency to passive compliance, to a heedless endurance, is something to keep one's eyes on—in sharp focus.

I myself can occasionally summon the courage to complain, but   9
I cannot, as I have intimated, complain softly. My own instinct is so
strong to let the thing ride, to forget about it—to expect that someone will take the matter up, when the grievance is collective, in my
behalf—that it is only when the provocation is at a very special key,
whose vibrations touch simultaneously a complexus of nerves, aller-
gies, and passions, that I catch fire and find the reserves of courage
and assertiveness to speak up. When that happens, I get quite carried away. My blood gets hot, my brow wet, I become unbearably
and unconscionably sarcastic and bellicose; I am girded for a total
showdown.

Why should that be? Why could not I (or anyone else) on that   10
railroad coach have said simply to the conductor, "Sir"—I take that
back: that sounds sarcastic—"Conductor, would you be good
enough to turn down the heat? I am extremely hot. In fact, I tend to
get hot every time the temperature reaches 85 degr—" Strike that
last sentence. Just end it with the simple statement that you are
extremely hot, and let the conductor infer the cause.

Every New Year's Eve I resolve to do something about the Mil-   11
quetoast in me and vow to speak up, calmly, for my rights, and for
the betterment of our society, on every appropriate occasion. Entering last New Year's Eve, I was fortified in my resolve because that
morning at breakfast I had had to ask the waitress three times for a
glass of milk. She finally brought it—after I had finished my eggs,
which is when I don't want it any more. I did not have the manliness
to order her to take the milk back, but settled instead for a cowardly
sulk, and ostentatiously refused to drink the milk—though I later
paid for it—rather than state plainly to the hostess, as I should have,
why I had not drunk it, and would not pay for it.

So by the time the New Year ushered out the Old, riding in on   12
my morning's indignation and stimulated by the gastric juices of
resolution that flow so faithfully on New Year's Eve, I rendered my
vow. Henceforward I would conquer my shyness, my despicable
disposition to supineness. I would speak out like a man against the
unnecessary annoyances of our time.

Forty-eight hours later, I was standing in line at the ski repair   13
store in Pico Peak, Vermont. All I needed, to get on with my skiing,
was the loan, for one minute, of a small screwdriver, to tighten a
loose binding. Behind the counter in the workshop were two men.
One was industriously engaged in servicing the complicated

requirements of a young lady at the head of the line, and obviously he would be tied up for quite a while. The other—"Jiggs," his work-mate called him—was a middle-aged man, who sat in a chair puffing a pipe, exchanging small talk with his working partner. My pulse began its telltale acceleration. The minutes ticked on. I stared at the idle shopkeeper, hoping to shame him into action, but he was impervious to my telepathic reproof and continued his small talk with his friend, brazenly insensitive to the nervous demands of six good men who were raring to ski.

Suddenly my New Year's Eve resolution struck me. It was now or never. I broke from my place in line and marched to the counter. I was going to control myself. I dug my nails into my palms. My effort was only partially successful: 14

"If you are not too busy," I said icily, "would you mind handing me a screwdriver?"   15

Work stopped and everyone turned his eyes on me, and I experienced that mortification I always feel when I am the center of centripetal shafts of curiosity, resentment, perplexity.   16

But the worst was yet to come. "I am sorry, sir," said Jiggs deferentially, moving the pipe from his mouth. "I am not supposed to move. I have just had a heart attack." That was the signal for a great whirring noise that descended from heaven. We looked, stricken, out the window, and it appeared as though a cyclone had suddenly focused on the snowy courtyard between the shop and the ski lift. Suddenly a gigantic army helicopter materialized, and hovered down to a landing. Two men jumped out of the plane carrying a stretcher, tore into the ski shop, and lifted the shopkeeper onto the stretcher. Jiggs bade his companion good-by, was whisked out the door, into the plane, up to the heavens, down—we learned—to a nearby army hospital. I looked up manfully—into a score of man-eating eyes. I put the experience down as a reversal.   17

As I write this, on an airplane, I have run out of paper and need to reach into my briefcase under my legs for more. I cannot do this until my empty lunch tray is removed from my lap. I arrested the stewardess as she passed empty-handed down the aisle on the way to the kitchen to fetch the lunch trays for the passengers up forward who haven't been served yet. "Would you please take my tray?" "Just a *moment*, sir!" she said, and marched on sternly. Shall I tell her that since she is headed for the kitchen *anyway*, it could not delay the feeding of the other passengers by more than two seconds necessary   18 to stash away my empty tray? Or remind her that not fifteen minutes ago she spoke unctuously into the loudspeaker the words undoubtedly devised by the airline's highly paid public relations counselor: "If there is anything I or Miss French can do for you to make your trip more enjoyable, *please* let us—" I have run out of paper.

I think the observable reluctance of the majority of Americans to   19 assert themselves in minor matters is related to our increased sense of helplessness in an age of technology and centralized political and economic power. For generations, Americans who were too hot, or too cold, got up and did something about it. Now we call the plumber, or the electrician, or the furnace man. The habit of looking after our own needs obviously had something to do with the assertiveness that characterized the American family familiar to readers of American literature. With the technification of life goes our direct responsibility for our material environment, and we are conditioned to adopt a position of helplessness not only as regards the broken air conditioner, but as regards the overheated train. It takes an expert to fix the former, but not the latter; yet these distinctions, as we withdraw into helplessness, tend to fade away.

Our notorious political apathy is a related phenomenon. Every   20 year, whether the Republican or the Democratic Party is in office, more and more power drains away from the individual to feed vast reservoirs in far-off places; and we have less and less say about the shape of events which shape our future. From this alienation of personal power comes the sense of resignation with which we accept the political dispensations of a powerful government whose hold upon us continues to increase.

An editor of a national weekly news magazine told me a few   21 years ago that as few as a dozen letters of protest against an editorial stance of his magazine was enough to convene a plenipotentiary meeting of the board of editors to review policy. "So few people complain, or make their voices heard," he explained to me, "that we assume a dozen letters represent the inarticulated views of thousands of readers." In the past ten years, he said, the volume of mail has noticeably decreased, even though the circulation of his magazine has risen.

When our voices are finally mute, when we have finally suppressed the natural instinct to complain, whether the vexation is   22 trivial or grave, we shall have become automatons, incapable of feeling. When Premier Khrushchev first came to this country late in

1959, he was primed, we are informed, to experience the bitter resentment of the American people against his tyranny, against his persecutions, against the movement which is responsible for the great number of American deaths in Korea, for billions in taxes every year, and for life everlasting on the brink of disaster; but Khrushchev was pleasantly surprised, and reported back to the Russian people that he had been met with overwhelming cordiality (read: apathy), except, to be sure, for "a few fascists who followed me around with their wretched posters, and should be horse-whipped."

I may be crazy, but I say there would have been lots more   23
posters in a society where train temperatures in the dead of winter are not allowed to climb to 85 degrees without complaint.

Meanings and Values

1. By what means, if any, does Buckley's scolding of the American people avoid being disagreeable?

2. Restate completely what you believe to be the meaning of the last sentence of paragraph 8.

3. Why do you think the author said to "strike that last sentence" of the quoted matter in paragraph 10?

4. Explain the connection between anti-Khrushchev posters and complaining about the heat in a train (par. 23).

5a. State in your own words the central theme of this selection. (See "Guide to Terms": *Unity*.)

 b. Does it seem to you that this is the best way to have developed the theme? If not, what might have been a better way?

Expository Techniques

1a. Which of the standard methods of introduction does the first paragraph demonstrate? (Guide: *Introductions*.)

 b. How successful is its use?

2a. What generality do Buckley's examples illustrate? (You may use his words or your own.)

 b. In what way, if at all, does this generality differ from his central theme?

 c. In this respect, how does the writing differ from most?

3. Why do you think the Khrushchev example is kept until last? (Guide: *Emphasis*.)

4. What seems to be the purpose, or purposes, of paragraphs 4 and 12?

5. Assuming that this piece is typical of Buckley's writing, what aspects of his style or tone will probably make his writing identifiable when you next encounter it? (Guide: *Style/Tone*.)

Diction and Vocabulary

1. Explain the meaning (in par. 22) of Khrushchev's being "met with overwhelming cordiality (read: apathy)."

2. Explain the allusion to Milquetoast in paragraph 11. (Guide: *Figures of Speech*.)

3a. Were you annoyed by Buckley's liberal use of "dictionary-type" words? To what extent? Why were you annoyed?

  b. Cite any such words that were used without good reason.

  c. To what extent is this use a matter of style?

4. Use a dictionary as needed to understand the meanings of the following words: virile, doleful, sibilant, discreet (par. 2); gauntlet, consigned (3); supine, faculties, dissolution, rectify (4); hectoring (5); purposive (7); unobtrusive, ambiguous (8); provocation, complexus, unconscionably, bellicose, girded (9); infer (10); ostentatiously (11); impervious, reproof (13); centripetal (16); deferentially (17); unctuously (18); technification (19); apathy, phenomenon, dispensations (20); stance, plenipotentiary, inarticulated (21); automatons (22).

Suggestions for Writing and Discussion

1. Discuss, if you can, the idea that readers of American literature are familiar with the "assertiveness that characterized the American family" (par. 19).

2. An apathy such as Buckley describes, if permitted to develop to its extreme, could have disastrous results. Explore what some of these might be.

3. Buckley is generally thought to be one of the most effective spokespeople for the conservative right. Explain how you could have guessed his political views by what he says in this largely nonpolitical essay. Be specific.

4. Does the response of the American public to recent social and political issues indicate an increase or decrease in apathy? Give examples. If you are familiar with some other country, Canada or Mexico, for instance, indicate whether its citizens are as apathetic as the people Buckley describes.

(NOTE: Suggestions for topics requiring development by use of EXAMPLE are on page 85, at the end of this section.)

BARBARA EHRENREICH

BARBARA EHRENREICH received a B.A. from Reed College and a
Ph.D. from Rockefeller University in biology. She has been active
in the women's movement and other movements for social change
for a number of years and has taught women's issues at several
universities, including New York University and the State University of New York—Old Westbury. She is a Fellow of the Institute
for Policy Studies in Washington, D.C., and is active in the Democratic Socialists of America. A prolific author, Ehrenreich is a regular columnist for *Ms.* and *Mother Jones* and has published articles
in a wide range of magazines, among them *Esquire,* the *Atlantic,*
Vogue, New Republic, the *Wall Street Journal, TV Guide, The New York
Times Magazine, Social Policy,* and *The Nation.* Her books include *For
Her Own Good: 150 Years of the Experts' Advice to Women* (with
Deirdre English) (1978); *The Hearts of Men: American Dreams and the
Flight from Commitment* (1983); *Remaking Love: The Feminization of
Sex* (with Elizabeth Hess and Gloria Jacobs) (1986); *Fear of Falling:
The Inner Life of the Middle Class* (1989); and *The Worst Years of Our
Lives: Irreverent Notes from a Decade of Greed* (1990).

What I've Learned from Men

The theme and strategies of this essay (first published in *Ms.*) are
similar in some striking ways to those of Buckley's piece. Nonetheless, the essays' perspectives are clearly different, reflecting the
social and political outlooks of their authors. Yet Ehrenreich, like
Buckley, provides numerous illustrations of the skillful use of
examples in support of a generality. In addition, she demonstrates
the role of examples in definition as she contrasts "lady" with
"woman."

For many years I believed that women had only one thing to learn   1
from men: how to get the attention of a waiter by some means short
of kicking over the table and shrieking. Never in my life have I
gotten the attention of a waiter, unless it was an off-duty waiter
whose car I'd accidentally scraped in a parking lot somewhere.
Men, however, can summon a maître d' just by thinking the word
"coffee," and this is a power women would be well advised to
study. What else would we possibly want to learn from them?
How to interrupt someone in mid-sentence as if you were performing an act of conversational euthanasia? How to drop a pair of
socks three feet from an open hamper and keep right on walking? How to make those weird guttural gargling sounds in the
bathroom?

But now, at mid-life, I am willing to admit that there are some   2
real and useful things to learn from men. Not from all men—in fact,
we may have the most to learn from some of the men we like the
least. This realization does not mean that my feminist principles
have gone soft with age: what I think women could learn from men
is how to get *tough*. After more than a decade of consciousness-
raising, assertiveness training, and hand-to-hand combat in the
battle of the sexes, we're still too ladylike. Let me try that again—
we're just too *damn* ladylike.

Here is an example from my own experience, a story that I   3
blush to recount. A few years ago, at an international conference
held in an exotic and luxurious setting, a prestigious professor
invited me to his room for what he said would be an intellectual discussion on matters of theoretical importance. So far, so good. I
showed up promptly. But only minutes into the conversation—held
in all-too-adjacent chairs—it emerged that he was interested in
something more substantial than a meeting of minds. I was disgusted, but not enough to overcome 30-odd years of programming
in ladylikeness. Every time his comments took a lecherous turn, I
chattered distractingly; every time his hand found its way to my
knee, I returned it as if it were something he had misplaced. This
went on for an unconscionable period (as much as 20 minutes); then
there was a minor scuffle, a dash for the door, and I was out—with
nothing violated but my self-esteem. I, a full-grown feminist, conversant with such matters as rape crisis counseling and sexual
harassment at the workplace, had behaved like a ninny—or, as I
now understand it, like a lady.

The essence of ladylikeness is a persistent servility masked as   4
"niceness." For example, we (women) tend to assume that it is our
responsibility to keep everything "nice" even when the person we
are with is rude, aggressive, or emotionally AWOL. (In the above
example, I was so busy taking responsibility for preserving the
veneer of "niceness" that I almost forgot to take responsibility for
myself.) In conversations with men, we do almost all the work: soci-
ologists have observed that in male-female social interactions it's the
woman who throws out leading questions and verbal encourage-
ments ("So how did you *feel* about that?" and so on) while the man,
typically, says "Hmmmm." Wherever we go, we're perpetually
smiling—the on-cue smile, like the now-outmoded curtsy, being one
of our culture's little rituals of submission. We're trained to feel
embarrassed if we're praised, but if we see a criticism coming at us
from miles down the road, we rush to acknowledge it. And when
we're feeling aggressive or angry or resentful, we just tighten up our
smiles or turn them into rueful little moues. In short, we spend a
great deal of time acting like wimps.

For contrast, think of the macho stars we love to watch. Think,   5
for example, of Mel Gibson facing down punk marauders in "The
Road Warrior" . . . John Travolta swaggering his way through the
early scenes of "Saturday Night Fever" . . . or Marlon Brando shrug-
ging off the local law in "The Wild One." Would they simper their
way through tight spots? Chatter aimlessly to keep the conversation
going? Get all clutched up whenever they think they might—just
might—have hurt someone's feelings? No, of course not, and
therein, I think, lies their fascination for us.

The attraction of the "tough guy" is that he has—or at least   6
seems to have—what most of us lack, and that is an aura of power
and control. In an article, feminist psychiatrist Jean Baker Miller
writes that "a woman's using self-determined power for herself is
equivalent to selfishness [and] destructiveness"—an equation that
makes us want to avoid even the appearance of power. Miller cites
cases of women who get depressed just when they're on the verge of
success—and of women who do succeed and then bury their
achievement in self-deprecation. As an example, she describes one
company's periodic meetings to recognize outstanding salespeople:
when a woman is asked to say a few words about her achievement,
she tends to say something like, "Well, I really don't know how it
happened. I guess I was just lucky this time." In contrast, the men

will cheerfully own up to the hard work, intelligence, and so on, to which they owe their success. By putting herself down, a woman avoids feeling brazenly powerful and potentially "selfish"; she also does the traditional lady's work of trying to make everyone else feel better ("She's not really so smart, after all, just lucky").

So we might as well get a little tougher. And a good place to start is by cutting back on the small acts of deference that we've been programmed to perform since girlhood. Like unnecessary smiling. For many women—waitresses, flight attendants, receptionists— smiling is an occupational requirement, but there's no reason for anyone to go around grinning when she's not being paid for it. I'd suggest that we save our off-duty smiles for when we truly feel like sharing them, and if you're not sure what to do with your face in the meantime, study Clint Eastwood's expressions—both of them.

Along the same lines, I think women should stop taking responsibility for every human interaction we engage in. In a social encounter with a woman, the average man can go 25 minutes saying nothing more than "You don't say?" "Izzat so?" and, of course, "Hmmmm." Why should we do all the work? By taking so much responsibility for making conversations go well, we act as if we had much more at stake in the encounter than the other party—and that gives him (or her) the power advantage. Every now and then, we deserve to get more out of a conversation than we put into it: I'd suggest not offering information you'd rather not share ("I'm really terrified that my sales plan won't work") and not, out of sheer politeness, soliciting information you don't really want ("Wherever did you get that lovely tie?"). There will be pauses, but they don't have to be awkward for *you*.

It is true that some, perhaps most, men will interpret any decrease in female deference as a deliberate act of hostility. Omit the free smiles and perky conversation-boosters and someone is bound to ask, "Well, what's come over *you* today?" For most of us, the first impulse is to stare at our feet and make vague references to a terminally ill aunt in Atlanta, but we should have as much right to be taciturn as the average (male) taxi driver. If you're taking a vacation from smiles and small talk and some fellow is moved to inquire about what's "bothering" you, just stare back levelly and say, the international debt crisis, the arms race, or the death of God.

There are all kinds of ways to toughen up—and potentially move up—at work, and I leave the details to the purveyors of

7

8

9

10

assertiveness training. But Jean Baker Miller's study underscores a fundamental principle that anyone can master on her own. We can stop acting less capable than we actually are. For example, in the matter of taking credit when credit is due, there's a key difference between saying "I was just lucky" and saying "I had a plan and it worked." If you take the credit you deserve, you're letting people know that you were confident you'd succeed all along, and that you fully intend to do so again.

Finally, we may be able to learn something from men about what to do with anger. As a general rule, women get irritated: men get *mad*. We make tight little smiles of ladylike exasperation; they pound on desks and roar. I wouldn't recommend emulating the full basso profundo male tantrum, but women do need ways of expressing justified anger clearly, colorfully, and, when necessary, crudely. If you're not just irritated, but *pissed off*, it might help to say so. 11

I, for example, have rerun the scene with the prestigious professor many times in my mind. And in my mind, I play it like Bogart. I start by moving my chair over to where I can look the professor full in the face. I let him do the chattering, and when it becomes evident that he has nothing serious to say, I lean back and cross my arms, just to let him know that he's wasting my time. I do not smile, neither do I nod encouragement. Nor, of course, do I respond to his blandishments with apologetic shrugs and blushes. Then, at the first flicker of lechery, I stand up and announce coolly, "All right, I've had enough of this crap." Then I walk out—slowly, deliberately, confidently. Just like a man. 12

Or—now that I think of it—just like a woman. 13

Meanings and Values

1. How are most women likely to respond to the opening paragraph? How are most men likely to respond? Why?

2. The author "blush[es] to recount" her encounter with the "prestigious professor" (par. 3). Why?

3a. Define the psychological and moral problem that women face in grasping and exercising power (outlined in paragraph 6).

  b. Does the explanation of the problem and its causes offered by Ehrenreich seem reasonable to you? Be ready to explain your answer and to cite examples from your experience, if possible.

4. Is the main purpose of this essay expository or argumentative? If you have read the Buckley piece earlier in this section, you may wish to compare his aim in writing with Ehrenreich's. (See "Guide to Terms": *Purpose, Argument*.)

Expository Techniques

1a. Why do you think the author chose to wait until paragraph 2 to state the essay's theme? (Guide: *Unity*.)

b. What purpose is served by the brief examples in paragraph 1, including those in the form of rhetorical questions? (Guide: *Rhetorical Questions*.)

2a. In your own words, state the problem identified in paragraph 2.

b. In what way is the example in paragraph 3 related to the statement of the problem in the preceding paragraph?

c. Tell how the example in paragraph 3 is central to the expository purposes of the essay.

3a. Besides paragraph 3, which other parts of the essay discuss the definition of "lady" and "woman"?

b. Examine the use of contrasting pairs of quotations in paragraphs 4, 8, and 10 and be ready to explain how the author uses them to make generalities more forceful or convincing.

4. If you have read Buckley's "Why Don't We Complain?" compare the strategies Ehrenreich and Buckley use to open and conclude their essays. (Guide: *Introductions, Closings*.)

Diction and Vocabulary

1a. Discuss the ways in which the diction in paragraph 3 emphasizes the contrast between the professor's reputation and intellectual achievements and his behavior. (Guide: *Diction*.)

b. Identify the contrasts in diction in paragraph 11, and indicate the ways in which parallelism adds emphasis to them. (Guide: *Parallel Structure*.)

2. List the connotations that "lady" is likely to have for most readers and compare them with the connotations the word acquires in the course of this selection. (Guide: *Connotation/Denotation*.)

3. The following words may be unfamiliar to many readers. Use your dictionary, if necessary, to discover their meanings: maître d', guttural (par. 1); adjacent, lecherous, unconscionable, conversant (3); servility, veneer (4); simper (5); self-deprecation, brazenly (6); deference (7); taciturn (9); basso profundo (11); blandishments (12).

Suggestions for Writing and Discussion

1. If you have read Buckley's essay in this section, compare the political and social values in Ehrenreich's essay with those in Buckley's.

2. To what extent are the explanations and advice in this selection applicable solely or primarily to women? To whom else might they apply?

3. How accurate are the examples Ehrenreich provides of the way men and women converse?

(NOTE: Suggestions for topics requiring development by use of EXAMPLE follow.)

Writing Suggestions for Section 1
Example

Use one of the following statements or another suggested by them as your central theme. Develop it into a unified composition, using examples from history, current events, or personal experience to illustrate your ideas. Be sure to have your reader-audience clearly in mind, as well as your specific purpose for the communication.

1. Successful businesses keep employees at their highest level of competence.

2. In an age of working mothers, fathers spend considerable time and effort helping raise the children.

3. Family life can create considerable stress.

4. Laws holding parents responsible for their children's crimes would (or would not) result in serious injustices.

5. Letting people decide for themselves which laws to obey and which to ignore would result in anarchy.

6. Many people find horror movies entertaining.

7. Service professions are often personally rewarding.

8. Religion in the United States is not dying.

9. Democracy is not always the best form of government.

10. A successful career is worth the sacrifices it requires.

11. "An ounce of prevention is worth a pound of cure."

12. The general quality of television commercials may be improving (or deteriorating).

13. An expensive car can be a poor investment.

14. "Some books are to be tasted; others swallowed; and some few to be chewed and digested." (Francis Bacon, English scientist-author, 1561–1626)

15. Most people are superstitious in one way or another.

16. Relationships within the family are much more important than relationships outside the family.

17. New government-sponsored social welfare programs are necessary in spite of their cost (or are not necessary enough to warrant the huge costs).

2

Analyzing a Subject by *Classification*

People naturally like to sort and classify things. The untidiest urchin, moving into a new dresser of his own, will put his handkerchiefs together, socks and underwear in separate stacks, and perhaps his toads and snails (temporarily) into a drawer of their own. He may classify animals as those with legs, those with wings, and those with neither. As he gets older, he finds that schoolteachers have ways of classifying *him*, not only into a reading group but, periodically, into an "A" or "F" category, or somewhere in between. On errands to the grocery store, he discovers the macaroni in the same department as the spaghetti, the pork chops somewhere near the ham. In reading the local newspaper, he observes that its staff has done some classifying for him, putting most of the comics together and seldom mixing sports stories with the news of bridal showers. Eventually he finds courses neatly classified in the college catalogue, and he knows enough not to look for biology courses under "Social Science." (Examples again—used to illustrate a "prevalence.")

Our main interest in classification here is its use as a structural pattern for explanatory writing. Many subjects about which either students or graduates may need to write will remain a hodgepodge of facts and opinions unless they can find some system of analyzing the material, dividing the subject into categories, and classifying individual elements into those categories. Here we have the distinction usually made between the rhetorical terms *division* and *classification*—for example, dividing "meat" into pork, beef, mutton, and fowl, then classifying ham and pork chops into the category of "pork." But this distinction is one we need scarcely pause for here; once the need for analysis is recognized, the dividing and classifying become inevitable companions and result in the single scheme of "classification" itself, as we have been discussing it. The original division into parts merely sets up the system that, if well chosen, best serves our purpose.

Obviously, no single system of classification is best for all purposes. Our untidy urchin may at some point classify girls according to athletic prowess, then later by size or shape or hair color. (At the same time, of course, the girls may be placing him into one or more categories.) Other people may need entirely different systems of classification: the music instructor classifies girls as sopranos, altos, contraltos; the psychologist, according to their behavior patterns; the sociologist, according to their ethnic origins.

Whatever the purpose, for the more formal uses of classification ("formal," that is, to the extent of most academic and on-the-job writing), we should be careful to use a logical system that is complete and that follows a consistent principle throughout. It would not be logical to divide Protestantism into the categories of Methodist, Baptist, and Lutheran, because the system would be incomplete and misleading. But in classifying Protestants attending some special conference—a different matter entirely—such a limited system might be both complete and logical. In any case, the writer must be careful that classes do not overlap: to classify the persons at the conference as Methodists, Baptists, Lutherans, and clergy would be illogical, because some are undoubtedly both Lutheran, for instance, and clergy.

In dividing and classifying, we are really using the basic process of outlining. Moreover, if we are dealing with classifiable *ideas*, the resulting pattern *is* our outline, which has been our aim all along— a basic organizational plan.

This process of classification frequently does, in fact, organize much less tangible things than the examples mentioned. We might wish to find some orderly basis for discussing the South's post–Civil War problems. Division might give us three primary categories of information: economic, political, and social. But for a full-scale consideration of these, the major divisions themselves may be subdivided for still more orderly explanation: the economic information may be further divided into agriculture and industry. Now it is possible to isolate and clarify such strictly industrial matters as shortage of investment capital, disrupted transportation systems, and lack of power development.

Any plan like this seems almost absurdly obvious, of course—*after* the planning is done. It appears less obvious, however, to inexperienced writers who are dealing with a jumble of information they must explain to someone else. This is when they should be aware of the patterns at their disposal, and one of the most useful of these, alone or combined with others, is classification.

Sample Paragraph (Annotated)

Background suggesting the topic of the paragraph.

Palmville is not a planned town that sprang full-blown from an architect's drawing board. After all, the town has been around since 1880, and for its first ninety years it grew more or less by chance. In 1970, however, M&T Realty developed a building plan that has been followed informally by most of the other major developers. As a result, the town

Topic announcing the division into four categories.

now has four main neighborhoods, each characterized by a different kind of housing, and each using the name originally assigned by M&T's urban planner. Brooktown is a neighborhood

Classification, with each category containing a presentation of characteristics.

of modest starter homes, each with three bedrooms, $1\frac{1}{2}$ baths, a small dining area, and a one-car garage. The plain occupied by the homes is bisected by Talley's Creek (now running mostly in culverts), and is the dustiest area in town, at least by general reputation. The houses in Kingston Hills are a bit more costly. Some have three bedrooms, some four, but all have dens, dining rooms, two-car garages, and yards big enough for an in-ground pool or an elaborate patio. The streets in Brooktown and Kingston Hills are straight, but those in Paddock Estates curve gracefully around the three-acre lots of custom-built homes. Buyers get to choose from eight basic plans ranging from sprawling ranches, to oversized capes, to French Colonial chateaus. Each basic plan must be modified inside and out both to suit the homeowner's taste and to make sure that each house appears different enough to justify the ad for the development: "Unique Executive Homes on three-acre lots." In contrast, Village Green, the center of the original village, offers charming restored Victorian homes and cottages mixed with modern reproductions of homes from the same period. The homes (or the styles) may be old, but the prices are contemporary, and almost as high as for the luxury homes in Paddock Estates.

Sample Paragraph (Classification)

Rock and roll is old enough now to have its generations. Some of you reading this may be part of the first (those who grew up in the fifties on Elvis and Chuck Berry), or the second (fans of the British Invasion and the Motown sound), or even the third generation (kids in the seventies for whom the members of Led Zeppelin were *eminences grises* and the Beatles were Paul McCartney's *old* band). But no matter what wave you rode in on, the chances are pretty good that your parents didn't listen to rock, that they in fact detested it and regarded everything you listened to with the utmost disdain. I can still recall my mother's reaction to the first 45 I ever bought with my own money, the Rolling Stones' "Paint it Black," with "Stupid Girl" on the flip side. Staring in outrage at the photograph that adorned the sleeve—Mick, Keith, and the boys in their foppish, Edwardian finest—she finally exclaimed, "I suppose *that's* how you want to look!"

From "Talking 'Bout Their Generation," *Parenting Magazine* (September 1988). Reprinted by permission.

Piano Recitals

Heather Farnum

Last night while I was sitting at the piano and relaxing by playing some old recital pieces, memories of playing in piano recitals as a child and high school student came flooding back to me. I remember looking at each pianist intently, watching how she or he presented a piece, and imagining myself sitting at the piano and playing in a similar way. I watched how each presented a selection—whether or not the person gave feeling to the music and was comfortable with playing it. Most of all, I watched how the pianist interpreted a piece, for there are several quite different ways to interpret the same selection for an audience.

Novice pianists, intermediate pianists, and top class pianists all approach the job of interpretation in different and characteristic ways. You can help me explain these differences if you will imagine a stage in a brightly-lit church hall or school auditorium. Stretched across the stage is a grand piano, set up so the audience of parents, friends, and fellow students can see the recitalist.

The first person to walk tentatively across the stage to polite applause is a novice pianist. Like all novices, this one either rushes through the piece or plays much too slowly. He bobs his head up and down trying to maintain the tempo, messes up notes, and plays too loudly or too softly, but seldom in between.

The best example of a novice pianist I can recall is Stephany Cody, a girl of about seven. For her first recital, Stephany played "Twinkle, Twinkle, Little Star" as loudly as she could, bobbing her head throughout the familiar piece. Every time she reached the "twinkle, twinkle, little star" she speeded up because she knew that part best. However, when she reached "up above the sky so gray," she slowed way down as she struggled through the less familiar notes.

Next across the stage is an intermediate pianist. Sitting down, she strives for a professional look in form and stature. Unlike the novice pianist, she has control over dynamics, yet she is more tense because she is more aware of the things she needs to do and the things that can go wrong.

John Cody (Stephany's ten-year-old brother) comes to my mind as an image of the intermediate pianist. For one of his recitals, John played a piece called "Festival of Arragon." He sat down at the piano with a serious disposition, like a professional. When he began playing, however, his form fell apart. His shoulders sagged and he held his head at an awkward angle because he was paying more attention to the correct tempo and the correct shade of loudness or softness than to the image he was presenting of himself and the music.

Last across the stage is an advanced pianist. She (or he) sits in a relaxed yet formal manner at the piano. When she plays, the dynamics and shades of sound are balanced and put the piece on display rather than the pianist. The tempo is even and steady, and the audience senses a performer in control with a strong stage presence.

My piano teacher, Ann Fitch, remains in my mind as an image of the advanced pianist. Whenever she sits at the piano, she is calm and relaxed; her disposition alone makes the audience feel relaxed and at ease—ready for the piece to begin. She plays with tempos and rhythms that are steady and gradual. Most of all, however, she makes the audience members feel they are living the music.

An advanced pianist like Ann goes even further with her performance. She plays with a mood and a stage presence that enables listeners to share the pianist's emotions. A top flight pianist can convey feelings of love, romance, anger, sadness, depression, and excitement and arrange them in ways that guide listeners to the heart of the music without overwhelming them. Finally, if advanced pianists have a secret, it is that they keep four questions always in mind:

1. What is the tempo I want to follow for this piece?
2. What mood do I wish to present?
3. What emotions do I want to convey?
4. How can I play so that the audience can live the piece of music at the same time I do?

JUDITH VIORST

JUDITH VIORST was born in Newark, New Jersey, and attended Rutgers University. Formerly a contributing editor of *Redbook* magazine, for which she wrote a monthly column, she has also been a newspaper columnist, and in 1970 she received an Emmy award for her contributions to a CBS television special. She has written numerous fiction and nonfiction books for children, including *Alexander and the Terrible, Horrible, No Good, Very Bad Day* (1982). Among her various books of verse and prose for adults are *It's Hard to Be Hip Over Thirty and Other Tragedies of Married Life* (1968) (a collection of poems), *Yes, Married: A Saga of Love and Complaint* (1972) (prose pieces), and, more recently, *If I Were in Charge of the World and Other Worries* (1981), *Love and Guilt and the Meaning of Life* (1984), and *Necessary Losses* (1986).

What, Me? Showing Off?

In "What, Me? Showing Off?" first published in *Redbook*, Viorst uses classification to explore a behavior that most of us notice readily enough in other people but may be reluctant to acknowledge in our own actions—showing off. Though its tone is breezy and it contains frequent touches of humor, this essay is carefully organized and serious in purpose. Besides classification, Viorst makes good use of examples, definition, brief narratives, and even a short dramatic episode.

We're at the Biedermans' annual blast, and over at the far end of the 1 living room an intense young woman with blazing eyes and a throbbing voice is decrying poverty, war, injustice and human suffering. Indeed, she expresses such anguish at the anguish of mankind that attention quickly shifts from the moral issues she is expounding to how very, very, very deeply she cares about them.

She's showing off. 2

Down at the other end of the room an insistently scholarly fel- 3
low has just used *angst, hubris,* Kierkegaard and *epistemology* in the
same sentence. Meanwhile our resident expert in wine meditatively
sips, then pushes away, a glass of unacceptable Beaujolais.

They're showing off. 4

And then there's us, complaining about how tired we are today 5
because we went to work, rushed back to see our son's school play,
shopped at the market and hurried home in order to cook gourmet,
and then needlepointed another dining-room chair.

And what we also are doing is showing off. 6

Indeed everyone, I would like to propose, has some sort of need 7
to show off. No one's completely immune. Not you. And not I. And
although we've been taught that it's bad to boast, that it's trashy to
toot our own horn, that nice people don't strut their stuff, seek attention or name-drop, there are times when showing off may be forgivable and maybe even acceptable.

But first let's take a look at showing off that *is* obnoxious, that's 8
not acceptable, that's never nice. Like showoffs motivated by a fierce,
I'm-gonna-blow-you-away competitiveness. And like narcissistic
showoffs who are willing to do anything to be—and stay—the center of attention.

Competitive showoffs want to be the best of every bunch. 9
Competitive showoffs must outshine all others. Whatever is being
discussed, they have more—expertise or money or even aggravation—and better—periodontists or children or marriages or recipes
for pesto—and deeper—love of animals or concern for human suffering or orgasms. Competitive showoffs are people who reside in a
permanent state of sibling rivalry, insisting on playing Hertz to
everyone else's Avis.

(You're finishing a story, for instance, about the sweet little card 10
that your five-year-old recently made for your birthday when the
CSO interrupts to relate how her daughter not only made her a
sweet little card, but also brought her breakfast in bed and saved her
allowance for months and months in order to buy her—obviously
much more beloved—mother a beautiful scarf for her birthday.
Grrr.)

Narcissistic showoffs, however, don't bother to compete 11
because they don't even notice there's anyone there to compete with.
They talk nonstop, they brag, they dance, they sometimes quote

Homer in Greek, and they'll even go stand on their head if attention should flag. Narcissistic showoffs want to be the star while everyone else is the audience. And yes, they are often adorable and charming and amusing—but only until around the age of six.

(I've actually seen an NSO get up and leave the room when the conversation shifted from his accomplishments. "What's the matter?" I asked when I found him standing on the terrace, brooding darkly. "Oh, I don't know," he replied, "but all of a sudden the talk started getting so superficial." *Aagh!*)   12

Another group of showoffs—much more sympathetic types—are showoffs who are basically insecure. And while there is no easy way to distinguish the insecure from the narcissists and competitors, you may figure out which are which by whether you have the urge to reassure or to strangle them.   13

Insecure showoffs show off because, as one close friend explained, "How will they know that I'm good unless I tell them about it?" And whatever the message—I'm smart, I'm a fine human being, I'm this incredibly passionate lover—showoffs have many different techniques for telling about it.   14

Take smart, for example.   15

A person can show off explicitly by using flashy words, like the hubris-Kierkegaard fellow I mentioned before.   16

Or a person can show off implicitly, by saying not a word and just wearing a low-cut dress with her Phi Beta Kappa key gleaming softly in the cleavage.   17

A person can show off satirically, by mocking showing off: "My name is Bill Sawyer," one young man announces to every new acquaintance, "and I'm bright bright bright bright bright."   18

Or a person can show off complainingly: "I'm sorry my daughter takes after me. Men are just so frightened of smart women."   19

Another way showoffs show off about smart is to drop a Very Smart Name—if this brain is my friend, goes the message, I must be a brain too. And indeed, a popular showing-off ploy—whether you're showing off smartness or anything else—is to name-drop a glittery name in the hope of acquiring some gilt by association.   20

The theory seems to be that Presidents, movie stars, Walter Cronkite and Princess Di could be friends, if they chose, with anyone in the world, and that if these luminaries have selected plain old Stanley Stone to be friends with, Stanley Stone must be one hell of a   21 guy. (Needless to say, old Stanley Stone might also be a very dreary fellow, but if Walt and Di don't mind him, why should I?)

Though no one that I know hangs out with Presidents and movie stars, they do (I too!) sometimes drop famous names. 22

As in: "I go to John Travolta's dermatologist." 23

Or: "I own the exact same sweater that Jackie Onassis wore in a newspaper photograph last week." 24

Or: "My uncle once repaired a roof for Sandra Day O'Connor." 25

Or: "My cousin's neighbor's sister-in-law has a child who is Robert Redford's son's best friend." 26

We're claiming we've got gilt—though by a very indirect association. And I think that when we do, we're showing off. 27

Sometimes showoffs ask for cheers to which they're not entitled. Sometimes showoffs earn the praise they seek. And sometimes folks achieve great things and nonetheless do not show off about it. 28

Now *that's* impressive. 29

Indeed, when we discover that the quiet mother of four with whom we've been talking intimately all evening has recently been elected to the state senate—*and she never even mentioned it!*—we are filled with admiration, with astonishment, with awe. 30

What self-restraint! 31

For we know damn well—*I* certainly know—that if we'd been that lucky lady, we'd have worked our triumph into the conversation. As a matter of fact, I'll lay my cards right on the table and confess that the first time some poems of mine were published, I not only worked my triumph into every conversation for months and months, but I also called almost every human being I'd ever known to proclaim the glad tidings both local and long distance. Furthermore—let me really confess—if a stranger happened to stop me on the street and all he wanted to know was the time or directions, I tried to detain him long enough to enlighten him with the news that the person to whom he was speaking was a Real Live Genuine Honest-to-God Published Poet. 32

Fortunately for everyone, I eventually—it took me awhile—calmed down. 33

Now, I don't intend to defend myself—I was showing off, I was bragging and I wasn't the slightest bit shy or self-restrained, but a golden, glowing, glorious thing had happened in my life and I had an overwhelming need to exult. Exulting, however (as I intend to argue farther on), may be a permissible form of showing off. 34

Exulting is what my child does when he comes home with an *A*   35
on his history paper ("Julius Caesar was 50," it began, "and his good
looks was pretty much demolished") and wants to read me the
entire masterpiece while I murmur appreciative comments at frequent intervals.

Exulting is what my husband does when he cooks me one of his   36
cheese-and-scallion omelets and practically does a tap dance as he
carries it from the kitchen stove to the table, setting it before me with
the purely objective assessment that this may be the greatest omelet
ever created.

Exulting is what my mother did when she took her first grand-   37
son to visit all her friends, and announced as she walked into the
room, "Is he gorgeous? Is that a gorgeous baby? Is that the most
gorgeous baby you ever saw?"

And exulting is what that mother of four would have done if   38
she'd smiled and said, "Don't call me 'Marge' any more. Call me
'Senator.'"

Exulting is shamelessly shouting our talents or triumphs to the   39
world. It's saying: I'm taking a bow and I'd like to hear clapping.
And I think if we don't overdo it (stopping strangers to say you've
been published is overdoing it), and I think if we know when to quit
("Enough about me. Let's talk about you. So what do you think
about me?" does not count as quitting), and I think if we don't get
addicted (i.e., crave a praise-fix for every poem or *A* or omelet), and
I think if we're able to walk off the stage (and clap and cheer while
others take their bows), then I think we're allowed, from time to
time, to exult.

Though showing off can range from very gross to very subtle,   40
and though the point of showing off is sometimes nasty, sometimes
needy, sometimes nice, showoffs always run the risk of being
thought immodest, of being harshly viewed as . . . well . . . showoffs.
And so for folks who want applause without relinquishing their
sense of modesty, the trick is keeping quiet and allowing someone
else to show off *for* you.

And I've seen a lot of marriages where wives show off for hus-   41
bands and where husbands, in return, show off for wives. Where
Joan, for instance, mentions Dick's promotion and his running time
in the marathon. And where Dick, for instance, mentions all the
paintings Joanie sold at her last art show. And where both of them

lean back with self-effacing shrugs and smiles and never once show off about themselves.

Friends also may show off for friends, and parents for their children, though letting parents toot our horns is risky. Consider, for example, this sad tale of Elliott, who was a fearless and feisty public-interest lawyer: 42

"My son," his proud mother explained to his friends, "has always been independent." (Her son blushed modestly.)   43

"My son," his proud mother continued, "was the kind of person who always knew his own mind." (Her son blushed modestly.)   44

"My son," his proud mother went on, "was never afraid. He never kowtowed to those in authority." (Her son blushed modestly.)   45

"My son," his proud mother concluded, "was so independent and stubborn and unafraid of authority that we couldn't get him toilet-trained—he wet his pants till he was past four." (Her son . . .)   46

But showing off is always a risk, whether we do it ourselves or whether somebody else is doing it for us. And perhaps we ought to consider the words Lord Chesterfield wrote to his sons: "Modesty is the only sure bait when you angle for praise."   47

And yes, of course he's right, we know he's right, he must be right. But sometimes it's so hard to be restrained. For no matter what we do, we always have a lapse or two. So let's try to forgive each other for showing off.   48

Meanings and Values

1a. Name the categories into which Viorst divides showoffs. (Note: In doing this you will need to decide if Viorst views people who say nothing about their achievements as a category of showoffs.)

b. Which of the categories does Viorst divide into subcategories? What are the subcategories?

2a. Where, if anywhere, do the categories in this essay overlap? For example, can showoffs who have a real achievement to brag about be *both* competitive and exulting?

b. If the categories overlap, is the result confusing and misleading? Why? Or is some overlap inevitable in any classification that attempts to explain human behavior?

3. According to the examples in paragraphs 36 and 37, exulting may sometimes mean exaggerating or stretching the truth. Do you agree with Viorst that exulting should be permissible even if it means inflating one's accomplishments? Be ready to defend your answer.

4a. What does Viorst imply about the personalities of narcissistic showoffs when she says, "they are often adorable and charming and amusing—but only until around the age of six" (par. 11)?

b. What message is the woman with the Phi Beta Kappa key conveying (par. 17)?

Expository Techniques

1a. In what order are the categories arranged? Worst to best? Most forgivable to least forgivable? Some other order?

b. Where and how is this arrangement announced to the reader?

2a. The introduction to this essay is relatively long (pars. 1–8). What does Viorst do to get readers interested in the subject? (See "Guide to Terms": *Introductions*.)

b. Where in the introduction does she announce the central theme? Where else in the essay does she speak directly about the central theme?

c. Where in the introduction does she indicate the plan of organization?

d. What role do the one-sentence paragraphs play in the introduction? Do they add to its effectiveness or detract from it? (Guide: *Evaluation*.)

3. At several places in the essay Viorst comments on its organization and summarizes the categories. Identify these places.

4a. Why does paragraph 10 seem to be addressed to a female reader?

b. Can the example be easily understood by male readers or might it alienate them?

c. In the rest of the essay does Viorst take care to balance examples more likely to appeal to men with those more likely to appeal to women? Be ready to support your answer.

5a. For some of the categories the discussion consists of a general definition followed by examples. Which discussions follow this arrangement?

b. Describe briefly the organization of the remaining discussions.

6a. Identify a section of the essay where Viorst uses parallel paragraphs and discuss their effect. (Guide: *Parallel Structure*.)

b. Do the same with parallel sentences.

c. Do the same with parallel sentence parts.

Diction and Vocabulary

1. What words or kinds of words does Viorst repeat frequently in the course of the essay? What purposes does the repetition serve?

2a. To what does the phrase "gilt by association" allude? (Guide: *Figures of Speech, Allusion.*)

  b. Identify as many as you can of the direct references and allusions to people, ideas, or events in the following paragraphs: pars. 3, 9, 11, 21, and 23–26. What purposes do these references serve?

3. How is irony (understatement) used in paragraph 36? (Guide: *Irony.*) How is exaggeration used in paragraph 32?

4. Viorst uses some devices that in many essays would seem excessively informal or careless: unusual or made-up words ("*Grrr,*" par. 10; "*Aagh,*" 12); informal phrases ("strut their stuff," 7); exclamation points; and parentheses surrounding an entire paragraph, among other things. In what ways do such devices contribute to the humor of the essay? to its overall tone? (Guide: *Style/Tone.*)

5. If you are unfamiliar with any of the following words, consult your dictionary as necessary: decrying, expounding (par. 1); *angst, hubris, epistemology* (3); narcissistic (8); periodontists, sibling (9); brooding (12); cleavage (17); dermatologist (23); enlighten (32); exult (34); appreciative (35); assessment (36); shamelessly, crave (39); gross, immodest, relinquishing (40); feisty (42); kowtowed (45).

Suggestions for Writing and Discussion

1. Are there times when it might be useful or appropriate to be a competitive (narcissistic, insecure) showoff? Be ready to justify your answer and to provide specific examples.

2. Prepare an essay of your own that classifies some other human behavior according to its acceptable and unacceptable forms, like losing one's temper, being afraid, or being envious.

3. At several places in the essay, the author pokes fun at her own behavior or that of members of her family. Discuss how important this strategy is to the success of the essay and to the willingness of readers to view their own behavior in the ways Viorst describes.

(NOTE: Suggestions for topics requiring development by use of CLASSIFICATION are on page 139, at the end of this section.)

RENEE E. TAJIMA is a filmmaker and writer. She produced a documentary for public television entitled "Adopted Son: The Death of Vincent Chin." Currently she is associate editor of *The Independent Film and Video Monthly* as well as a freelance writer. With Christine Choy she runs the Film News Now Foundation. Formerly editor of *Bridge: Asian American Perspectives,* Tajima has also edited *Journey Across Three Continents: Black and African Films, Asian American Film and Video,* and *Reel Change: Guide to Social Issue Media* (2d ed.).

Lotus Blossoms Don't Bleed: Images of Asian American Women

Categories are an important tool for thinking, but unless created with care, they can become unrepresentative stereotypes. Tajima's essay reminds us of the need to be aware of how the categories presented by film and television can shape our perceptions. And she demonstrates how restrictive and harmful stereotypes can be. The classification system here is somewhat complex, consisting of two different kinds of characters, "Lotus Blossoms" and "Dragon Ladies," that appear in several different types of movie roles.

In recent years the media have undergone spectacular technical   1
innovations. But whereas form has leaped toward the year 2000, it
seems that content still straddles the turn of the last century. A reigning
example of the industry's stagnation is its portrayal of Asian
women. And the only real signs of life are stirring far away from
Hollywood in the cutting rooms owned and operated by Asian
America's independent producers.

The commercial media are, in general, populated by stereo- 2
typed characterizations that range in complexity, accuracy, and
persistence over time. There is the hooker with a heart of gold
and the steely tough yet honorable mobster. Most of these characters
are white, and may be as one-dimensional as Conan the Barbarian
or as complex as R. P. McMurphy in *One Flew Over the Cuckoo's Nest*.

Images of Asian women, however, have remained consistently 3
simplistic and inaccurate during the sixty years of largely forgettable
screen appearances. There are two basic types: the Lotus Blossom
Baby (a.k.a. China Doll, Geisha Girl, shy Polynesian beauty), and
the Dragon Lady (Fu Manchu's various female relations, prostitutes,
devious madames). There is little in between, although experts
may differ as to whether Suzie Wong belongs to the race-blind
"hooker with a heart of gold" category, or deserves one all of
her own.

Asian women in American cinema are interchangeable in 4
appearance and name, and are joined together by the common
language of non-language—that is, uninterpretable chattering,
pidgin English, giggling, or silence. They may be specifically identified by nationality—particularly in war films—but that's where
screen accuracy ends. The dozens of populations of Asian and
Pacific Island groups are lumped into one homogeneous mass of
Mama-sans.

Passive Love Interests

Asian women in film are, for the most part, passive figures who exist 5
to serve men, especially as love interests for white men (Lotus Blossoms) or as partners in crime with men of their own kind (Dragon
Ladies). One of the first Dragon Lady types was played by Anna
May Wong. In the 1924 spectacular *Thief of Bagdad* she uses treachery
to help an evil Mongol prince attempt to win the Princess of Bagdad
from Douglas Fairbanks.

The Lotus Blossom Baby, a sexual-romantic object, has been the 6
prominent type throughout the years. These "Oriental flowers" are
utterly feminine, delicate, and welcome respites from their often
loud, independent American counterparts. Many of them are the
spoils of the last three wars fought in Asia. One recent television
example is Sergeant Klinger's Korean wife in the short-lived series
"AfterMash."

In the real world, this view of Asian women has spawned an   7
entire marriage industry. Today the Filipino wife is particularly in
vogue for American men who order Asian brides from picture cata-
logues, just as you might buy an imported cheese slicer from
Spiegel's. (I moderated a community program on Asian American
women recently. A rather bewildered young saleswoman showed
up with a stack of brochures to promote the Cherry Blossom companion service, or some such enterprise.) Behind the brisk sales of
Asian mail-order brides is a growing number of American men who
are seeking old-fashioned, compliant wives, women they feel are no
longer available in the United States.

Feudal Asian customs do not change for the made-for-movie   8
women. Picture brides, geisha girls, concubines, and hara-kari are all
mixed together and reintroduced into any number of settings. Take
for example these two versions of Asian and American cultural
exchange:

1. It's Toko Riki on Japan's Okinawa Island during the late   9
1940s in the film *Teahouse of the August Moon*. American occupation
forces nice guy Captain Fisby (Glenn Ford) gets a visit from Japanese yenta Sakini (Marlon Brando).

Enter Brando: "Hey Boss, I Sonoda has a present for you."   10

Enter the gift: Japanese actress Machiko Kyo as a geisha,   11
giggling.

Ford: "Who's she?"   12

Brando: "Souvenir . . . introducing Lotus Blossom geisha girl   13
first class."

Ford protests the gift. Kyo giggles.   14

Brando sneaks away with a smile: "Goodnight, Boss." Kyo,   15
chattering away in Japanese, tries to pamper a bewildered Ford who
holds up an instructive finger to her and repeats slowly, "Me . . . me
. . . no." Kyo looks confused.

2. It's San Francisco, circa 1981, in the television series   16
"The Incredible Hulk." Nice guy David Banner (Bill Bixby
a.k.a. The Hulk) gets a present from Chinese yenta Hyung
(Beulah Quo).

Enter Quo: "David, I have something for you."   17

Enter Irene Sun as Tam, a Chinese refugee, bowing her head   18
shyly.

Quo: "The Floating Lotus Company hopes you will be very   19
happy. This is Tam, your mail-order bride."

Bixby protests the gift. Sun, speaking only Chinese, tries to   20
pamper a bewildered Bixby who repeats slowly in an instructive
tone, "you . . . must . . . go!" Sun looks confused.

Illicit Interracial Love

On film Asian women are often assigned the role of expendability in   21
situations of illicit Asian-white love. In these cases the most expedi-
ent way of resolving the problems of miscegenation has been to get
rid of the Asian partner. Thus, some numbers of hyphenated (made-
for-television, wartime, wives-away-from-home) Asian women
have expired for the convenience of their home-bound soldier
lovers. More progressive-minded GI's of the Vietnam era have
returned to Vietnam years later to search for the offspring of these
love matches.

In 1985 the General Foods Gold Showcase proudly presented a   22
post-Vietnam version of the wilting Lotus Blossom on network television. "A forgotten passion, a child he never knew. . . . All his
tomorrows forever changed by *The Lady from Yesterday*." He is Vietnam vet Craig Weston (Wayne Rogers), official father of two, and
husband to Janet (Bonnie Bedelia). She is Lien Van Huyen (Tina
Chen), whom Weston hasn't seen since the fall of Saigon. She brings
the child, the unexpected consequence of that wartime love match,
to the United States. But Janet doesn't lose her husband, she gains a
son. As *New York Times* critic John J. O'Connor points out, Lien has
"the good manners to be suffering from a fatal disease that will conveniently remove her from the scene."

The geographic parallel to the objectification of Asian women is   23
the rendering of Asia as only a big set for the white leading actors.
What would "Shogun" be without Richard Chamberlain? The most
notable exception is the 1937 movie version of Pearl Buck's novel *The
Good Earth*. The story is about Chinese in China and depicted with
some complexity and emotion. Nevertheless the lead parts played
by Louise Rainer and Paul Muni follow the pattern of choosing
white stars for Asian roles, a problem which continues to plague
Asian actors.

One film that stands out as an exception because it was cast   24
with Asian people for Asian characters is *Flower Drum Song* (1961),
set in San Francisco's Chinatown. Unfortunately the film did little

more than temporarily take a number of talented Asian American actresses and actors off the unemployment lines. It also gave birth for a while to a new generation of stereotypes—gum-chewing Little Leaguers, enterprising businessmen, and all-American tomboys—variations on the then new model minority myth. *Flower Drum Song* hinted that the assimilated, hyphenated Asian American might be much more successful in American society than the Japanese of the 1940s and the Chinese and Koreans of the 1950s, granted they keep to the task of being white American first.

The women of *Flower Drum Song* maintain their earlier image   25
with few modernizations. Miyoshi Umeki is still a picture bride. And in *Suzie Wong* actress Nancy Kwan is a hipper, Americanized version of the Hong Kong bar girl without the pidgin English. But updated clothes and setting do not change the essence of these images.

In 1985 director Michael Cimino cloned Suzie Wong to TV news   26
anchor Connie Chung and created another anchor, Tracy Tzu (Ariane), in the disastrous exploitation film *Year of the Dragon.* In it Tzu is ostensibly the only positive Asian American character in a film that vilifies the people of New York's Chinatown. The Tzu character is a success in spite of her ethnicity. Just as she would rather eat Italian than Chinese, she'd rather sleep with white men than Chinese men. (She is ultimately raped by three "Chinese boys.") Neither does she bat an eye at the barrage of racial slurs fired off by her lover, lead Stanley White, the Vietnam vet and New York City cop played by Mickey Rourke.

At the outset Tzu is the picture of professionalism and sophisti-   27
cation, engaged in classic screen love/hate banter with White. The turning point comes early in the picture when their flirtatious sparring in a Chinese restaurant is interrupted by a gangland slaughter. While White pursues the culprits, Tzu totters on her high heels into a phone booth where she cowers, sobbing, until White comes to the rescue.

The standard of beauty for Asian women that is set in the   28
movies deserves mention. Caucasian women are often used for Asian roles, which contributes to a case of aesthetic imperialism for Asian women. When Asian actresses are chosen they invariably have large eyes, high cheekbones, and other Caucasian-like characteristics when they appear on the silver screen. As Judy Chu of the University of California, Los Angeles, has pointed out, much of

Anna May Wong's appeal was due to her Western looks. Chu unearthed this passage from the June 1924 *Photoplay* which refers to actress Wong, but sounds a lot like a description of Eurasian model/actress Ariane: "Her deep brown eyes, while the slant is not pronounced, are typically oriental. But her Manchu mother has given her a height and poise of figure that Chinese maidens seldom have."

Invisibility

There is yet another important and pervasive characteristic of Asian women on the screen, invisibility. The number of roles in the Oriental flower and Dragon Lady categories have been few, and generally only supporting parts. But otherwise Asian women are absent. Asian women do not appear in films as union organizers, or divorced mothers fighting for the custody of their children, or fading movie stars, or spunky trial lawyers, or farm women fighting bank foreclosures; Asian women are not portrayed as ordinary people.   29

Then there is the kind of invisibility that occurs when individual personalities and separate identities become indistinguishable from one another. Some memorable Asian masses are the islanders fleeing exploding volcanoes in *Krakatoa: East of Java* (1969) and the Vietnamese villagers fleeing Coppola's airborne weaponry in various scenes from *Apocalypse Now* (1979). Asian women populate these hordes or have groupings of their own, usually in some type of harem situation. In *Cry for Happy* (1961), Glenn Ford is cast as an American GI who stumbles into what turns out to be the best little geisha house in Japan.   30

Network television has given Asian women even more opportunities to paper the walls, so to speak. They are background characters in "Hawaii 5-0," "Magnum PI," and other series that transverse the Pacific. I've seen a cheongsam-clad maid in the soap "One Life to Live," and assorted Chinatown types surface whenever the cops and robbers shows revive scripts about the Chinatown Tong wars.   31

The most stunning exceptions to television's abuse of Asian images is the phenomenon of news anchors: Connie Chung (CBS) and Sasha Foo (CNN) have national spots, and Tritia Toyota (Los Angeles), Wendy Tokuda (San Francisco), Kaity Tong (New York),   32

Sandra Yep (Sacramento), and others are reporters in large cities. All of them cover hard news, long the province of middle-aged white men with authoritative voices. Toyota and Yep have been able to parlay their positions so that there is more coverage of Asian American stories at their stations. Because of their presence on screen— and ironically, perhaps because of the celebrity status of today's newscasters—these anchors wield much power in rectifying Asian women's intellectual integrity in the media. (One hopes *Year of the Dragon's* Tracy Tzu hasn't canceled their positive effect.)

Undoubtedly the influence of these visible reporters is fortified   33
by the existence of highly organized Asian American journalists. The West Coast-based Asian American Journalists Association has lobbied for affirmative action in the print and broadcast media. In film and video, the same types of political initiatives have spurred a new movement of independently produced works made by and about Asian Americans.

Small Gems from Independents

The independent film movement emerged during the 1960s as an   34
alternative to the Hollywood mill. In a broad sense it has had little direct impact in reversing the distorted images of Asian women, although some gems have been produced. . . . But now Asian American independents, many of whom are women, have consciously set out to bury sixty years of Lotus Blossoms who do not bleed and Mama-sans who do not struggle. These women filmmakers—most of whom began their careers only since the 1970s—often draw from deeply personal perspectives in their work: Virginia Hashii's *Jenny* Portrays a young Japanese American girl who explores her own Nikkei heritage for the first time; Christine Choy's *From Spikes to Spindles* (1976) documents the lives of women in New York's Chinatown; Felicia Lowe's *China: Land of My Father* (1979) is a film diary of the filmmaker's own first reunion with her grandmother in China; Renee Cho's *The New Wife* (1978) dramatizes the arrival of an immigrant bride to America; and Lana Pih Jokel's *Chiang Ching: A Dance Journey* traces the life of dancer-actress-teacher Chiang. All these films were produced during the 1970s and together account for only a little more than two hours of screen time. Most are first works with the same rough-edged quality that characterized early Asian American film efforts.

Women producers have maintained a strong presence during the 1980s, although their work does not always focus on women's issues. . . . Also in this decade veteran filmmakers Emiko Omori and Christine Choy have produced their first dramatic efforts. Omori's *The Departure* is the story of a Japanese girl who must give up her beloved traditional dolls in pre–World War II California. . . . In *Fei Tien: Goddess in Flight*, Choy tries to adapt a nonlinear cinematic structure to Genny Lim's play *Pigeons*, which explores the relationship between a Chinese American yuppie and a Chinatown "bird lady."

Perhaps the strongest work made thus far has been directed by a male filmmaker, Arthur Dong. *Sewing Woman* is a small, but beautifully crafted portrait of Dong's mother, Zem Ping. It chronicles her life from war-torn China to San Francisco's garment factories. Other films and tapes by Asian men include Michael Uno's *Emi* (1978), a portrait of the Japanese American writer and former concentration camp internee Emi Tonooka; the Yonemoto brothers' neonarrative *Green Card*, a soap-style saga of a Japanese immigrant artist seeking truth, love, and permanent residency in Southern California; and Steve Okazaki's *Survivors*, a documentary focusing on the women survivors of the atomic blasts over Hiroshima and Nagasaki. All these filmmakers are American-born Japanese. *Orientations*, by Asian Canadian Richard Fung, is the first work I've seen that provides an in-depth look at the Asian gay community, and it devotes a good amount of time to Asian Canadian lesbians.

Our Own Image

These film and videomakers, women and men, face a challenge far beyond creating entertainment and art. Several generations of Asian women have been raised with racist and sexist celluloid images. The models for passivity and servility in these films and television programs fit neatly into the myths imposed on us, and contrast sharply with the more liberating ideals of independence and activism. Generations of other Americans have also grown up with these images. And their acceptance of the dehumanization implicit in the stereotypes of expendability and invisibility is frightening.

Old images of Asian women in the mainstream media will likely remain stagnant for a while. After sixty years, there have been few signs of progress. However, there is hope because of the growing number of filmmakers emerging from our own communities. Wayne Wang in 1985 completed *Dim Sum,* a beautifully crafted feature film about the relationship between a mother and daughter in San Francisco's Chinatown. *Dim Sum,* released through a commercial distributor, could be the first truly sensitive film portrayal of Asian American women to reach a substantial national audience. In quality and numbers, Asian American filmmakers may soon constitute a critical mass out of which we will see a body of work that gives us a new image, our own image.

Meanings and Values

1a. What are the two main images of Asian women in Hollywood films (par. 3)?

b. What are the three main roles Asian women have played in Hollywood films? (Note: See paragraphs 5, 21, and 29.)

2. How do the roles Asian women play in recent independent productions differ from those generally created for them in Hollywood productions?

3a. How would you characterize the *overall* tone of this essay? (See "Guide to Terms": *Style and Tone.*)

b. Identify any sections of the essay where the tone varies noticeably.

4. Point out any passages in the essay that offer clear instances of irony, especially sarcasm or understatement. (Guide: *Irony.*)

Expository Techniques

1a. Does Tajima offer a clear definition of each category?

b. If not, how might the categories be introduced and defined more clearly?

2a. Are the categories in this essay distinct or is there some overlapping?

b. If the categories overlap, does the author acknowledge this? Where?

3a. Would this essay be more effective if it had fewer examples? A greater number? Explain. (Guide: *Evaluation.*)

b. Evaluate the examples in the following paragraphs for clarity and effectiveness: 8–20, 22, and 26–27.

c. Discuss whether the examples of work by independent filmmakers provide convincing evidence that these films go beyond the stereotypes.

Diction and Vocabulary

1. The names used to identify many of the standard character types are clichés. Point out the clichés used in this way in paragraphs 2 and 3.

2. Explain the meaning of the following terms: "cutting rooms" (par. 1); "Mama-sans" (4); "a cheongsam-clad maid" (31).

3. If you do not know the meanings of some of the following words, look them up in a dictionary: simplistic (par. 3); homogeneous (4); Mongol (5); compliant (7); yenta (9); objectification (23); vilifies (26); pervasive (29).

Suggestions for Writing and Discussion

1. Discuss how movies and television have stereotyped other ethnic or social groups. Are these stereotypes always negative? Are they always harmful?

2. Immigrant groups are often subjected to negative stereotyping. Draw on your own experience and knowledge for examples of this process or do research on immigrant groups that are now considered part of the mainstream but were once treated as outsiders.

(NOTE: Suggestions for topics requiring development by use of CLASSIFICATION are on page 139, at the end of this section.)

JUDITH STONE

JUDITH STONE has been a regular contributor to a number of magazines, including *Discover*. Her writings have been collected in *Light Matters: Essays in Science from Gravity to Levity* (1991). As the title suggests, Stone writes about science and scientific matters with both wit and detailed knowledge.

Personal Beast

From the play of words in its title through the rest of its many puns and humorous images, this essay looks critically and understandingly at our often exaggerated and absurd affection for pets—and the status they can confer on their owners. The essay first appeared as a column in *Discover* magazine.

For the past several millennia, dogs have pretty much had the Man's Best Friend market cornered. Lately, however, thanks to a sort of demographic Darwinism, several strong contenders for the title are nipping at the heels of the chosen species. 1

The dog emerged as protopet in Mesopotamia, where our nomadic ancestors first began living in villages about 12,000 to 14,000 years ago. (And if you think it's hard to paper-train a puppy, imagine having to use stone tablets.) 2

"Domestication was an urban event," explains Alan Beck, Ph.D., director of the University of Pennsylvania's Center for the Interaction of Animals and Society. "The garbage generated by these new high-density human communities probably attracted wolf packs; villagers may have bred the pups into pets with the idea of making peace with the pack. These domesticated creatures could bark a warning when nondomestic animals came around, and also 3 help with trash control. And perhaps one of the earliest reasons for breeding pets was for companionship; the desire to nurture is part of human culture." (Those days, when Hector was a pup, probably marked the first time in history that a human being uttered the words, "Aw, Ma, can't I keep it?")

Now a new kind of urbanization is creating a new kind of pet.   4 People are choosing animals that better fit a busier life and a smaller dwelling. Is there room for Fido in Mondo Condo, a world of two-income families with less time but more discretionary income? Folks want pets that are small and independent, pets that offer them a way to announce their individuality in a crowded, standardized world. Miniaturization, convenience, chic—the pet of the nineties has many of the same fine qualities as an under-the-counter microwave or a car phone. Here, hot off the Ark Nouveau, are the exotic animals that busy Americans simply must have.

Some of you may be seeking a companion that's low-mainte-   5 nance, affectionate, cute (though swaybacked and paunchy), and perfectly content curled up in front of the TV, pigging out on junk food. (Yeah, yeah, I know—you're already married to it. You're a scream, honestly.) I mean the Vietnamese pot-bellied pig, the nation's top-selling Asian import. A black, beagle-sized porker that's also called a Chinese house pig, it looks like a cross between a hog, a honey bear, and a hand puppet.

"If you can keep a poodle, you can keep one of these pigs," says   6 Fredericka Wagner, co-owner, with husband Bob, of Flying W Farms in Piketon, Ohio, which sends more of the little piggies to market than anyone in the country. "They're very appealing. Full grown, they weigh up to 45 or 50 pounds and stand about 12 to 13 inches high. They graze instead of root. Ordinary pigs have a long, straight snout; this one has a short, pushed-in, wrinkly nose. Its little ears stick straight up like a bat's and it has a straight tail that it wags like a dog's. It barks, too, and it can learn tricks—to come when it's called, sit up and beg, or roll over and play dead hog instead of dead dog." And it's easier to housebreak than a cat, Wagner says. Her three little pigs, Choo-Choo, Matilda, and Hamlet, like to sit around with the family and watch movies on TV (presumably *Porky's I* through *III*), and they enjoy supplementing their diet of Purina Pig Chow with candy, brownies, peanuts, and potato chips.

When the pigs arrived two years ago from Vietnam (by way of   7 Sweden and Canada, after three years of red tape), the Wagners already ran a midget menagerie, selling impossibly cute 18-inch miniature sheep (perfect for baby sweaters, easy to count for insomniacs), pygmy goats, miniature donkeys, and championship miniature Arabian horses. (Apparently there are no bonsai bovines, or the Wagners would have them.) "Miniature horses are bred down from larger horses—anything from huge Belgian draft horses to Shetland ponies—a process that can take a century," Wagner says. "In our experience, to reduce a horse from 48 inches to 34 inches takes six generations—about twenty years. You can do it in only three generations if you have a 30-inch stallion, but you'd have to dig a hole to put the mare in."

Wagner first heard about the pigs from a friend in California; reportedly they'd been imported by Vietnam veterans who recalled the friendly critters from their tours of duty. Though Wagner was instantly attracted to them, she wasn't sure she'd get the business off the ground. But the swine flew. "We can't keep up with the demand," she says. "In the first eighteen months we sold a hundred pigs." Wagner is boarish on pot-bellied pigs as an investment. "Not even the stock market will pay you back as fast as these pigs will. I've had several retired people buy them to supplement their income. They breed at six months [the pigs, not the retirees] and it takes three weeks, three months, and three days for them to have babies. By the time your gilt is a year old—a gilt is a pregnant sow—she's given you her first litter of pigs and you have your investment back three times over." Since you can only have gilt by association, those who want to breed pigs must buy an unrelated pair for $2,500. "We expect that to go up to $3,000, because the demand is so great," says Wagner, in hog heaven. "We've sold them to everyone from poets to princes—we shipped some overseas to a Saudi Arabian prince. Stephanie Zimbalist, the actress, has one." 8

Stephanie Zimbalist! A recommendation, indeed. But what about having the same pet as *Michael Jackson?* For part of his personal zoo (boa, deer, chimp/valet, glove, and, nearly, the Elephant Man), Jackson has chosen a taller order of hip creature, the llama. His is one of about 15,000 in the country. "But in years to come, we'll see more and more of them in the average home," says Florence Dicks, owner of the Llonesome Llama Ranch in Sumner, Washington. "They're great hiking companions, their wool is increasingly in demand, and they make wonderful pets. They've been part of 9 domestic life in South America for centuries. I think of them as one of life's necessities."

Dicks, who runs Llama Lluvs Unlltd., the world's only Llama-gram delivery service, notes that the recent lifting of a government ban on imports will increase the llama population; most American-born llamas are descended from a single herd owned by William Randolph Hearst.

"They're very gentle," Dicks says. "Many of my fifteen llamas lived in the house for their first year. They're easier to house-train than a cat." (You know how all weird meat is described as "sort of like chicken"? Apparently all weird pets are easier to housebreak than a cat.) Dicks explains, in more detail than necessary, that llamas are what's called communal voiders—a great name for a rock band. Spread some llama droppings where you want them to go, and, in the comradely way of communal voiders everywhere, they will use that spot forever after. "We've shared our bathroom with llamas for five years, and they've never had an accident," Dicks says. Okay, they squeeze the toothpaste from the top, but nobody's perfect.

"I train my llamas to hum—that's the noise they make—when they want to go outside," Dicks reports. "They communicate by tone variance. If they're relaxed, there's a musical quality to the hum. If they're stressed, you can hear the anxiety. I have a llama who hums with a rising inflection when he's curious."

Full-grown llamas can stand over six feet tall and weigh up to 500 pounds. A male costs between $1,500 and $15,000. (And at a recent auction, a male said to have outstanding stud qualities—he always sends a thank-you note—fetched $100,000). A gelded male will set you back $700 or $800, a female about $8,000. The only bad thing about llamas, Dicks says, is that you have to clip their toenails every three or four months. Which doesn't sound like a big deal if you're already sharing a bathroom.

But more and more of us have life-styles and living spaces—to use a pair of expressions even more nauseating than the word *pus*—that can't accommodate a dog, let alone a llama. I know I barely have room in my apartment for a pet peeve. Hence the proliferation among city dwellers of ferrets, dwarf rabbits, and birds. According to the American Veterinary Medical Association, birds are the fastest growing pet category. Their numbers increased 24 percent between 1983 and 1987, from 10.3 million to 12.8 million. Talking birds, like Amazon parrots, are especially sought after, reports veterinarian

Katherine Quesenberry, head of the exotic pet service of the Animal Medical Center of New York. (And I guess if you crossed these South American birds with llamas, you'd get Fernando Llamas, six-foot communal voiders that squawk, "You look *mah*velous." Cheep gag.)

The ferret, a more personable cousin of the weasel, has been   15
bred in captivity for a century, mostly for lab research. But its popularity as a pet has steadily risen over the last decade. Says Tina Ellenbogen, a Seattle veterinarian and information services director for the Delta Society, a national organization dedicated to the study of human-animal bonding, "People become attached to ferrets because they have a lot of personality. They're small, clean, and amusing." (It's sometimes hard to tell when people are talking about ferrets and when they're talking about Dudley Moore.) You can walk them on a harness or let them play on a ferrets wheel. They're easily litter-trained, says Ellenbogen—easier than a cat, I imagine—and statistically less likely to bite than a dog is. Males are unpleasant if you don't remove their stink glands, and females are sexually insatiable until you have them fixed, but hey.

Maybe you're a person who doesn't understand all the sound   16
and furry over mammals. Maybe you'd rather see something in cold blood.

The reptile of the hour is the African Old World chameleon.   17
"Having one is like owning a dinosaur!" says Gary Bagnall, head of California Zoological Supplies, one of the five largest reptile distributors in the country. "They look truly prehistoric. Their eyes move independently and they have 10-inch tongues with stickum at the end for catching insects. The base color is green, but they can blend into their surroundings by changing to yellow, orange, white, black, brown, and sometimes blue." The 6- to 10-inch chameleons start at $35; a foot-long variety, called Miller's chameleon, goes for $1,000. "We get only about four of them a year," Bagnall says. "There's a waiting list."

The nation's most sought-after amphibian, according to Bag-   18
nall, is the poison arrow frog, a tiny (less than an inch long), jewel-like native of South America that comes in orange and black, yellow and black, or blue. The really great thing about the poison arrow frog is that if you boil up about fifty of them, you get enough of the toxin they secrete to brew a dandy blowdart dip guaranteed to make hunting small jungle mammals a breeze.

Alive, the frogs, which cost from $35 to $200, require a lot of 19
attention, Bagnall warns. "They can't take extremes in temperature
or dryness, and their diet is restricted to very small insects. In fact,
you have to raise fruit flies for them." Most of us don't have time to
raise fruit flies for our families, let alone for a pet. But, paradoxically,
though exotic pet owners are getting busier, they're also getting
savvier and more dedicated.

"The whole pet industry has changed," says Bagnall. "Exotic 20
pet owners can't afford to be ignorant, because they're paying
more." Making a fatal mistake with a $3,500 miniature ram and ewe
is a whole different thing from accidentally offing a twenty-five-cent
baby turtle. (I'd like to take this opportunity to make a public
confession. I'm sorry, Shelly. I was only seven, and I didn't know
that painting your back with nail polish would kill you. Forgive
me, too, for digging you up two weeks after the funeral, but I was
curious to see if the rumors I'd heard about deterioration were
true. You didn't disappoint.) Continues Bagnall, "I can't speak for
birds and mammals, but the prices of even standard, bread-and-
butter reptiles—boas, garter snakes, pythons—have tripled over the
last three years because of government regulation of imports." But
the high prices seem to add to the mystique, he says. "Reptiles
attract people who want something not everybody has. Also, if
you're allergic to fur, they're a nice alternative." (And probably a
certain percentage of newly minted MBAs are even now saying to
their mentors, "Rep *ties?* I thought you said 'invest in some rep-
tiles!'") Bagnall adds that poison arrow frogs and Old World
chameleons are especially popular now because they've only
recently appeared in zoos. "And if a reptile shows up in a movie, its
popularity increases tenfold, like the Burmese python in *Raiders of
the Lost Ark.*"

Yes, it's a cachet as cachet can world. Perhaps all human 21
progress stems from the tension between two basic drives: to have
just what everyone else has and to have what no one has. Covet your
neighbor's ass? Get yourself a miniature one and watch him mewl
with envy. But be careful: Once an odd animal enters the mainstream, those on the cutting edge of the pet thing have to push for a
new personal beast. "Pygmy goats used to be really rare," Fredericka Wagner says with a sigh. "Now everyone has them." (Haven't
you noticed that the first question you're asked at the best restaurants these days is "May I check your goat?")

The proliferation of peculiar pets may necessitate a revamping   22
of terminology, says veterinarian Quesenberry. "The term *exotics* is
no longer valid. We're talking about animals that haven't historically been domesticated, but they're not wild anymore, either,
because they're being bred in captivity and exposed to humans from
an early age. Somebody has suggested using the term *special species*
for these animals, and reserving the term *exotics* for the zoo stuff."

If you're not ready to pay big bucks for little pigs, you'll be   23
happy to know that the classic exotic pet, the simple yet eloquent sea
monkey, retails for just $3.99. Remember sea monkeys? When some
of us were kids, during what scientists call the Late Cleaver-Brady
Epoch, sea monkeys were advertised in the backs of magazines, usually between the Mark Eden Bust Developer and the Can You Draw
This Elf School of Art. A smiling, bikini-clad creature with the head
of a monkey and the body of a seahorse promised the requisite
hours of fun for kids from eight to—if I recall the stats correctly—
eighty. Remember your disappointment when the "monkeys"
turned out to be brine shrimp, so infinitesimal that they could only
be clearly seen with the enclosed magnifying glass? Remember how
not one of them wore a bathing suit? Well, for the same low price, a
new generation of kids can learn a powerful lesson about the true
nature of existence (sometimes when you expect a bikini-clad
aquatic primate, you get a bunch of stupid, skinny-dipping germs).
And sea monkeys are easier to house-train than cats.

Meanings and Values

1a. In your own words, tell what Stone considers the main qualities of
    the pet of the 90s.

 b. Explain the differences she sees between contemporary pets (and
    owners) and those of the past.

2a. Identify the categories Stone presents in this essay.

 b. Are there any subcategories? If so, what are they?

 c. Do any of the categories overlap? If so, is the overlap confusing?

3. Does this essay have a serious purpose? If so, what is it?

Expository Techniques

1a. Can the second sentence in this essay be considered a thesis state-
    ment? If so, why? (See "Guide to Terms": *Thesis*.)

b. Are there any other sentences that might be considered additional thesis statements or repetitions and developments of the second sentence? Identify any such sentences and discuss their role in the essay.

2. Why does the author choose to begin the essay by discussing dogs? Would the essay have been more effective had she begun with a discussion of cats or of some other familiar kind of pet? (Guide: *Evaluation*.)

3. Discuss the role of the comments within the parentheses in paragraph 20. Explain the ways these comments are similar to or different from other parenthetical comments in the essay.

Diction and Vocabulary

1. What does "Mondo Condo" (par. 4) mean, and for what purpose does the writer use the phrase?

2. Identify the source of each of the following allusions, and discuss what each means: Hector (par. 3); Ark Nouveau (4); swine flew (8); in cold blood (16). (Guide: *Figures of Speech*.)

3. How does the word choice in the last sentence of paragraph 5 emphasize the meaning and create a pattern of sound? (Guide: *Emphasis, Diction*.)

4. If you do not know the meaning of some of the following words, look them up in the dictionary: nomadic (par. 2); discretionary (4); voiders (11); variance (12); gelded (13); insatiable (15); cachet (21).

Suggestions for Writing and Discussion

1. Try to come up with some other kinds of pets that might be included in Stone's classification or subdivide a single category of pets, such as cats, to create a classification that will introduce readers to unfamiliar members of the larger category.

2. Prepare an essay classifying leisure time activities or hobbies that contrasts those popular a decade or two ago with those popular now.

(NOTE: Suggestions for topics requiring development by use of CLASSIFICATION are on page 139, at the end of this section.)

BRENDA PETERSON

BRENDA PETERSON, a novelist and essayist, was born in 1950 on a forest ranger station in the Sierra Nevada Mountains. As a child she lived in many different places, especially in the Southeast. Currently, she lives in Seattle. Peterson received a B.A. in 1972 from the University of California-Davis. From 1972 to 1976 she worked as an editorial assistant at *The New Yorker* magazine. She has taught creative writing at Arizona State University and now works as an environmental writer. Her novels include *River of Light* (1978), *Becoming the Enemy* (1988), and *Duck and Cover* (1991). Her essays have been collected in *Living by Water: Essays on Life, Land and Spirit* (1990), and *Nature and Other Mothers* (1992).

Life Is a Musical

In this essay, Peterson offers several closely related classifications as a way of exploring the ways music can (and ought to) enrich and heal our emotional lives. This essay was first published in *Nature and Other Mothers*.

When the day is too gray, when the typewriter is too loud, after a 1 lovers' quarrel, when a sister calls with another family horror story, when the phone never stops and those unanswered messages blink on my machine like angry, red eyes—I tune out my life and turn up the music. Not my favorite public radio station but my own personal frequency—I have my own soul's station. It is somewhere on the dial between Mozart's *Magic Flute*, the gospel-stomping tiger growl of Miss Aretha Franklin, Motown's deep dance 'n' strut, and the singing story of Broadway musicals.

Whether it's Katie Webster's Swamp Boogie Queen singing 2 "Try a Little Tenderness," or a South American samba, whether it's the Persuasions crooning "Let It Be" or that throbbing baritone solo "Other Pleasures" from *Aspects of Love,* my musical solace is so complete it surrounds me in a mellifluous bubble like a placenta of sound. To paraphrase the visionary Stevie Wonder, I have learned to survive by making sound tracks in my own particular key of life.

For years now I've made what I call "tapes against terror" to hide me away from the noisy yak and call of the outside world. These homemade productions are dubbed Mermaid Music; sometimes I send them to friends for birthdays and feel the pleasure of playing personal disc jockey to accompany their lives too. Among my siblings, we now exchange music tapes instead of letters. It is particularly gratifying to hear my nieces and nephews singing along to my tapes, as another generation inherits our family frequency.

I trace making my musical escapes to a childhood of moving around. As we packed the cardboard boxes with our every belonging—sometimes we hadn't even bothered to unpack our dresses from those convenient hanging garment containers provided by the last moving company—the singing began. From every corner of the emptying house, we'd hear the harmonies: my father a walking bass as he heaved-ho in the basement; my mother's soprano sometimes shrill and sharp as the breaking glass in the kitchen; my little brother between pure falsetto and a tenor so perfect we knew he'd stopped packing his room simply to sing; my sisters and I weaving between soprano and first and second alto from our bedrooms as we traded and swapped possessions for our next life. At last gathered in the clean, white space that was once our house, we'd hold hands and sing "Auld Lang Syne." Piling into the station wagon, with the cat in a wooden box with slats for air holes, Mother would shift into a rousing hymn, "We'll Leave It All Behind," or sometimes, if she was mutinously happy to hightail it out of some small "burg" as she called them, she'd lead us into "Shuffle Off to Buffalo," substituting wherever we were moving for the last word. "Chattanooga Choo Choo" and "California, Here We Come" were her standard favorites for leave-taking. If, as we drove past our schools and our friends' houses for the last time, the harmonies in the backseat faltered, Mother might remind us that choirs of angels never stayed long in one place singing because the whole world needed music. Father might suggest some slower songs, as long as they weren't sad.

In all the shifting landscapes and faces of my childhood, what stays the same is the music. First, there was my mother's music, which seems now to have entered effortlessly into her children's minds as if we were tiny tape recorders: the mild, sweetly suave Mills Brothers, Mitch Miller's upbeat swing, the close sibling harmonies of the Andrews Sisters, and always the church music, the heartfelt Sunday singing, which is the only thing I ever miss since leaving that tight fellowship of Southern Baptist believers.

Ever since I can remember—certainly I have flashes of being   6
bounced around in the floating dark of my mother's womb as she tap-danced on the church organ pedals, sang at the top of her voice, and boogied across the keys—there has been this music. It is the only counterpoint to, the only salvation from a sermon that paralyzes the soul into submitting to a jealous God. From the beginning, music was an alternative to that hellfire terror. I can still hear it: a preacher's voice, first a boom, then a purr that raises into a hiss and howl to summon that holy hurricane of fire and brimstone. But after enduring the scourge of sins, there came the choir. Cooing and shushing, mercy at last fell upon those of us left on an Earth that this God had long ago abandoned. Listening to the full-bodied harmonies, I could close my eyes and heretically wonder, Wasn't Heaven still here?

Yessss, hallelujah, still here . . . Hush, can't you hear? the choir mur-   7
mured like so many mammies' lullabies. Then silence, as a small woman stepped forward, her rapt vibrato shimmering like humid heat lightning right before rain. Or a baritone dropping his woes and his dulcet voice low as a cello, caressing a whole congregation. If we were blessed that Sunday, there might be a shorter sermon and a "songfest" with harmonies we could hear in our heads, syncopating, counterpointing in a lovely braid of bright sound that beckoned us. *Sing now, brothers and sisters.* And we were many voices making one song. The fundamental fear was gone; weren't we already angels in Heaven?

Now that I am forty and have been what my family pityingly   8
refers to as "settled-down" for ten years, now that I am so far back-slid from the fellowship of the Southern Baptist believers, now that I no longer even make top ten on my mother's prayer list, now that the terror of Hell has been replaced by the terror of living, I still find myself calling upon my homemade choirs to accompany me in my car, to surround my study or kitchen and sing back the demons of daily life. Sometimes I've even caught myself slipping another tape

against terror into the stereo and singing a distracted riff of my mother's favorite, "We'll Leave It All Behind."

During the recent holy war between the United States and Iraq, with the apocalyptic rhetoric about "Satan" and "infidels" eerily reminiscent of southern revivals—Mermaid Music was working long hours to meet my own and my friends' wartime demands. To offset NPR's daily interviews with military experts commenting on the allied video-war air strikes with the zealous aplomb of sports-casters, I'd surrender to the tender tenor of Aaron Neville singing "With God on Our Side" or "Will the Circle Be Unbroken?" As I drove along freeways where phosphorescent orange bumper stick-ers shouted USA KICKS BUTT! or OPERATION DESERT STORM, as if it were a souvenir banner of a hot vacation spot, I wondered that there was no music for the Gulf War. Where were the songs like "My Buddy" or "It's a Long Way to Tipperary"? 9

During the last days of the war, I relied upon Bach's Violin Con-certo in D Minor, the fierce longing of Jacqueline DePres's cello, Fauré's Requiem and, as always, Mozart. On a particularly bad day, between the Pentagon press conferences—men with pointers, target maps, smart-bomb videos, and a doublespeak war doggerel that called bombing "servicing a target"—I made a beeline to my public library and checked out every musical from *Oklahoma* to *Miss Saigon*. I made a tape entitled "Life Is a Musical" and divided it into three sections: (1) Love Found in Strange Places, (2) Love Lost Every-where, and (3) Love Returns. It was astonishing how songs from vastly different time periods and places segued together. My favorite storyline riff is "Empty Chairs at Empty Tables," from *Les Misérables* to "The American Dream" from *Miss Saigon* to "Carefully Taught" from *South Pacific* to "Don't Cry for Me, Argentina," from *Evita* to "Bring Him Home" from *Les Misérables*. When I sent copies out to a select group of musicals-loving friends, it was as if we were all together at a candlelight mass or cross-continent communion, try-ing to imagine a war where bombs fell. 10

Playing my own tapes against terror is a way to document and summon back the necessities that mothered them. For example, "My Funny Valentine," with its Billie Holiday/Sarah Vaughan/Ella Fitzgerald/Alberta Hunter blues and ebullience is still a favorite, long after that lover has gone. Upon hearing that an old friend had bone cancer, I made him a tape called "Music to Heal By," which included the Delta Rhythm Boys' version of "Dry Bones." My friend 11 wrote to say it was the first time he'd laughed in a long time. Now he's making his own tapes. After a writer friend of mine drank herself to death, I felt so bereft—since, after all, we'd planned to retire to the Black Hole Nursing Home for Wayward Writers together— that I made a tape called "The Ten Commandments of Love, or Southern Baptists Beware!" It's every song I ever slow-danced to or memorized in the sweaty backseat of a borrowed car as my date and I broke Sunday school rules on Saturday night. Declared by my siblings and southern pals to have gone into "metal" (their word for platinum or gold), it includes Etta James's soaring "At Last," Sam Cooke's silky "Wonderful World," and a steamy duet of "634-5789" with Robert Cray and Tina Turner. It's a great tape for getting in the mood.

Since ancient times, the Chinese have believed that certain 12
sounds can balance and heal. In acupressure, for example, each organ has a sound. Listening to a healthy heart, an astute healer can hear laughter or, if there is disease, wind. The gallbladder shouts; the stomach speaks in a singsong, sometimes overly sympathetic voice; and the kidney, ever the perfectionist, groans. Sighs can be a sign of liver ailments, and the pitch of a person's voice can tell a story of that body's health just as well as a tongue. In some Taoist practices to enhance longevity, re-creating the sounds of certain organs can strengthen and tone them. For example, the *whuuuh whuuuh* sound of the kidney can revitalize the adrenals, fortifying the immune system. If one cannot take time to sing in the key of every organ, I'd suggest Chinese wind chimes like the ones that grace my back porch. When a strong salt wind blows off the beach, my chimes, which are perfectly pitched to a five-element Chinese scale, play an impromptu arpeggio—a momentary transport to some monastic garden, a Shangri-la of sound. Scientific studies report that the actual sound of nature resonates at the level of eight hertz; by comparison, a refrigerator reverberates at eighty hertz. Is it any wonder some of us need to return to a musical womb to retreat from such technological onslaughts to our nervous systems?

In fact, our time in the womb is not at all quiet; it is a noisy sym- 13
phony of voices, lower-tract rumbles, whirrings like waterfalls, and white noise. One of my friends found that if she played a tape of the roar of her sturdy Kirby vacuum cleaner, the sound immediately put her boisterous newborn twins to sleep. I have another friend whose entire house is wall-to-wall egg cartons, which absorb sound as well

as enhance his audiophilic tendencies. I've visited houses that sound like living inside an aquarium, where pleasant underwater burbles from elaborate tropical fish tanks drown out the world. I've also entered homes where cuckoo clocks, grandfather chimes, and deep gongs count the hours so that I felt I was inside a ticking time bomb. Consciously or unconsciously we all make sound tracks to underscore our lives.

Mermaid Music has allowed me to enter a reverie of song, a   14
backstage "smaller-than-life" sojourn away from all the stresses. Right now I'm at work on two dance tapes for a summer roll-up-the-rug party. Entitled "Bop till You Drop" and "Bad Girls," the tapes defy all hearers not to kick up their heels with such all-time hits as "Heat Wave" and "I Heard It Through the Grapevine," as well as the ever-popular "R-E-S-P-E-C-T." Of course, I've had requests for sequels and am at work on "Life Is a Musical II" divided into (1) "Falling," (2) "Feeling," and (3) "Forever Ruined/Recovery." It flows from "People Will Say We're in Love" to "Happy Talk" to "Just You Wait, Henry Higgins!"

My siblings say I should sell my tapes against terror on late-   15
night TV in the company of such classics as Veg-O-Matics and "Elvis Lives" medleys. The idea fills me with horror. After all, there are copyright violations cops who come like revenuers in the dark of the night to bust local moonshiners and music makers. I'd rather stay strictly small-time and nonprofit, like that long-ago lullaby service I had in college, a trio of nannies against nightmares. But if anyone out there in music land is making his or her own tapes against terror, I'd be open to an exchange. After all, it's better than bombs through the mail or collecting baseball cards.

So tune in, and maybe we'll find ourselves on the same fre   16
quency. On this lifelong Freeway of Love, I just want to be an Earth Angel with my Magic Flute. Because after all, Everybody Plays the Fool and Ain't Nobody's Business If I Do.

Meanings and Values

1. In a paragraph of your own, summarize what this essay has to say about music, human emotions, and the relationship between them.

2. What subject or subjects is Peterson classifying in this essay?

3. Explain what the writer means by the phrase "my soul's station" (par. 11).

4.   According to paragraph 9, what kind of music did the Gulf War fail to produce?

Expository Techniques

1a.   Which paragraph announces the purpose and theme of the essay? (See "Guide to Terms": *Purpose, Unity*.)

 b.   Can this essay be said to have a thesis statement? If so, where is it? (Guide: *Thesis*.)

2.   What pattern other than classification does the writer employ in paragraph 4? (Hint: See Section 6.)

3a.   What different subjects does Peterson classify in this essay?

 b.   How, if at all, does the writer keep these different classifications from overlapping in a confusing manner?

 c.   Would this essay be more effective if the writer had concentrated on only one or two of the classifications? Explain. (Guide: *Evaluation*.)

4.   What is the function of the clauses that open the first sentence in the essay? (Guide: *Syntax, Introductions*.)

Diction and Vocabulary

1.   Identify the extended comparison in paragraph 12 and explain its relation to the central theme of the essay. (Guide: *Figures of Speech, Unity*.)

2.   Identify those paragraphs in the essay that begin with transition words indicating that they will further develop the topic or ideas of the preceding paragraph. Discuss whether the transition words serve effectively to link paragraphs and ideas within the essay. (Guide: *Transitions*.)

3.   If you do not know the meaning of some of the following words, look them up in the dictionary: solace, mellifluous, placenta (par. 2); falsetto (4); suave (5); heretically (6); dulcet (7); riff (8); eerily, zealous, aplomb (9); segued (10); ebullience (11); astute (12); audiophilic (13).

Suggestions for Writing and Discussion

1.   Classify the kinds of music you like and the ways they are linked to particular emotions or situations. Discuss your classification with others to see how their classifications are similar or different.

2.   Prepare an essay classifying tastes in music, art, movies, sports, some other art form, or some other activity. If you can, explain why

differences in people's tastes in art or preferences for certain activities can be explained on basis of differences in character, background, or some other factor.

(NOTE: Suggestions for topics requiring development by use of CLASSIFICATION are on page 139, at the end of this section.)

DON KUNZ was born in Kansas City, Missouri. He received a B.A. in from Kansas State University, an M.A. from the University of Texas at Austin, and a Ph.D. in English from the University of Washington, Seattle. He is an essayist, short story writer, and poet as well as a professor of American literature and film. His work has appeared in a variety of publications including *Vietnam Generation, Literature/Film Quarterly, Confrontation, Change,* and *Midwest Poetry Review.*

Nutty Professors

Television and movies provide us with numerous examples of professional people: lawyers, scientists, nurses, doctors, police officers, and a host of others. Sometimes the portraits are realistic and complex; at other times they are exaggerated and simplistic, as is the case with mad scientists or mousey librarians. In this essay, a shorter form of an article first published in *Forum for Honors,* the author looks at one of the abiding stereotypes of television and film, the "nutty professor," and at what the different versions of this figure reveal about our attitudes towards power and knowledge.

My father didn't want me to become a professor, but I did it anyway. 1
He was afraid I would go crazy. At the time, I thought his fears were silly; after all, my professors in college did not seem to be insane. Since then, I have realized that my father's idea of professors was not based upon models from life but from popular culture—jokes, cartoons, movies, television. Certainly, the latter two media have been particularly influential in shaping attitudes toward professors in American culture. Three distinct professorial stereotypes stand out in the American mass media of the 1960s and 1970s, represented

Adapted from "Nutty Professors" by Don Kunz, *Forum for Honors,* Vol. XXI, No. 2, Summer/Fall 1992. Reprinted by permission.

by the televised stand-up comedy act of Professor Irwin Corey, the sit-com character, Professor Roy Hinkley of *Gilligan's Island*, and the feature-length film character, Professor Charles W. Kingsfield of *The Paper Chase*. While these three are neither the first nor the most recent mass media depictions, they seem to reveal most clearly a spectrum of professorial characterizations.

In the popular mind, all three professorial stereotypes are, to varying degrees, crazy, but their behavioral disorders stretch from a diverting idiocy, through a pathetically obsessive ineffectualness, and all the way to a sinister madness.

Although a Broadway and Hollywood actor, Irwin Corey is best known for his stand-up comedy act as Professor Irwin Corey, which he perfected in numerous televised guest appearances, including a regular stint on *The Andy Williams Show* during the 1969–70 season. Corey represents the professor as zany. In his abstracted and manic behavior, he is a distant cousin to the mad scientist but stripped of his lust for power. Professor Corey's appearance and behavior reassure us that the acquisition of much formal schooling reduces one to a state of benign idiocy. It is as if some twentieth-century Faust had been cheated by the Devil—*caveat emptor*—lost his soul in return for permanent brain damage and the shabbily costumed manner of a nineteenth-century undertaker in the last stages of delirium tremens.

Professor Corey's long, baggy, black swallow-tailed coat and unpressed droopy-seated drawers, his formal white shirt and black string bow tie identify him as an anachronism. These along with his matted, long, gray hair complete an unkempt appearance—the outward and visible sign of an intelligence distracted by its own processes. In this, he constitutes a paradoxical version of absent-mindedness: he looks so vacant because his mind is so full. Consequently, his costume and behavior reveal not only a creature living in another world but a bad advertisement for it, a warning: this is what happens to your body when you exercise your mind.

Professor Corey's mannerisms are like those of a man possessed. He has only two remarkable behavioral modes, and they are exact opposites. The first is a rapid, erratic flitting and cavorting around the stage punctuated by unpredictable sorties into the audience, by which he breaches the expected decorum of an actor and so enhances our sense of absurdity. Corey struts, stumbles, bounces up and down on his toes like a child learning to walk or runs jerkily like a Keystone Cop with a hot foot. His second posture is an ecstatic somnambulism: he is suddenly struck dumb, rooted to the spot, swaying back and forth from the ankles up as if summoning up an energy from the floor which blissfully rocks him to sleep. If the smile flickering upon Corey's face is any indication, these two extremes— eccentric locomotion and moments of trance-like nodding off—seem to derive from a kind of divine rapture. The gestural message which he acts out is that knowledge alters consciousness for the worse more effectively than either dexedrine or sominex. In either case, his bizarre behavior establishes an emotional distance between himself and his audience, inviting derisive laughter.

Orally, Professor Corey's forté is the extended nonsequitur 6 which stretches skeins of illogic to preposterous lengths. These speeches are a remarkable achievement. (Try talking for even five minutes without making any sense whatsoever.) It is a major creative act to assert one's freedom from the habit of rational discourse and grammatical structure. In this, Corey is a Lord of Misrule, a bringer of linguistic chaos. His oral performance parodies the extemporaneous lecturer. A clause is thrown out, qualified beyond recognition, and elaborated upon to distraction; a false analogy is developed, another unrelated clause appended, a new verb selected by way of correction, an absurd appositive, an obscurely self-congratulatory allusion, a metaphor which clouds rather than clarifies, a throat cleared, a mind changed, and a rhetorical question, an ejaculation that resembles a temper tantrum. His lecture becomes an absurd soliloquy by stylistic default.

Of the same kind as Professor Irwin Corey is Groucho Marx's 7 character, Professor Quincy Wagstaff, from *Horse Feathers* (1932). Marx's character is the most obvious precursor of Corey: his black swallow-tailed coat, peculiar walk, unpredictable antics, and nonsensical double talk mark him as a distant ancestor of the zany professor. But Groucho's trademark cigar makes an enormous difference. It signals an alert, shrewd, purposeful intelligence lurking behind the chaos it creates. Groucho's Professor Wagstaff is a confidence man toying with victims. His seemingly nonsensical blather meanders towards recognizable meaning—outrageous puns and clearly calculated punchlines. And he can be brief: during his extemporaneous biology lecture, for example, when he slaps his pointer across a diagram of a horse and finds it resting on the animal's backside, Professor Wagstaff remarks: "That reminds me, I haven't seen my son all day." Similarly, his seemingly spontaneous antics more often than not prove to be part of some scheme: as President of Huxley College he nonchalantly engineers a football victory over Darwin College. Groucho's Professor Wagstaff is a zany but not the pure form of it that Professor Corey has perfected.

Similar, too, is Jerry Lewis's character, Professor Julius Ferris 8
Kelp, from *The Nutty Professor* (1963), a nearly contemporaneous version of Corey's idiotic stereotype. His buckteeth, glasses, and poorly fitting '60s suitcoats establish a grotesque but not anachronistic appearance. He too trips, stumbles, and lurches about the set wreaking havoc, but he is not so much absent minded as accident prone—another in a long list of incompetent characters upon which Lewis exercised his comedic talent. Furthermore, when Lewis's Professor Kelp spouts nonsense, it is often the result of being distracted by the beautiful coed in his class (Miss Stella Purdy) rather than being lost in the labyrinth of his own thought processes like Corey. Finally, this nutty professor is reformed by Miss Purdy, who uncovers a decent, kind, intelligent man lurking within the bumbling, grotesque Professor Kelp, and marries him. Thus the film's plot, which is a sentimentalized version of Dr. Jekyll and Mr. Hyde or an academic version of Beauty and the Beast, does not allow Kelp to remain true to the professor as zany best exemplified by Corey.

Another different stereotype emerges with Professor Roy Hink- 9
ley, played by Russell Johnson on the television serial, *Gilligan's Island*. This professor does not work alone even though he is a castaway on the tropical island. His characterization is intimately tied to the needs of a situation comedy upon which the weekly episodes generate seemingly endless variations. In the cast, he is described by name and identified as a brilliant research scientist, but during the shows he remains nameless: he is "The Professor." This eradication of his individuality is complemented by his wooden manner: this professor is all twenty-four volumes of *The Encyclopedia Americana* disguised as a person. While The Professor's expertise runs primarily to the technical, he is something of a psychologist, a geologist, a linguist, and an anthropologist. He also knows chemical formulae, physical structures, historical dates, and mathematical probabilities. The Professor is simply a reference work for the other castaways from the USS Minnow to consult as their different backgrounds and interests inevitably entangle them in one ridiculous situation after another. Thus, Professor Hinkley finds himself delivering lessons to

the Skipper, First Mate Gilligan, movie star Ginger Grant, million-
aire Thurston Howell III and his wife Lovey, and Kansas general
store clerk Mary Ann.

As a source of factual knowledge, The Professor resembles a   10
modern Adam naming and classifying items for his innocent companions marooned on this South Pacific Eden. He provides a sense
of order, stability, and security with his authoritative pronounce-
ments, in which his fellows have implicit faith but no understanding. This is because most of what he says is polysyllabic jargon.
Ironically, his explanations confuse rather than clarify. Most of what
he says is prefaced by "you see." "You see, Skipper." "You see, Mary
Ann." "You see, Ginger." "You see, Gilligan." Still, Professor Hinkley is no more an eye opener than Professor Corey: he leaves his fellows lost in a fog of words, separated from him by an esoteric
vocabulary and the higher intelligence which it pretends to convey.

But, there any resemblance to Corey ends. Certainly, Gilligan's   11
professor does not fit the dumpy stereotype acted out by Corey. In
fact, Hinkley is handsome. Forty-ish, trim, tall, clean-shaven with a
square jaw, thick curly hair, bright eyes uncorrected by spectacles,
neither neck confined by tie nor shoulders burdened by white cotton
or tweed coat—this professor might as well be a bachelor executive
for IBM on a cruise. And what luck! There he is, stranded on a lush
tropical island with two beautiful women and a collection of easily
distracted fools. Why, then, does this seemingly virile man concentrate all his energy only upon fleeing this conventional earthly paradise and getting back to civilization? Because he is a brilliant
research scientist, because he is "The Professor." He *must* be crazy.

The study of science may have been a shot in the arm for civi-   12
lization, but it has immunized The Professor against the charms of
the wholesome Mary Ann and the narcissistic Ginger. His lack of
sexual awareness echoes Mary Ann's but proceeds from a different
cause. Mary Ann is from the mythological heartland of American
innocence, Kansas. The Professor is from the mythological world of
unreality, the state of academia. Mary Ann's Dogpatch consciousness is engrossed in making fruit salad not love. The Professor's
mind is absorbed by higher thought processes; for him sexual
naivete is an occupational hazard.

In the prime time of the television wasteland, the Edenic myth   13
has been garbled. It looks like the new Adam has been washed up
onto a slightly more populous Eden in the South Pacific. Before

beginning this life as a castaway, he has gorged himself on the fruit of knowledge in that more advanced earthly paradise, the American university, which has awarded him a Ph.D. But, this has caused rather than compromised his sexual innocence: talk about pure research! Furthermore, The Professor wants to use his scientific knowledge only to invent the means of his escape from the primal state which he has regained. Stripped as he is of most strong emotions and animal drives, The Professor is a wooden figure, more like the Tree of Knowledge itself waiting to be tapped by the other lost souls. In this, the bitter fruit he bears is that knowledge is not enough for deliverance from anything but temporary crises, a means of prolonging the hope of being restored to one's rightful home: Hollywood, I think. Perhaps, we are meant to see him as the new Adam playing God—a kind of *Deus ex Professorial*, which is to say, a perpetually failing *Deus ex Machina* of the tropical island's slapstick paradise. Time after time, his obscure bits of lore hold out the hope of escape from the island but are insufficient to bring it about. It is, after all, Gilligan's Island, where ineptness, accident, and misunderstanding prevail over accumulated fact, logical prediction, and understood relationship.

Rendered impotent in its specifically sexual sense by his distracted intelligence and in a more general sense by accident and circumstance, Gilligan's professor is a pathetic fool. His virile image and confident manner continually seduce his fellow travellers into the belief that knowledge is power, and despite his repeated failure, they never lose faith in him. Because all of his learning has betrayed Professor Hinkley into such a state of pathetic foolishness, we must understand that his impotence acts as a synecdoche: it warns us that higher education will prove ineffectual as a means by which to insure some control over the future. ¹⁴

Hinkley's most obvious precursor is Fred MacMurray's Professor Ned Brainard in *The Absent Minded Professor* (1961). Like Hinkley, Professor Brainard is a handsome, well-dressed man whom a beautiful woman finds attractive, and he is also a brilliant research scientist so obsessed with his work that he is more or less oblivious to her charms. In fact, Professor Brainard becomes so distracted by his chemical experiments that he forgets to attend his own wedding on three separate occasions. But unlike Hinkley, Brainard's obsessive lab work results in a practical invention which actually succeeds. He invents flubber, an anti-gravity device which ¹⁵

simultaneously redeems him in the eyes of Medfield College's basketball coach, its most successful entrepreneurial alumnus, the U.S. Defense Department, and his fiancée. By the end of the film Professor Brainard is no longer known as "Neddy the Nut." Unlike the Professor on Gilligan's Island, he evolves beyond the stereotype of the pathetically ineffectual fool whose dedication to knowledge condemns him to celibacy.

A more recent and inventive variation on the stereotype of the [16] professor as work-obsessed, life-oblivious failure may be found in *The National Lampoon's Animal House* (1978). At first, Donald Sutherland's Professor Dave Jennings of the English Department at Faber College seems Hinkley's opposite. Professor Jennings confesses to his class that Milton is boring, that he is teaching only to pay the bills while he works on his novel, and that after four years his novel is still "a piece of shit." Jennings hardly seems obsessed with his work. Furthermore, he smokes dope with members of his class and fornicates with one of his female students. Unlike the Professor on *Gilligan's Island*, the professor in *Animal House* is not oblivious to the pleasures of the flesh. Although Jennings may seem Hinkley's antistereotype, he is simply an imaginative variant. Professor Jennings admits that he finds Satan the most interesting character in *Paradise Lost*, and he invites his students to consider that Milton intends to say that being evil may be more fun than being good. Clearly, then, this literature professor simply has taken his work home with him. In a different way, Jennings is as obsessed as Hinkley and as much a failure. The presumably superior knowledge which he professes has left him dissipated as well as powerless.

In sharp contrast, John Houseman's Professor Charles W. [17] Kingsfield of *The Paper Chase* (1973) represents the kind of professor who seems to be firmly dictating the terms of the future. Unlike Professor Corey or Professor Hinkley, there is nothing amusing or pathetic about him. The feature-length film version illustrates this harsh professorial stereotype more clearly than the somewhat more sentimental television serial spin-off on CBS during the 1978–79 season, but even in that softened version, its rigid spine remains. As this professor's name, Kingsfield, his college, Harvard, and his field, law, all indicate—his is a patrician presence. In its atmosphere, the audience suffers all its fantasies of intellectual bankruptcy and speechless embarrassment. His high, balding forehead; his unblinking, cold and overly large eyes which have the reflecting power of ball bearings; his flaring and irregularly shaped nostrils; his ears that lay back like a temperamental thoroughbred ready to bite—all these evoke a dangerous personality. Kingsfield's overly long staring pretends to make a virtue of a threat, excusing it as scholarly scrutiny. He is stout but not portly, as if the muscle of youth gave way to a girdled hardness. The low-angled shots of him on his dais magnify his stature and stuffy malevolence. He mostly stands in one place. But if he moves, he paces slowly, deliberately, planting his heel first and then the rest as if crushing something slowly to test its hardness. But mostly, his minimal gestures create controlled silences during which others suffer.

Kingsfield's appearance is as neat as an establishment pinstripe. 18 His impeccable tailoring, precisely clipped speech, and royal bearing might mislead one to mistake him for an Englishman. But, he is without ruddy cheeks or heartiness or the hereditary generosity of British aristocracy. No, he is a self-made man, the embodiment of sound American business principles on a naturalistic model—merciless, powerful, remorseless—like a gangster with status and an icy sense of protocol made possible by money. Professor Kingsfield exudes the bearing and values of the corporation president who takes humorless pride in manufacturing the most efficient nerve gas or chemical defoliant or in bribing small brown or olive officials of emerging nations. He is an academic Daddy Warbucks unsoftened by Annie and her dog, Sandy.

Quite the opposite of Professor Irwin Corey, Professor Charles 19 W. Kingsfield's madness is sinister. His questions probe insistently like a knife into one's ignorance. In a way, Professor Kingsfield is sort of an intellectual rapist, bullying his virginal first year law class to submit to his vision of a world based exclusively upon contracts. Like all rapes, this one is an act not of sexual passion but of hostility.

Yet, there is innocence in all this despite Kingsfield's arrogant- 20 seeming maliciousness. He is the harsh father figure living in a world of legal theorizing and logical proof, a world of perfect integrity and absolute certainty, a world where feeling is superfluous or unaffordable. During the film, Kingsfield permits himself only one moment of humorous self-reproach when, having goaded the young protagonist to shout out in class, "you're a son of a bitch, Kingsfield," he replies with haughty composure, "that is the most intelligent thing you've said today." Otherwise, this professor is engaged in the heady business of bullying his youthful pretenders with impunity and sweeping serene as royalty through the preoccupied fields of his superior mind. He embodies the audience's fears of the intellectual—absolute knowledge, status, power, articulateness. Kingsfield stands for the unblinking, naked awareness of truth stripped of all hypocrisy, cant, sentimentality, tact, comforting anthropomorphism, fallacy or ambiguity. Who really wants to know what truth is, especially if he has to become like Kingsfield to possess it? It is better, as the film's youthful protagonist does, to make a paper airplane of the grade-report form and toss is off toward the crashing surf.

In the film, Kingsfield's one potentially redeeming feature is   21
that he has a beautiful daughter. One immediately suspects it must have been by artificial insemination, but never mind. There she is. This along with his establishment manner qualifies him nicely for the comic role of the heavy father. And so it is that his strong cerebral presence both threatens and adds savor to the carnal knowledge which his lovely daughter and most defiant student (appropriately enough named Hart) are regularly gaining of one another by hitting the sack instead of the books. The best part is that Kingsfield suspects but never knows this for sure. In one particularly exciting scene, Hart has just made love with Kingsfield's daughter while the professor is away consulting in Washington. Hart wanders naked through Kingsfield's study. He examines the memorabilia of greatness, signed photographs of and letters from the President of the United States and Justices of the Supreme Court. A car door slams. Hart peers through a curtain to see Kingsfield emerging from a car, briefcase in hand. But while the professor suspiciously enters his violated home as Hart flees, he does not discover him. Like Gilligan's professor, Kingsfield has no carnal knowledge, not even vicariously. No one would think of bringing him an apple.

Two recent variations of the malevolent professor epitomized   22
by Kingsfield may be found in *Back to School* (1987). Paxton Whitehead's Professor Barbay of Grand Lakes University is a pompous, legalistic, self-appointed guardian of high standards in the college of business. He delights in humiliating students in class, carrying out petty acts of vengeance against those who would challenge his authority, and dealing in the arcane and complex—like posing an oral examination question with twenty-seven parts. A more sinister and hysterical version of this type is the late Sam Kinison's Professor Terguson of Grand Lakes University's History Department.

Professor Terguson, a Vietnam War veteran recently released from a mental institution, bullies his class into accepting his obsessively held hypothetical explanation for what is wrong with America: that all its recent leaders have been wimps who didn't have the guts to bomb every other nation back to the stone age. Professor Terguson's wild-eyed, top-of-the-lungs, in-your-face screaming diatribe is an uncontrolled, raw, working-class version of the malevolent professor typified by the more aristocratic Charles W. Kingsfield of Harvard Law School.

Professor Irwin Corey, Professor Roy Hinkley, and Professor 23 Charles W. Kingsfield—these three different representations of professorial characters reveal a wide range of conventional depiction. The stereotype ranges from the harmless buffoon whose nonsensical antics divert an audience from the serious business of their lives to the stern authoritarian whose knowledge of legal contracts threatens to restrict and so enhances all their pleasures. What these popular conceptions of professors share is an audience that would regard them as representing different forms of insanity brought upon by excessive schooling.

My father formed his conclusion about professors before Corey 24 got his act together, before Hinkley became a castaway, before Kingsfield began to lay down the law. Never mind that: my father knew what the herd had whispered, and he wanted to warn me. Naturally, I don't think I have gone crazy by becoming a professor. If there is a craziness to be documented, perhaps it belongs to a collective consciousness in America which continues to invest belief in the illusion of the nutty professor.

Meanings and Values

1. Identify the categories of nutty professors that the writer presents and name the main examples he gives of each.

2. Are there any subcategories? If so, what are they and what specific nutty professors are presented as illustrations of them?

3. State what you believe to be the purpose and central theme of this essay. (See "Guide to Terms": *Purpose, Unity.*) Where are the purpose and theme stated directly to readers, if at all?

Expository Techniques

1a. Where and how does the writer introduce the main categories he will discuss in the essay?

b.   How does he remind readers of these categories in the course of the essay?

2.   Identify the transitions the writer uses at the beginnings and ends of paragraphs to help introduce categories or extended examples. (Guide: *Transition*.)

3.   Many of the examples in this essay are quite detailed. Could any of the details be cut without harming the essay? Which could be eliminated? Would the essay be harmed if details were left out? In what ways would it be weakened?

4a. What similarities are there between the way the essay opens and the way it concludes?

b.   Has the writer chosen an effective way to begin and end the essay? Why, or why not? (Guide: *Evaluation*.)

Diction and Vocabulary

1.   The writer uses the words "nutty" and "crazy" to refer to each of the kinds of professors he discusses, yet the meaning of these words changes for each category. In your own words, state the ways in which the professors in each of the main categories is "crazy."

2a. To what does each of the following allusions refer: Keystone Cop (5), Dr. Jekyll and Mr. Hyde (8), Dogpatch (12), and *Deus ex Machina* (13). (Guide: *Figures of Speech*.)

b.   Discuss the role each allusion plays in the passage in which it appears.

3.   If you do not know the meaning of some of the following words, look them up in a dictionary: zany, manic, benign, *caveat emptor*, delirium tremens (par. 3); drawers, anachronism, paradoxical (4); cavorting, ecstatic, somnambulism (5) forte, nonsequitur (6); precursor (7); eradication (9); polysyllabic (10); narcissistic, engrossed (12); synecdoche (14); dais (17); carnal (21).

Suggestions for Writing and Discussion

1.   Choose a stereotype familiar from television, movies, or books, and divide it into categories like those presented in this essay. You might want to consider the ways scientists, doctors, or athletes are treated in these media.

2.   Compare the categories identified in Tajima's "Lotus Blossoms Don't Bleed: Images of Asian American Women" (p. 102) with those discussed in "Nutty Professors." What similarities are there between the stereotypes each author identifies; what important differences are there?

(NOTE: Suggestions for topics requiring development by use of CLASSIFICATION follow.)

Writing Suggestions for Section 2
Classification

Use division and classification (into at least three categories) as your basic method of analyzing one of the following subjects from one interesting point of view. (Your instructor may have good reason to place limitations on your choice of subject.) Narrow the topic as necessary to enable you to do a thorough job.

1. College students.
2. College teachers.
3. Athletes.
4. Coaches.
5. Salespeople.
6. Hunters (or fishermen).
7. Parents.
8. Drug users.
9. Police officers.
10. Summer (or part-time) jobs.
11. Sailing vessels.
12. Game show hosts.
13. Friends.
14. Careers.
15. Horses (or other animals).
16. Television programs.
17. Motivations for study.
18. Methods of studying for exams.
19. Lies.
20. Selling techniques.
21. Tastes in clothes.
22. Contemporary music.
23. Love.
24. Ways to spend money.
25. Attitudes toward life.
26. Fast foods (or junk foods).
27. Smokers.
28. Investments.
29. Actors.
30. Books or magazines.

3

Explaining by Means of *Comparison* and *Contrast*

One of the first expository methods we used as children was *comparison*, noticing similarities of objects, qualities, and actions, or *contrast*, noticing their differences. We compared the color of the new puppies with that of their mother, contrasted our father's height with our own. Then the process became more complicated. Now we employ it frequently in college essay examinations or term papers when we compare or contrast forms of government, reproductive systems of animals, or ethical philosophies of humans. Later, in the business or professional world, we may prepare important reports based on comparison and contrast—between kinds of equipment for purchase, the personnel policies of different departments, or precedents in legal matters. Nearly all people use the process, though they may not be aware of this, many times a day—in choosing a head of lettuce, in deciding what to wear to school, in selecting a house, or a friend, or a religion.

In the more formal scholastic and professional uses of comparison and contrast, however, an ordered plan is needed to avoid having a mere list of characteristics or a frustrating jumble of similarities and differences. If authors want to avoid communication blocks that will prevent their "getting through" to their readers, they will observe a few basic principles of selection and development. These principles apply mostly to comparisons between two subjects only; if three or more subjects are to be considered, they should be grouped to make the discussion easy to follow.

A *logical* comparison or contrast can be made only between subjects of the same general type. (Analogy, a special form of comparison used for another purpose, is discussed in the next section.) For example, contrasting a pine and a maple could be useful or meaningful, but little would be gained, except exercise in sentence construction, by contrasting the pine and the pansy.

Of course, logical but informal comparisons that are merely incidental to the basic structure, and hence follow no special pattern, may be made in any writing. Several of the preceding selections make limited use of comparison and contrast; Viorst does some contrasting of types of showoffs, and Judith Stone uses some comparison between the long history of dogs as pets and today's more fashionable pets. But once committed to a formal, full-scale analysis by comparison and contrast, the careful writer ordinarily gives the subjects similar treatment. Points used for one should also be used for the other, and usually in the same order. All pertinent points should be explored—pertinent, that is, to the purpose of the comparison.

The purpose and the complexity of materials will usually suggest their arrangement and use. Sometimes the purpose is merely to point out *what* the likenesses and differences are, sometimes it is to show the *superiority* of one thing over another—or possibly to convince the reader of the superiority, as this is also a technique of argumentation. The purpose may be to explain the *unfamiliar* (wedding customs in Ethiopia) by comparing it to the *familiar* (wedding customs in Kansas). Or it may be to explain or emphasize some other type of *central idea*, as in most of the essays in this section.

One of the two basic methods of comparison is to present all the information on the two subjects, one at a time, and to summarize by combining their most important similarities and differences. This method may be desirable if there are few points to compare, or if the individual points are less important than the overall picture they present. Therefore, this procedure might be a satisfactory means of showing the relative difficulty of two college courses or of comparing two viewpoints concerning an automobile accident. (Of course, as in all other matters of expository arrangement, the last subject discussed is in the most emphatic position.)

However, if there are several points of comparison to be considered, or if the points are of individual importance, alternation of the material would be a better arrangement. Hence, in a detailed comparison of Oak Valley and Elm Hill hospitals, we might compare their sizes, locations, surgical facilities, staffs, and so on, always in the same order. To tell all about Oak Valley and then all about Elm Hill would create a serious communication block, requiring readers constantly to call on their memory of what was cited earlier or to turn back to the first group of facts again and again in order to make the meaningful comparisons that the author should have made for them.

Often the subject matter or the purpose itself will suggest a more casual treatment, or some combination or variation of the two basic methods. We might present the complete information on the first subject, then summarize it point by point within the complete information on the second. In other circumstances it may be desirable simply to set up the thesis of likeness or difference, and then to explain a *process* that demonstrates this thesis. And although expository comparisons and contrasts are frequently handled together, it is sometimes best to present all similarities first, then all differences—or vice versa, depending on the emphasis desired. In argument, the arrangement we choose is that which best demonstrates the superiority of one thing (or plan of action) over another. This may mean a point-by-point contrast or the presentation of a weaker alternative before a stronger one.

In any basic use of comparison (conveniently, the term is most often used in a general sense to cover both comparison and contrast), the important thing is to have a plan that suits the purpose and material thoughtfully worked out in advance.

Sample Paragraph (Annotated)

Similarity announced. Though differences are not mentioned, the word "Parents" points towards "children" and suggests that the next generation may have a different perspective.

A *contrast* that serves to emphasize how similar are the outlooks of the parents.

Parents who moved from Valley City to Palmville generally have one thing in common: they agree there is little reason to make the long drive back to the metropolis, except, perhaps, to commute to work, for special shopping, or to hear a big star in concert. The talk at neighborhood gatherings, at youth baseball games, and in the aisles at Kwik Shop often revolves around how good it is to live in Palmville and how happy everyone is to have left Valley City. A few voices can even be heard claiming that the two new malls, the industries moving to Caton Industrial

Park, and new groups like the Palmville Community Symphony mean "there just aren't good reasons to go to Valley City anymore." In contrast, most of the town's children have their eyes set on Valley City as a distant Oz with I-104 as the Yellow Brick Road. To most it means entertainment in the form of mammoth rock shows; shopping at W.P. Sowerby's Department Store or the three-tier Okono Mall; and days on the beach watching glamorous people and being seen, too. To many it means opportunity in the form of large universities, jobs with major corporations, or careers in advertising and fashion. And to a few it means escape: "Anywhere but Palmville." Both parents and children share a desire to strike out on their own, the first group to get away from Valley City, the second group to return.

Contrast announced.
(Note use of transition: "In contrast.")

Point-by-point presentation of similarities in outlook that also offers point-by-point differences from the parents.

The kids' own slogan used as vivid example.

Final comparison (similarity).

Sample Paragraph (Comparison/Contrast)

Large computers have some essential attributes of an intelligent brain: they have large memories, and they have gates whose connections can be modified by experience. However, the thinking of these computers tends to be narrow. The richness of human thought depends to a considerable degree on the enormous number of wires, or nerve fibers, coming into each gate in the human brain. A gate in a computer has two, or three, or at most four wires entering on one side, and one wire coming out the other side. In the brain of an animal, the gates may have thousands of wires entering one side, instead of two or three. In the human brain, a gate may have as many as 100,000 wires entering it. Each wire comes from another gate or nerve cell. This means that every gate in the human brain is connected to as many as 100,000 other gates in other parts of the brain. During the process of thinking innumerable gates open and close throughout the brain. When one of these gates "decides" to open, the decision is the result of a complicated assessment involving inputs from thousands of other gates. This circumstance explains much of the difference between human thinking and computer thinking.

Student Writer: Explaining by Means of Comparison and Contrast

The Day Care Choice

Susan Haeberle

Parents all agree that they want to raise their children in the very best way possible, yet the best way to raise one child may not be the best way for another. Some parents choose to stay home with their kids during the day; others choose to send their children to day care; and still others have no choice but to work and rely on day care providers. As with many choices in life, the day care/stay at home dilemma has no easy way out. Recognizing the differences between the choices—the strengths and weaknesses of each—and choosing with a child's best interest in mind is probably the best a parent can do.

What, then, are the pluses and minuses from the perspective of a child's needs and preferences? To begin with, children in day care centers benefit from learning important lessons that other children generally do not learn until they are older. A good day care center can teach children to compromise, for example. Children in day care must learn to share their toys; therefore, they also get used to not getting everything they want. I once observed two children in the day care center where I worked. They both wanted to play with the same toy. At our day care center we tried not to get involved in disputes between children unless absolutely necessary. These two children argued over the toy for a while, then decided to compromise by playing together.

In my time at the day care center, I also noticed that the kids learned to be quite independent because they were not with their parents all the time. Being with other children also sparks curiosity and creativity in many kids. They have to constantly make up games and other activities to keep themselves entertained. All the day care centers I know do not allow kids to sit passively before a TV; the children must therefore find their entertainment in social interaction and creative play.

Because they get used to a school setting before other children, the kids in day care often have a head start. They get used to obeying people besides their parents. They become accustomed to structured learning and to scheduled activities. One study of eight-year-olds and thirteen-year-olds showed that those who entered day care before age one were among the students performing best in school; those without out-of-home care were frequently among those performing worst moreover, school adjustment is rated highest for children who entered day care before the age of one.

While there are clear pluses for putting children in day care, there are also minuses. Children in day care do not get a lot of personal attention. They also do not get to spend a lot of time with their parents. When they do, parents often spoil the children. Under these conditions, children may act up in day care when they don't get what they want. Another drawback to day care is that when the children grow up, they may be very dependent on their friends. In my experience as a day care worker, I noticed children becoming very close to a few friends so that they did not play with a variety of kids.

Some people feel that putting children in day care means robbing them of their childhood by forcing them into a situation where they have to fend for themselves. It is also very difficult for children to get used to taking orders from two different sets of people. Usually the rules at home are very different from the rules at day care. Dr. Elliot Baker argues that children from birth to age three should be looked after by the same person. Group care, he says, can cause serious damage to their emotional development. He also says that shared care could have serious impacts on young children. Small children require the love and attention of one person, preferably the parent, until age three.

Keeping a child at home has its own drawbacks, however. Children at home may have to play by themselves much of the time. They can also become very attached to their parents. Whenever my young brother gets hurt he runs to his mom because he is so used to her catering to him. When a child gets older, behavior like this could have serious effects on him or her. In addition, an only child that is raised at home is used to playing by himself, so he may not want to play with others. For instance, one time my brother had his cousin over to play. Every time the cousin picked up one of the toys, my brother grabbed it out of his hand. This behavior is the opposite of the kind of cooperation learned in daycare.

On the other hand, children at home get the love and attention they need as babies. They frequently do not need much independence early on, for they can become independent as they grow up. A child who spends a lot of time playing alone is already developing independence. Closeness with a parent can also be important because personality develops to a considerable extent before age three. Children at home are also exposed to fewer diseases. As a day care worker, I often felt that everyone in the place was always sick. Finally, some people argue that a child deserves time at home to grow up before being forced into school and responsibility.

There are many different ways to raise a child, and most are neither completely good or bad. For those people who have no choice, putting a child into day care is certainly nothing to feel guilty about. For those people who have a choice, taking into account the needs and personality of an individual child, and not children in general, is the best way to make a decision.

MARK TWAIN

MARK TWAIN was the pen name of Samuel Clemens (1835–1910). He was born in Missouri and became the first author of importance to emerge from "beyond the Mississippi." Although best known for bringing humor, realism, and Western local color to American fiction, Mark Twain wanted to be remembered as a philosopher and social critic. Still widely read, in most languages and in all parts of the world, are his numerous short stories (his "tall tales," in particular), autobiographical accounts, and novels, especially *Adventures of Huckleberry Finn* (1884). Ernest Hemingway called the last "the best book we've had," an appraisal with which many critics agree.

Two Ways of Seeing a River

"Two Ways of Seeing a River" (editors' title) is from Mark Twain's "Old Times on the Mississippi," which was later expanded and published in book form as *Life on the Mississippi* (1883). It is autobiographical. The prose of this selection is vivid, as is all of Mark Twain's writing, but considerably more reflective in tone than most.

1

Now when I had mastered the language of this water and had come to know every trifling feature that bordered the great river as familiarly as I knew the letters of the alphabet, I had made a valuable acquisition. But I had lost something, too. I had lost something which could never be restored to me while I lived. All the grace, the beauty, the poetry, had gone out of the majestic river! I still kept in mind a certain wonderful sunset which I witnessed when steamboating was new to me. A broad expanse of the river was turned to blood; in the middle distance the red hue brightened into gold, through which a solitary log came floating, black and conspicuous; in one place a long, slanting mark lay sparkling upon the water; in another the surface was broken by boiling, tumbling rings that were as many-tinted as an opal; where the ruddy flush was faintest was a smooth spot that was covered with graceful circles and radiating lines, ever so delicately traced; the shore on our left was densely wooded, and the somber shadow that fell from this forest was broken in one place by a long, ruffled trail that shone like silver; and high above the forest wall a clean-stemmed dead tree waved a single leafy bough that glowed like a flame in the unobstructed splendor that was flowing from the sun. There were graceful curves, reflected images, woody heights, soft distances, and over the whole scene, far and near, the dissolving lights drifted steadily, enriching it every passing moment with new marvels of coloring.

I stood like one bewitched. I drank it in, in a speechless rapture. 2 The world was new to me and I had never seen anything like this at home. But as I have said, a day came when I began to cease from noting the glories and the charms which the moon and the sun and the twilight wrought upon the river's face; another day came when I ceased altogether to note them. Then, if that sunset scene had been repeated, I should have looked upon it without rapture and should have commented upon it inwardly after this fashion: "This sun means that we are going to have wind tomorrow; that floating log means that the river is rising, small thanks to it; that slanting mark on the water refers to a bluff reef which is going to kill somebody's steamboat one of these nights, if it keeps on stretching out like that; those tumbling 'boils' show a dissolving bar and a changing channel there; the lines and circles in the slick water over yonder are a warning that that troublesome place is shoaling up dangerously; that silver streak in the shadow of the forest is the 'break' from a new snag and he has located himself in the very best place he could have found to fish for steamboats; that tall dead tree, with a single living branch, is not going to last long, and then how is a body ever going to get through this blind place at night without the friendly old landmark?"

No, the romance and beauty were all gone from the river. All 3 the value any feature of it had for me now was the amount of usefulness it could furnish toward compassing the safe piloting of a steamboat. Since those days, I have pitied doctors from my heart. What does the lovely flush in a beauty's cheek mean to a doctor but a "break" that ripples above some deadly disease? Are not all her visible charms sown thick with what are to him the signs and symbols of hidden decay? Does he ever see her beauty at all, or doesn't he simply view her professionally and comment upon her unwholesome condition all to himself? And doesn't he sometimes wonder whether he has gained most or lost most by learning his trade?

Meanings and Values

1. No selection could better illustrate the intimate relationship of several skills with which students of writing should be familiar, especially the potentials in *point of view* (and attitude), *style,* and *tone.*

   a. What is the point of view in paragraph 1? (See "Guide to Terms": Point of View.)

   b. Where, and how, does it change in paragraph 2?

   c. Why is the shift important to the author's contrast?

   d. Show how the noticeable change of tone is related to this change in point of view. (Guide: *Style/Tone.*)

   e. Specifically, what changes in style accompany the shift in tone and attitude?

   f. How effectively do they all relate to the central theme itself? (Remember that such effects seldom just "happen"; the writer *makes* them happen.)

2a. Is the first paragraph primarily objective or subjective? (Guide: *Objective/Subjective.*)

   b. How about the latter part of paragraph 2?

   c. Are your answers to 2a and 2b related to point of view? If so, how?

3a. Does the author permit himself to engage in sentimentality? (Guide: *Sentimentality.*) If so, how could it have been avoided without damage to his theme's development?

   b. If not, what restraints does the author use?

4. Do you think the last sentence refers only to doctors? Why, or why not?

Expository Techniques

1a. Where do you find a second comparison or contrast? Which is it?

   b. Is the comparison/contrast made within itself, with something external, or both? Explain.

   c. Is this part of the writing closely enough related to the major contrast to justify its use? Why, or why not?

2a.   In developing the numerous points of the major contrast, would an alternating, point-to-point system have been better? Why, or why not?

b.   Show how the author uses organization within the groups to assist in the overall contrast.

3a.   What is the most noteworthy feature of syntax in paragraphs 1 and 2? (Guide: *Syntax*.)

a.   How effectively does it perform the function intended?

4.   What is gained by the apparently deliberate decision to use rhetorical questions only toward the end? (Guide: *Rhetorical Questions*.)

Diction and Vocabulary

1.   Why would the colloquialism in the last sentence of paragraph 2 have been inappropriate in the first paragraph? (Guide: *Colloquial Expressions*.)

2a.   Compare the quality of metaphors in the quotation of paragraph 2 with the quality of those preceding it. (Guide: *Figures of Speech*.)

b.   Is the difference justified? Why, or why not?

Suggestions for Writing and Discussion

1.   List other vocations in which you assume (or perhaps know) that the beauty and romance eventually give way to practical realities; state briefly, for each, why this hardening should be expected. How would one's attitude be apt to change from the beginning romantic appeal?

2.   Show how, if at all, Mark Twain's contrast might be used to show parallels to life itself—e.g., differences in the idealism and attitudes of youth and maturity.

3.   Explore the possibility, citing examples if possible, of being able to retain both the "rapture" and the "usefulness."

(NOTE: Suggestions for topics requiring development by use of COMPARISON and CONTRAST are on page 177, at the end of this section.)

BRUCE CATTON (1899–1978) was a Civil War specialist whose early career included reporting for various newspapers. In 1954 he received both the Pulitzer Prize for historical work and the National Book Award. He served as director of information for the United States Department of Commerce and wrote many books, including *Mr. Lincoln's Army* (1951), *Glory Road* (1952), *A Stillness at Appomattox* (1953), *The Hallowed Ground* (1956), *America Goes to War* (1958), *The Coming Fury* (1961), *Terrible Swift Sword* (1963), *Never Call Retreat* (1966), *Waiting for the Morning Train: An American Boyhood* (1972), and *Gettysburg: The Final Fury* (1974). For five years, Catton edited *American Heritage*.

Grant and Lee: A Study in Contrasts

"Grant and Lee: A Study in Contrasts" was written as a chapter of *The American Story*, a collection of essays by noted historians. In this study, as in most of his other writing, Catton does more than recount the facts of history: he shows the significance within them. It is a carefully constructed essay, using contrast and comparison as the entire framework for his explanation.

When Ulysses S. Grant and Robert E. Lee met in the parlor of a modest house at Appomattox Court House, Virginia, on April 9, 1865, to work out the terms for the surrender of Lee's Army of Northern Virginia, a great chapter in American life came to a close, and a great new chapter began. 1

These men were bringing the Civil War to its virtual finish. To be sure, other armies had yet to surrender, and for a few days the fugitive Confederate government would struggle desperately and 2

From *The American Story*, Earl Schenck Miers, editor. © 1956 by Broadcast Music, Inc. Copyright renewed 1984. Reprinted by permission of the U.S. Capitol Historical Society.

vainly, trying to find some way to go on living now that its chief support was gone. But in effect it was all over when Grant and Lee signed the papers. And the little room where they wrote out the terms was the scene of one of the most poignant, dramatic contrasts in American history.

They were two strong men these oddly different generals, and they represented the strengths of two conflicting currents that, through them, had come into final collision. 3

Back of Robert E. Lee was the notion that the old aristocratic concept might somehow survive and be dominant in American life. 4

Lee was tidewater Virginia, and in his background were family, culture, and tradition . . . the age of chivalry transplanted to a New World which was making its own legends and its own myths. He embodied a way of life that had come down through the age of knighthood and the English country squire. America was a land that was beginning all over again, dedicated to nothing much more complicated than the rather hazy belief that all men had equal rights and should have an equal chance in the world. In such a land Lee stood for the feeling that it was somehow of advantage to human society to have a pronounced inequality in the social structure. There should be a leisure class, backed by ownership of land; in turn, society itself should be keyed to the land as the chief source of wealth and influence. It would bring forth (according to this ideal) a class of men with a strong sense of obligation to the community; men who lived not to gain advantage for themselves, but to meet the solemn obligations which had been laid on them by the very fact that they were privileged. From them the country would get its leadership; to them it could look for the higher values—of thought, of conduct, or personal deportment—to give it strength and virtue. 5

Lee embodied the noblest elements of this aristocratic ideal. Through him, the landed nobility justified itself. For four years, the Southern states had fought a desperate war to uphold the ideals for which Lee stood. In the end, it almost seemed as if the Confederacy fought for Lee; as if he himself was the Confederacy . . . the best thing that the way of life for which the Confederacy stood could ever have to offer. He had passed into legend before Appomattox. Thousands of tired, underfed, poorly clothed Confederate soldiers, long since past the simple enthusiasm of the early days of the struggle, somehow considered Lee the symbol of everything for which they had been willing to die. But they could not quite put this feeling into 6 words. If the Lost Cause, sanctified by so much heroism and so many deaths, had a living justification, its justification was General Lee.

Grant, the son of a tanner on the Western frontier, was everything Lee was not. He had come up the hard way and embodied nothing in particular except the eternal toughness and sinewy fiber of the men who grew up beyond the mountains. He was one of a body of men who owed reverence and obeisance to no one, who were self-reliant to a fault, who cared hardly anything for the past but who had a sharp eye for the future. 7

These frontier men were the precise opposites of the tidewater aristocrats. Back of them, in the great surge that had taken people over the Alleghenies and into the opening Western country, there was a deep, implicit dissatisfaction with a past that had settled into grooves. They stood for democracy, not from any reasoned conclusion about the proper ordering of human society, but simply because they had grown up in the middle of democracy and knew how it worked. Their society might have privileges, but they would be privileges each man had won for himself. Forms and patterns meant nothing. No man was born to anything, except perhaps to a chance to show how far he could rise. Life was competition. 8

Yet along with this feeling had come a deep sense of belonging to a national community. The Westerner who developed a farm, opened a shop, or set up in business as a trader could hope to prosper only as his own community prospered—and his community ran from the Atlantic to the Pacific and from Canada down to Mexico. If the land was settled, with towns and highways and accessible markets, he could better himself. He saw his fate in terms of the nation's own destiny. As its horizons expanded, so did his. He had, in other words, an acute dollars-and-cents stake in the continued growth and development of his country. 9

And that, perhaps, is where the contrast between Grant and Lee becomes most striking. The Virginia aristocrat, inevitably, saw himself in relation to his own region. He lived in a static society which could endure almost anything except change. Instinctively, his first loyalty would go to the locality in which that society existed. He would fight to the limit of endurance to defend it, because in defending it he was defending everything that gave his own life its deepest meaning. 10

The Westerner, on the other hand, would fight with an equal 11 tenacity for the broader concept of society. He fought so because everything he lived by was tied to growth, expansion, and a constantly widening horizon. What he lived by would survive or fall with the nation itself. He could not possibly stand by unmoved in the face of an attempt to destroy the Union. He would combat it with everything he had, because he could only see it as an effort to cut the ground out from under his feet.

So Grant and Lee were in complete contrast, representing two 12 diametrically opposed elements in American life. Grant was the modern man emerging; beyond him, ready to come on the stage, was the great age of steel and machinery, of crowded cities and a restless burgeoning vitality. Lee might have ridden down from the old age of chivalry, lance in hand, silken banner fluttering over his head. Each man was the perfect champion of his cause, drawing both his strengths and his weaknesses from the people he led.

Yet it was not all contrast, after all. Different as they were—in 13 background, in personality, in underlying aspiration—these two great soldiers had much in common. Under everything else, they were marvelous fighters. Furthermore, their fighting qualities were really very much alike.

Each man had, to begin with, the great virtue of utter tenacity 14 and fidelity. Grant fought his way down the Mississippi Valley in spite of acute personal discouragement and profound military handicaps. Lee hung on in the trenches at Petersburg after hope itself had died. In each man there was an indomitable quality . . . the born fighter's refusal to give up as long as he can still remain on his feet and lift his two fists.

Daring and resourcefulness they had, too: the ability to think 15 faster and move faster than the enemy. These were the qualities which gave Lee the dazzling campaigns of Second Manassas and Chancellorsville and won Vicksburg for Grant.

Lastly, and perhaps greatest of all, there was the ability, at the 16 end, to turn quickly from war to peace once the fighting was over. Out of the way these two men behaved at Appomattox came the possibility of a peace of reconciliation. It was a possibility not wholly realized, in the years to come, but which did, in the end, help the two sections to become one nation again . . . after a war whose bitterness might have seemed to make such a reunion wholly impossible. No part of either man's life became him more than the part he played in their brief meeting in the McLean house at Appomattox. Their behavior there put all succeeding generations of Americans in their debt. Two great Americans, Grant and Lee—very different, yet under everything very much alike. Their encounter at Appomattox was one of the great moments of American history.

Meanings and Values

1a. Clarify the assertions that through Lee "the landed nobility justified itself" and that "if the Lost Cause . . . had a living justification," it was General Lee (par. 6).

b. Why are these assertions pertinent to the central theme?

2a. Does it seem reasonable that "thousands of tired, underfed, poorly clothed Confederate soldiers" (par. 6) had been willing to fight for the aristocratic system in which they would never have had even a chance to be aristocrats? Why, or why not?

b. Can you think of more likely reasons why they were willing to fight?

3. Under any circumstances today might such a social structure as the South's be best for a country? Explain.

4a. What countries of the world have recently been so torn by internal war and bitterness that reunion has seemed, or still seems, impossible?

b. Do you see any basic differences between the trouble in those countries and that in America at the time of the Civil War?

5a. The author calls Lee a symbol (par. 6). Was Grant also a symbol? If so, of what? (See "Guide to Terms": *Symbol*.)

b. How would you classify this kind of symbolism?

Expository Techniques

1. Make an informal list of paragraph numbers from 3 to 16, and note by each number whether the paragraph is devoted primarily to Lee, to Grant, or to direct comparison or contrast of the two. This chart will show you Catton's basic pattern of development. (Notice, for instance, how the broad information of paragraphs 4–6 and 7–9 seems almost to "funnel" down through the narrower summaries in paragraphs 10 and 11 and into paragraph 12, where the converging elements meet and the contrast is made specific.)

2. What new technique of development is started in paragraph 13?

3a. What is gained, or lost, by using one sentence for paragraph 3?

b. For paragraph 4?

4a. How many paragraphs does the introduction comprise?

b. How successfully does it fulfill the three basic requirements of a good introduction? (Guide: *Introductions.*)

5. Show how Catton has constructed the beginning of each paragraph so that there is a smooth transition from the one preceding it. (Guide: *Transition.*)

6. The author's conclusion is really only the explanation of one of his integral points—and this method, if not carefully planned, runs the risk of ending too abruptly and leaving the reader unsatisfied. How has Catton avoided this hazard? (Guide: *Closings.*)

7a. What seems to be the author's attitude toward Grant and Lee?

b. Show how his tone reflects this attitude. (Guide: *Style/Tone.*)

Diction and Vocabulary

1. Why would a use of colloquialisms have been inconsistent with the tone of this writing?

2a. List or mark all metaphors in paragraphs 1, 3, 5, 7–11, and 16. (Guide: *Figures of Speech.*)

b. Comment on their general effectiveness.

3. If you are not already familiar with the following words, study their meanings as given in the dictionary and as used in this essay: virtual, poignant (par. 2); concept (4); sinewy, obeisance (7); implicit (8); tenacity (11); diametrically, burgeoning (12); aspiration (13); fidelity, profound, indomitable (14); succeeding (16).

4. Explain how the word "poignant" aptly describes this contrast of two men (par. 2).

Suggestions for Writing and Discussion

1. Find, by minor research, an incident in the life of Grant or Lee that will, in suitable essay form, illustrate one of Catton's points.

2. Select some other dramatic moment in history and show its long-range significance.

3. Select some important moment in your life and show its long-range significance.

4. Explain how someone you know symbolizes a philosophy or way of life.

(NOTE: Suggestions for topics requiring development by use of COMPARISON and CONTRAST are on page 177, at the end of this section.)

ANNA QUINDLEN is a reporter and writer best know for her column which appears regularly in *The New York Times* and is nationally syndicated. After graduating from Barnard College in 1974, she worked as a general assignment and city hall reporter at *The New York Times*, as writer of the "About New York" column, as deputy metropolitan editor, and finally as the author of several columns, including "Life in the 30's" and "Public and Private." Her novel, *Object Lessons*, was published in 1991, and a children's book, *The Tree that Came to Stay*, appeared in 1991. Her columns have been collected in *Living Out Loud* (1987) and *Thinking Out Loud: On the Personal, the Political, the Public and the Private* (1993).

Men at Work

In "Men at Work," a column that first appeared in 1992, Quindlen uses strongly drawn images of "the five o'clock dad" and the new "eight o'clock dad" to explore the changing (and unchanging) roles of men as parents. In the course of this carefully crafted essay, Quindlen also highlights contrasts between women's and men's roles and expectations as well as conflicts within today's evolving notions of fatherhood.

Overheard in a Manhattan restaurant, one woman to another: "He's a terrific father, but he's never home."   1

The five o'clock dads can be seen on cable television these days,   2
just after that time in the evening the stay-at-home moms call the arsenic hours. They are sixties sitcom reruns, Ward and Steve and Alex, and fifties guys. They eat dinner with their television families and provide counsel afterward in the den. Someday soon, if things keep going the way they are, their likenesses will be enshrined in a

diorama in the Museum of Natural History, frozen in their recliner chairs. The sign will say, "Here sit lifelike representations of family men who worked only eight hours a day."

The five o'clock dad has become an endangered species. A corporate culture that believes presence is productivity, in which people of ambition are afraid to be seen leaving the office, has lengthened his workday and shortened his homelife. So has an economy that makes it difficult for families to break even at the end of the month. For the man who is paid by the hour, that means never saying no to overtime. For the man whose loyalty to the organization is measured in time at his desk, it means goodbye to nine to five.

To lots of small children it means a visiting father. The standard joke in one large corporate office is that the dads always say their children look like angels when they're sleeping because that's the only way they ever see them. A Gallup survey taken several years ago showed that roughly 12 percent of the men surveyed with children under the age of six worked more than sixty hours a week, and an additional 25 percent worked between fifty and sixty hours. (Less than 8 percent of the working women surveyed who had children of that age worked those hours.)

No matter how you divide it up, those are twelve-hour days. When the talk-show host Jane Wallace adopted a baby recently, she said one reason she was not troubled by becoming a mother without becoming a wife was that many of her married female friends were "functionally single," given the hours their husbands worked. The evening commuter rush is getting longer. The 7:45 to West Backofbeyond is more crowded than ever before. The eight o'clock dad. The nine o'clock dad.

There's a horribly sad irony to this, and it is that the quality of fathering is better than it was when the dads left work at five o'clock and came home to café curtains and tuna casserole. The five o'clock dad was remote, a "Wait till your father gets home" kind of dad with a newspaper for a face. The roles he and his wife had were clear: she did nurture and home, he did discipline and money.

The role fathers have carved out for themselves today is a vast improvement, a muddling of those old boundaries. Those of us obliged to convert behavior into trends have probably been a little heavy-handed on the shared childbirth and egalitarian diaper-changing. But fathers today do seem to be more emotional with their children, more nurturing, more open. Many say, "My father never told me he loved me," and so they tell their own children all the time that they love them.

When they're home.   8

There are people who think that this is changing even as we   9
speak, that there is a kind of perestroika of home and work that we will look back on as beginning at the beginning of the 1990s. A non-profit organization called the Families and Work Institute advises corporations on how to balance personal and professional obliga-tions and concerns, and Ellen Galinsky, its co-founder, says she has noticed a change in the last year.

"When we first started doing this the groups of men and of   10
women sounded very different," she said. "If the men complained at all about long hours, they complained about their wives' complaints. Now if the timbre of the voice was disguised I couldn't tell which is which. The men are saying: 'I don't want to live this way anymore. I want to be with my kids.' I think the corporate culture will have to begin to respond to that."

This change can only be to the good, not only for women but   11
especially for men, and for kids, too. The stereotypical five o'clock dad belongs in a diorama, with his "Ask your mother" and his "Don't be a crybaby." The father who believes hugs and kisses are sex-blind and a dirty diaper requires a change, not a woman, is infi-nitely preferable. What a joy it would be if he were around more.

"This is the man's half of having it all," said Don Conway-Long,   12
who teaches a course at Washington University in St. Louis about men's relationships that drew 135 students this year for thirty-five places. "We're trying to do what women want of us, what children want of us, but we're not willing to transform the workplace." In other words, the hearts and minds of today's fathers are definitely in the right place. If only their bodies could be there, too.

Meanings and Values

1a. The opening paragraph of this essay presents a brief scene. What does this scene suggest about the current roles of men and women? What does it suggest about the typical relationships of men and women?

 b. Discuss how the themes introduced briefly in paragraph 1 are devel-oped in detail in paragraph 4.

2a. In what ways can the "five o'clock dad" and the "eight o'clock dad" be said to symbolize different roles for fathers? (See "Guide to Terms": *Symbol*.)

 b. What indication is there in paragraphs 2, 5, and 11 that we should treat as symbols these images of different kinds of fathers? Explain.

3. What does the author mean by the following phrases: "presence is productivity" (par. 3) and "there is a kind of perestroika of home and work" (9).

4. In paragraph 6, Quindlen speaks of a situation as characterized by "a horribly sad irony." Do you agree that the situation can be considered ironic? Why, or why not? (Guide: *Irony*.)

Expository Techniques

1a. Discuss the role of paragraph 8 as a transition between different sections of the essay. (Guide: *Transition*.)

 b. How is paragraph 8 related to the essay's central theme? (Guide: *Unity*.)

 c. Is the paragraph too short to be effective? Should it be a full sentence rather than a fragment? Be ready to explain your answers. (Guide: *Evaluation*.)

2a. Identify the places in the essay where the word *home* appears. Then discuss the way this repetition serves to convey the essay's central theme(s) and unify it. (Guide: *Unity*.)

 b. What other words besides *and, the,* and the like does the author repeat frequently throughout the essay? In what ways does she use them to convey ideas and organize the discussion?

3. Discuss how Quindlen uses the following to create comparisons and contrasts and to organize the essay: differences in historical time period, differences in time of day, differences in gender, and differences between home and work.

Diction and Vocabulary

1. To what does the title allude? (Guide: *Figures of Speech-Allusion*.) What is the title's significance?

2. How does the writer use diction in paragraphs 6 and 11 to heighten contrasts? (Guide: *Diction*.) How do these paragraphs employ parallel sentence structures for the same purpose? (Guide: *Parallel Structure*.)

3. What is the "diorama" Quindlen imagines in paragraphs 2 and 11? Why is it an appropriate image for this essay?

Suggestions for Writing and Discussion

1. In what ways have roles of children changed over the last few decades? Do these changes parallel changes in the roles of men and women or of work and home?

2. Some people might view the appropriate identities and responsibilities for men and women in ways different than Quindlen does. Discuss these alternate perspectives and try to explain why and how they differ from Quindlen's.

(NOTE: Suggestions for topics requiring development by use of COMPARISON and CONTRAST are on page 177, at the end of this section.)

PHILLIP LOPATE

PHILLIP LOPATE was born in 1943 in New York City. He attended
Columbia University and received a BA in 1964. He has taught creative writing in the Teachers and Writers Collaborative program in
New York City and is currently on the faculties of the University
of Houston and Columbia University. His publications include *The
Eyes Don't Always Want to Stay Open* (1972) and *The Daily Round*
(1976) (poems); *Confessions of Summer* (1979), *Bachelorhood: Tales of
the Metropolis* (1981), and *The Rug Merchant* (1988) (fiction); *Being
with Children* (1975) (nonfiction); and *Against Joie de Vivre: Personal
Essays* (1989) (a collection of essays). His essays have appeared in
a variety of publications, including *New Age Journal*, *Texas Monthly*,
The New York Times Book Review, *Columbia*, *House and Garden*,
Vogue, *Esquire*, and *Interview*.

A Nonsmoker with a Smoker

In this essay, which first appeared in *New Age Journal*, Lopate uses
comparison and contrast to explore his own ambiguous feelings
about smoking—and about his relationship with a smoker. In the
course of the essay, he touches on many aspects of the
smoking/nonsmoking conflict, yet he offers a personal perspective
often lost in the public controversy.

Last Saturday night my girlfriend, Helen, and I went to a dinner 1
party in the Houston suburbs. We did not know our hosts, but were
invited on account of Helen's chum Barry, whose birthday party it
was. We had barely stepped into the house and met the other guests,
seated on a U-shaped couch under an A-framed ceiling, when Helen
lit a cigarette. The hostess froze. "Uh, could you please not smoke in
here? If you have to, we'd appreciate your using the terrace. We're
both sort of allergic."

Helen smiled understandingly and moved toward the glass 2
doors leading to the backyard in a typically ladylike way, as
though merely wanting to get a better look at the garden. But I
knew from that gracious "Southern" smile of hers that she was
miffed.

As soon as Helen had stepped outside, the hostess explained 3
that they had just moved into this house, and that it had taken weeks
to air out because of the previous owner's tenacious cigar smoke. A
paradigmatically awkward conversation about tobacco ensued: like
testifying sinners, two people came forward with confessions about
kicking the nasty weed; our scientist-host cited a recent study of
indoor air pollution levels; a woman lawyer brought up the latest
California legislation protecting nonsmokers; a roly-poly real estate
agent admitted that, though he had given up smokes, he still sat in
the smoking section of airplanes because "you meet a more interesting type of person there"—a remark his wife did not find amusing.
Helen's friend Barry gallantly joined her outside. I did not, as I
should have; I felt paralyzed.

For one thing, I wasn't sure which side I was on. I have never 4
been a smoker. My parents both chain-smoked, so I grew up accustomed to cloudy interiors and ever since have been tolerant of other
people's nicotine urges. To be perfectly honest, I'm not crazy about
inhaling smoke, particularly when I've got a cold, but that irritating
inconvenience pales beside the damage that would be done to my
pluralistic worldview if I did not defend smokers' rights.

On the other hand, a part of me wished Helen *would* stop smok- 5
ing. That part seemed to get a satisfaction out of the group's "banishing" her: they were doing the dirty work of expressing my
disapproval.

As soon as I realized this, I joined her in the garden. Presently a 6
second guest strolled out to share a forbidden toke, then a third. Our
hostess ultimately had to collect the mutineers with an announce-
ment that dinner was served.

At the table, Helen appeared to be having such a good time, jok- 7
ing with our hosts and everyone else, that I was unprepared for the
change that came over her as soon as we were alone in the car afterward. "I will never go back to that house!" she declared. "Those people have no concept of manners or hospitality, humiliating me the
moment I stepped in the door. And that phony line about 'sort of
allergic'!"

Normally, Helen is forbearance personified. Say anything that   8
touches her about smoking, however, and you touch the rawest of
nerves. I remembered the last time I foolishly suggested that she
"think seriously" about stopping. I had just read one of those newspaper articles about the increased possibility of heart attacks, lung
cancer, and birth deformities among women smokers, and I was
worried for her. My concern must have been maladroitly expressed,
because she burst into tears.

"Can't we even talk about this without your getting so sensi-   9
tive?" I had asked.

"You don't understand. Nonsmokers never understand that it's   10
a real addiction. I've tried quitting, and it was hell. Do you want me
to go around for months mean and cranky outside and angry inside?
You're right, I'm sensitive, because I'm threatened with having
taken away from me the thing that gives me the most pleasure in
life, day in, day out," she said. I shot her a look: careful, now. "Well,
practically the most pleasure. You know what I mean." I didn't. But
I knew enough to drop it.

I love Helen, and if she wants to smoke, knowing the risks   11
involved, that remains her choice. Besides, she wouldn't quit just
because I wanted her to; she's not that docile, and that's part of what
I love about her. Sometimes I wonder why I even keep thinking
about her quitting. What's it to me personally? Certainly I feel protective of her health, but I also have selfish motives. I don't like the
way her lips taste when she's smoked a lot. I associate her smoking
with nervousness, and when she lights up several cigarettes in a
row, I get jittery watching her. Crazy as this may sound, I also find
myself becoming jealous of her cigarettes. Occasionally, when I go to
her house and we're sitting on the couch together, if I see Helen eyeing the pack I make her kiss me first, so that my lips can engage hers
(still fresh) before the competition's. It's almost as though there were
another lover in the room—a lover who was around long before
I entered the picture, and who pleases her in mysterious ways I
cannot.

A lit cigarette puts a distance between us: it's like a weapon in   12
her hand, awakening in me a primitive fear of being burnt. The
memory is not so primitive, actually. My father used to smoke
absentmindedly, letting the ash grow like a caterpillar eating every
leaf in its path, until gravity finally toppled it. Once, when I was
about nine, my father and I were standing in line at a bakery, and he

accidentally dropped a lit ash down my back. Ever since, I've inwardly winced and been on guard around these little waving torches, which epitomize to me the dangers of intimacy.

I've worked hard to understand from the outside the satisfaction of smoking. I've even smoked "sympathetic" cigarettes, just to see what the other person was experiencing. But it's not the same as being hooked. How can I really empathize with the frightened but stubborn look Helen gets in her eyes when, despite the fact we're a little late going somewhere, she turns to me in the car and says, "I need to buy a pack of cigarettes first"? I feel a wave of pity for her. We are both embarrassed by this forced recognition of her frailty— the "indignity," as she herself puts it, of being controlled by something outside her will.

I try to imagine myself in that position, but a certain smugness keeps getting in the way (I don't have that problem and *am I glad*). We pay a price for our smugness. So often it flip-flops into envy: the outsiders wish to be included in the sufferings and highs of others, as if to say that only by relinquishing control and surrendering to some dangerous habit, some vice or dependency, would one be able to experience "real life."

Over the years I have become a sucker for cigarette romanticism. Few Hollywood gestures move me as much as the one in *Now Voyager*, when Paul Henreid lights two cigarettes, one for himself, the other for Bette Davis: these form a beautiful fatalistic bridge between them, a complicitous understanding like the realization that their love is based on the inevitability of separation. I am all the more admiring of this worldly cigarette gallantry because its experiential basis escapes me.

The same sort of fascination occurs when I come across a literary description of nicotine addiction, like this passage in Mailer's *Tough Guys Don't Dance:* "Over and over again I gave them up, a hundred times over the years, but I always went back. For in my dreams, sooner or later, I struck a match, brought flame to the tip, then took in all my hunger for existence with the first puff. I felt impaled on desire itself—those fiends trapped in my chest and screaming for one drag."

"Impaled on desire itself"! Such writing evokes a longing in me for the centering of self that tobacco seems to bestow on its faithful. Clearly, there is something attractive about having this umbilical relation to the universe—this curling pillar, this spiral staircase, this

prayer of smoke that mediates between the smoker's inner substance and the alien ether. Inwardness of the nicotine trance, sad
wisdom ("every pleasure has its price"), beauty of ritual, squan-
dered health—all those romantic meanings we read into the famous
photographic icons of fifties saints, Albert Camus or James Agee or
James Dean or Carson McCullers puffing away, in a sense they're
true. Like all people who return from a brush with death, smokers
have gained a certain power. They know their "coffin nails." With
Helen, each cigarette is a measuring of the perishable, an enactment
of her mortality, from filter to end-tip in fewer than five minutes. I
could not stand to be reminded of my own death so often.

Meanings and Values

1.   Tell why you think the writer made the title say *with* rather than *and*.

2.   Does the writer's portrayal of the party (pars. 1–6) make Helen's
     anger (7) seem justified? Why, or why not?

3a. To what parts of this essay might smokers and nonsmokers react in
     different ways?

 b. How might their reactions differ? Be specific in answering this
     question.

4.   What conclusion about smoking, if any, does the writer reach in the
     last paragraph of the essay?

Expository Techniques

1.   The focus of the essay shifts at the end of paragraph 3. What role
     does the last sentence in the paragraph play, and in what way does
     the focus shift?

2a. How would you characterize the tone and style in paragraph 1? In
     paragraph 3? (See "Guide to Terms": *Style and Tone.*)

 b. What contrast does the writer emphasize through the differences in
     tone and style between paragraphs 1 and 3?

3.   To what extent does the focus of paragraphs 7–11 lie on the question
     of smoking versus not smoking, and to what extent does it focus on
     the relationship between the writer and Helen? Be ready to defend
     your answer with specific evidence from the text.

4.   What is being compared in paragraph 11? How is this comparison
     related to the overall pattern of comparison in the essay?

5.   In what ways do paragraphs 13 and 14 contrast with 15 and 16?

6a. State in your own words the contrast the author makes in the last two sentences of the essay.

b. Do these sentences make an effective conclusion? (Guide: *Closings, Evaluation.*)

Diction and Vocabulary

1. Identify the informal diction in paragraph 1 and the formal diction in paragraph 3. (Guide: *Diction.*) Why has the writer created these contrasts in diction. (Hint: See "Expository Techniques," 2a and b.)

2. Identify the similes in paragraph 12, and tell what they suggest about the effect of smoking on personal relationships. (Guide: *Figures of Speech.*)

3. Explain how cigarettes act as symbols in paragraph 15. (Guide: *Symbol.*)

4. Identify the metaphors in paragraph 15. Discuss their meaning and their effect, both as individual metaphors and as a cluster. (Guide: *Figures of Speech.*)

5. If you do not know the meaning of some of the following words, look them up in a dictionary: tenacious, paradigmatically, ensued (par. 3); pluralistic (4); toke (6); forbearance, maladroitly (8); epitomize (12); fatalistic, complicitious (15).

Suggestions for Writing and Discussion

1. What habits, preferences, or activities other than smoking can cause difficulties in relationships? Are such differences and difficulties inevitable?

2. Have recent campaigns against smoking in public places taken into account adequately the perspective and interests of smokers? Should they pay attention to the rights of both smokers and nonsmokers?

3. If smoking, wearing a fur coat, or some other activity or belief offends you, should you let the person doing the activity know about your feelings? What steps can you take to communicate your feelings without offending the other person? Should you worry about upsetting the other person?

(NOTE: Suggestions for topics requiring development by use of COMPARISON and CONTRAST are on page 177, at the end of this section.)

ALICE WALKER

ALICE WALKER was born in Georgia in 1944, the youngest in a family of eight. Her parents were sharecroppers, and she attended rural schools as a child, going on eventually to attend Spelman College and Sarah Lawrence College, from which she graduated. She worked as an editor of *Ms.* magazine and taught at several colleges. At present she teaches at the University of California—Berkeley and lives in northern California. Her work as a poet, novelist, and essayist has been highly acclaimed, and one of her novels, *The Color Purple* (1982), received both a Pulitzer Prize and the American Book Award for fiction. Some of her other works are *Revolutionary Petunias and Other Poems* (1973); *In Love and Trouble* (1973), short stories; *Meridian* (1976), *The Temple of My Familiar* (1989), and *Possessing the Secret of Joy* (1992), novels; and *In Search of Our Mothers' Gardens* (1983) and *Living by the Word* (1988), essays.

Am I Blue?

Humans and horses might seem at first so different that any comparison would have to take the form of an analogy—a pairing of essentially unlike subjects whose limited similarities can be used for explanatory purposes (see Section 4). Walker's strategy in this essay from *Living by the Word* is just the opposite, however. She explains that despite their obvious differences, humans and animals are essentially alike, at least in important matters such as the capacity to love and to communicate.

> *"Ain't these tears in these* 1
> *eyes tellin' you?"*

For about three years my companion and I rented a small house in 2
the country that stood on the edge of a large meadow that appeared
to run from the end of our deck straight into the mountains. The

mountains, however, were quite far away, and between us and them there was, in fact, a town. It was one of the many pleasant aspects of the house that you never really were aware of this.

It was a house of many windows, low, wide, nearly floor to ceil- 3 ing in the living room, which faced the meadow, and it was from one of these that I first saw our closest neighbor, a large white horse, cropping grass, flipping its mane, and ambling about—not over the entire meadow, which stretched well out of sight of the house, but over the five or so fenced-in acres that were next to the twenty-odd that we had rented. I soon learned that the horse, whose name was Blue, belonged to a man who lived in another town, but was boarded by our neighbors next door. Occasionally, one of the children, usually a stocky teen-ager, but sometimes a much younger girl or boy, could be seen riding Blue. They would appear in the meadow, climb up on his back, ride furiously for ten or fifteen minutes, then get off, slap Blue on the flanks, and not be seen again for a month or more.

There were many apple trees in our yard, and one by the fence 4 that Blue could almost reach. We were soon in the habit of feeding him apples, which he relished, especially because by the middle of summer the meadow grasses—so green and succulent since January—had dried out from lack of rain, and Blue stumbled about munching the dried stalks half-heartedly. Sometimes he would stand very still just by the apple tree, and when one of us came out he would whinny, snort loudly, or stamp the ground. This meant, of course: I want an apple.

It was quite wonderful to pick a few apples, or collect those that 5 had fallen to the ground overnight, and patiently hold them, one by one, up to his large, toothy mouth. I remained as thrilled as a child by his flexible dark lips, huge, cubelike teeth that crunched the apples, core and all, with such finality, and his high, broad-breasted *enormity;* beside which, I felt small indeed. When I was a child, I used to ride horses, and was especially friendly with one named Nan until the day I was riding and my brother deliberately spooked her and I was thrown, head first, against the trunk of a tree. When I came to, I was in bed and my mother was bending worriedly over me; we silently agreed that perhaps horseback riding was not the safest sport for me. Since then I have walked, and prefer walking to horseback riding—but I had forgotten the depth of feeling one could see in horses' eyes.

I was therefore unprepared for the expression in Blue's. Blue   6
was lonely. Blue was horribly lonely and bored. I was not shocked
that this should be the case; five acres to tramp by yourself, endlessly, even in the most beautiful of meadows—and his was—cannot
provide many interesting events, and once rainy season turned to
dry that was about it. No, I was shocked that I had forgotten that
human animals and nonhuman animals can communicate quite
well; if we are brought up around animals as children we take this
for granted. By the time we are adults we no longer remember.
However, the animals have not changed. They are in fact *completed*
creations (at least they seem to be, so much more than we) who are
not likely to change; it is their nature to express themselves. What
else are they going to express? And they do. And, generally speaking, they are ignored.

After giving Blue the apples, I would wander back to the house,   7
aware that he was observing me. Were more apples not forthcoming
then? Was that to be his sole entertainment for the day? My partner's
small son had decided he wanted to learn how to piece a quilt; we
worked in silence on our respective squares as I thought . . .

Well, about slavery: about white children, who were raised by   8
black people, who knew their first all-accepting love from black
women, and then, when they were twelve or so, were told they must
"forget" the deep levels of communication between themselves and
"mammy" that they knew. Later they would be able to relate quite
calmly, "My old mammy was sold to another good family." "My old
mammy was _____ _____." Fill in the blank. Many more years
later a white woman would say: "I can't understand these Negroes,
these blacks. What do they want? They're so different from us."

And about the Indians, considered to be "like animals" by the   9
"settlers" (a very benign euphemism for what they actually were),
who did not understand their description as a compliment.

And about the thousands of American men who marry Japan-   10
ese, Korean, Filipina, and other non-English-speaking women and of
how happy they report they are, *"blissfully,"* until their brides learn
to speak English, at which point the marriages tend to fall apart.
What then did the men see, when they looked into the eyes of the
women they married, before they could speak English? Apparently
only their own reflections.

I thought of society's impatience with the young. "Why are they   11
playing the music so loud?" Perhaps the children have listened to

much of the music of oppressed people their parents danced to before they were born, with its passionate but soft cries for acceptance and love, and they have wondered why their parents failed to hear.

I do not know how long Blue had inhabited his five beautiful, 12 boring acres before we moved into our house; a year after we had arrived—and had also traveled to other valleys, other cities, other worlds—he was still there.

But then, in our second year at the house, something happened 13 in Blue's life. One morning, looking out the window at the fog that lay like a ribbon over the meadow, I saw another horse, a brown one, at the other end of Blue's field. Blue appeared to be afraid of it, and for several days made no attempt to go near. We went away for a week. When we returned, Blue had decided to make friends and the two horses ambled or galloped along together, and Blue did not come nearly as often to the fence underneath the apple tree.

When he did, bringing his new friend with him, there was a 14 different look in his eyes. A look of independence, of self-possession, of inalienable *horse*ness. His friend eventually became pregnant. For months and months there was, it seemed to me, a mutual feeling between me and the horses of justice, of peace. I fed apples to them both. The look in Blue's eyes was one of unabashed "this is *it*ness."

It did not, however, last forever. One day, after a visit to the city, 15 I went out to give Blue some apples. He stood waiting, or so I thought, though not beneath the tree. When I shook the tree and jumped back from the shower of apples, he made no move. I carried some over to him. He managed to half-crunch one. The rest he let fall to the ground. I dreaded looking into his eyes—because I had of course noticed that Brown, his partner, had gone—but I did look. If I had been born into slavery, and my partner had been sold or killed, my eyes would have looked like that. The children next door explained that Blue's partner had been "put with him" (the same expression that old people used, I had noticed, when speaking of an ancestor during slavery who had been impregnated by her owner) so that they could mate and she conceive. Since that was accomplished, she had been taken back by her owner, who lived somewhere else.

Will she be back? I asked. 16

They didn't know. 17

Blue was like a crazed person. Blue *was*, to me, a crazed person. 18
He galloped furiously, as if he were being ridden, around and
around his five beautiful acres. He whinnied until he couldn't. He
tore at the ground with his hooves. He butted himself against his
single shade tree. He looked always and always toward the road
down which his partner had gone. And then, occasionally, when he
came up for apples, or I took apples to him, he looked at me. It was
a look so piercing, so full of grief, a look so *human*, I almost laughed
(I felt too sad to cry) to think there are people who do not know that
animals suffer. People like me who have forgotten, and daily forget,
all that animals try to tell us. "Everything you do to us will happen
to you; we are your teachers, as you are ours. We are one lesson" is
essentially it, I think. There are those who never once have even considered animals' rights: those who have been taught that animals
actually want to be used and abused by us, as small children "love"
to be frightened, or women "love" to be mutilated and raped. . . .
They are the great-grandchildren of those who honestly thought,
because someone taught them this: "Women can't think," And "nig-
gers can't faint." But most disturbing of all, in Blue's large brown
eyes was a new look, more painful than the look of despair: the look
of disgust with human beings, with life; the look of hatred. And it
was odd what the look of hatred did. It gave him, for the first time,
the look of a beast. And what that meant was that he had put up a
barrier within to protect himself from further violence; all the apples
in the world wouldn't change that fact.

And so Blue remained, a beautiful part of our landscape, very 19
peaceful to look at from the window, white against the grass. Once
a friend came to visit and said, looking out on the soothing view:
"And it *would* have to be a white horse; the very image of freedom."
And I thought, yes, the animals are forced to become for us merely
"images" of what they once so beautifully expressed. And we are
used to drinking milk from containers showing "contented" cows,
whose real lives we want to hear nothing about, eating eggs and
drumsticks from "happy" hens, and munching hamburgers advertised by bulls of integrity who seem to command their fate.

As we talked of freedom and justice one day for all, we sat 20
down to steaks. I am eating misery, I thought, as I took the first bite.
And spit it out.

Meanings and Values

1a. In which paragraphs does Walker describe what she believes to be Blue's thoughts and feelings?

b. According to Walker, in what ways is Blue similar to a human? In what ways is he different?

2. What thematic purposes are served by the following phrases:

a. "human animals and nonhuman animals" (par. 6)

b. "who did not understand their description as a compliment" (par. 9)

c. "Am I Blue?" (title)

d. "If I had been born into slavery, and my partner had been sold or killed, my eyes would have looked like that." (par. 15)

e. "It gave him, for the first time, the look of a beast." (par. 18)

3. To what other groups does the author compare Blue and his relationships with humans in paragraphs 8–11?

Expository Techniques

1a. Why do you think Walker chose to wait until near the end of the essay (paragraph 18) for a detailed discussion of its theme? ("Guide to Terms": *Unity*.)

b. To what extent does the placement of this discussion give the essay an expository rather than an argumentative purpose? (Guide: *Argument*.)

2. Discuss how the "'images'" presented in paragraph 19 can be regarded as ironic symbols. (Guide: *Symbol, Irony*)

3a. Describe the way Walker alters the tempo of the sentences and builds to a climax in the concluding paragraph of the essay. (Guide: *Closings*.)

b. Some readers might consider the ending effective. Others might consider it overly dramatic or distasteful. Explain which reaction you consider most appropriate. (Guide: *Evaluation*.)

Diction and Vocabulary

1. Describe the ways in which Walker uses syntax and figurative language (simile) for thematic purposes in this passage: "Blue was like a crazed person. Blue *was*, to me, a crazed person" (par. 18). (Guide: *Syntax, Figures of Speech*.)

2. In speaking of the "'settlers,'" Walker says that this term is "a very benign euphemism for what they actually were" (par. 9). What does

she mean by this comment? What other terms might be applied to them (from Walker's point of view)? Why might she have chosen not to use such terms?

3a. The title of this essay is taken from a song of the same name. In terms of the content of the essay, to what ideas or themes does it refer? Can it be considered a paradox? (Guide: *Paradox.*)

b. The quotation from the song that opens the essay points to some of the ideas discussed in the essay. What are they?

Suggestions for Writing and Discussion

1. Prepare a paper of your own explaining the regulations that safeguard the rights of animals used in experiments or outlining some common abuses in animal experimentation.

2. Walker links racism and disregard for the rights of animals. Is she correct in doing this, or is the connection farfetched?

3. Should people adopt vegetarianism for moral as well as health reasons?

4. Many people claim that in attributing human personalities to animals, we are simply fooling ourselves or being egocentric in assuming that the real meaning of events can be understood in human terms. What do you think?

(NOTE: Suggestions for topics requiring development by use of COMPARISON and CONTRAST follow.)

Writing Suggestions for Section 3
Comparison and Contrast

Base your central theme on one of the following, and develop your composition primarily by use of comparison and/or contrast. Use examples liberally for clarity and concreteness, chosen always with your purpose and reader-audience in mind.

1. Two kinds of families.
2. The sea at two different times.
3. The innate qualities needed for success in two different careers.
4. The natural temperaments of two acquaintances.
5. Two musicians.
6. The teaching techniques of two instructors or former teachers.
7. Two methods of parental handling of teenage problems.
8. Two family attitudes toward the practice of religion.
9. Two "moods" of the same town at different times.
10. The personalities (or atmospheres) of two cities or towns of similar size.
11. Two politicians with different leadership styles.
12. Two people who approach problems in different ways.
13. Two different attitudes toward the same thing or activity: one "practical," the other romantic or aesthetic.
14. The beliefs and practices of two religions or denominations concerning one aspect of religion.
15. Two courses on the same subject: one in high school and one in college.
16. The differing styles of two players of some sport or game.
17. The hazards of frontier life and those of life today.
18. Two companies with very different styles or business philosophies.
19. Two recent movies or rock videos.
20. Two magazines focusing on similar subjects but directed at different audiences.
21. The "rewards" of two different kinds of jobs.
22. Two views of loyalty.

4

Using *Analogy* as an Expository Device

Analogy is a special form of comparison that is used for a specific purpose: to explain something abstract or difficult to understand by showing its similarity to something concrete or easy to understand. A much less commonly used technique than logical comparison (and contrast), analogy is, nonetheless, a highly efficient means of explaining some difficult concepts or of giving added force to the explanations.

Logical comparison is made between two members of the same general class, usually assuming the same kind of interest in the subject matter of both. But in analogy we are really concerned only with the subject matter of one, using a second just to help explain the first. The two subjects, quite incomparable in most respects, are never of the same general class; if they are, we then have logical comparison, not analogy.

If the analogy is to be effective, the writer should be able to assume that the reader is familiar enough with the easier subject, or can quickly be made so, that it really helps explain the more difficult one. A common example is the explanation of the human circulatory system, which we may have trouble comprehending, by comparing the heart and arteries with a pump forcing water through the pipes of a plumbing system. This analogy has been carried further to liken the effect of cholesterol deposits on the inner walls of the arteries to that of mineral deposits that accumulate inside water pipes and eventually close them entirely. Although there is little logical similarity between a steel pipe and a human artery, the *analogical* similarity would be apparent to most readers—but the analogy might cause even greater confusion for anyone who did not know about pumps.

Distinguishing between analogy and metaphor is sometimes difficult. The difference is basically in their purpose: the function of a metaphor is merely to *describe,* to create a brief, vivid image for the reader; the function of analogy is primarily one of exposition, *to explain*, rather than to describe. In this sense, however, the function of a metaphor is actually *to suggest* an analogy: instead of showing the similarities of the heart and the pump, a metaphor might simply refer to "that faithful pump inside my chest," implying enough of a comparison to serve its purpose as description. (We can see here why some people refer to analogy as "extended" metaphor.) The analogist, when trying to explain the wide selection of college subjects and the need for balance in a course of study, could use the easily understood principle of a cafeteria, which serves Jell-O and lemon meringue pie as well as meat and potatoes. If his purpose had been only to create an image, to describe, he might have referred simply to the bewildering variety in "the cafeteria of college courses"—and that would have been a metaphor. (For still another example of the more conventional type of analogy, see the explanation of *Unity*, in the "Guide to Terms.")

But as useful as analogy can be in exposition, it is a difficult technique to use in logical argument. The two subjects of an analogy, although similar in one or more ways useful for illustration, may be basically too different for any reliable conclusions to be drawn from their similarity.

Sample Paragraph (Annotated)

Introduces the *analogy*.

Residents of Palmville have a saying: "Living here is like living in a fishbowl." It certainly does seem like everybody's business (personal or not) is open to view from all sides. When the result is gossip about people's personal lives, this characteristic of Palmville life is not very pleasant. But it does have good sides. When Jake Mollicone grew

Uses the analogy to explain events and relationships.

depressed because of business problems and tried to commit suicide, "nosey" neighbors were right there to save his life and help him recover, physically and mentally. When the Statler twins tried to make extra money by delivering less heating fuel than the bill showed, the rumor mill put the police on the case right away. In addition, a recent editorial in the *Palmville Gazette* suggested that extending the familiar "fishbowl" analogy might be a good idea for Palmville. The editorial pointed out that most fish tanks can be homes to a wide variety of colorful species and that the recent growth of Palmville has likewise brought together people of different backgrounds and qualities in an interesting and healthy mix. The editorial also reminded readers that when a fish tank becomes too crowded, it turns into a dirty, unhealthy environment—and the inhabitants often try to eat each other. "The lesson is clear," the paper concluded, "that while some growth is enriching and beneficial, too much expansion would be the wrong thing for life in our 'fishbowl.'"

Editorial extends the analogy. More a speculation or warning than an argument.

Sample Paragraph (Analogy)

If distant galaxies are really receding from the earth, and if more distant galaxies are receding faster than nearby ones, a remarkable picture of the universe emerges. Imagine that the galaxies were raisins scattered through a rising lump of bread dough. As the dough expanded, the raisins would be carried farther and farther apart from each other. If you were standing on one of the raisins, how would things look? You wouldn't feel any motion yourself, of course, just as you don't feel the effects of the earth's motion around the sun, but you would notice that your nearest neighbor was moving away from you. This motion would be due to the fact that the dough between you and your nearest neighbor would be expanding, pushing the two of you apart.

Life Isn't Like Baseball

Kevin Nomura

My father loves baseball. So does my mom. My sister was a star soft-ball player in high school, and she is the regular shortstop on her col-lege team. When my father tried to sign me up for little league, however, I let him know that I would rather be playing soccer or ten-nis. It was about this time that he started trying to convince me that "Life is like baseball." I wasn't convinced the first time he told me, and I'm still not. Let me explain why.

Striking Out. People who think life is like baseball often talk about "striking out," "staying ahead on the count," or "taking a big swing." When you are up to bat in baseball, you get a lot of chances—not just three strikes but also four balls and any number of fouled off pitches. I have made some serious mistakes at work, at school, and in my love life, but while I have been lucky enough to get an occasional second chance, I have never gotten any more. When I have failed at something, I have never failed as completely, as obviously, and as publicly as a baseball player does striking out. I suppose that getting booed off the stage is like striking out, but when I sang off tune in my high school's production of "Bye, Bye Birdie," no one yelled at me or called me back to the dugout (woops, dressing room). Instead my parents told me they were proud of me no matter what, and the director told me ways to get through my part of the song fast.

Hitting a Home Run. People seldom strike out in real life, and they do not hit home runs either. When baseball fans talk about "hit-ting a home run" at work or in some other activity, they mean accomplishing something dramatic whose success and importance no one can deny. Who had a job that is big enough or important enough to allow for a home run? Can the manager of a MacDonald's hit a home run? Can a clerk in a department store or a steelworker do it? Who has a job that allows for dramatic and significant achieve-ment? Can a teacher create brilliant students overnight or an artist become famous for one drawing rather than a lifetime of careful, patient effort? I don't think so, or only so seldom that such an achievement is unrealistic for us mortals.

Like a Spitball. People who believe that life is like baseball often ignore those parts of the game that don't fit very well with everyday experience or that are not very pleasant. Is life like a spitball? Are successful people the ones who load things up with petroleum jelly or scuff them with emery boards, then lie when confronted with the evidence—and boast about their deception afterwards? And if some do, should we pretend their actions are good sport and hold them up as examples for the kids? Should we praise people for "stealing" and put the biggest thieves in the record books? Should we treat every botched move—every balk—as a serious error and a public humiliation. Would you like it if a slight slip on your part automatically allowed your competitors to advance a base and maybe even bring home the winning run?

I realize that I probably haven't convinced any real baseball fans to stop seeing life in terms of their game. I also realize that people will go on talking about "taking a good cut" or "winding up too long before the pitch." My younger brother says he agrees with me, but then he thinks that life is a slap shot.

BILL BRADLEY was born in 1943 in Crystal City, Missouri. He attended Princeton University, where he played basketball, and received a BA in 1965. From 1965–1968 he attended Oxford University as a Rhodes Scholar, earning an MA in 1968. In the years following (1967–1977) he played professional basketball with the New York Knicks. In 1979 he was elected U.S. Senator from New Jersey, a position he currently holds. Bradley has written an autobiography, *Life on the Run* (1976) as well as numerous articles in publications such as the *Wall Street Journal, Harper's, New Perspectives Quarterly,* and *The New York Times Book Review.*

How to Get the Big Picture

In this brief essay, Bradley starts with a childhood experience, then uses it as a key to understanding an important habit of mind. The essay first appeared in *Esquire.*

When I was a kid, I used to walk down the street, then stop in front   1
of a shop window. With my head still facing down the street—not looking into the window—I'd say to myself, *I can see that red blouse in the window. I can see a pair of black shoes. I can see that poster advertising vacations in France.*

Once, during my first week with the Knicks, I was late for din-   2
ner one night, and I shot out of my apartment building and ran across Eighth Avenue against the light. Out of the corner of my eye, I suddenly saw something—an MG—speeding right at me. I had just enough time to jump. I rolled over the top, then fell and hit the street. I came out of it with a bruised hip and wrist, but at least I didn't get run over. I remember thinking, *Thank God I saw that car. Yeah. I saw it because of my peripheral vision.*

Practicing my peripheral vision led me to the idea of seeing the   3
whole court in a basketball game. I discovered that I could look one

BILL BRADLEY, "How to Get the Big Picture." *Esquire,* October 1993, p. 57.

way and see things other players couldn't, and that made it easier
for me to pass or move.

This way of seeing the game naturally led to the idea of its being   4
a sort of radar in life or your profession, meaning constantly scanning to see all of the possible implications for any particular action.
My eyes have become a metaphor for a frame of mind.

Meanings and Values

1.   When Bradley talks about peripheral vision, he is also talking about
     a "way of seeing" or "frame of mind" (par. 4). In your own words,
     summarize the meaning of this analogy.

2.   Each of the paragraphs in the essay takes up a different subject. What
     are the subjects and how does the writer relate them to each other?
     (See "Guide to Terms": *Unity*.)

Expository Techniques

1a. How do the last sentence in paragraph 2 and the first sentences in
     paragraphs 3 and 4 help give focus to the essay? (Guide: *Unity*.)

 b. In what ways do these sentences act as transitions? (Guide:
     Transitions.)

2.   How does Bradley use concrete detail in paragraphs 1 and 2 to
     prevent the essay from becoming too abstract? (Guide: *Concrete/
     Abstract*.)

Diction and Vocabulary

1.   In the concluding sentence, Bradley speaks of his eyes as a
     "metaphor." Is his use of the term appropriate or would the term
     "analogy" be more exact? Explain. (See Introduction, pp. 179–180
     and Guide: *Figures of Speech*.)

2.   Discuss the ways both the diction and style in this essay move from
     relatively informal (in paragraph 1) to relatively formal (in para-
     graph 4). (Guide: *Style/Diction*.)

Suggestions for Writing and Discussion

1.   What special skills (like peripheral vision) or attitudes (like an
     awareness of possibilities) have you developed? When do you use
     them and for what purpose?

2. Bradley describes ways in which his outlook has helped him to win or to protect himself. What kinds of abilities or perspectives aid us in helping others or in building and strengthening communities?

(NOTE: Suggestions for topics requiring development by use of ANALOGY are on page 218, at the end of this section.)

LOREN C. EISELEY (1907–1977) was professor of anthropology and the history of science at the University of Pennsylvania, where he also served as provost from 1959 to 1961. He was a Guggenheim Foundation Fellow and was in charge of anthropological expeditions for various universities and for the Smithsonian Institution. Eiseley, a respected naturalist and conservationist, also served on many public service boards and commissions and was awarded many honorary degrees and medals. Widely published in both scholarly and popular magazines, Eiseley also wrote several books, including *The Immense Journey* (1957), *Darwin's Century* (1959), *The Firmament of Time* (1960), *The Unexpected Universe* (1969), and *The Night Country* (1971).

The Brown Wasps

"The Brown Wasps" was selected from Eiseley's book *The Night Country*. It is an essay with a simple theme, developed through a rather intricate web of simple analogies. In reading this selection, you will see why Eiseley was—and is—widely admired for his lucid, almost poetic style, as well as for his sensitive philosophical approach to all living things.

There is a corner in the waiting room of one of the great Eastern   1
stations where women never sit. It is always in the shadow and overhung by rows of lockers. It is, however, always frequented—not so much by genuine travelers as by the dying. It is here that a certain element of the abandoned poor seeks a refuge out of the weather, clinging for a few hours longer to the city that has fathered them. In a precisely similar manner I have seen, on a sunny day in midwinter, a few old brown wasps creep slowly over an abandoned wasp

nest in a thicket. Numbed and forgetful and frost-blackened, the hum of the spring hive still resounded faintly in their sodden tissues. Then the temperature would fall and they would drop away into the white oblivion of the snow. Here in the station it is in no way different save the city is busy in its snows. But the old ones cling to their seats as though these were symbolic and could not be given up. Now and then they sleep, their gray old heads resting with painful awkwardness on the backs of the benches.

Also they are not at rest. For an hour they may sleep in the gasping exhaustion of the ill-nourished and aged who have to walk in the night. Then a policeman comes by on his round and nudges them upright.   2

"You can't sleep here," he growls.   3

A strange ritual then begins. An old man is difficult to waken.   4
After a muttered conversation the policeman presses a coin into his hand and passes fiercely along the benches prodding and gesturing toward the door. In his wake, like birds rising and settling behind the passage of a farmer through a cornfield, the men totter up, move a few paces and subside once more upon the benches.

One man, after a slight, apologetic lurch, does not move at all.   5
Tubercularly thin, he sleeps on steadily. The policeman does not look back. To him, too, this has become a ritual. He will not have to notice it again officially for another hour.

Once in a while one of the sleepers will not awaken. Like the   6
brown wasps, he will have had his wish to die in the great droning center of the hive rather than in some lonely room. It is not so bad here with the shuffle of footsteps and the knowledge that there are others who share the bad luck of the world. There are also the whistles and the sounds of everyone, everyone in the world, starting on journeys. Amidst so many journeys somebody is bound to come out all right. Somebody.

Maybe it was on a like thought that the brown wasps fell away   7
from the old paper nest in the thicket. You hold till the last, even if it is only to a public seat in a railroad station. You want your place in the hive more than you want a room or a place where the aged can be eased gently out of the way. It is the place that matters, the place at the heart of things. It is life that you want, that bruises your gray old head with the hard chairs; a man has a right to his place.

But sometimes the place is lost in the years behind us. Or some-   8
times it is a thing of air, a kind of vaporous distortion above a heap

of rubble. We cling to a time and place because without them man is lost, not only man but life. This is why the voices, real or unreal, which speak from the floating trumpets at spiritualist seances are so unnerving. They are voices out of nowhere whose only reality lies in their ability to stir the memory of a living person with some fragment of the past. Before the medium's cabinet both the dead and the living revolve endlessly about an episode, a place, an event that has already been engulfed by time.

This feeling runs deep in life; it brings stray cats running over   9
endless miles, and birds homing from the ends of the earth. It is as though all living creatures, and particularly the more intelligent, can survive only by fixing or transforming a bit of time into space or by securing a bit of space with its objects immortalized and made permanent in time. For example, I once saw, on a flower pot in my own living room, the efforts of a field mouse to build a remembered field. I have lived to see this episode repeated in a thousand guises, and since I have spent a large portion of my life in the shade of a nonexistent tree, I think I am entitled to speak for the field mouse.

One day as I cut across the field, which at that time extended on   10
one side of our suburban shopping center, I found a giant slug feeding from a runnel of pink ice cream in an abandoned Dixie cup. I could see his eyes telescope and protrude in a kind of dim, uncertain ecstasy as his dark body bunched and elongated in the curve of the cup. Then, as I stood there at the edge of the concrete, contemplating the slug, I began to realize it was like standing on a shore where a different type of life creeps up and fumbles tentatively among the rocks and sea wrack. It knows its place and will only creep so far until something changes. Little by little as I stood there, I began to see more of this shore that surrounds the place of man. I looked with sudden care and attention at things I had been running over thoughtlessly for years. I even waded out a short way into the grass and the wild-rose thickets to see more. A huge black-belted bee went droning by and there were some indistinct scurryings in the underbrush.

Then I came to a sign which informed me that this field was to   11
be the site of a new Wanamaker suburban store. Thousands of obscure lives were about to perish, the spores of puffballs would go smoking off to new fields, and the bodies of little white-footed mice would be crunched under the inexorable wheels of the bulldozers.

Life disappears or modifies its appearances so fast that everything takes on an aspect of illusion—a momentary fizzing and boiling with smoke rings, like pouring dissident chemicals into a retort. Here man was advancing, but in a few years his plaster and bricks would be disappearing once more into the insatiable maw of the clover. Being of an archaeological cast of mind, I thought of this fact with an obscure sense of satisfaction and waded back through the rose thickets to the concrete parking lot. As I did so, a mouse scurried ahead of me, frightened of my steps if not of that ominous Wanamaker sign. I saw him vanish in the general direction of my apartment house, his little body quivering with fear in the great open sun on the blazing concrete. Blinded and confused, he was running straight away from his field. In another week scores would follow him.

I forgot the episode then and went home to the quiet of my living room. It was not until a week later, letting myself into the apartment, that I realized I had a visitor. I am fond of plants and had several ferns standing on the floor in pots to avoid the noon glare by the south window. 12

As I snapped on the light and glanced carelessly around the room, I saw a little heap of earth on the carpet and a scrabble of pebbles that had been kicked merrily over the edge of one of the flower pots. To my astonishment I discovered a full-fledged burrow delving downward among the fern roots. I waited silently. The creature who had made the burrow did not appear. I remembered the wild field then, and the flight of the mice. No house mouse, no *Mus domesticus,* had kicked up this little heap of earth or sought refuge under a fern root in a flower pot. I thought of the desperate little creature I had seen fleeing from the wild-rose thicket. Through intricacies of pipes and attics, he, or one of his fellows, had climbed to this high green solitary room. I could visualize what had occurred. He had an image in his head, a world of seed pods and quiet, of green sheltering leaves in the dim light among the weed stems. It was the only world he knew and it was gone. 13

Somehow in his flight he had found his way to this room with drawn shades where no one would come till nightfall. And here he had smelled green leaves and run quickly up the flower pot to dabble his paws in common earth. He had even struggled half the afternoon to carry his burrow deeper and had failed. I examined the hole, but no whiskered twitching face appeared. He was gone. I gathered 14 up the earth and refilled the burrow. I did not expect to find traces of him again.

Yet for three nights thereafter I came home to the darkened   15
room and my ferns to find the dirt kicked gaily about the rug and the burrow reopened, though I was never able to catch the field mouse within it. I dropped a little food about the mouth of the burrow, but it was never touched. I looked under beds or sat reading with one ear cocked for rustling in the ferns. It was all in vain; I never saw him. Probably he ended in a trap in some other tenant's room.

But before he disappeared, I had come to look hopefully for his   16
evening burrow. About my ferns there had begun to linger the insub-stantial vapor of an autumn field, the distilled essence, as it were, of a mouse brain in exile from its home. It was a small dream, like our dreams, carried a long and weary journey along pipes and through spider webs, past holes over which loomed the shadows of waiting cats, and finally, desperately, into this room where he had played in the shuttered daylight for an hour among the green ferns on the floor. Every day these invisible dreams pass us on the street, or rise from beneath our feet, or look out upon us from beneath a bush.

Some years ago the old elevated railway in Philadelphia was   17
torn down and replaced by a subway system. This ancient El with its barnlike stations containing nut-vending machines and scattered food scraps had, for generations, been the favorite feeding ground of flocks of pigeons, generally one flock to a station along the route of the El. Hundreds of pigeons were dependent upon the system. They flapped in and out of its stanchions and steel work or gathered in watchful little audiences about the feet of anyone who rattled the peanut-vending machines. They even watched people who jingled change in their hands, and prospected for food under the feet of the crowds who gathered between trains. Probably very few among the waiting people who tossed a crumb to an eager pigeon realized that this El was like a food-bearing river, and that the life which haunted its banks was dependent upon the running of the trains with their human freight.

I saw the river stop.   18

The time came when the underground tubes were ready; the   19
traffic was transferred to a realm unreachable by pigeons. It was like a great river subsiding suddenly into desert sands. For a day, for two days, pigeons continued to circle over the El or stand close to the red vending machines. They were patient birds, and surely this great

river which had flowed through the lives of unnumbered generations was merely suffering from some momentary drought.

They listened for the familiar vibrations that had always heralded an approaching train; they flapped hopefully about the head of an occasional workman walking along the steel runways. They passed from one empty station to another, all the while growing hungrier. Finally, they flew away. [20]

I thought I had seen the last of them about the El, but there was a revival and it provided a curious instance of the memory of living things for a way of life or a locality that has long been cherished. Some weeks after the El was abandoned, workmen began to tear it down. I went to work every morning by one particular station, and the time came when the demolition crews reached this spot. Acetylene torches showered passers-by with sparks, pneumatic drills hammered at the base of the structure, and a blind man who, like the pigeons, had clung with his cup to a stairway leading to the change booth, was forced to give up his place. [21]

It was then, strangely, momentarily, one morning that I witnessed the return of a little band of the familiar pigeons. I even recognized one or two members of the flock that had lived around this particular station before they were dispersed into the streets. They flew bravely in and out among the sparks and the hammers and the shouting workmen. They had returned—and they had returned because the hubbub of the wreckers had convinced them that the river was about to flow once more. For several hours they flapped in and out through the empty windows, nodding their heads and watching the fall of girders with attentive little eyes. By the following morning the station was reduced to some burned-off stanchions in the street. My bird friends had gone. It was plain, however, that they retained a memory for an insubstantial structure now compounded of air and time. Even the blind man clung to it. Someone had provided him with a chair, and he sat at the same corner staring sightlessly at an invisible stairway where, so far as he was concerned, the crowds were still ascending to the trains. [22]

I have said my life has been passed in the shade of a nonexistent tree, so that such sights do not offend me. Prematurely I am one of the brown wasps and I often sit with them in the great droning hive of the station, dreaming sometimes of a certain tree. It was planted sixty years ago by a boy with a bucket and a toy spade in a little Nebraska town. That boy was myself. It was a cottonwood sapling [23] and the boy remembered it because of some words spoken by his father and because everyone died or moved away who was supposed to wait and grow old under its shade. The boy was passed from hand to hand, but the tree for some intangible reason had taken root in his mind. It was under its branches that he sheltered; it was from this tree that his memories, which are my memories, led away into the world.

After sixty years the mood of the brown wasps grows heavier 24 upon one. During a long inward struggle I thought it would do me good to go and look upon that actual tree. I found a rational excuse in which to clothe this madness. I purchased a ticket and at the end of two thousand miles I walked another mile to an address that was still the same. The house had not been altered.

I came close to the white picket fence and reluctantly, with great 25 effort, looked down the long vista of the yard. There was nothing there to see. For sixty years that cottonwood had been growing in my mind. Season by season its seeds had been floating farther on the hot prairie winds. We had planted it lovingly there, my father and I, because he had a great hunger for soil and live things growing, and because none of these things had long been ours to protect. We had planted the little sapling and watered it faithfully, and I remembered that I had run out with my small bucket to drench its roots the day we moved away. And all the years since, it had been growing in my mind, a huge tree that somehow stood for my father and the love I bore him. I took a grasp on the picket fence and forced myself to look again.

A boy with the hard bird eye of youth pedaled a tricycle slowly 26 up beside me.

"What'cha lookin' at?" he asked curiously.   27

"A tree," I said.   28

"What for?" he said.   29

"It isn't there," I said, to myself mostly, and began to walk away 30 at a pace just slow enough not to seem to be running.

"What isn't there?" the boy asked. I didn't answer. It was obvi- 31 ous I was attached by a thread to a thing that had never been there, or certainly not for long. Something that had to be held in the air, or sustained in the mind, because it was part of my orientation in the universe and I could not survive without it. There was more than an animal's attachment to a place. There was something else, the attachment of the spirit to a grouping of events in time; it was part of our morality.

So I had come home at last, driven by a memory in the brain as 32
surely as the field mouse who had delved long ago into my flower
pot or the pigeons flying forever amidst the rattle of nut-vending
machines. These, the burrow under the greenery in my living room
and the red-bellied bowls of peanuts now hovering in midair in the
minds of pigeons, were all part of an elusive world that existed
nowhere and yet everywhere. I looked once at the real world about
me while the persistent boy pedaled at my heels.

It was without meaning, though my feet took a remembered 33
path. In sixty years the house and street had rotted out of my mind.
But the tree, the tree that no longer was, that had perished in its first
season, bloomed on in my individual mind, unblemished as my
father's words. "We'll plant a tree here, son, and we're not going to
move any more. And when you're an old, old man you can sit under
it and think how we planted it here, you and me, together."

I began to outpace the boy on the tricycle. 34

"Do you live here, Mister?" he shouted after me suspiciously. I 35
took a firm grasp on airy nothing—to be precise, on the bole of a
great tree. "I do," I said. I spoke for myself, one field mouse, and several pigeons. We were all out of touch but somehow permanent. It
was the world that had changed.

Meanings and Values

1a. How would you describe the tone of this selection? (See "Guide to
Terms": *Style/Tone*.)

   b. Are the tone and the pace suitable to the subject matter? Why, or
why not?

   c. Is Eiseley's style compatible with the tone?

2a. What was Eiseley's apparent purpose in writing this essay? (Guide:
Evaluation.) ("Purpose" is the key question in this evaluation: it is
significant that the essay was written for inclusion in a book.)

   b. How well did he achieve his purpose?

   c. Was it worthwhile?

3. Explain how the seats were "symbolic" to the old men (par. 1).
(Guide: *Symbol*.)

4. Paragraphs 2–5 give us a small but well-rounded picture of the policeman. Use your own words to describe him as fully as possible.

5a. Clarify the meaning, or meanings, of paragraph 8.

   b. How does spending much of his life "in the shade of a nonexistent
tree" entitle Eiseley to speak for the field mouse (par. 9)?

   c. What was it, precisely, that caused Eiseley's "obscure sense of satisfaction" (par. 11)? Why?

6a. Where would you place this essay on an objective-to-subjective continuum? Why? (Guide: *Objective/Subjective*.)

   b. Could you classify it as formal? Why, or why not? (Guide: *Essay*.)

7. Select at least one passage that would be, in the hands of many writers, particularly subject to sentimentalism. (Guide: *Sentimentalism*.) Explain why you consider it overly sentimental, or how Eiseley was able to avoid that fault.

Expository Techniques

1a. What are the three major analogies that are linked in this essay?

   b. Do they all have the same analogical purpose? If not, what is their relationship?

   c. With what particular act does Eiseley analogically equate his own return to Nebraska, or is it an outgrowth of the whole theme to that point?

   d. How effectively does each analogy achieve its purpose?

2a. The transition between paragraphs 7 and 8 is especially important. Why? (Guide: *Transitions*.)

   b. By what means does Eiseley assure a smooth connection?

3. Is unity damaged by the introduction of the boy toward the end? (Guide: *Unity*.) Show how it is damaged, or explain what you think was Eiseley's purpose in using him. (The fact that the child happened along in "real life" would not have justified including him here; the author *selects* his own details.)

4a. Study the second sentence of paragraph 23 and the first sentence of paragraph 24. What, exactly, do they have in common?

   b. What, if anything, is gained by this change?

5a. Did you find it difficult to get at the essence of Eiseley's meanings—in other words, did you find the essay hard to read? If so, try to determine just what caused your difficulties.

   b. Could these difficulties have been readily avoided by the author without sacrificing anything of quality or message?

   c. Do you think a more experienced reader than you would have had any difficulty at all?

Diction and Vocabulary

1a. How would you describe the diction of this writing? (Guide: *Diction.*)

 b. How would you describe the syntax? (Guide: *Syntax.*)

 c. Explain why the diction and syntax, and the pace of the writing, would, or would not, be appropriate for most college papers. For most newspaper writing.

2. Why does the author refer to the old "paper" nest in the thicket (par. 7)?

3a. Demonstrate the meaning of the term *metaphor* by use of one or more examples from this selection. (Guide: *Figures of Speech.*)

 b. The meaning of *simile.*

 c. The meaning of *personification.*

4. If you are not familiar with the meaning of any of the following words, consult your dictionary: sodden (par. 1); subside (4); vaporous (8); guises (9); runnel, wrack (10); inexorable, dissident, retort, insatiable, maw (11); dispersed (22).

Suggestions for Writing and Discussion

Plan and discuss, in oral or written form, one of the following passages, clarifying its meanings and implications.

1. "We cling to a time and place because without them man is lost, not only man but life."

2. "Life disappears or modifies its appearances so fast that everything takes on an aspect of illusion. . . ."

3. "Every day these invisible dreams pass us on the street, or rise from beneath our feet, or look out upon us from beneath a bush."

4. ". . . the attachment of the spirit to a grouping of events in time; it was part of our morality."

(NOTE: Suggestions for topics requiring development by use of ANALOGY are on page 218, at the end of this section.)

BILL McKIBBEN

In his writing, Bill McKibben focuses on matters of the environment and on the relationship of nature to human activity. He
examines the various media that surround and shape our lives, as
well as the flood of information and ideas that has grown so
rapidly in recent years His essays and articles have appeared in a
wide variety of magazines including *Vogue, Rolling Stone, Mother
Jones, Buzzworm's Earth Journal, The New York Times Magazine, The
New Yorker, Natural History, Good Housekeeping,* and *The New York
Review of Books.* He has written three books: *The End of Nature*
(1989), *The Age of Missing Information* (1992), and *Look at the Land;
Aerial Reflections on America* (with Alex Maclean) (1993). McKibben
lives in New York's Adirondack Mountains.

Sometimes You Just Have to Turn It Off

As the title suggests, McKibben draws his analogy from the almost
constant presence of televisions, tape recordings, radios, VCRs,
and other electronic equipment in our lives—and he then criticizes
this presence. This essay appeared in *Esquire.*

A man walks into a room, fumbles for the remote, and turns on the   1
TV. This is the quintessential act of modern life. It obliterates the
three rarest commodities of our age: silence, solitude, darkness.
Weather one hundred times a day. *SportsCenter.* CNN, *People,*
WFAN. "You give us twenty-two minutes, we'll give you the
world." MTV—no drifting away into reverie, too busy counting
thighs. Enough Sunday paper to last till evening. Blockbuster Video.
The Comedy Channel. The op-ed page. The Sharper Image cata-
logue, the computer bulletin board, the phone in the car-plane-toilet.
The fax unrolling, the pager chirping. Two weeks of previews for the

Academy Awards, the Academy Awards, three days of Academy Awards postmortem. Ours is the age of distraction.

I live in a house without a television, half a mile from the nearest neighbor, far enough out that no one will deliver us a daily newspaper. And yet the magazines and newsletters arrive with each morning's mail, and every time I plunk myself down on the sofa I reach for them. The radio fills the silence half the day.

Because our minds are jazzed. Because we fear boredom. Because we are so hooked on infodrug, on intravenous entertainment, that any break in the action seems unnatural, a vacuum. And yet each of us intuits this too: We are lacking something, something for which Siskel, Ebert, Safire, Keanu, Shaq, and Naughty by Nature are insufficient substitutes. Solitude, silence, darkness.

Some years ago I went on a long solo backpacking trip. Only a week, but that was as long as I'd ever been by myself, all alone except for an occasional chance meeting. The hiking was not hard; there was no high adventure. And for a day or two my mind still rang with the almost literal buzz of regular life. My opinions on presidential politics, the plots of shows I'd seen, my plans for the projects I'd take up next—I was my own little CNN, neurons chattering happily away. And I hardly noticed where I was hiking. My eyes were fixed on some invisible middle distance, the same place you look when you're driving a car on the highway.

But after a few days away my head started to quiet down. I started to notice my body—to notice, almost for the first time in my life, when I was really hungry as opposed to feeling like it was time for dinner. I started to notice the woods, notice them deeply—stop for long stretches to watch birds, stare at strange mushrooms, feel scaly bark. Feel the sun, feel it letting me stretch out. Feel the faint breeze lift the hairs on my back. See twilight turn detail to geometry and then to suggestion. Stare for hours.

And so what? That is a hard question to answer, hard because the answers are subtle, hard because they are easy to ridicule. I think the answer goes like this: There are other broadcasts, on wavelengths that do not appear on our cable boxes, other commentaries, which do not appear in the back pages of newspapers.

These natural broadcasts are timeless—the sense of the presence of the divine, for instance, that has marked human beings in every culture as far back as anthropologists can go and that we now try unsuccessfully to buy from televangelists or crystal merchants.

These broadcasts are low, resonant only in stillness. They are easily *jammed*—we don't have to be in the woods to hear them, but we have to be *quiet*.

What do these broadcasts concern? *Nothing new.* Nothing new. 8 Nothing novel. Only the most basic information, the sort that can ground us; that we are part, a seamless part, of something very much bigger, which is an almost incomprehensible notion for us. We have no dark, so we do not see the stars—the Hubble telescope sending back radio images of the big bang is no substitute for a score of nights under the blanket of stars or for the luminous enfolding of the northern lights.

All this sounds trippy. And is it not self-indulgent in a world 9 and an age that demand responsibility, attention? In point of cold, hard fact, there's no real danger of escaping information. It *would* be wrong to choose ignorance of the genocide underway in Bosnia. But day after day to stare distractedly at the latest scene of devastation, the latest dying child, the latest grieving mother? What we need is not additional information—we have, the least-informed of us, more information than a king two centuries ago—but more reflection, more silence and solitude and darkness to put in context what we know. What we know about Bosnia, what we know about our lives and our wives and our children.

Self-obsession is no risk, either. Self-obsession is what comes 10 through the TV set—the ceaseless preoccupation with keeping us from becoming bored for even an instant. Reminding us at every break that our immediate satisfaction is the purpose of a consumer society. Listening to this other broadcast, this low-level rumbling, *opens* us to the world. If it seems at first superficially dull—if meditation seems maddening, if the sunset seems to take a hell of a long time—at some deeper level the absence of distraction soon becomes a chuckling thrill.

We are past the point in human history where the deep currents 11 of existence belong to us by birthright—we have to fight to block out some of the endless rain of information, entertainment, stress. We have to fight *not* to turn on the TV, to walk into the room and savor the quiet. To get started we have to take the long view and remind ourselves that no one ever lay on his deathbed wishing he'd watched more *Matlock*.

Meanings and Values

1a. To what does "It" in the title of this essay refer?

 b. What is the analogy around which the essay is built?

 c. How does the author present the analogy in the title and the first paragraph?

2. According to McKibben (par. 3), what do we lack?

3a. How does the author manage to keep from sounding superior or arrogant as he criticizes our behavior?

 b. Characterize the tone of this essay and relate it to the overall purpose. (See "Guide to Terms": *Tone*.)

Expository Techniques

1a. What strategy does McKibben use to open the essay? (Guide: *Introductions*.)

 b. In what ways does the closing echo or modify the opening?

2a. What contrast does the essay explore in paragraphs 4 and 5?

 b. What senses does the writer appeal to in paragraph 4? In paragraph 5? Why would the writer choose to emphasize different senses in each paragraph?

 c. Which paragraph presents details that are more abstract and which presents details that are more concrete? (Guide: *Abstract/Concrete*.)

 d. What is the reason for the difference noted in question 2c?

Diction and Vocabulary

1a. What figure of speech does the author employ in the statement "I was my own little CNN," and for what reasons does he use it? (Guide: *Figures of Speech*.)

 b. Explain the use this essay makes of a rhetorical question in paragraph 6. (Guide: *Rhetorical Questions*.)

 c. Can paragraph 6 be said to present a paradox or a statement that might seem paradoxical for a moment? If so, what is it? (Guide: *Paradox*.)

2. Discuss the use of parallel sentence structures in paragraphs 3 and 6. (Guide: *Parallel Structure*.)

3. What unusual words or word combinations does the writer use in paragraphs 1 and 3? What is his purpose in using them?

Suggestions for Writing and Discussion

1.   Do you share McKibben's attitude toward the media that dominate our lives? Or do you think he is overstating his case?

2.   What is it about ourselves or about the media that makes us so dependent on them to fill up our time and take up our attention?

3.   In what ways (if at all) might our society change if we each spent more time alone in the natural world? Would the changes all be for the good?

(NOTE: Suggestions for topics requiring development by use of ANALOGY are on page 218, at the end of this section.)

Tom Wolfe was born in 1931 and grew up in Richmond, Virginia, was graduated from Washington and Lee University, and took his doctorate at Yale. After working for several years as a reporter for *The Washington Post*, he joined the staff of the *New York Herald Tribune* in 1962. He has won two Washington Newspaper Guild Awards, one for humor and the other for foreign news. Wolfe has been a regular contributor to *New York, Esquire*, and other magazines. His books include *The Kandy-Kolored Tangerine-Flake Streamline Baby* (1965), *The Electric Kool-Aid Acid Test* (1968), *The Pump House Gang* (1968), *Radical Chic and Mau-Mauing the Flak Catchers* (1970), *The New Journalism* (1973), *The Painted Word* (1975), *The Right Stuff* (1977), *In Our Time* (1980), *Underneath the I-Beams: Inside the Compound* (1981), *From Bauhaus to Our House* (1981), *The Purple Decades: A Reader* (1984), and *The Bonfire of the Vanities* (1986).

O Rotten Gotham—Sliding Down into the Behavioral Sink

"O Rotten Gotham—Sliding Down into the Behavioral Sink," as used here, is excerpted from a longer selection by that title in Wolfe's book *The Pump House Gang* (1968). Here, as he frequently does, the author investigates an important aspect of modern life—seriously, but in his characteristic and seemingly freewheeling style. It is a style that is sometimes ridiculed by scholars but is far more often admired. (Wolfe, as the serious student will discover, is always in complete control of his materials and methods, using them to create certain effects, to reinforce his ideas.) In this piece his analogy is particularly noteworthy for the extensive usage he is able to get from it.

I just spent two days with Edward T. Hall, an anthropologist, watching thousands of my fellow New Yorkers short-circuiting   1 themselves into hot little twitching death balls with jolts of their own adrenalin. Dr. Hall says it is overcrowding that does it. Overcrowding gets the adrenalin going, and the adrenalin gets them hyped up. And here they are, hyped up, turning bilious, nephritic, a queer, autistic, sadistic, barren, batty, sloppy, hot-in-the-pants, chancred-on-the-flankers, leering, puling, numb—the usual in New York, in other words, and God knows what else. Dr. Hall has the theory that overcrowding has already thrown New York into a state of behavioral sink. Behavioral sink is a term from ethology, which is the study of how animals relate to their environment. Among animals, the sink winds up with a "population collapse" or "massive die-off." O rotten Gotham.

It got to be easy to look at New Yorkers as animals, especially   2
looking down from some place like a balcony at Grand Central at the rush hour Friday afternoon. The floor was filled with the poor white humans, running around, dodging, blinking their eyes, making a sound like a pen full of starlings or rats or something.

"Listen to them skid," says Dr. Hall.   3

He was right. The poor old etiolate animals were out there skid-   4
ding on their rubber soles. You could hear it once he pointed it out. They stop short to keep from hitting somebody or because they are disoriented and they suddenly stop and look around, and they skid on their rubber-soled shoes, and a screech goes up. They pour out onto the floor down the escalators from the Pan-Am Building, from 42nd Street, from Lexington Avenue, up out of subways, down into subways, railroad trains, up into helicopters—

"You can also hear the helicopters all the way down here," says   5
Dr. Hall. The sound of the helicopters using the roof of the Pan-Am Building nearly fifty stories up beats right through. "If it weren't for this ceiling"—he is referring to the very high ceiling in Grand Central—"this place would be unbearable with this kind of crowding. And yet they'll probably never 'waste' space like this again."

They screech! And the adrenal glands in all those poor white   6
animals enlarge, micrometer by micrometer, to the size of cantaloupes. Dr. Hall pulls a Minox camera out of a holster he has on his belt and starts shooting away at the human scurry. The Sink!

Dr. Hall has the Minox up to his eye—he is a slender man, calm,   7
52 years old, young-looking, an anthropologist who has worked with Navajos, Hopis, Spanish-Americans, Negroes, Trukese. He was the most important anthropologist in the government during the

crucial years of the foreign aid program, the 1950s. He directed both the Point Four training program and the Human Relations Area Files. He wrote *The Silent Language* and *The Hidden Dimension*, two books that are picking up the kind of "underground" following his friend Marshall McLuhan started picking up about five years ago. He teaches at the Illinois Institute of Technology, lives with his wife, Mildred, in a high-ceilinged town house on one of the last great residential streets in downtown Chicago, Astor Street; he has a grown son and daughter, loves good food, good wine, the relaxed, civilized life—but comes to New York with a Minox at his eye to record!—perfect—The Sink.

We really got down in there by walking down into the Lexington Avenue line subway stop under Grand Central. We inhaled those nice big fluffy fumes of human sweat, urine, effluvia, and sebaceous secretions. One old female human was already stroked out on the upper level, on a stretcher, with two policemen standing by. The other humans barely looked at her. They rushed into line. They bellied each other, haunch to paunch, down the stairs. Human heads shone through the gratings. The species North European tried to create bubbles of space around themselves, about a foot and a half in diameter— 8

"See, he's reacting against the line," says Dr. Hall. 9

—but the species Mediterranean presses on in. The hell with bubbles of space. The species North European resents that, this male human behind him presses forward toward the booth . . . *breathing* on him, he's disgusted, he pulls out of the line entirely, the species Mediterranean resents him for resenting it, and neither of them realizes what the hell they are getting irritable about exactly. And in all of them the old adrenals grow another micrometer. 10

Dr. Hall whips out the Minox. Too perfect! The bottom of The Sink. 11

It is the sheer overcrowding, such as occurs in the business sections of Manhattan five days a week and in Harlem, Bedford-Stuyvesant, southeast Bronx every day—sheer overcrowding is converting New Yorkers into animals in a sink pen. Dr. Hall's argument runs as follows: all animals, including birds, seem to have a built-in inherited requirement to have a certain amount of territory, space, to lead their lives in. Even if they have all the food they need, and there are no predatory animals threatening them, they cannot tolerate crowding beyond a certain point. No more than two 12 hundred wild Norway rats can survive on a quarter acre of ground, for example, even when they are given all the food they can eat. They just die off.

But why? To find out, ethologists have run experiments on all   13
sorts of animals, from stickleback crabs to Sika deer. In one major experiment, an ethologist named John Calhoun put some domesticated white Norway rats in a pen with four sections to it, connected by ramps. Calhoun knew from previous experiments that the rats tend to split up into groups of ten to twelve and that the pen, therefore, would hold forty to forty-eight rats comfortably, assuming they formed four equal groups. He allowed them to reproduce until there were eighty rats, balanced between male and female, but did not let it get any more crowded. He kept them supplied with plenty of food, water, and nesting materials. In other words, all their more obvious needs were taken care of. A less obvious need—space—was not. To the human eye, the pen did not even look especially crowded. But to the rats, it was crowded beyond endurance.

The entire colony was soon plunged into a profound behavioral   14
sink. "The sink," said Calhoun, "is the outcome of any behavioral process that collects animals together in unusually great numbers. The unhealthy connotations of the term are not accidental: a behavioral sink does act to aggravate all forms of pathology that can be found within a group."

For a start, long before the rat population reached eighty, a sta-   15
tus hierarchy had developed in the pen. Two dominant male rats took over the two end sections, acquired harems of eight to ten females each, and forced the rest of the rats into the two middle pens. All the overcrowding took place in the middle pens. That was where the "sink" hit. The aristocrat rats at the end grew bigger, sleeker, healthier, and more secure the whole time.

In The Sink, meanwhile, nest building, courting, sex behavior,   16
reproduction, social organization, health—all of it went to pieces. Normally, Norway rats have a mating ritual in which the male chases the female, the female ducks down into a burrow and sticks her head up to watch the male. He performs a little dance outside the burrow, then she comes out, and he mounts her, usually for a few seconds. When The Sink set in, however, no more than three males—the dominant males in the middle sections—kept up the old customs. The rest tried everything from satyrism to homosexuality or else gave up on sex altogether. Some of the subordinate males

spent all their time chasing females. Three or four might chase one female at the same time, and instead of stopping at the burrow entrance for the ritual, they would charge right in. Once mounted, they would hold on for minutes instead of the usual seconds.

Homosexuality rose sharply. So did bisexuality. Some males would mount anything—males, females, babies, senescent rats, anything. Still other males dropped sexual activity altogether, wouldn't fight and, in fact, would hardly move except when the other rats slept. Occasionally, a female from the aristocrat rats' harems would come over the ramps and into the middle sections to sample life in The Sink. When she had had enough, she would run back up the ramp. Sink males would give chase up to the top of the ramp, which is to say, to the very edge of the aristocratic preserve. But one glance from one of the king rats would stop them cold and they would return to The Sink. [17]

The slumming females from the harems had their adventures and then returned to a placid, healthy life. Females in The Sink, however, were ravaged, physically and psychologically. Pregnant rats had trouble continuing pregnancy. The rate of miscarriages increased significantly, and females started dying from tumors and other disorders of the mammary glands, sex organs, uterus, ovaries, and Fallopian tubes. Typically, their kidneys, livers, and adrenals were also enlarged or diseased or showed other signs associated with stress. [18]

Child-rearing became totally disorganized. The females lost the interest or the stamina to build nests and did not keep them up if they did build them. In the general filth and confusion, they would not put themselves out to save offspring they were momentarily separated from. Frantic, even sadistic competition among the males was going on all around them and rendering their lives chaotic. The males began unprovoked and senseless assaults upon one another, often in the form of tail-biting. Ordinarily, rats will suppress this kind of behavior when it crops up. In The Sink, male rats gave up all policing and just looked out for themselves. The "pecking order" among males in The Sink was never stable. Normally, male rats set up a three-class structure. Under the pressure of overcrowding, however, they broke up into all sorts of unstable subclasses, cliques, packs—and constantly pushed, probed, explored, tested one another's power. Anyone was fair game, except for the aristocrats in the end pens. [19]

Calhoun kept the population down to eighty, so that the next   20
stage, "population collapse" or "massive die-off," did not occur. But
the autopsies showed that the pattern—as in the diseases among the
female rats—was already there.

The classic study of die-off was John J. Christian's study of Sika   21
deer on James Island in the Chesapeake Bay, west of Cambridge,
Maryland. Four or five of the deer had been released on the island,
which was 280 acres and uninhabited, in 1916. By 1955 they had
bred freely into a herd of 280 to 300. The population density was
only about one deer per acre at this point, but Christian knew that
this was already too high for the Sikas' inborn space requirements,
and something would give before long. For two years the number of
deer remained 280 to 300. But suddenly, in 1958, over half the deer
died; 161 carcasses were recovered. In 1959 more deer died and the
population steadied at about 80.

In two years, two-thirds of the herd had died. Why? It was not   22
starvation. In fact, all the deer collected were in excellent condition,
with well-developed muscles, shining coats, and fat deposits
between the muscles. In practically all the deer, however, the
adrenal glands had enlarged by 50 percent. Christian concluded that
the die-off was due to "shock following severe metabolic disturbance, probably as a result of prolonged adrenocortical hyperactivity.... There was no evidence of infection, starvation, or other
obvious cause to explain the mass mortality." In other words, the
constant stress of overpopulation, plus the normal stress of the cold
of the winter, had kept the adrenalin flowing so constantly in the
deer that their systems were depleted of blood sugar and they died
of shock.

Well, the white humans are still skidding and darting across the   23
floor of Grand Central. Dr. Hall listens a moment longer to the skidding and the darting noises, and then says, "You know, I've been on
commuter trains here after everyone has been through one of these
rushes, and I'll tell you, there is enough acid flowing in the stomachs
in every car to dissolve the rails underneath."

Just a little invisible acid bath for the linings to round off the   24
day. The ulcers the acids cause, of course, are the one disease people
have already been taught to associate with the stress of city life. But
over-crowding, as Dr. Hall sees it, raises a lot more hell with the
body than just ulcers. In everyday life in New York—just the usual,
getting to work, working in massively congested areas like 42nd

Street between Fifth Avenue and Lexington, especially now that the Pam-Am Building is set in there, working in cubicles such as those in the editorial offices at Time-Life, Inc., which Dr. Hall cites as typical of New York's poor handling of space, working in cubicles with low ceilings and, often, no access to a window, while construction crews all over Manhattan drive everybody up the Masonite wall with air-pressure generators with noises up to the boil-a-brain decibel level, then rushing to get home, piling into subways and trains, fighting for time and for space, the usual day in New York—the whole now-normal thing keeps shooting jolts of adrenalin into the body, breaking down the body's defenses and winding up with the work-a-daddy human animal stroked out at the breakfast table with his head apoplexed like a cauliflower out of his $6.95 semi-spread Pima-cotton shirt, and nosed over into a plate of No-Kolresto egg substitute, signing off with the black thrombosis, cancer, kidney, liver, or stomach failure, and the adrenals ooze to a halt, the size of eggplants in July.

One of the people whose work Dr. Hall is interested in on this score is Rene Dubos at the Rockefeller Institute. Dubos's work indicates that specific organisms, such as the tuberculosis bacillus or a pneumonia virus, can seldom be considered "the cause" of a disease. The germ or virus, apparently, has to work in combination with other things that have already broken the body down in some way—such as the old adrenal hyperactivity. Dr. Hall would like to see some autopsy studies made to record the size of adrenal glands in New York, especially of people crowded into slums and people who go through the full rush-hour-work-rush-hour cycle every day. He is afraid that until there is some clinical, statistical data on how overcrowding actually ravages the human body, no one will be willing to do anything about it. Even in so obvious a thing as air pollution, the pattern is familiar. Until people can actually see the smoke or smell the sulphur or feel the sting in their eyes, politicians will not get excited about it, even though it is well known that many of the lethal substances polluting the air are invisible and odorless. For one thing, most politicians are like the aristocrat rats. They are insulated from The Sink by practically sultanic buffers—limousines, chauffeurs, secretaries, aides-de-camp, doormen, shuttered houses, high-floor apartments. They almost never ride subways, fight rush hours, much less live in the slums or work in the Pam-Am Building.

Meanings and Values

1a. Who are members of the "species Mediterranean"?

b. Who belong to the "species North European"?

c. What could account for their difference in space requirements (pars. 8–10)?

2. Is this writing primarily objective or subjective? (See "Guide to Terms": *Objective/Subjective.*) Why?

3a. Do you get the impression that the author is being unkind, "making fun" of the harried New Yorkers?

b. How, if at all, does he prevent such an impression?

4a. Compare Wolfe's style, tone, and point of view with those of Catton (Section 3). (Guide: *Style/Tone* and *Point of View.*)

b. Do these features necessarily make one author less effective than another in achieving his purposes? Explain.

Expository Techniques

1a. Using whatever criteria we have available for judging the success of analogy, appraise the effectiveness of this one.

b. Does the author work it *too* hard? Be prepared to defend your answer.

2. What are the benefits of the frequent return to what Dr. Hall is doing or saying (e.g., in pars. 3, 5, 7, 9, 11, and 23)?

3. Paragraph 12 has a useful function beyond the simple information it imparts—a sort of organic relation to the coming development. Explain how this is accomplished.

4. How is the switch to Sika deer (par. 21) prepared for, and a bumpy transition avoided?

5. The preceding three questions are related in some manner to the problems of transition. How, if at all, are such problems also matters of coherence? (Guide: *Coherence.*)

6. Wolfe is adept at creating just the effect he wants, and the careful student of writing can detect a subtle change of style and pace with each change of subpurpose. (Guide: *Style/Tone.*)

a. Analyze stylistic differences, with resulting effects, between the description of chaos at Grand Central and the information about Dr. Hall in paragraph 7.

b. Analyze such differences between the Grand Central scene and the account of the laboratory experiment with rats.

c. Analyze the differences between the Grand Central scene and the final paragraph.

7. Explain how the style of the more descriptive portions is also a matter of emphasis. (Guide: *Emphasis*.)

8a. Illustrate as many as possible of the elements of effective syntax (itself a matter of style) by examples from this selection. (Guide: *Syntax*.)

b. What is gained or lost by the unusual length and design of the last sentence of paragraph 24? (We can be sure that it did not "just happen" to Wolfe—and equally sure that one of such length would be disastrous in most writing.)

Diction and Vocabulary

1. What is the significance of the word "Gotham"?

2a. Why do you think the author refers (deliberately, no doubt) to "my fellow New Yorkers" in the first sentence?

b. What soon could have been the effect if he had not taken such a step?

3. Why does he consistently, after paragraph 2, refer to the people as "poor white humans," "poor human animals," etc.?

4. In paragraph 14 he refers to the connotations of the word "sink." What are its possible connotations? (Guide: *Connotation/Denotation*.)

5. Cite examples of verbal irony to be found in paragraphs 5, 8, and 24. (Guide: *Irony*.)

6. Which of the elements of style mentioned in your answer to question 4a of "Meanings and Values" are also matters of diction?

7. Consult your dictionary as needed for full understanding of the following words: autistic, puling (par. 1); etiolate (4); effluvia, sebaceous (8); pathology (14); satyrism (16); senescent (17); decibel, thrombosis (24); lethal (25).

Suggestions for Writing and Discussion

1. Carrying Wolfe's analogy still further, trace the steps by which a rise in serious crime must result from the overcrowding of "poor human animals."

2. If you are familiar with another city, particularly during rush hours, which appears to you much like New York in this respect, describe it.

3. If you are familiar with some area of high-density population that has solved its problem of overcrowding, explain the solution.

4. What practical steps can the *individual* take, if forced to live and/or work in overcrowded conditions, to avoid becoming the victim of his or her own adrenals?

(NOTE: Suggestions for topics requiring development by use of ANALOGY are on page 218, at the end of this section.)

PATRICIA RAYBON

Patricia Raybon was born in 1949. She attended Ohio State University (BA, 1971) and the University of Colorado (MA, 1977). For a number of years she was a newspaper reporter, writer, and editor. Currently she is an associate professor at the University of Colorado School of Journalism and Mass Communication. Her work has been published in a wide variety of magazines and newspapers, including *The New York Times Magazine* and *USA Today*.

Letting in Light

The analogy around which this essay is built is a subtle but particularly effective one. To observe it at work, consider the following relationships as you read: washing windows *equals* women's work *equals* letting in light. By the end of the essay, Raybon may have changed your mind about activities that many people no longer consider particularly important or valuable. This essay first appeared in *The New York Times Magazine*.

The windows were a gift or maybe a bribe—or maybe a bonus—for 1
falling in love with such a dotty old house. The place was a wreck.
A showoff, too. So it tried real hard to be more. But it lacked so
much—good heat, stable floors, solid walls, enough space. A low
interest rate.

But it had windows. More glass and bays and bows than people 2
on a budget had a right to expect. And in unlikely places—like the
window inside a bedroom closet, its only view a strawberry patch
planted by the children next door.

None of it made sense. So we bought the place. We saved up 3
and put some money down, then toasted the original builder—no
doubt some brave and gentle carpenter, blessed with a flair for the
grand gesture. A romantic with a T-square.

We were young then and struggling. Also, we are black. We 4
looked with irony and awe at the task now before us. But we did not
faint.

The time had come to wash windows.   5

Yes, I do windows. Like an amateur and a dabbler, perhaps, but 6
the old-fashioned way—one pane at a time. It is the best way to pay
back something so plain for its clear and silent gifts—the light of
day, the glow of moon, hard rain, soft snow, dawn's early light.

The Romans called them *specularia*. They glazed their windows 7
with translucent marble and shells. And thus the ancients let some
light into their world.

In my own family, my maternal grandmother washed win- 8
dows—and floors and laundry and dishes and a lot of other things
that needed cleaning—while doing day work for a rich, stylish red-
head in her Southern hometown.

To feed her five children and keep them clothed and happy, to 9
help them walk proudly and go to church and sing hymns and have
some change in their pockets—and to warm and furnish the house
her dead husband had built and added onto with his own hands—
my grandmother went to work.

She and her third daughter, my mother, put on maids' uniforms 10
and cooked and sewed and served a family that employed my
grandmother until she was nearly 80. She called them Mister and
Missus—yes, ma'am and yes, sir—although she was by many years
their elder. They called her Laura. Her surname never crossed their
lips.

But her daughter, my mother, took her earnings from the cook- 11
ing and serving and window washing and clothes ironing and went
to college, forging a life with a young husband—my father—that
granted me, their daughter, a lifetime of relative comfort.

I owe these women everything.   12

They taught me hope and kindness and how to say thank you. 13

They taught me how to brew tea and pour it. They taught me 14
how to iron creases and whiten linen and cut hair ribbon on the bias
so it doesn't unravel. They taught me to carve fowl, make butter
molds and cook a good cream sauce. They taught me "women's
work"—secrets of home, they said, that now are looked on mostly
with disdain: how to sweep, dust, polish and wax. How to mow,
prune, scrub, scour and purify.

They taught me how to wash windows.   15

Not many women do anymore, of course. There's no time. Life   16
has us all on the run. It's easier to call a "window man," quicker to
pay and, in the bargain, forget about the secret that my mother and
her mother learned many years before they finally taught it to me:

Washing windows clears the cobwebs from the corners. It's   17
plain people's therapy, good for troubles and muddles and other
consternations. It's real work, I venture—honest work—and it's a
sound thing to pass on. Mother to daughter. Daughter to child.
Woman to woman.

This is heresy, of course. Teaching a girl to wash windows is   18
now an act of bravery—or else defiance. If she's black, it's an act of
denial, a gesture that dares history and heritage to make something
of it.

But when my youngest was 5 or 6, I tempted fate and ancestry   19
and I handed her a wooden bucket. Together we would wash the
outdoor panes. The moment sits in my mind:

She works a low row. I work the top. Silently we toil, soaping   20
and polishing, each at her own pace—the only sounds the squeak of
glass, some noisy birds, our own breathing.

Then, quietly at first, this little girl begins to hum. It's a non-   21
sense melody, created for the moment. Soft at first, soon it gets
louder. And louder. Then a recognizable tune emerges. Then she is
really singing. With every swish of the towel, she croons louder and
higher in her little-girl voice with her little-girl song. "This little light
of mine—I'm gonna let it shine! Oh, this little light of mine—I'm
gonna let it shine!" So, of course, I join in. And the two of us sere-
nade the glass and the sparrows and mostly each other. And too
soon our work is done.

"That was fun," she says. She is innocent, of course, and does   22
this work by choice, not by necessity. But she's not too young to look
at truth and understand it. And her heart, if not her arm, is resolute
and strong.

Those years have passed. And other houses and newer win-   23
dows—and other "women's jobs"—have moved through my life. I
have chopped and puréed and polished and glazed. Bleached and
folded and stirred. I have sung lullabies.

I have also marched and fought and prayed and taught and tes-   24
tified. Women's work covers many bases.

But the tradition of one simple chore remains. I do it without   25
apology.

Last week, I dipped the sponge into the pail and began the gen-   26
tle bath—easing off the trace of wintry snows, of dust storms and
dead, brown leaves, of too much sticky tape used to steady paper
pumpkins and Christmas lights and crepe-paper bows from holidays now past. While I worked, the little girl—now 12—found her
way to the bucket, proving that her will and her voice are still up to
the task, but mostly, I believe, to have some fun.

We are out of step, the two of us. She may not even know it. But   27
we can carry a tune. The work is never done. The song is two-part
harmony.

Meanings and Values

1a.   Why do windows make the house attractive (pars. 1–2)?

 b.   What do they seem to symbolize in paragraphs 1–4? 26? (See "Guide
      to Terms": *Symbol*.) Do they take on symbolic meanings anywhere
      else in the essay? If so, what are these other meanings?

2.   According to the essay, why might the writer (and other people)
      view window washing as a negative, unnecessary, or demeaning
      act? Be specific in your answer and point to passages that support
      your conclusions.

3.   What positive reasons for washing windows does the author give in
      the course of the essay? Be specific.

4a.   Where in the essay does the author equate washing windows with
      "women's work"?

 b.   In the course of the essay, the writer points out that washing win-
      dows means letting in light. Are we to take the idea of letting in light
      simply and literally, or might it have deeper meanings?

 c.   If it has deeper meanings, point to passages that suggest these mean-
      ings and summarize in your own words the ideas being conveyed.

Expository Techniques

1.   How does Raybon call attention to a particular subject in the opening
      sentences of paragraphs 1 and 2? (Guide: *Emphasis*.)

2.   Explain the role paragraph 5 plays as a transition. Is it effective?
      (Guide: *Transitions, Evaluation*.)

3a.   Point out the parallel sentence structures in paragraphs 13–15.
      (Guide: *Parallel Structure*.)

 b.   What does the writer achieve with this use of parallelism?

   c.   Explain why the last parallel sentence (par. 15) focuses on window washing.

4.   Identify the transitions in paragraphs 16 and 23 and discuss their function within the essay as a whole.

Diction and Vocabulary

1.   To what extent should the phrase "clears the cobwebs from the corners" (par. 17) be taken literally? To what extent can it be regarded as a metaphor? Explain. (Guide: *Figures of Speech*.)

2a.   Explain how the phrase "A romantic with a T-Square" might be regarded as presenting a paradox. (Guide: *Paradox*.)

   b.   In what ways might the author, the "we" of paragraphs 3–4, and the house itself be accurately described as "A romantic with a T-Square"?

3.   The song quoted in paragraph 21 is an allusion (Guide: *Figures of Speech*.) To what does it allude? What does this allusion suggest about the meaning of light for the writer?

4.   Are we to take the last sentences of the essay literally as a statement about singing? If not, what figurative or metaphoric meaning might they carry? Explain. (Guide: *Figures of Speech*.)

Suggestions for Writing and Discussion

1.   What kinds of work or other activities have traditionally been regarded as "women's work" or "women's jobs"? What have been regarded as "men's work"?

2.   Do you believe that the perspective offered in this essay is contrary to the changes made possible by the "women's movement"? Why, or why not? Or, do you think it offers a useful warning about holding onto essential values amid change? What sort of position might Raybon take in current discussions over roles for men and women (and children)?

(NOTE: Suggestions for topics requiring development by use of ANALOGY follow.)

Writing Suggestions for Section 4
Analogy

In any normal situation, the analogy is chosen to help explain a theme-idea that already exists—such as those in the first group below. But for classroom training, which is bound to be somewhat artificial, it is permissible to work from the other direction, to develop a theme that fits a preselected analogy-symbol.

1. State a central theme about one of the following general topics or a suitable one of your own, and develop it into a composition by use of an analogy of your own choosing.

   a. A well-organized school system.

   b. Starting a new business or other enterprise.

   c. The long-range value of programs for underprivileged children.

   d. Learning a new skill.

   e. The need for cooperation between management and labor.

   f. Today's intense competition for success.

   g. Dealing with stress.

   h. The results of ignorance.

2. Select an analogy-symbol from the list below and fashion a theme that it can illustrate. Develop your composition as instructed.

   a. A freeway at commuting time.

   b. Building a road through a wilderness.

   c. Building a bridge across a river.

   d. A merry-go-round.

   e. A wedding.

   f. A car wash.

   g. Flood destruction of a levee.

   h. The tending of a young orchard.

   i. An animal predator stalking prey.

   j. A baseball game.

   k. A juggling act.

   l. An oasis.

   m. A duel.

   n. An airport.

5

Explaining Through *Process Analysis*

Process analysis explains how the steps of an operation lead to its completion. Although in one narrow sense it may be considered a kind of narration, process analysis has an important difference in purpose, and hence in approach. Other narration is mostly concerned with the story itself, or with a general concept illustrated by it, but process tells of methods that end in specified results. We might narrate a story about a rifle—its purchase, its role in colorful episodes, perhaps its eventual retirement from active service. (We could, for other purposes, *define* "rifle," or *classify* the types of rifles, and no doubt *compare* and *contrast* these types and *illustrate* by examples.) But showing how a rifle works, or how it is manufactured, or how it should be cared for—this is process, and it sometimes becomes the basic pattern of an exposition.

Most writers are especially concerned with two kinds of process, both of them apparent in the preceding example of rifles: the directional, which explains how to *do* something (how to shoot a gun or how to clean it); and the informational, which explains how something is or was *done* (how guns are manufactured). The directional process can range from the instructions on a shampoo bottle to a detailed plan showing how to make the United Nations more effective, and will often contain detailed justification for individual steps or for the process itself. The informational process, on the other hand, might explain the steps of a wide variety of operations or actions, of mental or evolutionary processes, with no how-to-do-it purpose at all—how someone went about choosing a college or how the planet Earth was formed. Informational process analysis has been seen in earlier selections: Staples explained how he keeps from frightening other people when he takes his evening walks, and Wolfe explained how the experiment with Norway rats was conducted.

Most process analyses are organized into simple, chronological steps. Indeed, the exact order is sometimes of greatest importance, as in a recipe. But occasionally there are problems in organization. The step-by-step format may need to be interrupted for descriptions, definitions, and other explanatory asides. If the process is a proposed solution, part of a problem-solution argument, then it may be necessary to justify each of the steps in turn and dismiss alternatives. And, still more of a problem, some processes defy a strict chronological treatment, because several things occur simultaneously. To explain the operating process of a gasoline engine, for example, the writer would be unable to convey at once everything that happens at the same time. Some way must be found to present the material in *general* stages, organized as subdivisions, so that the reader can see the step-by-step process through the confusion of interacting relationships.

Another difficulty in explaining by process analysis is estimating what knowledge the reader may already have. Presuming too little background may quickly lead to boredom or even irritation, with a resulting communication block; presuming too much will almost certainly leave the reader bewildered. Like a chain dependent on its weakest link for its strength, the entire process analysis can fail because of one unclear point that makes the rest incomprehensible.

Sample Paragraph (Annotated)

Process to be analyzed.

Palmville has an unusual form of city government, at least compared with other cities in the state. Instead of an elected mayor, it has an appointed city manager responsible for all city operations and employees. This

Background on the process.

arrangement is by no means unusual, yet Palmville also has no city council or board of supervisors. Instead, it has a Board of Proposers and a Town Meeting. How, then, are laws passed,

Reason for process analysis.

budgets approved, and appointments made? Members of the Board of

Beginning of *informational* process. How the unusual procedure works. Begins chronologically then covers some of the key features of the process.

Proposers draw up proposals for new laws, regulations, hiring, and budgets, but they do not vote on the proposals. They send the proposals to the Town Meeting for a vote. Town Meetings are scheduled four times a year in the auditorium of the Civic Center. Only people who come to the meeting are eligible to vote on the proposals; they must be registered voters who live within the city limits. Upcoming Town Meetings are publicized through the local media. The system worked well when Palmville was a small town and there was little business to be done.

Problems and need for change in future.

Now the meetings last 8–10 hours; even so, important business often ends up being postponed until the next meeting. Although most Palmville residents enjoy the direct participation in government that the system allows, they have also begun to recognize the need for change.

Sample Paragraph (Process Analysis)

It's not the wind, though, that's the most dangerous part of a hurricane. It's the water, especially when something called the "storm surge" occurs. As the low-pressure eye of the hurricane sits over the ocean, the sea level literally rises into a dome of water. For every inch drop in barometric pressure, the ocean rises a foot higher. Now, out at sea, that means nothing. The rise is not even noticeable. But when that mound of water starts moving toward land, the situation becomes crucial. As the water approaches a shallow beach, the dome of water rises. It may rise ten to fifteen feet in an hour and span fifty miles. Like a marine bulldozer, the surge may rise up twenty feet high, crash onto land, and wash everything away. Then with six- to eight-foot waves riding atop this mound of water, the storm surge destroys buildings, trees, cars, and anything else in its path. It's this storm surge that accounts for 90 percent of the deaths during a hurricane.

Losing Weight

Karin Gaffney

Across the board, regardless of age, gender, race, or background, most people spend time trying to lose weight (Williamson, et al.). Some people want to lose only five or ten pounds while others worry about getting rid of seventy-five pounds or more. As a result, weight loss is both a universal concern and a highly individualized matter.

Losing weight must mean a lot to Americans. After all, they spend over three billion dollars on weight loss programs each year ("Rating" 353). If you think you need to diet, think again. Many people think they are overweight because they compare themselves to impossibly thin models or imagine themselves in the slimmest of new fashions. So if you think you need to diet, consult a doctor and other reliable sources of health information. Then go on a good weight loss program—if you really need one.

Why should you be careful about going on a diet? A study in 1988 by the Centers for Disease Control concluded that any change of weight either up or down led to a higher rate of heart disease in the people studied ("Losing" 350). This does not necessarily mean that you should forget about dieting, however, because weight loss can also help you avoid other health problems ("Losing" 348, 350).

To lose weight, some people turn to commercial diets and hospital programs, yet the majority rely on self help. For those people who are trying to lose weight on their own, I can offer some general advice along with a simple weight-loss program. The simple advice is no different from what most of us have already heard, but it probably still needs to be repeated: 1) cut down on high fat foods, 2) eat moderate portions of healthy food, and 3) get regular exercise. Above all, consult your doctor not only to determine whether you should diet but to make sure your dietary and exercise programs are appropriate for you (and not for the models and athletes who appear on exercise tapes or talk about their health and muscle power diets in magazines).

A person who is overweight probably has a diet heavy in fat (Beitz 281). A calorie of fat in food becomes part of body fat much more easily than does a calorie of carbohydrate, which is easily burned as energy (Delaney 46). In other words, the body often keeps the fat it takes in but the carbohydrates it uses up. Moreover, a gram of fat has about 2.25 times as many calories as one gram of carbohydrate or protein does (Beitz 281).

The first step in a healthy weigh-loss plan is to reduce the fat in your diet. If you eliminate high-fat foods such as ice creams, cheese, hamburgers, and butter from your diet, your body will respond immediately to the change. Low-fat substitutes, such as low-fat milk, can also have a positive effect, as can steps like cutting the fat off meat or taking the skin off poultry ("Losing" 352).

The second step is to eat more foods that are low in fat but high in fiber and carbohydrates. Here are several choices:

1. Potatoes (baked, not fried, and without butter or sour cream)
2. Beans (pinto, kidney, lentils, and so on)
3. Whole grains (cereals, pastas, breads)
4. Fresh fruits
5. Skim milk (and skim milk products).

When you eat foods like these, your blood sugar levels stabilize and you get "filled up," yet you take in only about one-half the number of calories that fatty alternatives provide (Delaney 44–45).

The third step is to snack wisely. Limit your snacks, of course, and choose from foods like the following: string cheese, corn-on-the-cob (without butter), vegetables, angel food cake, pita bread, soft pretzels, fruits, bagels, nonfat yogurt, juice, animal crackers, or fig bars ("30 Low Fat" 3). Food companies have also been adding fat-free items to grocery shelves in recent years, so when you shop, look for low-fat frozen desserts, low-fat cookies, and the like.

The fourth step is to exercise regularly. Exercise can burn up to 200–300 calories per day (Delaney 46). You may also be surprised to learn that exercise can decrease your weight even if you do not radically change your eating habits. Regular exercise increases basal metabolism, the energy needed just to stay alive. One half of the calories in a person's diet, for example, can go to basal metabolism.

Exercise can increase the basal metabolism rate so that a person can lose more calories by just living and breathing. The amount of muscle a person has also affects basal metabolism. A person with more muscle has a higher basal metabolism and burns up more of the calories in food through this means. ("Losing" 357).

Your exercise routine does not have to be strenuous or exhausting like that of an Olympic trainee. Moderate exercise, such as one-half hour to an hour of good paced walking is beneficial. If you need an incentive to start your exercise program, remember that a person who goes from a non-exerciser to a moderate exerciser will notice the results more than someone going from moderate to advanced. There are other side benefits to exercise as well. For example, people who exercise regularly develop adult diabetes 40 percent less frequently than non-exercisers do ("Losing" 351).

The fifth step is to set reasonable goals for weight loss. Concentrate on losing a pound or two at a time, and try to maintain this small weight loss before continuing ("Losing" 350). This approach will help make you confident of your ability to lose weight and help you avoid the yo-yo effect of losing a lot of weight, then gaining it right back.

The final step is to keep several key points in mind.

1. Make eating right and exercising (not dieting) the focus of your attention and effort.
2. Concentrate on maintaining your healthy lifestyle so that you can make your weight loss permanent and benefit over the long term from good eating and exercise habits.
3. Remember that you are an individual and that the advice offered here may or may not apply to you. Always consult a doctor who knows you and your medical history.

List of Works Cited

Beitz, Donald C. "Nutrition." *McGraw-Hill Yearbook of Science and Technology*. 1993.

Delaney, Lisa. "The 'No-Hunger' Weight-Loss Plan." *Prevention* Sept. 1993: 43–46.

"Losing Weight: What Works, What Doesn't." *Consumer Reports* June 1993: 347–352.

"Rating the Diets." *Consumer Reports* June 1993: 353–357.

"30 Low Fat Foods to Grab." *Thinline* Sept./Oct. 1993: 3.

Williamson, David F., Mary K Serdula, Robert F. Auclay, Alan Levy, and Tim Byers. "Weight Loss Attempts in Adults: Goals, Duration, and Rate of Weight Loss." *American Journal of Public Health* Sept. 1992: pp. 82–89.

DONALD M. MURRAY

DONALD M. MURRAY, born in 1924 in Boston, until recently taught writing at the University of New Hampshire. He has served as an editor of *Time* and, in 1954, was awarded the Pulitzer Prize for editorials written for the *Boston Herald*. Among his published works are novels, books of nonfiction, stories, poetry, and both textbooks and articles on the teaching of writing.

The Maker's Eye:
Revising Your Own Manuscripts

"The Maker's Eye: Revising Your Own Manuscripts," first published in slightly different form in *The Writer*, provides an example of directional process. The author presents his information in chronological steps, most of them supported by direct quotations from professional writers. Much of the advice is applicable to student writing as well as to professional work.

When students complete a first draft, they consider the job of writing done—and their teachers too often agree. When professional writers complete a first draft, they usually feel that they are at the start of the writing process. When a draft is completed, the job of writing can begin. 1

That difference in attitude is the difference between amateur and professional, inexperience and experience, journeyman and craftsman. Peter F. Drucker, the prolific business writer, calls his first draft "the zero draft"—after that he can start counting. Most writers share the feeling that the first draft, and all of those which follow, are opportunities to discover what they have to say and how best they can say it. 2

To produce a progression of drafts, each of which says more   3
and says it more clearly, the writer has to develop a special kind of
reading skill. In school we are taught to decode what appears on the
page as finished writing. Writers, however, face a different category
of possibility and responsibility when they read their own drafts. To
them the words on the page are never finished. Each can be changed
and rearranged, can set off a chain reaction of confusion or clarified
meaning. This is a different kind of reading, which is possibly more
difficult and certainly more exciting.

Writers must learn to be their own best enemy. They must   4
accept the criticism of others and be suspicious of it; they must
accept the praise of others and be even more suspicious of it. Writers cannot depend on others. They must detach themselves from
their own pages so that they can apply both their caring and their
craft to their own work.

Such detachment is not easy. Science fiction writer Ray Brad-   5
bury supposedly puts each manuscript away for a year to the day
and then rereads it as a stranger. Not many writers have the discipline or the time to do this. We must read when our judgment may
be at its worst, when we are close to the euphoric moment of
creation.

Then the writer, counsels novelist Nancy Hale, "should be crit-   6
ical of everything that seems to him most delightful in his style. He
should excise what he most admires, because he wouldn't thus
admire it if he weren't . . . in a sense protecting it from criticism."
John Ciardi, the poet, adds, "The last act of the writing must be to
become one's own reader. It is, I suppose, a schizophrenic process,
to begin passionately and to end critically, to begin hot and to end
cold; and, more important, to be passion-hot and critic-cold at the
same time."

Most people think that the principal problem is that writers are   7
too proud of what they have written. Actually, a greater problem for
most professional writers is one shared by the majority of students.
They are overly critical, think everything is dreadful, tear up page
after page, never complete a draft, see the task as hopeless.

The writer must learn to read critically but constructively, to cut   8
what is bad, to reveal what is good. Eleanor Estes, the children's
book author, explains: "The writer must survey his work critically,
coolly, as though he were a stranger to it. He must be willing to
prune, expertly and hard-heartedly. At the end of each revision, a

manuscript may look . . . worked over, torn apart, pinned together, added to, deleted from, words changed and words changed back. Yet the book must maintain its original freshness and spontaneity."

Most readers underestimate the amount of rewriting it usually takes to produce spontaneous reading. This is a great disadvantage to the student writer, who sees only a finished product and never watches the craftsman who takes the necessary step back, studies the work carefully, returns to the task, steps back, returns, steps back, again and again. Anthony Burgess, one of the most prolific writers in the English-speaking world, admits, "I might revise a page twenty times." Roald Dahl, the popular children's writer, states, "By the time I'm nearing the end of a story, the first part will have been reread and altered and corrected at least 150 times. . . . Good writing is essentially rewriting. I am positive of this." 9

Rewriting isn't virtuous. It isn't something that ought to be done. It is simply something that most writers find they have to do to discover what they have to say and how to say it. It is a condition of the writer's life. 10

There are, however, a few writers who do little formal rewriting, primarily because they have the capacity and experience to create and review a large number of invisible drafts in their minds before they approach the page. And some writers slowly produce finished pages, performing all the tasks of revision simultaneously, page by page, rather than draft by draft. But it is still possible to see the sequence followed by most writers most of the time in rereading their own work. 11

Most writers scan their drafts first, reading as quickly as possible to catch the larger problems of subject and form, then move in closer and closer as they read and write, reread and rewrite. 12

The first thing writers look for in their drafts is *information*. They know that a good piece of writing is built from specific, accurate, and interesting information. The writer must have an abundance of information from which to construct a readable piece of writing. 13

Next writers look for *meaning* in the information. The specifics must build to a pattern of significance. Each piece of specific information must carry the reader toward meaning. 14

Writers reading their own drafts are aware of *audience*. They put themselves in the reader's situation and make sure that they deliver information which a reader wants to know or needs to know in a manner which is easily digested. Writers try to be sure that they 15 anticipate and answer the questions a critical reader will ask when reading the piece of writing.

Writers make sure that the *form* is appropriate to the subject and the audience. Form, or genre, is the vehicle which carries meaning to the reader, but form cannot be selected until the writer has adequate information to discover its significance and an audience which needs or wants that meaning. 16

Once writers are sure the form is appropriate, they must then look at the *structure*, the order of what they have written. Good writing is built on a solid framework of logic, argument, narrative, or motivation which runs through the entire piece of writing and holds it together. This is the time when many writers find it most effective to outline as a way of visualizing the hidden spine by which the piece of writing is supported. 17

The element on which writers may spend a majority of their time is *development.* Each section of a piece of writing must be adequately developed. It must give readers enough information so that they are satisfied. How much information is enough? That's as difficult as asking how much garlic belongs in a salad. It must be done to taste, but most beginning writers underdevelop, underestimating the reader's hunger for information. 18

As writers solve development problems, they often have to consider questions of *dimension*. There must be a pleasing and effective proportion among all the parts of the piece of writing. There is a continual process of subtracting and adding to keep the piece of writing in balance. 19

Finally, writers have to listen to their own voices. *Voice* is the force which drives a piece of writing forward. It is an expression of the writer's authority and concern. It is what is between the words on the page, what glues the piece of writing together. A good piece of writing is always marked by a consistent, individual voice. 20

As writers read and reread, write and rewrite, they move closer and closer to the page until they are doing line-by-line editing. Writers read their own pages with infinite care. Each sentence, each line, each clause, each phrase, each word, each mark of punctuation, each section of white space between the type has to contribute to the clarification of meaning. 21

Slowly the writer moves from word to word, looking through language to see the subject. As a word is changed, cut, or added, as a construction is rearranged, all the words used before that moment 22 and all those that follow that moment must be considered and reconsidered.

Writers often read aloud at this stage of the editing process, muttering or whispering to themselves, calling on the ear's experience with language. Does this sound right—or that? Writers edit, shifting back and forth from eye to page to ear to page. I find I must do this careful editing in short runs, no more than fifteen or twenty minutes at a stretch, or I become too kind with myself. I begin to see what I hope is on the page, not what actually is on the page.

This sounds tedious if you haven't done it, but actually it is fun. Making something right is immensely satisfying, for writers begin to learn what they are writing about by writing. Language leads them to meaning, and there is the joy of discovery, of understanding, of making meaning clear as the writer employs the technical skills of language.

Words have double meanings, even triple or quadruple meanings. Each word has its own potential for connotation and denotation. And when writers rub one word against the other, they are often rewarded with a sudden insight, an unexpected clarification.

The maker's eye moves back and forth from word to phrase to sentence to paragraph to sentence to phrase to word. The maker's eye sees the need for variety and balance, for a firmer structure, for a more appropriate form. It peers into the interior of the paragraph, looking for coherence, unity, and emphasis, which make meaning clear.

I learned something about this process when my first bifocals were prescribed. I had ordered a larger section of the reading portion of the glass because of my work, but even so, I could not contain my eyes within this new limit of vision. And I still find myself taking off my glasses and bending my nose towards the page, for my eyes unconsciously flick back and forth across the page, back to another page, forward to still another, as I try to see each evolving line in relation to every other line.

When does this process end? Most writers agree with the great Russian writer Tolstoy, who said, "I scarcely ever reread my published writings, if by chance I come across a page, it always strikes me: all this must be rewritten; this is how I should have written it."

The maker's eye is never satisfied, for each word has the potential to ignite new meaning. This article has been twice written all the way through the writing process, and it was published four years ago. Now it is to be republished in a book. The editors make a few small suggestions, and then I read it with my maker's eye. Now it has been re-edited, re-revised, re-read, re-re-edited, for each piece of writing to the writer is full of potential and alternatives.

A piece of writing is never finished. It is delivered to a deadline,   30
torn out of the typewriter on demand, sent off with a sense of accomplishment and shame and pride and frustration. If only there were a couple more days, time for just another run at it, perhaps then. . . .

Meanings and Values

1a. What is the author's point of view in this selection? (See "Guide to Terms": *Point of View*.)

 b. What is the relationship between his tone and the point of view? (Guide: *Style/Tone*.)

2a. What, if anything, prevents this selection from being as fascinating to read as some of the other pieces already studied?

 b. Could (or should) Murray have done anything else to enliven his process analysis? If so, what might it be?

3a. What was the author's purpose in writing this selection? (Guide: *Evaluation*.)

 b. How well did he succeed?

 c. Was it worth doing?

Expository Techniques

1a. What standard techniques of introduction does this author use in his opening paragraph? (Guide: *Introductions*.)

 b. How well does this paragraph meet the requirements of a good introduction?

2.   Into which of the two basic types of process analysis can this selection be classed? Why?

3.   What, if anything, is gained by the frequent use of quotations from professional writers?

4a. Are the distinctions among his eight steps of rewriting (pars. 13–20) made clear enough? Be specific.

 b. Does anything about the order of these eight steps seem peculiar to you? If so, explain.

5a. Cite examples of parallel structure from paragraphs 21 and 26. (Guide: *Parallel Structure*.)

 b. What is gained by such usage?

Diction and Vocabulary

1a. Cite several uses of figurative language and state what kind they are. (Guide: *Figures of Speech.*)

 b. What is the main advantage in their use?

2a. What, if anything, do you find unusual about saying "a majority of their time" (par. 18)?

 b. What other way, if any, do you prefer?

3. Is it clear to you how "each word has its own potential for connotation and denotation" (par. 25)? (Guide: *Connotation/Denotation.*) If it is, explain the assertion.

4. Use the dictionary as necessary to understand the meanings of the following words: prolific (par. 2); euphoric (5); excise, schizophrenic (6); spontaneity (8); genre (16); potential (29).

Suggestions for Writing and Discussion

1a. Who was the reader-audience the author apparently had in mind in writing this process analysis?

 b. Explain fully why it would, or would not, be worth all the suggested time and trouble just to produce papers for your college courses.

2. Discuss the assertion that "writers begin to learn what they are writing about by writing" (par. 24). If it seems more logical (for you) to learn what you are writing about some other way, what is it?

(NOTE: Suggestions for topics requiring development by PROCESS ANALYSIS are on page 267, at the end of this section.)

ANN FARADAY

ANN FARADAY studied at University College in London, where she
received her Ph.D. in psychology. After additional research and
training in the analysis of dreams, she developed her own method
of interpretation. Much of her time is now spent lecturing on this
approach to understanding dreams and on conducting research.
She is the author of two books on analyzing and understanding
dreams: *Dream Power* (1972) and *The Dream Game* (1974).

Unmasking Your Dream Images

Finding the right or best way to interpret dreams has been a concern of psychologists and other people for many years. In this
selection from *The Dream Game,* Faraday uses process analysis
along with examples to explain her approach.

There would not *be* a dream from the unconscious except as the person is   1
confronting some issue in his conscious life—some conflict, anxiety, baffle-
ment, fork in the road, puzzle or situation of compelling curiosity. That is,
the incentive for dreaming—what cues off my particular dream on a particular night—is my need to "make something" of the world I am living in at
the moment.

—Rollo May

[If you wish to understand and use your dreams, you can begin by   2
writing] down at least a few recent dreams along with notes of their
themes (falling, being chased, meeting famous people, or whatever).. . . If you are able to relate your dreams to the events or
thoughts of the day—without which any dream interpretation is
incomplete—then several of your dreams should be clear to you.
The majority of dreams, however, depict strange and even weird

images and characters and usually do require further work before their meanings emerge. To tie the events and thoughts of the day to these dreams is particularly important because there are always several possible interpretations of each dream symbol, and only you can find the "correct" interpretation by relating it to something that was on your mind or in your heart as you fell asleep.

In deciding whether a dream image should be understood literally or symbolically, the rules are: 3

1. If the dream character—human, animal, vegetable, or mineral—is a *real* person or thing in your life or on your mind at the time of the dream, then it should be considered literally in the first instance and taken symbolically when and only when a literal interpretation makes no sense. (Even Jung, the archexponent of elaborate dream symbolism, was insistent that dreams of a husband, wife, child, neighbor, colleague, the dog, and anyone with whom we are in intimate contact at the time of the dream almost always refer to the individuals themselves rather than to anything more subtle.) I know from my own experience that it is a mistake to interpret a dream of your car failing as a symbol of failing *drive* in yourself until you have checked the car, since the dream may well be throwing up subliminal perceptions of something wrong with the engine which you have been too busy to notice during the course of the day. 4

2. If a dream character or image cannot be taken literally as a real person or thing in your life, then it symbolizes either someone or something in your external life, or a part of your own personality which your heart is bringing to your attention. (Jung referred to the former as an *objective* interpretation, and to the latter as a *subjective* interpretation.) 5

In looking for the meaning of any symbolic dream image, always check first to discover whether or not it symbolizes someone or something external to yourself at the time of the dream, for we dream about the world outside us just as much as we dream of our private inner world. For example, if you dream of Vincent Price, and the real Vincent Price does not figure personally in your life at the moment, then look around to see if anyone else would fit the name. Is there perhaps a Mr. or Mrs. Price or a Vincent in your present life to whom the dream could refer? If not, then you must ask yourself what Vincent Price means to you. It could be something like costliness (a pun on his name) or showmanship (an association based on his qualities), or whatever else he may mean to you personally. Is 6 there someone in your present life—husband, wife, colleague, neighbor, and so on—who has behaved in an extravagant (or showy or entertaining) way during the previous day or two? If there is, then your dream is probably expressing concern about your relationship with this particular person.

If you can think of no such person, then you have to consider   7
the possibility that Vincent Price might be a part of yourself—which is nice if you admire him, and not so good if you dislike him! Have you behaved extravagantly or shown off during the past day or two? Always remember that the dream exaggerates in order to bring its point home to you; if you dream of a fascist and it turns out to represent part of your own personality, don't get too upset, for the dream is merely saying that you *feel* you behaved a bit like a fascist in the recent past, which may mean no more than some unpleasant thought about your Jewish neighbor or a dictatorial attitude toward your teenage son. If you continually dream of fascists and there are none in your life, either literally or figuratively, then it is probably fair to say that you have an inner conflict about this subject—but once again, you must remember that the dream merely reflects *your feeling* about yourself and your behavior, and your friends may not see you in this light at all. As Erich Fromm writes in his book *The Forgotten Language*, "Dreams are like a microscope through which we look at the hidden occurrences in our soul."

. . . I shall take several dreams from my collection to demon-   8
strate in a practical way the various techniques you can use to discover the identities of your dream characters and images. I have chosen these few examples from thousands of dreams in order to stress what I consider the most important points in dream interpretation, but they cannot be more than guidelines at this point in the dream game. . . . I cannot interpret your dreams: you must do it for yourself; my aim is to help you make a start. Even after applying all the rules and suggestions given in this [essay], you will almost certainly find that some dreams still elude you. Don't worry about this too much; it happens to all of us. But do continue to write down your dreams, together with the events and thoughts of the day, for many of them may become clearer to you as you get to know the meanings of certain recurring symbols over a series of dreams. Very often you will find that a certain elusive symbol in one dream reveals its meaning quite openly in another dream. When this starts happening, you are ready to complete your dream glossary. . . .

The other principles to be borne in mind at this stage in the 9 dream game are [as follows]:

3. Even though dreams may take us back to childhood or con- 10 cern themselves with future possibilities, they are always triggered by something on our minds or in our hearts at the time of the dream. People or things that were once very intimate parts of our lives— parents, siblings, childhood home, or friends—cannot be taken liter- ally in our dreams if we are no longer directly involved with them. A dream does not indulge in reminiscence for its own sake. Such characters and images appear in our dreams either because they rep- resent the voices of the past which still live on in us and influence our present behavior, or to tell us that something in our present sit- uation reminds us of a similar situation in the past.

4. The feeling tone of a dream is always important and some- 11 times gives the clue to the meaning of a dream symbol. For example, if I dream of a dog passing me in the street wagging its tail and feel very dejected in the dream because it does not respond to my friendly call, the clue to the dream's meaning may come in remem- bering how upset I was at my husband's behavior the previous evening at a "cocktail" party—and my dream could be reflecting my heart's thought that he was so concerned with playing the "gay dog" that he failed to pay me any attention.

5. If you happen to know from reading books that some partic- 12 ular symbol occurs commonly in people's dreams and has been stated by experts to have a universal meaning, by all means take this as a *suggestion* of what the symbol *might* mean if it occurs in your own dream, for our dreams pick up and utilize symbols from any- where in order to make their point. Never assume that it must have this particular meaning, however, for there might be other more per- sonal associations that are more important to you which actually determine how your dreaming mind uses this particular symbol. Since the majority of people in the West were brought up in a house, for example, a dream house is likely to mean "living space"—a sym- bol of your personality itself—but even this symbol can have differ- ent meanings in different circumstances. Always check what the symbol means to you—and always check on a possible literal mean- ing in the first instance.

6. If the same dream image or character recurs frequently in 13 your dreams, then it is likely to have a similar meaning throughout a series of dreams, and for this reason it is helpful to compile a

dream glossary of your own recurring symbols. You should not be surprised to discover, however, that on occasion this particular symbol has a different meaning, and can sometimes be merely part of the background with no great significance. Any symbol is influenced to a great extent by the symbols it is grouped with in any one dream, and we should always see it in the context of the dream as a whole.

7. Dreams do not come to tell us what we already know about 14 the people in our lives or about ourselves, so if at first sight a dream seems to be doing no more than this, look deeper. At the very least, it may be clarifying the thoughts of the heart by putting them in vivid picture language or urging us to do something about a long-standing problem—but the dream may have an altogether deeper meaning which we can discover by looking again at its symbols.

8. A dream symbol is correctly interpreted when and only when 15 it makes sense to the dreamer in terms of his present life situation and moves him to change his life constructively. Someone else may see a different possible interpretation, but this is only what your dream would mean *to him had he* dreamed it. Dreams do not arise arbitrarily from some universal reservoir: they arise out of the dreamer's present life experience and are meaningful to him alone. While I cannot say that the *purpose* of dreams is to move us to change our lives, I do insist that a "correct" interpretation—which means an effective interpretation—shows the way. For this reason, I suggest that anyone working on a dream successfully should conclude by writing down *briefly* what the dream means and *what he is going to do about it.* Jung made a habit of asking his patients, after they had worked together on a dream, "Now, *in one sentence*, what is the meaning of the dream?" [My colleagues and I] follow this rule in all our dream work, though we allow two or three sentences if neces-sary. And we conclude by asking the dreamer what practical action the dream message could lead him to take.

9. A dream is incorrectly (ineffectively) interpreted if the inter- 16 pretation leaves the dreamer disappointed or diminished. Many psychotherapists still insist that they know the correct interpretation of your dream and believe that the message which makes sense to you may not be the one you need to see at any given moment in time—apparently quite oblivious of the fact that their colleagues, on the basis of the same dream, may be seeing quite different things for you. You must learn to trust your *own* feelings and judgment.

Meanings and Values

1a. According to the quotation at the beginning of this selection, what is the purpose of dreaming?

b. Why does Faraday think most people need to learn how to interpret their dreams?

2. In your words, explain the distinction Faraday draws in paragraph 4 between interpreting dreams literally and interpreting them symbolically. (You may wish to look up the meaning of the terms *literally* and *symbolically*.)

3a. Having read this selection, do you consider the procedure explained by the author to be useful and accurate, fanciful and unreliable, or somewhere in between?

b. Is your evaluation based on the information presented in the essay? The way the essay is written? Your view of dreams and dream interpretation? Some combination? Explain. (See "Guide to Terms": *Evaluation*.)

Expository Techniques

1a. Drawing on specific evidence from the essay for support, explain why you think this selection is a directional process, an informational process, or a mixture of the two.

b. If you consider it a combination, identify those paragraphs that are primarily directional, primarily informational, and a mixture of the two.

2a. Do the numbers indicate steps in the process? If not, what do they identify?

b. Are the numbers used effectively? (Guide: *Evaluation*.)

3a. Identify both the brief and extended examples in these paragraphs: 4, 6, 10, and 15.

b. Choose two of these paragraphs and discuss whether the examples are intended as illustrations for explanatory statements or as a way of showing readers how to do something.

4a. Where in the selection does the author mention other ways of interpreting dreams than the approach she thinks is correct?

b. For what purpose does she mention these alternative approaches?

Diction and Vocabulary

1. Choose one of the longer paragraphs in this essay and explain why you think the diction is either abstract or concrete. (Guide: *Diction, Concrete/Abstract.*)

2. Consult the dictionary as needed for a full understanding of the following words, especially as they are used in this selection: subliminal (par. 4); objective, subjective (5); fascist, figuratively (7); elusive (8); arbitrarily (15).

Suggestions for Writing and Discussion

1. Discuss what dreams mean to you and how you go about interpreting them.

2. There are many different explanations of why dreams occur and what they mean. See if you can find any explanations in recent books or magazines and report on them to your classmates or in an essay.

(NOTE: Suggestions for topics requiring development by use of PROCESS ANALYSIS are on page 267, at the end of this section.)

L. RUST HILLS

L. Rust Hills is a writer and editor, perhaps best known for his work as fiction editor for *Esquire*. He has published several collections of contemporary fiction. His essays have appeared in a variety of magazines, including *Esquire*, *Harper's*, *McCall's*, and *The New Yorker*.

How to Eat an Ice-Cream Cone

This essay was first published in 1968. Its humorous observations of the way people behave are still accurate and penetrating, though its view of roles within a family may seem slightly dated to some readers. For ice cream lovers (most of us, that is), Hills's directions may be either a revelation or a source of debate.

Before you even get the cone, you have to do a lot of planning about it. We'll assume that you lost the argument in the car and that the family has decided to break the automobile journey and stop at an ice-cream stand for cones. Get things straight with them right from the start. Tell them that after they have their cones there will be an imaginary circle six feet away from the car, and that no one—man, woman, or especially child—will be allowed to cross the line and reenter the car until his ice-cream cone has been entirely consumed and he has cleaned himself up. Emphasize: Automobiles and ice-cream cones don't mix. Explain: Melted ice cream, children, is a fluid which is eternally sticky. One drop of it on a car-door handle spreads to the seat covers, to trousers, and thence to hands, and then to the steering wheel, the gear shift, the rear-view mirror, all the knobs of the dash-board—spreads everywhere and lasts forever,

spreads from a nice old car like this, which might have to be abandoned because of stickiness, right into a nasty new car, in secret
ways that even scientists don't understand. If necessary, even make
a joke: "The family that eats ice-cream cones together, sticks
together." Then let their mother explain the joke and tell them you
don't mean half of what you say, and no, we won't be getting a
new car.

Blessed are the children who always eat the same flavor of ice   2
cream or always know beforehand what kind they will want. Such
good children should be quarantined from those who say "I want to
wait and see what flavors there are." It's hard to just listen, while a
beautiful young child who has always been perfectly happy with a
plain vanilla ice-cream cone is subverted by a young schoolmate
who has been invited along for the weekend, a pleasant and polite
child, perhaps, but spoiled by permissive parents and flawed by an
overactive imagination. This schoolmate has a flair for contingency
planning: "Well, I'll have banana, if they have banana, but if they
don't have banana, then I'll have peach, if it's fresh peach, and if
they don't have banana or fresh peach, I'll see what else they have
that's like that, like maybe fresh strawberry or something, and if
they don't have that or anything like that that's good, I'll just have
chocolate marshmallow chip or chocolate ripple or something like
that." Then—turning to one's own once simple and innocent child,
now already corrupt and thinking fast—the schoolmate invites a
similar rigmarole: "What kind are *you* going to have?"

I'm a great believer in contingency planning. But none of this is   3
realistic. Few adults, and even fewer children, are able to make up
their mind beforehand what kind of ice-cream cone they'll want. It
would be nice if they could be all lined up in front of the man who's
making up the cones and just snap smartly, when their turn came,
"Strawberry, please," "Vanilla, please," "Chocolate, please." But of
course it never happens like that. There is always a great discussion,
a great jostling and craning of necks and leaning over the counter to
see down into the tubs of ice cream, and much intrapersonal consul-
tation—"What kind are *you* having?"—back and forth, as if that
should make any difference. Until finally the first child's turn comes
and he asks the man, "What kinds do you have?"

Now this is the stupidest question in the world, because there is   4
always a sign posted saying what kinds of ice cream they have. As I
tell the children, that's what they put the sign up there for, so you

won't have to ask what kinds of ice cream they have. The man gets sick of telling everybody all the different kinds of ice cream they have, so they put a sign up there that says. You're supposed to read it, not ask the man.

"All right, but the sign doesn't say strawberry." 5

"Well, that means they don't have strawberry." 6

"But there *is* strawberry, right there." 7

"That must be raspberry or something." (Look again at the sign. 8 Raspberry isn't there either.)

When the child's turn actually comes, he says, "Do you have 9 strawberry?"

"Sure." 10

"What other kinds do you have?" 11

The trouble is, of course, that they put up the sign that says 12 what flavors they have, with little cardboard inserts to put in or take out flavors, way back when they first opened the store. But they never change the sign—or not often enough. They always have flavors that aren't on the list, and often they don't have flavors that *are* on the list. Children know this—whether innately or from earliest experience it would be hard to say. The ice-cream man knows it too. Even grown-ups learn it eventually. There will always be chaos and confusion and mind-changing and general uproar when ice-cream cones are being ordered, and there has not been, is not, and will never be any way to avoid it.

Humans are incorrigibly restless and dissatisfied, always in 13 search of new experiences and sensations, seldom content with the familiar. It is this, I think, that accounts for others wanting to have a taste of your cone, and wanting you to have a taste of theirs. "Do have a taste of this fresh peach, it's delicious," my wife used to say to me, very much (I suppose) the way Eve wanted Adam to taste her delicious apple. An insinuating look of calculating curiosity would film my wife's eyes—the same look those beautiful, scary women in those depraved Italian films give a man they're interested in. "How's *yours?*" she would say. For this reason, I always order chocolate chip now. Down through the years, all those close enough to me to feel entitled to ask for a taste of my cone—namely my wife and step-children—have learned what chocolate chip tastes like, so they have no legitimate reason to ask me for a taste. As for tasting other people's cones, never do it. The reasoning here is that if it tastes good, you'll wish you'd had it; if it tastes bad, you'll have had a taste of something that tastes bad; if it doesn't taste either good or bad, then you won't have missed anything. Of course no person in his right mind ever *would* want to taste anyone else's cone, but it is useful to have good, logical reasons for hating the thought of it.

Another important thing. Never let the man hand you the ice- 14 cream cones for the whole group. There is no sight more pathetic than some bumbling, disorganized papa holding four ice-cream cones in two hands, with his money still in his pocket, when the man says, "Eighty cents." What does he do then? He can't hand the cones back to the man to hold while he fishes in his pocket for the money, for the man has just given them to *him*. He can start passing them out to the kids, but at least one of them will have gone to the car to see how the dog is doing or have been sent in back by his mother to wash his hands or something. And even if Papa does get them distributed, he's still going to be left with his own cone in one hand, while he tries to get his money with the other. Meanwhile, of course, the man is very impatient, the next group asking him: "What flavors do you have?"

No, never let the man hand you the cones of others. Make him 15 hand each one to each kid individually. That way, too, you won't get disconcerting tastes of butter pecan and black raspberry on your own chocolate chip. And insist that he tell you how much it all costs and settle with him *before* he hands you your own cone. Make sure everyone has got paper napkins and everything *before* he hands you your own cone. Get *everything* straight before he hands you your own cone.

Then, when the moment finally comes, reach out and take it 16 from him. Strange, magical, *dangerous* moment! Consider what it is that you are about to be handed: It is a huge irregular mass of ice cream, faintly domed at the top from the metal scoop which dug it out and then insecurely perched it on the uneven top edge of a hollow inverted cone made out of the most brittle and fragile of materials. Clumps of ice cream hang over the side, very loosely attached to the main body. There is always much more ice cream than the cone could hold, even if the ice cream were tamped down into the cone, which of course it isn't. And the essence of ice cream is that it melts. It doesn't just stay there teetering in this irregular, top-heavy mass, it also *melts*. And it melts fast. And it doesn't just melt, it melts into a stickiness that cannot be wiped off. The only thing one person could hand to another that might possibly be more dangerous is a live hand grenade on which the pin had been pulled five seconds earlier. And of course if anybody offered you that, you could say, "Oh. Uh, well—no thanks."

Ice-cream men handle cones routinely, and are inured. They are like professionals who are used to handling sticks of TNT; their movements quick and skillful. An ice-cream man may attempt to pass a cone to you casually, almost carelessly. Never accept a cone on this basis! Keep your hand at your side, overcoming the instinct by which everyone's hand goes out—almost automatically—whenever he is proffered something delicious and expected. The ice-cream man will look up at you, startled, questioning. Lock his eyes with your own, and *then*, slowly, calmly, and above all, deliberately, take the cone from him.

Grasp the cone firmly but gently between thumb and forefinger, two thirds of the way up. Then dart swiftly away to an open area, away from the jostling crowd at the stand. Then take up the classic ice-cream-cone-eating stance: feet from one to two feet apart, body bent forward from the waist at a twenty-five-degree angle, right elbow well up, right forearm horizontal, at a level with your collarbone and about twelve inches from it. But don't start eating yet! Check first to see what emergency repairs may be necessary. Sometimes a sugar cone will be so crushed or broken or cracked that all you can do is gulp at the thing like a savage, getting what you can of it, as you look frantically around for a trash basket.

Sometimes, of course, a cracked cone can be brought through— but this takes nerve as well as skill. Checking the cone for possible trouble can be done in a second or two, if one knows where to look and does it systematically. A trouble spot some people overlook is the bottom tip of the cone. This may have been broken off. Or the flap of the cone material at the bottom, usually wrapped over itself in that funny spiral construction, may be folded in a way that is imperfect and leaves an opening. No need to say that through this opening—in a matter of perhaps thirty or at most ninety seconds— will begin to pour hundreds of thousands of atoms of sticky melted ice cream. In this case you must instantly get the paper napkin in your left hand under the bottom of the cone to stem the forthcoming flow, or be doomed to eat the cone far too rapidly. It is a grim moment. No one wants to eat a cone under that kind of pressure, but neither does he want to end up with the bottom of the cone stuck to a messy napkin. There's an alternative, one that takes both skill and courage: Forgoing any cradling of the cone, grasp it more firmly between thumb and forefinger and extend the other fingers so that they are out of the way of the dripping from the bottom; then increase the waist-bend angle from twenty-five degrees to thirty-five degrees, and then eat the cone, *allowing* it to drip out of the bottom onto the ground in front of you! Experienced and thoughtful cone-eaters acclaim the successful execution of this dangerous acceptance of the broken-tip challenge.

So far, we have been discussing irregularities in the cone itself. But of course there is the ice cream to worry about too. In this area immediate action is sometimes needed on three fronts at once. Frequently the ice cream will be mounted on the cone in a way that is perilously lopsided. This requires immediate corrective action to move it back into balance—a slight pressure downward with the teeth and lips to seat the ice cream more firmly in and on the cone—but not so hard, of course, as to break the cone. On other occasions, gobs of ice cream will be hanging loosely from the main body, about to fall to the ground (bad) or onto one's hand (far, far worse). This requires instant action too: snapping at the gobs with the split-second timing of a frog in a swarm of flies. But sometimes trickles of ice cream will already (already!) be running down the cone toward one's fingers, and one must quickly raise the cone, tilting one's face skyward, and lick with an upward motion to push the trickles away from the fingers and (as much as possible) into the mouth.

Which to do first? Every ice-cream cone is like every other ice-cream cone in that it has the potential to present all three problems, but each ice-cream cone is paradoxically unique in that it will present the problems in a different order of emergency, and hence require a different order of solutions. And it is (thank God!) an unusual ice-cream cone that will present all three problems in *exactly* the same degree of emergency. It is necessary to make an instantaneous judgment as to where the greatest danger is, and *act!* The whole thing will be a mess before you've even tasted it. If it isn't possible to decide between any given two of the basic three emergencies—lopsided mount, dangling gobs, already running trickles—then make an arbitrary adjudication: Assign a "heads" value to one and a "tails" value to the other, then flip a coin to decide which is to be tended to first. Don't for heaven's sake, *actually* flip a coin—you'd have to dig in your pockets for it. (Unless you had it ready in your hand before you were handed the cone, in case this sort of problem developed.) There isn't remotely enough time for anything like that. Just decide *in your mind* which came up—heads or tails—and then try to remember as fast as you can which of the problems it was that had been assigned to the winning side of the coin.

In trying to make wise and correct decisions about the ice-cream 22 cone in your hand, you should always try to keep your ultimate objective in mind. The first objective is to get the cone under control. Secondarily, one will want to eat the cone calmly and with pleasure. Real pleasure, of course, lies not simply in enjoying the taste of the ice-cream cone, but in eating it *right,* which is where the ultimate objective comes in.

Let us assume that you have darted to your open space and 23 made your necessary emergency repairs. The cone is still dangerous, of course—still, so to speak, "live." But you can now proceed with it in an orderly fashion. First revolve the cone through the full 360 degrees, turning the cone by moving the thumb away from you and the forefinger toward you, so the cone moves counterclockwise. Snap at the loose gobs of ice cream as you do this. Then, with the cone still "wound," which will require the wrist to be bent at the full right angle toward you, apply pressure with the mouth and tongue to accomplish overall realignment, straightening and settling the whole mess. Then, unwinding the cone back through the full 360 degrees, remove any trickles of ice cream. Now, have a look at the cone. Some supplementary repairs may be necessary, but the cone is now defused.

At this point, you can risk a glance around you to see how badly 24 the others are doing with their cones. Then, shaking your head with good-natured contempt for the mess they're making, you can settle down to eating yours. This is done by eating the ice cream off the top, at each bite pressing down cautiously, so that the ice cream settles farther and farther into the cone, being very careful not to break the cone. Of course, you never take so much ice cream into your mouth at once that it hurts your teeth; and for the same reason never let unmelted ice cream into the back of your mouth. If these procedures are followed correctly, you should shortly arrive at the ideal, your ultimate objective, the way an ice-cream cone is always pictured as being, but never actually is when it is handed to you. The ice cream should now form a small dome whose large circumference exactly coincides with the large circumference of the cone itself: a small skullcap that fits exactly on top of a larger, inverted dunce cap.

Like the artist, who makes order out of chaos, you have taken an unnatural, abhorrent, irregular, chaotic form like this:

and from it you have sculpted an ordered, ideal shape that might be envied by Praxiteles or even Euclid:

Now at last you can begin to take little nibbles of the cone itself, being very careful not to crack it. Revolve the cone so that its rim remains level as it descends, while you eat both ice cream and cone. Because it is in the geometrical nature of things, the inverted cone shape, as you keep nibbling the top off it, still remains a cone *shape;* and because you are constantly reforming with your tongue the little dome of ice cream on top, it follows in logic—and in actual practice, if you are skillful and careful—that as you eat the cone on down it continues to look exactly the same, so that at the very end you will hold between your thumb and forefinger a tiny, idealized replica of an ice-cream cone, a harmless thing perhaps an inch high. 25

Then, while the others are licking their sticky fingers, preparatory to wiping them on their clothes, or going back to the ice-cream stand for more paper napkins to try to clean themselves up—*then* you can hold the miniature cone up for everyone to see, and pop it gently into your mouth. 26

Meanings and Values

1a. Different groups of readers might focus on different facets of this essay. Some might be interested in the directions it offers, for example, while others might enjoy the humor. List the different features or topics in the essay that you think might attract readers' attention.

  b. Do you think that readers today are more likely to pay attention to different parts of the essay than readers did when the essay first appeared? Are they likely to react to the essay in any different ways? Be ready to explain your answers in detail.

  c. Identify the main purpose(s) of this essay. Is your answer likely to differ from the answer readers might have given in 1968? Why, or why not? (See "Guide to Terms": *Unity.*)

2a. To what extent should this essay be considered ironic? (Guide: *Irony.*)

b. Identify any passage you consider to be especially ironic and explain the kind of irony the writer employs (mild understatement, sarcasm, or irony of situation—see Guide: *Irony*).

3. Is the writer critical of any particular kinds of people or practices? If so, which ones? Is his criticism mild or harsh. Explain.

Expository Techniques

1a. In which paragraph does Hills actually begin giving directions on how to eat an ice-cream cone?

b. What other directions or explanations does he offer beforehand? Be specific.

c. What is gained, or lost, by waiting so long to begin the directions for eating a cone?

2. Identify those kinds of information Hills presents that make his directions for eating a cone especially effective. (If you consider the directions ineffective, identify those kinds of information that are missing or presented in a confusing manner.) (Guide: *Evaluation*.)

3. Describe the sentence strategies Hills uses to create emphasis and humor in the following paragraphs: 1, 3, 15, 22, and 25.

4. Identify the transitions that open each of the following paragraphs. Tell whether each identifies a step in a process, introduces a new topic, or performs some other role: 14, 16, 19, 20, 21, 23, 24, 25, and 26.

5. What strategy does Hills use to conclude his essay? Is it effective? How else might he have ended the piece? (Guide: *Closings, Evaluation*.)

Diction and Vocabulary

1. What allusion begins paragraph 2, and why does the author use it? Is the beginning of the paragraph likely to be effective even if a reader does not recognize the allusion? Why, or why not? (Guide: *Figures of Speech*.)

2a. What contrasts in diction and style does Hills create in paragraph 13, and how do they contribute to the humorous approach in the paragraph? (Guide: *Diction, Style/Tone*.)

b. Identify the allusion in the paragraph and tell how it is supposed to add to the humor. Does the humor seem dated in any way? If so, why?

c. In what ways can this paragraph be seen as ironic? Explain. (Guide: *Irony*.)

d. Can any other sections of the essay be viewed as predominantly ironic? If so, which ones?

3.   If you do not know the meaning of any of the following words, look
     them up in a dictionary: subverted, contingency (par. 2); innately
     (12); incorrigibly, insinuating (13); disconcerting (15); adjudication
     (21); abhorrent (24).

Suggestions for Writing and Discussion

1.   What things other than ice-cream cones come in irregular forms that
     people often try to convert into regular, idealized forms? Is the desire
     to make things regular something natural to humans, or is it some-
     thing we learn?

2.   Is eating an ice-cream cone worth all the time and attention Hills
     gives it? Is there some broader attitude towards everyday activities
     he is trying to encourage readers to adopt? What other ordinary ac-
     tivities do you think would benefit from this kind of attention?

3.   If you are convinced you know the right way or the best way to do
     something, share your approach with others in an essay.

(NOTE: Suggestions for topics requiring development by use of PROCESS ANALYSIS are
on page 267, at the end of this section.)

LAURA MANSNERUS

LAURA MANSNERUS is a journalist and writer of magazine feature articles. Her work has been published in *The New York Times, The New York Times Magazine, Working Woman,* and *McCall's.*

Count to 10 and Pet the Dog

Anger and stress are so often parts of our daily lives that we seldom stop to consider the ways they can harm us. In this article from *The New York Times Magazine,* Mansnerus looks at some recent and controversial research for steps that we can take to improve our health and prolong our lives.

If every negative emotion given a name—fear, depression, loneliness, dread, anxiety, resentment and more—sets in motion some physiological disturbance, it cannot bode well for those chronically afflicted by any of them. One in particular is suspect, though, implicated especially in heart disease, and that is anger.

Of all the emotional facets that heart patients might show, this one appears most prominent. Their anger tends to be unusually frequent and unusually intense. Such findings have led researchers not just to conclude that the angry are more vulnerable to sickness of various sorts, but also to prescribe ways of harnessing, dispelling and even banishing the emotion. While the "fight or flight" response might have been a survival tool in the Stone Age, the tendency to see threats all around has outlived its usefulness.

You know you're in trouble "if you're always getting into arguments and fights and you feel you're embattled because of all the stupid people in the world," says Dr. Redford Williams of the Duke University Medical Center, who, with his wife, Virginia, a historian, wrote "Anger Kills."

The antidote for anger most frequently prescribed is a dose of introspection and self-restraint. 4

The message is roughly this: Quell your anger and thus reduce the stress-induced hormones in your bloodstream, alleviate the insult to your body and decrease your risk of illness. If Step 1 can be accomplished, the others will follow. 5

This notion is appealing. In the last decade, many psychologists, some psychiatrists and a few cardiologists have tried behavior modification for people at high risk of heart disease. There is no easy protocol, however, in part because, as with so much else in medicine, the experts cannot even agree on terminology. 6

The semantic difficulties were present from the time that Dr. Meyer Friedman and Dr. Ray H. Rosenman, cardiologists in San Francisco, identified a pattern of behavior they dubbed "Type A." That was in 1958, and their portrait of the coronary-prone personality has been relentlessly analyzed ever since. Now, some specialists say stress of all kinds is dangerous, others say only anger—or, to use the word preferred by one camp of researchers, hostility—is dangerous. Some regard hostility as a personality trait, and others speak of it as a physiological disorder. There are corresponding differences over diagnosis: Some say the questionnaires used to determine a person's "hostility level" are useful instruments, and others insist on physical examinations to detect certain tics and speech patterns that tend to be associated with excessive anger. 7

As director of Duke's Behavioral Medicine Research Center, Dr. Williams, an internist and a psychiatrist, has spent 15 years trying to home in on the lethal elements of the Type A personality. He has implicated hostility—which he distinguishes from the hurried, even time-obsessed components of the Type A—and subdivided it into three more precise rubrics: anger, cynicism and aggressiveness. 8

Dr. Williams has devised strategies for controlling hostility, such as reading a newspaper or magazine when you're caught in a long line. Dr. Friedman, not convinced that the driven personality he named 35 years ago can be compartmentalized, leads "Type A counseling." And then there are less formal "anger management" and "stress management" programs, everything from retreats for corporate executives to workshops in church basements. 9

All arise from the premise that "mood precedes organic change," in the words of Dr. John A. Larson, director of the Institute of Stress Medicine at Norwalk Hospital in Norwalk, Conn., who 10 conducts behavior modification workshops on the Friedman model. "In this case, anger precedes plaque in the arteries."

Indeed, it seems to. But so do high cholesterol levels, high blood   11
pressure and smoking, which are recognized as the most important
risk factors. The body's immediate reaction to anger is often an ele-
vation in blood pressure, but no one has documented a link between
sustained hypertension and an angry personality. Dr. Williams notes
all kinds of ways these conditions might aggravate one another, but
says that "most of us feel that stress will be officially sanctioned as a
risk factor like sedentary life style, smoking and so on."

How a lifetime's flare-ups play into the many other causes of   12
heart disease is a well-worked mind/body puzzle, still far from
solution. How one's outlook can aid the workings of the heart is
even less well understood. Can the body be talked out of anger?
Probably. Can the ailing thereby reduce their risks? Possibly. Can
the still-healthy do so? Hardly anyone is even guessing.

Dr. Larson believes that anger is an increasingly common state   13
of mind in America, one strain in a "stress disorder." Clearly, many
ordinary people agree. When he and his colleagues recruited subjects for a study by Dr. Friedman, placing a newspaper ad seeking
"the best-stressed men in Fairfield County," their call packed the
hospital auditorium. About 200 area residents are now research subjects, the experimental group attending behavior modification workshops and the control group receiving only occasional mailings of
health advice.

Dr. Larson runs similar workshops for paying patients, who   14
meet for 10-week semesters at the hospital. In a course called
"Changing Points of View," Dr. Larson, towering, lean and almost
hypnotically soft-spoken, leads exercises in deep breathing and
visualization. Among the 14 men and 2 women gathered around a
hospital conference table one evening, chests rose and fell to the
incantation: "Direct your attention to your feet on the floor. . . . Be
aware of the air going in your nostrils cool and going out warm. . . .
Visualize a place you like to be. . . . Experience it and see the objects
there, the forms and shadows. Take another deep breath and experience the sounds, the surf, the wind, leaves, a babbling brook."

Most people at the table had had heart attacks or veered per-   15
ilously close. Some just described themselves as angry. One man
said by way of introduction, "I'm here to learn to suffer fools
gladly."

This is a strong theme for Dr. Friedman, Dr. Williams and   16
others, though their emphasis varies. Dr. Williams focuses on reducing hostility but also talks about the importance of social supports.
Dr. Friedman attacks not just hostility but also the sense of urgency
he once named "the hurry sickness." Dr. Dean Ornish, director of
the Preventive Medicine Research Center in Sausalito, Calif., asks a
commitment of body as well as soul; the book that sets out his program contains 148 pages of low-fat recipes.

Their advice about hostility is basically the same: Recognize and   17
defuse hostile thoughts. Call on your sense of compassion and forgive-
ness. Nurture relationships. Above all, recast your view of the world.

They acknowledge that the recasting is not simply a matter of   18
will. They also acknowledge that a hostile personality is in part a
product of genetic accident and upbringing, and is aggravated by
some circumstances, like living in a big city or being poor.

But Dr. Williams says none of that precludes change. Stress "is   19
an interaction between the person and the environment," he says. "It
is not just a function of what's out there. It's a function of how the
person is dealing with what's out there."

He emphasizes extending oneself to others. He speaks warmly   20
of a workshop technique that pairs people off as talker and listener;
the listener is not allowed to interrupt. "All you've done is keep your
mouth shut," he says. "It doesn't take great psychological insight,
but it leads to empathy, to tolerance." He talks about caring for pets:
"It's a relationship. Even if it's a goldfish, if you talk to the damned
thing, it's probably good for you." He talks about living each day as
if it were your last. Not even the crankiest people, he says, express a
desire to spend their final hours getting even with enemies.

If such urgings sound like platitudes, their authors acknowl-   21
edge that. As Dr. Friedman puts it, if you took all the self-help books
in the universe and condensed them into a paragraph, "it would
pretty much be the Sermon on the Mount."

What these doctors hope to check is a process older than the   22
species. It starts with a perceived threat, the root of all hostility,
which causes the body's fight-or-flight response. The adrenal glands
send adrenalin, noradrenalin and cortisol into the bloodstream,
quickening the heartbeat and raising blood pressure. The sympathetic nervous system helps direct blood to the muscles, constricting
arteries to the internal organs.

What happens in the coronary arteries is less clear. One likely 23
scenario is that the inner lining is damaged by a surge in blood flow,
and a protective clot covers any injured tissue. Cholesterol is drawn
to the spot from fat cells released into the bloodstream for quick
energy, which are not all reabsorbed. The release of stress hormones
makes blood platelets stickier, which might lead to the accumulation
of plaque.

This process occurs over and over in people who are angered 24
often. And so it might work in people under any frequent stress. But
in the chronically angry, the damage is amplified because the
response itself is sharper.

Researchers have measured the physiological response to anger 25
in several ways. One was the measure taken by Dr. Gail Ironson,
a psychiatrist, in her study of cardiac patients in a veterans hospital
in Palo Alto, Calif. While the pumping efficiency of their hearts
was gauged, the patients pedaled stationary bicycles, performed
mental arithmetic, gave speeches defending themselves against an
accusation of shoplifting and recounted a recent event that still
made them mad.

Dr. Ironson found this about their hearts: The physical exercise 26
increased pumping efficiency a bit, and the arithmetic and speeches
had no effect, but the warmed-over anger impaired pumping efficiency by an average of 5 percent. Results for a healthy control group
showed no impairment at all.

As for the subjects' minds, she found some information in ques- 27
tionnaires describing how angry they got in a variety of mundane
situations. "Those who got angry at the most things were almost
always the cardiac patients," Dr. Ironson says. "It goes beyond
anger," she adds, noting a hostile, even vengeful tone in both written and oral responses.

Still, many medical researchers and physicians are skeptical of 28
any mass prescription of behavioral counseling, even if it is harmless
at worst. Probably the great majority of cardiologists are in this category. So is Peter G. Kaufmann, chief of behavioral medicine at the
National Heart, Lung and Blood Institute. "The link between negative emotions and heart disease is not firmly established," he says.
"The nature of it is not nailed down."

Dr. Toshihiko Maruta of the Mayo Clinic also believes there's 29
something there, even after leading a study of clinic patients that
found no link between their scores on the M.M.P.I. hostility scale

and their subsequent incidence of heart disease. "As a psychiatrist, I don't hesitate to say that struggle and turmoil and conflict is capable of being one of the contributing factors of coronary heart disease," he says. "I don't have much doubt about it."

Dr. Maruta does doubt that the relationship is direct, and he doubts that the emotional turmoil can be headed off easily: "We're talking about hostility as a character trait, something enduring. Otherwise, there's no sense in measuring it from a point 20 years ago and relating that to the incidence of disease today. If we talk about it as an enduring pattern, by definition it's very difficult to change. It's not something you change in a two- or three-day workshop. You have to work with a patient much longer." 30

There are, of course, those who say that while researchers hunt their "mechanisms"—the biologic processes at work in disease—medicine should do whatever seems to work. 31

Suppose you're a hostile person, and you're motivated to soften your relationship with the world. In Dr. Williams's scheme, your cynicism—to say nothing of your skepticism—already looms large. Will you be moved by people telling you to be conciliatory? 32

"The best answer I can give is my own experience," says Dr. Williams. "I have changed over the years. As I did the research, I came to think, 'This is me I'm describing here.' Maybe it wasn't the rest of the world screwing up all the time. I think most people would agree that I have changed in how I treat people." 33

Dr. Friedman has a less encouraging answer. He acknowledges that the Type A's in his counseling groups are highly inclined to change their behavior. They are willing to show up for group meetings. They are likely to be believers in psychotherapy (though Dr. Friedman says, crisply, "We don't do couch stuff") and beneficiaries of medical plans that might pay for it. Still, he says, they generally remain true to their fundamental crankiness. "They pick on us whenever they can," he says. "They complain." 34

And how does Dr. Friedman reach people who are not convinced that they have reason to worry about their health? 35

"Oh," he replies. "We don't." 36

Meanings and Values

1.   What can readers learn from this article? In what specific ways can they benefit from the advice it presents?

2.   Is the purpose of this process analysis informative, directional, or both? Cite specific portions of the essay to support your answer.

3.   Where in the essay does the author present objections to the linking of anger and heart disease? Why does he give them so much attention?

4.   Although the writer and many of the researchers she cites see a clear link between anger and heart disease, some readers might disagree. What parts of the essay might these readers find either less than completely convincing or not convincing at all? What is there in the essay or missing from the essay that might justify their doubts? Explain.

5.   What information, evidence, or reasoning does the writer present in paragraphs 14 to 27 to convince readers that the advice being offered is sound and worth following? Does she make use of any of the techniques characteristic of argument? (See "Guide to Terms": *Argument*.)

Expository Techniques

1a. Which paragraphs in the first half of this essay are devoted primarily to explaining the need to pay attention to anger?

 b. Which paragraphs describe past difficulties convincing people to pay attention to anger?

 c. Which paragraphs in the essay discuss current attempts to help people deal with anger in healthy ways?

 d. Which paragraphs explore the negative consequences of anger?

 e. Which paragraphs present objections to current research on the relationship between anger and heart disease?

 f. Are these different groups of paragraphs arranged in any particular order? If so, what is it?

2.   How do the questions in paragraph 12 help to link one section of the essay to another? Be specific in your answer. (Guide: *Transition*.)

3.   What role does paragraph 17 play in the essay? Is it necessary or would the essay be just as effective without it? (Guide: *Evaluation*.)

4.   Where in the essay does the writer employ comparison-contrast and cause-effect as expository patterns? (See Sections 3 and 6.) Discuss the use she makes of these patterns.

Diction and Vocabulary

1a. In the opening paragraph of this essay, the writer uses relatively formal language. Rewrite the paragraph using less formal diction.
(Guide: *Diction*.)

 b. Which version of the paragraph, formal or less formal, do you think
best serves the purposes of the essay? Explain. (Guide: *Evaluation*.)

 c. Why might the writer have chosen such formal diction?

2. To what extent can the title be considered a cliche? (Guide: *Cliches*.)
Is the title effective? Why, or why not?

3. Compare this essay to the student paper in the introduction to
Section 5 (pp. 223–226). Where would you place each on a formal-
informal continuum? (Guide: *Essay*.)

4. If you do not know the meaning of some of the following words,
look them up in a dictionary: physiological (par. 1); introspection (4);
alleviate (5); protocol (6); rubrics (8); sedentary (11); precludes (19);
platitudes (21); vengeful (27).

Suggestions for Writing and Discussion

1. What are some unnecessary kinds of anger or stress in students'
lives? What steps might students (or instructors) take to eliminate
them?

2. Are there times when anger is necessary and when expressing it may
be good for your health and well being? Are all kinds of stress bad?
Is sorrow an emotion to be avoided? Consider writing about the positive side of emotions that are often viewed negatively.

3. What other health problems besides heart disease are common today? Do some research and prepare a paper reporting on one such
problem and ways to avoid it.

(NOTE: Suggestions for topics requiring development by use of PROCESS ANALYSIS are
on page 267, at the end of this section.)

JESSICA MITFORD

JESSICA MITFORD was born in 1917, the daughter of an English peer. Her brother was sent to Eton, but she and her six sisters were educated at home by their mother. At the age of nineteen Mitford left home, eventually making her way to the United States in 1939. She made her home in San Francisco and she became an American citizen in 1944. She did not begin her writing career until she was thirty-eight. Her books are *Lifeitselfmanship* (1956); her autobiography, *Daughters and Rebels* (1960); the bestseller *The American Way of Death* (1963); *The Trial of Dr. Spock* (1969); *Kind and Usual Punishment* (1973), a devastating study of the American penal system; *A Fine Old Conflict* (1977); and *Poison Penmanship* (1979). Mitford's articles have appeared in the *Atlantic*, *Harper's*, and *McCall's*.

To Dispel Fears of Live Burial

"To Dispel Fears of Live Burial" (editors' title) is a portion of *The American Way of Death*, a book described in *The New York Times* as a "savagely witty and well-documented exposé." The "savagely witty" style, evident in this selection, does not obscure the fact of its being a tightly organized, step-by-step process analysis.

Embalming is indeed a most extraordinary procedure, and one must 1 wonder at the docility of Americans who each year pay hundreds of millions of dollars for its perpetuation, blissfully ignorant of what it is all about, what is done, how it is done. Not one in ten thousand has any idea of what actually takes place. Books on the subject are extremely hard to come by. They are not to be found in most libraries or bookshops.

In an era when huge television audiences watch surgical opera- 2 tions in the comfort of their living rooms, when, thanks to the animated cartoon, the geography of the digestive system has become familiar territory even to the nursery school set, in a land where the satisfaction of curiosity about almost all matters is a national pastime, the secrecy surrounding embalming can, surely, hardly be attributed to the inherent gruesomeness of the subject. Custom in this regard has within this century suffered a complete reversal. In the early days of American embalming, when it was performed in the home of the deceased, it was almost mandatory for some relative to stay by the embalmer's side and witness the procedure. Today, family members who might wish to be in attendance would certainly be dissuaded by the funeral director. All others, except apprentices, are excluded by law from the preparation room.

A close look at what does actually take place may explain in large measure the undertaker's intractable reticence concerning a procedure that has become his major *raison d'être*. Is it possible he fears that public information about embalming might lead patrons to wonder if they really want this service? If the funeral men are loath to discuss the subject outside the trade, the reader may, understandably, be equally loath to go on reading at this point. For those who have the stomach for it, let us part the formaldehyde curtain. . . .

The body is first laid out in the undertaker's morgue—or rather, Mr. Jones is reposing in the preparation room—to be readied to bid the world farewell.

The preparation room in any of the better funeral establishments has the tiled and sterile look of a surgery, and indeed the embalmer-restorative artist who does his chores there is beginning to adopt the term "dermasurgeon" (appropriately corrupted by some mortician-writers as "demisurgeon") to describe his calling. His equipment, consisting of scalpels, scissors, augers, forceps, clamps, needles, pumps, tubes, bowls and basins, is crudely imitative of the surgeon's as is his technique, acquired in a nine- or twelve-month post-high-school course in an embalming school. He is supplied by an advanced chemical industry with a bewildering array of fluids, sprays, pastes, oils, powders, creams, to fix or soften tissue, shrink or distend it as needed, dry it here, restore the moisture there. There are cosmetics, waxes and paints to fill and cover features, even plaster of Paris to replace entire limbs. There are ingenious aids to prop and stabilize the cadaver: A Vari-Pose Head Rest, the Edwards Arm and Hand Positioner, the Repose Block (to support the shoulders during the embalming), and the Throop Foot Positioner, which resembles an old-fashioned stocks.

Mr. John H. Eckels, president of the Eckels College of Mortuary Science, thus describes the first part of the embalming procedure: "In the hands of a skilled practitioner, this work may be done in a comparatively short time and without mutilating the body other than by slight incision—so slight that it scarcely would cause serious inconvenience if made upon a living person. It is necessary to remove the blood, and doing this not only helps in the disinfecting, but removes the principal cause of disfigurements due to discoloration." 6

Another textbook discusses the all-important time element: "The earlier this is done, the better, for every hour that elapses between death and embalming will add to the problems and complications encountered. . . ." Just how soon should one get going on the embalming? The author tells us, "On the basis of such scanty information made available to this profession through its rudimentary and haphazard system of technical research, we must conclude that the best results are to be obtained if the subject is embalmed before life is completely extinct—that is, before cellular death has occurred. In the average case, this would mean within an hour after somatic death." For those who feel that there is something a little rudimentary, not to say haphazard, about this advice, a comforting thought is offered by another writer. Speaking of fears entertained in early days of premature burial, he points out, "One of the effects of embalming by chemical injection, however, has been to dispel fears of live burial." How true; once the blood is removed, chances of live burial are indeed remote. 7

To return to Mr. Jones, the blood is drained out through the veins and replaced by embalming fluid pumped in through the arteries. As noted in *The Principles and Practices of Embalming*, "Every operator has a favorite injection and drainage point—a fact which becomes a handicap only if he fails or refuses to forsake his favorites when conditions demand it." Typical favorites are the carotid artery, femoral artery, jugular vein, subclavian vein. There are various choices of embalming fluid. If Flextone is used, it will produce a "mild, flexible rigidity. The skin retains a velvety softness, the tissues are rubbery and pliable. Ideal for women and children." It may be blended with B. and G. Products Company's Lyf-Lyk tint, which is guaranteed to reproduce "nature's own skin texture . . . the velvety 8 appearance of living tissue." Suntone comes in three separate tints: Suntan; Special Cosmetic Tint, a pink shade "especially indicated for young female subjects"; and Regular Cosmetic Tint, moderately pink.

About three to six gallons of dyed and perfumed solution of formaldehyde, glycerin, borax, phenol, alcohol and water are soon circulating through Mr. Jones, whose mouth has been sewn together with a "needle directed upward between the upper lip and gum and brought out through the left nostril," with the corners raised slightly "for a more pleasant expression." If he should be bucktoothed, his teeth are cleaned with Bon Ami and coated with colorless nail polish. His eyes, meanwhile, are closed with flesh-tinted eye caps and eye cement.   9

The next step is to have at Mr. Jones with a thing called a trocar. This is a long, hollow needle attached to a tube. It is jabbed into the abdomen, poked around the entrails and chest cavity, the contents of which are pumped out and replaced with "cavity fluid." This done, and the hole in the abdomen sewn up, Mr. Jones's face is heavily creamed (to protect the skin from burns which may be caused by leakage of the chemicals), and he is covered with a sheet and left unmolested for a while. But not for long—there is more, much more, in store for him. He has been embalmed, but not yet restored, and the best time to start the restorative work is eight to ten hours after embalming, when the tissues have become firm and dry.   10

The object of all this attention to the corpse, it must be remembered, is to make it presentable for viewing in an attitude of healthy repose. "Our customs require the presentation of our dead in the semblance of normality . . . unmarred by the ravages of illness, disease or mutilation," says Mr. J. Sheridan Mayer in his *Restorative Art.* This is rather a large order since few people die in the full bloom of health, unravaged by illness and unmarked by some disfigurement. The funeral industry is equal to the challenge: "In some cases the gruesome appearance of a mutilated or disease-ridden subject may be quite discouraging. The task of restoration may seem impossible and shake the confidence of the embalmer. This is the time for intestinal fortitude and determination. Once the formative work is begun and affected tissues are cleaned or removed, all doubts of success vanish. It is surprising and gratifying to discover the results which may be obtained."   11

The embalmer, having allowed an appropriate interval to   12
elapse, returns to the attack, but now he brings into play the skill and
equipment of sculptor and cosmetician. Is a hand missing? Casting
one in plaster of Paris is a simple matter. "For replacement purposes,
only a cast of the back of the hand is necessary; this is within the ability of the average operator and is quite adequate." If a lip or two, a
nose or an ear should be missing, the embalmer has at hand a variety of restorative waxes with which to model replacements. Pores
and skin texture are simulated by stippling with a little brush, and
over this cosmetics are laid on. Head off? Decapitation cases are
rather routinely handled. Ragged edges are trimmed, and head
joined to torso with a series of splints, wires and sutures. It is a good
idea to have a little something at the neck—a scarf or high collar—
when time for viewing comes. Swollen mouth? Cut out tissue as
needed from inside the lips. If too much is removed, the surface con-
tour can easily be restored by padding with cotton. Swollen necks
and cheeks are reduced by removing tissue through vertical
incisions made down each side of the neck. "When the deceased
is casketed, the pillow will hide the suture incisions . . . as an
extra precaution against leakage, the suture may be painted with
liquid sealer."

The opposite condition is more likely to present itself—that   13
of emaciation. His hypodermic syringe now loaded with massage cream, the embalmer seeks out and fills the hollowed and
sunken areas by injection. In this procedure the backs of the
hands and fingers and the under-chin area should not be
neglected.

Positioning the lips is a problem that recurrently challenges the   14
ingenuity of the embalmer. Closed too tightly, they tend to give a
stern, even disapproving expression. Ideally, embalmers feel, the
lips should give the impression of being ever so slightly parted, the
upper lip protruding slightly for a more youthful appearance. This
takes some engineering, however, as the lips tend to drift apart. Lip
drift can sometimes be remedied by pushing one or two straight
pins through the inner margin of the lower lip and then inserting
them between the two front upper teeth. If Mr. Jones happens to
have no teeth, the pins can just as easily be anchored in his Armstrong Face Former and Denture Replacer. Another method to maintain lip closure is to dislocate the lower jaw, which is then held in its
new position by a wire run through holes which have been drilled

through the upper and lower jaws at the midline. As the French are fond of saying, *il faut souffrir pour être belle.*[1]

If Mr. Jones has died of jaundice, the embalming fluid will very likely turn him green. Does this deter the embalmer? Not if he has intestinal fortitude. Masking pastes and cosmetics are heavily laid on, burial garments and casket interiors are color-correlated with particular care, and Jones is displayed beneath rose-colored lights. Friends will say, "How *well* he looks." Death by carbon monoxide, on the other hand, can be rather a good thing from the embalmer's viewpoint: "One advantage is the fact that this type of discoloration is an exaggerated form of a natural pink coloration." This is nice because the healthy glow is already present and needs but little attention.

The patching and filling completed, Mr. Jones is now shaved, washed and dressed. Cream-based cosmetic, available in pink, flesh, suntan, brunette and blond, is applied to his hands and face, his hair is shampooed and combed (and, in the case of Mrs. Jones, set), his hands manicured. For the horny-handed son of toil special care must be taken; cream should be applied to remove ingrained grime, and the nails cleaned. "If he were not in the habit of having them manicured in life, trimming and shaping is advised for better appearance—never questioned by kin."

Jones is now ready for casketing (this is the present participle of the verb "to casket"). In this operation, his right shoulder should be depressed slightly "to turn the body a bit to the right and soften the appearance of lying flat on the back." Positioning the hands is a matter of importance, and special rubber positioning blocks may be used. The hands should be cupped slightly for a more lifelike, relaxed appearance. Proper placement of the body requires a delicate sense of balance. It should lie as high as possible in the casket, yet not so high that the lid, when lowered, will hit the nose. On the other hand, we are cautioned, placing the body too low "creates the impression that the body is in a box."

Jones is next wheeled into the appointed slumber room where a few last touches may be added—his favorite pipe placed in his hand or, if he was a great reader, a book propped into position. (In the case of little Master Jones a Teddy bear may be clutched.) Here he will hold open house for a few days, visiting hours 10 A.M. to 9 P.M.

15

16

17

18

1. You have to suffer if you want to be beautiful (Editors' note).

Meanings and Values

1a. What is the author's tone? (See "Guide to Terms": *Style/Tone*.)

b. Try to analyze the effect this tone had, at first reading, on your impressions of the subject matter itself.

c. Form a specific comparison between this effect of tone and the effect of "tone of voice" in spoken language.

2. Why was it formerly "almost mandatory" for some relative to witness the embalming procedure (par. 2)?

3a. Do you believe that public information about this procedure would cost mortuaries much embalming business (par. 3)? Why, or why not?

b. Why *do* people subject their dead to such a process?

4. Use the three-part system of evaluation to judge the success of this process analysis. (Guide: *Evaluation*.)

Expository Techniques

1a. What is the central theme? (Guide: *Unity*.)

b. Which parts of the writing, if any, do not contribute to the theme, thus damaging unity?

c. What other elements of the writing contribute to, or damage, unity?

2a. Beginning with paragraph 4, list or mark the transitional devices that help to bridge paragraphs. (Guide: *Transition*.)

b. Briefly explain how coherence is aided by such interparagraph transitions.

3. In this selection, far more than in most, emphasis can best be studied in connection with style. In fact, the two are almost indistinguishable here, and few, if any, of the other methods of achieving emphasis are used at all. (Guide: *Emphasis* and *Style/Tone*.) Consider each of the following stylistic qualities (some may overlap; others are included in diction) and illustrate, by examples, how each creates emphasis.

a. Number and selection of details—e.g., the equipment and "aids" (par. 5).

b. Understatement—e.g., the "chances of live burial" (par. 7).

c. Special use of quotations—e.g., "that the body is in a box" (par. 17).

d. Sarcasm and/or other forms of irony—e.g., "How *well* he looks" (par. 15). (Guide: *Irony*.)

Diction and Vocabulary

1. Much of the essay's unique style (with resulting emphasis) comes from qualities of diction. Use examples to illustrate the following. (Some may be identical to those of the preceding answer, but they need not be.)

   a. Choice of common, low-key words to achieve sarcasm through understatement—e.g., "This is nice . . . " (par. 15).

   b. Terms of violence—e.g., "returns to the attack" (par. 12).

   c. Terms of the living—e.g., "will hold open house" (par. 18).

   d. The continuing use of "Mr. Jones."

2a. Illustrate the meaning of "connotation" with examples of quotations from morticians. (Guide: *Connotation/Denotation*.)

   b. Are these also examples of "euphemism"?

   c. Show how the author uses these facts to her own advantage—i.e., again, to achieve emphasis.

3a. Comment briefly on the quality and appropriateness of the metaphor that ends the introduction. (Guide: *Figures of Speech*.)

   b. Is this, in any sense, also an allusion? Why, or why not?

4. Use the dictionary as needed to understand the meanings of the following words: docility, perpetuation (par. 1); inherent, mandatory (2); intractable, reticence, *raison d'être* (3); ingenious (5); rudimentary, cellular, somatic (7); carotid artery, femoral artery, subclavian vein (8); semblance (11); simulated, stippling, sutures (12); emaciation (13); dispel (7, title).

Suggestions for Writing and Discussion

1. What evidence can you find that "the satisfaction of curiosity about almost all matters is a national pastime" (par. 2)? Is this a good thing or not? Why?

2. Burial customs differ widely from country to country, sometimes from area to area in this country. If you can, describe one of the more distinctive customs and, if possible, show its sources—e.g., the climate, "old country" tradition.

3. What do you foresee as near- and far-future trends or radical changes in American burial practices? Why?

4. You may wish to develop further your answers to question 3 of "Meanings and Values"—the rationale of a large majority of people who do use this mortuary "service" for their departed relatives.

5. If you like, explain your personal preferences and the reasons for them.

(NOTE: Suggestions for topics requiring development by PROCESS ANALYSIS follow.)

Writing Suggestions for Section 5
Process Analysis

1. From one of the following topics develop a central theme into an *informational* process analysis, showing:

   a. How you selected a college.

   b. How you selected your future career or major field of study.

   c. How your family selected a home.

   d. How an unusual sport is played.

   e. How religious faith is achieved.

   f. How gasoline is made.

   g. How the air (or water) in _____ becomes polluted.

   h. How lightning kills.

   i. How foreign policy is made.

   j. How political campaigns are financed.

   k. How _____ Church was rebuilt.

   l. How fruit blossoms are pollinated.

   m. How a computer chip is designed or made.

2. Select a specific reader-audience and write a *directional* process analysis on one of the following topics, showing:

   a. How to *do* any of the processes suggested by topics 1a–e. (This treatment will require a different viewpoint, completely objective, and may require a different organization.)

   b. How to overcome shyness.

   c. How to overcome stage fright.

   d. How to make the best use of study time.

   e. How to write a college composition.

   f. How to sell an ugly house.

   g. How to prepare livestock or any other entry for a fair.

   h. How to start a club (or some other kind of recurring activity).

6

Analyzing *Cause-and-Effect* Relationships

Unlike process analysis, which merely tells *how*, causal analysis seeks to explain *why*. The two may be combined, but they need not be—many people have driven a car successfully after being told how to do it, never knowing or caring why the thing moved when they turned a key and worked a pedal or two.

Some causes and effects are not very complicated; at least their explanation requires only a simple statement. A car may sit in the garage for a while because its owner has no money for a license tag, and sometimes this is explanation enough. But frequently a much more thorough analysis is required, and this may even become the basic pattern of an exposition.

To explain fully the causes of a war or a depression or election results, the writer must seek not only *immediate* causes (the ones encountered first) but also *ultimate* causes (the basic, underlying factors that help to explain the more apparent ones). Business or professional people, as well as students, often have a pressing need for this type of analysis. How else could they fully understand or report on a failing sales campaign, diminishing church membership, a local increase in traffic accidents, or teenage use of drugs? The immediate cause of a disastrous warehouse fire could be faulty electrical wiring, but this might be attributed in turn to the company's unwise economy measures, which might be traced even further to undue pressures on the management to show large profits. The written analysis might logically stop at any point, of course, depending entirely on its purpose and the reader-audience for which it is intended.

Similarly, both the immediate and ultimate *effects* of an action or situation may, or may not, need to be fully explored. If a five percent pay raise is granted, what will be the immediate effect on the cost of production, leading to what ultimate effects on prices and, in some cases, on the economy of a business, a town, or perhaps the entire nation?

In earlier sections of this book we have seen several examples of causal analysis. In Section 1, for instance, Buckley gives some attention to both immediate and ultimate causes of American apathy, and in Section 4, Wolfe is concerned with both immediate and ultimate effects of overcrowding.

Causal analysis is one of the chief techniques of reasoning; and if the method is used at all, the reader must always have confidence in its thoroughness and logic. Here are some ways to avoid the most common faults in causal reasoning:

1. Never mistake the fact that something happens with or after another occurrence as evidence of a causal relationship—for example, that a black cat crossing the road caused the flat tire a few minutes later, or that a course in English composition caused a student's nervous breakdown that same semester.

2. Consider all possibly relevant factors before attributing causes. Perhaps studying English did result in a nervous breakdown, but the cause may also have been ill health, trouble at home, the stress of working while attending college, or the anguish of a love affair. (The composition course, by providing an "emotional" outlet, may even have helped postpone the breakdown!)

3. Support the analysis by more than mere assertions: offer evidence. It would not often be enough to *tell* why Shakespeare's wise Othello believed the villainous Iago—the dramatist's lines should be used as evidence, possibly supported by the opinions of at least one literary scholar. If you are explaining that capital punishment deters crime, do not expect the reader to take your word for it—give before-and-after statistics or the testimony of reliable authorities.

4. Be careful not to omit any links in the chain of causes or effects unless you are certain that the readers for whom the writing is intended will automatically make the right connections themselves—and this is frequently a dangerous assumption. To unwisely omit one or more of the links might leave the reader with only a vague, or even erroneous, impression of the causal connection, possibly invalidating all that follows and thus making the entire writing ineffective.

5. Be honest and objective. Writers (or thinkers) who bring their old prejudices to the task of causal analysis, or who fail to see the probability of *multiple* causes or effects, are almost certain to distort their analyses or to make them so superficial, so thin, as to be almost worthless.

Ordinarily the method of causal analysis is either to work logically from the immediate cause (or effect) down toward the most basic, or to start with the basic and work up toward the immediate. But after at least analyzing the subject and deciding what the purpose requires in the paragraph or entire composition, the writer will usually find that a satisfactory pattern suggests itself.

Sample Paragraph (Annotated)

A question introduces the phenomenon to be explained.

Why has Palmville grown so rapidly over the past decade? In response to a survey conducted last year by the Chamber of Commerce, most new residents said the reason they moved to Palmville was to escape from the living conditions in Valley City and its nearest suburbs, especially congestion, air pollution, and high housing costs.

An *ultimate cause,* though a negative one.

The ultimate cause does not provide a satisfactory explanation for the choice of Palmville.

Other towns nearby have not grown as rapidly as Palmville, however. On the survey, people also indicated why they chose to move here rather than to other towns in Nocatowie County, such as Lopestown, El Caton, or Fillmore Glen.

Immediate causes.

Use of the survey adds authority to the explanation.

People say they came to Palmville because of the location. Interstate 104 runs through the town on its way to Valley City, making commuting possible, though taxing. They came because M&T Realty spent a good deal on ads in the *Valley City Times* telling about affordable three-bedroom homes in the town. They came for the good schools and the nearby lakes and parks.

Taken together, the immediate causes provide a satisfactory explanation for the choice of Palmville.

Finally, almost all those surveyed said that they came in part because they were already familiar with the name of the town from the region's most famous agricultural product: The Palmville Onion.

Sample Paragraph (Cause/Effect)

Rap [music] started in discos, not the midtown glitter palaces like Studio 54 or New York, New York, but at Mel Quinn's on 42nd Street and Club 371 in the Bronx, where a young Harlemite who called himself D. J. Hollywood spun on the weekends. It wasn't unusual for black club jocks to talk to their audiences in the jive style of the old personality deejays. Two of the top black club spinners of the day, Pete (D. J.) Jones and Maboya, did so. Hollywood, just an adolescent when he started, created a more complicated, faster style, with more rhymes than his older mentors and call-and-response passages to encourage reaction from the dancers. At local bars, discos, and many illegal after-hours spots frequented by street people, Hollywood developed a huge word-of-mouth reputation. Tapes of his parties began appearing around the city on the then new and incredibly loud Japanese portable cassette players flooding into America. In Harlem, Kurtis Blow, Eddie Cheeba, and D. J. Lovebug Star-ski; in the Bronx, Junebug Star-ski, Grandmaster Flash, and Melle Mel; in Brooklyn, three kids from the projects called Whodini; and in Queens,

Russell and Joey, the two youngest sons from the middle-class Simmons household—all shared a fascination with Hollywood's use of the rhythmic breaks in his club mixes and his verbal dexterity. These kids would all grow up to play a role in the local clubs and, later, a few would appear on the national scene to spread Hollywood's style. Back in the 1970s, while disco reigned in the media, the Black Main Streets of New York were listening to D. J. Hollywood, and learning.

Nelson George, *The Death of Rhythm and Blues*.

Student Writing; Analyzing Cause-and-Effect
Relationships

Students Who Cheat

Timothy Dunbar

College students feel many pressures, especially the pressure to get
the best grades possible. Getting good grades is a major focus for
many students' lives, and these students often resort to many different strategies to keep their grade point averages high in order to get
into the best graduate or professional programs and to land the best
jobs. The main strategy all too many of them choose is cheating, and
the number who make this choice is startling (Kibler B1).

Students in high schools and colleges alike resort to cheating to
get ahead. In a recent survey of almost nine thousand high school
and college students, sixty-one percent of the high schoolers and
thirty-two percent of the college students admitted to cheating on an
exam once in the previous year. Researchers have pointed out that
other general surveys done at ten-year intervals have found cheating
on the rise for the past thirty years. The survey also found considerable evidence of lying and common dishonesty (Schroeder 74). If
this apparent trend towards cheating and dishonest behavior continues, the consequence could be a gloomy future for our society.

But why do so many students turn to cheating as a way to succeed? There seem to be so many other paths to good grades. Effective study skills, improvement in memorization, better time
management, and better use of available resources are all valid
options for students to consider. Despite the available options, however, research indicates that academic dishonesty is becoming the
strategy of choice for a growing number of students, and academic
institutions need to learn why students choose this option rather
than more appropriate ones (Kibler B1). Some people suggest that
high schools and colleges need to examine the problem more carefully than they have in the past. For example, many studies of cheating have focused on what academic institutions should do to
discourage dishonest behavior without examining possible causes of

the behavior in any depth. Such recommendations include improving teaching techniques, designing assignments and tests that make it harder to cheat, reducing the size of classes, and discussing the moral and ethical repercussions of cheating. Even though each of these approaches probably has some value, none has had clearly positive results, and none of the attempts to reduce cheating has tried to identify its real causes or focus on them.

Laziness, pressure, fear, and lack of commitment are among the motivations people point to as the causes of cheating. Each of these may hold true in individual cases. On the other hand, none of them offer a satisfactory explanation for widespread cheating. Are we to believe, for example, that students as a whole have suddenly become so lazy that they prefer cheating to reading, notetaking, and cramming? If so, why haven't college professors noticed the phenomenon and begun writing articles about the alarming increase in student laziness? Doesn't it seem more likely that most lazy students would ignore their grades rather than take the time and effort to raise them through cheating?

I think it is more likely that a general decline in ethics has something to do with the increase in cheating. Perhaps the moral standards children develop at home and while they are at school are not doing their job. Christina Hoff Somers thinks that college students today are learning too much about pregnancy, abortion, capital punishment, DNA research, and not enough about private decency, honesty, personal responsibility, and honor. She argues that topics such as hypocrisy, self-deception, cruelty, or selfishness are rarely taught as much as they should be. Somers further argues that morality must come from a balance between social morality and private morality. It would seem that personal survival dominates the morality of too many students today because too many are willing to be dishonest if doing so will help them accomplish an objective. For example, a recent survey in *U.S. News and World Report* asked college students if they would steal from their employer. Thirty-four percent said they would. No wonder they are also willing to cut corners in college.

Cheating probably also has psychological causes. William and Pamela Kibler state in their article that cheating is often related to low self-esteem. They think that it is a way for students with low self-esteem to achieve their goals and avoid failure. If an individual is tempted to cheat, someone with low self-esteem probably finds it easier to yield to the temptation. Students who cheat often perceive themselves as being incapable of meeting the challenges that are brought before them. They see cheating as a way of gaining control over their lives.

If many or most students who cheat do so because they see it as a morally and psychologically acceptable option, perhaps the best way to deal with the problem is to help these students see its negative consequences. Cheating is often self-defeating. Students who get their grades through dishonest means often have a false image of what they know and can do. As a result, they often find themselves unable to handle real academic challenges or problems they encounter later in their jobs and professions. If cheating gets you into a prestigious and demanding graduate program or law school, then when you get there you will probably be overwhelmed by the demands. Your only way out may be to continue cheating on your tests and written work, but with each act of dishonesty the risk of discovery and its consequences grow greater. There are long-term consequences to cheating that students often do not realize when they focus on the short-term rewards.

In the long run, dishonesty harms those who practice it. It also harms honest people by stealing the credit they deserve for their hard work, their intelligence, and their integrity. To deal effectively with cheating, therefore, we also need to encourage and support honest behavior. We need to enlist teachers, families, and community leaders in an attempt to develop the kind of moral fiber that encourages honesty and that helps people avoid harming themselves and others through dishonest behavior.

Works Cited

Kibler, William L., and Pamela Vannoy Kibler. "When Students Resort to Cheating." *Chronicle of Higher Education* 14 July 1993: B1–B2.

Schroeder, Ken. "Give and Take, Part II." *Education Digest* 58.6 (1993): 73–74.

Somers, Christina Hoff. "Teaching the Virtues." *Public Interest* 111 (1993): 3–13.

BOB GREENE, born in 1947, in Columbus, Ohio, is a columnist for *The Chicago Tribune* and writes regularly for *Esquire* magazine. His daily reports and commentary are syndicated to more than 120 other newspapers in the United States. His articles have appeared in *Newsweek, Harper's, Rolling Stone, New Times, The New York Times,* and other publications, and his commentary has been featured on the CBS television and radio networks. Greene has written numerous books, including *We Didn't Have None of Them Fat Funky Angels on the Walls of Heartbreak Hotel* (1971), *Billion Dollar Baby* (1974), *Johnny Deadline, Reporter* (1976), *Good Morning, Merry Sunshine* (1984), *Cheeseburgers* (1985), *Be True to Your School: A Diary of 1964* (1986), and *Homecoming: When the Soldiers Returned from Vietnam* (1989).

Thirty Seconds

Much has been written about the broad influence of television on our lives and culture. In this essay, however, Bob Greene looks at some of the specific consequences a television commercial had for a man who participated in it. In doing so, he also attests to the remarkable power of the medium. "Thirty Seconds" first appeared in Greene's "American Beat" column in *Esquire*.

It's funny how a man can live his whole life—a life filled with heroism and downfalls, fatherhood and courage and pain and introspection—and no one notices. No one outside the man's family and his small group of friends.

It's funny what television can do. Take the same man. Film a TV commercial that is brilliantly conceived and executed, and the man becomes known and revered in every corner of the nation. He is the same person; nothing at all about him has changed. Nothing except the most important thing of all: he has been televised.

Novelists can write one hundred thousand words, two hundred   3
thousand words, and not cause a ripple. For Bill Demby, it took only fifty-seven words, written by someone else and spoken by an announcer during a thirty-second television commercial, to totally revise his life.

Here are the words: "When Bill Demby was in Vietnam, he   4
dreamed of coming home and playing a little basketball. A dream that all but died when he lost both legs to a Vietcong rocket. But then researchers discovered that a Du Pont plastic could make truly life-like artificial limbs. Now Bill's back, and some say he hasn't lost a step."

There was a tag-line promoting Du Pont. The fifty-seven words   5
about Bill Demby and the Du Pont tag line weren't what was so significant, of course. What was significant was the film footage of Demby—his artificial legs visible to the camera—competing in a game of playground basketball with able-bodied men. It began airing in the fall of 1987, and it became one of those commercials that people think about and talk to their friends about. It won a Clio award from the advertising industry; Demby was featured on the ABC program 20/20. He went from being completely anonymous to truly famous in a matter of weeks.

When I caught up with him he was heading for a small college   6
in the Midwest to make an address to the students. The basketball arena had been reserved for the event because an overflow crowd was expected.

"I walked into a McDonald's the other day to get something to   7
eat," Bill Demby said. "This guy said hello to me and I said hi back. I thought he was just a friendly guy. But then he said, 'I liked the commercial.'"

Demby, now thirty-eight, was driving a truck on a road outside   8
Quang Tri, Vietnam, on March 26, 1971, when a Vietcong rocket hit the vehicle. A twenty-year-old Army private at the time, he lost both legs below the knee. He spent the next year in Walter Reed hospital in Washington, and then tried to put his life back together.

Nothing very spectacular happened. He had problems with   9
alcohol and drugs. A promising athlete before going to Vietnam, Demby—with the help of artificial legs—began trying to play sports

again. He was in Nashville in 1987 at a basketball tournament sponsored by the U.S. Amputee Athletic Association when he was
invited to audition for a Du Pont commercial. Du Pont had manufactured some of the materials used in certain prostheses, and had
sent representatives of its advertising agency to the amputee
tournament.

"I was very wary about doing it," Demby said. "I knew that on 10
television, they can go into the cutting room and put things together
any way they want. As far as the world was concerned at that point,
Bill Demby didn't exist. As an amputee, usually I kept to myself."

Demby and four other disabled men wearing prostheses played 11
basketball with personnel from the BBD&O ad agency looking on,
and all five men submitted to informal interviews. Before long,
Demby was told that he had been selected from the five to be the star
of the Du Pont spot.

He was far from thrilled. "Actually, I called them up and said I 12
was not interested in doing the commercial," Demby said.

I asked him why that was. For the first time in our conversation, 13
he seemed to hesitate, as if a little embarrassed. Finally he said:

"I don't like to take my pants off in front of people." Meaning 14
he doesn't like people to look at his artificial legs. Any people, much
less millions upon millions of television viewers.

But in the end he decided to say yes. The commercial was shot 15
on a basketball court in New York City, on Columbus Avenue
between Seventy-sixth and Seventy-seventh streets, in late August
1987. "They told us that we were just supposed to play basketball,
and that they'd film it," Demby said. "The other guys weren't
actors—they were just players from the neighborhood. Players without physical disabilities.

"We played basketball from 7:00 in the morning until 6:30 at 16
night. I got very tired. They had rented a room for me at the War-
wick Hotel, and when the filming was over I just went to my room,
took a shower, and fell asleep with the television set on. When I
woke up the next morning the TV was still going. I didn't think
much about what had happened. I just thought I had played some
pickup basketball and they had filmed it, and now I would go back
to my regular life. I went home that day. I felt that nothing had
changed."

The advertising agency put the commercial together quickly. 17
Demby and his family, who live near Washington, D.C., received a

telephone call advising them to watch the CBS *Sunday Morning* broadcast on September 13, 1987. That was the day the commercial first aired.

"My wife and daughter and I sat in front of the TV set," Demby said. "The commercial came on. The wonderful feeling . . . there are no words to describe it."   18

The first time Demby realized that something unusual was up came within a few weeks. "I was walking down the street in Washington, and this real huge guy started staring right into my eyes. I was kind of scared. He said, 'It's you. It's you.' I didn't know what he was talking about. I thought that maybe he was going to rob me or something. I said, 'No, no.' And then the guy said, 'You're the one in the commercial. It's the best one I've ever seen.'"   19

Since that moment, Demby has become used to the public recognition. Sometimes he doesn't much like it. "On occasion it still surprises me when people look at me," he said. "It shouldn't, but it does. Once in a while when someone will ask me about the commercial I'll find myself saying, 'No, that was my twin brother.'"   20

There are other times, though . . .   21

"A man came up to me—a man who had been having a lot of troubles. He explained the details of his troubles. He told me he had given up on everything. He said that seeing me in the commercial had turned him around. He thanked me for changing his life. Me.   22

"I walked away so that he wouldn't see me cry."   23

Soon everything was happening for Demby. He went to a New York Knicks basketball game—he had never even been inside Madison Square Garden before—and the crowd gave him a long standing ovation. Moses Malone and Patrick Ewing shook his hand.   24

He began to be invited to speak before large groups, such as the college audience he was on his way to address when I joined him. The *20/20* segment was filmed. The irony, of course, was that he was the same man he had been for the almost twenty years after he had returned from Vietnam. But because of those thirty seconds on the Du Pont commercial (a sixty-second version also ran), for the first time in his life people were treating him as if he were special.   25

"It was very hard to get used to," Demby said. He was interviewed by newspapers and magazines; suddenly people saw him as a symbol of bravery and hope. He knew that if the commercial had   26 not been broadcast, the same people would stare right through him as though he were invisible. Now they adored him.

Not everything made him feel great. "For a long time, I had   27
been hesitant to tell people that I had lost my legs in Vietnam," he said. "I'd always wear long pants, even when I was playing sports. But now everyone knows what my legs look like.

"And my past problem with alcohol and PCP . . . that was my   28
private problem, and now it's out. My daughter was eight years old, and she didn't know about it. She probably never would have, if the commercial hadn't been filmed and people hadn't started talking about me. She was very hurt by it. I tried to explain. I told her, 'It was just a bad part in Daddy's life. He was weak.'"

There is one aspect of the commercial that Demby virtually   29
never volunteers to talk about. The standard line is that the film crew just shot the pickup basketball game and edited the footage down. The most emotional moment in the commercial comes when Demby is knocked to the ground, hard, by an opposing player. On his back, he stares up. Then he gets to his feet. It is one of those magical television instants—a second or two of film that gives the audience goose bumps and stays with them for a long time.

"That didn't happen during the game," Demby said. "We had   30
been playing all day, and finally the director, Rick Levine, called me aside. He said he needed something else. He asked me if I would mind if he had one of the players knock me down."

It must have been quite a question. Imagine saying to a man   31
with artificial legs: "Listen, we know you've been playing basketball for hours, but would it be okay if we had you jump in the air and then we pushed you to the concrete so that you land on your back? We'll only need to do it a few times."

Demby thought about it and said yes. He figured that Levine   32
must know what he was doing. It paid off; without that sequence—especially the expression in Demby's eyes after he hits the ground—the commercial would lose its strongest surge of visceral humanity and power. Still, though: imagine asking the question.

Now, with all that has happened to Demby, you have to remind   33
yourself that there were four other finalists for the starring role in the commercial, and that if BBD&O had selected any one of those four, today no one would know who Bill Demby is. Demby said that

he has not heard from or seen the other four since auditioning. He got the thirty seconds; they didn't.

He does his best to keep it in perspective. There are days now 34 when he feels it would be impossible to be any more famous and respected. "But I know that just as fast as this has come, it can leave. It could turn out to be a very temporary thing.

"I have a tendency to think we're all sort of crazy. The idea that 35 thirty seconds could completely change a man's life." He tries not to lose sight of the fact that with or without the commercial, he would still be Bill Demby.

He is finally accepting the idea that strangers will approach him 36 and tell him how much they admire him. "That's just society, though," he said. "That's just people reacting to what they've seen on their television screen.

"I keep having this thought. One of these days the commercial 37 is going to stop running. They all do.

"And not long after that, someone is going to say to someone 38 else, 'Hey, do you remember that guy—the amputee who played basketball in that commercial?'

"And the other guy will hesitate for a second and then say, 39 'Yeah, I think so. What was his name?'"

Meanings and Values

1a. List both the positive and the negative effects of the commercial.

  b. Explain why you think the author wants us to consider the commercial on the whole as either harmful or beneficial.

2a. Is the primary focus of this essay on what happened to Bill Demby as a result of the commercial? Or is it on the power of television to affect our lives and attitudes? Be ready to support your answer with evidence from the essay.

  b. How would you describe the main purpose or purposes of the essay? (See "Guide to Terms": *Purpose.*)

  c. If you believe the essay has more than one important purpose, explain why it should (or should not) be considered unified. (Guide: *Unity.*)

3. The subject of this essay is one that many writers might be tempted to handle in a sentimental manner. To what extent does Greene's treatment avoid sentimentality, if at all? (Guide: *Sentimentality.*)

4. Do you remember seeing this commercial on television? Does your memory of the commercial and its effectiveness agree with Greene's account?

Expository Techniques

1. In which parts of the essay does Greene discuss causes? Effects?

2. Should paragraphs 1–3 or 1–6 be considered the introduction to this essay? Why?

3a. Identify the uses of parallelism in the first two paragraphs of the essay. (Guide: *Parallel Structure.*)

  b. How does the author use parallel structures to emphasize the central theme of the essay? (Guide: *Emphasis.*)

4. At several places in the essay, Greene talks about the men who were considered for the commercial but not chosen. To what extent do these discussions detract from the essay's unity or contribute to its central theme? (Guide: *Unity.*)

5. In what ways does Green's frequent use of quotations from Bill Demby add to the effectiveness of the essay? (Guide: *Evaluation.*)

Diction and Vocabulary

1. Discuss how Greene uses diction and sentence structure to create drama and tension in paragraphs 29, 31, and 32. (Guide: *Diction, Syntax.*)

2. If you do not know the meaning of any of the following words, look them up in the dictionary: introspection (par. 1); protheses (9); visceral (32).

Suggestions for Writing and Discussion

1. The commercial described in this essay may represent a growing interest in the effects of the Vietnam war on both those who fought in it and those who did not. What other evidence of this growing interest can you identify?

2. Is Demby's prediction about his anonymity after the commercial stops running likely to come true (pars. 37–39)? Why, or why not?

3. If you believe television is as powerful as Greene suggests, can you cite some other examples of its effects?

(NOTE: Suggestions for topics requiring development by analysis of CAUSE AND EFFECT are on pages 308–309, at the end of this section.)

SUSAN PERRY AND JIM DAWSON

SUSAN PERRY is a former staff writer for Time-Life, Inc., and now works full-time as a freelance writer specializing in health, business, and women's issues. Her articles have appeared in such publications as *Ms., The Washington Post,* and the *Minneapolis Star.* JAMES DAWSON is a science reporter who writes regularly for the *Minneapolis Star-Tribune.* Recently Perry and Dawson co-authored *The Secrets Our Body Clocks Reveal* (1988).

What's Your Best Time of Day?

This essay, published as a magazine article, is drawn from *The Secrets Our Body Clocks Reveal.* The piece opens with examples of some puzzling behaviors, looks at their causes in the rhythms of our bodies, then examines some further effects of these rhythms. Along the way it provides some practical advice for taking the best advantage of the biological patterns that help govern our lives. As might be expected, the authors draw on a variety of patterns to accomplish these tasks, including classification, process, and the use of examples.

Every fall, Jane, a young mother and part-time librarian, begins to 1 eat more and often feels sleepy. Her mood is also darker, especially when she awakens in the morning; it takes all her energy just to drag herself out of bed. These symptoms persist until April, when warmer weather and longer days seem to lighten her mood and alleviate her cravings for food and sleep.

Joseph, a 48-year-old engineer for a Midwestern computer com- 2 pany, feels cranky early in the morning. But as the day progresses, he becomes friendlier and more accommodating.

All living organisms, from mollusks to men and women, exhibit   3
biological rhythms. Some are short and can be measured in minutes
or hours. Others last days or months. The peaking of body temperature, which occurs in most people every evening, is a daily rhythm.
The menstrual cycle is a monthly rhythm. The increase in sexual
drive in the autumn—not in the spring, as poets would have us
believe—is a seasonal, or yearly, rhythm.

The idea that our bodies are in constant flux is fairly new—and   4
goes against traditional medical training. In the past, many doctors
were taught to believe the body has a relatively stable, or homeostatic, internal environment. Any fluctuations were considered random
and not meaningful enough to be studied.

As early as the 1940s, however, some scientists questioned the   5
homeostatic view of the body. Franz Halberg, a young European scientist working in the United States, noticed that the number of white
blood cells in laboratory mice was dramatically higher and lower at
different times of day. Gradually, such research spread to the study
of other rhythms in other life forms, and the findings were sometimes startling. For example, the time of day when a person receives
X-ray or drug treatment for cancer can affect treatment benefits and
ultimately mean the difference between life and death.

This new science is called chronobiology, and the evidence sup-   6
porting it has become increasingly persuasive. Along the way, the
scientific and medical communities are beginning to rethink their
ideas about how the human body works, and gradually what had
been considered a minor science just a few years ago is being studied in major universities and medical centers around the world.
There are even chronobiologists working for the National Aeronau-
tics and Space Administration, as well as for the National Institutes
of Health and other government laboratories.

With their new findings, they are teaching us things that can   7
literally change our lives—by helping us organize ourselves so we
can work *with* our natural rhythms rather than against them. This
can enhance our outlook on life as well as our performance at work
and play.

Because they are easy to detect and measure, more is known of   8
daily—or circadian (Latin for "about a day")—rhythms than other
types. The most obvious daily rhythm is the sleep/wake cycle. But
there are other daily cycles as well: temperature, blood pressure,
hormone levels. Amid these and the body's other changing rhythms,

you are simply a different person at 9 A.M. than you are at 3 P.M. How you feel, how well you work, your level of alertness, your sensitivity to taste and smell, the degree with which you enjoy food or take pleasure in music—all are changing throughout the day.

Most of us seem to reach our peak of alertness around noon. 9 Soon after that, alertness declines, and sleepiness may set in by midafternoon.

Your short-term memory is best during the morning—in fact, 10 about 15 percent more efficient than at any other time of day. So, students, take heed: when faced with a morning exam, it really does pay to review your notes right before the test is given.

Long-term memory is different. Afternoon is the best time for 11 learning material that you want to recall days, weeks or months later. Politicians, business executives or others who must learn speeches would be smart to do their memorizing during that time of day. If you are a student, you would be wise to schedule your more difficult classes in the afternoon, rather than in the morning. You should also try to do most of your studying in the afternoon, rather than late at night. Many students believe they memorize better while burning the midnight oil because their short-term recall is better during the wee hours of the morning than in the afternoon. But short-term memory won't help them much several days later, when they face the exam.

By contrast, we tend to do best on cognitive tasks—things that 12 require the juggling of words and figures in one's head—during the morning hours. This might be a good time, say, to balance a checkbook.

Your manual dexterity—the speed and coordination with 13 which you perform complicated tasks with your hands—peaks during the afternoon hours. Such work as carpentry, typing or sewing will be a little easier at this time of day.

What about sports? During afternoon and early evening, your 14 coordination is at its peak, and you're able to react the quickest to an outside stimulus—like a baseball speeding toward you at home plate. Studies have also shown that late in the day, when your body temperature is peaking, you will *perceive* a physical workout to be easier and less fatiguing—whether it actually is or not. That means you are more likely to work harder during a late-afternoon or early-evening workout, and therefore benefit more from it. Studies involving swimmers, runners, shot-putters and rowing crews have shown consistently that performance is better in the evening than in the morning.

In fact, all of your senses—taste, sight, hearing, touch and smell—may be at their keenest during late afternoon and early evening. That could be why dinner usually tastes better to us than breakfast and why bright lights irritate us at night. 15

Even our perception of time changes from hour to hour. Not only does time seem to fly when you're having fun, but it also seems to fly even faster if you are having that fun in the late afternoon or early evening, when your body temperature is also peaking. 16

While all of us follow the same general pattern of ups and downs, the exact timing varies from person to person. It all depends on how your "biological" day is structured—how much of a morning or night person you are. The earlier your biological day gets going, the earlier you are likely to enter—and exit—the peak times for performing various tasks. An extreme morning person and an extreme night person may have circadian cycles that are a few hours apart. 17

Each of us can increase our knowledge about our individual rhythms. Learn how to listen to the inner beats of your body; let them set the pace of your day. You will live a healthier—and happier—life. As no less an authority than the Bible tells us, "To every thing there is a season, and a time to every purpose under heaven." 18

Meanings and Values

1. In what ways are the patterns illustrated or discussed in the first three paragraphs similar to each other?

2. According to the explanations in this essay, what are the best times to undertake the following activities, and why:

   a. play a sport

   b. balance a checkbook

   c. learn a speech

   d. prepare for an exam

Expository Techniques

1. What functions do the examples that open the essay perform for readers? (See "Guide to Terms": *Introductions*.)

2a. Where in the essay do the authors use classification and for what purposes is it employed?

b. Where and for what purposes do the authors use process analysis?

3. Would this essay be more effective if discussions of the causes and the effects were more clearly separated? Why, or why not? (Guide: *Evaluation*.)

4. Discuss the arrangement of paragraphs 9–12, paying special attention to parallel structures and transitions within and between paragraphs. (Guide: *Unity, Parallel Structure*.)

Diction and Vocabulary

1. In what ways does the diction in paragraphs 1 and 2 emphasize the contrasts being illustrated? (Guide: *Diction*.)

2. Discuss how the authors provide explanations of the following scientific or otherwise unfamiliar terms in the text so that readers will not have to pause to look them up: homeostatic (par. 4); circadian (8); cognitive tasks (12); manual dexterity (13).

3. Does the allusion that concludes the essay seem appropriate? Why, or why not? Try looking up the passage in the Bible (Ecclesiastes 3:1) to see if its original meaning is similar to the one it has in the context of this essay.

Suggestions for Writing and Discussion

1. Do your experiences confirm what the authors say about the cycles that guide our behavior? Provide examples that either support or contradict the essay's conclusions.

2. How might typical academic or work schedules be altered to take into account the patterns described in this selection? What common practices seem particularly in need of change given the information provided here?

(NOTE: Suggestions for topics requiring development by analysis of CAUSE AND EFFECT are on pages 308–309, at the end of this section.)

LINDA HASSELSTROM

LINDA HASSELSTROM is an essayist, poet, and environmental writer who is also a rancher in western South Dakota. Her books include *Caught by One Wing* (1984) and *Roadkill* (1987) (poetry); *Windbreak: A Woman Rancher on the Northern Plains* (1987) and *Going over East* (1987) (journals and nonfiction); and *Land Circle: Writings Collected from the Land* (1991) (essays and poetry). Her essays have appeared in many magazines such as *High Country News, Northern Lights, North American Review, Working Parents, Whole Earth Review,* and *Utne Reader* as well as newspapers such as the *Los Angeles Times* and *The Christian Science Monitor.*

A Peaceful Woman Explains Why She Carries a Gun

This version of the essay "Why One Peaceful Woman Carries a Pistol" first appeared in the *Utne Reader.* In it, Hasselstrom takes a subject (gun ownership) usually dealt with in terms of general principles (the right to bear arms) or social trends and explores it in terms of a particular person in a particular setting. This focus on the individual leads to an analysis of cause and effect relationships that readers are likely to find either invigorating or disquieting, or both.

I am a peace-loving woman. But several events in the past 10 years have convinced me I'm safer when I carry a pistol. This was a personal decision, but because handgun possession is a controversial subject, perhaps my reasoning will interest others. 1

I live in western South Dakota on a ranch 25 miles from the nearest large town; for several years I spent winters alone here. As a free-lance writer, I travel alone a lot—more than 100,000 miles by car in the last four years. With women freer than ever before to travel 2 alone, the odds of our encountering trouble seem to have risen. And help, in the West, can be hours away. Distances are great, roads are deserted, and the terrain is often too exposed to offer hiding places.

A woman who travels alone is advised, usually by men, to pro-   3 tect herself by avoiding bars and other "dangerous situations," by approaching her car like an Indian scout, by locking doors and windows. But these precautions aren't always enough. I spent years following them and still found myself in dangerous situations. I began to resent the idea that just because I am female, I have to be extra careful.

A few years ago, with another woman, I camped for several   4 weeks in the West. We discussed self-defense, but neither of us had taken a course in it. She was against firearms, and local police told us Mace was illegal. So we armed ourselves with spray cans of deodorant tucked into our sleeping bags. We never used our improvised Mace because we were lucky enough to camp beside people who came to our aid when men harassed us. But on one occasion we visited a national park where our assigned space was less than 15 feet from other campers. When we returned from a walk, we found our closest neighbors were two young men. As we gathered our cooking gear, they drank beer and loudly discussed what they would do to us after dark. Nearby campers, even families, ignored them; rangers strolled past, unconcerned. When we asked the rangers point-blank if they would protect us, one of them patted my shoulder and said, "Don't worry, girls. They're just kidding." At dusk we drove out of the park and hid our camp in the woods a few miles away. The illegal spot was lovely, but our enjoyment of that park was ruined. I returned from the trip determined to reconsider the options available for protecting myself.

At that time, I lived alone on the ranch and taught night classes   5 in town. Along a city street I often traveled, a woman had a flat tire, called for help on her CB radio, and got a rapist who left her beaten. She was afraid to call for help again and stayed in her car until morning. For that reason, as well as because CBs work best along line-of-sight, which wouldn't help much in the rolling hills where I live, I ruled out a CB.

As I drove home one night, a car followed me. It passed me on   6 a narrow bridge while a passenger flashed a blinding spotlight in my face. I braked sharply. The car stopped, angled across the bridge, and four men jumped out. I realized the locked doors were useless if they broke the windows of my pickup. I started forward, hoping to knock their car aside so I could pass. Just then another car appeared, and the men hastily got back in their car. They continued to follow me, passing and repassing. I dared not go home because no one else was there. I passed no lighted houses. Finally they pulled over to the roadside, and I decided to use their tactic: fear. Speeding, the pickup horn blaring, I swerved as close to them as I dared as I roared past. It worked; they turned off the highway. But I was frightened and angry. Even in my vehicle I was too vulnerable.

Other incidents occurred over the years. One day I glanced out   7
a field below my house and saw a man with a shotgun walking toward a pond full of ducks. I drove down and explained that the land was posted. I politely asked him to leave. He stared at me, and the muzzle of the shotgun began to rise. In a moment of utter clarity I realized that I was alone on the ranch, and that he could shoot me and simply drive away. The moment passed; the man left.

One night, I returned home from teaching a class to find deep   8
tire ruts in the wet ground of my yard, garbage in the driveway, and a large gas tank empty. A light shone in the house; I couldn't remember leaving it on. I was too embarrassed to drive to a neighboring ranch and wake someone up. An hour of cautious exploration convinced me the house was safe, but once inside, with the doors locked, I was still afraid. I kept thinking of how vulnerable I felt, prowling around my own house in the dark.

My first positive step was to take a kung fu class, which teaches   9
evasive or protective action when someone enters your space without permission. I learned to move confidently, scanning for possible attackers. I learned how to assess danger and techniques for avoiding it without combat.

I also learned that one must practice several hours every day to   10
be good at kung fu. By that time I had married George; when I practiced with him, I learned how *close* you must be to your attacker to use martial arts, and decided a 120-pound woman dare not let a six-foot, 220-pound attacker get that close unless she is very, very good at self-defense. I have since read articles by several women who were extremely well trained in the martial arts, but were raped and beaten anyway.

I thought back over the times in my life when I had been   11
attacked or threatened and tried to be realistic about my own behavior, searching for anything that had allowed me to become a victim.

Overall, I was convinced that I had not been at fault. I don't believe myself to be either paranoid or a risk-taker, but I wanted more protection.

With some reluctance I decided to try carrying a pistol. George   12
had always carried one, despite his size and his training in martial arts. I practiced shooting until I was sure I could hit an attacker who moved close enough to endanger me. Then I bought a license from the county sheriff, making it legal for me to carry the gun concealed.

But I was not yet ready to defend myself. George taught me that   13
the most important preparation was mental: convincing myself I could actually *shoot a person.* Few of us wish to hurt or kill another human being. But there is no point in having a gun—in fact, gun possession might increase your danger—unless you know you can use it. I got in the habit of rehearsing, as I drove or walked, the precise conditions that would be required before I would shoot someone.

People who have not grown up with the idea that they are capa-   14
ble of protecting themselves—in other words, most women—might have to work hard to convince themselves of their ability, and of the necessity. Handgun ownership need not turn us into gunslingers, but it can be part of believing in, and relying on, *ourselves* for protection.

To be useful, a pistol had to be available. In my car, it's within   15
instant reach. When I enter a deserted rest stop at night, it's in my purse, with my hand on the grip. When I walk from a dark parking lot into a motel, it's in my hand, under a coat. At home, it's on the headboard. In short, I take it with me almost everywhere I go alone.

Just carrying a pistol is not protection; avoidance is still the best   16
approach to trouble. Subconsciously watching for signs of danger, I believe I've become more alert. Handgun use, not unlike driving, becomes instinctive. Each time I've drawn my gun—I have never fired it at another human being—I've simply found it in my hand.

I was driving the half-mile to the highway mailbox one day   17
when I saw a vehicle parked about midway down the road. Several men were standing in the ditch, relieving themselves. I have no objection to emergency urination, but I noticed they'd dumped several dozen beer cans in the road. Besides being ugly, cans can slash a cow's feet or stomach.

The men noticed me before they finished and made quite a per-   18
formance out of zipping their trousers while walking toward me. All

four of them gathered around my small foreign car, and one of them demanded what the hell I wanted.

"This is private land. I'd appreciate it if you'd pick up the beer cans." 19

"What beer cans?" said the belligerent one, putting both hands 20 on the car door and leaning in my window. His face was inches from mine, and the beer fumes were strong. The others laughed. One tried the passenger door, locked; another put his foot on the hood and rocked the car. They circled, lightly thumping the roof, discussing my good fortune in meeting them and the benefits they were likely to bestow upon me. I felt very small and very trapped and they knew it.

"The ones you just threw out," I said politely. 21

"I don't see no beer cans. Why don't you get out here and show 22 them to me, honey?" said the belligerent one, reaching for the handle inside my door.

"Right over there," I said, still being polite, "—there, and over 23 there." I pointed with the pistol, which I'd slipped under my thigh. Within one minute the cans and the men were back in the car and headed down the road.

I believe this incident illustrates several important principles. 24 The men were trespassing and knew it; their judgment may have been impaired by alcohol. Their response to the polite request of a woman alone was to use their size, numbers, and sex to inspire fear. The pistol was a response in the same language. Politeness didn't work; I couldn't match them in size or number. Out of the car, I'd have been more vulnerable. The pistol just changed the balance of power. It worked again recently when I was driving in a desolate part of Wyoming. A man played cat-and-mouse with me for 30 miles, ultimately trying to run me off the road. When his car passed mine with only two inches to spare, I showed him my pistol, and he disappeared.

When I got my pistol, I told my husband, revising the old Colt 25 slogan, "God made men *and women,* but Sam Colt made them equal." Recently I have seen a gunmaker's ad with a similar sentiment. Perhaps this is an idea whose time has come, though the pacifist inside me will be saddened if the only way women can achieve equality is by carrying weapons.

We must treat a firearm's power with caution. "Power tends to 26 corrupt, and absolute power corrupts absolutely," as a man (Lord

Acton) once said. A pistol is not the only way to avoid being raped or murdered in today's world, but, intelligently wielded, it can shift the balance of power and provide a measure of safety.

Meanings and Values

1a. State in your own words the phenomenon Hasselstrom analyzes in this essay.

b. Does she explain causes, effects, or both? Identify specific portions of the essay to support your answer.

2a. What attitudes towards gun ownership does Hasselstrom probably anticipate her readers will bring to the essay? Be specific.

b. Where in the essay, if at all, does she acknowledge likely attitudes?

c. What point(s) of view towards gun ownership does she encourage readers to adopt? Where does she announce this outlook?

3. How would you characterize the writer's purpose? Explanation? Argument? Self-justification? (See "Guide to Terms": *Purpose*.)

Expository Techniques

1a. Identify the main examples presented in this essay.

b. Why, if at all, are we justified in considering this essay as primarily concerned with explaining causes and effects when so much of it is devoted to examples?

2a. In what ways does the writer use strategies of comparison and contrast in paragraphs 9–11 to consider and dismiss alternatives to gun owning (See Section 3)?

b. Explain why her tactics in these paragraphs are successful or unsuccessful. (Guide: *Evaluation*.)

3a. What generalities concerning when and how to use a gun correctly does the writer present in paragraphs 12–26?

b. Where in the paragraphs does she announce the generalities?

c. For which does she provide supporting examples?

d. Which of the examples, if any, also illustrate causes or effects of gun ownership?

Diction and Vocabulary

1. Discuss the writer's use of connotation in paragraphs 4, 6–8, and 17–23 to create emotional emphasis that makes her reasons for

owning a gun seem plausible and convincing. (Guide: *Connotation/ Denotation.*)

2. Tell how the writer's use of qualification and her word choice in the opening paragraph help keep the essay from becoming predominantly argumentative. (Guide: *Qualification, Diction.*)

3. How might this essay have been different had the writer not made such frequent use of "I" in presenting examples and explanations?

Suggestions for Writing and Discussion

1. Explore another issue like gun control over which there has been considerable public debate, writing about it from a personal perspective, exploring causes and effects, and providing explanation rather than argument.

2. Are people's attitudes about issues like animal rights, gun control, economic issues, and education likely to differ according to where they live or according to their economic and social status? What other factors might affect people's outlooks in substantial ways?

(NOTE: Suggestions for topics requiring development by analysis of CAUSE AND EFFECT are on pages 308–309, at the end of this section.)

PAUL THEROUX

Self-Propelled

"Self-Propelled" first appeared as an essay in *The New York Times Magazine* on April 25, 1993. In it, Theroux searches for the causes of behaviors that many people, including some of the participants, consider virtually impossible to explain. Searching for our own motivations and those of other people is one of the most frequent and rewarding uses for cause and effect as a pattern of thinking and writing.

When my French publisher, Robert Laffont, asked me whom in the whole of France I wished to meet, I said, "d'Aboville," whose book "Seul" ("Alone") had just appeared. The next day at a cafe in the shadow of Saint-Sulpice, I said to d'Aboville's wife, Cornelia, "He is my hero." She replied softly, with feeling, "Mine too." 1

It is a commonplace that almost anyone can go to the moon: you pass a physical and NASA puts you in a projectile and shoots you there. It is perhaps invidious to compare an oarsman with an astronaut, but rowing across the Pacific Ocean alone in a small boat, as 2 the Frenchman Gerard d'Aboville did in 1991, shows old-fashioned bravery. Yet even those of us who go on journeys in eccentric circles, simpler and far less challenging than d'Aboville's, seldom understand what propels us. Ed Gillet paddled a kayak 63 days from California to Maui a few years ago and cursed himself much of the way for not knowing why he was making such a reckless crossing. Astronauts have a clear, scientific motive, but adventurers tend to evade the awkward questions why.

D'Aboville was 46 when he single-handedly rowed a 26-foot 3 boat of his own design from Japan to Washington State in 1991. He had previously (in 1980) rowed across the Atlantic, also from west to east, Cape Cod to Brittany. But the Atlantic was a piece of cake compared with his Pacific crossing, one of the most difficult and dangerous in the world. For various reasons, d'Aboville set out very late in the season and was caught first by heavy weather and finally tumultuous storms—40-foot waves and 80-mile-an-hour winds. Many times he was terrified, yet halfway through the trip—which had no stops (no islands at all in that part of the Pacific)—when a Russian freighter offered to rescue him, "I was not even tempted." He turned his back on the ship and rowed on. The entire crossing, averaging 7,000 strokes a day, took him 134 days. I wanted to ask him why he had taken this enormous personal risk.

D'Aboville, short and compactly built, is no more physically 4 prepossessing than another fairly obscure and just as brave long-distance navigator, the paddler Paul Caffyn of New Zealand. Over the past decade or so, Caffyn has circumnavigated Australia, Japan, Great Britain and his own New Zealand through the low-pressure systems of the Tasman Sea in his 17-foot kayak.

In a memorable passage in his book, "The Dark Side of the 5 Wave," Caffyn is battling a horrible chop off the North Island and sees a fishing boat up ahead. He deliberately paddles away from the boat, fearing that someone on board will see his flimsy craft and ask him where he is going: "I knew they would ask me why I was doing it, and I did not have an answer."

I hesitated to spring the question on d'Aboville. I asked him 6 first about his preparations for the trip. A native of Brittany, he had always rowed, he said. "We never used outboard motors—we rowed boats the way other children pedaled bicycles." Long ocean crossings interested him, too, because he loves to design highly specialized boats.

His Pacific craft was streamlined—it had the long seaworthy   7
lines of a kayak, and a high-tech cockpit with a roll-up canopy that
could seal in the occupant in rough weather. A pumping system,
using sea water as ballast, easily righted the boat in the event of
capsizing. The boat had few creature comforts but all necessities—a
stove, a sleeping place, roomy hatches for dehydrated meals
and drinking water. D'Aboville also had a video camera and
filmed himself rowing, in the middle of nowhere, humming
the Alan Jackson country-and-western song "Here in the Real
World." D'Aboville sang it and hummed it for months but did not
know any of the words, or indeed the title, until I recognized it on
his video.

"That is a very hard question," he said, when I asked him why   8
he had set out on this seemingly suicidal trip—one of the longest
ocean crossings possible, at one of the worst times of the year. He
denied that he had any death wish. "And it is not like going over a
waterfall in a barrel." He had prepared himself well. His boat was
well found. He is an excellent navigator, "Yes, I think I have
courage," he said when I asked him point-blank whether he felt he
was brave.

It was the equivalent, he said, of scaling the north face of a   9
mountain, typically the most difficult ascent. But this lonely four-
and-a-half-month ordeal almost ended in his death by drowning,
when a severe storm lashed the Oregon-Washington coast as
d'Aboville approached it, upside down, in a furious sea. The video
of his last few days at sea, taken by a Coast Guard vessel, is so frightening that d'Aboville wiped tears from his eyes watching it with me.
"At this time last year I was in the middle of it." He quietly ignored
my questions about the 40-foot waves. Clearly upset at the memory,
he said, "I do not like to talk about it."

"Only an animal does useful things," he said at last, after a long   10
silence. "An animal gets food, finds a place to sleep, tries to keep
comfortable. But I wanted to do something that was not useful—not
like an animal at all. Something only a human being would do."

The art of it, he was saying—such an effort was as much esthetic   11
as athletic. And that the greatest travel always contains within it the
seeds of a spiritual quest, or else what's the point? The English
explorer Apsley Cherry-Garrard would have agreed with this. He
went to Antarctica with Scott in the ship "Terra Nova" and made a
six-week crossing of a stretch of Antarctica in 1912, on foot, in the

winter, when that polar region is dark all day and night, with a whipping wind and temperature of 80 below.

"Polar exploration is at once the cleanest and most isolated way   12 of having a bad time which has been devised" are the first words of his narrative. On his trek, which gave him the title for his book, "The Worst Journey in the World," he wrote: "Why do some human beings desire with such urgency to do such things: regardless of the consequences, voluntarily, conscripted by no one but themselves? No one knows. There is a strong urge to conquer the dreadful forces of nature, and perhaps to get consciousness of ourselves, of life, and of the shadowy workings of our human minds. Physical capacity is the only limit. I have tried to tell how, and when, and where? But why. That is a mystery."

But there is no conquering, d'Aboville says. *Je n'ai pas vaincu le*   13 *Pacifique, il m'a laissé passer.* "I did not conquer the Pacific," he said afterward. "It let me go across."

Meanings and Values

1. Why does Theroux consider d'Aboville a hero? In what ways, if at all does he portray d'Aboville as a person whose qualities or actions we ought to imitate?

2. What causes or effects does Theroux seek to explain in this essay? In your opinion, does he succeed or not? Why? (See "Guide to Terms": *Evaluation.*)

3. What causes for their actions do the adventurers (and Theroux) consider and reject? What explanations do they accept?

Expository Techniques

1. Explain the probable significance of the contrast Theroux makes near the beginning of the essay between adventurers and astronauts. Would the contrast have a different effect if it appeared later in the essay, perhaps at the end?

2. What strategy does the writer employ to begin this essay? What strategy does he use to conclude it? (Guide: *Introductions, Closings.*)

3a. Where in the essay does Theroux indicate that a particular adventurer or adventurers in general have no explanation for their actions?

  b. Tell how such statements are related to the essay's central theme and indicate what, if at all, they contribute to its unity. (Guide: *Unity.*)

4a. In what ways does the writer present d'Aboville and the other adventurers so that they do not seem foolhardy, eccentric, or careless?

b. Explain why, in your own opinion, Theroux is either likely or unlikely to convince most readers that the adventurers are to be taken
seriously and not dismissed as foolish thrill seekers or people with
distorted values and psychological instability.

Diction and Vocabulary

1. Discuss how the quotations from d'Aboville and the other adventurers that Theroux uses create the impression that they are calm, rational, and intelligent people. Pay particular attention to the tone and
the word choice in the quotations. (Guide: *Style/Tone, Diction.*)

2. Tell how the parallel sentence structures in paragraph 10 emphasize
the point d'Aboville is trying to make. (Guide: *Parallel Structures.*)

3. Why might Theroux have chosen to quote d'Aboville in French in
the last paragraph when he did not do so in the rest of the essay? Explain why you think his use of French either adds to or detracts from
the essay's effectiveness. (Guide: *Evaluation.*)

4. If you do not know the meaning of some of the following words,
look them up in a dictionary: invidious (par. 2); prepossessing (4);
chop (5); esthetic (11); conscripted (12).

Suggestions for Writing and Discussion

1. List as many other activities as you can that people in general consider dangerous or foolhardy but that participants see as reaffirming
their human qualities or offering some similar reward.

2. Prepare an essay justifying your participation in some risk-taking
or potentially dangerous activity such as skydiving, mountain-
climbing, or dirt-bike racing. As an alternative, consider justifying
your participation in time-consuming and mentally challenging
activities such as tournament level chess, crossword puzzle solving,
or jigsaw puzzle assembly.

(NOTE: Suggestions for topics requiring development by analysis of CAUSE AND EFFECT
are on pages 308–309, at the end of this section.)

WILLIAM SEVERINI KOWINSKI

WILLIAM SEVERINI KOWINSKI grew up in Greensburg, Pennsylvania. In 1964, the year before the first mall was built in Greensburg, he left to attend Knox College in Illinois. While attending Knox he spent a semester studying in the fiction and poetry workshops at the University of Iowa. Kowinski was a writer and editor for the Boston *Phoenix* and the Washington *Newsworks* and has written articles for a number of national newspapers and magazines including *Esquire, New Times,* and *The New York Times Magazine.* His book *The Malling of America: An Inside Look at the Great Consumer Paradise* (1985) is based on his travels to malls throughout the United States and Canada.

Kids in the Mall: Growing Up Controlled

Over the past twenty years, the number, size, and variety of suburban shopping malls have grown at astonishing rates, replacing, in many cases, both plazas and urban shopping districts. They are now important economic and cultural forces in American and Canadian society. In this chapter from *The Malling of America,* Kowinski looks at some of the ways malls have affected the teenagers who spend much of their time shopping, working, or just hanging around at the mall.

Butch heaved himself up and loomed over the group. "Like it was different 1 for me," he piped. "My folks used to drop me off at the shopping mall every morning and leave me all day. It was like a big free baby-sitter, you know? One night they never came back for me. Maybe they moved away. Maybe there's some kind of a Bureau of Missing Parents I could check with."

—Richard Peck

Secrets of the Shopping Mall, a
novel for teenagers

From his sister at Swarthmore, I'd heard about a kid in Florida   2
whose mother picked him up after school every day, drove him
straight to the mall, and left him there until it closed—all at his
insistence. I'd heard about a boy in Washington who, when his
family moved from one suburb to another, pedaled his bicycle
five miles every day to get back to his old mall, where he once
belonged.

These stories aren't unusual. The mall is a common experience   3
for the majority of American youth; they have probably been going
there all their lives. Some ran within their first large open space, saw
their first fountain, bought their first toy, and read their first book in
a mall. They may have smoked their first cigarette or first joint or
turned them down, had their first kiss or lost their virginity in the
mall parking lot. Teenagers in America now spend more time in the
mall than anywhere else but home and school. Mostly it is their
choice, but some of that mall time is put in as the result of two-
paycheck and single-parent households, and the lack of other viable
alternatives. But are these kids being harmed by the mall?

I wondered first of all what difference it makes for adolescents   4
to experience so many important moments in the mall. They are,
after all, at play in the fields of its little world and they learn its
ways; they adapt to it and make it adapt to them. It's here that these
kids get their street sense, only it's mall sense. They are learning the
ways of a large-scale artificial environment: its subtleties and flexi-
bilities, its particular pleasures and resonances, and the attitudes it
fosters.

The presence of so many teenagers for so much time was not   5
something mall developers planned on. In fact, it came as a big surprise. But kids became a fact of mall life very early, and the International Council of Shopping Centers found it necessary to
commission a study, which they published along with a guide to
mall managers on how to handle the teenage incursion.

The study found that "teenagers in suburban centers are bored   6
and come to the shopping centers mainly as a place to go. Teenagers
in suburban centers spent more time fighting, drinking, littering and
walking than did their urban counterparts, but presented fewer
overall problems." The report observed that "adolescents congre-
gated in groups of two to four and predominantly at locations
selected by them rather than management." This probably had
something to do with the decision to install game arcades, which

allow management to channel these restless adolescents into naturally contained areas away from major traffic points of adult shoppers.

The guide concluded that mall management should tolerate 7 and even encourage the teenage presence because, in the words of the report, "The vast majority support the same set of values as does shopping center management." *The same set of values* means simply that mall kids are already preprogrammed to be consumers and that the mall can put the finishing touches to them as hard-core, lifelong shoppers just like everybody else. That, after all, is what the mall is about. So it shouldn't be surprising that in spending a lot of time there, adolescents find little that challenges the assumption that the goal of life is to make money and buy products, or that just about everything else in life is to be used to serve those ends.

Growing up in a high-consumption society already adds ines- 8 timable pressure to kids' lives. Clothes consciousness has invaded the grade schools, and popularity is linked with having the best, newest clothes in the currently acceptable styles. Even what they read has been affected. "Miss [Nancy] Drew wasn't obsessed with her wardrobe," noted *Wall Street Journal.* "But today the mystery in teen fiction for girls is what outfit the heroine will wear next." Shopping has become a survival skill and there is certainly no better place to learn it than the mall, where its importance is powerfully reinforced and certainly never questioned.

The mall as a university of suburban materialism, where Valley 9 Girls and Boys from coast to coast are educated in consumption, has its other lessons in this era of change in family life and sexual mores and their economic and social ramifications. The plethora of products in the mall, plus the pressure on teens to buy them, may contribute to the phenomenon that psychologist David Elkind calls "the hurried child": kids who are exposed to too much of the adult world too quickly, and must respond with a sophistication that belies their still-tender emotional development. Certainly the adult products marketed for children—form-fitting designer jeans, sexy tops for preteen girls—add to the social pressure to look like an adult, along with the home-grown need to understand adult finances (why mothers must work) and adult emotions (when parents divorce).

Kids spend so much time at the mall partly because their par- 10 ents allow it and even encourage it. The mall is safe, it doesn't seem to harbor any unsavory activities, and there is adult supervision; it is, after all, a controlled environment. So the temptation, especially for working parents, is to let the mall be their babysitter. At least the kids aren't watching TV. But the mall's role as a surrogate mother may be more extensive and more profound.

Karen Lansky, a writer living in Los Angeles, has looked into   11
the subject and she told me some of her conclusions about the effects on its teenaged denizens of the mall's controlled and controlling environment. "Structure is the dominant idea, since true 'mall rats' lack just that in their homelives," she said, "and adolescents about to make the big leap into growing up crave more structure than our modern society cares to acknowledge." Karen pointed out some of the elements malls supply that kids used to get from their families, like warmth (Strawberry Shortcake dolls and similar cute and cuddly merchandise), old-fashioned mothering ("We do it all for you," the fast-food slogan), and even home cooking (the "homemade" treats at the food court).

The problem in all this, as Karen Lansky sees it, is that while   12
families nurture children by encouraging growth through the assumption of responsibility and then by letting them rest in the bosom of the family from the rigors of growing up, the mall as a structural mother encourages passivity and consumption, as long as the kid doesn't make trouble. Therefore all they learn about becoming adults is how to act and how to consume.

Kids are in the mall not only in the passive role of shoppers—   13
they also work there, especially as fast-food outlets infiltrate the mall's enclosure. There they learn how to hold a job and take responsibility, but still within the same value context. When *CBS Reports* went to Oak Park Mall in suburban Kansas City, Kansas, to tape part of their hour-long consideration of malls, "After the Dream Comes True," they interviewed a teenaged girl who worked in a fast-food outlet there. In a sequence that didn't make the final program, she described the major goal of her present life, which was to perfect the curl on top of the ice-cream cones that were her store's specialty. If she could do that, she would be moved from the lowly soft-drink dispenser to the more prestigious ice-cream division, the curl on top of the status ladder at her restaurant. These are the achievements that are important at the mall.

Other benefits of such jobs may also be overrated, according to   14
Laurence D. Steinberg of the University of California at Irvine's social ecology department, who did a study on teenage employment.

Their jobs, he found, are generally simple, mindlessly repetitive and boring. They don't really learn anything, and the jobs don't lead anywhere. Teenagers also work primarily with other teenagers; even their supervisors are often just a little older than they are. "Kids need to spend time with adults," Steinberg told me. "Although they get benefits from peer relationships, without parents and other adults it's one-sided socialization. They hang out with each other, have age-segregated jobs, and watch TV."

Perhaps much of this is not so terrible or even so terribly differ-   15
ent. Now that they have so much more to contend with in their lives, adolescents probably need more time to spend with other adolescents without adult impositions, just to sort things out. Though it is more concentrated in the mall (and therefore perhaps a clearer target), the value system there is really the dominant one of the whole society. Attitudes about curiosity, initiative, self-expression, empathy, and disinterested learning aren't necessarily made in the mall; they are mirrored there, perhaps a bit more intensely—as through a glass brightly.

Besides, the mall is not without its educational opportunities.   16
There are bookstores, where there is at least a short shelf of classics at great prices, and other books from which it is possible to learn more than how to do sit-ups. There are tools, from hammers to VCRs, and products, from clothes to records, that can help the young find and express themselves. There are older people with stories, and places to be alone or to talk one-on-one with a kindred spirit. And there is always the passing show.

The mall itself may very well be an education about the future.   17
I was struck with the realization, as early as my first forays into Greengate,[1] that the mall is only one of a number of enclosed and controlled environments that are part of the lives of today's young. The mall is just an extension, say, of those large suburban schools— only there's Karmelkorn instead of chem lab, the ice rink instead of the gym: It's high school without the impertinence of classes.

Growing up, moving from home to school to the mall—from   18
enclosure to enclosure, transported in cars—is a curiously continuous process, without much in the way of contrast or contract with unenclosed reality. Places must tend to blur into one another. But

---

[1]Greengate Mall in Greensburg, Pennsylvania, where Kowinski began his research on malls (Editors' note).

whatever differences and dangers there are in this, the skills these adolescents are learning may turn out to be useful in their later lives. For we seem to be moving inexorably into an age of pre-planned and regulated environments, and this is the world they will inherit.

Still, it might be better if they had more of a choice. One   19 teenaged girl confessed to *CBS Reports* that she sometimes felt she was missing something by hanging out at the mall so much. "But I'm here," she said, "and this is what I have."

Meanings and Values

1.   Why do malls have a marked effect on children and teenagers?

2a.   Do teenagers who spend their time in malls display any obviously unusual behavior? If so, in what ways do they behave?

b.   If not, how might one describe their behavior?

3a.   What question does this essay attempt to answer? Where in the essay is the question asked?

b.   Other than providing an answer to the question, what purpose or purposes does this selection have? (See "Guide to Terms": *Purpose.*)

4a.   What does Kowinski see as the major effects of malls on teenagers?

b.   What other, less important effects (if any) does he identify?

c.   Discuss whether or not the author presents enough evidence to convince most readers that he has correctly identified the effects.

5a.   Where in the essay does Kowinski consider causes other than the mall environment for the attitudes and behaviors of teenagers?

b.   Explain how the alternative explanation either undermines or adds to his view of the malls.

Expository Techniques

1.   What strategies does the author employ in the introduction (pars. 1–3) to help convince readers of the importance of reading and thinking about what happens to teenagers as a result of the time they spend at malls? (Guide: *Introductions.*)

2.   Discuss how the author uses examples, quotations from authorities, and various strategies of emphasis in paragraphs 8, 9, 11, 13, and 14 to indicate whether or not the effects of malls can be considered harmful. (Guide: *Emphasis.*)

3a.   Which section of the essay are devoted *primarily* to exploring the effects of the mall environment?

b. Which are devoted *primarily* to discussing whether or not the effects are harmful?

c. What use does the author make of qualification in presenting his conclusions in paragraphs 15 and 17–19? (Guide: *Qualification.*)

d. Explain why this strategy adds to or weakens your confidence in his conclusions.

4. Explain how parallelism in paragraphs 17 and 18 helps emphasize similarities in the environments. (Guide: *Parallel Structure.*)

Diction and Vocabulary

1a. Who is the Nancy Drew alluded to in paragraph 8? (Guide: *Allusion.*)

b. What is the purpose of this allusion?

2a. What transitional devices are used to tie together paragraphs 7–9? (Guide: *Transition.*)

b. Which are used to link paragraphs 10–13?

3. If you do not know the meaning of some of the following words, look them up in the dictionary: loomed, piped (par. 1); viable (3); resonances, fosters (4); incursion (5); inestimable (8); mores, ramifications, plethora (9); surrogate (10); denizens (11); nurture (12); socialization (14); impositions, empathy, disinterested (15); kindred (16); forays, impertinence (17); inexorably (18).

Suggestions for Writing and Discussion

1. Were malls as important to you as they were to some of the people Kowinski describes in his essay? Based on your experience and observations, does Kowinski appear to be overstating the effects of malls on teenagers?

2. Prepare an essay exploring the roles malls have played in your social life. If you grew up in a town without a mall, write about some other place in which you and people your age gathered.

3. If you have read Marie Winn's essay "Television Addiction" in Section 7, apply her definition of *addiction* in an essay of your own on malls ("Mall Addiction," perhaps) or on some other influential force in contemporary life like cars or rock music.

(NOTE: Suggestions for topics requiring development by analysis of CAUSE AND EFFECT follow.)

Writing Suggestions for Section 6
Cause and Effect

Analyze the immediate and ultimate causes and/or effects of one of the following subjects, or another suggested by them. (Be careful that your analysis does not develop into a mere listing of superficial "reasons.")

1. The ethnic makeup of a neighborhood.
2. Some *minor* discovery or invention.
3. The popularity of some modern singer or other celebrity.
4. The popularity of some fad of clothing or hair style.
5. The widespread fascination for antique cars (or guns, furniture, dishes, etc.).
6. The widespread enjoyment of fishing or hunting.
7. Student cheating.
8. Too much pressure (on you or an acquaintance) for good school grades.
9. Your being a member of some minority ethnic or religious group.
10. Your association, as an outsider, with members of such a group.
11. The decision of some close acquaintance to enter the religious life.
12. Some unreasonable fear or anxiety that afflicts you or someone you know well.
13. The reluctance of many women today to enter what used to be primarily women's professions such as nursing.
14. Your tendency toward individualism.
15. The popularity of computer games.
16. The mainstreaming of handicapped children.
17. The appeal of careers that promise considerable financial rewards.
18. The appeal of a recent movie or current television series.
19. The willingness of some people to sacrifice personal relationships for professional success.
20. The disintegration of a marriage or family.
21. A family's move (or reluctance to move) to a new home.
22. A candidate's success in a local or national election.

23. A recent war or international conflict.
24. A trend in the national economy.
25. The concern with diet and physical fitness.
26. Worry about crime.
27. Attention to gender roles.

7

Using *Definition* to Help Explain

Few writing faults can cause a more serious communication block between writer and reader than using key terms that can have various meanings or shades of meaning. To be useful rather than detrimental, such terms must be adequately defined.

Of the two basic types of definition, only one is our special concern as a pattern of exposition. But the other, the simpler form, is often useful to clarify meanings of concrete or noncontroversial terms. This simple process is similar to that used most in dictionaries: either providing a synonym (for example, cinema: a motion picture), or placing the word in a class and then showing how it differs from others of the same class (for example, metheglin: an alcoholic liquor made of fermented honey—here the general class is "liquor," and the differences between metheglin and other liquors are that it is "alcoholic" and "made of fermented honey").

With many such abstract, unusual, or coined terms, typical readers are too limited by their own experiences and opinions (and no two sets are identical) for writers to expect understanding of the exact sense in which the terms are used. They have a right, of course, to use such abstract words any way they choose—as long as their readers know what that way is. The importance of making this meaning clear becomes crucial when the term is used as a key element of the overall explanation. And sometimes the term being defined is even more than a key element: it may be the subject itself, for purposes of either explanation or argument.

Extended definition, unlike the simple, dictionary type, follows no set and formal pattern. Often readers are not even aware of the process. Because it is an integral part of the overall subject, extended definition is written in the same tone as the rest of the exposition (or argument), usually with an attempt to interest the readers, as well as to inform or persuade them.

There are some expository techniques peculiar to definition alone. The purpose may be served by giving the *background* of the term. Or the definition may be clarified by *negation*, sometimes called "exclusion" or "differentiation," by showing what is *not* meant by the term. Still another way is to enumerate the *characteristics* of what is defined, sometimes isolating an essential one for special treatment.

To demonstrate the possibilities in these patterns, we can use the term *juvenile delinquency*, which might need defining in some contexts since it certainly means different things to different people. (Where do we draw the line, for instance, between "childish pranks" and antisocial behavior, or between delinquent and nondelinquent experimentation with sex or marijuana?) We might show how attitudes toward juvenile crime have changed: "youthful high spirits" was the label for some of our grandfathers' activities that would be called "delinquency" today. Or we could use negation, eliminating any classes of juvenile wrongdoing not considered delinquency in the current discussion. Or we could simply list characteristics of the juvenile delinquent or isolate one of these—disrespect for authority or lack of consideration for other people—as a universal.

But perhaps the most dependable techniques for defining are the basic expository patterns already studied. Writers could illustrate their meaning of *juvenile delinquency* by giving *examples* from their own experience, from newspaper accounts, or from other sources. (Every one of the introductions to the eleven sections of this book, each a definition, relies greatly on illustration by example.) They could analyze the subject by *classification* of types or degrees of delinquency. They could use the process of *comparison* and *contrast*, perhaps between delinquent and nondelinquent youth. Showing the *causes* and *effects* of juvenile crime could help explain their attitudes toward it, and hence its meaning for them. They might choose to use *analogy*, perhaps comparing the child to a young tree growing grotesque because of poor care and attention. Or a step-by-step analysis of the *process* by which a child becomes delinquent might, in some cases, help explain the intended meaning.

Few extended definitions would use all these methods, but the extent of their use must always depend on three factors: (1) the term itself, since some are more elusive and subject to misunderstanding than others; (2) the function the term is to serve in the writing, since it would be foolish to devote several pages to defining a term that serves only a casual or unimportant purpose; and (3) the prospective reader-audience, since writers want to avoid insulting the intelligence or background of their readers, yet want to go far enough to be sure of their understanding.

But this, of course, is a basic challenge in any good writing—analyzing the prospective readers and writing for the best effect on *them*.

Sample Paragraph (Annotated)

The subject to be defined is clearly announced. After all, few readers are likely to know what *Buhna* means, let alone *Buhna Bash*.

Some of the *characteristics*.

Background of the term.

Negation or *exclusion* to indicate what the term does not mean.

Analogy with a brief example.

Every year on August 17, Palmville celebrates Buhna Bash, also known as Buhna Days or the Buhna Festival. Most of the day revolves around picnics, sports (including baseball, volleyball, and tennis tournaments), and the Palmville Onion Parade. The latter is presided over by the Onion of Ceremonies (winner of a costume contest). Where did the name Buhna come from? In part from Karl Buhler, the town's first settler, who helped incorporate the city in 1880. And in part from Salvador Nana, who was the first farmer in the region to cultivate the now-famous large, sweet onion called the Palmville Onion. The day may be a Bash, but it is a bash without alcohol and with plenty of laughter and exercise. For Palmville residents, Buhna Bash is like New Year's because it is a time of high spirits and hope for the coming year—often accompanied by optimistic resolutions.

Sample Paragraph (Definition)

This is *orienteering*, a mixture of marathon, hike, and scavenger hunt, a cross-country race in which participants must locate a series of markers set in unfamiliar terrain by means of map and compass. The course, which may range from an acre of city park to twenty square miles of wilderness, is dotted with anywhere from four to fifteen "controls," red-and-white flags whose general locations are marked on the map by small circles. At each control there is a paper punch that produces a distinctive pattern on a card the racer carries. In most events the order in which the card must be punched is fixed; the route taken to reach each control, however, is up to the participant.

Excerpt from "Marathoning with Maps" by Linton Robinson from *Science*, published by The American Association for the Advancement of Science. Reprinted by permission.

Student Writing: Using Definition to Explain

Stars

Lori L'Heureux

How many of us as children longed to be famous when we grew up? Many of us admired a certain celebrity and wanted to be just like him or her when we got older. We wanted to be a star.

The word "star," used to describe a celebrity, first came into use around 1830. Before this there was no special term to label performers who, on their own, could draw large numbers of spectators to a performance or an athletic contest. The lack of a term for such a celebrity probably reflected a greater emphasis on the performance or athletic event than on the individual performer or athlete. But as the role of talented individuals became more important, a word for it was needed. Many words, old or newly fashioned, might have served, but the noun borrowed from gazing at the night sky somehow captured the emerging role (Braudy 9).

Stars, indeed, have an enormous impact on our lives. They are recognized throughout society, observed closely onstage and off, thought about, talked about, emulated, even dreamed about. Stardom is a vital force in our culture.

Because so many people perceive the work stars do as a form of upgraded play, they understand only imperfectly the work life of celebrity entertainers. According to Jib Fowles, many stars resent the stereotypes that have been created for them over the last century. Many people, thinking that the majority of stars spend the hours of the day at leisure, imagine them living a lavish lifestyle characterized by money and glamour. Stars are thought to be greedy and to associate only with people whose social status matches their own. Stars are frequently imagined as leading relaxed lives: this one reclining in a chaise lounge, reading a script; that one stretched out on a massage table, getting worked on by a team's trainer; several others poolside and prone. But in reality, the life of most stars is quite the opposite (Fowles 59).

I conducted a survey of my own to see if most people hold these misconceptions of celebrities' lives. I asked fifteen people to tell me what type of lives they felt celebrities lead. Twelve people said that stars were rich and had easy careers. Only three said celebrities led hard lives in the public eye and had difficult jobs. Two people added that they were never tempted to become stars (L'Heureux).

But what exactly is a star? Is there a downside to being constantly in the public eye? Is being a star really a lot of work? What is the cost of being famous?

It must be understood that being a star is a social role that an individual adopts. Every day of our lives, we, too, take on social roles; we accept the obligations and behaviors of being an employee, a parent, a spouse, and so forth. Celebrity performers are similar; they wake up in the morning and step into the star role.

A star's talent delights audiences of all ages. A star acts or sings or cracks jokes or even just poses, and does these things with such style that we are fascinated and refreshed. We pay attention to stars because their performances are so successful at entertaining us. Because the audience for television shows, films, and recordings has become so large and so appreciative, the acclamation a star receives has become greater and more ferocious in recent decades. Through ticket sales, high ratings, and fan mail, an audience makes known its jubilant or waning response to a star's performance. When the response is good, the flow of good tidings certifies a star in public regard and elevates him or her to a special glory. At some moments for certain stars and their captivated fans, the reaction can be manic, as when the Beatles first toured the U.S. in 1964.

Becoming a star is sometimes a difficult task. Trying to become known in the industry, to be liked by directors, and to get parts, hopefuls embark on endless rounds of auditions. Most will spend more time at auditions than they ever will before the camera. Athletes struggling to become star players generally spend many years in the minor leagues (or the equivalent) waiting for a call to the "show."

Meanwhile, between roles, struggling actors have to sustain themselves. Usually this means menial jobs of one sort or another. For example, Marilyn Monroe labored in a wartime defense plant where she packed parachutes. For aspiring athletes, a job in the off season is generally a necessity.

Fame may require much in the way of disappointment, strain, and heartache. Since so many people are striving to become stars, and since so few will make it, the typical aspirant's work life is a ceaseless round of rejection and exclusion. He or she may attempt to maintain motivation with visions of ultimate stardom, but the daily experience of trudging from audition to audition can prove devastating. Celebrity George C. Scott commented about acting, "I think it is a psychologically damaging profession, just too much rejection to cope with every day of your life."

Aspirants may initially set themselves on the path to stardom because, in their rosy view, fame promises freedom beyond compare. But in fact the job of the celebrity performer is subject to suffocating impositions and strangling constraints. Asked what it means to become a star, Cary Grant replied, "Does it mean happiness? Yeah, for a couple of days. And then what happens? You find out that your life is not your own anymore, and that you're on show every time you step out on the street."

According to Yoti Lane, such a reaction is altogether typical, for "one of the most characteristic symptoms of having actually become a celebrity is a certain disillusionment, which sets in—after the first thrill of seeing one's name in headlines—upon discovering the obligations and inconveniences of being known by everyone everywhere" (Lane 130).

Underestimated by the public, a star's work is one of the most strenuous occupations that a person can have. Fred Astaire commented, "People will come up to me and say, 'Boy, it must have been fun making those old MGM musicals.' Fun? I suppose you could have considered them that—if you like beating your brains and feet out." Knocking oneself out to deliver first-rate performances to the public, time after time, is the fate of those ensconced in the star role. The occupation calls for extraordinary effort and ceaseless toil.

For most stars the preparation for performing begins with a general readiness. Professional athletes work out countless hours to maintain their physical condition. Singers exercise their voices daily, practicing their delivery and keeping their vocal cords in shape. Actors take classes to strengthen their performance or spend time carefully observing others.

From a base of readiness, the star prepares for the performance. The rock band practices its songs for a concert; the comedian works on new material; and the actor concentrates on a new character to become familiar with it. Actors must go over their lines again and again, working to get them right. Before going on, the star has to be costumed and made up, a process that can be very time-consuming.

The hard work for a star truly begins when he or she must concentrate on the task at hand. What a performer must do is create wonderfully and completely, on cue. The star has been engaged to deliver, within the framework of the performance, the right act at the right moment. The audience expects the comedian to have the perfect punchline, the centerfielder to catch the ball in the sun, and the actress to cry when required.

Being a star can also be dangerous. Actor Sylvester Stallone calculates that in making some of his action films he has broken his nose three times, his hand twice, and has suffered a concussion and a ruptured stomach. Also a danger to stars is their public. Fan letters pour in by the thousands each day, and the letter writers often want to enter into some sort of transaction with their idols. This can be dangerous when fans strive to encounter a star in person, pushing and shoving for contact, or when outraged fans try to injure a star.

For the privilege of staring at a star, fans will follow an entertainer into parties, restaurants, and even bathrooms. Sometimes stars have to live with the unremitting presence of fans camped at their front doors. The romance and obsession that are in a fan's mind can lead them to stalk an idol. Brooke Shields was the object of the affections of one Mark Bailey who attempted to break into her New Jersey home; the judge put him on five years' probation. While David Letterman was on the West Coast, a mentally ill woman who claimed to be his wife installed herself in his East Coast home (Fowles 310).

The media can also invade the privacy of a star. Interviews may seem endless and prove to be very draining. The press tends to emphasize personal questions that make the subject of an interview understandably uncomfortable. Magazines such as *The National Enquirer* strive to create rumors about different stars, often relying on questionable sources and rumors that later prove to be unfounded. A personal problem that any of us could easily encounter and that most of us would like to face in privacy frequently ends up on the front pages of newspapers, creating stress and embarrassment for the celebrity and threatening his or her career.

Even if their lives do not fit within stereotypes, stars are not people who lead normal lives. Celebrities are widely admired and often receive considerable money for their work, yet they must face situations that the general public does not fully understand. Stars face danger; give up their privacy; and work long, hard hours. Referring to celebrities as "stars" is quite appropriate because their lives are as far from ours as the stars are distant from the ground we stand on.

Works Cited

Braudy, Leo. *Frenzy of Renown: Fame and Its History.* New York: Oxford UP, 1986.

Fowles, Jib. *Starstruck.* Chicago: Smithsonian, 1992.

Lane, Yoti. *The Psychology of the Actor.* Westport, CT: Greenwood, 1959.

L'Heureux, Lori. Survey. November 7–10, 1993.

MARIE WINN

MARIE WINN was born in Czechoslovakia, and emigrated with her family to the United States, where she attended the New York City schools. She graduated from Radcliffe College and also attended Columbia University. Winn has written eleven books, all of them about children, and has been a frequent contributor to *The New York Times*, the *Wall Street Journal* and various other newspapers and periodicals. Her most recent books are *Children Without Childhood* (1983) and *Unplugging the Plug-In Drug* (1987).

Television Addiction

"Television Addiction" is the title of a chapter in Marie Winn's highly regarded book *The Plug-In Drug* (1977), and our selection is an excerpt from that chapter. It will be seen that a careful definition of the term *addiction*, and a careful application of it to TV viewing, particularly by the young, is of utmost importance to the author's main point, as indicated by the book's title. The selection is a fairly typical use of extended definition.

The word "addiction" is often used loosely and wryly in conversation. People will refer to themselves as "mystery book addicts" or "cookie addicts." E. B. White writes of his annual surge of interest in gardening: "We are hooked and are making an attempt to kick the habit." Yet nobody really believes that reading mysteries or ordering seeds by catalogue is serious enough to be compared with addictions to heroin or alcohol. The word "addiction" is here used jokingly to denote a tendency to overindulge in some pleasurable activity.

People often refer to being "hooked on TV." Does this, too, fall into the lighthearted category of cookie eating and other pleasures that people pursue with unusual intensity, or is there a kind of television viewing that falls into the more serious category of destructive addiction?

When we think about addiction to drugs or alcohol, we frequently focus on negative aspects, ignoring the pleasures that accompany drinking or drug-taking. And yet the essence of any serious addiction is a pursuit of pleasure, a search for a "high" that normal life does not supply. It is only the inability to function without the addictive substance that is dismaying, the dependence of the organism upon a certain experience and an increasing inability to function normally without it. Thus a person will take two or three drinks at the end of the day not merely for the pleasure drinking provides, but also because he "doesn't feel normal" without them.

An addict does not merely pursue a pleasurable experience and need to experience it in order to function normally. He needs to *repeat* it again and again. Something about that particular experience makes life without it less than complete. Other potentially pleasurable experiences are no longer possible, for under the spell of the addictive experience, his life is peculiarly distorted. The addict craves an experience and yet he is never really satisfied. The organism may be temporarily sated, but soon it begins to crave again.

Finally a serious addiction is distinguished from a harmless pursuit of pleasure by its distinctly destructive elements. A heroin addict, for instance, leads a damaged life: his increasing need for heroin in increasing doses prevents him from working, from maintaining relationships, from developing in human ways. Similarly an alcoholic's life is narrowed and dehumanized by his dependence on alcohol.

Let us consider television viewing in the light of the conditions that define serious addictions.

Not unlike drugs or alcohol, the television experience allows the participant to blot out the real world and enter into a pleasurable and passive mental state. The worries and anxieties of reality are as effectively deferred by becoming absorbed in a television program as by going on a "trip" induced by drugs or alcohol. And just as alcoholics are only inchoately aware of their addiction, feeling that they control their drinking more than they really do ("I can cut it out any time I want—I just like to have three or four drinks before dinner"), people similarly overestimate their control over television watching. Even as they put off other activities to spend hour after hour watching television, they feel they could easily resume living in a different, less passive style. But somehow or other while the television set is present in their homes, the click doesn't sound. With television pleasures available, those other experiences seem less attractive, more difficult somehow.

A heavy viewer (a college English instructor) observes: 8

"I find television almost irresistible. When the set is on, I cannot   9 ignore it. I can't turn it off. I feel sapped, will-less, enervated. As I reach out to turn off the set, the strength goes out of my arms. So I sit there for hours and hours."

The self-confessed television addict often feels he "ought" to   10 do other things—but the fact that he doesn't read and doesn't plant his garden or sew or crochet or play games or have conversations means that those activities are no longer as desirable as television viewing. In a way a heavy viewer's life is as imbalanced by his television "habit" as a drug addict's or an alcoholic's. He is living in a holding pattern, as it were, passing up the activities that lead to growth or development or a sense of accomplishment. This is one reason people talk about their television viewing so ruefully, so apologetically. They are aware that it is an unproductive experience, that almost any other endeavor is more worthwhile by any human measure.

Finally it is the adverse effect of television viewing on the   11 lives of so many people that defines it as a serious addiction. The television habit distorts the sense of time. It renders other experiences vague and curiously unreal while taking on a greater reality for itself. It weakens relationships by reducing and sometimes eliminating normal opportunities for talking, for communicating.

And yet television does not satisfy, else why would the viewer   12 continue to watch hour after hour, day after day? "The measure of health," writes Lawrence Kubie, "is flexibility . . . and especially the freedom to cease when sated."[1] But the television viewer can never be sated with his television experiences—they do not provide the true nourishment that satiation requires—and thus he finds that he cannot stop watching.

[1]Lawrence Kubie, *Neurotic Distortion and the Creative Process* (Lawrence: University of Kansas Press, 1958).

Meanings and Values

1. Would you classify this as formal or informal writing? Why? (See "Guide to Terms": *Essay*.)

2. Is it primarily objective or subjective? Why? (Guide: *Objective/ Subjective*.)

3. Using our three-question method, evaluate this selection, giving particular attention to the third question. (Guide: *Evaluation*.)

4a. What do you think would be Winn's reply to the assertion that television is such an important element in contemporary culture that time spent watching it is seldom wasted?

b. Do you think you would agree with her answer? Explain.

Expository Techniques

1a. What is the first technique of definition used in this selection? Where is it used?

b. Why is it important to get this aspect of the subject over first?

2a. Which paragraphs are devoted to an enumeration of the characteristics of addiction?

b. What are the characteristics of addiction, according to the author?

3a. What major pattern of exposition does the latter half of the selection utilize?

b. How important is definition of the term prior to this development? Why?

c. Would it have been better if the author had presented a more orderly, point-by-point discussion of this latter material? Why, or why not?

Diction and Vocabulary

1a. Is there anything distinctive about Winn's diction, as demonstrated in this piece? (Guide: *Diction*.) (You may wish to compare it with that of Wolfe in Section 4.)

b. Does your answer to question 1a indicate that Winn's style is inferior in some way? Explain.

2. Use the dictionary as necessary to understand the meanings of the following words: wryly (par. 1); organism (3); sated (4); inchoately (7); enervated (9).

Suggestions for Writing and Discussion

1. Even assuming that a person has a terrible TV habit, what does it really matter (to the person or to others) whether the habit qualifies as an addiction?

2. What other pastimes can you think of that fit, or nearly fit, Winn's criteria for addiction? Do they have any redeeming qualities that TV viewing does not offer?

3. Why do people often worry about the amount of time spent watching TV but seldom about the amount of time spent reading books or magazines? Explain.

(NOTE: Suggestions for topics requiring development by use of DEFINITION are on page 360, at the end of this section.)

ROGER WELSCH

ROGER WELSCH was a professor of English and anthropology at the University of Nebraska-Lincoln when he decided to move to a small tree farm in the central Plains. Since then he has made a living as a writer and television and radio columnist and has begun his "rural education." His essays on rural life have been collected in *It's Not the End of the Earth but You Can See It from Here: Tales of the Great Plains* (1990) and he writes a regular column for *Natural History* magazine. His other books include *Treasury of Nebraska Pioneer Folklore* (1966); *Shingling the Fog and Other Plains Lies* (1980); *Mister, You Got Yourself a Horse: Tales of Old-Time Horse Trading* (1981); *Omaha Tribal Myths and Trickster Tales* (1981); *Touching the Fire* (1992); and *Cather's Kitchens: Foodways in Literature and Life* (1987) and *Catfish at the Pump: Humor and the Frontier* (1987) (both with Linda K. Welsch).

Gypsies

As the title suggests, this essay offers a definition of a group of people rather than a term or concept. In addition, one of Welsch's tasks is to redefine a group whose reputation over the centuries has often been less than positive.

I was once talking with a Lakota wise man, Richard Fool Bull, wondering at his ability to sense what seemed to me to be mystic occurrences. Magic things seemed to happen to him fairly regularly. A hundred years ago they would have been called "visions" by the Indians. A thousand years ago they would have been called "miracles" even in our culture, but Mr. Fool Bull accepted them as a normal part of life. 1

"They *are* a normal part of life," he laughed when I expressed my amazement. "They happen all the time." 2

"To you maybe, Mr. Fool Bull, but not to me."   3

"Oh yes, to you too," he said, nodding seriously. "That is the   4
sad thing about white culture. You see, Roger, it is not a matter of me
being trained to see such things; *you* have been trained not to see
them."

That's not a new idea. In anthropology classes it is a common   5
teaching trick, for example, to tell students that there are still peoples
of this world who do not know the connection between sexual
intercourse and pregnancy. That usually excites astonishment in
the class—how can anyone not understand a cause-and-effect that
obvious?

The professor lets the students throw around their obvious cul-   6
tural superiority for a few minutes and then asks, "What is the result
of eating asparagus?" It is rare that anyone responds with a serious
response. "Your urine smells to high heaven for a couple of hours,
that's what. Now, why is it you think these people are so stupid
because they have not realized an association that spans nine
months while you have never figured out a very obvious cause-and-
effect relationship that takes place over only a few minutes?" The
fact of the matter is, very obvious things, most not at all mystical,
happen around us all the time and we manage to remain totally
oblivious to them.

I enjoy the regular—every few months or so—articles that   7
appear in the Omaha or Rising City newspapers that run pretty
much along these lines:

The Bleaker County Savings and Loan lost an estimated $900 in an unusual
fraud perpetrated against teller Judy Hockworthy last Thursday. According
to Ms. Hockworthy six or seven swarthy people—probably Indians or Iranians—came in to the office at 48th and Caldwell Streets looking for change
for the parking meter and a fifty-dollar bill with an L in the serial number.

Ms. Hockworthy reported that the men spoke broken English and the
women were dressed in loose, colorful clothing. The men had seventeen
one-hundred-dollar bills for which they wanted the change for the parking
meter and the fifty-dollar bills.

After several changes of the bills, the alleged defrauders left the office and
drove away in late-model pickup trucks, all with campers on the beds and
all with Illinois license plates.

The police have no suspects.

I love those stories. For one thing, I think it's wonderful that   8
these skilled con men get away with what they do in large part
because they have plenty of money in their hands when they enter

the bank. The thesis in our society, evidently, is, "Anyone who has lots of money is obviously to be trusted" when every indication should tell us exactly the opposite.

But there is a deeper, philosophical reason for my affection for these enduring, widespread petty bilkers. You see, I like coyotes. I don't care if coyotes take 15 percent of the lambs and calves on western ranges. To me coyotes represent something very important—that creatures under the pressure of full warfare can survive. Out here coyotes are hunted with high-power rifles, traps, exploding baits, poison, airplanes, calls, chumming, and mobs. And yet survive. They *prosper!* That prospect gives coyotes like me a lot of hope, you see.

Well, newspaper stories like that are about human coyotes, I guess. Gypsies. That's who those "Indians or Iranians" are, Gypsies. Through a thousand years of resistance, through wars and contempt and murder and expulsion, the Gypsies survive. Before Hitler murdered the Jews, he murdered the Gypsies.

And yet here they are, still with us, and so skillfully concealed that most Americans haven't the foggiest notion they are still here.

Before I forget, let me tell you what happened in Germany. The Gypsies were almost totally eradicated in Germany, and do you know what happened after the Second World War? The Gypsies *swarmed* into Germany. Where would they be safer than where they had only a few years before been pariahs? They could still be hated in England or Sweden, but not in Germany. Gypsy caravans parked illegally under Autobahn overpasses and in department-store parking lots because the gypsies knew that here, where they had been most abused, now they would be most tolerated.

I admired especially the ones camped illegally under the overpasses. Can you imagine a better place to set up camp? Families sat at picnic tables and enjoyed supper even when it was raining like crazy or when the sun was blazing, peacefully watching the traffic whiz by. Overpass railings were festooned with wet laundry, a kind of Gypsy flag of resistance.

Gypsies are still visible throughout Europe, where their distinctive clothing and wagons and a long tradition make them easily recognized by the citizens of the countries they travel. In America Gypsies are almost invisible. Americans see them not as "Gypsies" but "slightly peculiar, dark people—maybe Iranians or Indians." The average American perceives their pickup trucks with inevitable camper toppers and "For Sale" signs as something strange—but almost never as "Gypsies"!

What I love about American Gypsies is that they are seen only rarely, and then briefly, like comets. I, for one, feel graced when I have the chance to see them, even if only in passing on the highway.

Fremont, Nebraska, used to be a popular place for Gypsies to stop and for all I know may still be. It is on Highway 30, the Lincoln Highway, and that was the main artery for cross-country travel for many years. For the still nomadic Gypsies, the long, open stretches of the Lincoln Highway must have been like a hometown. And Fremont is about halfway across America, so it was a logical meeting and resting place for the eternal travelers.

As a boy I once read a newspaper report of a time when two rival Gypsy bands wound up at a Gypsy cemetery in Fremont at the same time—both paying respect, as I recall, to the hallowed memory of the same patriarch of the tribe. The result was memorable. My recollection is that something like four hundred shots were fired, and when the police finally sorted things out after the pitched battle, they amassed a huge pile of knives, clubs, guns, brass knuckles, and other weapons of choice.

Now, I am not a violent guy and you probably wonder what possible saving grace I could deduce from a violent encounter like that. Well, what I found *glorious* about it was that not a single person was hurt. It was all posturing, maneuvering, threatening, and bluster. Coyotes at play.

I've spoken with quite a few people in Fremont about the Gypsies in the old days, and there are a lot of stories. The Gypsies often asked to camp at farms and farmers would usually give them permission in order to avoid later retribution, but they made sure the chickens and children were put to bed early and the mother and father stayed up late to keep an eye on things.

Older farm women who remember when Gypsies would camp near their farmsteads tell me that the Gypsy women and children would often come to the house asking for eggs or milk and they were usually given those simple things. Later inspection revealed that the next day tools, cooking utensils, dogs, and even horses or cows showed up missing—or perhaps I should say didn't show up missing.

Today, savvy merchants close up the store the minute they hear that the Gypsies are in town. For those too slow or inexperienced to close up shop, the experience is usually that ten or twelve women with voluminous clothing sweep into the store and scatter throughout the aisles. Merchandise disappears within the ample folds of the clothing. The ensuing shouting, arguing, and linguistic confusion makes it impossible for the merchant, security, or even the police to sort out one woman from another, let alone retrieve pilfered goods, and the inventory is shot to hell for the rest of the year.

All except the new car and truck dealers. They love to see the   22
Gypsies come to town. The Gypsies frequently buy new vehicles in Fremont, and their mode of operation is always the same. They come onto the lot, point to the vehicle they want, ask how much it is, and without any haggling whatsoever pay the price in cash.

Now, I know what's going to happen when folks read this.   23
Latter-day Gypsies are going to say that I have slandered their people, that Gypsies never steal, that all the stories are fictions, that Gypsies actually travel around the world doing good deeds wherever they can. Well, anyone who tries to sell that sort of nonsense does the Gypsies a gross disservice. By lying about their people, they deny their heritage. I have no sympathy for people like that. Just as surely as Gypsies have leavened the cultural loaf of western civilization with their music, art, and food, they have enriched us all with their irrepressible resistance to change, their thousands of years of resistance to authority and order not their own.

There will be non-Gypsies who say I am a real jerk for suggest-   24
ing that common thievery is anything but common thievery and the Gypsies should learn to behave like Americans if they intend to live in this glorious land of the free, home of the brave. They should learn that nothing is more rewarding than money earned by the sweat of your brow—sort of like Ivan Boesky or Donald Trump or Don King, I guess. No, the Gypsies offer another alternative—survival by wit.

I don't condone cheating and thievery normally, but in the case   25
of the Gypsies it is a cultural inheritance and its cleverness makes me glad to be a member of the same species as the Gypsies.

I used to think that one of the things I wanted to do in my life   26
was to spend an afternoon or evening in a Gypsy camp. My fantasy was that I would spot a bunch of Gypsy pickup trucks in a small park some day, somewhere on the Plains—I know what to look for, after all. I imagined that what I would do on that occasion is walk into the camp with a couple of chickens and maybe a battered banjo

I wouldn't mind losing over my shoulder. That way I could trade the chickens for something to eat—something *Gypsy*—and play my banjo in exchange for some of their legendary music.

Unfortunately, the closest I have come to realizing that fantasy is one time when some friends and I stopped for a picnic lunch in a public parking place at a large park in South Dakota. We were eating and I was eyeing ten or twelve pickup campers on the other side of the parking lot. I suspected they might be Gypsies.

As we were eating, two five- or six-year-old children approached us from the direction of the trucks. They were beautiful children—dark-skinned with enormous, black eyes. Obviously they were Gypsies. "Would you like a cookie?" I asked them.

They nodded yes.

I held out the sack, but to my surprise they backed away a couple steps. No, they explained, they would not take the cookies as a gift. They would accept them only if they could buy them from me.

Hummm. Maybe these weren't Gypsies. Gypsies steal, I thought. They don't *buy*. I was put mentally off balance.

"How much you want for the cookies, Mister?" one of the children asked.

These were great big chocolate chip cookies, and I had a big bag of about sixty or seventy of them; they had cost me maybe eight dollars early that morning at the grocery store. "Tell you what, young man," I said. "How about a penny. Will you pay a penny for a cookie this big?"

He smiled and nodded yes, and I felt like a real prince for being such a nice guy with these kids. And I felt like a real dope for all the things I had said in the past about Gypsies being—how shall I say it?—shrewd operators.

The little boy handed me a penny, and I gave him a cookie. His little friend handed me a penny, and I gave him a cookie too. Gosh, what a pleasant little vignette, I thought.

Then suddenly, out of nowhere, I was surrounded by eighty little children, all with pennies, all wanting cookies. So we wound up selling our entire supper, all of it—cookies, sandwiches, candy bars, chips, everything, for something like eighty-five cents!

These folks were Gypsies, all right—kids and all. I had been had, but good. I had fallen for exactly the routine I had watched other people fall for for decades—my junior deceivers had confused me with their impressive wealth, they had let me believe that I was being the clever party to the exchange, they had come at me from a direction I would have never thought of looking into, and when it was all over, I still wasn't sure what had happened to me, how much I had lost, how it had ever developed, why I had been such a dope.

And I loved it. Every minute of it. I have savored the moment 38 over and over for these twenty years now. Outwitted by the Gypsies, I was, and not just by Gypsies but by two five-year-old Gypsies.

I still keep an old banjo around the house, and a few chickens, 39 just in case.

Meanings and Values

1. In your own words, summarize Welsch's attitudes towards Gypsies.

2. How would you characterize the tone of this essay? (See "Guide to Terms": *Style/Tone*.)

3. How would you characterize the purpose of this essay? (Guide: *Purpose*.)

4. Estimate the importance of tone in helping the essay achieve its purpose.

Expository Techniques

1. Tell where the essay makes use of each of the following definition techniques:

   a. background

   b. negation

   c. enumeration

   d. analogy

2. Welsch mentions other definitions of Gypsies as part of his attempt to redefine the group and change readers' attitudes. Where does he mention these other definitions and what are they?

3a. At first, paragraphs 1–7 may appear to be only loosely related to the rest of the essay. Discuss whether they contribute to or undermine the unity of the selection. (Guide: *Unity*.)

   b. How, if at all, can these paragraphs be considered part of an effective introduction?

4. What is the central theme of this essay, and in what ways is it communicated to readers?

5.   Which examples in the body of the essay are most successful in creat-
      ing admiration (or at least respect) for Gypsies? Which are least suc-
      cessful? Why? (Guide: *Evaluation*.)

Diction and Vocabulary

1.   Study the word choice in paragraphs 10 and 13 and explain how
      Welsch uses it to invite sympathy and admiration for his subjects.
      Pay special attention to repetition and to the connotation of words.
      (Guide: *Connotation/Denotation*.)

2a.   What are the synonyms Welsch offers in paragraphs 1–6 for the phe-
      nomenon he refers to first as "mystic occurrences"?

 b.   Offer a definition of the phenomenon yourself using any of the defi-
      nition strategies discussed in the introduction to Section 7.

3.   If you do not know the meaning of any of the following words, look
      them up in a dictionary: bilkers (par. 9); festooned (13); patriarch,
      amassed (17); posturing (18); retribution (19); vignette (35).

Suggestions for Writing and Discussion

1.   Try to think of any other group (or practices) that might be defended
      in a manner similar to the way Welsch defends Gypsies. List the
      kinds of things you might cover in an essay on the topic.

2.   At several places in the essay, Welsch defends his outlook against
      possible criticisms (see paragraphs 23–25). What other criticisms
      might there be of his outlook in the essay?

(NOTE: Suggestions for topics requiring development by use of DEFINITION are on page
360, at the end of this section.)

RICHARD BEN CRAMER

RICHARD BEN CRAMER was born in 1950 in Rochester, New York. He received a B.A. in 1971 from Johns Hopkins University and an M.S. in 1971 from Columbia University. He worked as a reporter for the *Baltimore Sun* and the *Philadelphia Inquirer,* then as a foreign correspondent in Europe, Africa, and the Middle East. He won several awards for his reporting, including a Pulitzer Prize in 1979. His work has appeared in numerous magazines and periodicals, including the *New York Times, Esquire,* and *Rolling Stone.* His two books are *Ted Williams: The Season of the Kid* (1991) and *What It Takes: The Way to the White House* (1992).

Know Your Way Home

In this essay, which was first published in *Esquire* in October of 1993, Cramer explores some of the meanings of *home,* a word that for most of us is rich in personal and cultural associations. Cramer, however, looks at some of the meanings it has for people from the Baby Boom generation. Not every Baby Boomer will agree with Cramer's definitions, of course, and people from other generations (or backgrounds) may even look at them as mistaken paths that others would do well to avoid.

In England, recently, I learned the real definition of *parochial.* A law 1 in the time of Elizabeth I restricted you to your own parish. If you did leave, and ran into trouble elsewhere, you were literally whipped home: That is to say, the beadles of each parish between you and your place of birth would flog you through their territory, then hand you over at the boundary to the lash-bearing beadles of the neighboring parish . . . until you were, safely (for them), back in your slot.

I suspect it was success in colonial America (and, perhaps, in 2 other sparsely peopled adventurelands) that spawned the idea of picking your own home—searching it out, as conviction or economy required. It was certainly Americans who turned this innovation into a way of life, first as frontier farmers and ranchers, later as industrial cowpokes—followin' them fact'ry dogies where they roamed.

But it was only our own post-war generation (with the meat-ax 3 of sharper American success) that cleaved altogether the ideas of Necessity and Home. Now we *selected* our hometown (wasn't that our right?) . . . off a menu as wide as the world. Maybe we talked about a job there (not that there weren't jobs elsewhere)—but it was really about a friend there, or some girl who was nice to us in a bar . . . the weather, the way the mountains looked . . . the college community gave it such "tone" . . . or it made us feel cool to say we lived there. We were operating so far from our forebears' experience that we had to make up lame-brained words like *lifestyle*. Now everybody had to (you know, uh, like) . . . *find his own space!*

We got to the point—with our Boogie boards on the crest of the 4 potent baby-boom wave—we thought we could surf over Home, completely. If Home was supposed to be wherever we chose to make it . . . well, it was only a small step (and self-regard required it) to say that wherever we were was Home.

We were arrived upon a glorious age: The world was our 5 oyster . . . not necessarily to be eaten (though, God knows, we've tried) . . . but we were raised to the conviction that wherever we— we favored grains of sand—lodge our grit, there we become pearls.

And in this all-freedom all-power, I was Homeless. 6

I don't mean I slept on a steam grate. I had apartments, I had 7 houses—splendid places, too. By age twenty, at college, I had an old Maryland farmhouse (with acreage!) that would have contented any settler through most of America's history.

Me, I graduated and moved on. Settling was definitely *not* the 8 point—it smacked of *settling for*, second-best. It never occurred to me to move back to where I was born. My friends had scattered. That was my parents' home . . . anyway, what about that oyster world? Home was something dorks like Glen Campbell moaned about. We all lived in a yellow submarine. I made a bet with one girl: The first of us to have two out of the following three—kid, insurance, mortgage—would have to buy the other a sailboat. I knew she'd welsh.

I picked a job that would keep me on the move. Newspapering 9 was about impermanence. You'd never have two workdays the same. The stories would carry you all over the world. I started in Baltimore (two apartments, one house) and Annapolis (a hundred hotel rooms); then Philadelphia (an apartment); New York (one apartment, a storage box); Cairo (an office apartment); London (one flat I barely saw); Rome (*un attico*). By that time, I didn't even say I had a home. I had a bureau. In fact, by Boogie-board all-power, I was the bureau . . . until I was out of the newspaper business, and I had to decide where to live.

This was a new concept. Of course, I'd always said I lived some- 10
where. I lived in Cairo . . . it made me feel cool to say so. But I didn't really live anywhere, except in the stories—everywhere at once. Now I was supposed to pick a home—for me. There wasn't even much for me to consult. So I did what any sensible man of my age did. I decided I'd live . . . wherever my girlfriend wanted.

I haven't mentioned the girlfriend. She was the reason I came 11
back from Rome, and the reason I was faced with this crisis of all-freedom, this question of self, of Home. Not that she was much threat to saddle me with a domestic establishment. This girl didn't even own a skillet.

But a strong decorating sense she had. So we moved to New 12
York, to a place that was strong on decoration. It was what the French call *mignon*—though at the time, I didn't know that word. For example, the bedroom window looked out on a patio with lights that shone aloft through plants from underneath the wooden deck—you could see this semi-Polynesian effect (we called it Hawaii) *from the bed* . . . which was a decorating coup, as there was no room to be off the bed, and you couldn't go out to the patio because it was really someone's roof and couldn't take the weight of an actual human. Another example: The living room (which was pretty much the only real room) had a curved wall. This softening of standard form was a decorating coup . . . insofar as it softened (in fact, disguised past the start of the lease) the hard fact that much of this living room had been eaten away for the closet and bath. I also learned there that mirrors are a decorating-coup substitute for light and space. This living room had mirrors. In fact, when I paced it off—continuously for a year—it was the size of an upmarket Japanese car. I think it was in that place I first said, "I want a home." Understandably, the girlfriend did not react. I talked to myself quite a bit that year.

Or it may have been in our second place in New York—it was 13
bigger, I picked it—I started talking about Home. I brought the word

up with the landlord, an Israeli gent . . . in summer, urging him to scrape the rime off the windows . . . in winter, I suggested the place would be better with heat. "Eli, don't you understand?" I'd wail into the phone. "This is my home!" His reply was concision itself *"I get tsuris, yourrent guzzup."* So I'd transfer wailing to the girlfriend: "I want a home!"

"What's this?" she'd say.   14

"Tsuris."   15

But Eli had a point—it wasn't my home. He knew, as well as I   16
did: I'd be gone before the bum who slept in the downstairs doorway. The fact was, the girlfriend and I had no more home than the
bum. And no idea what Home was: We kept getting it confused with
the best place to live.

"How about Paris?" the girlfriend would say. (She thought   17
Paris had the strongest decorating sense.)

"How 'bout Moscow?" (I still had a lingering confusion   18
between Home and story.)

Said the girlfriend: "Get a life."   19

I got a book—which maintained the confusion for six years   20
more. We moved around, hauling the book. The girlfriend came
along to edit and argue.

"I want a home."   21

"Shut up. Finish the book."   22

We married, had a child. I finished the book. We had to decide   23
where to live. The wife announced: "Paris."

"Yes, dear." (Strangely, it turned out, at the end of six years'   24
labor, I owed.)

She leased an apartment on the basis of a snapshot that showed   25
a gilded mirror. I contracted to pay for this decorating coup by
working in Paris for a sixty-year-old magazine. We called movers—
we had skillets now, furniture, a million books, and (by the movers'
count) three million four hundred twenty-two thousand articles for
child care and entertainment. Those I carried to Paris.

That was January—when I learned the word *mignon*. It means   26
cute. Our apartment was *mignon*. The living room (pretty much—
well, you get the idea. . .) featured that gilded mirror because there
was no light or space. In fact, when I paced it off . . . well, I couldn't,
because of a Lego castle and a Brio train set. But I knew what to do.

I got an airline ticket to America. After two days in the country, 27
I bought an old farmhouse, with acreage, in Maryland. I took some

photos—I hoped they'd display potential for strong decoration. Then I got back on the airplane, to show the photos to the wife. I said: "This is home."

"What?" 28

"Home." 29

And when our year in Paris has passed, we'll go back there— 30
Home. Our place. We'll stay. We won't have any choice. After twenty-two years of patient work, I have acquired one-tenth the acreage I had in college, at one hundred times the price. In fact, by my calculation, if I continue working for the sixty-year-old magazine, I will fully own this house three years after my death.

I don't mind. I look at all those zeros on my mortgage as chain- 31
like between the noble ideas of Necessity and Home.

I tell my wife: We'll still travel. . . . Hey! The world is our oys- 32
ter! But I've no doubt, if we do leave, for work, for wanderlust—somehow, soon . . . life will whip us home.

Meanings and Values

1a. What specific terms or concepts does the writer define in this essay?

 b. In what ways are these terms or concepts related to each other?

2. Explain what each of the following phrases means:

 a. "safely . . . back in your slot" (par. 1)

 b. "We got to the point—with our Boogie boards on the crest of the potent baby-boom wave—we thought we could surf over Home, completely." (par. 4)

 c. ". . . I was the bureau. . . ." (par. 9)

 d. "I got a book—which maintained the confusion for six years more." (par. 20)

 e. "I look at all those zeros on my mortgage as chainlike between the noble ideas of Necessity and Home." (par. 31)

3a. What incorrect or mistaken definitions of *home* does the writer offer in the course of this selection? What definition or definitions, if any, does he want readers to accept as correct or appropriate?

 b. What strategies are used in the selection to identify correct and incorrect definitions?

Expository Techniques

1a. This essay is arranged in part as a story, or narrative (see Section 9). In what ways can its primary pattern be considered one of definition despite the presence of narrative elements? Be sure to support your answer with specific evidence from the text.

b. What definitions strategies does the essay employ? (See Introduction: *Definition*.)

2. Discuss how the following short paragraphs act as transitions: 6, 19, and 23. (See *"Guide to Terms"*: Transitions.)

3a. The first sentence of paragraph 3 states an idea that is discussed at length in the rest of the essay. Tell how this statement and the idea it presents are related to the essay's central theme. (Guide: *Unity*.)

b. What role does this sentence play in helping readers recognize the selection's purpose and in unifying the essay? (Guide: *Purpose, Unity*.)

Diction and Vocabulary

1a. At many places in the essay, the writer mixes informal and formal language. Identify examples of slang, colloquial language, and formal language in paragraphs 2, 4, and 13. (Guide: *Colloquial Expressions*.)

b. For each paragraph, discuss the writer's apparent purposes for mixing the levels of language and explain why you find the mixture effective or ineffective. (Guide: *Evaluation*.)

2. Point out any foreign terms used in the essay. Tell what impression of the writer they create and how most readers are likely to react to their presence.

3a. Identify the metaphor in paragraph 5 and discuss its meaning. (Guide: *Figures of Speech*.)

b. Where else in the selection does the metaphor appear? Tell how it helps unify the piece. (Guide: *Unity*.)

4. If you do not know the meaning of some of the following terms, look them up in a dictionary: beadles (par. 1); cleaved (3); coup (25); wanderlust (32).

Suggestions for Writing and Discussion

1. Discuss your own and your classmates' attitudes towards home, hometowns and neighborhoods, and moving from familiar to unfamiliar places. Look for both agreements and disagreements within the group.

2.   Do the values expressed by this writer from the baby boom genera-
     tion differ from those likely to be expressed by people from other
     generations, either older or younger? What conflicting values, if any,
     characterize the different generations?

(NOTE: Suggestions for topics requiring development by use of DEFINITION are on page
360, at the end of this section.)

KESAYA NODA

KESAYA E. NODA was born in California and raised in rural New Hampshire. She did not learn Japanese until she graduated from high school, but she then spent two years living and studying in Japan. After college, she wrote *The Yamato Colony*, based on her research into the history of the California community to which her grandparents came as immigrants and in which her parents were raised. Following this, she worked and traveled in Japan for another year. Noda earned a master's degree from the Harvard Divinity School. She now teaches at Lesley College in Cambridge, Massachusetts.

Growing Up Asian in America

The act of definition in this essay is one of self-definition, both of an individual and, by implication, of a cultural group. This complex task is accomplished in an especially clear manner. In reading, pay attention to the different kinds of expository patterns Noda employs, including comparison and narration. Note, too, how clearly she makes the different pieces of the essay fit together.

Sometimes when I was growing up, my identity seemed to hurtle   1
toward me and paste itself right to my face. I felt that way, encountering the stereotypes of my race perpetuated by non-Japanese people (primarily white) who may or may not have had contact with other Japanese in America. "You don't like cheese, do you?" someone would ask. "I know your people don't like cheese." Sometimes questions came making allusions to history. That was another aspect of the identity. Events that had happened quite apart from the me who stood silent in that moment connected my face with an incomprehensible past. "Your parents were in California? Were they

in those camps during the war?" And sometimes there were phrases or nicknames: "Lotus Blossom." I was sometimes addressed or referred to as racially Japanese, sometimes as Japanese American, and sometimes as an Asian woman. Confusions and distortions abounded.

How is one to know and define oneself? From the inside—within a context that is self defined, from a grounding in community and a connection with culture and history that are comfortably accepted? Or from the outside—in terms of messages received from the media and people who are often ignorant? Even as an adult I can still see two sides of my face and past. I can see from the inside out, in freedom. And I can see from the outside in, driven by the old voices of childhood and lost in anger and fear.

I Am Racially Japanese

A voice from my childhood says: "You are other. You are less than. You are unalterably alien." This voice has its own history. We have indeed been seen as other and alien since the early years of our arrival in the United States. The very first immigrants were welcomed and sought as laborers to replace the dwindling numbers of Chinese, whose influx had been cut off by the Chinese Exclusion Act of 1882. The Japanese fell natural heir to the same anti-Asian prejudice that had arisen against the Chinese. As soon as they began striking for better wages, they were no longer welcomed.

I can see myself today as a person historically defined by law and custom as being forever alien. Being neither "free white," nor "African," our people in California were deemed "aliens, ineligible for citizenship," no matter how long they intended to stay here. Aliens ineligible for citizenship were prohibited from owning, buying, or leasing land. They did not and could not belong here. The voice in me remembers that I am always a *Japanese* American in the eyes of many. A third-generation German American is an American. A third-generation Japanese American is a Japanese American. Being Japanese means being a danger to the country during the war and knowing how to use chopsticks. I wear this history on my face.

I move to the other side. I see a different light and claim a different context. My race is a line that stretches across ocean and time to link me to the shrine where my grandmother was raised. Two high, white banners lift in the wind at the top of the stone steps leading to the shrine. It is time for the summer festival. Black characters are written against the sky as boldly as the clouds, as lightly as kites, as sharply as the big black crows I used to see above the fields in New Hampshire. At festival time there is liquor and food, ritual, discipline, and abandonment. There is music and drunkenness and invocation. There is hope. Another season has come. Another season has gone.

I am racially Japanese. I have a certain claim to this crazy place   6
where the prayers intoned by a neighboring Shinto priest (standing in for my grandmother's nephew who is sick) are drowned out by the rehearsals for the pop singing contest in which most of the villagers will compete later that night. The village elders, the priest, and I stand respectfully upon the immaculate, shining wooden floor of the outer shrine, bowing our heads before the hidden powers. During the patchy intervals when I can hear him, I notice the priest has a stutter. His voice flutters up to my ears only occasionally because two men and a woman are singing gustily into a microphone in the compound, testing the sound system. A prerecorded tape of guitars, samisens, and drums accompanies them. Rock music and Shinto prayers. That night, to loud applause and cheers, a young man is given the award for the most *netsuretsu*—passionate, burning—rendition of a song. We roar our approval of the reward. Never mind that his voice had wandered and slid, now slightly above, now slightly below the given line of the melody. Netsuretsu. Netsuretsu.

In the morning, my grandmother's sister kneels at the foot of   7
the stone stairs to offer her morning prayers. She is too crippled to climb the stairs, so each morning she kneels here upon the path. She shuts her eyes for a few seconds, her motions as matter of fact as when she washes rice. I linger longer than she does, so reluctant to leave, savoring the connection I feel with my grandmother in America, the past, and the power that lives and shines in the morning sun.

Our family has served this shrine for generations. The family's   8
need to protect this claim to identity and place outweighs any individual claim to any individual hope. I am Japanese.

I Am a Japanese American

"Weak." I hear the voice from my childhood years. "Passive," I hear.   9
Our parents and grandparents were the ones who were put into

those camps. They went without resistance; they offered cooperation as proof of loyalty to America. "Victim," I hear. And, "Silent."

Our parents are painted as hard workers who were socially uncomfortable and had difficulty expressing even the smallest opinion. Clean, quiet, motivated, and determined to match the American way; that is us, and that is the story of our time here.

"Why did you go into those camps," I raged at my parents, frightened by my own inner silence and timidity. "Why didn't you do anything to resist? Why didn't you name it the injustice it was?" Couldn't our parents even think? Couldn't they? Why were we so passive?

I shift my vision and my stance. I am in California. My uncle is in the midst of the sweet potato harvest. He is pressed, trying to get the harvesting crews onto the field as quickly as possible, worried about the flow of equipment and people. His big pickup is pulled off to the side, motor running, door ajar. I see two tractors in the yard in front of an old shed; the flat bed harvesting platform on which the workers will stand has already been brought over from the other field. It's early morning. The workers stand loosely grouped and at ease, but my uncle looks as harried and tense as a police officer trying to unsnarl a New York City traffic jam. Driving toward the shed, I pull my car off the road to make way for an approaching tractor. The front wheels of the car sink luxuriously into the soft, white sand by the roadside and the car slides to a dreamy halt, tail still on the road. I try to move forward. I try to move back. The front bites contentedly into the sand, the back lifts itself at a jaunty angle. My uncle sees me and storms down the road, running. He is shouting before he is even near me.

"What's the matter with you," he screams. "What the hell are you doing?" In his frenzy, he grabs his hat off his head and slashes it through the air across his knee. He is beside himself. "Don't you know how to drive in sand? What's the matter with you? You've blocked the whole roadway. How am I supposed to get my tractors out of here? Can't you use your head? You've cut off the whole roadway, and we've got to get out of here."

I stand on the road before him helplessly thinking, "No, I don't know how to drive in sand. I've never driven in sand."

"I'm sorry, uncle," I say, burying a smile beneath a look of sincere apology. I notice my deep amusement and my affection for him with great curiosity. I am usually devastated by anger. Not this time.

During the several years that follow I learn about the people 16
and the place, and much more about what has happened in this
California village where my parents grew up. The issei, our grandparents, made this settlement in the desert. Their first crops were
eaten by rabbits and ravaged by insects. The land was so barren that
men walking from house to house sometimes got lost. Women came
here too. They bore children in 114 degree heat, then carried the
babies with them into the fields to nurse when they reached the end
of each row of grapes or other truck farm crops.

I had had no idea what it meant to buy this kind of land and 17
make it grow green. Or how, when the war came, there was no space
at all for the subtlety of being who we were—Japanese Americans.
Either/or was the way. I hadn't understood that people were literally afraid for their lives then, that their money had been frozen in
banks; that there was a five-mile travel limit; that when the early
evening curfew came and they were inside their houses, some of
them watched helplessly as people they knew went into their barns
to steal their belongings. The police were patrolling the road, interested only in violators of curfew. There was no help for them in the
face of thievery. I had not been able to imagine before what it must
have felt like to be an American—to know absolutely that one is an
American—and yet to have almost everyone else deny it. Not only
deny it, but challenge that identity with machine guns and troops of
white American soldiers. In those circumstances it was difficult to
say, "I'm a Japanese American." "American" had to do.

But now I can say that I am a Japanese American. It means I 18
have a place here in this country, too. I have a place here on the East
Coast, where our neighbor is so much a part of our family that my
mother never passes her house at night without glancing at the
lights to see if she is home and safe; where my parents have hauled
hundreds of pounds of rocks from fields and arduously planted
Christmas trees and blueberries, lilacs, asparagus, and crab apples;
where my father still dreams of angling a stream to a new bed so that
he can dig a pond in the field and fill it with water and fish. "The
neighbors already came for their Christmas tree?" he asks in December. "Did they like it? Did they like it?"

I have a place on the West Coast where my relatives still farm, 19
where I heard the stories of feuds and backbiting, and where I saw
that people survived and flourished because fundamentally they
trusted and relied upon one another. A death in the family is not just

a death in a family; it is a death in the community. I saw people help each other with money, materials, labor, attention, and time. I saw men gather once a year, without fail, to clean the grounds of a ninety-year-old woman who had helped the community before, during, and after the war. I saw her remembering them with birthday cards sent to each of their children.

I come from a people with a long memory and a distinctive   20
grace. We live our thanks. And we are Americans. Japanese Americans.

I Am a Japanese American Woman

Woman. The last piece of my identity. It has been easier by far for   21
me to know myself in Japan and to see my place in America than it has been to accept my line of connection with my own mother. She was my dark self, a figure in whom I thought I saw all that I feared most in myself. Growing into womanhood and looking for some model of strength, I turned away from her. Of course, I could not find what I sought. I was looking for a black feminist or a white feminist. My mother is neither white nor black.

My mother is a woman who speaks with her life as much as   22
with her tongue. I think of her with her own mother. Grandmother had Parkinson's disease and it had frozen her gait and set her fingers, tongue, and feet jerking and trembling in a terrible dance. My aunts and uncles wanted her to be able to live in her own home. They fed her, bathed her, dressed her, awoke at midnight to take her for one last trip to the bathroom. My aunts (her daughters-in-law) did most of the care, but my mother went from New Hampshire to California each summer to spend a month living with grandmother, because she wanted to and because she wanted to give my aunts at least a small rest. During those hot summer days, mother lay on the couch watching the television or reading, cooking foods that grandmother liked, and speaking little. Grandmother thrived under her care.

The time finally came when it was too dangerous for grand-   23
mother to live alone. My relatives kept finding her on the floor beside her bed when they went to wake her in the mornings. My mother flew to California to help clean the house and make arrangements for grandmother to enter a local nursing home. On her last day at home, while grandmother was sitting in her big, overstuffed

armchair, hair combed and wearing a green summer dress, my mother went to her and knelt at her feet. "Here, Mamma," she said. "I've polished your shoes." She lifted grandmother's legs and helped her into the shiny black shoes. My grandmother looked down and smiled slightly. She left her house walking, supported by her children, carrying her pocket book, and wearing her polished black shoes. "Look, Mamma," my mom had said, kneeling. "I've polished your shoes."

Just the other day, my mother came to Boston to visit. She had   24
recently lost a lot of weight and was pleased with her new shape and her feeling of good health. "Look at me, Kes," she exclaimed, turning toward me, front and back, as naked as the day she was born. I saw her small breasts and the wide, brown scar, belly button to pubic hair, that marked her because my brother and I were both born by Caesarean section. Her hips were small. I was not a large baby, but there was so little room for me in her that when she was carrying me she could not even begin to bend over toward the floor. She hated it, she said.

"Don't I look good? Don't you think I look good?"   25

I looked at my mother, smiling and as happy as she, thinking of   26
all the times I have seen her naked. I have seen both my parents naked throughout my life, as they have seen me. From childhood through adulthood we've had our naked moments, sharing baths, idle conversations picked up as we moved between showers and closets, hurried moments at the beginning of days, quiet moments at the end of days.

I know this to be Japanese, this ease with the physical, and it   27
makes me think of an old, Japanese folk song. A young nursemaid, a fifteen-year-old girl, is singing a lullaby to a baby who is strapped to her back. The nursemaid has been sent as a servant to a place far from her own home. "We're the beggars," she says, "and they are the nice people. Nice people wear fine sashes. Nice clothes."

> *If I should drop dead,*
> *bury me by the roadside!*
> *I'll give a flower*
> *to everyone who passes.*
>
> *What kind of flower?*
> *The cam-cam-camellia {tsun-tsun-tsubaki}*
> *watered by Heaven:*
> *alms water.*[1]

---

[1]Patia R. Isaku, *Mountain Storm, Pine Breeze: Folk Song in Japan* (Tucson: University of Arizona Press, 1981), 41.

The nursemaid is the intersection of heaven and earth, the intersection of the human, the natural world, the body, and the soul. In this song, with clear eyes, she looks steadily at life, which is sometimes so very terrible and sad. I think of her while looking at my mother, who is standing on the red and purple carpet before me, laughing, without any clothes.

I am my mother's daughter. And I am myself.

I am a Japanese American woman.

Epilogue

I recently heard a man from West Africa share some memories of his childhood. He was raised Muslim, but when he was a young man, he found himself deeply drawn to Christianity. He struggled against this inner impulse for years, trying to avoid the church yet feeling pushed to return to it again and again. "I would have done *anything* to avoid the change," he said. At last, he became Christian. Afterwards he was afraid to go home, fearing that he would not be accepted. The fear was groundless, he discovered, when at last he returned—he had separated himself, but his family and friends (all Muslim) had not separated themselves from him.

The man, who is now a professor of religion, said that in the Africa he knew as a child and a young man, pluralism was embraced rather than feared. There was "a kind of tolerance that did not deny your particularity," he said. He alluded to zestful, spontaneous debates that would sometimes loudly erupt between Muslims and Christians in the village's public spaces. His memories of an atheist who harangued the villagers when he came to visit them once a week moved me deeply. Perhaps the man was an agricultural advisor or inspector. He harassed the women. He would say:

"Don't go to the fields! Don't even bother to go to the fields. Let God take care of you. He'll send you the food. If you believe in God, why do you need to work? You don't need to work! Let God put the seeds in the ground. Stay home."

The professor said, "The women laughed, you know? They just laughed. Their attitude was, 'Here is a child of God. When will he come home?'"

The storyteller, the professor of religion, smiled the most fantastic, tender smile as he told this story. "In my country, there is a deep affirmation of the oneness of God," he said. "The atheist and the women were having quite different experiences in their encounter, though the atheist did not know this. He saw himself as quite separate from the women. But the women did not see themselves as being separate from him. 'Here is a child of God,' they said. 'When will he come home?'"

Meanings and Values

1. Define in your own words each of the identities Noda outlines for herself.

2. How can the last section of the essay, "Epilogue" (pars. 31–34), be said to harmonize these identities or at least to suggest a way of building bridges among them?

3. Discuss how the opening section of this essay (pars. 1–2) explains the author's need to define herself and suggests indirectly that each of us needs to go through a similar process.

Expository Techniques

1a. Apart from definition, what expository technique does Noda use to organize this essay as a whole?

 b. What expository pattern does she employ in paragraphs 3–8?

 c. What pattern does she use in paragraphs 9–20?

 d. What pattern or patterns organize paragraphs 21–28?

 e. What pattern helps conclude the essay in paragraphs 31–34?

2. This essay makes use of a variety of expository patterns. Explain why it is accurate (or inaccurate) to refer to the overall pattern as one of definition. Be ready to defend your answer with evidence from the text.

3a. Tell how paragraph 2 helps predict and justify the organization of the essay.

 b. Why is this kind of paragraph a useful part of the essay?

 c. For what kinds of essays might a paragraph like this be neither useful nor necessary?

4. Discuss the use of subtitles in organizing the essay. In what ways are they linked to the overall definition pattern? (See "Guide to Terms": *Unity*.)

Diction and Vocabulary

1. Each of the major sections in the body of the essay uses a different cluster of terms to explore and define a particular part of the author's identity. Tell what the clusters of terms are in each section.

2. Tell how the diction in paragraphs 22–28 contributes to their effectiveness. (Consider also the contribution made by the choice of details.) (Guide: *Diction*.)

3. If you do not know the meanings of some of the following terms, look them up in a dictionary: context (par. 2); influx (3); invocation (5); Shinto, samisens (6); issei (16); arduously (18); pluralism, spontaneous, harangued (32).

Suggestions for Writing and Discussion

1. If you believe that all people have multiple identities, try defining yours in an essay. If you can, try harmonizing them as well, or at least discuss the relationships among them.

2. At the end of the essay, Noda endorses a kind of "pluralism." To what extent is our society already guided by such an attitude? Do we often look at people and events with an opposite attitude? Give some examples. What might be some of the practical consequences (good and bad) of a thoroughgoing pluralism in our society? Is such an attitude really possible for a large society to adopt?

(NOTE: Suggestions for topics requiring development by use of DEFINITION are on page 360, at the end of this section.)

CECIL HELMAN

Cecil Helman is a physician, anthropologist, painter, poet, essayist, and short story writer. He was born in South Africa in 1944,
and after completing medical school at the University of Cape
Town, he studied social anthropology at the University of London.
He currently practices medicine in north London and teaches at
Middlesex Medical School, Brunel University, and University Col-
lege in London. He has published three books: *The Exploding News-
paper* (1988), *Culture, Health and Illness: An Introduction for Health
Professionals* (1990), and *The Body of Frankenstein's Monster: Essays in
Myth and Medicine* (1991).

Half-Green, Half-Black

In this essay from his collection *The Myth of Frankenstein's Monster*,
Helman begins by exploring the meaning of *placebo effect* as it
applies to drugs. From this relatively familiar ground, he expands
the meaning of the concept to include matters of mental and spiritual health. In doing so, he demonstrates the growing awareness in
contemporary medical science of the relationship of body, mind,
and spirit.

The story is apocryphal, but somehow true.

1

It goes like this: an anxious woman patient is given regular pre-
scriptions by her doctor for a certain well-known tranquillizer—a little capsule which is half-black and half-green in colour. One day she
tells the doctor (in some versions it is a relative or friend): 'Usually I
take my capsule at bedtime with the green end first, and it works
just fine. I have a long deep sleep, and I wake up rested and relaxed
the next morning. But last night, for some odd reason, I swallowed
it down with the *black* end first. And then it didn't work at all, and

2

I had awful insomnia. I was up half the night tossing about, with nerves and panic, and palpitations too.'

A certain enigmatic power seems to be condensed into the green end of that little gelatin capsule—an invisible power that originates not in the medication, but in the woman herself. It consists, above all, of the healing, soothing strengths of her own mind, and of her belief in herself and in others—a belief so powerful that it can cure the body, and calm the mind. Projected onto one half of the tranquillizer capsule, it is the phenomenon that modern medicine now calls the *placebo effect*.

Whether it is a pill or a potion, almost anything you believe in can become a placebo. In medical practice, placebos are usually pills made entirely of sugar, or capsules that are empty inside. Although they look authentic, and have a convincing taste, they are really counterfeit drugs, cunning and plausible copies of the real thing. It is solely the patient's belief in their power and function that turns these inactive substances into a powerful medicine. But the placebo effect can also be found elsewhere—hidden, for example, in the healing powers of a smile, or a touch, in a gesture or a word, or even in the intricate rituals of a diagnostic test.

Research has shown how all manner of ailments have been helped by a belief in placebos. They are reported to have relieved angina pectoris and pain, helped hay fever and headaches, suppressed several types of coughs, lowered high blood pressures, healed ulcers in the stomach and the duodenum, and soothed the aching throb of rheumatoid arthritis. Many depressed, nervous and insomniac people—and even some schizophrenics—have been helped by the placebo effect.

Sometimes its unusual power can lie hidden in the actual shape, colour or name of a remedy or medication. Studies have shown how some tranquillizer tablets coloured green have calmed the nerves of anxious patients, but not when those same tablets were coloured yellow; while other scientists have shown how some depressed patients felt happier after swallowing down a yellow tablet, but not when that tablet was crimson or green. And certain headaches, too, have only been helped by pain-killing tablets when a famous brand-name was printed on their packet, but not when that packet was unlabelled and plain.

But these many types of placebo are not only healing in their effects—for they can cause discomfort, and even dependency upon them. Tell some suggestible people that they will feel weak or dizzy, impotent or ill, from a little pill made entirely of sugar, and some of them surely will.

Thus the placebo effect, with its many names and actions, and the many masks on its hundred faces, is part of a very powerful magic—the universal magic of belief. Its mechanism is mysterious, and its origins obscure, but in the long historical drama of human healing, it has always been the leading actor. 8

Friedrich Anton Mesmer, born in 1734 near Lake Konstanz, was the son of a gamekeeper, and a student in Vienna of the uncomfortably named Fr Maximilian Hell. He was a qualified physician, and the holder of no less than four doctorates, one of them in astrology. In later years he moved on to Paris where, under the patronage of Marie-Antoinette, he wrote his long and rambling *Dissertation on Animal Magnetism*. As a fashionable faith healer in pre-Revolutionary France, he became one of the most famous practitioners in history of the art of the placebo effect. 9

All of the universe, believed Dr. Mesmer, was composed of a unitary and ubiquitous gas, which he termed the 'aestheric continuum', and which he claimed was dominated by the forces of magnetism. Any disturbance in the delicate balance of these magnetic forces of the universe, often under the influence of a disordered mind, could cause human suffering, disease and even death. 10

His famous trances of healing took place in a large room lined with stained glass and mirrors, overflowing with flowers and incense, and filled with the sounds of soft music. In its centre stood a large tub full of iron filings, with iron bars protruding from its side. Rows of wealthy patients sat in silent expectation around the tub, clasping each other's hands, or gripping onto the ends of the iron rods. Suddenly a slight *frisson* would ripple around the room as the great 'magnetist' himself entered, dressed in a lilac silk robe, and carrying in his hand a special iron rod, held aloft like a wand. Slowly he would pass around the circle, staring fixedly into each of their faces, while making arcane, mathematical movements with both of his hands—until at last, in a rustle of silk, a circle of swooning ladies would sink slowly to the floor. 11

In this way, many of his patients' ailments were healed by his invisible 'mesmerism', including the several forms of hysteria, as well as various pains and paralyses, convulsions, blindness, and even 'congestion' of the liver and the spleen. 12

It was an age in France when the tinderboxes of revolution were 13
already beginning to spark. In this incendiary atmosphere, a puzzled Louis XVI convened a panel of experts—not to study the social unrest gathering around him, but rather to examine the curious cures of Dr. Mesmer. Among the members of this panel were Benjamin Franklin, Lavoisier and the soon-to-be-infamous Dr. Guillotin. By 1784 they had sceptically concluded that most of the cures were not caused by Mesmer's 'animal magnetism' as he had claimed, but solely by the suggestibility of his patients. That was the end of the matter, but there was a curious addendum to their report: 'It is impossible not to admit', they said, 'that some great force acts upon and masters the patients,' and that this invisible force 'appears to reside in the magnetiser.'

What was this mysterious 'great force' that resided in Dr. Mesmer, and what is it now—two hundred years later? Above all, it is 14
the magnetic charisma of the healer's personality, which in every generation needs for its power a potent placebo-blend of mesmerism and faith, as well as a ritual milieu of healing and care. It arises always from the centre of an ancient matrix of human beliefs—beliefs in the workers of wonders and miracles, in faith healers and holy waters, in magic cures and in magic curses, and in the healing touch of the Seventh Son of a Seventh Son.

Phineas Parkhurst Quimby, a famous and flamboyant faith 15
healer born in 1802 in New England, and—like Mesmer—bearer of another 'great force', once put it thus: 'I tell the patient his troubles, and what he thinks is his disease, and my explanation is the cure. If I succeed in correcting his errors I change the fluids in the system, and establish the patient in health. The truth is the cure.'

Quimby's 'truth' is thus the universal self-assurance of all healers, from psychoanalysts to shamans: their belief in their own expla- 16
nations, and in their metamorphic power over matter and mind. Everywhere, in their clinics or temples of healing, the main task of their many techniques is to shape, mould and give *meaning* to the raw clay of human suffering—to somehow order the turmoil of their patients' perceptions, the terror of disorder, and the chaos of fear. Around all of this they erect a scaffolding of reassurance, an intricate cage of concepts to which only they have the key.

Over the centuries, wise doctors and traditional healers have 17
always seen themselves as the allies, and not the enemies, of the healing powers of the self. They have seen their task as cooperating

with all those remedies concealed in the brain and the blood, as working with the shamans of the white blood cells, and the logical gurus of the immunological system.

Yet though many healers have shown how belief can heal 18 ulcers, soothe pain, lower the blood pressure, and calm a frightened brain, the placebo effect still remains as the uninvited and invisible guest at the celebratory banquets of modern medical science. In textbooks and in journals, its curious power encounters only the collective sneer of the medical profession. There it is described as '*only* the placebo effect'—not as a 'real' drug or effect, but '*just* a placebo'. It is still spoken of by most of the medical world as if it were only a bogus and confusing element, merely a false phenomenon in the smooth machinery of high-technology healing.

Yet somehow, despite all of this, it still remains as an enigmatic 19 gap at the centre of the rational paradigm of modern medicine. Right there, in the very heart of medical theory, there is a numberless, unpredictable and uncontrollable void. But look more closely at the shape of that void, for over the years the sneers of science have seeped right into it, and filled it up like plaster in a mould. Slowly as it sets we recognize its familiar shape, the curious symmetry of its bumps and projections, the emerging limbs, heart, nose, eyes, ears, ideas and memory, and hear—from somewhere within it—the faint sounds of a human voice.

It is Act One, Scene One. A doctor's office, somewhere in the 20 Western world, sometime this century. It is a clean, hygienic room, with a faint bouquet of expensive disinfectant. There are bright fluorescent lights on the ceiling, and a framed diploma hangs on the wall. Shining instruments lie scattered on the shelves of a glass cabinet, like the iron rods of Anton Mesmer. On another shelf stands a double row of plump textbooks, their Latin names lettered in gold.

Gathered behind the doctor's desk are the ancestral portraits of 21 legendary doctors, a gilt-framed genealogy that stretches all the way from Hippocrates, Galen and Maimonides up to Pasteur, Harvey and Sir William Osler.

In the corner of the office there is a wash-basin, a square of shin- 22 ing tiles, and a pair of clean white towels hanging from a rail.

Now there is a tentative knock on the door. Slowly it opens, and 23 an anxious patient enters the room, and glances around him. A man, or a woman, rises smiling from behind the large cluttered desk with a hand outstretched. The doctor wears a white coat, or a smart grey suit, and his silver spectacles are worn over a mask of detached benevolence. Around his neck hangs the two-headed serpent of Aesculapius, each of its plastic mouths waiting to whisper its message into his attentive ear. A beeper and a golden row of pens stand stiffly to attention in his pocket. On the desk lie a silver ophthalmoscope in its box, and three cardboard obelisks of medical files.

As he takes his seat at the centre of this theatre of medical magic, the patient inhales deeply of the heady, disinfected air. Some-where deep inside himself, a frightened child creeps into the early morning warmth of its parents' bed.   24

He looks around the room, and as he does so his eye gathers together the mystical ciphers of the power of Science, forming them slowly and calmly into a grammar of belief. Now he takes another, and deeper breath, and then, with a sigh, begins to speak . . .   25

The doctor's office, like Mesmer's great room of flowers and incense, or the crowded halls of Phineas Quimby, is a sort of secular Lourdes, a shrine to the faith of the cities and suburbs. Here, like the guru in his long limousine, or the shaman in his fur and paint, he supplies the pieces missing from our personal jig-saw, and ritually re-assembles the broken fragments of our humpty-dumpty world. In this familiar ambience of healing and trust, the charisma of his power surrounds all of the drugs, both real and placebo, prescribed for his patients, and coats them thinly with an invisible layer of belief.   26

Wrapped in this ritual envelope, the tranquillizers or sleeping tablets that his patients carry away with them become a symbolic tonic, fuel, food or friend, at the very centre of their impoverished lives. The bottles of bright-coloured antibiotics that he dispenses become the medical 'magic bullets' fired at their enemies, those tiny Germs or Viruses hidden somewhere within themselves. While all those hundreds of heart drugs, pain-killers and blood-pressure tablets so regularly prescribed, weave themselves slowly, day by day, into the ordered fabric of patients' lives—and there become the emblems of their disability, their magnets for empathy, and the cir-cular metaphors for their doctor's love.   27

Like the black end of the tranquillizer capsule, there is a dark side to the placebo effect. It is the harmful, pathogenic effect of both belief and trust, and is called the *nocebo* effect—from the Latin *noceo*, I hurt.   28

The most awesome example of this effect—the killing power of 29
a public curse—is the phenomenon anthropologists call 'voodoo
death', 'hex death', or even 'magical death'. They tell how it has happened in Africa, Australia, the Caribbean, and elsewhere. There is
something of the stuff of horror films about their tales—the sort that
flicker on the television screen on a wet winter's night—or of the
wild recollections of elderly travellers.

On the cinema screen, its usual image is that of the voodoo 30
priest, a dark man squatting near the flames of a midnight fire, as he
rummages among the entrails of a decapitated rooster. Beside him
on the hot Caribbean earth lie the little manikins of wood or of wax,
pierced all over with pins. Several scenes later (and here the hairs
begin to rise at the back of our necks), we hear those familiar, irregular screams as they echo among the rows of little wooden shacks,
and watch as the camera pans past the faces of the terrified crowd,
and then sinks down slowly towards the victim—the man found
dead and goggle-eyed in his bed, with not a mark on his petrified
body.

This is the familiar nocebo of Hollywood, the fatal power of a 31
celluloid curse—but in the canons of true anthropology, although
the dénouement is often the same, the picture is much less dramatic.
In that same heat of the tropical air, a certain man realizes that he is
doomed, cursed publicly for a particular crime or moral transgres-
sion by the words of a powerful priest, witch, shaman or sorcerer,
acting on behalf of the tribe. Slowly over the next few days, his clans-
men and kin withdraw from him, shaking their heads, and avoiding
his eyes. 'Shortly thereafter,' writes the French anthropologist
Claude Lévi-Strauss, 'sacred rites are held to dispatch him to the
realm of shadows. First brutally torn from all of his family and social
ties and excluded from all functions and activities through which he
experienced self-awareness, then banished by the same forces from
the world of the living, the victim yields to the combined terror, the
sudden total withdrawal of the multiple reference systems provided
by the support of the group.' The man is now socially dead, an object
of fear and taboo, his corporeal self merely a shadowy hallucination
in the eyes of the tribe. Shortly thereafter, his body too will die, in an
expected and yet mysterious way.

Some years later, though many thousands of miles away, and 32
far from the tropics, an old woman is torn away suddenly by her
children from her tiny room, her little shrine of memories. Against

her wishes they place her in an Old Aged 'Home' in another city, in a huge and anonymous building that can never be her home. And very soon afterwards she too dies, suddenly and mysteriously, and is found cold and staring in a little room bare except for a Bible, a torn nightdress, and a brace of family photographs that stare silently through her from the bedside table.

And meanwhile, elsewhere in that same distant city, a white-coated high priest or sorcerer enters a hospital room, and with the needle of a sterilized syringe pierces a certain patient's body here and there, peers through it with a special machine, and then rummages for an answer among those medical entrails of paper and celluloid—the patient's blood test results and his X-Ray plates. The doctor in the white coat looks down at the sick man and then, slowly and gravely, he shakes his head. With a swallowed sigh, the patient's friends and kin gathered around the bed mumble their excuses and then leave the room, one by one. Something invisible happens to the patient then, when he is alone again—something final, cellular and microscopic—as with a sob and staring eyes he turns his face stiffly to the wall.

Like the old woman sent to the Old Aged 'Home', or a retarded child hidden away in an institution, or the man told he has HIV—the antibody of death—floating in his bloodstream, the patient's name soon fades and dies away under the magical curse of a diagnostic word. To the rest of society he slowly becomes the undead, the half-forgotten inhabitant of a limbo land, the Land of Nocebo, the one that lies just beyond the horizons of life.

But in the meantime, back in the bedroom, it is already the following night. Carefully the apocryphal woman has swallowed down her tranquillizer capsule with a glass of water, this time with the green end first.

Carried downwards by the waves of peristalsis, and the wash of water, the capsule meanders from side to side like a confused submarine, voyaging down the long oesophagus towards the stomach. But along with that capsule the woman has swallowed something else: its colour, its texture and emblematic shape, and the mystical name printed upon the packet. And with all of these she has also swallowed the makers and marketers of the capsule, smiling at her from their clean white laboratories. And she has also gulped down the healing charisma of the doctor, the grave glance of his face as he bends over the cluttered desk writing the prescription, and the kindly curl of his mouth as he raises his silvered head and hands it over to her. And along with him are swallowed also all the rituals and symbolic powers of Medical Science, encoded in the talismans of the doctor's office, from the circle of diplomas on his wall to the glitter of his arcane instruments.

Now all of this concoction of symbols and certainties, gulped   37
down with a mouthful of water, begins to seep slowly out of her stomach and into her psyche. Though the capsule has not yet reached the intestine, its site of absorption, the fingers of a soft languor are already beginning to relax the tension of her muscles, loosening the tight knots in her terrified brain.

Meanwhile, deep down in her stomach, the peristaltic waves   38
turn the capsule round and around, so that now it shoots down into the small intestine, black end first. But the woman is unaware of this. For already she is fast asleep, dreaming of a wide calm field, emerald as an aquarium, and of the green bushes and shrubs that have begun to sprout all around her, out of the black, shiny gelatin earth.

Meanings and Values

1a. Which parts of this piece are devoted to exploring the positive meanings and consequences of the *placebo effect?*

 b. Which parts explore the negative meanings and consequences?

2. Besides the pill in the anecdote that opens the selection, what else in the essay is presented as half-green and half-black?

3. In which paragraphs does the writer emphasize differences between medical science and the power of personal or religious belief? In which does he show how modern medical practice makes use of the power of belief?

Expository Techniques

1a. Where does Helman first state the topic and the main idea to be developed in the essay?

 b. In which sentence or sentences does he make clear that the main purpose of the essay is to define? (See "Guide to Terms": *Purpose.*)

2. What is added to the definition of *placebo effect* by the story of Mesmer (pars. 9–14)?

3a. Discuss the writer's use of the following strategies, paying attention to what each contributes to the definition: comparison, example, negation, and cause and effect. (See *Definition: Introduction.*)

b.   Explain the use of analogy in the following paragraphs: 19, 26, 28, 36.

4.   Where and for what purposes are the story of the woman and the green and black capsule employed? How are the different appearances of this story related? (Guide: *Introductions, Closings*.)

Diction and Vocabulary

1.   At several places in this selection, Helman points out that the placebo effect and the nocebo effect are frequently associated with religious belief. Explain how he uses both the denotations and connotations of words in paragraphs 10, 14, 16, 26, 32, and 34 to suggest such connections.

2.   Explain what each of the following passages means. Pay special attention to the strategies noted in parentheses after each passage.

a.   "the shamans of the white blood cells" (par. 17) (metaphor) (Guide: *Figures of Speech*.)

b.   "Around his neck hangs the two-headed serpent of Aesculapius, each of its plastic mouths waiting to whisper its message into his attentive ear." (par. 23) (metaphor, allusion) (Guide: *Figures of Speech*.)

c.   "And along with him are swallowed also all the rituals and symbolic powers of Medical Science, encoded in the talismans of the doctor's office, from the circle of diplomas on his wall to the glitter of his arcane instruments." (par. 36) (connotation) (Guide: *Connotation and Denotation*.)

3.   If you do not know the meaning of some of the following terms, look them up in a dictionary: apocryphal (par. 1); palpitations (2); enigmatic (3); plausible (4); angina pectoris (5); ubiquitous (10); frisson, arcane (11); incendiary (13); metamorphic (10); shamans, gurus (17); paradigm, symmetry (19); ambience, charisma (26); denouement, corporeal (31); languor (37).

Suggestions for Writing and Discussion

1.   In what significant ways other than the ones Helman discusses can our beliefs affect our physical and mental condition? To what extent can we consciously control our state of mind and its emotional or physical consequences?

2.   If it became possible to use medication to get rid of all emotional pain, depression, anger, and similar emotions, do you think that widespread use of such a medication would be a good idea? What would be some of the likely consequences?

(NOTE: Suggestions for topics requiring development by use of DEFINITION follow.)

Writing Suggestions for Section 7
Definition

Develop a composition for a specified purpose and audience, using whatever methods and expository patterns will help convey a clear understanding of your meaning of one of the following terms:

1. Country music.
2. Conscience.
3. Religion.
4. Bigotry.
5. Success.
6. Empathy.
7. Family.
8. Hypocrisy.
9. Humor.
10. Sophistication.
11. Naiveté.
12. Cowardice.
13. Wisdom.
14. Integrity.
15. Morality.
16. Greed.
17. Social poise.
18. Intellectual (the person).
19. Pornography.
20. Courage.
21. Patriotism.
22. Equality (or equal opportunity).
23. Loyalty.
24. Stylishness (in clothing or behavior).
25. Fame.
26. Obesity.
27. Cheating.
28. Hero.
29. Feminine.
30. Masculine.

8

Explaining with the Help of *Description*

Exposition, as well as argument, can be made more vivid, and hence more understandable, with the support of description. Most exposition does contain some elements of description, and at times description carries almost the entire burden of the explanation, becoming a basic pattern for the expository purpose.

Description is most useful in painting a word-picture of something concrete, such as a scene or a person. Its use is not restricted, however, to what we can perceive with our senses; we can also describe (or attempt to describe) an abstract concept, such as an emotion or a quality or a mood. But most attempts to describe fear, for instance, still resort to the physical—a "coldness around the heart," perhaps—and in such concrete ways communicate the abstract to the reader.

In its extreme forms, description is either *objective* or *impressionistic* (subjective), but most of its uses are somewhere between these extremes. Objective description is purely factual, uncolored by any feelings of the author; it is the type used for scientific papers and most business reports. But impressionistic description, as the term implies, at least tinges the purely factual with the author's personal impressions; instead of describing how something *is,* objectively, the author describes how it *seems,* subjectively. Such a description might refer to the "blazing heat" of an August day. Somewhat less impressionistic would be "extreme heat." But the scientist would describe it precisely as "64 degrees Celsius," and this would be purely objective reporting, unaffected by the impressions of the author. (No examples of the latter are included in this section, but many textbooks for other courses utilize the technique of pure objective description, as do encyclopedias. The McPhee essay in Further

Readings provides some good examples of objective description, although not entirely unmixed with colorful impressionistic details.)

The first and most important job in any descriptive endeavor is to select the details to be included. There are usually many from which to choose, and writers must constantly keep in mind the kind of picture they want to paint with words—for *their* purpose and *their* audience. Such a word-picture need not be entirely visual; in this respect writers have more freedom than artists, for writers can use strokes that will add the dimensions of sound, smell, and even touch. Such strokes, if made to seem natural enough, can help create a vivid and effective image in the reader's mind.

Most successful impressionistic description focuses on a single *dominant impression*. Of the many descriptive details ordinarily available for use, the author selects those that will help create a mood or atmosphere or emphasize a feature or quality. But more than the materials themselves are involved, for even diction can often assist in creating the desired dominant impression. Sometimes syntax is also an important factor, as in the use of short, hurried sentences to help convey a sense of urgency or excitement.

Actual structuring of passages is perhaps less troublesome in description than in most of the other patterns. But some kind of orderliness is needed for the sake of both readability and a realistic effect. (Neither objective nor impressionistic description can afford not to be realistic, in one manner or another.) In visual description, orderliness is usually achieved by presenting details as the eye would find them—that is, as arranged in space. We could describe a person from head to toe, or vice versa, or begin with the most noticeable feature and work from there. A scenic description might move from near to far or from far to near, from left to right or from right to left. It might also start with a broad, overall view, gradually narrowing to a focal point, probably the most significant feature of the scene. These are fairly standard kinds of description; but as the types and occasions for using description vary widely, so do the possibilities for interesting treatment. In many cases, writers are limited only by their own ingenuity.

But ingenuity should not be allowed to produce *excessive* description, an amazingly certain path to reader boredom. A few well-chosen details are better than profusion. Economy of words is desirable in any writing, and description is no exception. Appropriate use of figurative language and careful choice of strong nouns and verbs will help prevent the need for strings of modifiers, which are wasteful and can seem amateurish.

Even for the experienced writer, however, achieving good description remains a constant challenge; the beginner should not expect to attain this goal without working at it.

Sample Paragraph (Description)

Background.

Interpretation of the photograph.

Generally objective description of the photograph, though "almost smell" is certainly impressionistic.

The details of the photograph are presented objectively, but the description is filled with impressionistic observations about the dancer's moods and the emotional "temperature" of the scene.

The theme of this year's Amateur Photography Contest sponsored by the Palmville *Gazette* was "Snapshots of Palmville." There were two "Top Shot" award winners. Emily Grezibel looked to the past with a black-and-white photograph of Ericson's Feed Store. The peeling white paint on the front of the old clapboard building gleams in the hot midday sun and little puffs of dust follow the footsteps of the elderly farmer in dark bib overalls as he passes in front of the Blue Seal Feeds sign. One can almost smell the dust and the scents of feed, fertilizer, and oil hanging in the air. The title sums up the photograph's theme: "Fading." Brian Alonzo's color photograph "Saturday Night" is the other winner. Taken in the parking lot of the Palmville Mall, it shows a group of teenagers dancing to the music of a boom box sitting on the hood of a shiny, cherry-red convertible. Several of the couples dancing in the foreground appear to be singing along with the music and the dancers are frozen in the middle of joyous, athletic dance steps. Other teenagers sit on hoods of bright blue, turquoise, and yellow cars in a semicircle behind the dancers, clapping and smiling. The silent yet exciting sounds of the music seem to radiate

The central theme of the paragraph is the contrast between the generations and their outlooks.

from the entire picture. The whole scene is illuminated by the arc lights of the parking lot, making the picture seem a festival celebrating the energy and hopefulness of the next generation of Palmville citizens.

Sample Paragraph (Description)

It's no winter without an ice storm. When Robert Frost gazed at bowed-over birch trees and tried to think that boys had bent them playing, he knew better: "Ice-storms do that." They do that and a lot more, trimming disease and weakness out of the tree—the old tree's friend, as pneumonia used to be the old man's. Some of us provide life-support systems for our precious shrubs, boarding them over against the ice, for the ice storm takes the young or unlucky branch or birch as well as the rotten or feeble. One February morning we look out our windows over yards and fields littered with kindling, small twigs and great branches. We look out at a world turned into one diamond, ten thousand carats in the line of sight, twice as many facets. What a dazzle of spinning refracted light, spider webs of cold brilliance attacking our eyeballs! All winter we wear sunglasses to drive, more than we do in summer, and never so much as after an ice storm, with its painful glaze reflecting from maple and birch, granite boulder and stone wall, turning electric wires into bright silver filaments. The snow itself takes on a crust of ice, like the finish of a clay pot, that carries our weight and sends us swooping and sliding. It's worth your life to go for the mail. Until sand and salt redeem the highway, Route 4 is quiet. We cancel the appointment with the dentist, stay home, and marvel at the altered universe, knowing that midday sun will strip ice from tree and roof and restore our ordinary white winter world.

Bright Light

Carey Braun

The sun woke me by sneaking its way through the narrow cracks of the vertical blinds. I squinted at the bright sun, then kept my eyes closed and enjoyed its warmth on my face and shoulders. After a time, I slid across the bed to the window and peeked through the blinds to look out on a day that reminded me of *my* version of Andrew Lloyd Webber's song, "*Light* changes everything"—or at least the sun does.

What better place to see light, feel light, and become one with the sun, I thought, than at the beach. I rushed out of bed, got dressed, had a bite of breakfast, grabbed my bathing suit and suntan lotion, and headed for the beach.

As I stepped out of the car in the parking lot, I felt a sun-warmed breeze across my face. It blew my hair across my cheek and made me wonder what it would be like to be a bird, able to skim across the waves of wind with the sun on my back. I hurried down the walkway. On each side of the path, dilapidated summer cottages managed to look fresh and new in the early morning rays. Crossing the sand, I stepped gingerly on the hot sand, a recognition that even this early in the day we need to shape our actions to the sun's heat and power.

I sat on the blanket and rubbed the suntan lotion over my body. My skin shined, reflecting the sun's rays and making me seem for a moment like a second source of light. But soon I began to feel like a frying pan that would sizzle if a drop of water hit me. In the background I could hear the sound of many boom boxes blending together forming a light-hearted hymn that took away thoughts of everything else but this time and place. People were splashing the water, sending luminous drops into the air and breaking the surface of the water into a million mirroring pieces. During brief breaks in the music and the sounds of splashing, I could hear the sound of birds singing.

The sun's heat relaxed me so that I fell asleep. When I woke, there was sweat covering my face and my arms and refracting the sun's rays. If I looked just right, I could see rainbow dots on the surface of my skin. I woke up slowly and decided to head for the cool, refreshing water in front of me. I could feel my body temperature dropping as it moved into the water. As I dove into a wave, chills went through my body like shock waves. I was ready to move back to the beach and the sun.

I couldn't taste the sun, but as I walked back to my blanket, I licked the salt off my lips which had dried quickly in the heat. Salt, I decided, must be the taste of light, at least this morning. The salt on my skin made it feel like stretched leather, tight across my cheekbones and shoulders and stiffening at my joints. I walked across the glinting sand, through midday air heated to luminous, shimmering waves to the outdoor shower.

As I let the water wash away the salt, I looked at the sky and realized that the sun was beginning to descend. The subtle change in light made me feel cooler even though the sand was just as hot as I returned to my blanket. As the light turned to afternoon, people began looking at each other, perhaps noticing the growing shadows and the loss of brilliance. Light now turned to haze, luminous and bright, but still haze. People began straggling up the sand, looking as if their energy, too, had begun to wane. The music left and the song that remained was the crash of waves, glinting here and there as the growing fog broke to let through a stray ray.

I gathered my belongings and shook all the sand off. As I drove away, I took one last look in the mirror to mourn the passing of the sun's power and light; startled by the electrifying colors of reds, yellow, and oranges spreading from the horizon through the sky, I realized once again the power of light to change everything.

SHARON CURTIN

SHARON CURTIN, a native of Douglas, Wyoming, was raised in a family of ranchers and craftspeople. Curtin, a feminist and political leftist, has worked as a nurse in New York and California but now devotes most of her time to writing and to operating a small farm in Virginia.

Aging in the Land of the Young

"Aging in the Land of the Young" is the first part of Curtin's article by that title, as it appeared in the *Atlantic* in July 1972. It is largely a carefully restructured composite of portions of her book *Nobody Ever Died of Old Age,* also published in 1972. It illustrates the subjective form of description, generally known as impressionistic description.

Old men, old women, almost 20 million of them. They constitute 10   1
percent of the total population, and the percentage is steadily growing. Some of them, like conspirators, walk all bent over, as if hiding
some precious secret, filled with self-protection. The body seems to
gather itself around those vital parts, folding shoulders, arms, pelvis
like a fading rose. Watch and you see how fragile old people come
to think they are.

Aging paints every action gray, lies heavy on every movement,   2
imprisons every thought. It governs each decision with a ruthless
and single-minded perversity. To age is to learn the feeling of no
longer growing, of struggling to do old tasks, to remember familiar
actions. The cells of the brain are destroyed with thousands of unfelt

tiny strokes, little pockets of clotted blood wiping out memories and abilities without warning. The body seems slowly to give up, randomly stopping, sometimes starting again as if to torture and tease with the memory of lost strength. Hands become clumsy, frail transparencies, held together with knotted blue veins.

Sometimes it seems as if the distance between your feet and the floor were constantly changing, as if you were walking on shifting and not quite solid ground. One foot down, slowly, carefully force the other foot forward. Sometimes you are a shuffler, not daring to lift your feet from the uncertain earth but forced to slide hesitantly forward in little whispering movements. Sometimes you are able to "step out," but this effort—in fact the pure exhilaration of easy movement—soon exhausts you. 3

The world becomes narrower as friends and family die or move away. To climb stairs, to ride in a car, to walk to the corner, to talk on the telephone; each action seems to take away from the energy needed to stay alive. Everything is limited by the strength you hoard greedily. Your needs decrease, you require less food, less sleep, and finally less human contact; yet this little bit becomes more and more difficult. You fear that one day you will be reduced to the simple acts of breathing and taking nourishment. This is the ultimate stage you dread, the period of helplessness and hopelessness, when independence will be over. 4

There is nothing to prepare you for the experience of growing old. Living is a process, an irreversible progression toward old age and eventual death. You see men of eighty still vital and straight as oaks; you see men of fifty reduced to gray shadows in the human landscape. The cellular clock differs for each one of us, and is profoundly affected by our own life experiences, our heredity, and perhaps most important, by the concepts of aging encountered in society and in oneself. 5

The aged live with enforced leisure, on fixed incomes, subject to many chronic illnesses, and most of their money goes to keep a roof over their heads. They also live in a culture that worships youth. 6

A kind of cultural attitude makes me bigoted against old people; it makes me think young is best; it makes me treat old people like outcasts. 7

Hate that gray? Wash it away! 8
Wrinkle cream. 9

Monkey glands. 10

Face-lifting. 11

Look like a bride again. 12

Don't trust anyone over thirty. 13

I fear growing old. 14

Feel Young Again! 15

I am afraid to grow old—we're all afraid. In fact, the fear of 16
growing old is so great that every aged person is an insult and a
threat to the society. They remind us of our own death, that our
body won't always remain smooth and responsive, but will someday betray us by aging, wrinkling, faltering, failing. The ideal way
to age would be to grow slowly invisible, gradually disappearing,
without causing worry or discomfort to the young. In some ways
that does happen. Sitting in a small park across from a nursing home
one day, I noticed that the young mothers and their children gathered on one side, and the old people from the home on the other.
Whenever a youngster would run over to the "wrong" side, chasing
a ball or just trying to cover all the available space, the old people
would lean forward and smile. But before any communication could
be established, the mother would come over, murmuring embarrassed apologies, and take her child back to the "young" side.

Now, it seemed to me that the children didn't feel any particu- 17
lar fear and the old people didn't seem to be threatened by the children. The division of space was drawn by the mothers. And the
mothers never looked at the old people who lined the other side of
the park like so many pigeons perched on the benches. These well-
dressed young matrons had a way of sliding their eyes over, around,
through the old people; they never looked at them directly. The old
people may as well have been invisible; they had no reality for the
youngsters, who were not permitted to speak to them, and they
offended the aesthetic eye of the mothers.

My early experiences were somewhat different; since I grew up 18
in a small town, my childhood had more of a nineteenth-century flavor. I knew a lot of old people, and considered some of them friends.
There was no culturally defined way for me to "relate" to old people, except the rules of courtesy which applied to all adults. My
grandparents were an integral and important part of the family and
of the community. I sometimes have a dreadful fear that mine will
be the last generation to know old people as friends, to have a sense

of what growing old means, to respect and understand man's mortality and his courage in the face of death. Mine may be the last generation to have a sense of living history, of stories passed from generation to generation, of identity established by family history.

Meanings and Values

1. What is the general tone of this writing? (See "Guide to Terms": *Style/Tone.*)

2. If you find it depressing to read about aging, try to analyze why (especially in view of the fact that you are very likely many years from the stage of "a fading rose").

3. Why do you suppose it is more likely to be the mothers than the children who shun old people (pars. 16–17)?

4a. Has this author avoided the excesses of sentimentality? (Guide: *Sentimentality.*) If not, where does she fail?

   b. If she does avoid sentimentality, try to discover how.

Expository Techniques

1a. Why should this writing be classed as primarily impressionistic, rather than objective?

   b. What is the dominant impression?

2a. Analyze the role that selection of details plays in creating the dominant impression.

   b. Provide examples of the type of details that could have been included but were not. Are such omissions justifiable?

3a. Paragraph 5 ends the almost pure description to begin another phase of the writing. What is it?

   b. How has the author provided for a smooth transition between the two? (Guide: *Transition.*)

4a. What particular method of gaining emphasis has been used effectively in one portion of the selection? (Guide: *Emphasis.*)

   b. How might the material have been presented if emphasis were not desired?

5. Which previously studied patterns of exposition are also used in this writing? Cite paragraphs where each may be found.

Diction and Vocabulary

1a. The author sometimes changes person—e.g., "they" to "you" after paragraph 2. Analyze where the changes occur.

 b. What justification, if any, can you find for each change?

2a. Which two kinds of figures of speech do you find used liberally to achieve this description? (Guide: *Figures of Speech.*)

 b. Cite three or more examples of each.

 c. As nearly as you can tell, are any of them clichés? (Guide: *Clichés.*)

Suggestions for Writing and Discussion

1. If Curtin is correct in her fears expressed in the last two sentences, what could be the consequences for society in general?

2. Discuss the pros and cons of placing old people in rest homes, rather than letting them live alone or taking them to live with the family. What other alternatives, if any, does the family have?

3. If you know some very old person who (apparently) is not as affected by aging as the ones the author describes, what seems to account for this difference?

4. If many people at age sixty-five to seventy-five are still efficient at their jobs, as is often argued, what practical reasons are there for forcing retirement at that age?

(NOTE: Suggestions for topics requiring development by use of DESCRIPTION are on page 403, at the end of this section.)

JOYCE MAYNARD

JOYCE MAYNARD was born in 1953 and spent her childhood in Durham, New Hampshire, where her father taught at the nearby University of New Hampshire. At 19, while she was still a sophomore at Yale University, her first book appeared: *Looking Backward: A Chronicle of Growing Up Old in the Sixties* (1973). Maynard was a reporter for *The New York Times* and currently writes a syndicated newspaper column. She also writes monthly for *Parenting* magazine and has published two novels, *Baby Love* (1981) and *To Die For* (1992). Many of her columns were reprinted in the collection *Domestic Affairs* (1987).

The Yellow Door House

Permanence, continuity, and change are some of the ideas explored through description in this essay, originally published as one of the author's columns. Comparison plays an important part in the exposition as well, particularly in juxtaposing Maynard's memories of the house with its present reality.

I've known only two homes in my life: the one I live in now, with my 1 husband and children, and another one, just sixty miles from here, where I grew up. My father's dead now, and even before that, my parents were divorced and my mother moved away from our old house. But though she rents the house out nine months of the year and hasn't spent a winter there for thirteen years, she hasn't sold our old house yet. It's still filled with our old belongings from our old life. And though my mother has another house now, and a good life, with another man, in a new place, she still comes back to the old house for a couple of months every summer. Every year I ask her, "Have you considered putting the house on the market?" And every summer the answer is "not yet."

My children call the place where I grew up the yellow door   2
house. They love the place, with its big, overgrown yard, the old
goldfish pond, the brick walkway, the white picket fence. On the
front door there's a heavy brass knocker my sons like to bang on to
announce their arrival for visits with their grandmother, and French
windows on either side that I was always cautioned against breaking as a child. (As now I caution my children.) There's a brass mail
slot I used to pass messages through to a friend waiting on the other
side. Now my daughter Audrey does the same.

It's a big house, a hip-roofed colonial, with ceilings higher than   3
anybody needs, and a sweeping staircase rising up from the front
hall, with a banister that children more adventurous than my sister
and I (mine, for instance) are always tempted to slide on. There are
plants everywhere, paintings my father made, Mexican pottery, and
a band of tin Mexican soldiers—one on horseback, one playing the
flute, one the tuba. We bought those soldiers on the first trip I ever
made to New York City. They cost way too much, but my mother
said we could get them if we took the bus home instead of flying. So
we did.

One room of the yellow door house is wood paneled and lined   4
with books. There used to be a big overstuffed armchair in it that
I'd settle into with my cookies and milk, when I came home
from school, to do my homework or watch "Leave It to Beaver."
(That chair is in my house now.) There's a porch with a swing
out back, and a sunny corner in the kitchen where I always ate
my toast—grilled in the oven, sometimes with cinnamon sugar
and sometimes jam, but always the way my mother made it, but-
tered on both sides. My mother is a wonderful, natural cook,
who would announce, on a typical night, three different dessert
possibilities, all homemade. Now I wouldn't think of eating a third
piece of blueberry pie. But the old habits return when I walk into
my mother's kitchen. The first thing I do is go see what's in the
refrigerator.

It's been fourteen years since I lived in the yellow door house,   5
but I could still make my way around it blindfolded. There are
places where the house could use some work now, and my mother
never was the best housekeeper. I open a drawer in the big Welsh
dresser in the dining room, looking for a safety pin, and so much
spills out (though not safety pins) that I can't close it again. A person
can choose from five different kinds of cookies in this house. There's

a whole closetful of fabric scraps and antique lace. Eight teapots. But no yardstick, no light bulbs, no scissors.

My children's favorite place in the house is the attic. The front 6 half used to be the studio where my father painted, at night, when he came home from his job as an English teacher. The paintings and paints are long gone now; but my father was a lover of art supplies and hopelessly extravagant when it came to acquiring them, so every once in a while, even now, thirteen years since he's been here, I'll come upon a box of unopened pastels, or watercolor pencils, or the kind of art gum eraser he always used. I'll pick up a stub of an oil pastel and hold it up to my nose, and a wave of feeling will wash over me that almost makes my knees weak. Cadmium yellow light. Cerulean blue. Suddenly I'm ten years old again, sitting on the grass in a field a couple of miles down the road from here, with a sketch pad on my lap and my father beside me, drawing a picture of Ski Jump Hill.

Beyond the room that was my father's studio is the part of our 7 attic where my mother—a hoarder, like me—has stored away just about every toy we ever owned, and most of our old dresses. A ripped Chinese umbrella, a broken wicker rocker, a hooked rug she started and never finished, an exercise roller, purchased around 1947, meant to undo the damage of all those blueberry pies. Songs I wrote when I was nine. My sister's poems. My mother's notes from college English class. My father's powerfully moving proclamations of love to her, written when she was eighteen and he was thirty-eight, when she was telling him she couldn't marry him and he was telling her she must.

Every time we come to the yellow door house to visit, Audrey 8 and Charlie head for the attic—and though we have mostly cleaned out my old Barbies now (and a Midge doll, whose turned-up nose had been partly nibbled off by mice), we never seem to reach the end of the treasures: My homemade dollhouse furniture (I packed it away, room by room, with notes enclosed, to the daughter I knew I would someday have, describing how I'd laid out the rooms.) An old wooden recorder. A brass doll bed. Wonderfully detailed doll clothes my mother made for us every Christmas (at the time, I longed for store-bought). One year she knit a sweater, for a two-inch-tall bear, using toothpicks for knitting needles. Another year she sewed us matching skirts from an old patchwork quilt.

The little town where I grew up (and where I used to know just   9
about everyone) has been growing so fast that my mother hardly
knows anyone on our street anymore. A house like hers has become
so desirable that within days of her arrival this summer, my mother
got a call from a realtor asking if she'd be interested in selling. He
named as a likely asking price a figure neither one of us could
believe. My parents bought the house, thirty years ago, for a fifth of
that amount, and still, they sometimes had to take out loans to meet
the mortgage payments.

For years now, I have been telling my mother that it makes lit-   10
tle sense to hold on to the yellow door house (and to worry about
tenants, make repairs, put away the Mexican tin soldiers every
Labor Day and take them out again every Fourth of July). But I suddenly realized, hearing about this realtor's call, that when the day
comes that my mother sells the house, I will be deeply shaken. I
doubt if I will even want to drive down our old street after that, or
even come back to the town, where I scarcely know anybody anymore. I don't much want to see some other family inventing new
games, new rituals, in our house. Don't want to know where they
put their Christmas tree, or what sort of paintings they hang on their
walls. It would be crazy—impossible—to pack up and haul away all
those dress-up clothes and bits of costume jewelry and boxes of old
book reports and crumbs of pastels. But neither do I relish the
thought of someday having to throw them out.

My mother's yellow door house is a perfect place to play hide-   11
and-seek, and last weekend, when I was there visiting with my three
children, that's what my two sons and I did. I found a hiding place
in the wood-paneled room, behind the couch. I scrunched myself up
so small that several minutes passed without my sons' finding me,
even though they passed through the room more than once.

Many families have rented the house since my mother ceased to   12
make it her full-time home, but the smell—I realized—hasn't
changed. Listening to my children's voices calling out to me through
the rooms, I studied a particular knothole in the paneling, and it
came back to me that this knothole had always reminded me of an
owl. I ran my finger over the wood floors and the upholstery on the
side of the couch, and noted the dust my mother has always tended
to leave in corners. I heard the sewing machine whirring upstairs:
my mother, sewing doll clothes with Audrey. I smelled my mother's
soup on the stove. And for a moment, I wanted time to freeze.

But then I let myself make a small noise. "We found you, we 13
found you," my boys sang out, falling into my arms. And then we
all had lunch, with my mother's chocolate chip cookies for dessert—
and headed back to the house I live in now. Whose door is green.

Meanings and Values

1. Where in the opening paragraph does Maynard introduce the
   themes of change and continuity?

2. List the kinds of memories the objects in the attic call up in the
   author's mind (pars. 6–8).

3. What does the author believe will be lost if her mother sells the
   house?

4a. What is meant by the phrase "I wanted time to freeze" in paragraph
    12?

 b. What actions does the author take in the next paragraph that under-
    mine this wish and the values implied by it?

Expository Techniques

1a. Identify the subjects Maynard describes in each of the paragraphs
    following the opening.

 b. Do these paragraphs generally focus on a single scene (or subject) or
    on several? Be ready to support your answer with examples from the
    text.

 c. Can the descriptions in paragraphs 4 and 10 be considered unified?
    Why, or why not? (See "Guide to Terms": *Unity*.)

2. What use does Maynard make of comparison in paragraphs 2, 12,
   and 13 to convey themes of continuity, permanence, and change?

Diction and Vocabulary

1a. Identify the concrete diction in paragraph 6 and discuss how it con-
    tributes to the effectiveness of the passage. (Guide: *Evaluation*.)

 b. What are the technical terms used in the passage, and how do they
    contribute to its effect? (Guide: *Diction*.)

2a. Why does the author mention the television program "Leave It to
    Beaver" (par. 4)?

 b. In what ways has her life been similar to the life of the family de-
    picted in the series? In what ways has it differed?

Suggestions for Writing and Discussion

1. Do many people today have a chance to return to the homes and apartments in which they grew up? Is it likely that many spent their entire childhoods living in a single house or apartment? How are the childhood memories of people whose families moved often likely to differ from those of Maynard? Are their values likely to differ also?

2. Prepare an essay describing one or more places where you lived as a child. In the course of the description deal with questions of change, loss, growth, continuity, and related matters.

(NOTE: Suggestions for topics requiring development by use of DESCRIPTION are on page 403, at the end of this section.)

GEORGE SIMPSON, born in Virginia in 1950, received his B.A. in journalism from the University of North Carolina. He went to work for *Newsweek* in 1972 and in 1978 became public affairs director for that magazine. Before joining *Newsweek,* Simpson worked for two years as a writer and editor for the *Carolina Financial Times* in Chapel Hill, North Carolina, and as a reporter for the *News-Gazette* in Lexington, Virginia. He received the Best Feature Writing award from Sigma Delta Chi in 1972 for a five-part investigative series on the University of North Carolina football program. He has written stories for *The New York Times, Sport, Glamour,* the *Winston-Salem Journal,* and *New York.*

The War Room at Bellevue

"The War Room at Bellevue" was first published in *New York* magazine. The author chose, for good reason, to stay strictly within a time sequence as he described the emergency ward. This essay is also noteworthy for the cumulative descriptive effect, which was accomplished almost entirely with objective details.

Bellevue. The name conjures up images of an indoor war zone: the   1
wounded and bleeding lining the halls, screaming for help while
harried doctors in blood-stained smocks rush from stretcher to
stretcher, fighting a losing battle against exhaustion and the crushing number of injured. "What's worse," says a longtime Bellevue
nurse, "is that we have this image of being a hospital only for . . ."
She pauses, then lowers her voice; "for crazy people."

Though neither battlefield nor Bedlam is a valid image, there is   2
something extraordinary about the monstrous complex that spreads
for five blocks along First Avenue in Manhattan. It is said best by the

head nurse in Adult Emergency Service: "If you have any chance for survival, you have it here." Survival—that is why they come. Why do injured cops drive by a half-dozen other hospitals to be treated at Bellevue? They've seen the Bellevue emergency team in action.

9:00 P.M. It is a Friday night in the Bellevue emergency room.   3 The after-work crush is over (those who've suffered through the day, only to come for help after the five-o'clock whistle has blown) and it is nearly silent except for the mutter of voices at the admitting desk, where administrative personnel discuss who will go for coffee. Across the spotless white-walled lobby, ten people sit quietly, passively, in pastel plastic chairs, waiting for word of relatives or to see doctors. In the past 24 hours, 300 people have come to the Bellevue Adult Emergency Service. Fewer than 10 percent were true emergencies. One man sleeps fitfully in the emergency ward while his heartbeat, respiration, and blood pressure are monitored by control consoles mounted over his bed. Each heartbeat trips a tiny bleep in the monitor, which attending nurses can hear across the ward. A half hour ago, doctors in the trauma room withdrew a six-inch stiletto blade from his back. When he is stabilized, the patient will be moved upstairs to the twelve-bed Surgical Intensive Care Unit.

9:05 P.M. An ambulance backs into the receiving bay, its red and   4 yellow lights flashing in and out of the lobby. A split second later, the glass doors burst open as a nurse and an attendant roll a mobile stretcher into the lobby. When the nurse screams, "Emergency!" the lobby explodes with activity as the way is cleared to the trauma room. Doctors appear from nowhere and transfer the bloodied body of a black man to the treatment table. Within seconds his clothes are stripped away, revealing a tiny stab wound in his left side. Three doctors and three nurses rush around the victim, each performing a task necessary to begin treatment. Intravenous needles are inserted into his arms and groin. A doctor draws blood for the lab, in case surgery is necessary. A nurse begins inserting a catheter into the victim's penis and continues to feed in tubing until the catheter reaches the bladder. Urine flows through the tube into a plastic bag. Doctors are glad not to see blood in the urine. Another nurse records pulse and blood pressure.

The victim is in good shape. He shivers slightly, although the   5 trauma room is exceedingly warm. His face is bloodied, but shows no major lacerations. A third nurse, her elbow propped on the treatment table, asks the man a series of questions, trying to quickly outline his medical history. He answers abruptly. He is drunk. His left side is swabbed with yellow disinfectant and a doctor injects a local anesthetic. After a few seconds another doctor inserts his finger into the wound. It sinks in all the way to the knuckle. He begins to rotate his finger like a child trying to get a marble out of a milk bottle. The patient screams bloody murder and tries to struggle free.

Meanwhile in the lobby, a security guard is ejecting a derelict who has begun to drink from a bottle hidden in his coat pocket. "He's a regular, was in here just two days ago," says a nurse. "We checked him pretty good then, so he's probably okay now. Can you believe those were clean clothes we gave him?" The old man, blackened by filth, leaves quietly.

9:15 P.M. A young Hispanic man interrupts, saying his pregnant girl friend, sitting outside in his car, is bleeding heavily from her vagina. She is rushed into an examination room, treated behind closed doors, and rolled into the observation ward, where, much later in the night, a gynecologist will treat her in a special room—the same one used to examine rape victims. Nearby, behind curtains, the neurologist examines an old white woman to determine if her headaches are due to head injury. They are not.

9:45 P.M. The trauma room has been cleared and cleaned mercilessly. The examination rooms are three-quarters full—another overdose, two asthmatics, a young woman with abdominal pains. In the hallway, a derelict who has been sleeping it off urinates all over the stretcher. He sleeps on while attendants change his clothes. An ambulance—one of four that patrol Manhattan for Bellevue from 42nd Street to Houston, river to river—delivers a middle-aged white woman and two cops, the three of them soaking wet. The woman has escaped from the psychiatric floor of a nearby hospital and tried to drown herself in the East River. The cops fished her out. She lies on a stretcher shivering beneath white blankets. Her eyes stare at the ceiling. She speaks clearly when an administrative worker begins routine questioning. The cops are given hospital gowns and wait to receive tetanus shots and gamma globulin—a hedge against infection from the befouled river water. They will hang around the E.R. for another two hours, telling their story to as many as six other policemen who show up to hear it. The woman is rolled into an examination room, where a male nurse speaks gently: "They tell me you fell into the river." "No," says the woman, "I jumped. I have to commit suicide." "Why?" asks the nurse. "Because I'm insane and I can't help [it]. I have to die." The nurse gradually discovers the woman has a history of psychological problems. She is given dry bedclothes and placed under guard in the hallway. She lies on her side, staring at the wall.

The pace continues to increase. Several more overdose victims   9
arrive by ambulance. One, a young black woman, had done a striptease on the street just before passing out. A second black woman is semiconscious and spends the better part of her time at Bellevue alternately cursing at and pleading with the doctors. Attendants find a plastic bottle coated with methadone in the pocket of a Hispanic O.D. The treatment is routinely the same, and sooner or later involves vomiting. Just after doctors begin to treat the O.D., he vomits great quantities of wine and methadone in all directions. "Lovely business, huh?" laments one of the doctors. A young nurse confides that if there were other true emergencies, the overdose victims would be given lower priority. "You can't help thinking they did it to themselves," she says, "while the others are accident victims."

10:30 P.M. A policeman who twisted his knee struggling with an   10
"alleged perpetrator" is examined and released. By 10:30, the lobby is jammed with friends and relatives of patients in various stages of treatment and recovery. The attendant who also functions as a translator for Hispanic patients adds chairs to accommodate the overflow. The medical walk-in rate stays steady—between eight and ten patients waiting. A pair of derelicts, each with battered eyes, appear at the admitting desk. One has a dramatically swollen face laced with black stitches.

11:00 P.M. The husband of the attempted suicide arrives. He   11
thanks the police for saving his wife's life, then talks at length with doctors about her condition. She continues to stare into the void and does not react when her husband approaches her stretcher.

Meanwhile, patients arrive in the lobby at a steady pace. A   12
young G.I. on leave has lower-back pains; a Hispanic man complains of pains in his side; occasionally parents hurry through the adult E.R. carrying children to the pediatric E.R. A white woman of about 50 marches into the lobby from the walk-in entrance. Dried blood covers her right eyebrow and upper lip. She begins to perform. "I was assaulted on 28th and Lexington, I was," she says grandly, "and I don't have to take it *anymore.* I was a bride 21 years ago and, God, I was beautiful then." She has captured the attention of all present.

"I was there when the boys came home—on Memorial Day—and I don't have to take this kind of treatment."

As midnight approaches, the nurses prepare for the shift change. They must brief the incoming staff and make sure all reports are up-to-date. One young brunet says, "Christ, I'm gonna go home and take a shower—I smell like vomit."

11:50 P.M. The triage nurse is questioning an old black man about chest pains, and a Hispanic woman is having an asthma attack, when an ambulance, its sirens screaming full tilt, roars into the receiving bay. There is a split-second pause as everyone drops what he or she is doing and looks up. Then all hell breaks loose. Doctors and nurses are suddenly sprinting full-out toward the trauma room. The glass doors burst open and the occupied stretcher is literally run past me. Cops follow. It is as if a comet has whooshed by. In the trauma room it all becomes clear. A half-dozen doctors and nurses surround the lifeless form of a Hispanic man with a shotgun hole in his neck the size of your fist. Blood pours from a second gaping wound in his chest. A respirator is slammed over his face, making his chest rise and fall as if he were breathing. "No pulse," reports one doctor. A nurse jumps on a stool and, leaning over the man, begins to pump his chest with her palms. "No blood pressure," screams another nurse. The ambulance driver appears shaken, "I never thought I'd get here in time," he stutters. More doctors from the trauma team upstairs arrive. Wrappings from syringes and gauze pads fly through the air. The victim's eyes are open yet devoid of life. His body takes on a yellow tinge. A male nurse winces at the gunshot wound. "This guy really pissed off somebody," he says. This is no ordinary shooting. It is an execution. IV's are jammed into the body in the groin and arms. One doctor has been plugging in an electrocardiograph and asks everyone to stop for a second so he can get a reading. "Forget it," shouts the doctor in charge. "No time." "Take it easy, Jimmy," someone yells at the head physician. It is apparent by now that the man is dead, but the doctors keep trying injections and finally they slit open the chest and reach inside almost up to their elbows. They feel the extent of the damage and suddenly it is all over. "I told 'em he was dead," says one nurse, withdrawing. "They didn't listen." The room is very still. The doctors are momentarily disgusted, then go on about their business. The room clears quickly. Finally there is only a male nurse and the still-warm body, now waxy-yellow, with huge ribs exposed on both sides of the chest and giant holes in both sides of the neck. The nurse speculates that this is yet another murder in a Hispanic political struggle that has brought many such victims to Bellevue. He marvels at the extent of the wounds and repeats, "This guy was really blown away."

Midnight. A hysterical woman is hustled through the lobby into   15
an examination room. It is the dead man's wife, and she is nearly delirious. "I know he's dead, I know he's dead," she screams over and over. Within moments the lobby is filled with anxious relatives of the victim, waiting for word on his condition. The police are everywhere asking questions, but most people say they saw nothing. One young woman says she heard six shots, two louder than the other four. At some point, word is passed that the man is, in fact, dead. Another woman breaks down in hysterics; everywhere young Hispanics are crying and comforting each other. Plainclothes detectives make a quick examination of the body, check on the time of pronouncement of death, and begin to ask questions, but the bereaved are too stunned to talk. The rest of the uninvolved people in the lobby stare dumbly, their injuries suddenly paling in light of a death.

12:30 A.M. A black man appears at the admissions desk and says   16
he drank poison by mistake. He is told to have a seat. The ambulance brings in a young white woman, her head wrapped in white gauze. She is wailing terribly. A girl friend stands over her, crying, and a boyfriend clutches the injured woman's hands, saying, "I'm here, don't worry, I'm here." The victim has fallen downstairs at a friend's house. Attendants park her stretcher against the wall to wait for an examination room to clear. There are eight examination rooms and only three doctors. Unless you are truly an emergency, you will wait. One doctor is stitching up the eyebrow of a drunk who's been punched out. The friends of the woman who fell down the stairs glance up at the doctors anxiously, wondering why their friend isn't being treated faster.

1:10 A.M. A car pulls into the bay and a young Hispanic asks if   17
a shooting victim has been brought here. The security guard blurts out, "He's dead." The young man is stunned. He peels his tires leaving the bay.

1:20 A.M. The young woman of the stairs is getting stitches in a   18
small gash over her left eye when the same ambulance driver who brought in the gunshot victim delivers a man who has been stabbed in the back on East 3rd Street. Once again the trauma room goes

from 0 to 60 in five seconds. The patient is drunk, which helps him endure the pain of having the catheter inserted through his penis into his bladder. Still he yells, "That hurts like a bastard," then adds sheepishly, "Excuse me, ladies." But he is not prepared for what comes next. An X-ray reveals a collapsed right lung. After just a shot of local anesthetic, the doctor slices open his side and inserts a long plastic tube. Internal bleeding had kept the lung pressed down and prevented it from reinflating. The tube releases the pressure. The ambulance driver says the cops grabbed the guy who ran the eight-inch blade into the victim's back. "That's not the one," says the man. "They got the wrong guy." A nurse reports that there is not much of the victim's type blood available at the hospital. One of the doctors says that's okay, he won't need surgery. Meanwhile blood pours from the man's knife wound and the tube in his side. As the nurses work, they chat about personal matters, yet they respond immediately to orders from either doctor. "How ya doin'?" the doctor asks the patient. "Okay," he says. His blood spatters on the floor.

So it goes into the morning hours. A Valium overdose, a woman who fainted, a man who went through the windshield of his car. More overdoses. More drunks with split eyebrows and chins. The doctors and nurses work without complaint. "This is nothing, about normal, I'd say," concludes the head nurse. "No big deal." 19

Meanings and Values

1a. What is the author's point of view? (See "Guide to Terms": *Point of View*.)

 b. How is this reflected by the tone? (Guide: *Style/Tone*.)

2. Does Simpson ever slip into sentimentality—a common failing when describing the scenes of death and tragedy? (Guide: *Sentimentality*.) If so, where? If not, how does he avoid it?

3a. Cite at least six facts learned from reading this piece that are told, not in general terms, but by specific, concrete details—e.g., that a high degree of cleanliness is maintained at Bellevue, illustrated by "the spotless white-walled lobby" (par. 3) and "the trauma room has been cleared and cleaned mercilessly" (par. 8).

 b. What are the advantages of having facts presented in this way?

Expository Techniques

1. How do you think the author went about selecting details, from among the thousands that must have been available to him?

2a. Do you consider the writing to be primarily objective or impressionistic?

  b. Clarify any apparent contradictions.

  c. What is the dominant impression, if any?

3. What is the value of using a timed sequence in such a description?

4. Does it seem to you that any of this description is excessive—i.e., unnecessary to the task at hand?

5a. List, in skeletal form, the facts learned about the subject from reading the two-paragraph introduction.

  b. How well does it perform the three basic purposes of an introduction? (Guide: *Introductions.*)

6. What is the significance of the rhetorical question in paragraph 2? (Guide: *Rhetorical Questions.*) Why is it rhetorical?

7. Is the short closing effective? (Guide: *Closings.*) Why, or why not?

Diction and Vocabulary

1a. Cite the clichés in paragraphs 4, 5, 8, and 14. (Guide: *Clichés.*)

  b. What justification, if any, can you offer for their use?

2. Cite the allusion in paragraph 2, and explain its meaning and source. (Guide: *Figure of Speech.*)

3a. Simpson uses some slang and other colloquialisms. Cite as many of these as you can. (Guide: *Colloquial Expressions.*)

  b. Is their use justified? Why, or why not?

4. Why is "alleged perpetrator" placed in quotation marks (par. 10)?

Suggestions for Writing and Discussion

1. Explain why "neither battlefield nor Bedlam is a valid image" of the emergency room at Bellevue (pars. 1, 2).

2. Do you think it is right and/or understandable that O.D.'s should be given lower priorities than "true emergencies" (par. 9)? Defend your views.

3. If you have had a job that to the outsider might seem hectic or hazardous, or both, were the personnel also able to "chat about personal matters" while the work was in progress? What were the circumstances?

(NOTE: Suggestions for topics requiring development by use of DESCRIPTION are on page 403, at the end of this section.)

LUIS J. RODRIGUEZ

Luis J. Rodriguez was born in El Paso, Texas in 1954 but spent his childhood and youth in Watts and East Los Angeles. While he was growing up, Rodriguez was both a gang member and an aspiring writer. At sixteen he began writing an account of his experiences with poverty and gang life in Los Angeles, an account which eventually became *Always Running—La Vida Loca: Gang Days in L.A.* (1993). His award-winning writing has also appeared in *Poems Across the Pavement* (1989), *The Concrete River* (1991), and articles in such magazines and newspapers as *The Chicago Review, TriQuarterly, Left Curve, Milestones, El Grito, The Los Angeles Times,* and *The National Catholic Reporter.* He currently lives in Chicago, where he runs the Tia Chucha Press, and he works with groups throughout the country seeking to reduce gang violence.

The Ice Cream Truck

In "The Ice Cream Truck,"[1] a selection from *Always Running,* Rodriguez links descriptions of several "ruins" (places, things, and people) with a loose narrative. Taken together, the descriptions help explain what it was like to grow up in a community shaped—or distorted—by poverty and careless violence.

> "You *cholos* have great stories about climbing fences."
>
> —a barrio boxing coach

The Hills blistered below a haze of sun and smog. Mothers with wet   1
strands of hair across their foreheads flung wash up to dry on
weathered lines. Sweat-drenched men lay on their backs in the
gravel of alleys, beneath broken-down cars propped up on cinder
blocks. *Charrangas* and *corridos* splashed out of open windows.

[1]Editors' title

Suddenly from over a hill, an ice cream truck raced by with 2 packs of children running beside it. A hurried version of "Old McDonald Had A Farm" chimed through a speaker bolted on the truck's roof. The truck stopped long enough for somebody to toss out dozens of sidewalk sundaes, tootie-fruities and half-and-half bars to the children who gathered around, thrusting up small, dirt-caked hands that blossomed open as their shrieks blended with laughter.

Then the truck's transmission gears growled as it continued up 3 the slope, whipped around a corner and passed a few of us *vatos* assembled on a field off Toll Drive. We looked over toward the echoes of the burdensome chimes, the slip and boom of the clutch and rasp of gears as the ice cream truck entered the dead-end streets and curves of Las Lomas.

"*Orale, ése, ¿qué está pasando?*" a dude named Little Man asked 4 while passing a bottle of Tokay wine to Clavo.

"It's Toots and the *gaba,* you know, Axel," Clavo replied. "They 5 just stole an ice cream truck on Portrero Grande Drive."

"*¡Qué cábula!*" Little Man said. "They sure is crazy." 6

We continued to talk and drink until the day melted into night. 7

Little Man and one of the López brothers, Fernie, all Tribe, were 8 there in the field with me and my *camaradas* Clavo, Chicharrón, and Wilo. The four of us were so often together that the list of our names became a litany. We spray-painted our *placas* on the walls, followed by *AT* for Animal Tribe or *SSG* for South San Gabriel.

Everyone called me Chin because of my protruding jawbone. I 9 had it tattooed on my ankle.

We sat around a small roasting pit Chicharrón made from 10 branches and newspaper. Around us were ruins, remains of a home which had been condemned and later ravaged by fire. We assembled inside the old cement foundation with its scattered sections of brick and concrete walls splattered with markings and soot with rusted re-enforcing bars protruding from stone blocks.

We furnished the lot with beat-up couches and discarded sofas. 11 Somebody hung plastic from a remaining cinder-block wall to a low branch so homeboys could sleep there—and miss most of any rain— when there was nowhere else to go. It was really a vacant lot but we called all such lots "the fields."

Even as we talked, there was Noodles, a wino and old *tecato*, 12 crashed out on the sofa.

"Get up Noodles, time for some *refín*," Chicharrón exclaimed as 13 he placed stolen hot dogs and buns on the fire. Wilo threw a dirt clod at the sofa and Noodles mumbled some incoherent words.

"*Orale*, leave the *vato* alone, *ése*," Little Man said. 14

But Noodles got up, spittle dripping from his mouth. 15

"Hey *ése*, Noodles is awake, and man is he pissed," Wilo said. 16

"How can you tell?" Chicharrón asked. 17

"When he moves fast and you can't understand what he's say- 18 ing, then he's pissed," Wilo answered. "When he moves slow and you still can't understand what he's saying, he's all right."

Noodles staggered toward us, his arms flailing, as if boxing— 19 huffing, puffing and dropping mucus from his nose.

"Get the hell out of here, *pinche*," Wilo said as he stood up and 20 pushed the wino aside.

"You thinks youse are tuss dues . . . you ain't so tuss," Noodles 21 said, throwing sloppy left hooks and uppercuts into the air.

Wilo placed his hand over Noodles' head, whose wiry body 22 looked like a strand from a dirty mop. Wilo was also thin and slippery. The rest of us laughed and laughed at the two *flaquillos* goofing around.

"Ah leave the *vato* alone, homeboy," Clavo suggested. "Let's 23 break out another bottle."

As we cooked, shared wine and told stories of *jainas* and the 24 little conquests, of fights for honor, homeys and the 'hood, a gray Mercury sedan with its headlights turned off crept up the road. Wilo was the closest up the slope to the street. He looked over at the Mercury, then frowned.

"Anybody recognize the *ranfla?*" Wilo inquired. 25

"*Chale*," Chicharrón responded. "It looks too funky to be gang- 26 bangers."

"Unless that's what they want it to look like." 27

Wilo moved up the slope from the field, followed by Clavo, 28 Chicharrón and Little Man. Fernie stayed back with Noodles and me. Wilo and Clavo were the first ones to hit the street as the Mercury delayed a turn around a curve.

Clavo moved to one side of the Mercury, its occupants covered 29 in darkness. He stretched out his arms and yelled out: "Here stand The Animal Tribe—*¡y qué!*"

The Mercury stopped. A shadow stepped out of a bashed-in   30
side door, a sawed-off shotgun in his hands. Another shadow
pushed an automatic rifle out the side window.

"Sangra Diablos! *¡Qué rifa!*" the dude with the shotgun yelled   31
out. Then a blast snapped at the night air.

Wilo and Chicharrón fell back down the slope. Automatic gun-   32
fire followed them as they rolled in the dirt. The bullets skimmed off
tree branches, knocked over trash cans and ricocheted off walls.
Wilo ended up face-down; Chicharrón landed on his butt. Noodles
knelt behind the sofa, whimpering. The cracking sounds stopped.
The Mercury sped off, its tires throwing up dirt and pebbles
behind it.

I could see the car speeding down another hill. I ran up the   33
slope, slipping and sliding toward the road. On the street, Little Man
kneeled over Clavo, who lay sprawled on the ground and trembling.
Half of Clavo's face was shot full of pellets, countless black, stream-
ing round holes; his eye dripping into the dirt.

Wilo and the others climbed up and rushed up to Little Man.   34
Fernie began jumping up and down like he had been jolted with
lightning, letting out *gritos*. I kept looking at Clavo's face, thinking
something stupid like how he was such a dummy, always taking
chances, all the time being "the dude." Then I squatted on the
ground, closed my eyelid and let a tear stream down the side of
my face.

Windows flung upwards. Doors were pushed aside. People   35
bolted out of their homes. Mothers cursed in Spanish from behind
weather-beaten picket fences.

As Clavo was taken to the hospital, Fernie talked about getting   36
all the Tribe together, about meeting later that night, about guns and
warfare and *"ya estuvo"*—that's it. A war, fought for generations
between Lomas and Sangra, flared up again.

Later, as I walked down the hills on the way back home, sirens   37
tore across the sky and a sheriff's helicopter hovered nearby, beam-
ing a spotlight across shacks and brush, over every hole and crevice
of the neighborhood.

I mounted a fence which wound around a dirt embankment,   38
hoping to get out of the helicopter's sights. I looked over the other
side and there overturned at the bottom of the gully, to be ravaged
by scavengers for parts, to be another barrio monument, lay an ice
cream truck.

Meanings and Values

1a. In what way are the attitudes and behaviors of the groups of people in paragraphs 1 (adults), 2 (children), and 24 (youths) alike? In what ways do they differ?

b. What commentary on the behavior and values of the young men is implied by the description of Noodles and his behavior?

2a. Can the ice cream truck be considered a symbol, especially at the end of the selection? (See "Guide to Terms": *Symbol*.)

b. If so, explain its meaning. If not, tell why the writer chose to have it appear at the beginning and again in paragraph 38.

3a. In what ways can each of the following be considered ruined or de-cayed: the ice cream truck, the home where the youths gather, Noo-dles, the Animal Tribe after the confrontation, and the neighborhood as a whole?

b. How is emphasis on decay and ruin in each of these cases related to the selection's central theme? (Guide: *Unity*.)

Expository Techniques

1a. Identify the main subject or subjects being described in each of the following sections of the piece: paragraphs 1–3, 4–9, 10–11, 12–23, 24–32, 33–36, and 37–38.

b. What indications are there in the text that the writer wants us to re-gard these as different units of the piece? (Hint: Look for shifts in time or place and for transitions.) (Guide: *Transitions*.)

2a. What aspects of the scene or the characters does Rodriguez focus on in paragraphs 1–3? 13–23? 32–34? 36–37?

b. What might account for the differences (or similarities) in the de-scriptive techniques the writer employs in each of these sections?

3a. Where in the essay does the author state or come close to stating the central theme?

b. Should the central theme have been stated more (or less) directly? Why?

c. If readers were asked to state the central theme of this piece, would their statements probably be similar or dissimilar? Be ready to ex-plain your reasoning.

Diction and Vocabulary

1a. This selection employs a number of Spanish words and phrases. Do you think that their presence will make the piece hard for most readers to understand? Why, or why not? Explain your reasoning and support it with specific examples from the text.

b. For what purpose might Rodriguez have included so many Spanish terms? (Guide: *Purpose.*)

c. If you have read Gloria Anzaldua's "Tlilli, Tlapalli," (pp. 572–582), compare her use of Spanish words and phrases with Rodriguez's use.

2. Discuss the contribution of specific, concrete language to the descriptions in paragraphs 1–2 and 10–11. (Guide: *Concrete.*)

3. Identify two paragraphs from different parts of the selection in which Rodriguez uses slang and comment on the contributions of the language to the portrait of the scene or person being described. (Guide: *Slang.*)

Suggestions for Writing and Discussion

1. Compare Rodriguez's description of gang members and their community with those frequently presented on television and in films and newspapers.

2. If you were to write about your own childhood or high school years, how might your descriptions be similar to or different from those of Rodriguez?

3. To what extent is Rodriguez critical of the people he portrays and to what extent is he sympathetic towards them?

(NOTE: Suggestions for topics requiring development by use of DESCRIPTION are on page 403, at the end of this section.)

E. B. WHITE

E. B. WHITE, distinguished essayist, was born in Mount Vernon, New York, in 1899 and died in 1985 in North Brooklin, Maine. A graduate of Cornell University, White worked as a reporter and advertising copywriter, and in 1926 he joined the staff of the *New Yorker* magazine. After 1937 he did most of his writing at his farm in Maine, for many years contributing a regular column, "One Man's Meat," to *Harper's* magazine and freelance editorials for the "Notes and Comments" column of the *New Yorker*. White also wrote children's books, two volumes of verse, and, with James Thurber, *Is Sex Necessary?* (1929). With his wife, Katherine White, he compiled *A Subtreasury of American Humor* (1941). Collections of his own essays include *One Man's Meat* (1942), *The Second Tree from the Corner* (1953), *The Points of My Compass* (1962), and *Essays of E. B. White* (1977). In 1959 he revised and enlarged William Strunk's *The Elements of Style*, a textbook still widely used in college classrooms. White received many honors and writing awards for his crisp, highly individual style and his sturdy independence of thought.

Once More to the Lake

In this essay White relies primarily on description to convey his sense of the passage of time and the power of memory. The vivid scenes and the clear yet expressive prose in this essay are characteristic of his writing.

August 1941

One summer, along about 1904, my father rented a camp on a lake 1
in Maine and took us all there for the month of August. We all got
ringworm from some kittens and had to rub Pond's Extract on our
arms and legs night and morning, and my father rolled over in a

canoe with all his clothes on; but outside of that the vacation was a success and from then on none of us ever thought there was any place in the world like that lake in Maine. We returned summer after summer—always on August 1 for one month. I have since become a salt-water man, but sometimes in summer there are days when the restlessness of the tides and the fearful cold of the sea water and the incessant wind that blows across the afternoon and into the evening make me wish for the placidity of a lake in the woods. A few weeks ago this feeling got so strong I bought myself a couple of bass hooks and a spinner and returned to the lake where we used to go, for a week's fishing and to revisit old haunts.

I took along my son, who had never had any fresh water up his   2
nose and who had seen lily pads only from train windows. On the journey over to the lake I began to wonder what it would be like. I wondered how time would have marred this unique, this holy spot—the coves and streams, the hills that the sun set behind, the camps and the paths behind the camps. I was sure that the tarred road would have found it out, and I wondered in what other ways it would be desolated. It is strange how much you can remember about places like that once you allow your mind to return into the grooves that lead back. You remember one thing, and that suddenly reminds you of another thing. I guess I remembered clearest of all the early mornings, when the lake was cool and motionless, remembered how the bedroom smelled of the lumber it was made of and of the wet woods whose scent entered through the screen. The partitions in the camp were thin and did not extend clear to the top of the rooms, and as I was always the first up I would dress softly so as not to wake the others, and sneak out into the sweet outdoors and start out in the canoe, keeping close along the shore in the long shadows of the pines. I remembered being very careful never to rub my paddle against the gunwale for fear of disturbing the stillness of the cathedral.

The lake had never been what you would call a wild lake. There   3
were cottages sprinkled around the shores, and it was in farming country although the shores of the lake were quite heavily wooded. Some of the cottages were owned by nearby farmers, and you would live at the shore and eat your meals at the farmhouse. That's what our family did. But although it wasn't wild, it was a fairly large and undisturbed lake and there were places in it that, to a child at least, seemed infinitely remote and primeval.

I was right about the tar: it led to within half a mile of the shore.   4
But when I got back there, with my boy, and we settled into a camp
near a farmhouse and into the kind of summertime I had known, I
could tell that it was going to be pretty much the same as it had been
before—I knew it, lying in bed the first morning, smelling the bedroom and hearing the boy sneak quietly out and go off along the
shore in a boat. I began to sustain the illusion that he was I, and
therefore, by simple transposition, that I was my father. This sensation persisted, kept cropping up all the time we were there. It was
not an entirely new feeling, but in this setting it grew much stronger.
I seemed to be living a dual existence. I would be in the middle of
some simple act, I would be picking up a bait box or laying down a
table fork, or I would be saying something, and suddenly it would
be not I but my father who was saying the words or making the gesture. It gave me a creepy sensation.

We went fishing the first morning. I felt the same damp moss   5
covering the worms in the bait can, and saw the dragonfly alight on
the tip of my rod as it hovered a few inches from the surface of the
water. It was the arrival of this fly that convinced me beyond any
doubt that everything was as it always had been, that the years were
a mirage and that there had been no years. The small waves were the
same, chucking the rowboat under the chin as we fished at anchor,
and the boat was the same boat, the same color green and the ribs
broken in the same places, and under the floorboards the same freshwater leavings and débris—the dead helgramite, the wisps of moss,
the rusty discarded fishhook, the dried blood from yesterday's
catch. We stared silently at the tips of our rods, at the dragonflies
that came and went. I lowered the tip of mine into the water, tentatively, pensively dislodging the fly, which darted two feet away,
poised, darted two feet back, and came to rest again a little farther
up the rod. There had been no years between the ducking of this
dragonfly and the other one—the one that was part of memory. I
looked at the boy, who was silently watching his fly, and it was my
hands that held his rod, my eyes watching. I felt dizzy and didn't
know which rod I was at the end of.

We caught two bass, hauling them in briskly as though they   6
were mackerel, pulling them over the side of the boat in a busi-
nesslike manner without any landing net, and stunning them with a
blow on the back of the head. When we got back for a swim before
lunch, the lake was exactly where we had left it, the same number of

inches from the dock, and there was only the merest suggestion of a breeze. This seemed an utterly enchanted sea, this lake you could leave to its own devices for a few hours and come-back to, and find that it had not stirred, this constant and trustworthy body of water. In the shallows, the dark, water-soaked sticks and twigs, smooth and old, were undulating in clusters on the bottom against the clean ribbed sand, and the track of the mussel was plain. A school of minnows swam by, each minnow with its small individual shadow, doubling the attendance, so clear and sharp in the sunlight. Some of the other campers were in swimming, along the shore, one of them with a cake of soap, and the water felt thin and clear and unsubstantial. Over the years there had been this person with the cake of soap, this cultist, and here he was. There had been no years.

Up to the farmhouse to dinner through the teeming, dusty field, the road under our sneakers was only a two-track road. The middle track was missing, the one with the marks of the hooves and the splotches of dried, flaky manure. There had always been three tracks to choose from in choosing which track to walk in; now the choice was narrowed down to two. For a moment I missed terribly the middle alternative. But the way led past the tennis court, and something about the way it lay there in the sun reassured me; the tape had loosened along the backline, the alleys were green with plantains and other weeds, and the net (installed in June and removed in September) sagged in the dry noon, and the whole place steamed with midday heat and hunger and emptiness. There was a choice of pie for dessert, and one was blueberry and one was apple, and the waitresses were the same country girls, there having been no passage of time, only the illusion of it as in a dropped curtain—the waitresses were still fifteen; their hair had been washed, that was the only difference—they had been to the movies and seen the pretty girls with the clean hair. 7

Summertime, oh, summertime, pattern of life indelible, the fade-proof lake, the woods unshatterable, the pasture with the sweetfern and the juniper forever and ever, summer without end; this was the background, and the life along the shore was the design, their tiny docks with the flagpole and the American flag floating against the white clouds in the blue sky, the little paths over the roots of the trees leading from camp to camp and the paths leading back to the outhouses and the can of lime for sprinkling, and at the souvenir counters at the store the miniature birch-bark canoes and 8 the postcards that showed things looking a little better than they looked. This was the American family at play, escaping the city heat, wondering whether the newcomers in the camp at the head of the cove were "common" or "nice," wondering whether it was true that the people who drove up for Sunday dinner at the farmhouse were turned away because there wasn't enough chicken.

It seemed to me, as I kept remembering all this, that those times 9 and those summers had been infinitely precious and worth saving. There had been jollity and peace and goodness. The arriving (at the beginning of August) had been so big a business in itself, at the railway station the farm wagon drawn up, the first smell of the pine-laden air, the first glimpse of the smiling farmer, and the great importance of the trunks and your father's enormous authority in such matters, and the feel of the wagon under you for the long ten-mile haul, and at the top of the last long hill catching the first view of the lake after eleven months of not seeing this cherished body of water. The shouts and cries of the other campers when they saw you, and the trunks to be unpacked, to give up their rich burden. (Arriving was less exciting nowadays, when you sneaked up in your car and parked it under a tree near the camp and took out the bags and in five minutes it was all over, no fuss, no loud wonderful fuss about trunks.)

Peace and goodness and jollity. The only thing that was wrong 10 now, really, was the sound of the place, an unfamiliar nervous sound of the outboard motors. This was the note that jarred, the one thing that would sometimes break the illusion and set the years moving. In those other summertimes all motors were inboard; and when they were at a little distance, the noise they made was a seda-tive, an ingredient of summer sleep. They were one-cylinder and two-cylinder engines, and some were make-and-break and some were jump-spark, but they all made a sleepy sound across the lake. The one-lungers throbbed and fluttered, and the twin-cylinder ones purred and purred, and that was a quiet sound, too. But now the campers all had outboards. In the daytime, in the hot mornings, these motors made a petulant, irritable sound; at night, in the still evening when the afterglow lit the water, they whined about one's ears like mosquitoes. My boy loved our rented outboard, and his great desire was to achieve single-handed mastery over it, and authority, and he soon learned the trick of choking it a little (but not too much), and the adjustment of the needle valve. Watching him I would remember the things you could do with the old one-cylinder engine with the heavy flywheel, how you could have it eating out of your hand if you got really close to it spiritually. Motorboats in those days didn't have clutches, and you would make a landing by shutting off the motor at the proper time and coasting in with a dead rudder. But there was a way of reversing them, if you learned the trick, by cutting the switch and putting it on again exactly on the final dying revolution of the flywheel, so that it would kick back against compression and begin reversing. Approaching a dock in a strong following breeze, it was difficult to slow up sufficiently by the ordinary coasting method, and if a boy felt he had complete mastery over his motor, he was tempted to keep it running beyond its time and then reverse it a few feet from the dock. It took a cool nerve, because if you threw the switch a twentieth of a second too soon you would catch the flywheel when it still had speed enough to go up past center, and the boat would leap ahead, charging bull-fashion at the dock.

    We had a good week at the camp. The bass were biting well and   11
the sun shone endlessly, day after day. We would be tired at night and lie down in the accumulated heat of the little bedrooms after the long hot day and the breeze would stir almost imperceptibly outside and the smell of the swamp drift in through the rusty screens. Sleep would come easily and in the morning the red squirrel would be on the roof, tapping out his gay routine. I kept remembering everything, lying in bed in the mornings—the small steamboat that had a long rounded stern like the lip of a Ubangi, and how quietly she ran on the moonlight sails, when the older boys played their mandolins and the girls sang and we ate doughnuts dipped in sugar, and how sweet the music was on the water in the shining night, and what it had felt like to think about girls then. After breakfast we would go up to the store and the things were in the same place—the minnows in a bottle, the plugs and spinners disarranged and pawed over by the youngsters from the boys' camp, the Fig Newtons and the Beeman's gum. Outside, the road was tarred and cars stood in front of the store. Inside, all was just as it had always been, except there was more Coca-Cola and not so much Moxie and root beer and birch beer and sarsaparilla. We would walk out with the bottle of pop apiece and sometimes the pop would backfire up our noses and hurt. We explored the streams, quietly, where the turtles slid off the sunny logs and dug their way into the soft bottom; and we lay on the

town wharf and fed worms to the tame bass. Everywhere we went I had trouble making out which was I, the one walking at my side, the one walking in my pants.

One afternoon while we were there at that lake a thunderstorm 12 came up. It was like the revival of an old melodrama that I had seen long ago with childish awe. The second-act climax of the drama of the electrical disturbance over a lake in America had not changed in any important respect. This was the big scene, still the big scene. The whole thing was so familiar, the first feeling of oppression and heat and a general air around camp of not wanting to go very far away. In mid-afternoon (it was all the same) a curious darkening of the sky, and a lull in everything that had made life tick; and then the way the boats suddenly swung the other way at their moorings with the coming of a breeze out of the new quarter, and the premonitory rumble. Then the kettle drum, then the snare, then the bass drum and cymbals, then crackling light against the dark, and the gods grinning and licking their chops in the hills. Afterward the calm, the rain steadily rustling in the calm lake, the return of light and hope and spirits, and the campers running out in joy and relief to go swimming in the rain, their bright cries perpetuating the deathless joke about how they were getting simply drenched, and the children screaming with delight at the new sensation of bathing in the rain, and the joke about getting drenched linking the generations in a strong indestructible chain. And the comedian who waded in carrying an umbrella.

When the others went swimming, my son said he was going in, 13 too. He pulled his dripping trunks from the line where they had hung all through the shower and wrung them out. Languidly, and with no thought of going in, I watched him, his hard little body, skinny and bare, saw him wince slightly as he pulled up around his vitals the small, soggy, icy garment. As he buckled the swollen belt, suddenly my groin felt the chill of death.

Meanings and Values

1a.   Why does White decide to return to the lake?

  b.   Can the lake be considered a personal symbol for White? (See "Guide to Terms": *Symbol*.) If so, what does it symbolize?

2.   In what ways have the lake and its surroundings remained the same since White's boyhood? Be specific. In what ways have they changed?

3a. At one point in the essay White says, "I seemed to be living a dual existence" (par. 4). What is the meaning of this statement?

b. How does this "dual existence" affect his point of view in the essay? (Guide: *Point of View.*)

c. Is the "dual existence" emphasized more in the first half of the essay or the second half? Why?

4a. Where would you place this essay on an objective-to-subjective continuum? (Guide: *Objective/Subjective.*)

b. Is this a formal or an informal essay? Explain. (Guide: *Essay.*)

5a. After spending a day on the lake, White remarks, "There had been no years" (par. 6). What other direct or indirect comments does he make about time and change? Be specific.

b. How are these comments related to the central theme of the essay? (Guide: *Unity.*)

6a. What is the tone of the essay? (Guide: *Style/Tone.*)

b. Does the tone change or remain the same throughout the essay?

7a. What is meant by the closing phrase of the essay, "suddenly my groin felt the chill of death" (par. 13)?

b. Is this an appropriate way to end the essay? Why, or why not?

Expository Techniques

1. If you agree that the lake is a personal symbol for White, explain how he enables readers to understand its significance. (Guide: *Symbol.*)

2a. In the first part of the essay White focuses on the unchanged aspects of the lake; in the second part he begins acknowledging the passage of time. Where does this shift in attitude take place?

b. What strategies, including transitional devices, does White use to signal to the reader the shift in attitude? Be specific.

3. How does White use the discussion of outboard motors and inboard motors (par. 10) to summarize the differences between life at the lake in his youth and at the time of his return with his son? Explain.

4. Many of the descriptive passages in this essay convey a dominant impression, usually an emotion or mood. Choose a paragraph from the essay and discuss how the author's choice of details, variety of syntax, and diction help create a dominant impression. Be specific. (Guide: *Syntax and Diction.*)

5a. In many places the author combines description and comparison. Select a passage from the essay and discuss in detail how he combines the patterns.

b. In what ways is the combination of description and comparison appropriate to the theme and the point of view of the essay?

6. White has often been praised for the clarity and variety of his prose style. To what extent are these qualities the result of syntax and of the variety of strategies he uses to achieve emphasis? (Choose a sample paragraph, such as 6, 9, or 12, to illustrate your answer.) (Guide: *Emphasis and Syntax.*)

Diction and Vocabulary

1. To what extent are the qualities of White's style mentioned in your answer to question 6 of "Expository Techniques" matters of diction? (Guide: *Diction.*)

a. How much do the connotations of the words used in paragraph 8 contribute to the dominant impression the author is trying to create? (Guide: *Connotation/Denotation.*) In paragraph 10?

2a. Why would the author refer to the person with the cake of soap as "this cultist" (par. 6)?

b. In what sense can a tennis court steam "with midday heat and hunger and emptiness" (par. 7)?

3. What kind of paradox is presented in this passage: ". . . the waitresses were the same country girls, there having been no passage of time, only the illusion of it as in a dropped curtain—the waitresses were still fifteen; their hair had been washed, that was the only difference—they had been to the movies and seen the pretty girls with the clean hair" (par. 7)? (Guide: *Paradox.*)

4a. Is the diction in this passage sentimental: "Summertime, oh, summertime, pattern of life indelible, the fade-proof lake, the woods unshatterable, the pasture with the sweetfern and the juniper forever and ever, summer without end . . . " (par. 8)? (Guide: *Sentimentality.*)

b. If so, why would the author choose to use this style in the passage?

c. Does the passage contain an allusion? If so, what is alluded to and why? (Guide: *Figures of Speech.*)

5. Study the author's uses of the following words, consulting the dictionary as needed: incessant, placidity (par. 1); gunwale (2); primeval (3); transposition (4); helgramite, pensively (5); petulant (10); premonitory (12); languidly (13).

Suggestions for Writing and Discussion

1. Choose some place you remember from your childhood and have seen recently, and write a description of it comparing its present appearance with your memories of it.

2. Prepare a description of some object or place that symbolizes the passage of time and try to control the tone of your description so it reflects your attitudes toward time and change.

3. Discuss your relationship with your parents (or your children) insofar as that relationship includes experiences similar to the ones White describes in "Once More to the Lake."

4. If you have taken a summer vacation like the one recorded by White, compare your experiences and the setting to those in the essay. How much has our civilization—and our vacations—changed since the time of the events in the essay?

(NOTE: Suggestions for topics requiring development by use of DESCRIPTION follow.)

Writing Suggestions for Section 8
Description

1. Primarily by way of impressionistic description that focuses on a single dominant impression, show and explain the mood, or atmosphere, of one of the following:

   a. A country fair.

   b. A ball game.

   c. A rodeo.

   d. A wedding.

   e. A funeral.

   f. A busy store.

   g. A ghost town.

   h. A cave.

   i. A beach in summer (or winter).

   j. An antique shop.

   k. A party.

   l. A family dinner.

   m. A traffic jam.

   n. Reveille.

   o. An airport (or a bus depot).

   p. An automobile race (or a horse race).

   q. A home during one of its rush hours.

   r. The last night of holiday shopping.

   s. A natural scene at a certain time of day.

   t. The campus at examination time.

   u. A certain person at a time of great emotion—e.g., joy, anger, grief.

2. Using objective description as your basic pattern, explain the functional qualities or the significance of one of the following:

   a. A house for sale.

   b. A public building.

   c. A dairy barn.

   d. An ideal workshop (or hobby room).

   e. An ideal garage.

   f. A fast-food restaurant.

   g. The layout of a town (or airport).

   h. The layout of a farm.

   i. A certain type of boat.

   j. A sports complex.

9

Using *Narration* as an Expository Technique

Attempts to classify the functions of narration seem certain to develop difficulties and end in arbitrary and sometimes fuzzy distinctions. These need not distress us, however, if we remember that narration remains narration—a factual or fictional report of a sequence of events—and that our only reason for trying to divide it into categories is to find some means of studying its uses.

In a sense, as we have already seen in Section 5, exposition by process analysis makes one important, if rather narrow, use of narration, since it explains in sequence how specific steps lead to completion of some process. At the other extreme is narration that has very little to do with exposition: the story itself is the important thing, and instead of a series of steps leading obviously to a completed act, events *develop* out of each other and build suspense, however mild, through some kind of conflict. This use of narration includes the novel and the short story, as well as some news and sports reporting. Because we are studying exposition, however, we must avoid getting too involved with these uses of narration; they require special techniques, the study of which would require a whole course or, in fact, several courses.

Between the extremes of a very usable analysis of process and very intriguing narration for the story's sake—and often seeming to blur into one or the other—is narration for *explanation*'s sake, to explain a concept that is more than process and that might have been explained by one of the other patterns of exposition. Here only the form is narrative; the function is expository.

Fortunately, the average student seldom needs to use narration for major explanatory purposes, as it has been used in each of the following selections. But to learn the handling of even minor or localized narration, the best procedure (short of taking several college courses, or at least one that concentrates on the narrative form) is simply to observe how successful writers use it to perform various functions. Localized narration can sometimes be helpful in developing any of the other major patterns of exposition—e.g., as in the Buckley essay (Section 1) or in Catton's (Section 3).

The most common problems can be summarized as follows:

1. *Selection of details.* As in writing description, the user of narration always has far more details available than can or should be used. Good unity demands the selection of only those details that are most relevant to the purpose and the desired effect.

2. *Time order.* The writer can use straight chronology, relating events as they happen (the usual method in minor uses of narration), or the flashback method, leaving the sequence temporarily in order to go back and relate some now-significant happening of a time prior to the main action. If flashback is used, it should be deliberate and for a valid reason—not merely because the episode was neglected at the beginning.

3. *Transitions.* The lazy writer of narration is apt to resort to the transitional style of a three-year-old: ". . . and then we . . . and then she . . . and then we. . . ." Avoiding this style may tax the ingenuity, but invariably the result is worth the extra investment of time and thought.

4. *Point of view.* This is a large and complex subject if dealt with fully, as a course in narration would do. Briefly, however, the writer should decide at the beginning whether the reader is to experience the action through a character's eyes (and ears and brain) or from an overall, objective view. This decision makes a difference in how much can be told, whose thoughts or secret actions can be included. The writer must be consistent throughout the narrative and include only information that could logically be known through the adopted point of view.

5. *Dialogue.* Presumably the writer already knows the mechanics of using quotations. Beyond these, the problems are to make conversation as natural-sounding as possible and yet to keep it from rambling through many useless details—to keep the narrative moving forward by *means* of dialogue.

As in most patterns of writing, the use of expository narration is most likely to be successful if the writer constantly keeps the purpose and audience in mind, remembering that the only reason for using the method in the first place—for doing *any* writing—is to communicate ideas. Soundness, clarity, and interest are the best means of attaining this goal.

Sample Paragraph (Annotated)

Central theme announced (reason for the narrative).

Narrative in generally chronological order.

Told from an "objective" point of view, not through the eyes of participants.

The story of Palmville's oil well is often told to newcomers in order to reveal the character of the town and, incidentally, to explain why city government policy is set by a Town Meeting rather than by a city council. In 1953, several successful oil wells were drilled in neighboring Yutawpa County, setting off an "Oil Rush" in this part of the state. The mayor at the time, Norbert Flax, was gripped by "Oil Fever" and devised a plan for city-funded drilling in what is now Anna May Wong Park. A citizen's group led by Herbert and Ellie Gomez opposed the plan, arguing that it would simply waste taxpayers' money. Recognizing that the mayor had the City Council on his side, Ellie and Herbert organized a campaign against the proposal, built around the theme of greater citizen participation in government and complete with marches, placards, and chants of "Par-Ti-Ci-Pa-Tion!" The wells were dry, the city had to triple the tax rate to pay off the debt, and growth in population and jobs was stunted for two decades. Since the debacle, citizen participation has been a key element in Palmville's government, the town has a city manager rather than a mayor, and all major policy decisions are made by the Town Meeting.

Sample Paragraph (Narration)

For anyone who has looked up from the sullen South Georgia shore [island near Antarctica] towards the soaring, razor-edged peaks and the terrible chaos of glaciers topped by swirling clouds and scoured by mighty winds, the knowledge of the crossing made by these three men adds a wider dimension to an already awe-inspiring sight. How they did it, God only knows, but they crossed the island in thirty-six hours. They were fortunate that the weather held, although many times great banks of fog rolled in from the open sea, creeping towards them over the snow and threatening to obscure their way. Confronted by precipices of ice and walls of rock they had often to retrace their steps adding many miles to the journey. They walked almost without rest. At one point they sat down in an icy gully, the wind blowing the drift around them, and so tired were they that Worsely and Crean fell asleep immediately. Shackleton, barely able to keep himself awake, realized that to fall asleep under such conditions would prove fatal. After five minutes he woke the other two, saying that they had slept for half an hour.

Edwin Mickleburgh, *Beyond the Frozen Sea: Visions of Antarctica*. New York: St. Martin's Press, 1987.

Student Writing: Using Narration as an Expository Technique

Fighting Fat

Dennis Santos

"Fat-so, Fat-so!" The words echoed through my head and still do. I was not slightly overweight or husky as a child. I was fat: short fat legs, chubby cheeks, the whole nine yards. I couldn't help noticing how fat I was; the kids in school told me so. But though I was never able to shut them up, I learned to recognize my strength and their weakness.

I am in the second grade; it's recess time and everyone is playing freeze tag. I'm "it" and Hector Mohica taunts me while all the "frozen" people laugh like hyenas. Hector was the fastest in the second grade, and I was the slowest. I know I can't catch him, so I run in frustration hoping to save face. The recess bell rings, and everyone stops and turns slowly to return to school. I keep running and bang into Hector, sending him to the ground. As he sits looking stunned, I whisper, "That's what a fat-so will do to you."

The next day is Wednesday when library is followed by gym. Mrs. Shea is reading *Amelia Bedelia Plays Baseball,* but I'm not paying attention; I'm thinking about being called "fat-so" during gym. In gym we line up to pick teams for whiffle ball, and Mike Laporte gets picked as the first captain. I keep hoping that Hector won't be the second captain, but Mr. Britt picks him anyway. Girl, boy, girl, boy, it goes on, and I am still standing there waiting to be chosen. My friend Larry tells Hector to pick me. "No, he's a fat-so," says Hector loudly, and I am the last one chosen.

When I get up to bat, Hector's pitching. The first pitch, whistling like a tea kettle, zips by my swinging bat. The second pitch hits me, and everyone laughs. As I jog to first, I decide I'd rather have a pitch hit me than face the humiliation of being a fat boy striking out. Several outs later and Hector is up to bat. He hits the first pitch and it pops up and lands in my hands. As I come in from the outfield, Hector says, "Nice catch fat-so." Fed up and frustrated, I respond, "Hector, you're dead after school," and hit my right fist into the palm of my left hand.

After school, I find Hector waiting for me with John Delarosa and Lemul Smith. I'm worried, but at least I have my brother with me, a seventh-grader. We walk as far away from Hector as we can, but he follows me chanting the hated words. Just as I'm about to cry, my brother turns around and tells Hector to stop. No luck. "Just fight him," my brother says, "Show him what you can do." I start to take my jacket off, but Hector wastes no time and punches me on the side of the head. I feel a slight vibration go through my head, like the tuning fork in music class. I swing my jacket, which is still on one arm, and use it to wrestle him to the ground. After a lot of pinching and hair pulling, I end up on top with my knees on Hector's shoulders. He squirms to get out, but I am too strong and too heavy. My brother tells me to punch him, but I settle for two "I give ups" and a sense of my own achievement. I get to my feet and turn to watch Hector running away, yelling at the top of his lungs, "Fat-so, fat-so." "Loud-mouth idiot," I think, and walk home with my brother, laughing.

MARTIN GANSBERG

MARTIN GANSBERG, born in Brooklyn, New York, in 1920, received a Bachelor of Social Sciences degree from St. John's University. He has been an editor and reporter for *The New York Times* since 1942, including a three-year period as editor of its international edition in Paris. He also served on the faculty of Fairleigh Dickinson University. Gansberg has written for many magazines, including *Diplomat, Catholic Digest, Facts,* and *U.S. Lady.*

38 Who Saw Murder Didn't Call the Police

"38 Who Saw Murder. . . " was written for the New York Times in 1964, and for obvious reasons it has been anthologized frequently since then. Cast in a deceptively simple news style, it still provides material for serious thought, as well as a means of studying the use and technique of narration.

For more than half an hour 38 respectable, law-abiding citizens in Queens watched a killer stalk and stab a woman in three separate attacks in Kew Gardens.

Twice their chatter and the sudden glow of their bedroom lights interrupted him and frightened him off. Each time he returned, sought her out, and stabbed her again. Not one person telephoned the police during the assault; one witness called after the woman was dead.

That was two weeks ago today.

Still shocked is Assistant Chief Inspector Frederick M. Lussen, in charge of the borough's detectives and a veteran of 25 years of homicide investigations. He can give a matter-of-fact recitation on many murders. But the Kew Gardens slaying baffles him—not because it is a murder, but because the "good people" failed to call the police.

"As we have reconstructed the crime," he said, "the assailant had three chances to kill this woman during a 35-minute period. He returned twice to complete the job. If we had been called when he first attacked, the woman might not be dead now." 5

This is what the police say happened beginning at 3:20 A.M. in the staid, middle-class, tree-lined Austin Street area: 6

Twenty-eight-year-old Catherine Genovese, who was called Kitty by almost everyone in the neighborhood, was returning home from her job as manager of a bar in Hollis. She parked her red Fiat in a lot adjacent to the Kew Gardens Long Island Rail Road Station, facing Mowbray Place. Like many residents of the neighborhood, she had parked there day after day since her arrival from Connecticut a year ago, although the railroad frowns on the practice. 7

She turned off the lights of her car, locked the door, and started to walk the 100 feet to the entrance of her apartment at 82–70 Austin Street, which is in a Tudor building, with stores in the first floor and apartments on the second. 8

The entrance to the apartment is in the rear of the building because the front is rented to retail stores. At night the quiet neighborhood is shrouded in the slumbering darkness that marks most residential areas. 9

Miss Genovese noticed a man at the far end of the lot, near a seven-story apartment house at 82–40 Austin Street. She halted. Then, nervously, she headed up Austin Street toward Lefferts Boulevard, where there is a call box to the 102nd Police Precinct in nearby Richmond Hill. 10

She got as far as a street light in front of a bookstore before the man grabbed her. She screamed. Lights went on in the 10-story apartment house at 82–67 Austin Street, which faces the bookstore. Windows slid open and voices punctuated the early-morning stillness. 11

Miss Genovese screamed: "Oh, my God, he stabbed me! Please help me! Please help me!" 12

From one of the upper windows in the apartment house, a man called down: "Let that girl alone!" 13

The assailant looked up at him, shrugged and walked down Austin Street toward a white sedan parked a short distance away. Miss Genovese struggled to her feet. 14

Lights went out. The killer returned to Miss Genovese, now try- 15
ing to make her way around the side of the building by the parking
lot to get to her apartment. The assailant stabbed her again.

"I'm dying!" she shrieked. "I'm dying!" 16

Windows were opened again, and lights went on in many 17
apartments. The assailant got into his car and drove away. Miss
Genovese staggered to her feet. A city bus, Q-10, the Lefferts Boulevard line to Kennedy International Airport, passed. It was 3:35 A.M.

The assailant returned. By then, Miss Genovese had crawled to 18
the back of the building, where the freshly painted brown doors to
the apartment house held out hope for safety. The killer tried the
first door; she wasn't there. At the second door, 82–62 Austin Street,
he saw her slumped on the floor at the foot of the stairs. He stabbed
her a third time—fatally.

It was 3:50 by the time the police received their first call, from a 19
man who was a neighbor of Miss Genovese. In two minutes they
were at the scene. The neighbor, a 70-year-old woman, and another
woman were the only persons on the street. Nobody else came
forward.

The man explained that he had called the police after much 20
deliberation. He had phoned a friend in Nassau County for advice
and then he had crossed the roof of the building to the apartment of
the elderly woman to get her to make the call.

"I didn't want to get involved," he sheepishly told the police. 21

Six days later, the police arrested Winston Moseley, a 29-year- 22
old business-machine operator, and charged him with homicide.
Moseley had no previous record. He is married, has two children
and owns a home at 133–19 Sutter Avenue, South Ozone Park,
Queens. On Wednesday, a court committed him to Kings County
Hospital for psychiatric observation.

When questioned by the police, Moseley also said that he had 23
slain Mrs. Annie May Johnson, 24, of 146–12 133rd Avenue, Jamaica,
on Feb. 29 and Barbara Kralik, 15, of 174–17 140th Avenue,
Springfield Gardens, last July. In the Kralik case, the police are
holding Alvin L. Mitchell, who is said to have confessed to that
slaying.

The police stressed how simple it would have been to have got- 24
ten in touch with them. "A phone call," said one of the detectives,
"would have done it." The police may be reached by dialing "O" for
operator or SPring 7-3100.

Today witnesses from the neighborhood, which is made up of   25
one-family homes in the $35,000 to $60,000 range with the exception
of the two apartment houses near the railroad station, find it difficult
to explain why they didn't call the police.

A housewife, knowingly if quite casually, said, "We thought it   26
was a lover's quarrel." A husband and wife both said, "Frankly, we
were afraid." They seemed aware of the fact that events might have
been different. A distraught woman, wiping her hands on her apron,
said, "I didn't want my husband to get involved."

One couple, now willing to talk about that night, said they   27
heard the first screams. The husband looked thoughtfully at the
bookstore where the killer first grabbed Miss Genovese.

"We went to the window to see what was happening," he said,   28
"but the light from our bedroom made it difficult to see the street."
The wife, still apprehensive, added: "I put out the light and we were
able to see better."

Asked why they hadn't called the police, she shrugged and   29
replied: "I don't know."

A man peeked out from the slight opening in the doorway to his   30
apartment and rattled off an account of the killer's second attack.
Why hadn't he called the police at the time? "I was tired," he said
without emotion. "I went back to bed."

It was 4:25 A.M. when the ambulance arrived to take the body of   31
Miss Genovese. It drove off. "Then," a solemn police detective said,
"the people came out."

Meanings and Values

1a. What is Gansberg's central (expository) theme?

  b. How might he have developed this theme without using narration at
      all? Specify what patterns of exposition he could have used instead.

  c. Would any of them have been as effective as narration *for the pur-
      pose?* Why, or why not?

2. Show how this selection could be used as an illustration in an
    explanatory discussion of abstract and concrete writing. (See "Guide
    to Terms": *Concrete/Abstract.*)

3a. Why has this narrative account of old news (the murder made its
     only headlines in 1964) retained its significance to this day?

  b. Are you able to see in this event a paradigm of any larger condition
      or situation? If so, explain, using examples as needed to illustrate
      your ideas.

4. If you have read Wolfe's essay (Section 4), do you think Dr. Hall would have been surprised at this New York case of noninvolvement? Why, or why not?

Expository Techniques

1a. What standard introductory technique is exemplified in the first paragraph? (Guide: *Introductions*.)

b. How effective do you consider it?

c. If you see anything ironic in the fact stated there, explain the irony. (Guide: *Irony*.)

2a. Where does the main narration begin?

b. What, then, is the function of the preceding paragraphs?

3a. Study several of the paragraph transitions within the narration itself to determine Gansberg's method of advancing the time sequence (to avoid overuse of "and then"). What is the technique?

b. Is another needed? Why, or why not?

4a. What possible reasons do you see for the predominant use of short paragraphs in this piece?

b. Does this selection lose any effectiveness because of the short paragraphs?

5. Undoubtedly, the author selected with care the few quotations from witnesses that he uses. What principle or principles do you think applied to his selection?

6. Explain why you think the quotation from the "solemn police detective" was, or was not, deliberately and carefully chosen to conclude the piece. (Guide: *Closings*.)

7a. Briefly identify the point of view of the writing. (Guide: *Point of View*.)

b. Is it consistent throughout?

c. Show the relation, as you see it, between this point of view and the author's apparent attitude toward his subject matter.

8a. Does he permit himself any sentimentality? If so, where? (Guide: *Sentimentality*.)

b. If not, specifically what might he have included that would have slipped into melodrama or sentimentality?

Diction and Vocabulary

1a. Why do you think the author used no difficult words in this narration?

b.   Do you find the writing at all belittling to college people because of this fact? Why, or why not?

Suggestions for Writing and Discussion

1.   Use both developed and undeveloped examples to show the prevalence, among individuals, of an anti-involvement attitude today. Or, if you prefer, show that this accusation is unjustified.

2.   If this narration can be regarded as a paradigm (see question 3b of "Meanings and Values"), select one example from the larger subject and develop it on whatever theme you choose. Your example could be from international affairs, if you like (and if you don't mind becoming the center of a controversy)—e.g., the recent cries of "Murder!" from numerous small countries. If you prefer, go into more distant (and therefore less controversial) history for your example.

3.   If such a crime as the Genovese murder were happening in an area or a situation where police were not so instantly available, what do you think an observer should do about it? What would *you* do? Justify your stand fully.

(NOTE: Suggestions for topics requiring development by NARRATION are on page 442, at the end of this section.)

RITA WILLIAMS

RITA WILLIAMS graduated from the California Institute of the Arts
with a Master of Fine Arts degree. Her short stories have appeared
in a variety of anthologies and magazines. She also writes op-ed
articles, book reviews, and theater reviews for the *LA Weekly*. At
present she is working on a book of essays, a novel about her family of African-American hunting guides in the Rocky Mountains,
and a screenplay about an uncle who was a Civil War Veteran.

The Quality of Mercy

In this essay Williams looks at some of the complicated relationships between race and crime. Though her subject is one that lends
itself easily to argument and anger, Williams keeps the essay's
focus on exposition. She reports her anger and frustration as well
as those of the young men who confront her; then she considers its
meaning.

It's 10:30 on a Saturday night, and I am trying to drive up La   1
Cienega, but even at this hour, the turgid flow of traffic is maddening. I decide to cut over to Crescent Heights, which should move
faster. As I swing right onto Airdrome, a pedestrian steps in front of
my car. This strikes me as very wrong, but I stop.

When the guy moves around toward my side, I see why it feels   2
odd. He is a young, black kid, braced in a combat stance, and he is
pointing a gun at me. Before the fear slams my senses shut, I regis-
ter a baby face with dimples, a sensuous, pink mouth, and a Batman
cap with the bill sideways on his head. His eyes are what make me
lose hope. He looks bored.

Panic wrestles with paralysis as I contemplate flooring it and   3
running him down. But he would definitely shoot me, and I can tell

from the size of the barrel that if he gets off even one round, it will
be lethal.

He walks toward my door, and the closer he gets, the more I feel   4
my system become drowsy with fear.

But my thoughts surge through a list of protests so naive that it   5
surprises me. Having worked for years to transform my own black
rage into something constructive, I had not realized I felt entitled to
some kind of immunity. Instead, I am now staring down the cannon
of this kid who is acting out *his* black rage.

Then two more guys appear, quiet as eels, a foot from the door.   6
I sense rather than see them, because I can't tear my eyes away from
the escape route ahead. I struggle not to slide completely into shock.
My unlocked car door swings open.

"Get out," the kid demands. His voice is close behind me to the   7
left. The muscles at the base of my head twitch as he gently rests the
gun barrel at the base of my brainstem. I fantasize the trajectory of
the bullet passing through the left rear of my skull and exploding
out my right temple. I know I should do exactly as he says, but I'm
too scared to move.

Then I remember something familiar about this kid's stance. His   8
teachers were probably cops. He has that same paramilitary detachment. Long ago, I was taught that when a jacked-up cop shakes
you down, you keep your hands in plain sight and don't make
any fast moves. That lesson was learned fighting for the civil rights
of kids such as these. I hope now it will work to protect me from
them.

Then another buried lesson surfaces. I was backpacking in   9
Wyoming and had fallen asleep in the afternoon. I awoke at dusk to
find a young mountain lion on a ledge above me. Somehow I knew
that I must not look it in the eye or give in to my panicky impulse to
tear off down the mountain. So I acted as if I were unaware of any
danger. Once the lion had satisfied itself that I was neither a threat
nor a source of food, it vanished. My hope, now, is to maintain a posture of active passivity. So I continue staring ahead.

"I *said* get out of the car, bitch," the kid snaps.   10

The layers of contempt in the word *bitch* make me wonder   11
whether the plan is rape. I notice my legs cramp. I decide that exposing my entire body to his rage would be suicidal, so I don't move
at all. But I have another problem. I'm angry. And that has to be
contained.

I decide that I am not going to be punished for whatever it is   12
these kids hate women for. When I realize that such puny resistance
as I will offer may be effective, it gives me courage. This is not the
first group of bullies I have faced. At the WASP prep school I
attended in rural Colorado, "nigger" was the nicest name they called
me. It got so virulent I used to eat my meals on a tray in the lavatory.
But one day I saw myself in the mirror, cowering on the can, scarf-
ing down my lunch. And I realized this was the bottom. Nothing
they could say to me could be worse than this, so I took my tray into
the lunchroom.

From then on, it was open season. They went at me with a   13
renewed vengeance. Then one evening before study hall, I once
more lost my nerve. I just couldn't stand it, so I walked away from
school—which could have gotten me expelled. They loved it. And
that was it. I picked up a rock and decided to fight. And to my surprise, the chase ended, the name-calling stopped. Now, even though
these kids are black, it feels just like my old hometown.

The first kid drags a jagged fingernail across my throat as he   14
tries to yank me out of the car. But even though I haven't moved, I
am no longer immobile. My grip on the steering wheel tightens,
even as his pulling me slams my head against the roof of the car.
After a halfhearted go at it, he stops and moves away from the
car. There is whispering among the boys, and I pick up the
phrase "Bitch must be crazy." I pray that I won't slide into hysterical laughter.

This standoff has gone on far too long. The cars passing behind   15
me on brightly lit La Cienega sound so deliciously ordinary. I can
hear the clicking of the traffic signal as the lights cycle from green to
amber to red. Then I hear the guy who has been standing the farthest
away approach the car. He croons, "Ah, man. Man, this is a sister.
We can't be ripping off no sister."

I don't get it. Then I realize that, in the dark, they could not tell   16
that I was black. But in this epidemic of black-on-black violence, I
would never expect my race to protect me. If anything, it should
make them rip me off with impunity.

But the compassion flowing toward me from this young man is   17
unmistakable. He has interceded for me. And I'm sure that he is taking a tremendous risk by doing so. I also know that this delicate
dynamic could shift back in a breath. But I have to look at him anyway. "Thank you," I say, then floor it.

It's a good thing the car finds the way back home, because I   18
can't remember how to get there. When I am finally safe, I only want
to immerse myself in the mundane. I definitely do not want to call
the police. But somebody else might be in danger. So I have to do
something.

"Yes, officer," I say to the policeman who comes on the line. "I   19
want to report an attempted, I don't know what, robbery or assault
or. . ."

"Where did this happen, ma'am?"   20

"Over in Los Angeles, on Airdrome right off La Cienega."   21

"Sorry, ma'am. You'll have to call the Wilshire Division. We   22
don't handle L.A. stuff in this precinct. You need to call this number
and tell them what happened." The line goes dead.

Then the effort of holding myself together collapses, and I start   23
shivering.

While I make some tea, I chide myself to gain perspective.   24
That desk sergeant was not a therapist and my little incident,
which ended well, will seem tame to him, given the calls he
must field on a Saturday night in L.A. But I try the number he
gave me.

"Wilshire District. Please hold."   25

I listen to a tape, which tells me to "Please hold during this   26
recording." Then a male voice answers.

"Wilshire Division."   27

"I want to report a holdup tonight."   28

"Where did it happen?" I fill in the details. "So why didn't you   29
just keep on driving?"

"Officer, he had this huge gun. I was certain he was going to   30
blow me away if I moved at all."

"Yeah, well, why did you stop in the first place?"   31

"I stop for pedestrians." Mine was clearly the stupidest phone   32
call he had received that evening.

"Well, what do you want to do?" he asks. "You want us to send   33
somebody out there to talk to you, or what?"

"Look, I just wanted to report what happened in case they   34
should try to hurt anyone else. I don't have any idea how the police
department handles these things, so you tell me."

"You weren't hurt, right?"   35

"No," I say, "unless you think having a gun held to your head   36
is hurtful."

He puts me on hold. When he comes back on five minutes later, 37
he says, "Call the dispatch commander and have them send out a
patrol car. I'm going to transfer you now."

"Wait," I say. "What's that number in case I get disconnected?" 38

He tells me the number, transfers me and I get disconnected. 39
When I call back, the recording I listened to earlier repeats itself
eight times. Now the voice is that of a woman, a black woman. Hope
for understanding, maybe even some empathy, comes back.

"You wish to make a report?" she asks. 40

"Please," I say. 41

"What was the location of the incident?" 42

I give her the information. Then I notice her tone shift when I 43
tell her that the one kid let me go because I was a "sister."

"These kids were black?" 44

"Yes," I reply, and before I can say anything else, she interrupts 45
me. "Will that be all?"

I can't quite let it go. So I ask her, "What do you think of how I 46
handled this situation?"

"Listen, lady, anybody who'd drive around in L.A. at night 47
without their door locked is crazy and, second, you ought to have
run those fools down. Then we could have sent a cruiser to take
them to the morgue. You can believe they would have done the
same to you. I don't understand you stopping in the first place."

I feel dumb. She does have a point. My door should have been 48
locked, but ... I prepare to launch into a self-defensive diatribe,
when it hits me that this black woman, and the cops I spoke to
before, and the kids who tried to hold me up would all concur that
I have been the fool this evening. And that she can't hear me any
more than they could have. So I decide to let it rest.

She tells me that she will send a cruiser out, but since I can't 49
identify any suspects, I shouldn't expect much.

Meanings and Values

1. In your own words, tell what Williams is trying to *explain* through
   this narrative.

2. Is her purpose primarily to explain or to tell an involving story?
   What specific evidence of her purpose does the essay provide? (See
   "Guide to Terms": *Purpose*.)

3a. In which paragraphs of the essay does she comment on the *expository*
   meaning of the narrative?

b. According to these statements, what meaning or meanings does the narrative have?

Expository Techniques

1a. Why do you think Williams waits until the fifth paragraph to reveal her own ethnic identity? What does she gain or lose by waiting so long to do so? (Guide: *Evaluation.*)

b. Explain how the somewhat indirect phrase she uses to identify her ethnicity, "Having worked for years to transform my own black rage into something constructive," helps her develop the central theme of the piece. (Guide: *Unity.*)

2. The subject Williams discusses could easily be the subject of an argumentative essay. Tell how her use of narrative in developing the essay helps keep it from becoming an argumentative essay rather than an expository essay. (See Section 11: *Argument.*)

3a. For what purpose(s) does Williams employ description in paragraph 2?

b. What does her use of dialogue in paragraphs 17–24 add to the essay?

c. Discuss her use of repetition in the first sentence of paragraph 7 and the single sentence of paragraph 10 as a way of framing her thoughts at the time and introducing her explanations of the events.

d. Discuss the use of a similar "framing" technique in paragraphs 10–15.

Diction and Vocabulary

1a. Identify and explain the differences in style and tone between the language used by the young men (pars. 7, 10, and 13–15) and that used by the dispatch commander (pars. 40–47). (Guide: *Style/Tone.*)

b. In what ways are either or both of these like or unlike the language she uses in the rest of the essay? Explain the extent to which these similarities or dissimilarities in language reflect differences in outlook.

2. Where in the essay does the writer make use of slang herself and for what purpose(s)? (Guide: *Slang.*)

3. Identify the simile in paragraph 6 and discuss its meaning. (Guide: *Figures of Speech.*)

4. If you do not know the meaning of some of the following words, look them up in a dictionary: sensuous (par. 2); trajectory (7); virulent, cowering (12); mundane (18); diatribe (48).

Suggestions for Writing and Discussion

1. Discuss the extent to which crime within ethnic communities or communities based on class is a greater (or lesser problem) than crime which crosses such lines. Does crime within a group affect only that group or the society as a whole?

2. Prepare a paper narrating your experience as a victim (or victimizer) and explain what it reveals about relationships among people or about power, rage, and fear.

(NOTE: Suggestions for topics requiring development by NARRATION are on page 442, at the end of this section.)

SANDRA CISNEROS

A novelist, poet, and short story writer, SANDRA CISNEROS was born in 1954 in Chicago. Growing up, she spent time in both Chicago and Mexico City. She studied at the University of Iowa and taught at California State University-Chico. Her published works include two collections of short stories, *The House on Mango Street* (1984) and *Woman Hollering Creek* (1991), and a collection of poetry *My Wicked, Wicked Ways* (1987).

Only Daughter

In "Only Daughter," an essay published in *Glamour* magazine, Cisneros tells of her struggle to win approval from her father for her career as a writer. Cisneros makes use of several short narratives in exploring the reasons for her desire to become a writer and for her father's puzzlement over her unwillingness to take on the traditional role he had envisioned for her. Her use of descriptive detail to create characters and settings is also worth noting.

Once, several years ago, when I was just starting out my writing career, I was asked to write my own contributor's note for an anthology I was part of. I wrote: "I am the only daughter in a family of six sons. *That* explains everything."

Well, I've thought about that ever since, and yes, it explains a lot to me, but for the reader's sake I should have written: "I am the only daughter in a *Mexican* family of six sons." Or even: "I am the only daughter of a Mexican father and a Mexican-American mother." Or: "I am the only daughter of a working-class family of nine." All of these had everything to do with who I am today.

I was/am the only daughter and *only* a daughter. Being an only daughter in a family of six sons forced me by circumstance to spend a lot of time by myself because my brothers felt it beneath them to play with a *girl* in public. But that aloneness, that loneliness, was good for a would-be writer—it allowed me time to think and think, to imagine, to read and prepare myself.

Being only a daughter for my father meant my destiny would 4
lead me to become someone's wife. That's what he believed. But when I was in the fifth grade and shared my plans for college with him, I was sure he understood. I remember my father saying, "*Que bueno, ni'ja,* that's good." That meant a lot to me, especially since my brothers thought the idea hilarious. What I didn't realize was that my father thought college was good for girls—good for finding a husband. After four years in college and two more in graduate school, and still no husband, my father shakes his head even now and says I wasted all that education.

In retrospect, I'm lucky my father believed daughters were 5
meant for husbands. It meant it didn't matter if I majored in something silly like English. After all, I'd find a nice professional eventually, right? This allowed me the liberty to putter about embroidering my little poems and stories without my father interrupting with so much as a "What's that you're writing?"

But the truth is, I wanted him to interrupt. I wanted my father 6
to understand what it was I was scribbling, to introduce me as "My only daughter, the writer." Not as "This is only my daughter. She teaches." *Es maestra*—teacher. Not even *profesora.*

In a sense, everything I have ever written has been for him, to 7
win his approval even though I know my father can't read English words, even though my father's only reading includes the brown-ink *Esto* sports magazines from Mexico City and the bloody ¡*Alarma!* magazines that feature yet another sighting of *La Virgen de Guadalupe* on a tortilla or a wife's revenge on her philandering husband by bashing his skull in with a *molcajete* (a kitchen mortar made of volcanic rock). Or the *fotonovelas,* the little picture paperbacks with tragedy and trauma erupting from the characters' mouths in bubbles.

My father represents, then, the public majority. A public who is 8
uninterested in reading, and yet one whom I am writing about and for, and privately trying to woo.

When we were growing up in Chicago, we moved a lot because 9
of my father. He suffered bouts of nostalgia. Then we'd have to let go our flat, store the furniture with mother's relatives, load the station wagon with baggage and bologna sandwiches and head south. To Mexico City.

We came back, of course. To yet another Chicago flat, another   10
Chicago neighborhood, another Catholic school. Each time, my
father would seek out the parish priest in order to get a tuition
break, and complain or boast: "I have seven sons."

He meant *siete hijos*, seven children, but he translated it as   11
"sons." "I have seven sons." To anyone who would listen. The Sears
Roebuck employee who sold us the washing machine. The short-
order cook where my father ate his ham-and-eggs breakfasts. "I
have seven sons." As if he deserved a medal from the state.

My papa. He didn't mean anything by that mistranslation, I'm   12
sure. But somehow I could feel myself being erased. I'd tug my
father's sleeve and whisper: "Not seven sons. Six! and *one daughter*."

When my oldest brother graduated from medical school, he ful-   13
filled my father's dream that we study hard and use this—our
heads, instead of this—our hands. Even now my father's hands are
thick and yellow, stubbed by a history of hammer and nails and
twine and coils and springs. "Use this," my father said, tapping his
head, "and not this," showing us those hands. He always looked
tired when he said it.

Wasn't college an investment? And hadn't I spent all those   14
years in college? And if I didn't marry, what was it all for? Why
would anyone go to college and then choose to be poor? Especially
someone who had always been poor.

Last year, after ten years of writing professionally, the financial   15
rewards started to trickle in. My second National Endowment for
the Arts Fellowship. A guest professorship at the University of
California, Berkeley. My book, which sold to a major New York
publishing house.

At Christmas, I flew home to Chicago. The house was throb-   16
bing, same as always; hot *tamales* and sweet *tamales* hissing in my
mother's pressure cooker, and everybody—my mother, six brothers,
wives, babies, aunts, cousins—talking too loud and at the same time,
like in a Fellini film, because that's just how we are.

I went upstairs to my father's room. One of my stories had just   17
been translated into Spanish and published in an anthology of
Chicano writing, and I wanted to show it to him. Ever since he
recovered from a stroke two years ago, my father likes to spend
his leisure hours horizontally. And that's how I found him,
watching a Pedro Infante movie on Galavisión and eating rice
pudding.

There was a glass filmed with milk on the bedside table. There were several vials of pills and balled Kleenex. And on the floor, one black sock and a plastic urinal that I didn't want to look at but looked at anyway. Pedro Infante was about to burst into song, and my father was laughing. 18

I'm not sure if it was because my story was translated into Spanish, or because it was published in Mexico, or perhaps because the story dealt with Tepeyac, the *colonia* my father was raised in and the house he grew up in, but at any rate, my father punched the mute button on his remote control and read my story. 19

I sat on the bed next to my father and waited. He read it very slowly. As if he were reading each line over and over. He laughed at all the right places and read lines he liked out loud. He pointed and asked questions: "Is this So-and-so?" "Yes," I said. He kept reading. 20

When he was finally finished, after what seemed like hours, my father looked up and asked: "Where can we get more copies of this for the relatives?" 21

Of all the wonderful things that happened to me last year, that was the most wonderful. 22

Meanings and Values

1a. In what ways did being the only daughter affect the author's life as she was growing up? As an adult?

  b. In what ways did being only a daughter affect her as a child? In college and graduate school? As an adult?

2a. Cisneros says, "In a sense, everything I have ever written has been for him, to win his approval. . . ." What evidence of this motivation does she give in the essay?

  b. What other motivations for writing does she suggest in the essay, either consciously or unintentionally?

3. Does the ending sentence of the essay seem genuine in tone or forced? Be ready to explain the grounds for your answer. (See "Guide to Terms": *Style/Tone.*)

Expository Techniques

1a. This essay consists of several short narratives. What are they?

  b. In what manner are they linked to provide an overall narrative structure for the essay?

2. Tell what use Cisneros makes of repetition and parallel phases to organize the discussion in paragraphs 3 and 4. (Guide: *Parallel Structure*.)

3. What do the details about his reading (par. 7) reveal about the father's attitudes towards men and women and towards social roles in general?

4a. What do the details the author includes in the final narrative (pars. 16–17) reveal about her attitude towards her family? Towards her father?

b. What do these details contribute to the tone of the paragraphs? (Guide: *Tone*.)

Diction and Vocabulary

1. How does the language the author uses to talk about her life as a student, a college professor, and a writer (pars. 5, 14–15) differ from that she uses to talk about her father and her family (pars. 6–7, 11–12, and 16–18)? (Guide: *Diction*.)

2a. Explain what the Spanish words used in paragraphs 4, 6, 16, and 19 add to passages in which they occur.

b. Would the essay be less effective without the use of such terms? Why, or why not?

Suggestions for Writing and Discussion

1. Are tensions between parental expectations and children's chosen roles common in most contemporary families? Are they generally similar to the kind of tensions Cisneros describes? Do they follow some other typical pattern or patterns?

2. To what extent are Cisneros's experiences characteristic of immigrant families rather than other families? To what extent do they represent particular class or ethnic patterns?

3. What social, cultural, economic, or personal factors affect most college students' choice of career roles? Are families, peers, or media images likely to be most influential in career choices?

(NOTE: Suggestions for topics requiring development by NARRATION are on page 442, at the end of this section.)

GEORGE ORWELL

GEORGE ORWELL (1903–1950), whose real name was Eric Blair, was a British novelist and essayist, well known for his satire. He was born in India and educated at Eton in England; he was wounded while fighting in the Spanish Civil War. Later he wrote the books *Animal Farm* (1945), a satire on Soviet history, and *1984* (1949), a vivid picture of life in a projected totalitarian society. He was, however, also sharply aware of injustices in democratic societies and was consistently socialistic in his views. Many of Orwell's essays are collected in *Critical Essays* (1946), *Shooting an Elephant and Other Essays* (1950), and *Such, Such Were the Joys* (1953).

A Hanging

"A Hanging" is typical of Orwell's essays in its setting—Burma—and in its subtle but biting commentary on colonialism, on capital punishment, even on one aspect of human nature itself. Although he is ostensibly giving a straightforward account of an execution, the author masterfully uses descriptive details and dialogue to create atmosphere and sharply drawn characterizations. The essay gives concrete form to a social message that is often delivered much less effectively in abstract generalities.

It was in Burma, a sodden morning of the rains. A sickly light, like yellow tinfoil, was slanting over the high walls into the jail yard. We were waiting outside the condemned cells, a row of sheds fronted with double bars, like small animal cages. Each cell measured about ten feet by ten and was quite bare within except for a plank bed and a pot for drinking water. In some of them brown, silent men were squatting at the inner bars, with their blankets draped round them. 1

These were the condemned men, due to be hanged within the next week or two.

One prisoner had been brought out of his cell. He was a Hindu,   2
a puny wisp of a man, with a shaven head and vague liquid eyes. He had a thick, sprouting mustache, absurdly too big for his body, rather like the mustache of a comic man on the films. Six tall Indian warders were guarding him and getting him ready for the gallows. Two of them stood by with rifles and fixed bayonets, while the others handcuffed him, passed a chain through his handcuffs and fixed it to their belts, and lashed his arms tight to his sides. They crowded very close about him, with their hands always on him in a careful, caressing grip, as though all the while feeling him to make sure he was there. It was like men handling a fish which is still alive and may jump back into the water. But he stood quite unresisting, yielding his arms limply to the ropes, as though he hardly noticed what was happening.

Eight o'clock struck and a bugle call, desolately thin in the wet   3
air, floated from the distant barracks. The superintendent of the jail, who was standing apart from the rest of us, moodily prodding the gravel with his stick, raised his head at the sound. He was an army doctor, with a grey toothbrush mustache and a gruff voice. "For God's sake, hurry up, Francis," he said irritably. "The man ought to have been dead by this time. Aren't you ready yet?"

Francis, the head jailer, a fat Dravidian in a white drill suit and   4
gold spectacles, waved his black hand. "Yes sir, yes sir," he bubbled. "All iss satisfactorily prepared. The hangman iss waiting. We shall proceed."

"Well, quick march, then. The prisoners can't get their breakfast   5
till this job's over."

We set out for the gallows. Two warders marched on either side   6
of the prisoner, with their rifles at the slope; two others marched close against him, gripping him by arm and shoulder, as though at once pushing and supporting him. The rest of us, magistrates and the like, followed behind. Suddenly, when we had gone ten yards, the procession stopped short without any order or warning. A dreadful thing had happened—a dog, come goodness knows whence, had appeared in the yard. It came bounding among us with a loud volley of barks and leapt round us wagging its whole body, wild with glee at finding so many human beings together. It was a large woolly dog, half Airedale, half pariah. For a moment it

pranced around us, and then, before anyone could stop it, it had made a dash for the prisoner, and jumping up tried to lick his face. Everybody stood aghast, too taken aback even to grab the dog.

"Who let that bloody brute in here?" said the superintendent angrily. "Catch it, someone!" 7

A warder detached from the escort, charged clumsily after the 8 dog, but it danced and gambolled just out of his reach, taking everything as part of the game. A young Eurasian jailer picked up a handful of gravel and tried to stone the dog away, but it dodged the stones and came after us again. Its yaps echoed from the jail walls. The prisoner, in the grasp of the two warders, looked on incuriously, as though this was another formality of the hanging. It was several minutes before someone managed to catch the dog. Then we put my handkerchief through its collar and moved off once more, with the dog still straining and whimpering.

It was about forty yards to the gallows. I watched the bare 9 brown back of the prisoner marching in front of me. He walked clumsily with his bound arms, but quite steadily, with that bobbing gait of the Indian who never straightens his knees. At each step his muscles slid neatly into place, the lock of hair on his scalp danced up and down, his feet printed themselves on the wet gravel. And once, in spite of the men who gripped him by each shoulder, he stepped lightly aside to avoid a puddle on the path.

It is curious; but till that moment I had never realized what it 10 means to destroy a healthy, conscious man. When I saw the prisoner step aside to avoid the puddle, I saw the mystery, the unspeakable wrongness, of cutting a life short when it is in full tide. This man was not dying, he was alive just as we are alive. All the organs of his body were working—bowels digesting food, skin renewing itself, nails growing, tissues forming—all toiling away in solemn foolery. His nails would still be growing when he stood on the drop, when he was falling through the air with a tenth-of-a-second to live. His eyes saw the yellow gravel and the grey walls, and his brain still remembered, foresaw, reasoned—even about puddles. He and we were a party of men walking together, seeing, hearing, feeling, understanding the same world; and in two minutes, with a sudden snap, one of us would be gone—one mind less, one world less.

The gallows stood in a small yard, separate from the main 11 grounds of the prison, and overgrown with tall prickly weeds. It was a brick erection like three sides of a shed, with planking on top, and above that two beams and a crossbar with the rope dangling. The hangman, a greyhaired convict in the white uniform of the prison, was waiting beside his machine. He greeted us with a servile crouch as we entered. At a word from Francis the two warders, gripping the prisoner more closely than ever, half led, half pushed him to the gallows and helped him clumsily up the ladder. Then the hangman climbed up and fixed the rope round the prisoner's neck.

We stood waiting, five yards away. The warders had formed in a rough circle round the gallows. And then, when the noose was fixed, the prisoner began crying out to his god. It was a high, reiterated cry of "Ram! Ram! Ram! Ram!" not urgent and fearful like a prayer or cry for help, but steady, rhythmical, almost like the tolling of a bell. The dog answered the sound with a whine. The hangman, still standing on the gallows, produced a small cotton bag like a flour bag and drew it down over the prisoner's face. But the sound, muffled by the cloth, still persisted, over and over again: "Ram! Ram! Ram! Ram! Ram!" 12

The hangman climbed down and stood ready, holding the lever. Minutes seemed to pass. The steady, muffled crying from the prisoner went on and on, "Ram! Ram! Ram!" never faltering for an instant. The superintendent, his head on his chest, was slowly poking the ground with his stick; perhaps he was counting the cries, allowing the prisoner a fixed number—fifty, perhaps, or a hundred. Everyone had changed colour. The Indians had gone grey like bad coffee, and one or two of the bayonets were wavering. We looked at the lashed, hooded man on the drop, and listened to his cries—each cry another second of life; the same thought was in all our minds; oh, kill him quickly, get it over, stop that abominable noise! 13

Suddenly the superintendent made up his mind. Throwing up his head he made a swift motion with his stick. "Chalo!" he shouted almost fiercely. 14

There was a clanking noise, and then dead silence. The prisoner had vanished, and the rope was twisting on itself. I let go of the dog, and it galloped immediately to the back of the gallows; but when it got there it stopped short, barked, and then retreated into a corner of the yard, where it stood among the weeds, looking timorously out at us. We went round the gallows to inspect the prisoner's body. He was dangling with his toes pointed straight downwards, very slowly revolving, as dead as a stone. 15

The superintendent reached out with his stick and poked the 16 bare brown body; it oscillated slightly. "*He's* all right," said the superintendent. He backed out from under the gallows, and blew out a deep breath. The moody look had gone out of his face quite suddenly. He glanced at his wrist-watch. "Eight minutes past eight. Well, that's all for this morning, thank God."

The warders unfixed bayonets and marched away. The dog, 17 sobered and conscious of having misbehaved itself, slipped after them. We walked out of the gallows yard, past the condemned cells with their waiting prisoners, into the big central yard of the prison. The convicts, under the command of warders armed with lathis, were already receiving their breakfast. They squatted in long rows, each man holding a tin pannikin, while two warders with buckets marched around ladling out rice; it seemed quite a homely, jolly scene, after the hanging. An enormous relief had come upon us now that the job was done. One felt an impulse to sing, to break into a run, to snigger. All at once everyone began chattering gaily.

The Eurasian boy walking beside me nodded towards the way 18 we had come, with a knowing smile: "Do you know, sir, our friend (he meant the dead man) when he heard his appeal had been dismissed, he pissed on the floor of his cell. From fright. Kindly take one of my cigarettes, sir. Do you not admire my new silver case, sir? From the boxwallah, two rupees eight annas. Classy European style."

Several people laughed—at what, nobody seemed certain. 19

Francis was walking by the superintendent, talking garrulously: 20 "Well, sir, all has passed off with the utmost satisfactoriness. It was all finished—flick! Like that. It iss not always so—oah, no! I have known cases where the doctor was obliged to go beneath the gallows and pull the prissoner's legs to ensure decease. Most disagreeable!"

"Wriggling about, eh? That's bad," said the superintendent. 21

"Ach, sir, it iss worse when they become refractory! One man, I 22 recall, clung to the bars of hiss cage when we went to take him out. You will scarcely credit, sir, that it took six warders to dislodge him, three pulling at each leg. We reasoned with him, 'My dear fellow,' we said, 'think of all the pain and trouble you are causing to us!' But no, he would not listen! Ach, he wass very troublesome!"

I found that I was laughing quite loudly. Everyone was laugh- 23 ing. Even the superintendent grinned in a tolerant way. "You'd better all come out and have a drink," he said quite genially. "I've got a bottle of whisky in the car. We could do with it."

We went through the big double gates of the prison into the road. "Pulling at his legs!" exclaimed a Burmese magistrate suddenly, and burst into a loud chuckling. We all began laughing again. At that moment Francis' anecdote seemed extraordinarily funny. We all had a drink together, native and European alike, quite amicably. The dead man was a hundred yards away. 24

Meanings and Values

1. What was the real reason for the superintendent's impatience?

2. On first impression it may have seemed that the author gave undue attention to the dog's role in this narrative.

 a. Why was the episode such a "dreadful thing" (par. 6)?

 b. Why did the author think it worth noting that the dog was excited at "finding so many human beings together"?

 c. Of what significance was the dog's trying to lick the prisoner's face?

3. Explain how the prisoner's stepping around a puddle could have given the author a new insight into what was about to happen (par. 10).

4. Why was there so much talking and laughing after the hanging was finished?

5. What is the broadest meaning of Orwell's last sentence?

Expository Techniques

1. Cite examples of both objective and impressionistic description in the first paragraph.

2a. What is the primary time order used in this narrative?

 b. If there are any exceptions, state where.

3. Considering the relatively few words devoted to them, several of the characterizations in this essay are remarkably vivid—a result, obviously, of highly discriminating selection of details from the multitude of those that must have been available to the author. For each of the following people, list the character traits that we can observe, and state whether these impressions come to us through details of description, action, and/or dialogue.

 a. The prisoner.

 b. The superintendent.

c. Francis.

d. The Eurasian boy.

4a. Why do you think the author included so many details of the preparation of the prisoner (par. 2)?

b. Why did he include so many details about the dog and his actions?

c. What is gained by the assortment of details in paragraph 10?

5. The tone of writing such as this can easily slip into sentimentality or even melodrama without the author's realizing what is happening. (See *"Guide to Terms"*: *Sentimentality*.) Select three places in this narrative where a less-skilled writer might have had such trouble, and note by what restraints Orwell avoided sentimentality.

Diction and Vocabulary

1. A noteworthy element of Orwell's style is his occasional use of figurative language. Cite six metaphors and similes, and comment on their choice and effectiveness.

2. Orwell was always concerned with the precise effects that words could give to meaning and style.

a. Cite at least six nonfigurative words that seem to you particularly well chosen for their purpose.

b. Show what their careful selection contributes to the description of atmosphere or to the subtle meanings of the author.

c. How is this attention to diction a matter of style? (Guide: *Style/Tone*.)

Suggestions for Writing and Discussion

1. Select *one* of the points of controversy over capital punishment and present both sides with equal objectivity.

2. Consider the dilemma of a person whose "duty" seems to require one course of action and whose "conscience" just the opposite course. Use concrete illustrations to show how serious such dilemmas can be.

3. Examine the moral right, or lack of it, of the people of one country to impose their laws on the people of another country.

4. Discuss one benefit of colonialism to the people colonized. Use specific illustrations.

5. Explain how, in your own experience, a seemingly minor incident led to much deeper insight into a matter not fully understood before.

(NOTE: Suggestions for topics requiring development by NARRATION are on page 442, at the end of this section.)

DONALD HALL

DONALD HALL, poet, essayist, biographer, literary critic, and text-book writer, was born in Connecticut in 1928. In 1975, he left his teaching position at the University of Michigan to move to a farm in New Hampshire and devote his time to writing. Among his more than forty books of poetry, prose, and anthologies are *Kicking the Leaves* (1978) and *The Happy Man* (1986), poems; *String Too Short to Be Saved* (1961), *Seasons at Eagle Pond* (1987), and *Here at Eagle Pond* (1990), prose; *The Oxford Book of Children's Verse in America* (1985), anthology; and *Writing Well* (7th edition, 1991, with Sven Birkerts) and *A Writer's Reader* (6th edition, 1991, with Donald Emblen), textbooks.

The Embrace of Old Age

The title of this essay from *Here at Eagle Pond* takes on several different meanings for readers by the end of the selection. Likewise, the insights into youth and aging that Hall offers become richer and more complex as the essay progresses and even more apparent on rereading. Most interesting, perhaps, is the distance between what Hall saw as a youth and what he knows now.

When I spent my summers here [Wilmot, New Hampshire] as a boy, 1
my grandparents took me everywhere they went. We had no car. We didn't hitch up the horse to go to a drive-in movie, but we rode behind Riley to church on Sunday morning, and on Sunday night returned in the buggy for Christian Endeavor. We attended annual social events, in July the Church Fair and in August Old Home Day. Although my grandparents lived without anything that passes for entertainment in the 1990s—no car, no television, no VCR, no

restaurants, no cocktail parties—they were remarkably cheerful. My grandfather especially had a fortunate temperament. He liked his work, and a little amusement went a long way. Occasionally we hitched up Riley for a special occasion: a family reunion, an auction, an eightieth birthday party, a funeral, a long-delayed visit to a dying cousin. When I was fourteen years old we went to Willard and Alice Buzzle's diamond wedding anniversary.

In preparation, my grandmother made three blueberry pies and a bagful of ginger snaps; my grandfather dusted the horse carriage, wiped off the harness, and curried Riley. Because the buggy's iron rims rattled on its wooden wheels—a dry August—we drove it across the railroad tracks to Eagle Pond and urged Riley against his better judgment to wade, pulling the carriage into shallow water. We sat there for a few minutes as I delighted in the strangeness, sitting still in the buggy in the pond's shallows while the wood swelled tight inside the rims. Then we drove back to the farm to dress and set out. 2

Willard and Alice were older than my grandparents, who were in their sixties. I remembered the Buzzles from Old Home Day: They were *old*. Alice had been seventeen when she was married, which made her ninety-two on her seventy-fifth wedding anniversary. Willard was exactly one hundred, married the day he turned twenty-five, which of course made today's celebration double. Diamond wedding anniversaries were rare enough; today we added a simultaneous one hundredth birthday party. Three weekly newspapers sent photographer-reporters to the Danbury Grange. 3

Horses and buggies were uncommon on the roads, though horse farmers were not unknown in 1943. The war kept traffic down, but a few dark square cars passed us on Route 4. My grandfather kept the buggy's right wheels on the shoulder, and I watched sand spin off the wheels like Fourth of July nightworks fountains. When we arrived at the Grange Hall, it was decorated red, white, and blue. As we alighted my grandfather spoke in Riley's ear and tied him loosely to a young maple, so that he could bend his neck to eat grass. Inside, the Grange walls were covered with photographs of past Grange presidents, and there was an American flag beside the stage in the front, the drawn curtain showing a view of Mount Kearsage painted by a local artist in 1906. We were early, of course, and so was everyone else. My grandmother cut her pies and set the pieces out on a long table covered with pies and cookies. Willard and Alice's 4 sons Clarence and Frank scurried about, old men who moved with the sprightly energy of children anxious to please. Then a shout from the door told us that the bridal couple had arrived. I looked out to see Willard's Model A parked at the front door, driven by their surviving daughter Ada. Bride and bridegroom tottered up the steps, walking with canes held in outside hands so that they could join inside arms. They gripped each other fiercely, as if each were convinced that the other needed help. Willard looked the frailer as he climbed the Grange steps on his hundredth birthday and his seventy-fifth wedding anniversary, wavering over the worn wood stairs.

At the opened double doors Clarence and Frank took charge,   5
each grasping one parent, and led them into the hall, where my grandmother at the organ belted out the Wedding March. Now the ancient small parents, on the arms of ancient small sons, with ancient daughter in the rear, walked slowly the length of the hall between the folding chairs set up for the ceremony, waving and acknowledging our waves like conquerors returned from the war that was not over. When Alice and Willard reached the end of the hall, my grandmother's fingers switched to "Happy Birthday." Everyone sang while a huge cake, big enough for everyone present, was wheeled into the crowd, topped with a hundred candles and the figurines of a bride and groom. Willard and Alice conspired with Ada, Clarence, and Frank to blow out the candles, taking many breaths, after a pause for a wish.

And I thought, What could they wish for? Not for a long life!   6
Maybe for an easy winter? I studied Willard's infirmity. The skin of his hands was brown with liver spots, flesh hung like turkey wattles from his neck, and everything about him shook: his arms, his head on its frail stem, and his bony knees visibly trembling against his trouser legs. I felt horror—as if it were indecent to be alive with no future, each day merely a task for accomplishment. My vision of old age shook me as Willard shook.

Our minister, Kate's brother my uncle Luther, was host and   7
master of ceremonies for half an hour of reminiscences and songs: "The Old Oaken Bucket," "When You and I Were Young, Maggie," "Down by the Old Mill Stream." Luther read two telegrams, one for the wedding and one for the birthday, from President Franklin Delano Roosevelt. When we broke to eat I heaped my paper plate with hermits and brownies and cherry pie, not forgetting a piece of

wedding cake. Returning for seconds, I gathered the last piece of my grandmother's blueberry.

Then I was bored. I was rarely bored in my grandparents' company but today they paid me no mind. They had done introducing me and I had done with comments on how tall I was. Now they stood with other old people recollecting together. And I felt separate, separated especially because I understood that I was the *only one* in this crowd able to see clearly the futility and ugliness of old age.

So I prowled around the building, exploring the stage behind the painted curtain, finding a closet full of ancient costumes, trying on a top hat and derby. Then I opened a door I had not entered before, a green room to the side of the stage, and walked into the dimness without sensing the presence of others. In low light from a shaded window I saw two bodies embracing as they leaned against a wardrobe. I was embarrassed, I suppose because notions of embracing had begun to occupy me day and night. I started to back out, then saw that it was Willard and Alice who clung to each other, having crept from their thronged relatives and neighbors to this privacy. Their twin canes leaned on a box while their arms engaged each other. For a quick moment it was as if I saw, beyond the ancients in the green room, a young couple, seventy-five years back, who found a secret place to kiss and hug in.

Then I heard what she said: "Alice, Alice, Alice." She spoke urgently, "Alice, Alice," as if she were warning herself of something. At that moment I felt my grandfather's hand on my shoulder—it was time to go home; he had sought me out—and when I looked up I saw that he had heard. It was not until we were driving home that he mentioned it. I listened as he spoke—his voice controlled, as if he made a neutral observation, about the weather perhaps, that although the day was bright he wouldn't be surprised if it rained— saying, "Kate, Willard didn't know who Alice was."

Meanings and Values

1a. How would you describe the tone of the essay as it is established by the title and the opening paragraph? (See "Guide to Terms": *Style/Tone*.)

 b. How does the tone shift in the last paragraph?

2a. In your own words, state the central theme of the selection. (Guide: *Unity*.)

b. Identify those places where the writer seems to state the central theme either directly or ironically. (Guide: *Irony.*)

c. Would the selection be more or less effective if the writer had chosen to state the central theme more clearly near the beginning of the essay? Why, or why not? (Guide: *Evaluation.*)

Expository Techniques

1a. Many of the details and observations in paragraphs 2, 3, and 8 are typical of a fourteen-year-old boy. Which are they? (Guide: *Persona.*)

b. What evidence is there that the narrative is presented to a considerable extent from the perspective of a fourteen-year-old? (Guide: *Point of View.*)

c. To what extent does the point of view shape the presentation of events in paragraph 9? How does the writer signal to us that a youthful perspective is at work?

d. In what ways are the power and the surprise of the concluding paragraph the result of the use of this point of view?

2a. Reread the essay to identify any clues it contains that foreshadow the eventual revelation about Willard.

b. Explain why most readers are not likely to notice these clues during the first encounter with the essay.

c. Why might the selection have been less effective in conveying its theme if the author had provided more obvious foreshadowing?

Diction and Vocabulary

1. Discuss how the diction and the choice of details in paragraphs 2–5 and 6 create a sense of an old-fashioned festival. (Guide: *Diction.*)

2. Examine and discuss Hall's use of the following in paragraph 6:

 a. Rhetorical questions. (Guide: *Rhetorical Questions.*)

 b. Diction.

 c. Varied sentence structure and length.

 d. Simile. (Guide: *Figures of Speech.*)

3. Identify the figure of speech in the following sentence and discuss its relationship to the essay's central theme: "Now the ancient small parents, on the arms of ancient small sons, with ancient daughter in the rear, walked slowly the length of the hall between the folding chairs set up for the ceremony, waving and acknowledging our waves like conquerors returned from the war that was not over" (par. 5).

Suggestions for Writing and Discussion

1. If you have read Sharon Curtin's "Aging in the Land of the Young" (pp. 368–371), compare its treatment of old age and attitudes toward the elderly with the treatment provided in this essay.

2. In class, discuss how present-day relationships between children (or teenagers) and the elderly compare to the close relationship Hall had with his grandparents.

(NOTE: Suggestions for topics requiring development by NARRATION follow.)

Writing Suggestions for Section 9
Narration

Use narration as at least a partial pattern (e.g., in developed examples or in comparison) for one of the following expository themes or another suggested by them. Avoid the isolated personal account that has little broader significance. Remember, too, that development of the essay should itself make your point, without excessive moralizing.

1. People can still succeed without a college education.

2. The frontiers are not all gone.

3. When people succeed in communicating, they can learn to get along with each other.

4. Even with "careful" use of capital punishment, innocent people can be executed.

5. Sports don't always build character.

6. Physical danger can make us more aware of ourselves and our values.

7. Conditioning to the realities of the job is as important to the police officer as professional training.

8. It is possible for employees themselves to determine when they have reached their highest level of competence.

9. Wartime massacres are not a new development.

10. "Date rape" and sexual harassment on the job are devastating and generally unexpected.

11. Both heredity and environment shape personality.

12. Physical and mental handicaps can be overcome in some ways, but they are still a burden.

13. Toxic wastes pose a problem for many communities.

14. Hunting is a worthwhile and challenging sport.

15. Lack of money places considerable stress on a family or a marriage.

16. Exercise can become an obsession.

17. People who grow up in affluent surroundings don't understand what it is like to worry about money, to be hungry, or to live in a dangerous neighborhood.

18. Some jobs are simply degrading, either because of the work or because of the fellow workers.

10

Reasoning by Use of
Induction and *Deduction*

Induction and Deduction, important as they are in argumentation, may also be useful methods of exposition. They are often used simply to explain a stand or conclusion, without any effort or need to win converts.

Induction is the process by which we accumulate evidence until, at some point, we can make the "inductive leap" and thus reach a useful *generalization*. The science laboratory employs this technique; hundreds of tests and experiments and analyses may be required before the scientist will generalize, for instance, that a disease is caused by a certain virus. It is also the primary technique of the prosecuting attorney who presents pieces of inductive evidence, asking the jury to make the inductive leap and conclude that the accused did indeed kill the victim.

Even the commonplace "process of elimination" also may be considered a form of induction. If it can be shown, for instance, that "A" does not have the strength to swing the murder weapon, that "B" was in a drunken sleep at the time of the crime, and that "C" had recently become blind and could not have found her way to the boathouse, then we may be ready for the inductive leap—that the foul deed must have been committed by "X," the only other person on the island. (The use of this kind of induction implies an added obligation, of course, to make certain that all the possibilities but *one* have been eliminated: if we fail to note that "Y," a visitor on a neighboring island, and his boat were unaccounted for that evening, then our conclusion is invalid.)

On a more personal level, of course, we all learned to use induction at a very early age. We may have disliked the taste of orange juice, winter squash, and carrots, and we were not too young to make a generalization: orange-colored food tastes bad.

Whereas induction is the method of reaching a potentially useful generalization (for example, Professor Melville always gives an "F" to students who cut his class three times), *deduction* is the method of *using* such a generality, now accepted as a fact (for example, if we cut this class again today, we will get an "F"). Working from a generalization already formulated—by ourselves, by someone else, or by tradition—we may deduce that a specific thing or circumstance that fits into the generality will act the same. Hence, if convinced that orange-colored food tastes bad, we will be reluctant to try pumpkin pie.

A personnel manager may have discovered over the years that electronics majors from Central College are invariably well trained in their field. His induction may have been based on the evidence of observations, records, and the opinions of fellow Rotary members; and, perhaps without realizing it, he has made the usable generalization about the training of Central College electronics majors. Later, when he has an application from Nancy Ortega, a graduate of Central College, his *de*ductive process will probably work as follows: Central College turns out well-trained electronics majors; Ortega was trained at Central; therefore, Ortega must be well trained. Here he has used a generalization to apply to a specific case.

Put in this simplified form (which, in writing, it seldom is),[1] the deductive process is also called a "syllogism"—with the beginning generality known as the "major premise" and the specific that fits into the generality known as the "minor premise." For example:

> *Major premise*—Orange-colored food is not fit to eat.
> *Minor premise*—Pumpkin pie is orange-colored.
> *Conclusion*—Pumpkin pie is not fit to eat.

Frequently, however, the validity of one or both of the premises may be questionable, and here is one of the functions of *in*duction: to give needed support—with evidence such as opinions of experts,

---

[1]Neither induction nor deduction is confined to a particular order of presentation. If we use specific evidence to *reach* a generalization, it is induction regardless of which part is stated first in a written or spoken account. (Very likely, both a prosecutor's opening remarks and a medical researcher's written reports first present their generalizations and then the inductive evidence by which they have been reached.) But if we use a generality in which to *place* a specific, it is still deduction, however stated. (Hence the reasoning of the personnel manager might be: "Ortega must be well trained because she was educated at C.C., and there's where they really know how to do it.")

and results of experiments or surveys—to the *de*ductive syllogism, whether stated or implied. Deductive reasoning, in whatever form presented, is only as sound as both its premises. The child's conviction that orange-colored food is not fit to eat was not necessarily true; therefore, the conclusion about pumpkin pie is not very trustworthy. The other conclusions, that we will automatically get an "F" by cutting Melville's class and that Ortega is well trained in electronics, can be only as reliable as the original generalizations that were used as deductive premises. If the generalizations themselves were based on flimsy or insufficient evidence, any future deduction using them is likely to be erroneous.

These two faults are common in induction: (1) the use of *flimsy* evidence—mere opinion, hearsay, or analogy, none of which can support a valid generalization—instead of verified facts or opinions of reliable authorities; and (2) the use of *too little* evidence, leading to a premature inductive leap.

The amount of evidence needed in any situation depends, of course, on purpose and audience. The success of two Central College graduates might be enough to convince some careless personnel director that all Central electronics graduates would be good employees, but two laboratory tests would not convince medical researchers that they had learned anything worthwhile about a disease-causing virus. The authors of the Declaration of Independence, in justifying their argument for rebellion to a wide variety of readers and listeners, explained why they considered the king tyrannical, by listing twenty-eight despotic acts of his government, each of which was a verifiable fact, a matter of public record.

Induction and deduction are highly logical processes, and any trace of weakness can seriously undermine an exposition that depends on their reasonableness. (Such weakness can, of course, be even more disastrous in argument.) Although no induction or deduction ever reaches absolute, 100 percent certainty, we should try to get from these methods as high a degree of *probability* as possible. (We can never positively prove, for instance, that the sun will rise in the east tomorrow, but thousands of years of inductive observation and theorizing make the fact extremely probable—and certainly sound enough for any working generalization.)

Students using induction and deduction in compositions, essay examinations, or term papers—showing that Stephen Crane was a naturalistic writer, or that our national policies are unfair to revolutionary movements—should always assume that they will have a skeptical audience that wants to know the logical basis for *all* generalizations and conclusions.

Sample Paragraph (Annotated)

The report to the committee follows an *inductive* pattern.

The evidence presented in the body of the paragraph becomes the basis for an *inductive generalization.*

Two *inductive generalizations.*

The generalizations become the basis for an informal *deductive* syllogism pointing toward an action that probably needs to be taken.

Having built four new elementary schools in the last five years, members of the Palmville School Board were convinced they had solved the problem with overcrowding that had plagued the public schools ever since the mid-1970s. As a result, they were disappointed when School Superintendent Marisa LaRoux made her mid-July Projected Enrollment Report. She pointed out that the town's population has expanded by several hundred more families than were projected because the good weather this year spurred home building and the low mortgage rates encouraged buyers. In addition, more families are deciding to have two or more children, bringing the average number of children per family to 1.9, much higher than the figure of 1.65 used in the past to calculate demands for school services. The superintendent also admitted that the decades-old policy of calculating a family of two as a family without children has proven to be a serious mistake because it ignored the many children growing up in single-parent families. Based on this information, the superintendent concluded that the overcrowding problem would continue this year and probably for many years in the future. Chairperson Clifton Washington summed up the school board's response this way: "The schools are overcrowded now, and if more students are going to be coming to us asking for instruction, then we'd better get back into the school-building business."

Sample Paragraph (Induction)

Roaming the site, I can't help noticing that when men start cooking, the hardware gets complicated. Custom-built cookers—massive contraptions of cast iron and stainless steel—may cost $15,000 or more; they incorporate the team's barbecue philosophy. "We burn straight hickory under a baffle," Jim Garts, coleader of the Hogaholics, points out as he gingerly opens a scorching firebox that vents smoke across a water tray beneath a 4-by-8-foot grill. It's built on a trailer the size of a mobile home. Other cookers have been fashioned from a marine diesel engine; from a '76 Datsun, with grilling racks instead of front seats, a chimney above the dash, and coals under the hood; and as a 15-foot version of Elvis Presley's guitar (by the Graceland Love Me Tenderloins). It's awesome ironmongery.

Daniel Cohen, "Cooking-off for Fame and Fortune," *Smithsonian,* September 1988, p. 132.

Sample Paragraph (Deduction)

It is an everyday fact of life that competitors producing similar products assert that their own goods or services are better than those of their rivals. Every product advertised—from pain relievers to fried chicken—is claimed to be better than its competitors. If all these companies sued for libel, the courts would be so overloaded with cases that they would grind to a halt. For years courts dismissed criticisms of businesses, products, and performances as expressions of opinion. When a restaurant owner sued a guidebook to New York restaurants for giving his establishment a bad review, he won a $20,000 verdict in compensatory damages and $5 in punitive damages. But this was overturned by the court of appeals. The court held that, with the exception of one item, the allegedly libelous statements were expressions of opinion, not fact. Among these statements were that the "dumplings, on our visit, resembled bad ravioli . . . chicken with chili was rubbery and the rice . . . totally insipid. . . ." Obviously, it would be impossible to prove the nature of the food served at that particular meal. What is tender to one palate may be rubbery to another. The one misstatement of fact, that the Peking duck was served in one dish instead of three, was in my opinion, a minor and insignificant part of the entire review. Had the review of the restaurant been considered as a whole. . . , this small misstatement of fact would have been treated as *de minimis*. That is a well-established doctrine requiring that minor matters not be considered by the courts. In this case, the court held that the restaurant was a public figure and had failed to prove actual malice.

Reprinted from *A Chilling Effect, The Mounting Threat of Libel and Invasion of Privacy Actions to the First Amendment* by Lois G. Forer, by permission of W. W. Norton & Company, Inc. Copyright © 1987 by Lois G. Forer.

Student Writing: Reasoning by Use of Induction and Deduction

Mad about MADD

Sheilagh Brady

On May 3, 1980, Cari Lightner was walking through a suburban neighborhood on her way to a church carnival in Fair Oaks, California, when she was killed by a hit-and-run drunk driver. The driver was Clarence Busch, forty-six years old with four prior arrests for drunk driving. Busch had just been released on bail for a hit-and-run drunk-driving charge a week before.

Cari's mother, Candy Lightner, was thirty three at the time, a divorced mother of two other children working as a real estate agent. She was told by two police officers investigating the accident that Busch would probably receive little jail time, if any, because "'That's the way the system works'" (Lightner and Hathaway 224).

Faced with these circumstances, many of us might have concluded that the only possible responses were despair and frustrated rage. Candy Lightner reached another conclusion. Mulling over the police officers' words during dinner the same night, Lightner conceived of the organization that eventually became MADD, Mothers Against Drunk Driving. She felt the need to do something to take way her pain. MADD became a way for her to use her anger and to come to terms with the death of her daughter. For the next five years, Lightner devoted her time and effort to the creation of MADD.

Lightner moved to Dallas, Texas, the eventual headquarters of MADD, to begin working on organizing the new group. In March, 1983, NBC aired a documentary, "Mothers Against Drunk Driving: The Candy Lightner Story." According to James B. Jacobs, MADD chapters doubled across the United States by 1985, and in the same year *Time* magazine reported that there were 320 chapters nationwide, and 600,00 volunteers and donors (Otto 41).

MADD's response to drunk driving has been to emphasize jail sentences and legislation. MADD members get angry when people feel "that a killer drunk driver deserves a lesser penalty than other homicidal offenders" (Jacobs). MADD has been successful in focusing public attention on the problems associated with drinking and driving and mobilizing legal changes to create stiffer penalties for drunk driving. MADD aims to have these stiffer penalties made mandatory and plea bargaining abolished (Voas and Lacey 126–127).

Not only has MADD focused public attention but it has also had considerable effect on local, state, and federal governments. In 1988, S. Ungerleider and S.A. Bloch did an evaluation of MADD which has been summarized as concluding that MADD was "more successful in state legislatures where a large number of laws were enacted in an effort to produce more sever sanctions for the drunk driving offense" (Voas and Lacey 137).

Yet according to Dave Russel, a member of the Rhode Island Chapter of MADD, the past few years have been difficult. During the 1980s legislation was passed quickly because of the sudden public support through pressure groups concerned about drinking and driving. Since then, the progress of drunk-driving legislation has slowed considerably. Russel says that the number of deaths per year has steadily decreased since 1980 but that alcohol related accidents still take close to 19,000 lives each year. As a response to this situation, MADD chapters nationally have concluded that there is still a need for more drunk-driving legislation, even if legislators do not see it.

Having reached this conclusion, MADD chapters nationwide have decided to submit three different bills annually to their state legislatures. Some states have turned these bills into laws, but many have not. Just what are these MADD chapters proposing? Are the laws they want enacted reasonable or unreasonable?

One bill aims to reduce the BAC (Blood Alcohol Content) level from .10 to .08 as the legal limit of intoxication. In 1988 in a report focusing on BAC levels, researchers Moskowitz and Robinson found that although theoretically impairment begins with the first drink, significant impairment occurs in most people at .05 BAC or lower. At the Surgeon General's Workshop, December 14–16, 1988, C. Everett Koop called for lowering the BAC limit in all states to .08, as did the National Highway Transportation Safety Administration in reports sent to the United States Congress. According to MADD national office, lowering the BAC level to .09 will reduce drunk driving by making it more likely that drunk drivers will be caught, and also acting to discourage driving under the influence. If research evidence and reliable authorities suggest reducing the BAC level from .10 to .08 will save lives, then most of us are likely to conclude that the legislative proposal seems reasonable.

Another bill is the ALR Bill or the Administrative License Revocation. This law would eliminate the period between the arrest of a drunk driver and the hearing suspending the license. Right now, in many states, that period is supposed to be around thirty days, but inevitably becomes much longer, a delay which allows the drunk driver to continue driving for that much longer legally under a valid license. The ALR would be a process that would allows the police officer to take the drunk driver's license if there is a refusal to take the breathalyzer test. In return, the driver would be given a temporary permit, good for ten to fifteen days, following an appearance at a hearing. If the driver does not appear for the hearing or cannot provide reasonable evidence for refusing the test, the license is suspended. In the case of a "no show," the driver must appear later to answer to the charge against him or her, but what is important is that the license will have already been suspended.

The Administrative License Revocation was recommended by the Presidential Commission on Drunk Driving which developed the National commission Against Drunk Driving. According to several researchers, "administrative revocation has widespread support among researchers, highway safety experts, and the public in general because it has been shown to be an effective administrative action that protects innocent drivers" in an experiment conducted in California, Washington, and Minnesota (Peck, Sadler, and Perrine). Most of us would probably conclude that ALR is a reasonable procedure, yet seventeen states have not yet turned the ALR bill into a law.

Last, MADD chapters propose annually an Open Container Law requiring that open containers of alcohol not be allowed in the passenger compartments of vehicles. According to MADD's national chapter, it is fundamental to separate drinking and driving because this separation is essential to the public interest and to the public's understanding of the crisis created by drunk driving. MADD argues that banning open containers of alcoholic beverages in a vehicle is one way to make sure drivers do not start drinking while driving or to become even more intoxicated while driving.

Moskowitz and Robinson, in *Effects of Low Doses of Alcohol on Driving Skills*, report that drinking while driving is dangerous because ingesting even a small amount of alcohol begins the impairment process. For most of us, the Open Container Law probably also seems quite reasonable.

Even though the bills proposed by MADD chapters are likely to seem reasonable to most people, many states have not turned them into laws. At the same time, the combination of alcohol and driving remains a problem. 19,000 deaths per year may be lower than in previous years, but this is still too many avoidable tragedies. One appropriate response is for each of us to become involved in working for a solution. If MADD's three proposals seem reasonable to you, if they are not yet law in your state, and if you want these policies in place to protect you, your family, and your friends, call your local MADD chapter and ask what you can do to help.

Works Cited

Lightner, Candy and Nancy Hathaway. "The Other Side of Sorrow." *Ladies Home Journal* Sept. 1990: 158, 224–225.

Jacobs, James B. *Drunk Driving: An American Dilemma*. Chicago: U of Chicago P, 1989.

Moskowitz, H. and Robinson, C.D. *Effects of Low Doses of Alcohol on Driving Skills*. Washington: National Highway Traffic Safety Administration, 1988.

Otto, Freidrich. "Seven Who Succeeded." *Time* 7 Jan., 1985: 40–43, 45.

Peck, Raymond C., Sadler, D.D., and Perrine, M.W. "The Comparative Effectiveness of Alcohol Rehabilitation and Licensing Control Actions for Drunk Driving Offenders: A Review of the Literature." *Alcohol, Drugs and Driving: Abstracts and Reviews* 1 (1985): 15–39.

Russel, Dave. Personal Interview. 19 Nov., 1993.

Voas, Robert B. and John H. Lacey. "Drunk Driving Enforcement, Adjudication, and Sanctions in the United States In Robert E. Mann and R. Jean Wilson, eds. *Drinking and Driving: Advances in Research and Prevention*. New York: Guilford, 1990.

BARBARA EHRENREICH

BARBARA EHRENREICH received a B.A. from Reed College and a Ph.D. from Rockefeller University in biology. She has been active in the women's movement and other movements for social change for a number of years and has taught women's issues at several universities, including New York University and the State University of New York—Old Westbury. She is a Fellow of the Institute for Policy Studies in Washington, D.C., and is active in the Democratic Socialists of America. A prolific author, Ehrenreich is a regular columnist for *Ms.* and *Mother Jones* and has published articles in a wide range of magazines, among them *Esquire*, the *Atlantic*, *Vogue*, *New Republic*, the *Wall Street Journal*, *TV Guide*, the *New York Times Magazine*, *Social Policy*, and *The Nation*. Her books include *For Her Own Good: 150 Years of the Experts' Advice to Women* (with Deirdre English) (1978); *The Hearts of Men: American Dreams and the Flight from Commitment* (1983); *Remaking Love: The Feminization of Sex* (with Elizabeth Hess and Gloria Jacobs) (1986); *Fear of Falling: The Inner Life of the Middle Class* (1989); and *The Worst Years of Our Lives: Irreverent Notes from a Decade of Greed* (1990).

Star Dreck

Ehrenreich's humorous example of inductive and deductive reasoning offers some pointed criticisms of our values. It also points out the ease with which logic can be twisted and misdirected. Thus the essay serves as a caution for both writers and readers.

When I was a kid, we knew very little about the stars, and much of what we did know was imprecise and speculative in nature. But such is the beauty of the human mind—forever reaching, forever grasping—that we now know far more than we can possibly absorb or usefully apply, and certainly far more than I ever expected to know in my own lifetime: not only what they eat for breakfast and what their favorite colors are, but their secret self-doubts and worries, their hair-management problems, and the names and locations of their unclaimed progeny.

As in all expanding fields, we are faced with what the scholars   2
call an "information explosion," which is already taxing the resources of the available media. In the old days, there were only a few specialized journals, with titles like *Silver Screen* and *Swooning Starlets.* But today there are dozens of publications, such as *People* and *Us,* which make fast-breaking discoveries accessible even to the person of limited educational attainment. For the intellectual elite, we have such challenging sources as *Vanity Fair* and *Interview,* which provide the depth of analysis that is sadly lacking on *Entertainment Tonight.*

Of course there are still a few throwbacks who have failed to   3
appreciate our expanding knowledge of the stars. They point out that most Americans are profoundly ignorant—prone to believe that Botswana is in Florida or that the *Yellow Pages* is a "great book." But retro-pedants like Allan Bloom never bother to quiz us on Burt and Loni's baby problem, or the tribulations of Cher's unfortunately monikered "Bagel Boy." They forget that, as far as the majority of the world's population is concerned, star trivia *is* Western civilization.

I don't want to boast, but I do try to keep abreast. Once, for   4
example, I had the opportunity to shake the bejeweled hand of a very major star. But I didn't—not because I was shy; but because *I knew too much about her;* her former husband's megavitamin problem, her hairdresser's recent breakdown, her ill-concealed rivalry with Joan Collins. There was simply nothing left to say.

Theory, as usual, lags behind the frenetic accumulation of new   5
data, but already a few broad paradigmatic principles are beginning to emerge. There are three of them, just as there are three fundamental forces (not counting the fourth), three Stooges, and three Rambos. The first one is: all stars are related to each other.

It didn't used to be this way in the old days, when the average   6
star was the abused daughter of an alcoholic Mississippian. But in the last two decades, the stars have undergone a sudden and astonishing genetic convergence: there's Jamie Lee Curtis (daughter of Janet Leigh and Tony), Carrie Fisher (daughter of Debbie Reynolds and Eddie), Michael Douglas (son of Kirk), Jeff Bridges (son of

Lloyd), Charlie Sheen (son of Martin), Emilio Estevez (brother of Charlie), and so on. Frankly, no one knows what this means, although the search is on for the "star gene," which could then be transferred, by familiar bioengineering techniques, to piglets, mice, and intestinal bacteria.

The second principle, which is again the result of very recent research, is that *all stars work out.* Whether this is a response to the inevitable muscular weakening caused by inbreeding, or merely an attempt to fill in the empty hours between interviews for *Premiere,* no one knows, but it all began with Jane (daughter of Henry, sister of Peter).

The third and final principle, which we owe in part to the dedicated researchers at *Star* and similar journals, is that all stars—and especially those who do not work out—have had near-fatal encounters with cocaine (Richard Dreyfuss), alcohol (Don Johnson), food (Elizabeth Taylor), or the lack of it (Dolly Parton). Here again, inbreeding may be at work, but the net result is the unique life cycle of the star, which is not dissimilar to the classic saga of the hero as charted by Joseph Campbell: birth, abuse, the struggle against substances at Betty Ford—followed by redemption and inspiring appearances in "Just Say No" ads.

But as our knowledge increases, so does our frustration. Americans, after all, do not like knowing things (such as the location of Botswana) that they cannot do anything about. So, I say, give us some way of applying our ever-growing knowledge: let us *vote* on the lives of the stars!

After all, we're better informed about the lives of the stars than we are about such dreary matters as deficit management and the balance of trade. In fact, we are probably in a better position to make star decisions than the stars themselves. Consider that tragic misstep: Bruce's marriage to Julianne—which led to the dullest album of his career and the temporary removal of his earring. One hundred million American women were prepared to say, "No, don't do it. Wait for a Jersey Girl. Or, better yet, wait for me to move to Jersey and become one!" But we couldn't do a thing.

Imagine if we could have a referendum on Barbra and Don (hold out, Barb, he's just a bimbo!). Or a plebiscite on Michael Jackson's pigmentation (he'd be able to wear one of those "Black by Popular Demand" T-shirts!). Imagine the debates, the mass rallies and marches, the furious exchanges in the op-ed pages!

But of course the stars wouldn't accept that. They might rebel.   12
They'd go underground—get fat, go back to the substances of their
youth, and hide out in unmarked mobile homes in Culver City. I
guess there are some things that humankind just wasn't meant to
tinker with—some things that will always fill our souls with helpless
awe, and show us how insignificant and meaningless our own lives
are in the grand scheme of things. And no matter how much we may
learn about them, that is the function of the stars.

Meanings and Values

1. What two meanings does the word "stars" have in the opening
    paragraph?

2. What process of reasoning is illustrated (in fragmented form) in
    paragraph 9?

3. Try to identify as many targets of the author's ironic criticism as you
    can in paragraphs 9–12. (Hint: The most important targets are our
    own habits and values.)

4a. Is it possible to identify a central theme for this essay? If so, what is
    it?

 b. If not, can the essay still be considered unified? (See "Guide to
    Terms": *Unity.*) What are some of its important themes?

Expository Techniques

1. In which paragraph does the author introduce the first of her gener-
    alizations, derived, she suggests, from a process of induction?

2. In which paragraphs does she announce and illustrate the rest of the
    deductive generalizations?

3a. From what kinds of sources are most of the examples in the essay
    probably drawn? Be specific.

 b. Do you consider it likely that Ehrenreich means to poke fun at these
    sources? Why?

4a. What reasons do we have for suspecting that the speaker in this
    essay is not the author?

 b. Describe the character and attitudes of the persona created for this
    essay. (Guide: *Persona.*)

Diction and Vocabulary

1. How does the pun in the opening paragraph (a play on the word "stars") serve to surprise readers and undermine their sense of what the essay is about?

2a. In several passages in the essay, Ehrenreich uses scholarly and scientific language to discuss topics often found in gossip columns or popular magazines. Locate several examples of this use of language.

  b. For what purpose or purposes does the author employ this contrast between content and style? (Guide: *Style.*)

3a. There are numerous allusions in paragraphs 5, 7, and 8. Identify their sources. (Note: Some of the allusions refer to scholars and scientific theories.)

  b. What general purpose do these allusions serve?

4. If you do not know the meaning of some of the following words, look them up in the dictionary: progeny (par. 1); pedants, tribulations (3); frenetic, paradigmatic (5); plebiscite (11).

Suggestions for Writing and Discussion

1. Do you object to Ehrenreich's poking fun at magazines like *People?* What can be said in favor of them?

2. What does this essay have to say about the things people in our country value most? Do you think this view of our values is an accurate one?

3. If this essay can use reasoning to reach absurd conclusions, shouldn't we consider reasoning an unreliable method for making decisions?

(NOTE: Suggestions for topics requiring development by INDUCTION and DEDUCTION are on page 480, at the end of this section.)

JO COUDERT

Jo COUDERT was born in Williamsport, Pennsylvania, and grew up in Radburn, New Jersey. She attended Dean Academy in Franklin, Massachusetts and Smith College. Coudert's work as a writer has taken many forms, including plays, nonfiction books, and essays. Her published books include *Advice from a Failure* (1965), *The Alcoholic in Your Life* (1970), *Go Well: The Story of a House* (1974), and *The I Never Cooked Before Cookbook* (1963), and she is working on two more, *The Ditchdigger's Daughter* and *Inside Information for Women*. Her essays appear often in magazines like *Women's Day* and *Reader's Digest*, and she has had several of her plays produced.

Don't Come as You Are

By paying attention to what people around her are wearing, Coudert notices the important messages clothing choices send. As she points out, our clothing influences other people whether we wish it to or not. Her essay first appeared in *Woman's Day*.

It's Saturday evening. The silver is polished, flowers are on the table, a rib roast is in the oven—and two guests arrive wearing shorts. Not designer shorts or Bermudas, mind you, but the kind you save for playing soccer on a muddy field.

Friends recommend a dentist who seems efficient and pleasant. No law says dentist *have* to wear white coats, but a frayed pullover and unlaced hi-tops? I begin to wonder about his professional standards.

Business acquaintances kindly include a friend in their invitation—and he calls for me in an unironed shirt. I express hope that he has a jacket in the car, and he answers indignantly, "But this is a Brooks Brothers shirt!"

You're probably thinking, "Oh, well, that's how kids dress these   4
days." But these were all people with a healthy number of miles on
their odometers. They were people who once gave thought to the
circumstances and dressed accordingly, but now come as they are.
You see them everywhere, even in church. At midnight Mass last
Christmas Eve, I spotted a couple wearing out-at-the-knee blue
jeans.

When did people start believing that it didn't matter what they   5
had on? When did they stop taking pride in being well-dressed?
When did clothes become an affront as well as an adornment?

And why? It can't be just a matter of comfort. Men, it seems, are   6
the worst at dressing down when the occasion calls for dressing up,
but it's hard to believe that a jacket and pressed slacks offer so much
less comfort than a sweatshirt and jeans. And while comfort led
women to abandon the torture of girdles and spike heels, how much
discomfort is posed by a loose skirt?

Clothes are not just something we put on to cover our naked-   7
ness; they are a part of the atmosphere. Restaurateurs know this as
well as anyone. A friend, visiting San Francisco for the first time on
business, was eager to dine at the famed "Top of the Mark," but concerned about how she'd fare as a woman alone. She dressed in her
best, added a string of inherited pearls, asked for a good table—and
was shown to one with a glittering view. In contrast, a couple who
rode the elevator with her were seated near the kitchen door. They
hadn't bothered to change out of their rumpled sightseeing attire.

Clothes can influence not only how you're treated but how you   8
treat other people. I, who am ordinarily the politest of people,
rushed out the other day in a dirty jacket to make a deadline for
delivering a painting to an art show. When I got there, I realized that
a woman I'd been wanting to make friends with was running the
show. But, ashamed of how I looked, I pretended not to recognize
her. How rude I must have seemed—and was—simply because of
how poorly I was dressed.

A happier story is one a neighbor tells about her two children.   9
Dressed in new Easter outfits, they set off for Sunday school. Henry,
6, usually given to beating up on his sister, held out his hand to
escort her down the steps. Sarah, 4, accustomed to screams of rage at
her brother, laid her gloved hand in his and thanked him gravely.
Feeling themselves to look like a miniature lady and gentleman, they
behaved the same way.

My sister, who teaches school, tells me that she puts on high 10
heels on days when she needs to be very clear about her authority
over the class. Whether we think about it or not, we all know that
clothes communicate. Sometimes they communicate feelings we're
not even aware of—like hostility. When a weekend guest wore the
same blue jeans and shirt for an elegant brunch on Sunday morning
that she'd worn for a tramp in the woods on Saturday afternoon,
what were her hosts to think? Justifiably, they felt put down: *You and
your friends don't matter enough to go to the trouble of looking nice.*

I felt the same way when a relative invited herself over on a 11
Sunday, then showed up in her gardening outfit. "I know you're
having guests for dinner," she said offhandedly, "but it was raining
and I decided not to change my clothes."

I was hurt and I was angry. Clothes can honor the occasion and 12
enhance it. Or they can insult and bring it down. It isn't the fit of the
clothes—well-cut jeans with a good-looking blouse and jewelry are
welcome at any party of mine. It's the fit between the clothes and the
occasion that counts.

Clothes are important. They can go a long way toward making 13
you feel really good about yourself. When you look marvelous, you
delight yourself—and you give pleasure to the people around you.
There used to be an ad for stockings with the tag line: *You owe it to
your audience.* Let's get back to thinking we owe it to our audience
to have our clothes match the occasion. Even more, we owe it to
ourselves.

Meanings and Values

1a. What inductive generalization does Coudert advance, then dismiss,
in paragraph 4?

  b. How might this strategy increase the willingness of most readers to
accept whatever generalization the writer eventually endorses?

2a. From paragraph 7 on, Coudert presents a series of limited generalizations and applies each, deductively, to interpret typical behaviors.
Identify these limited generalizations.

  b. What generalization does the writer offer in paragraph 10? Can it be
considered a statement of the essay's theme which also sums up the
more limited generalizations Coudert offers in surrounding paragraphs? Why, or why not? (See "Guide to Terms": *Unity*.)

  c. Does Coudert present adequate evidence to support her conclusions
about the importance of appearance? Do you find her conclusions

convincing? Why, or why not? What might determine whether or not other readers find her reasoning convincing? (Guide: *Evaluation*.)

Expository Techniques

1a. What strategy does the writer use to begin this essay? Why is it particularly appropriate for an essay employing inductive reasoning? (Guide: *Introductions*.)

b. What strategy does she use to conclude the essay? (Guide: *Closings*.)

2. To what extent do the limited generalizations Coudert offers from paragraph 7 on (see 2a, above) act as topic sentences for the paragraphs in which they are presented?

3a. Tell what purposes the rhetorical questions in paragraphs 5 and 6 serve. (Guide: *Rhetorical Questions*.)

b. Could these purposes be better served in some other way? If so, what other strategy might be more effective?

Diction and Vocabulary

1a. Locate Coudert's descriptions of acceptable and unacceptable clothing and take note of the kinds of words she uses to describe each.

b. How do both the denotations and the connotations of the words she uses to describe acceptable kinds of dress differ from those she uses for the unacceptable? (Guide: *Connotation* and *Denotation*.)

2a. Where would you place the style of this essay on a continuum from formal to informal? (Guide: *Style/Tone*.)

b. How much does the writer's use of formal or informal language contribute to the formality or informality of its style? Be ready to support your answer with specific examples from the text. (Guide: *Diction*.)

Suggestions for Writing and Discussion

1. Discuss different kinds of clothing college students (or other people) wear and the messages they try to send with their choices. Are such messages easy to interpret or are they often misinterpreted?

2. The language we use can be appropriate or inappropriate for a situation in much the same way as the clothes we wear. Prepare an essay examining the different levels of language, from informal to formal, that a college student is likely to employ.

(NOTE: Suggestions for topics requiring development by INDUCTION and DEDUCTION are on page 480, at the end of this section.)

PETE HAMILL

PETE HAMILL was born in 1935 in Brooklyn, New York. He attended Pratt Institute and the University of the Americas. After spending time as a sheet metal worker and an advertising designer, he began working as a reporter. During his career he has written for the *Saturday Evening Post*, *Newsday*, the *New York Post*, and the *New York Daily News*. He is now a columnist for the *Village Voice*. Hamill has published novels and screenplays and written numerous articles for magazines such as *Cosmopolitan*, *The New York Times Magazine*, *Playboy*, and the *Reader's Digest*.

The Neverglades

This essay (from *Esquire* magazine) offers several inductive generalizations and a syllogism with an imaginative twist: Its conclusion is not (yet) clear. Along with the clear pattern of reasoning, the author offers vivid, carefully chosen language and details.

I first saw the Everglades in the spring of 1954. I was a kid then, poorly disguised as a sailor of the United States Navy, and my guide was the craziest woman I've ever known. She had a bottle-green 1940 Ford, and one morning in Pensacola she told me to take a week's leave. She was going to show me Key West. I did what I was told and off we went. She drove, barrel-assing south along the coast from Pensacola, swearing at truck drivers and tourists, drinking Jax beer all the way. We slept on a deserted beach, with palm fronds rattling above us in the breeze. We danced to Hank Williams and Webb Pierce in a shitkicker bar in citrus country and had to fight our way out. We had coconut juice for breakfast. We looked at garish sunsets in the gigantic Gulf evenings. Since there was no radio, she talked all the way. I never laughed as much again.

Then, before dawn, at Naples, she turned onto the Tamiami Trail. And stopped talking. 2

In memory, a lavender wash covered the world. We parked and 3 stepped out of the car. I looked out at a flat, empty prairie, its monotony relieved by the occasional silhouettes of nameless trees against the blank early-morning sky.

"What is this?" I asked. "Where are we?" 4

"Listen," she whispered. 5

And I heard them, far off, almost imperceptible at first: thin, 6 high, and then like the sound of a million whips cutting the air. They came over the edge of the horizon and then the sky was black with them. Birds. Thousands of them. Tens of thousands. Maybe a million. I shivered in fear and awe. The woman held my city-boy's hand. And then the vast dense flock was gone. The great molten ball of the sun oozed over the horizon.

"We're in The Everglades," she said. 7

I don't know what happened to that wild and lovely woman. 8 I'm certain that old '40 Ford was long ago hammered into scrap. But that moment in The Everglades has stayed with me across all the decades. It was as if someone had torn a hole in time that morning, and for one scary moment I stepped into the beginnings of the earth, before man, before cement and gasoline, before history. The Everglades are like that: so primeval that they can make you feel as if you are the first human ever to see them. Eventually, we made it to U.S. 1 and hurtled down the old two-lane highway, over the sea and into the luminous terrain of the Keys.

But I couldn't get The Everglades out of my head. Back in Pen- 9 sacola, I found and read a copy of Marjory Stoneman Douglas's lyrical 1947 book, *The Everglades: River of Grass*. I saw Budd Schulberg's wonderful movie, *Wind Across The Everglades*. In the years that followed, I drove across them again, took small boats down into Florida Bay, where the waters of the Glades empty, traveled with a tour guide into the eerie stands of mangrove at the edge of the land. Then, somehow, life became too busy for wandering through wild places. Twenty years went by. When I saw the Glades again, it was from twenty-thousand feet, on my way somewhere else.

Still, they were always *there*, part of America, part of my youth, 10 a wet, uncharted vastness in my imagination. Occasionally, I would read stories about the problems of the Glades and how they were drying up. Once in a while, there would be a piece on television, showing thousands of acres on fire. More and more frequently, there were predictions that the whole system might be dying. I decided I'd better go back before The Everglades joined all the other marvels that have been beaten out of the world I knew while I was young.

The first stop was Miami, which, like every other city in south- 11
ern Florida, lives off this ecosystem. "If The Everglades die, Miami dies, too," said Joe Podgor, of Friends of The Everglades. "It's as simple as that."

I moved around the next few days, and it was clear even to a 12
man with urban astigmatism that Podgor and the others were right: The Glades are in trouble.

The facts are easy enough to find. Over many thousands of 13
years, nature created a splendid system here. Fresh water from summer rains gathered in small lakes in central Florida (near Orlando). This water drained into the Kissimmee River, which in turn fed Lake Okeechobee, a shallow body of fresh water that covers 730 square miles. The overflow spilled over the southern lip of the lake and formed a fifty-mile-wide river that moved slowly and subtly south, 150 miles across southern Florida to the sea above the Keys. This was a slow process; the river moved down a gradual slope of one and a half inches to the mile before reaching Florida Bay. Clouds sucked moisture from these rich wetlands, blew north, and rained upon the lakes and rivers in a perpetual natural cycle. The great insight of Marjory Stoneman Douglas was to recognize The Everglades as a wide, shallow, sheetlike river, not a swamp.

Water is at the heart of the system. It feeds the Biscayne Aquifer, 14
the gigantic underground cavern that supplies fresh water to Miami and other thirsty coastal towns. And it has given life to a magnificent array of creatures. When the first Spaniards arrived in 1513, an estimated five million alligators lived in the Glades, along with uncounted crocodiles; this lush habitat is one of the few on earth where these cousins exist together. The sloughs (freshwater rivers running through the saw-grass prairies) were thick with largemouth bass and bluegills. There were herds of deer, thousands of raccoons, opossums, otter, mink, and black bear and fox, along with the beautiful Florida panther. There were twenty-six kinds of snakes. In the bays and rivers you could see the manatee, huge and homely and

shy. In Florida Bay, there were stone crabs, dolphins, sharks, and barracuda. And always, there were the birds.

I wasn't the first human to see the sky blacken with birds; I only 15 felt that way. Once they came in the millions: dozens of species, including flamingos, great white herons, ibis, snowy egrets, pelicans, roseate spoonbills, and bald eagles with seven-foot wingspans, living in nests that were nine feet deep. When John James Audubon passed through in 1832, he was astonished. A century later, a drive along the eighty-five miles of the Tamiami Trail from Miami to Naples left cars encrusted with *guano*.

Most of those birds are gone now—in the past fifty years, about 16 90 percent have vanished—along with many of the other living creatures. Only 10 percent of the ibis are left; the wood stork could be completely gone by the year 2000. There are only thirty known Florida panthers left alive; many fell to disease caused by the destruction of the ecosystem; many to speeding automobiles. Fisherman can no longer eat catfish or largemouth bass; they are loaded with mercury. The manatee had been smashed and shredded in the hundreds by powerboats. Ninety percent of the alligators are gone; in the 1880s alone, two and a half million were slaughtered for their hides. It is more and more difficult to see crocodiles, too; it's believed that only six hundred remain.

The problem, of course, was—and is—man. 17

Man came to The Everglades. Man stripped away the wild 18 orchids. Man hunted down the egrets for their plumes to satisfy the fashions of the turn of the last century. Man walked into the forests with saws and axes in the Forties and Fifties and destroyed the stands of knot-free cypress trees (cousins of the redwood). Man carted away the corpses of mahogany trees and live oak and gumbo-limbo, which had stood on hammocks above the saw-grass, providing shelter for raccoons and otter and deer. Man saw The Everglades as a mere swamp to be drained, planted, lived upon, tamed. He attacked and attacked and attacked.

A small band—Ernest Coe, Marjory Douglas, Art Marshall— 19 saw early that disaster was imminent. Beginning in the 1930s, they lobbied politicians. In 1947, President Truman finally set aside 1.4 million acres for The Everglades National Park. This was only a fraction of the original four thousand square miles that made up the natural Everglades, but it at least offered sanctuary to the creatures who had been so ferociously mauled by the bloody hand of man.

Now even this vast, silent preserve is threatened. "Some people   20
think it's already too late to save The Everglades," Joe Podgor said
one night at dinner. "I hope they're wrong. But if they're right, then
all of southern Florida is doomed."

The fatal wounds would be self-inflicted. In the Fifties, when I   21
first passed through the region, about a million people depended
upon water generated by The Everglades. Today the population is
4.5 million, with another 600 arriving every day. "Florida is adding
one Tampa to its population every year," Podgor explained, "and
they all use water." If the consequences are alarming, the images are
banal: millions of people bathing, flushing, filling swimming pools,
washing dogs. Few of them believe they could be transforming this
great green place into a desert. But they are. According to the South
Florida Water Management Corporation, per capita water use in the
area is two hundred gallons of fresh water a *day*. That water is
sucked up from the Biscayne Aquifer. It travels south from Okeechobee through canals. It is drained from The Everglades. It is manufactured in desalinization plants. And still, there is not enough.

To supply that water, man tampered with nature. First, an   22
immense dike was constructed around Lake Okeechobee, back in
the 1920s; the purpose of this earthen manacle was to prevent flooding and to reclaim part of The Everglades for agriculture. In some
ways, it worked. More than two million acres were drained and
planted and developed for human itinerants lusting for the sun.
Everybody cheered, particularly the real estate racketeers. The Tamiami Trail was constructed in the 1920s, effectively placing another
dike across the Glades, and a second highway, Alligator Alley, was
erected across the great slow river in the Sixties. Canals and dikes
were sliced south into the saw grass. Then, in the early '60s, after
Castro took Cuba, the sugar barons came upon the land. Eventually,
more than 430,000 acres of sugarcane were planted in the drained
Everglades south of Okeechobee, their existence subsidized by huge
government handouts (and free water, paid for by the city dwellers),
their overflow of phosphorus and nitrogen pumped back into the
lake. The spirit of this was essentially: *Up yours Fidel, we'll grow our
own sugar!*

North of the lake, a vast dairy industry began to thrive; it, too,   23
dumped its waste into the waters. After Disney World arrived, in
1971, even more millions of water-sucking bipeds were drawn to the
region, with the real estate developers and civic boosters prancing in

orgasmic frenzies of welcome. Worst of all, the loopy geniuses of the U.S. Army Corps of Engineers decided to straighten out the lazy curves of the Kissimmee River, gouging a new course through the savanna and palmetto trees, transforming it by 1971 into a fifty-two-mile concrete ditch that was romantically named C-38.

The result of all this: disaster. Vast algae blooms soon appeared in the lake. Hundreds of thousands of fish died. Even the developers could see that Okeechobee was being choked by chemicals and cow shit. Some citizens rose in anger; there were articles, studies, meetings, protests.

In 1983, under Governor Bob Graham, the state decided to take action. For the first time in the nation's history, a major water project was put in reverse. The Kissimmee was partially restored to its old course, complete with marshes to filter the nutrients (the total cost will be $275 million); the sugar barons were told to stop pumping swill into the lake. It was a good beginning; it wasn't enough.

For everybody involved knew that there was one certain way to save The Everglades, and nobody would dare try it. They needed only to force the principles of capitalism on the sugar barons. That is, cut the $3-billion-a-year federal subsidy in the world marketplace. Out in the world, sugar sells for thirteen to fourteen cents a pound; our domestic sugar barons are getting twenty-four cents a pound. This is all done under the familiar theory of socialism for the owners, capitalism for the workers. And in Florida, those workers are underpaid migrants from the Caribbean. The Florida sugar growers were allowed to pump their discharges into a part of the Glades reserved for wildlife; the theory was that these marshes would act as a sieve.

But that didn't happen. Phosphorus and other nutrients began creating cattails, which are foreign to the area, and are now growing at the rate of four acres a day; saw grass and other native plants are being choked to death by these intruders, and the entire food chain has been disrupted. Worse, the slow, steady flow of water downstream is being stopped, starving the lower Glades. All of this has been compounded by a long drought, which some feel was caused by the disruption of the ecosystem. No wading birds have nested in the Loxahatchee National Wildlife Refuge for two years; a few years ago there were thirty thousand. In addition, the once-rich Everglades muck, upon which the farms and sugar plantations were built, is drying up and blowing away; of the original fifteen, only five feet of this primeval soil remains, and by the end of the century, the rest of it could be gone. That would leave a rocky limestone desert, no longer suitable for agriculture, but almost certain to be transformed into another plastic extension of Condoland. By the time that happens, The Everglades could be dead.

Walking along the Anhinga Trail in the park not long ago, I saw   28 a lone alligator dozing on the banks of a canal. In the Taylor Slough, there were pond lilies and spears of green pickerelweed and dense coverings of water lettuce, which in the natural order of things, would die, decay, and become part of the muck and the peat below. In the distance, a dozen unseen birds chattered in their different idioms, while insects droned and chirped. I touched a blade of saw grass, its fine toothy edges raw against my fingers. This was no longer the great wild place I first glimpsed as a boy. But it was enough, one small fragment left to us that told the awesome tale of the beginning of the world. If we let this die, it would be an obscenity.

Meanings and Values

1. This essay offers an inductive generalization at the end of paragraphs 11–12. What is it?

2a. How does the evidence in the preceding paragraphs contribute to the generalization?

 b. What role is played by the evidence in paragraphs 1–10?

3. Can paragraph 17 be considered an inductive generalization? If so, where does the author present the evidence on which it is based?

4a. State in your own words the syllogism underlying paragraph 20.

 b. Does the author believe the conclusion is inevitable?

 c. If not, what does he think can be done?

Expository Techniques

1. What strategy does Hamill use in paragraphs 1–7 to open the essay? (See "Guide to Terms": *Introductions*.)

2. What pattern of exposition is employed in paragraphs 13–14?

3. What expository pattern shapes the relationship of paragraphs 15–16?

4. Paragraph 15 echoes an earlier section of the essay. What is the purpose of this strategy?

5. Discuss the special roles played by paragraphs, 2, 4, 5, and 17. What contributes to their effectiveness?

6. What use does Hamill make of cause-effect analysis in the latter part of the essay?

Diction and Vocabulary

1a. Discuss how the author uses diction to emphasize the contrasts between paragraphs 1 and 3. (Guide: *Diction.*)

b. How does the sentence structure contribute to this effect? (Guide: *Syntax.*)

2. Examine the following paragraphs to see how Hamill uses concrete details and word choice to create scenes that are like paintings: 3, 6, and 28. (Guide: *Concrete/Abstract.*)

3. Examine the strategy Hamill uses to introduce the sentences in paragraph 18. What emphasis does it provide? (Guide: *Emphasis.*)

4. If you do not know the meaning of some of the following words, look them up in a dictionary: wash (par. 3); primeval, luminous (8); ecosystem (11); astigmatism (12); aquifer (14); banal (21); bipeds, orgasmic (23); sieve (26).

Suggestions for Writing and Discussion

1. Do some research into the current state of the Everglades to determine how well efforts to preserve it are succeeding.

2. Examine and report on the effects of development and/or preservation on an area familiar to you.

3. Is it important to preserve historical sites as well as natural sites? Can some of the arguments in favor of one effort be used to support the other?

(NOTE: Suggestions for topics requiring development by INDUCTION and DEDUCTION are on page 480, at the end of this section.)

PATRICIA KEAN

PATRICIA KEAN is a writer living in New York City. She attended
Georgetown University, receiving a B.A. in English, and the University of Wisconsin-Madison, earning an M.A. in English. After
spending time teaching and working in publishing, she began her
career as a free-lance writer specializing in education issues. Her
articles and essays have appeared in magazines and newspapers
like *Lingua Franca*, *The New York Times*, and *Newsday*.

Blowing Up the Tracks

Segregating students by ability ("tracking"), Kean explains, often
means separating them on the basis of class, race, parental influence, or questionable testing procedures rather than real ability or
potential. Though her explanations may not please everyone, she
offers careful reasoning and detailed evidence to support her
observations and she also reports on school districts that have
abandoned tracking. This essay was first published in the *Washington Monthly*.

It's morning in New York, and some seventh graders are more equal   1
than others.

Class 7–16 files slowly into the room, prodded by hard-faced   2
men whose walkie-talkies crackle with static. A pleasant looking
woman shouts over the din, "What's rule number one?" No reply.
She writes on the board. "Rule One: Sit down."

Rule number two seems to be an unwritten law: Speak slowly.   3
Each of Mrs. H's syllables hangs in the air a second longer than nec-
essary. In fact, the entire class seems to be conducted at 16 RPM.
Books come out gradually. Kids wander about the room aimlessly.
Twelve minutes into class, we settle down and begin to play
"O. Henry Jeopardy," a game which requires students to supply

one-word answers to questions like: "O. Henry moved from North Carolina to what state—Andy? Find the word on the page."

The class takes out a vocabulary sheet. Some of the words they 4 are expected to find difficult include: popular, ranch, suitcase, arrested, recipe, tricky, ordinary, humorous, and grand jury.

Thirty minutes pass. Bells ring, doors slam. 5

Class 7–1 marches in unescorted, mindful of rule number one. 6 Paperbacks of Poe smack sharply on desks, notebooks rustle, and kids lean forward expectantly, waiting for Mrs. H. to fire the first question. What did we learn about the writer?

Hands shoot into the air. Though Edgar Allan Poe ends up 7 sounding a lot like Jerry Lee Lewis—a booze-hound who married his 13-year-old cousin—these kids speak confidently, in paragraphs. Absolutely no looking at the book allowed.

We also have a vocabulary sheet, drawn from "The Tell-Tale 8 Heart," containing words like: audacity, dissimulation, sagacity, stealthy, anxiety, derision, agony, and supposition.

As I sit in the back of the classroom watching these two very dif- 9 ferent groups of seventh graders, my previous life as an English teacher allows me to make an educated guess and a chilling prediction. With the best of intentions, Mrs. H. is teaching the first group, otherwise known as the "slow kids," as though they are fourth graders, and the second, the honors group, as though they are high school freshmen. Given the odds of finding a word like "ordinary" on the SAT's, the children of 7–16 have a better chance of standing before a "grand jury" than making it to college.

Tracking, the practice of placing students in "ability groups" 10 based on a host of ill-defined criteria—everything from test scores to behavior to how much of a fuss a mother can be counted on to make—encourages even well-meaning teachers and administrators to turn out generation after generation of self-fulfilling prophecies. "These kids know they're no Einsteins," Mrs. H. said of her low-track class when we sat together in the teacher's lounge. "They know they don't read well. This way I can go really slowly with them."

With his grades, however, young Albert would probably be 11 hanging right here with the rest of lunch table 7–16. That's where I discover that while their school may think they're dumb, these kids are anything but stupid. "That teacher," sniffs a pretty girl wearing lots of purple lipstick. "She talks so slow. She thinks we're babies.

She takes a year to do anything." "What about that other one?" a girl named Ingrid asks, referring to their once-a-week student teacher. "He comes in and goes like this: Rail (pauses) road. Rail (pauses) road. Like we don't know what railroad means!" The table breaks up laughing.

Outside the walls of schools across the country, it's slowly   12
become an open secret that enforced homogeneity benefits no one. The work of researchers like Jeannie Oakes of UCLA and Robert Slavin of Johns Hopkins has proven that tracking does not merely reflect differences—it causes them. Over time, slow kids get slower, while those in the middle and in the so-called "gifted and talented" top tracks fail to gain from isolation. Along the way, the practice resegregates the nation's schools, dividing the middle from the lower classes, white from black and brown. As the evidence piles up, everyone from the Carnegie Corporation to the National Governors Association has called for change.

Though some fashionably progressive schools have begun to   13
reform, tracking persists. Parent groups, school boards, teachers, and administrators who hold the power within schools cling to the myths and wax apocalyptic about the horrors of heterogeneity. On their side is the most potent force known to man: bureaucratic inertia. Because tracking puts kids in boxes, keeps the lid on, and shifts responsibility for mediocrity and failure away from the schools themselves, there is little incentive to change a nearly-century old tradition. "Research is research," the principal told me that day, "This is practice."

Back Track

Tracking has been around since just after the turn of the century. It   14
was then, as cities teemed with immigrants and industry, that education reformers like John Franklin Bobbitt began to argue that the school and the factory shared a common mission, to "work up the raw material into that finished product for which it was best adapted." By the twenties, the scientific principles that ruled the factory floor had been applied to the classroom. They believed the IQ test—which had just become popular—allowed pure science, not the whims of birth or class, to determine whether a child received the type of education appropriate for a future manager or a future laborer.

It hasn't quite worked out that way. Driven by standardized   15
tests, the descendants of the old IQ tests, tracking has evolved into a
kind of educational triage premised on the notion that only the least
wounded can be saved. Yet when the classroom operates like a bat-
tleground, society's casualties mount, and the results begin to seem
absurd: Kids who enter school needing more get less, while the
already enriched get, well, enricher. Then, too, the low-track graduates of 70 years ago held a distinct advantage over their modern
counterparts: If tracking prepared them for mindless jobs, at least
those jobs existed.

The sifting and winnowing starts as early as pre-K. Three-year   16
old Ebony and her classmates have won the highly prized "gifted
and talented" label after enduring a battery of IQ and psychological
tests. There's nothing wrong with the "regular" class in this Harlem
public school. But high expectations for Ebony and her new friends
bring tangible rewards like a weekly field trip and music and computer lessons.

Meanwhile, regular kids move on to regular kindergartens   17
where they too will be tested, and where it will be determined that
some children need more help, perhaps a "pre-first grade" developmental year. So by the time they're ready for first grade reading
groups, certain six-year-olds have already been marked as "sparrows"—the low performers in the class.

In the beginning, it doesn't seem to matter so much, because the   18
other reading groups—the robins and the eagles—are just a few feet
away and the class is together for most of the day. Trouble is, as they
toil over basic drill sheets, the sparrows are slipping farther behind.
The robins are gathering more challenging vocabulary words, and
the eagles soaring on to critical thinking skills.

Though policies vary, by fourth grade many of these groups   19
have flown into completely separate classrooms, turning an innocent three-tier reading system into three increasingly rigid academic
tracks—honors, regular, and remedial—by middle school.

Unless middle school principals take heroic measures like buy-   20
ing expensive software or crafting daily schedules by hand, it often
becomes a lot easier to sort everybody by reading scores. So kids
who do well on reading tests can land in the high track for math, science, social studies, even lunch, and move together as a self-
contined unit all day. Friendships form, attitudes harden. Kids on
top study together, kids in the middle console themselves by

making fun of the "nerds" above and the "dummies" below, and kids on the bottom develop behavioral problems and get plenty of negative reinforcement.

By high school, many low-track students are locked out of what Jeannie Oakes calls "gatekeeper courses," the science, math, and foreign language classes that hold the key to life after twelfth grade. Doors to college are slamming shut, though the kids themselves are often the last to know. When researcher Anne Wheelock interviewed students in Boston's public schools, they'd all insist they were going to become architects, teachers, and the like. What courses were they taking? "Oh, Keyboarding II, Earth Science, Consumer Math. This would be junior year and I'd ask, 'Are you taking Algebra?' and they'd say no." 21

Black Marks

A funny thing can happen to minority students on the way to being tracked. Even when minority children score high, they often find themselves placed in lower tracks where counselors and principals assume they belong. 22

In Paula Hart's travels for The Achievement Council, a Los Angeles-based educational advocacy group, she comes across district after district where black and Latino kids score in the 75th percentile for math, yet never quite make it into Algebra I, the classic gatekeeper course. A strange phenomenon occurs in inner city areas with large minority populations—high track classes shrink, and low track classes expand to fit humble expectations for the entire school population. 23

A few years ago, Dr. Norward Roussell's curiosity got the best of him. As Selma, Alabama's first black school superintendent, he couldn't help but notice that "gifted and talented" tracks were nearly lily white in a district that was 70 percent black. When he looked for answers in the files of high school students, he discovered that a surprising number of low track minority kids had actually scored higher than their white top track counterparts. 24

Parents of gifted and talented students staged a full-scale revolt against Roussell's subsequent efforts to establish logical standards for placement. In four days of public hearings, speaker after speaker said the same thing: We're going to lose a lot of our students to other schools. To Roussell, their meaning was clear: Put black kids in the 25 high tracks and we pull white kids out of the system. More blacks and more low-income whites did make it to the top under the new criteria, but Roussell himself was left behind. The majority-white school board chose not to renew his contract, and he's now superintendent in Macon County, Alabama, a district that is overwhelmingly black.

Race and class divisions usually play themselves out in a more 26 subtle fashion. Talk to teachers about how their high track kids differ from their low track kids and most speak not of intelligence, but of motivation and "family." It seems that being gifted and talented is hereditary after all, largely a matter of having parents who read to you, who take you to museums and concerts, and who know how to work the system. Placement is often a matter of who's connected. Jennifer P., a teacher in a Brooklyn elementary school saw a pattern in her class. "The principal put all the kids whose parents were in the PTA in the top tracks no matter what their scores were. He figures that if his PTA's happy, he's happy."

Once the offspring of the brightest and the best connected have 27 been skimmed off in honors or regular tracks, low tracks begin to fill up with children whose parents are not likely to complain. These kids get less homework, spend less class time learning, and are often taught by the least experienced teachers, because avoiding them can become a reward for seniority in a profession where perks are few.

With the courts reluctant to get involved, even when tracking 28 leads to racial segregation and at least the appearance of civil rights violations, changing the system becomes an arduous local battle fought school by school. Those who undertake the delicate process of untracking need nerves of steel and should be prepared to find resistance from every quarter, since, as Slavin notes, parents of high-achieving kids will fight this to the death. One-time guidance counselor Hart learned this lesson more than a decade ago when she and two colleagues struggled to introduce a now-thriving college curriculum program at Los Angeles' Banning High. Their efforts to open top-track classes to all students prompted death threats from an unlikely source—their fellow teachers.

Off Track Betting

Anne Wheelock's new book, *Crossing the Tracks*, tells the stories of 29 schools that have successfully untracked or never tracked at all. Schools that make the transition often achieve dramatic results. True to its name, Pioneer Valley Regional school in Northfield, Massachusetts was one of the first in the nation to untrack. Since 1983, the number of Pioneer Valley seniors going on to higher education jumped from 37 to 80 percent. But, the author says, urban schools continue to lag behind. "We're talking about unequal distribution of reform," Wheelock declares. "Change is taking place in areas like Wellesley, Massachusetts and Jericho, Long Island. It's easier to untrack when kids are closer to one another to begin with."

It's also easier for educators to tinker with programs and make   30
cosmetic adjustments than it is to ask them to do what bureaucrats hate most: give up one method of doing things without having another to put in its place. Tracking is a system; untracking is a leap of faith. When difficult kids can no longer be dumped in low tracks, new ways must be found to deal with disruptive behavior: early intervention, intensive work with families, and lots of tutoring. Untracking may also entail new instructional techniques like cooperative group learning and peer tutoring, but what it really demands is flexibility and improvisation.

It also demands that schools—and the rest of us—admit that   31
some kids will be so disruptive or violent that a solution for dealing with them must be found *outside* of the regular public school system. New York City seems close to such a conclusion. Schools Chancellor Joseph Fernandez is moving forward with a voluntary "academy" program, planning separate schools designed to meet the needs of chronic troublemakers. One of them, the Wildcat Academy, run by a non-profit group of the same name, plans to enroll 150 students by the end of the year. Wildcat kids will attend classes from nine to five, wear uniforms, hold part-time jobs, and be matched with mentors from professional fields. Districts in Florida and California are conducting similar experiments.

Moving away from tracking is not about taking away from the   32
gifted and talented and giving to the poor. That, as Wheelock notes, is "political suicide." It's not even about placing more black and Latino kids in their midst, a kind of pre-K affirmative action. Rather, it's about raising expectations for everyone. Or, as Slavin puts it: "You can maintain your tracking system. Just put everyone into the top track."

That's not as quixotic as it sounds. In fact, it's long been   33
standard practice in the nation's Catholic schools, a system so backward it's actually progressive. When I taught in an untracked

parochial high school, one size fit all—with the exception of the few we expelled for poor grades or behavior. My students, who differed widely in ability, interest, and background, nevertheless got Shakespeare, Thoreau, and Langston Hughes at the same pace, at the same time—and lived to tell the tale. Their survival came, in part, because my colleagues and I could decide if the cost of keeping a certain student around was too high and we had the option of sending him or her elsewhere if expulsion was warranted.

The result was that my honor students wrote elegant essays and   34
made it to Ivy League schools, right on schedule. And far from being held back by their "regular" and "irregular" counterparts, straight-A students were more likely to be challenged by questions they would never dream of asking. "Why are we studying this?" a big-haired girl snapping gum in the back of the room wondered aloud one day. Her question led to a discussion that turned into the best class I ever taught.

In four years, I never saw a single standardized test score. But   35
time after time I watched my students climb out of whatever mental category I had put them in. Tracking sees to it that they never get that chance. Flying directly in the face of Yogi Berra's Rule Number One, it tells kids it's over before it's even begun. For ultimately, tracking stunts the opportunity for growth, the one area in which all children are naturally gifted.

Meanings and Values

1. List the differences between class 7–16 and class 7–1 as they are described in paragraphs 2–8.

2a. In what ways can paragraphs 9 and 12 be said to offer inductive generalizations?

  b. Can paragraph 1 be viewed as an inductive generalization even though it comes at the beginning of the essay, before the evidence on which it is based? Why, or why not?

3. Discuss how the remainder of the essay can be said to follow deductively from paragraphs 12 and 13.

4. Does this essay remain expository throughout, or are there portions that might be classified as argumentative? If so, what are they? (See "Guide to Terms": *Argument*.)

Expository Techniques

1. What relatively unusual strategy does the writer use to open this essay? Why do you think she chose it? (Guide: *Introductions.*)

2. Paragraph 12 announces topics taken up later in the essay. What are they, and where is each one discussed in the body of the essay?

3a. Where in the essay does the writer use the following expository patterns: comparison, definition, and cause-effect?

b. For what purposes are each of these patterns employed?

4. How does Kean create sympathy for students harmed by tracking in her discussion of them in paragraphs 11, 17–18, 20–21, and 23–24? Does she avoid sentimentality? (Guide: *Sentimentality.*) If not, does it undermine the effectiveness of the paragraphs? Why, or why not?

Diction and Vocabulary

1. Explain how the contrasting vocabulary lists (pars. 4 and 8) serve to characterize the two groups. What does each set of words say about the kinds of careers and other situations teachers expect the students in a class to face in the future? (Hint: Pay attention to the words within quotation marks in paragraph 9.)

2a. How does the writer use diction in paragraphs 3 and 6 to characterize the different groups of students? (Guide: *Diction.*)

b. In speaking of "a big-haired girl snapping gum" (par. 34), the author draws on a negative stereotype. What is the stereotype, and what use does she make of it in the paragraph?

3. If you do not know the meaning of some of the following words, look them up in a dictionary: audacity, dissimulation, sagacity, stealthy, derision, supposition (par. 8); apocalyptic, heterogeneity (13); perks (27); chronic (31).

Suggestions for Writing and Discussion

1. Compare Kean's accounts with your experience of learning in a tracked or untracked program (or both). How accurate and trustworthy are her evidence and her conclusions?

2. The testing procedures used to place students in different tracks and to test their fitness for college work have been the subject of controversy for many years. Prepare an essay of your own reporting on one aspect of the controversy, such as racial bias, gender bias, or weakness in predicting actual performance.

3. If you have read Richard Lynn's "Why Johnny Can't Read, But Yoshio Can" (pp. 512–518), discuss the extent to which the reforms he proposes would discourage or encourage tracking.

(NOTE: Suggestions for topics requiring development by INDUCTION and DEDUCTION follow.)

Writing Suggestions for Section 10
Induction and Deduction

Choose one of the following unformed topics and shape your central theme from it. This could express the view you prefer or an opposing view. Develop your composition primarily by use of induction, alone or in combination with deduction. Unless otherwise directed by your instructor, be completely objective and limit yourself to exposition, rather than engaging in argumentation.

1. Little League baseball (or the activities of 4-H clubs, Boy Scouts, Girl Scouts, etc.) as a molder of character.

2. Conformity as an expression of insecurity.

3. Pop music as a mirror of contemporary values.

4. The status symbol as a motivator to success.

5. The liberal arts curriculum and its relevance to success in a career.

6. Student opinion as the guide to better educational institutions.

7. The role of public figures (including politicians, movie stars, and business people) in shaping attitudes and fashions.

8. The values of education, beyond dollars and cents.

9. Knowledge and its relation to wisdom.

10. The right of individuals to select the laws they obey.

11. Television commercials as a molder of morals.

12. The "other" side of one ecological problem.

13. The value of complete freedom from worry.

14. Homosexuality as in-born or as voluntary behavior.

15. Raising mentally retarded children at home.

16. Fashionable clothing as an expression of power (or a means of attaining status).

11

Using Patterns for *Argument*

Argument and exposition have many things in common. They both use the basic patterns of exposition; they share a concern for the audience; and they often deal with similar subjects, including social trends (changing relationships between men and women, the growth of the animal rights movement), recent developments (the creation of new strains of plants through genetic manipulation, medical treatment of the terminally ill), and issues of widespread concern (the quality of education, the effects of pollution). As a result, the study of argument is a logical companion to the study of exposition. Yet the two kinds of writing have very different purposes.

Expository writing shares information and ideas; it explores issues and explains problems. In exposition we select facts and ideas to give an accurate picture of a subject and arrange them as clearly as we can, emphasizing features likely to interest readers. To explain the importance of knowing how to use computers, for instance, an essay might provide examples of the roles of computers in business, industry, education, and research; it might describe the uses of computers for personal budgeting, recordkeeping, and entertainment; and it might emphasize that more everyday tasks than we realize are already heavily dependent on computers.

Argumentative writing, however, has a different motivation. It asks readers to choose one side of an issue or take a particular action, whether it is to buy a product, vote for a candidate, or build a new highway. In argument we select facts and ideas that provide strong support for our point of view and arrange this evidence in the most logical and persuasive order, taking care to provide appropriate background information and to acknowledge and refute opposing points of view. The evidence we choose is determined to a great extent by the attitudes and needs of the people we are trying to convince. For example, suppose we want to argue successfully that a high school or college ought to give all students advanced training in computer use. Our essay would need to provide examples of benefits to students that are great enough to justify the considerable expenses for equipment and staff. (Examples of greatly increased job opportunities and improved learning skills would make good evidence; discussions of how computers can be used for personal recordkeeping and managing household finances would not be likely to persuade school officials facing tight budgets.) And an effective essay would also answer possible objections to the proposal: Will only a limited number of students really benefit from advanced computer training? Are computers developing so rapidly that only large businesses and specialized institutes can afford to provide up-to-date training?

At the heart of an argumentative essay is the opinion we want readers to share or the action we want them to take. In argument this central theme is called the *thesis* or *proposition* and is often expressed concisely in a *thesis statement* designed to alert readers to the point of the argument. Some writers like to arrive at a sharply focused thesis early in the process of composing and use it to guide the selection and arrangement of evidence. Others settle on a tentative ("working") thesis, which they revise as the essay takes shape. In either case, checking frequently to see that factual evidence and supporting ideas or arguments are clearly linked to the thesis is a good way for writers to make sure their finished essays are coherent, unified arguments.

The purpose of a simple argumentative essay often falls into one of three categories. Some essays ask readers to agree with a value judgment ("The present city government is corrupt and ineffective"). Others propose a specific action ("Money from the student activity fee at this college should be used to establish and staff a fitness program available to all students"). And still others advance an opinion quite different from that held by most people ("Contrary to what many people believe, investing in stocks and bonds is not just for the wealthy—it is for people who want to become wealthy, too"). In situations calling for more complex arguments, however, writers should feel free to combine these purposes as long as the relationship among them is made clear to the reader. In a complex argument, for instance, we might *first* show that the city government is inefficient and corrupt and *then* argue that it is better to change the city charter to eliminate the opportunities for the abuse of power than it is to try to vote a new party into office or to support a reform faction within the existing political machine.

Another distinction is normally made between *logical argument* (usually called, simply, *argument*) and *persuasive argument* (usually termed *persuasion*). Whereas logical argument appeals to reason, persuasive argument appeals to the emotions. The aim of both, however, is to convince, and they are nearly always blended into whatever mixture seems most likely to do the convincing. After all, reason and emotion are both important human elements—and we may have to persuade someone even to listen to our logic. The emphasis on one or the other, of course, should depend on the subject and the audience.

Some authorities make a slightly different distinction: they say we argue merely to get people to change their minds, and we use persuasion to get them to *do* something about it—for example, to vote a Republican ticket, not just agree with the party platform. But this view is not entirely inconsistent with the other. We can hardly expect to change a *mind* by emotional appeal, but we can hope to get someone to *act* because of it.

The choice of supporting evidence for an argument depends in part on the subject and in part on the audience and situation. There is a good deal of evidence to support the argument that industry should turn to labor-saving machines and new work arrangements to increase its competitiveness. Company executives looking for ways to increase profits are likely to find almost all of this evidence persuasive, but workers and union leaders worried about loss of jobs and cuts in wages will probably be harder to persuade. Writers addressing the second group would need to choose evidence to show that industrial robots and work rules calling for fewer people would lead to increased sales, not lower wages and fewer jobs. And if the changes might actually cause layoffs, writers would have to show that without the changes a company might be forced to shut down entirely, throwing everyone out of work.

Variety in evidence gives the writer a chance to present an argument fully and at the same time helps persuade readers. Examples, facts and figures, statements from authorities, personal experience or the experience of other people—all these can be valuable sources of support. The basic patterns of exposition, too, can be viewed as ways to support arguments. For instance, to persuade people to take sailing (hang-gliding, skin-diving) lessons, we might tell the story of the inexperienced sailor who almost drowned even though she was sailing in a "safe" boat on a small lake. Or we might combine this narrative with a discussion of how lack of knowledge causes sailing accidents, with a classification of the dangers facing beginning sailors, or with examples of things that can go wrong while sailing. Most writers choose to combine patterns on the grounds that variety helps convince readers, just as three pieces of evidence are more convincing than one—as long as all three point to the same conclusion.

All the expository patterns can also be used to arrange factual evidence and supporting ideas or arguments, though some patterns are more useful than others. Entire arguments structured as narratives are rare, except for stories designed to show what the world will be like if we do not change our present nuclear, military, or technological policies. But example, comparison and contrast, cause and effect, definition, and induction or deduction are frequently used to organize arguments. A series of *examples* can be an effective way of showing that a government social policy does not work and in fact hurts the people it is supposed to serve. *Cause and effect* can organize argument over who is to blame for a problem or over the possible consequences of a new program. *Comparison* and *contrast* can guide choices among competing products, among ways of disposing of toxic waste, or among directions for national economic policy. *Definition* is helpful when a controversy hinges on the interpretation of a key term or when the meaning of an important word is itself the subject of disagreement. *Induction* and *deduction* are useful in argument because they provide the kind of careful, logical reasoning necessary to convince many readers, especially those who may at first have little sympathy for the writer's opinion.

An argument need not be restricted to a single pattern. The choice of a pattern or a combination of patterns depends on the subject, the specific purpose, and the kinds of evidence needed to convince the audience to which the essay is directed. Some arguments about complicated, significant issues make use of so many patterns that they can be called *complex arguments*.

In addition to using the patterns of exposition, most argumentative essays also arrange evidence according to its potential impact on the audience. Three of the most common arrangements are ascending order, refutation-proof, and con-pro. In *ascending order*, the strongest, most complex, or most emotionally moving evidence comes last, where it can build on the rest of the evidence in the essay and is likely to have the greatest impact on the reader. *Refutation-proof* acknowledges opposing points of view early in the essay and then goes on to show why the author's outlook is superior. *Con-pro* presents an opposing point of view and then refutes it, continuing until all opposition has been dealt with and all positive arguments voiced; this strategy is particularly useful when there is strong opposition to the writer's thesis. The strategies can be combined, of course, as in a refutation-proof essay that builds up to its strongest evidence.

Accuracy and fairness in argument are not only morally correct, they can also be a means of persuasion. Accuracy in the use of facts, figures, quotations, and references can encourage readers to trust what an author has to say. And writers who are able to acknowledge and refute opposing arguments fairly and without hostility add strength to their own arguments and may even win the respect of those who disagree with them.

But the most important elements of effective argument are careful choice of evidence and clear, logical reasoning. It is never possible to arrive at absolute proof—argument, after all, assumes that there are at least two sides to the matter under discussion—yet a carefully constructed case will convince many readers. At the same time, a flaw in logic can undermine an otherwise reasonable argument and destroy a reader's confidence in its conclusions. The introduction to Section 10, "Reasoning by Use of *Induction* and *Deduction*," discusses some important errors to avoid in reasoning or in choosing evidence. Here are some others:

Post hoc ergo propter hoc ("After this therefore because of this")—Just because one thing happened *after* does not mean that the first event caused the second. In arguing without detailed supporting evidence that a recent drop in the crime rate is the result of a newly instituted anticrime policy, a writer might be committing this error, because there are other equally plausible explanations: a drop in the unemployment rate, for example, or a reduction in the number of people in the fifteen to twenty-five age bracket, the segment of the population that is responsible for a high proportion of all crimes.

Begging the question—A writer "begs the question" when he or she assumes the truth of something that is still to be proven. An argument that begins this way, "The recent, unjustified rise in utility rates should be reversed by the state legislature," assumes that the rise is "unjustified," though this important point needs to be proven.

Ignoring the question—A writer may "ignore the question" by shifting attention away from the issue at hand to some loosely related or even irrelevant matter: for example, "Senator Jones's plan for encouraging new industries cannot be any good because in the past he has opposed tax cuts for corporations" (this approach shifts attention away from the merits of Senator Jones's proposal). A related problem is the *ad hominem* (toward the person) argument, which substitutes a personal attack for a discussion of the issue in question.

In composing argumentative essays, therefore, writers need to pay attention not only to what is necessary to convince an audience but also to the integrity of the evidence and arguments they advance in support of a thesis.

Sample Paragraph (Annotated)

The issue is outlined briefly.

> The latest state proposal to divert more water from agricultural to residential uses might be expected to gain support from rapidly urbanizing Palmville. Speaking through their Town

Thesis statement.

> Meeting, however, the citizens of the town argue that the state should not meddle with arrangements that have contributed so much to the economic and social health of the region. The

Evidence and *supporting arguments.* (These five points will themselves need much more evidence, of course, in presenting the actual argument.)

> report of the Town Meeting contained these arguments: (1) Farming in the Palmville area constitutes an important element in the state's food supply which would be expensive to replace. (2) Farms and support industries provide a large proportion of the jobs of Palmville residents. (3) The farms are an important part of the social fabric of the town and the region, providing, among other things, healthful summer

employment for many of the town's youth. (4) Diverting water from the farms would cause many to be sold to real estate developers, thus increasing the population *and* the demand for water. (5) The town's zoning plan will limit growth over the next decade and should slow the increasing demand for water. Whether state officials will be persuaded by these arguments remains to be seen, but Palmville residents hope to prevent changes that might threaten the community they have built so carefully.

Sample Paragraphs (Argument)

Still, the nearly two decades since Congress created Earth Day have left no doubt that our system of environmental regulation badly needs an overhaul. Overloaded with unrealistic deadlines and sweeping legislation during the 1970s, battered by budget cuts during the '80s, the Environmental Protection Agency now needs to devise a regulatory approach that's flexible and effective, and that relies as much on market-based incentives as rigid penalties. As perverse as this may sound, the EPA needs to stop trying to ban pollution and start letting companies pay for the privilege of polluting.

The basic idea is to turn pollution into a cost that, like any other expense, the company will want to minimize. This can be done directly by imposing a fee or tax on the pollutants released into the environment. It can be done indirectly by making companies pay for pollution permits. The government could even auction off the permits (a nice "revenue enhancer"). Alternatively, companies with low pollution levels could sell pollution rights to companies with poorer controls—financially rewarding the "clean" companies and penalizing the laggards. All of these schemes would force companies to pay for their pollution, giving them an incentive to find and use the most cost-effective preventive technology.

From "Grime and Punishment," *The New Republic,* February 20, 1989. Reprinted by permission.

Rain Forest Destruction

Stanis Terenzi

There are many environmental issues being discussed and debated today. In my opinion, one of the most important issues is rain forest destruction. Rain forests are one of the most productive ecosystems on the planet. People often don't understand the importance of the forests. Many products come directly from the forests, such as nuts, coffee beans, fruits, and lumber. In addition, our daily activities often involve some product from the rain forests. Yet rain forest destruction is becoming a major problem for the world. More then half of all the forests have already been destroyed. With every tree that is cut, we deny ourselves and future generations the wealth of benefits that are supplied by the rain forests and no other ecosystem (Caldera 83). If rain forest destruction isn't stopped or at least controlled, the world's tropical rain forests will dissapear within the next few decades (Raven 379), with disastrous results.

One question people ask is "Who cares about the trees?" Commercial logging accounts for 21 percent of tropical deforestation. Rain forests are being harvested for export. Most tropical countries allow commercial logging to proceed at a much faster than sustainable rate because the more trees that are harvested, the more money the country makes (Raven 380). This may seem all fine and dandy because we need the products from the trees: paper, pencils, furniture, or even the wood to build our houses. But if these rates continue to increase, there soon will be a shortage of timber, affecting tropical countries economically and the timber industry worldwide, an industry central to most people's lives.

In many tropical countries, overpopulation is a problem, and rain forests seem to provide an answer in the form of land for living, farming, or grazing. Treated carefully, rain forests can provide a partial answer for overpopulated countries, but over 12 percent of their forests have been cleared for grazing. The forests are often cleared by means of fire because these countries cannot afford the machinery to cut the trees down. Trees that are burned are useless for logging and pulp industries, so they are just wasted. Not only are the trees uselessly burned but also the land can only be grazed on for six to ten years, after which time, shrubby plants take over the range (Raven 380). In addition, the poverty-stricken people often practice monoculturing, which is the planting of one type of crop over an area. Monoculturing creates more problems of its own. With only one crop planted, all the nutrients are quickly excreted from the soil, and within a few years the soil is longer good for farming (Raven 379). This depletion is occurring at a much quicker rate today than it ever has in the past. Grazing and monoculturing are short term remedies for poverty-stricken areas, but in the long run, they create even more problems. If rain forests are destroyed for these purposes, large numbers of people will have nowhere to farm, graze, or even to live.

Rain forests hold over 50 percent of the world's species; that is rain forests are the most diverse ecosystems on earth. Deforestation, however, accounts for a rate of extinction averaging more than one hundred species a day. The great majority of these species will not have been collected or studied in any way. No comparable rate of extinction has occurred since sixty-five million years ago when more than half of the species of earth, including the dinosaurs, became extinct. Many people ask, "So What? Who cares about these species that don't affect us?" Scientifically we are losing the opportunity to understand and benefit from diverse ecosystems. Our children and our grandchildren will be denied the opportunity to utilize many of the plants and animals that could benefit their lives (Caldera 86).

Among the most important benefits of rain forests, now and in the future, are drugs for use as medicines. One quarter of all prescription drugs come from the forests. In addition, researchers speculate that there are three thousand plants that show a potential for fighting cancer, but only one percent of them have been examined. The plant resources of the forests also promise cures for many other diseases. If the tropical forests are destroyed, these cures may never be found. A single plant can hold 400,000 or more different genes, and just one gene could lead scientists to a cure. Yet once a plant species is gone, its chance to provide a cure is lost forever (Caldera 86).

No one knows what life will be like without the precious rain forests. We rely on them much more than most of us recognize. That is why we need to put an end to the indiscriminate destruction of the tropical rain forests before it is too late to save them and their resources. I know that I wouldn't want to be around when all the rain forests are gone.

Works Cited

Caldera, Anna Maria. *Endangered Environments*. New York: Mallard, 1991.

Raven, Peter. *Environment*. New York: Saunder, 1993.

BRIAN JARVIS

BRIAN JARVIS was born in St. Louis in 1976. He attended Ladue Horton Watkins High School and is currently a student at the University of Texas at Austin. His essays, articles, and opinion pieces have been published in the *Chicago Tribune, Pittsburgh Post, San Francisco Chronicle, St. Louis Post-Dispatch, Cleveland Plain Dealer*, and the "My Turn" section of *Newsweek*. He is currently working on a novel and training to be an American Gladiator.

Against the Great Divide

Jarvis begins his essay with a series of examples that illustrate what he views as a problem that is an unfortunate consequence of racism. He delays somewhat in offering his solution to the problem, and this delay gives him time to indicate that he does not blame either of the parties involved and finds their behaviors understandable. In proposing a specific action to overcome the problem, Jarvis begins with the local (his own school) and then broadens his focus with examples that suggest actions schools throughout the nation can take. This essay was first published as a "My Turn" column in *Newsweek*, as were the two essays that follow it.

I always notice one thing when I walk through the commons at my high school: the whites are on one side of the room and the blacks are on the other. When I enter the room, I think I'm at an African nationalist meeting. The atmosphere is lively, the clothes are colorful, the voices are loud, the students are up and about, the language is different and there's not a white face to be seen. But the moment I cross the invisible line to the other side, I feel I've moved to another country. There are three times as many people, the voices are softer, 1 the clothes more subdued. Everyone's sitting or lying down, and one has as much chance of seeing a black student as a Martian.

The commons is a gathering spot where students relax on 2 benches and talk with friends. They also buy candy and soda, watch TV and make phone calls. It's a place where all sorts of things happen. But you'll never find a white student and a black student talking to each other.

After three years, I still feel uncomfortable when I have to walk 3 through the "black" side to get to class. It's not that any black students threaten or harass me. They just quietly ignore me and look in the other direction, and I do the same. But there's one who sometimes catches my eye, and I can't help feeling awkward when I see him. He was a close friend from childhood.

Ten years ago, we played catch in our backyards, went bike rid- 4 ing and slept over at one another's houses. By the fifth grade, we went to movies and amusement parks, and bunked together at the same summer camps. We met while playing on the same Little League team, though we attended different grade schools. We're both juniors now at the same high school. We usually don't say anything when we see each other, except maybe a polite "Hi" or "Hey." I can't remember the last time we talked on the phone, much less got together outside of school.

Since entering high school, we haven't shared a single class or 5 sport. He plays football, a black-dominated sport, while I play tennis, which is, with rare exception, an all-white team. It's as if fate has kept us apart; though, more likely, it's peer pressure.

In the lunchroom, I sit with my white friends and my childhood 6 friend sits with his black ones. It's the same when we walk through the hallways or sit in the library. If Michael Jackson thinks, "It don't matter if you're black or white," he should visit my high school.

I wonder if proponents of desegregation realized that even if 7 schools were integrated, students would choose to remain apart. It wasn't until 1983 that St. Louis's voluntary city-suburban desegregation program was approved. Today, my school has 25 percent black students. While this has given many young people the chance for a better education, it hasn't brought the two races closer together.

In high school, I've become friends with Vietnamese-Americans, 8 Korean-Americans, Iranian-Americans, Indian-Americans, Russian-Americans and exchange students from France and Sweden. The only group that remains at a distance is the African-Americans.

I've had only a handful of black students in all my classes and only one black teacher (from Haiti).

Crucial course: In its effort to put students through as many   9
academic classes as possible and prepare them for college, my school seems to have overlooked one crucial course: teaching black and white students how to get along, which in my opinion, would be more valuable than all the others. It's not that there haven't been efforts to improve race relations. Last fall, a group of black and white students established a program called Students Organized Against Racism. But at a recent meeting, SOAR members decided that the separation of blacks and whites was largely voluntary and there was little they could do about it. Another youth group tried to help by moving the soda machine from the "white" side of the commons to the "black" side, so that white students would have to cross the line to get a Coke. But all that's happened is that students buy their sodas, then return to their own territory.

Last summer, at a youth camp called Miniwanca in Michigan, I   10
did see black and white teens get along. I don't mean just tolerate one another. I mean play sports together, dance together, walk on the beach together and become friends. The students came from all races and backgrounds, as well as from overseas. Camp organizers purposely placed me in a cabin and activity group that included whites, blacks, Southerners, Northerners and foreigners, none of whom I'd met before.

For 10 days, I became great friends with a group of strangers, at   11
least half of whom were black. One wouldn't know that racism existed at that idyllic place, where we told stories around camp-fires, acted in plays and shared our deepest thoughts about AIDS, parents, abortion and dating. Everyone got along so well there that it was depressing for me to return to high school. But at the same time, it made me hopeful. If black and white teenagers could be friends at leadership camp, couldn't they mix in school as well?

Schools need to make it a real priority to involve whites and   12
blacks together as much as possible. This would mean more multi-cultural activities, mandatory classes that teach black history and discussions of today's racial controversies. Teachers should mix whites and blacks more in study groups so they *have* to work together in and out of school. (Students won't do it on their own.) And most important, all students should get a chance to attend a

camp like Miniwanca. Maybe the Clinton administration could find a way to help finance other camps like it.

As it is now, black and white teenagers just don't know one another. I think a lot about my friend from childhood—what he does on weekends, what he thinks about college, what he wants to do with his life. I have no answers, and it saddens me. 13

Meanings and Values

1. State in your own words the problem that Jarvis identifies and indicate whether you think it is a significant problem nationwide.

2a. Does Jarvis offer evidence in the form of examples and reasoning to convince most readers that the problem is serious enough to require action?

b. What examples does he present to demonstrate the seriousness of the problem? Which are most effective? Least effective? Why? (See "Guide to Terms": *Evaluation*.)

3a. Where does Jarvis first state his proposition?

b. Where does he repeat it in greater detail?

c. Should the detailed repetition of the proposition be followed by supporting examples and reasons? Why, or why not?

Argumentative Techniques

1a. Does this essay contain a thesis statement? If so, where is it? If not, where and how does the writer make readers aware of his proposition? (See *Introduction*, Section 11.)

b. Do you think Jarvis should have let readers know earlier in the essay the course of action he is proposing? Why, or why not? (Guide: *Evaluation*.) What reasons might he have had for waiting so long to announce his proposal?

2a. How would you describe the tone of this essay? (Guide: *Style/Tone*.)

b. What strategies does the writer use to create this tone?

c. In what ways is the tone appropriate for the purposes of the essay?

Diction and Vocabulary

1. Discuss how the words Jarvis uses in paragraphs 1–9 to describe the behavior of both groups indicate his sympathetic view towards each and avoid blaming either one for the problem. (Guide: *Diction*.)

2. Jarvis uses words that are probably familiar to most high school and college students. Would the likely effect of the essay on readers differ in any way had he chosen more "dictionary-type" words? Explain any possible differences in effect.

Suggestions for Writing and Discussion

1. If it is true, as Jarvis suggests, that racial separation is greater in high school than in elementary school, what might account for the phenomenon?

2. Some people argue that all-female high schools are particularly healthy for women's development. Others argue that historically black colleges play important roles in educating people who go on to play important roles in the society at large. Prepare a paper arguing for (or against) separation or separate development in high school or college education.

(NOTE: Suggestions for topics requiring development by use of ARGUMENT are on page 545, at the end of this section.)

MICHAEL PERRY

MICHAEL PERRY was born in 1964 in Wisconsin and raised on a small dairy farm near New Auburn. Beginning at sixteen, he worked five summers as a cowboy in Elk Mountain, Wyoming. Perry has also worked as a manual laborer, heavy machinery operator, EMT (ambulance), proofreader, surgical nurse, and rehabilitation nurse. In 1987, he earned a B.S. in nursing from the University of Wisconsin-Eau Claire. At present, he is working full time as a writer. His publications include essays and humor pieces in publications such as *Newsweek, Christian Science Monitor, Capper's, Cowboy Magazine,* and *Emergency,* as well as poetry and short stories in a variety of magazines and journals, including *Pinehurst Journal, Lost Creek Letters, Midwest Poetry Review,* and *Wisconsin Academy Review.*

The Dilemma of a Good Samaritan

Most of us probably believe it is our duty to go to the aid of someone who has been injured, and in many states the laws offer special protection to people who act as "good Samaritans." Though the extended example Perry presents demonstrates his belief in the importance of helping others, it also provides support for his provocative argument that the time may have come for us to revise our values to meet new and frightening realities. This essay first appeared in the "My Turn" column in *Newsweek,* as did those that precede and follow it.

It might have been worse. Had I not reacted so quickly, instinctively 1 pumping the brakes and yanking the wheel to the right, I could have run over the body. Then I would always have wondered if it was I who had killed him. There is irony in this thought, considering the consequences I would assume as a result of my stopping to aid a stranger on a moonless fall night.

Pulling my car to a safe area, I clicked my hazard lights on and parked so that my headlights illuminated the accident scene. As I stepped out of the vehicle a stiff wind bit through my T-shirt, whisking away the last vestiges of warmth provided by the heater. Reaching into the back seat, I grabbed a flashlight, a reflective vest and a pair of rubber gloves from the first-aid kit that accompanies me on all my trips (I am a licensed emergency medical technician).

The victim lay on his left side, a pool of blood under his head. "He's dead," said one of the bystanders. Almost as soon as she had spoken the words, however, I saw the body shudder, the ribs rising with the unmistakable motion of a drawn breath. Although his breathing was regular, the man was unconscious and unresponsive. When I shined a light in his eyes, his widely dilated pupils barely flickered.

The accident site was in a remote location. By the time I heard the first siren, the pupils no longered flickered and the breaths were no longer coming on their own. I put an oral airway (a piece of equipment that helps unconscious victims breathe) in place. A sheriff's deputy and another bystander began to perform CPR.

When the ambulance arrived, I helped the crew as best I could. While they loaded the cot, I gave my name and address to a deputy. Shivering noticeably as a result of both the cold and the unexpected excitement, I was eager to get back to my car and the comfort of the heater. As I walked to my idling vehicle, the ambulance pulled away. In the brightly lit interior, volunteer EMTs bent over the body of the man whose crumpled car rested against a signpost in the median.

Because I have worked as an EMT for several years, the habit of washing my hands after every call is ingrained in me. A few miles up the road, I pulled into a 24-hour service station and let myself into the restroom.

The advent of the AIDS virus has made the wearing of rubber gloves *de rigueur* in all medical fields. Unfortunately, situations are more hazardous in an uncontrolled environment, and the thin latex is easily torn. Tonight was no different; the tip of my right pinkie finger was covered with blood. Turning on the tap, I washed away most of the blood. The dried fluid at the base and sides of the fingernail, however, was tenacious. Only after liberal dollops of liquid soap and vigorous scrubbing did the last red-brown traces disappear. Convinced I had done the best I could under the circumstances, I dried my hands and resumed my journey.

The following evening, I was laughing with friends when the 8 phone rang. It was the sheriff's department.

"Mike, there is a very strong possibility that the gentleman 9 involved in the accident last night was HIV-positive," said the voice on the other end of the line. "If he was, you will need to be tested. When his blood work is completed, we'll let you know." A rush of adrenaline hit me in the gut. I found myself shivering, just as I had the night before.

"How about the driver of the car?" I asked, my voice steadier 10 than my knees. "He didn't make it." It was the answer I expected.

The week since the phone call has passed. The victim's tests are 11 back. The results? Positive.

I have been exposed to HIV, the virus that causes AIDS. For the 12 next year, I will have to undergo periodic blood tests to determine whether I have contracted the virus. Although the odds are strongly in my favor, I will never be sure. The nagging uncertainty will always be there.

I am not resentful of the man who died on the freeway that 13 night. Nor do I regret my actions. They are the actions I felt morally and legally bound to take; I would do the same thing tomorrow. I am also not fearful of the future. My exposure was not what the experts term "significant" (a relative term, to be sure). The skin on my finger had no cuts or obvious breaks. The virus itself is very unstable; as soon as the blood dried, it was dead.

Snap decision: While the initial phone call left me with weak 14 knees and butterflies, they were gone after a few minutes. I'm both a realist and a pragmatist, and I know my life is better spent worrying about things I can control, so I am not preoccupied day and night by this new development.

I can't help reflecting that my experience is yet another conse- 15 quence of the AIDS epidemic. In the past, the average person on the street would hardly hesitate to lend assistance to an injured person. Now, fears both founded and unfounded threaten to quell this spirit. The decision to give care has been transformed from a snap decision to a daunting ethical dilemma. Can we blame the individual who out of fear for his or her own well-being chooses to walk away?

Even those of us trained in the art of rescue receive one guiding   16
principle from the earliest days of our education: the rescuer must
place self-protection over foolhardy action. It's a principle generally
intended for easily observed on-scene circumstances. Who's to say if
it is any less valid for an invisible virus?

Sadly, the emergence of AIDS has resulted in a highly emo-   17
tional division of "us versus them." It is not my intent to contribute
to this cleft. Indeed, it is my hope that by sharing my experience I
can show that the dark hand of this modern-day plague continues to
stretch out to touch all of us, in many ways. We must set aside misconceptions and the temptation to establish blame, uniting in the
battle to overcome this intractable disease. If we fail, we will continue to succumb.

The spirit of the good Samaritan is already ill.   18

Meanings and Values

1a.   In your own words, state the "dilemma of a good Samaritan."

 b.   Does the writer make any explicit statement of the dilemma any-
      where in the essay? If so, where? If not, in what ways does he present
      it to readers?

2.   For what opinion (proposition) is Perry arguing in this essay? How
      does it differ from the outlook most readers are likely to bring to the
      essay?

3a.   Perry opens the essay by saying "It might have been worse." What
      does he mean by this phrase?

 b.   Does the statement also have an ironic meaning? If so, what is it?
      (See "Guide to Terms": *Irony.*)

Argumentative Techniques

1a.   Perry waits until well into the essay to announce the proposition for
      which he is arguing. In which paragraph(s) does he finally present
      the proposition?

 b.   Why might he have chosen to wait for so long?

 c.   Does the delay make the argument confusing and undermine its per-
      suasiveness? In what ways? If not, what strategies does the author
      employ to avoid confusing readers?

2a.   Explain the role of the questions at the end of paragraphs 14 and 15?

 b.   Why might the author have chosen rhetorical questions to perform
      this role? (Guide: *Rhetorical Questions.*)

3a. Where does the extended example presented in the essay begin? Where does it end?

b. At what point does the writer interrupt the example to comment on its relevance to the argument he is developing in the essay?

Diction and Vocabulary

1a. To what does the word "Samaritan" (title, par. 17) allude? (Guide: *Figures of Speech*.)

b. Tell how this allusion serves to present an opposing point of view, different from the one Perry eventually endorses.

2. How does the language Perry uses convey his lack of anger at the victim or the situation? What indication is there, if any, that he might have taken extra care with the language to avoid a possible adverse reaction from some readers? (Guide: *Diction*.)

3. If you do not know the meaning of some of the following words, look them up in a dictionary: *de rigueur*, tenacious (par 7); pragmatist (14); cleft, intractable (17).

Suggestions for Writing and Discussion

1. What dangers might people face when offering help to someone who has been in an accident? What good reasons might they have for continuing to offer help (or withholding it) in the face of these dangers?

2. Other than AIDS, what diseases currently pose a real danger to people in developed countries? Why has modern medicine failed to eradicate these diseases? What diseases are dangers in undeveloped countries, and what might be done to lessen their threat?

(NOTE: Suggestions for topics requiring development by use of ARGUMENT are on page 545, at the end of this section.)

BARBARA L. KELLER

Born in Dayton, Ohio in 1953, BARBARA KELLER received a B.S. in zoology and chemistry from Southeastern Louisiana University in 1979 and did graduate work in biochemistry at Louisiana Technical University. She studied law at Louisiana State University, receiving her J.D. in 1989. Before her career as a lawyer, she worked in medical research and medicine. Currently, she has a private practice as an attorney, working largely in the area of special education and disability law. Keller began publishing poetry in high school and college, and she produced technical and scientific papers when she worked as a researcher. As a lawyer, she has written for law reviews on topics such as surrogate motherhood contracts, medical technology, and legal ethics. She is currently at work on a non-fiction book about raising an autistic child as well as two novels. She has also completed three childrens' books.

Frontiersmen Are History

Tackling a familiar issue like gun control with fresh insight can be a difficult job, but Barbara Keller's essay succeeds at it. Keller goes beyond well-worn pro and con stances and asks readers to consider the cultural values that shape our attitudes towards guns. Even if you do not agree with her that "We've outgrown the frontier spirit and the need of weapons for survival," you can learn from the strategies of argument Keller uses to make her case. This essay was first published in the "My Turn" column of *Newsweek,* as were the two that precede it.

Late on a recent Friday night, I had a personal introduction to terror. 1
My 11-year-old daughter and I were playing Scrabble. My husband had just phoned to let us know he was grounded in Dallas by bad weather. A moment later my front doorbell rang loudly and

repeatedly. I stood up, wondering who in God's name was ringing at 1 o'clock in the morning. Then I heard the sound of shattering glass. Someone was breaking into my house.

As I grabbed my daughter and dashed out the side door to my neighbor's to call the police, she began to cry. "Mom! What about the boys?" My three sons—3, 4 and a mentally handicapped 8-year-old—were asleep upstairs. I had made a split-second decision to leave them and run for help. To go to them, or the phone, would have taken me right into harm's way. Being eight months pregnant, I couldn't carry them two at a time to safety. The minutes it took until the police arrived seemed like years. I wasn't permitted to enter the house until the officers had secured it. I stood on the sidewalk, fearing for my sons' safety and worrying about their reaction if they awoke to find armed policemen trooping through their bedroom. Blessedly, the boys slept through it, and the would-be intruders ran off without entering the house. 2

In the aftermath of what was for me a horribly traumatic experience, my husband and I considered and once again rejected the idea of buying a gun for protection. Police officers have told me a gun is not a particularly good defense strategy, especially where there are small children in the home. If the gun isn't loaded—or the ammunition isn't very nearby—it's not likely to be much help in a situation needing a fast reaction. Yet if it *is* loaded and handy, it poses a serious threat to children—and others. 3

Like most residents of Baton Rouge, I have strong views on gun control. Unlike most, I am for it. You have to understand that this is Louisiana. We have been characterized humorously, but I fear accurately, as a society of good ole boys who consider the shotguns displayed in the back of the pickup as a God-given right and a status symbol. We don't much care for being told what to do, especially by the government. During the recent trial of Rodney Peairs, acquitted of killing a Japanese exchange student who he mistakenly thought was invading his home last Halloween, a local news program conducted a telephone poll on the question of gun control. At that time, 68 percent of the respondents opposed stricter controls. Such measures routinely fail in our legislature, as they do in Congress. 4

One result is that we have criminals armed with semiautomatic and assault weapons and a police force that is seriously outgunned. Our options, as I see them, are three: maintain the status quo; make it more difficult for criminals to obtain these weapons, or provide 5 them to the police as well. The status quo is to me unacceptable, and the notion of a police force armed with assault rifles roaming the streets of Baton Rouge does not bring solace to my soul. It terrifies me. That leaves the option of gun control.

Why does this prospect engender such hysteria? I do not pro- 6 pose to outlaw guns—only to make them more difficult to obtain. No one with a criminal record or history of violent mental illness— and no child—should by law be able to purchase a gun. And *no one* has a compelling need to buy an assault weapon.

Tempting fate: None of this may make a hill of beans of differ- 7 ence, directly, in the case of a homeowner protecting himself from real or perceived threats. But indirectly it can. We should rethink our cultural heritage and the historical gunslinger's mentality of "a Smith & Wesson beats four aces." We've outgrown the frontier spirit and the need of weapons for survival. In Baton Rouge, I am a defi- nite oddity in not allowing my children, including my normal, ram- bunctious little boys, to play at shooting people. I don't want my children to think of guns as problem solvers. Nor do I favor the sim- plistic depictions of good guys versus bad guys.

What really frightens me is that if I were faced with the prospect 8 of imminent harm to myself or my children and had a gun at the ready, I would reach for it, despite my feelings against using firearms for personal protection. Panic is a compelling emotion and basically incompatible with reason. It is tempting fate severely to keep a powerful weapon available to deal with panic-inducing cir- cumstances. The police are trained in when and how to shoot, and innocent people can still fall victim to an officer's adrenaline surge.

I will for a very long time remember the sound of glass break- 9 ing and feel all over again the fear mingled with disbelief of that recent Friday night. If I'd owned a gun, I undoubtedly would have used it—probably to my own detriment. I do not know if the young men who so thoroughly violated my sense of safety were armed. I do know that if I'd had a gun, and had actually confronted them, they would have been more likely to harm me, and my children. It would have been I who escalated the potential for violence, and I would have had to live with the consequences—just like Rodney Peairs.

Although I have felt the terror of helplessness, owning a hand- 10 gun is something I cannot do. And the "Shoot first, ask questions later" approach is an attitude I don't want to teach my children.

Guns are like cars. We are so inured to their power we tend to treat them irresponsibly. We see them as commodities that we have a right to own and use as we please. Instead, we should limit the "right to bear arms" so that only trained, responsible citizens can buy guns for sport, recreation and protection—while those who would be most likely to use weapons detrimentally will have a much harder time getting them. Most of all, we need to reconsider our entire love affair with guns and the ways that this passion destroys innocent lives.

Meanings and Values

1a. Where does Keller state her general stand on gun control, and what position does she take?

b. What specific propositions does Keller argue in favor of in this essay?

c. Where does she state the proposition(s)?

2a. What does she believe are the effects of a lack of gun control?

b. What effect(s) does she believe gun control will have?

3. In what ways can paragraphs 1–4 be considered an explanation of the issue she is addressing? In what ways can they be considered a refutation of opposing points of view? (See *Introduction,* Section 11.)

Argumentative Techniques

1. Why would the author choose to explain the reasoning that caused her not to buy a gun (par. 3) before presenting her arguments on the broader question of gun control? Explain why you find this strategy effective or not. (See "Guide to Terms": *Evaluation.*)

2. What kinds of evidence does the writer present in this essay? What kinds does she omit or use only sparingly? (Guide: *Argument.*)

3. What strategy is used to conclude this essay? (Guide: *Closings.*)

Diction and Vocabulary

1a. Take note of the places in which Keller presents her evidence or reasoning using the word "I."

b. Discuss how this strategy adds to (or detracts from) the persuasiveness of the argument. (Guide: *Evaluation.*)

2. Explain how Keller uses the connotation of words in paragraphs 4–7 to undermine the position of those who disagree with her view of gun control. (Guide: *Connotation* and *Denotation*.)

3. If you do not know the meaning of some of the following terms, look them up in the dictionary: engender (par. 6); rambunctious, simplistic (7); disbelief (9); inured (10).

Suggestions for Writing and Discussion

1. To what extent are argument about gun control actually arguments about the prevalence of crime in our society?

2. Prepare a paper drawing on your experiences with guns or crime (or both) and arguing for your point of view on gun control.

3. Crimes committed with guns are not the only violent acts that people are concerned about. What other kinds of violence pose real problems today? What can be done to reduce or eliminate these problems?

(NOTE: Suggestions for topics requiring development by use of ARGUMENT are on page 545, at the end of this section.)

JOANNE JACOBS

JOANNE JACOBS was born in Highland Park, Illinois in 1952. She attended Stanford University, receiving a B.A. in English and Creative Writing in 1974. She began her writing career in high school as editor of the newspaper, yearbook, and literary magazine. In college she was editor of the *Stanford Daily*. She has worked as a freelance writer and an editor on a variety of magazines and newspapers. Currently, she is on the editorial board of the *San Jose Mercury News*.

Producing Multiple-Choice Students

Students and teachers alike often complain about grades and grading procedures. But are the alternatives any better? In this essay, first published as a newspaper column, Jacobs argues that some fashionable new evaluation procedures may turn out to be less useful and more confusing than their proponents envision.

Field day, Ravinia School, 1958. The kindergartners lined up, waiting to be called for the roughly 100-yard dash, our big event. Our only event. Mrs. Lawson went down the rows, handing out green ribbons.

"How can we get ribbons now?" someone asked. "We haven't had the race yet." The ribbons were for participation, Mrs. Lawson explained. Everybody got one—which made sense, since everybody was required to participate. I was a lousy runner—not only slow, but also with a marked tendency to run diagonally, thereby turning the race into a 120-yard dash. There was no way I was going to win a ribbon.

Yet I bitterly resented that stupid green ribbon. The adults were   3
telling us to pretend to be winners of a foot race that we hadn't run.
We hadn't even participated. I can remember my fellow kindergartners hotly debating whether a second-place ribbon was red or yellow; we knew blue was first. We had a sense of standards. By the
end of the day, the trash cans were filled with half-eaten hot dogs,
paper plates and green ribbons.

The "report card of the future"—already adopted by some   4
school districts for younger students—is the "narrative progress
report," which drops letter grades in favor of words. I don't see any
reason why elementary school or even junior high school students
must get letter grades, if teachers have the time to write individual
evaluations instead. After all, there's no need to have class rankings
in the fifth grade.

But in deciding whether the new report cards are an education   5
fad or a meaningful change, we need to remember that the primary
purpose of K-8 progress reports is to convey information about student achievement in a way parents and students can understand.
Whether the evaluation is based on tests, written work, projects,
portfolios or whatever, the report card should show clearly whether
a student is meeting, exceeding or falling behind expectations for the
grade level.

Hardened cynic that I am, I suspect the narrative part of the nar-   6
rative report card will end up as "Maya enjoyed our gardening project!" or "Muhammed is friendly and helpful!"

Since the new report cards are supposed to enhance self-esteem,   7
teachers will be encouraged to gloss over deficiencies. Maya enjoyed
the garden project, but did she learn how plants grow, or just have
a good time squirting water on her friends? Muhammed is friendly,
but how's he doing academically?

Water flows downhill (ask Maya), and people tend to do what   8
is easiest. If teachers can't get students to meet academic standards,
the easy way out is to substitute subjective standards. Vague wording helps. If it is not clear how much of the science curriculum Maya
has mastered, nothing is unsatisfactory, and nobody needs to
improve.

Of course, the futuristic report cards are supposed to be more   9
descriptive, not more vague. But even when teachers try to be truth-
ful, the terminology may be confusing, especially to parents who are
not fluent in English and educationese.

Euphemisms vary from district to district: In San Jose, 10 Calif., elementary schools, what was once an "excellent," "outstanding" or A student in language arts, might now be an "independent" learner, while a B student might be dubbed "confident," a C-plus student "capable," C– "developing," D "limited" and F "emergent."

Most parents can understand the forward-looking "needs to 11 improve," or translate "satisfactory" into Spanish. How do parents with minimal English or minimal education decode the new lingo?

"Independent" means fourth-grader Juanita is "a self-motivated, 12 confident reader who pursues his-her own interest through reading" and is capable of reading in all subjects and researching topics. (If Juanita can read very well, but isn't a very independent person, I think she's still "independent.")

But if her parents are "limited" English readers, they may think 13 their daughter is being criticized for not obeying the teacher, or that she has an independent personality, but needs to buckle down to be "capable" in reading, missing the fact that "independent" means excellent, while "capable" means average.

The Trans are told their son is a "developing" writer. Is he 14 developing quickly or slowly? (Yes, you would hope all students were developing.) If the Trans are "developing" readers, they may be misled. Even native English speakers could be fooled when they're told Johnny is an "emergent" reader. It doesn't mean that Johnny has achieved a breakthrough. It means Johnny can't read.

In the San Jose district, by the way, it's better to be "confident" 15 than "capable." The district's explanation of its assessment scale stresses how a student feels—is she confident? Enthusiastic? Comfortable? Reluctant? It persistently confuses confidence with competence.

Of course, the report card can be explained in the parent-teacher 16 conference—assuming that working parents can make the conference, and that non-English-speaking parents will show up with a translator—usually their child—in tow.

While these report cards are most common in elementary 17 schools, San Jose is considering using the new style in junior high and high schools. This is supposed to be part of the move from multiple-choice tests to "authentic" performance assessments, also known as "outcomes" assessment, but it's a separate issue: A portfolio of a student's work can earn a B or a "confident." It had better

earn something that will be comprehensible to a college admissions
director or a future employer.

What counts is whether students are held to objective standards   18
and whether information about their achievement is conveyed in a
clear and useful fashion. My sixth-grade daughter loves letter
grades. I pointed out that she might feel differently if she wasn't a
very good student. "No," she said, emphatically. "I like to know
how I'm doing. If I got a D in something, then I'd know I had to
work really hard to bring it up to a C."

That's what report cards have to do, whether they use letters or   19
words. How many kids have the same determination to do well, but
don't know they're getting a green ribbon?

Meanings and Values

1a. What cause and effect does Jacobs present in paragraphs 1–3?

 b. How are these paragraphs related to the rest of the essay?

2a. List what the writer views as the likely negative consequences of the
new method of grading.

 b. List the arguments she thinks can be made in favor of the new
method of grading.

 c. List what she presents as the positive outcomes of the old method of
grading.

Argumentative Techniques

1a. Does Jacobs state the essay's proposition directly in the form of a
thesis statement or does she imply it in the course of the discussion?

 b. If she states it directly, which sentence or sentences present the
thesis?

 c. If she implies it, where and how does she do so?

2. In which paragraphs does Jacobs acknowledge and refute opposing
arguments?

3a. In what ways can paragraphs 6, 14, 15, and 16 be considered ironic?

 b. Tell whether you think the irony in these paragraphs makes readers
more or less likely to accept the writer's arguments and be ready to
explain your answer.

Diction and Vocabulary

1a. In several paragraphs Jacobs points out that the words used to evaluate student work can be ambiguous or confusing because they have a variety of different meanings. In which paragraphs does she point out problems that may result from the variety of denotations or connotations a particular word may have? (See "Guide to Terms": *Connotation* and *Denotation*.) In which does she envision problems that come from difficulties parents have in understanding English? And in which does she describe ambiguities that arise because the reader has no idea of the specific situations to which a word refers?

b. In your experience, which of these problems seem most likely to occur and which least likely? Why?

2a. Discuss Jacobs's use of concrete language in paragraph 3 as a way of creating a negative reaction to the "grading" system used for the race. (Guide: *Abstract/Concrete*.)

b. In what ways does Jacob's use the green ribbons as a symbol later in the essay? (Guide: *Symbol*.)

Suggestions for Writing and Discussion

1. What alternatives to traditional grading systems do you think are worth considering and why? What arguments can you make in favor of traditional methods?

2. Jacobs uses irony in advancing her argument about grading. What are the potential dangers of using irony in argumentative writing? What are some of the positive contributions this strategy can make?

3. Can the arguments Jacobs makes in favor of traditional methods of grading also be used to argue for the importance of standardized tests such as the SAT or ACT? Prepare an essay of your own arguing for or against some aspect of standardized testing.

(NOTE: Suggestions for topics requiring development by use of ARGUMENT are on page 545, at the end of this section.)

RICHARD LYNN

RICHARD LYNN was born in London, England, in 1930. He received
a B.A. from King's College, Cambridge, in 1953 and was awarded
a Ph.D. in 1956. He has taught at Exeter University and the Economic and Social Research Institute, Dublin, and is currently a professor of psychology at the University of Ulster. Among his books
are *Personality and National Character* (1971), *An Introduction to the
Study of Personality* (1971), *The Entrepreneur* (1974), and, most
recently, *Educational Achievement in Japan* (1988).

Why Johnny Can't Read, but Yoshio Can

This essay was first published in the *National Review,* a magazine
noted for its advocacy of conservative social, economic, and political policies. In the selection, Lynn compares the Japanese educational system to those of the United States and England in order to
argue for changes in the latter two systems. Of particular interest
in this essay is the way the comparison pattern lends itself to arguments urging the adoption of policies that have worked in another
setting.

There can be no doubt that American schools compare poorly with   1
Japanese schools. In the latter, there are no serious problems with
poor discipline, violence, or truancy; Japanese children take school
seriously and work hard. Japanese educational standards are high,
and illiteracy is virtually unknown.

   The evidence of Japan's high educational standards began to   2
appear as long ago as the 1960s. In 1967 there was published the first

of a series of studies of educational standards in a dozen or so economically developed nations, based on tests of carefully drawn representative samples of children. The first study was concerned with achievement in math on the part of 13- and 18-year-olds. In both age groups the Japanese children came out well ahead of their coevals in other countries. The American 13-year-olds came out second to last for their age group; the American 18-year-olds, last. In both age groups, European children scored about halfway between the Japanese and the Americans.

Since then, further studies have appeared, covering science as well as math. The pattern of results has always been the same: the Japanese have generally scored first, the Americans last or nearly last, and the Europeans have fallen somewhere in between. In early adolescence, when the first tests are taken, Japanese children are two or three years ahead of American children; by age 18, approximately 98 per cent of Japanese children surpass their American counterparts.   3

Meanwhile, under the Reagan Administration, the United States at least started to take notice of the problem. In 1983 the President's report, *A Nation at Risk*, described the state of American schools as a national disaster. A follow-up report issued by the then-secretary of education, Mr. William Bennett, earlier this year[1] claims that although some improvements have been made, these have been "disappointingly slow."   4

An examination of Japan's school system suggests that there are three factors responsible for its success, which might be emulated by other countries: a strong national curriculum, stipulated by the government; strong incentives for students; and the stimulating effects of competition between schools.   5

The national curriculum in Japan is drawn up by the Department of Education. It covers Japanese language and literature, math, science, social science, music, moral education, and physical education. From time to time, the Department of Education requests advice on the content of the curriculum from representatives of the teaching profession, industry, and the trade unions. Syllabi are then drawn up, setting out in detail the subject matter that has to be taught at each grade. These syllabi are issued to school principals, who are responsible for ensuring that the stipulated curriculum is   6

1. 1988, the year this essay was first published (Editors' note).

taught in their schools. Inspectors periodically check that this is being done.

The Japanese national curriculum ensures such uniformly high   7
standards of teaching that almost all parents are happy to send their children to the local public school. There is no flight into private schools of the kind that has been taking place in America in recent years. Private schools do exist in Japan, but they are attended by less than 1 per cent of children in the age range of compulsory schooling (six to 15 years).

This tightly stipulated national curriculum provides a striking   8
contrast with the decentralized curriculum of schools in America. Officially, the curriculum in America is the responsibility of school principals with guidelines from state education officials. In practice, even school principals often have little idea of what is actually being taught in the classroom.

America and Britain have been unusual in leaving the curricu-   9
lum so largely in the hands of teachers. Some form of national curriculum is used throughout Continental Europe, although the syllabus is typically not specified in as much detail as in Japan. And now Britain is changing course: legislation currently going through Parliament will introduce a national curriculum for England and Wales, with the principal subjects being English, math, science, technology, a foreign language, history and geography, and art, music, and design. It is envisioned that the new curriculum will take up approximately 70 per cent of teaching time, leaving the remainder free for optional subjects such as a second foreign language, or extra science.

Under the terms of the new legislation, school children are   10
going to be given national tests at the ages of seven, 11, 14, and 16 to ensure that the curriculum has been taught and that children have learned it to a satisfactory standard. When the British national curriculum comes into effect, America will be left as the only major economically developed country without one.

11

To achieve high educational standards in schools it is necessary to have motivated students as well as good teachers. A national curriculum acts as a discipline on teachers, causing them to teach efficiently, but it does nothing to provide incentives for students, an area in which American education is particularly weak.

One of the key factors in the Japanese education system is that 12
secondary schooling is split into two stages. At the age of 11 or 12,
Japanese children enter junior high school. After three years there,
they take competitive entrance examinations for senior high schools.
In each locality there is a hierarchy of public esteem for these senior
high schools, from the two or three that are regarded as the best in
the area, through those considered to be good or average, down to
those that (at least by Japanese standards) are considered to be poor.

The top schools enjoy national reputations, somewhat akin to 13
the famous English schools such as Eton and Harrow. But in England the high fees exacted by these schools mean that very few parents can afford them. Consequently there are few candidates for
entry, and the entrance examinations offer little incentive to work
for the great mass of children. By contrast, in Japan the elite senior
high schools are open to everyone. While a good number of these
schools are private (approximately 30 per cent nationwide, though
in some major cities the figure is as high as 50 per cent), even these
schools are enabled, by government subsidies, to keep their fees
within the means of a large proportion of parents. The public schools
also charge fees, but these are nominal, amounting to only a few
hundred dollars a year, and loans are available to cover both fees
and living expenses.

Thus children have every expectation of being able to attend the 14
best school they can qualify for; and, hence, the hierarchical rankings
of senior high schools act as a powerful incentive for children
preparing for the entrance examinations. There is no doubt that
Japanese children work hard in response to these incentives. Starting as early as age ten, approximately half of them take extra tuition
on weekends, in the evenings, and in the school holidays at supplementary coaching establishments known as *juku*, and even at that
early age they do far more homework than American children. At
about the age of 12, Japanese children enter the period of their lives
known as *examination hell:* during this time, which lasts fully two
years, it is said that those who sleep more than five hours a night
have no hope of success, either in school or in life. For, in addition to
conferring great social and intellectual status on their students, the
elite senior high schools provide a first-rate academic education,
which, in turn, normally enables the students to get into one of the
elite universities and, eventually, to move into a good job in industry or government.

Although Japanese children are permitted to leave school at the   15
age of 15, 94 per cent of them proceed voluntarily to the senior high
schools. Thus virtually all Japanese are exposed in early adolescence
to the powerful incentive for academic work represented by the
senior-high-school entrance examinations. There is nothing in the
school systems of any of the Western countries resembling this powerful incentive.

The prestige of the elite senior high schools is sustained by the   16
extensive publicity they receive from the media. Each year the top
hundred or so schools in Japan are ranked on the basis of the percentage of their pupils who obtain entry to the University of Tokyo,
Japan's most prestigious university. These rankings are widely
reported in the print media, and the positions of the top twenty
schools are announced on TV news programs, rather like the scores
made by leading sports teams in the United States and Europe. At a
local level, more detailed media coverage is devoted to the academic
achievements of all the schools in the various localities, this time
analyzed in terms of their pupils' success in obtaining entry to the
lesser, but still highly regarded, local universities.

Thus, once Japanese 15-year-olds have been admitted to their   17
senior high schools, they are confronted with a fresh set of incentives
in the form of entrance examinations to universities and colleges,
which are likewise hierarchically ordered in public esteem. After the
University of Tokyo, which stands at the apex of the status hierarchy, come the University of Kyoto and ten or so other highly prestigious universities, including the former Imperial Universities in the
major provincial cities and the technological university of Hitosub-
ashi, whose standing and reputation in Japan resembles that of the
Massachusetts Institute of Technology in the United States.

Below these top dozen institutions stand some forty or so less   18
prestigious but still well-regarded universities. And after these come
numerous smaller universities and colleges of varying degrees of
standing and reputation.

To some extent the situation in Japan has parallels in the United   19
States and Europe, but there are two factors that make the importance of securing admission to an elite university substantially
greater in Japan than in the West. In the first place, the entire Japanese system is geared toward providing lifelong employment, both in
the private sector and in the civil service. It is practically unheard of
for executives to switch from one corporation to another, or into

public service and then back into the private sector, as in the United States and Europe. Employees are recruited directly out of college, and, needless to say, the major corporations and the civil service recruit virtually entirely from the top dozen universities. The smaller Japanese corporations operate along the same lines, although they widen their recruitment net to cover the next forty or so universities in the prestige hierarchy. Thus, obtaining entry to a prestigious university is a far more vital step for a successful career in Japan than it is in the United States or Europe.

Secondly, like the elite senior high schools, the elite universities are meritocratic. The great majority of universities are public institutions, receiving substantial government subsidies. Again, as with the senior high schools, fees are quite low, and loans are available to defray expenses. In principle and to a considerable extent in practice, any young Japanese can get into the University of Tokyo, or one of the other elite universities, provided only that he or she is talented enough and is prepared to do the work necessary to pass the entrance examinations. Knowing this, the public believes that *all* the most talented young Japanese go to one of these universities—and, conversely, that anyone who fails to get into one of these schools is necessarily less bright. Avoiding this stigma is, of course, a further incentive for the student to work hard to get in.

The third significant factor responsible for the high educational standards in Japan is competition among schools. This operates principally among the senior high schools, and what they are competing for is academic reputation. The most prestigious senior high school in Japan is Kansei in Tokyo, and being a teacher at Kansei is something like being a professor at Harvard. The teachers' self-esteem is bound up with the academic reputation of their schools—a powerful motivator for teachers to teach well.

In addition to this important factor of self-esteem, there is practical necessity. Since students are free to attend any school they can get into, if a school failed to provide good-quality teaching, it would no longer attract students. In business terms, its customers would fade away, and it would be forced to close. Thus the essential feature of the competition among the Japanese senior high schools is that it exposes the teachers to the discipline of the free-enterprise system. In the case of the public senior high schools, the system can be regarded as a form of market socialism in which the competing institutions are state-owned but nevertheless compete against each other

20

21

22

for their customers. Here the Japanese have been successfully operating the kind of system that Mikhail Gorbachev may be feeling his
way toward introducing in the Soviet Union. The Japanese private
senior high schools add a further capitalist element to the system
insofar as they offer their educational services more or less like firms
operating in a conventional market.

The problem of how market disciplines can be brought to bear   23
on schools has been widely discussed in America and also in Britain
ever since Milton Friedman raised it a quarter of a century or so ago,
but solutions such as Friedman's voucher proposal seem as distant
today as they did then. Although the proposal has been looked at
sympathetically by Republicans in the United States and by Conser-
vatives in Britain, politicians in both countries have fought shy of
introducing it. Probably they have concluded that the problems of
getting vouchers into the hands of all parents, and dealing with
losses, fraud, counterfeits, and so forth, are likely to be too great for
the scheme to be feasible.

The Japanese have evolved a different method of exposing   24
schools to market forces. Subsidies are paid directly to the schools on
a per-capita basis in accordance with the number of students they
have. If a school's rolls decline, so do its incomes, both from subsidies and from fees. This applies to both the public and private senior
high schools, although the public schools obviously receive a much
greater proportion of their income as subsidies and a smaller proportion from fees.

A similar scheme is being introduced in Britain. The Thatcher   25
government is currently bringing in legislation that will permit public schools to opt out of local-authority control. Those that opt out
will receive subsidies from the central government on the basis of
the number of students they have. They will then be on their own, to
sink or swim.

There is little doubt that this is the route that should be followed   26
in America. The exposure of American schools to the invigorating
stimulus of competition, combined with the introduction of a
national curriculum and the provision of stronger incentives for students, would work wonders. Rather than complaining about Japanese aggressiveness and instituting counterproductive protectionist
measures, Americans ought to be looking to the source of Japan's
power.

Meanings and Values

1. What is the issue or problem Lynn identifies in paragraphs 1–4?

2. Summarize briefly the main reasons Lynn offers for the success of the Japanese school system.

3a. How does the curriculum in Japanese schools contrast with those in American and British schools?

   b. How does the Japanese system motivate students to excel, in contrast to the American and British systems?

4a. One possible weakness in this argument is that the author pays little attention to opposing points of view. Think of some reasonable objections a North American reader might have to the Japanese educational system. Try to identify some practical difficulties that stand in the way of the reforms the author proposes based on the Japanese model.

   b. Explain how you think the author might respond to these objections and possible problems.

Argumentative Techniques

1. What kinds of evidence does the author offer to demonstrate the seriousness of the problem he describes in the opening of the essay? (See Guide to Terms: *Argument*.)

2. Why might the author have chosen to summarize his main supporting arguments in paragraph 5, early in the essay?

3a. Discuss the strategies Lynn employs in paragraphs 11 and 21, which act as transitions between major segments of the essay. (Guide: *Transition*.)

   b. Tell how these two paragraphs, along with paragraphs 5 and 6, contribute to the overall coherence of the essay. (Guide: *Coherence*.)

4. How would you describe the tone of the essay? In what ways does it add to the persuasiveness of the argument? (Guide: *Tone*.)

Diction and Vocabulary

1a. Examine the diction in paragraphs 7, 14, and 22 to decide whether it is designed to appeal primarily to readers' emotions, reason, or both. (See the introduction to Section 11, p. 427, and Guide: *Diction*.)

   b. On the whole, would you characterize the writing in this selection as objective or subjective? Why? (Guide: *Objective/Subjective*.)

2. Identify the uses Lynn makes of parallel structures and contrasts in diction to emphasize the seriousness of the problem described in paragraphs 2 and 3. (Guide: *Parallel Structure.*)

3. Point out the transitional devices used in paragraphs to emphasize contrasts between the Japanese educational system and those of Britain and America. (Guide: *Transition.*)

Suggestions for Writing and Discussion

1. In what other ways do you think North Americans can learn from the economic or social systems of other countries? In discussing this issue, pay particular attention to countries such as Japan that have been especially successful in the last decade.

2. Prepare an essay in which you take issue with the recommendations in this essay and propose some educational reforms of your own that you believe would be just as effective—or even more so.

3. Using comparison as a strategy, argue for some solutions to a local problem such as disposal of solid waste, improvement of the transportation system, better administration of school athletics, or control of drug and alcohol abuse.

(NOTE: Suggestions for topics requiring development by use of ARGUMENT are on page 545, at the end of this section.)

BARBARA LAWRENCE

BARBARA LAWRENCE was born in Hanover, New Hampshire. After receiving a B.A. in French literature from Connecticut College, she worked as an editor on *McCall's, Redbook, Harper's Bazaar,* and the *New Yorker.* During this period she also took an M.A. in philosophy from New York University. Currently a professor of humanities at the State University of New York's College at Old Westbury, Lawrence has published criticism, poetry, and fiction in *Choice, Commonweal, Columbia Poetry, The New York Times,* and the *New Yorker.*

Four-Letter Words Can Hurt You

"Four-Letter Words Can Hurt You" first appeared in *The New York Times* and was later published in *Redbook.* In arguing against the "earthy, gut-honest" language often preferred by her students, Lawrence also provides a thoughtful, even scholarly, extended definition of *obscenity* itself. To accomplish her purpose, the author makes use of several other patterns as well.

Why should any words be called obscene? Don't they all describe natural human functions? Am I trying to tell them, my students demand, that the "strong, earthy, gut-honest"—or, if they are fans of Norman Mailer, the "rich, liberating, existential"—language they use to describe sexual activity isn't preferable to "phony-sounding, middle-class words like 'intercourse' and 'copulate?'" "Cop You Late!" they say with fancy inflections and gagging grimaces. "Now, what is *that* supposed to mean?" 1

Well, what is it supposed to mean? And why indeed should one 2
group of words describing human functions and human organs be
acceptable in ordinary conversation and another, describing presumably the same organs and functions, be tabooed—so much so, in
fact, that some of these words still cannot appear in print in many
parts of the English-speaking world?

The argument that these taboos exist only because of "sexual 3
hangups" (middle-class, middle-age, feminist), or even that they are
a result of class oppression (the contempt of the Norman conquerors
for the language of their Anglo-Saxon serfs), ignores a much more
likely explanation, it seems to me, and that is the sources and functions of the words themselves.

The best known of the tabooed sexual words, for example, 4
comes from the German *ficken*, meaning "to strike"; combined
according to Partridge's etymological dictionary *Origins*, with the
Latin sexual verb *futuere:* associated in turn with the Latin *fustis*, "a
staff or cudgel"; the Celtic *buc*, "a point, hence to pierce"; the Irish
bot, "the male member"; the Latin *battuere*, "to beat"; the Gaelic
batair, "a cudgeller"; the Early Irish *bualaim*, "I strike"; and so forth.
It is one of what etymologists sometimes called "the sadistic group
of words for the man's part in copulation."

The brutality of this word, then, and its equivalents ("screw," 5
"bang," etc.) is not an illusion of the middle class or a crotchet
of Women's Liberation. In their origins and imagery these
words carry undeniably painful, if not sadistic, implications, the
object of which is almost always female. Consider, for example,
what a "screw" actually does to the wood it penetrates; what
a painful, even mutilating, activity this kind of analogy suggests.
"Screw" is particularly interesting in this context, since the noun,
according to Partridge, comes from words meaning "groove," "nut,"
"ditch," "breeding sow," "scrofula" and "swelling," while the
verb, besides its explicit imagery, has antecedent associations to
"write on," "scratch," "scarify," and so forth—a revealing fusion
of a mechanical or painful action with an obviously denigrated
object.

Not all obscene words, of course, are as implicitly sadistic or 6
denigrating to women as these, but all that I know seem to serve a
similar purpose: to reduce the human organism (especially the
female organism) and human functions (especially sexual and procreative) to their least organic, most mechanical dimension; to

substitute a trivializing or deforming resemblance for the complex human reality of what is being described.

Tabooed male descriptives, when they are not openly denigrating to women, often serve to divorce a male organ or function from any significant interaction with the female. Take the word "testes," for example, suggesting "witnesses" (from the Latin *testis*) to the sexual and procreative strengths of the male organ; and the obscene counterpart of this word, which suggests little more than a mechanical shape. Or compare almost any of the "rich," "liberating" sexual verbs, so fashionable today among male writers, with that much-derived Latin word "copulate" ("to bind or join together") or even that Anglo-Saxon phrase (which seems to have had no trouble surviving the Norman Conquest) "make love." 7

How arrogantly self-involved the tabooed words seem in comparison to either of the other terms, and how contemptuous of the female partner. Understandably so, of course, if she is only a "skirt," a "broad," a "chick," a "pussycat" or a "piece." If she is, in other words no more than her skirt, or what her skirt conceals; no more than a breeder, or the broadest part of her; no more than a piece of a human being or a "piece of tail." 8

The most severely tabooed of all the female descriptives, incidentally, are those like a "piece of tail," which suggests (either explicitly or through antecedents) that there is no significant difference between the female channel through which we are all conceived and born and the anal outlet common to both sexes—a distinction that pornographers have always enjoyed obscuring. 9

This effort to deny women their biological identity, their individuality, their humanness, is such an important aspect of obscene language that one can only marvel at how seldom, in an era preoccupied with definitions of obscenity, this fact is brought to our attention. One problem, of course, is that many of the people in the best position to do this (critics, teachers, writers) are so reluctant today to admit that they are angered or shocked by obscenity. Bored, maybe, unimpressed, aesthetically displeased, but—no matter how brutal or denigrating the material—never angered, never shocked. 10

And yet how eloquently angered, how piously shocked many of these same people become if denigrating language is used about any minority group other than women; if the obscenities are racial or ethnic, that is, rather than sexual. Words like "coon," "kike," "spic," "wop," after all, deform identity, deny individuality and humanness 11

in almost exactly the same way that sexual vulgarisms and obscenities do.

No one that I know, least of all my students, would fail to ques-   12
tion the values of a society whose literature and entertainment
rested heavily on racial or ethnic pejoratives. Are the values of a
society whose literature and entertainment rest as heavily as ours on
sexual pejoratives any less questionable?

Meanings and Values

1a. Explain the meaning of *irony* by use of at least one illustration from
     the latter part of this essay. (See "Guide to Terms": *Irony.*)

b.   What kind of irony is it?

2a. Inasmuch as the selection itself includes many of the so-called
     "strong, earthy, gut-honest" words, could anyone logically call it
     obscene? Why, or why not?

b.   To what extent, if at all, does the author's point of view help deter-
     mine your answer to question 2a? (Guide: *Point of View.*)

3a. Compose, in your own words, a compact statement of Lawrence's
     thesis. (Guide: *Thesis.*)

b.   Are all parts of the essay completely relevant to this thesis? Justify
     your answer.

c.   Does the writing have unity?

4.   Evaluate this composition by use of our three-question system.
     (Guide: *Evaluation.*)

Argumentative Techniques

1.   What is the purpose of this essay? (Guide: *Purpose.*)

2a. What objection to her opinion does the author refute in paragraph 3,
     and how does she refute it? (Guide: *Refutation.*)

b.   Where else in the essay does she refute opposing arguments?

3a. Are the evidence and supporting arguments in this essay arranged
     in a refutation-proof pattern?

b.   If not, describe the arrangement of the essay.

4a. Which of the methods "peculiar to definition alone" (see the intro-
     duction to Section 7) does the author employ in developing this
     essay?

b.   Which of the regular patterns of exposition does she also use?

c. Explain your reasons and cite examples to justify your answers to 4a and 4b.

5a. Which of the standard techniques of introduction are used? (Guide: *Introductions.*)

b. Which methods are used to close the essay? (Guide: *Closing.*)

Diction and Vocabulary

1a. How, if at all, is this discussion of words related to *connotation*? (Guide: *Connotation/Denotation.*)

b. To what extent would connotations in this matter depend on the setting and circumstances in which the words are used? Cite illustrations to clarify your answer.

2. In view of the fact that the author uses frankly many of the "gut-honest" words, why do you suppose she plainly avoids others, such as in paragraphs 4 and 7?

3. The author says that a "kind of analogy" is suggested by some of the words discussed (par. 5). If you have studied Section 4 of this book, does her use of the term *analogy* seem in conflict with what you believed it to mean? Explain.

4. Study the author's uses of the following words, consulting the dictionary as needed: existential, grimaces (par. 1); etymological, cudgel (4); sadistic (4–6); crotchet, scrofula, explicit, antecedent, scarify (5); denigrated (5–7, 10–11); aesthetically (10); pejoratives (12).

Suggestions for Writing and Discussion

1. Why is it the so-called middle class that is so often accused of having sexual hangups—and hence all sorts of sex-related taboos?

2. Probably most people using obscene language (obscene, at least, by Lawrence's definition) are not aware of the etymology of the words. Can they, therefore, be accused of denigrating women—or is ignorance a suitable defense, as it is not in legal matters?

3. Does the author make a justifiable comparison between obscene words and ethnic pejoratives? Using illustrations for specificity, carry the comparison further to show why it is sound, or explain why you consider it a weak comparison.

(Note: Suggestions for topics requiring development by use of argument are on page 545, at the end of this section.)

MARTIN LUTHER KING, JR.

MARTIN LUTHER KING, JR. (1929–1968), was a Baptist minister, the president of the Southern Christian Leadership Conference, and a respected leader in the nationwide movement for equal rights for blacks. He was born in Atlanta, Georgia, and earned degrees from Morehouse College (A.B., 1948), Crozer Theological Seminary (B.D., 1951), Boston University (Ph.D., 1955), and Chicago Theological Seminary (D.D., 1957). He held honorary degrees from numerous other colleges and universities and was awarded the Nobel Peace Prize in 1964. Some of his books are *Stride Toward Freedom* (1958), *Strength to Love* (1963), and *Why We Can't Wait* (1964). King was assassinated April 4, 1968, in Memphis, Tennessee.

Letter from Birmingham Jail[1]

This letter, written to King's colleagues in the ministry, is a reasoned explanation for his actions during the civil rights protests in Birmingham. It is a good example of both persuasion and logical argument. Here the two are completely compatible, balancing each other in rather intricate but convincing and effective patterns.

[1]This response to a published statement by eight fellow clergymen from Alabama (Bishop C. C. J. Carpenter, Bishop Joseph A. Durick, Rabbi Hilton L. Grafman, Bishop Paul Hardin, Bishop Holan B. Harmon, the Reverend George M. Murray, the Reverend Edward V. Ramage, and the Reverend Earl Stallings) was composed under somewhat constricting circumstances. Begun on the margins of the newspaper in which the statement appeared while I was in jail, the letter was continued on scraps of writing paper supplied by a friendly Negro trusty, and concluded on a pad my attorneys were eventually permitted to leave me. Although the text remains in substance unaltered, I have indulged in the author's prerogative of polishing it for publication.—King's note.

MY DEAR FELLOW CLERGYMEN:

While confined here in the Birmingham city jail, I came across   1
your recent statement calling my present activities "unwise and
untimely." Seldom do I pause to answer criticism of my work and
ideas. If I sought to answer all the criticisms that cross my desk, my
secretaries would have little time for anything other than such cor-
respondence in the course of the day, and I would have no time for
constructive work. But since I feel that you are men of genuine good
will and that your criticisms are sincerely set forth, I want to try to
answer your statement in what I hope will be patient and reasonable
terms.

I think I should indicate why I am here in Birmingham, since   2
you have been influenced by the view which argues against "outsiders coming in." I have the honor of serving as president of the
Southern Christian Leadership Conference, an organization operating in every southern state, with headquarters in Atlanta, Georgia.
We have some eighty-five affiliated organizations across the South,
and one of them is the Alabama Christian Movement for Human
Rights. Frequently we share staff, educational, and financial
resources with our affiliates. Several months ago the affiliate here in
Birmingham asked us to be on call to engage in a nonviolent direct-
action program if such were deemed necessary. We readily con-
sented, and when the hour came, we lived up to our promise. So I,
along with several members of my staff, am here because I was
invited here. I am here because I have organizational ties here.

But more basically, I am in Birmingham because injustice is   3
here. Just as the prophets of the eighth century B.C. left their villages
and carried their "thus saith the Lord" far beyond the boundaries of
their home towns, and just as the Apostle Paul left his village of Tar-
sus and carried the gospel of Jesus Christ to the far corners of the
Greco-Roman world, so am I compelled to carry the gospel of freedom beyond my own home town. Like Paul, I must constantly
respond to the Macedonian call for aid.

Moreover, I am cognizant of the interrelatedness of all commu-   4
nities and states. I cannot sit idly by in Atlanta and not be concerned
about what happens in Birmingham. Injustice anywhere is a threat
to justice everywhere. We are caught in an inescapable network of
mutuality, tied in a single garment of destiny. Whatever affects one
directly, affects all indirectly. Never again can we afford to live with
the narrow, provincial "outside agitator" idea. Anyone who lives

inside the United States can never be considered an outsider within its bounds.

You deplore the demonstrations taking place in Birmingham. But your statement, I am sorry to say, fails to express a similar concern for the conditions that brought about the demonstrations. I am sure that none of you would want to rest content with the superficial kind of social analysis that deals merely with effects and does not grapple with underlying causes. It is unfortunate that demonstrations are taking place in Birmingham, but it is even more unfortunate that the city's white power structure left the Negro community with no alternative. 5

In any nonviolent campaign there are four basic steps: collection of the facts to determine whether injustices exist; negotiation; self-purification; and direct action. We have gone through all these steps in Birmingham. There can be no gainsaying the fact that racial injustice engulfs this community. Birmingham is probably the most thoroughly segregated city in the United States. Its ugly record of brutality is widely known. Negroes have experienced grossly unjust treatment in the courts. There have been more unsolved bombings of Negro homes and churches in Birmingham than in any other city in the nation. These are the hard, brutal facts of the case. On the basis of these conditions, Negro leaders sought to negotiate with the city fathers. But the latter consistently refused to engage in good-faith negotiation. 6

Then, last September, came the opportunity to talk with leaders of Birmingham's economic community. In the course of the negotiations, certain promises were made by the merchants—for example, to remove the stores' humiliating racial signs. On the basis of these promises, the Reverend Fred Shuttlesworth and the leaders of the Alabama Christian Movement for Human Rights agreed to a moratorium on all demonstrations. As the weeks and months went by, we realized that we were the victims of a broken promise. A few signs, briefly removed, returned; the others remained. 7

As in so many past experiences, our hopes had been blasted, and the shadow of deep disappointment settled upon us. We had no alternative except to prepare for direct action, whereby we would present our very bodies as a means of laying our case before the conscience of the local and the national community. Mindful of the difficulties involved, we decided to undertake a process of self-purification. We began a series of workshops on nonviolence, and 8 we repeatedly asked ourselves: "Are you able to accept blows without retaliating?" "Are you able to endure the ordeal of jail?" We decided to schedule our direct-action program for the Easter season, realizing that except for Christmas, this is the main shopping period of the year. Knowing that a strong economic-withdrawal program would be the by-product of direct action, we felt that this would be the best time to bring pressure to bear on the merchants for the needed change.

Then it occurred to us that Birmingham's mayoral election was coming up in March, and we speedily decided to postpone action until after election day. When we discovered that the Commissioner of Public Safety, Eugene "Bull" Connor, had piled up enough votes to be in the run-off, we decided again to postpone action until the day after the run-off so that the demonstrations could not be used to cloud the issues. Like many others, we waited to see Mr. Connor defeated, and to this end we endured postponement after postponement. Having aided in this community need, we felt that our direct-action program could be delayed no longer. 9

You may well ask, "Why direct action? Why sit-ins, marches, and so forth? Isn't negotiation a better path?" You are quite right in calling for negotiation. Indeed, this is the very purpose of direct action. Nonviolent direct action seeks to create such a crisis and foster such a tension that a community which has constantly refused to negotiate is forced to confront the issue. It seeks so to dramatize the issue that it can no longer be ignored. My citing the creation of tension as part of the work of the nonviolent-resister may sound rather shocking. But I must confess that I am not afraid of the word "tension." I have earnestly opposed violent tension, but there is a type of constructive, nonviolent tension which is necessary for growth. Just as Socrates felt that it was necessary to create a tension in the mind so that individuals could rise from the bondage of myths and half-truths to the unfettered realm of creative analysis and objective appraisal, so must we see the need for nonviolent gadflies to create the kind of tension in society that will help men rise from the dark depths of prejudice and racism to the majestic heights of understanding and brotherhood. 10

The purpose of our direct-action program is to create a situation so crisis-packed that it will inevitably open the door to negotiation. I therefore concur with you in your call for negotiation. Too long has 11

our beloved Southland been bogged down in a tragic effort to live in
monologue rather than dialogue.

One of the basic points in your statement is that the action that   12
I and my associates have taken in Birmingham is untimely. Some
have asked: "Why didn't you give the new city administration time
to act?" The only answer that I can give to this query is that the new
Birmingham administration must be prodded about as much as the
outgoing one, before it will act. We are sadly mistaken if we feel that
the election of Albert Boutwell as mayor will bring the millennium
to Birmingham. While Mr. Boutwell is a much more gentle person
than Mr. Connor, they are both segregationists, dedicated to main-
tenance of the status quo. I have hoped that Mr. Boutwell will be
reasonable enough to see the futility of massive resistance to desegregation. But he will not see this without pressure from devotees of
civil rights. My friends, I must say to you that we have not made a
single gain in civil rights without determined legal and nonviolent
pressure. Lamentably, it is an historical fact that privileged groups
seldom give up their privileges voluntarily. Individuals may see the
moral light and voluntarily give up their unjust posture; but, as
Reinhold Niebuhr has reminded us, groups tend to be more
immoral than individuals.

We know through painful experience that freedom is never vol-   13
untarily given by the oppressor; it must be demanded by the
oppressed. Frankly, I have yet to engage in a direct-action campaign
that was "well timed" in the view of those who have not suffered
unduly from the disease of segregation. For years now I have heard
the word "Wait!" It rings in the ear of every Negro with piercing
familiarity. This "Wait" has almost always meant "Never." We must
come to see, with one of our distinguished jurists, that "justice too
long delayed is justice denied."

We have waited for more than 340 years for our constitutional   14
and God-given rights. The nations of Asia and Africa are moving
with jetlike speed toward gaining political independence, but we
still creep at horse-and-buggy pace toward gaining a cup of coffee at
a lunch counter. Perhaps it is easy for those who have never felt the
stinging darts of segregation to say, "Wait." But when you have seen
vicious mobs lynch your mothers and fathers at will and drown
your sisters and brothers at whim; when you have seen hate-filled
policemen curse, kick, and even kill your black brothers and sisters;
when you see the vast majority of your twenty million Negro

brothers smothering in an airtight cage of poverty in the midst of an affluent society; when you suddenly find your tongue twisted and your speech stammering as you seek to explain to your six-year-old daughter why she can't go to the public amusement park that has just been advertised on television, and see tears welling up in her eyes when she is told that Funtown is closed to colored children, and see ominous clouds of inferiority beginning to form in her little mental sky, and see her beginning to distort her personality by developing an unconscious bitterness toward white people; when you have to concoct an answer for a five-year-old son who is asking, "Daddy, why do white people treat colored people so mean?"; when you take a cross-country drive and find it necessary to sleep night after night in the uncomfortable corners of your automobile because no motel will accept you; when you are humiliated day in and day out by nagging signs reading "white" and "colored"; when your first name becomes "nigger," your middle name becomes "boy" (however old you are) and your last name becomes "John," and your wife and mother are never given the respected title "Mrs."; when you are harried by day and haunted by night by the fact that you are a Negro, living constantly at tiptoe stance, never quite knowing what to expect next, and are plagued with inner fears and outer resentments; when you are forever fighting a degenerating sense of "nobodiness"—then you will understand why we find it difficult to wait. There comes a time when the cup of endurance runs over, and men are no longer willing to be plunged into the abyss of despair. I hope, sirs, you can understand our legitimate and unavoidable impatience.

You express a great deal of anxiety over our willingness to 15 break laws. This is certainly a legitimate concern. Since we so diligently urge people to obey the Supreme Court's decision of 1954 outlawing segregation in the public schools, at first glance it may seem rather paradoxical for us consciously to break laws. One may well ask: "How can you advocate breaking some laws and obeying others?" The answer lies in the fact that there are two types of laws: just and unjust. I would be the first to advocate obeying just laws. One has not only a legal but a moral responsibility to obey just laws. Conversely, one has a moral responsibility to disobey unjust laws. I would agree with St. Augustine that "an unjust law is no law at all."

Now, what is the difference between the two? How does one 16 determine whether a law is just or unjust? A just law is a man-made code that squares with the moral law or the law of God. An unjust law is a code that is out of harmony with the moral law. To put it in the terms of St. Thomas Aquinas: An unjust law is a human law that is not rooted in eternal law and natural law. Any law that uplifts human personality is just. Any law that degrades human personality is unjust. All segregation statutes are unjust because segregation distorts the soul and damages the personality. It gives the segregator a false sense of superiority and the segregated a false sense of inferiority. Segregation, to use the terminology of the Jewish philosopher Martin Buber, substitutes an "I-it" relationship for an "I-thou" relationship and ends up relegating persons to the status of things. Hence segregation is not only politically, economically, and sociologically unsound, it is morally wrong and sinful. Paul Tillich has said that sin is separation. Is not segregation an existential expression of man's tragic separation, his awful estrangement, his terrible sinfulness? Thus it is that I can urge men to obey the 1954 decision of the Supreme Court, for it is morally right; and I can urge them to disobey segregation ordinances, for they are morally wrong.

Let us consider a more concrete example of just and unjust laws.   17
An unjust law is a code that a numerical or power majority group compels a minority group to obey but does not make binding on itself. This is *difference* made legal. By the same token, a just law is a code that a majority compels a minority to follow and that it is willing to follow itself. This is *sameness* made legal.

Let me give another explanation. A law is unjust if it is inflicted   18
on a minority that, as a result of being denied the right to vote, had no part in enacting or devising the law. Who can say that the legislature of Alabama which set up that state's segregation laws was democratically elected? Throughout Alabama all sorts of devious methods are used to prevent Negroes from becoming registered voters, and there are some counties in which, even though Negroes constitute a majority of the population, not a single Negro is registered. Can any law enacted under such circumstances be considered democratically structured?

Sometimes a law is just on its face and unjust in its application.   19
For instance, I have been arrested on a charge of parading without a permit. Now, there is nothing wrong in having an ordinance which requires a permit for a parade. But such an ordinance becomes unjust when it is used to maintain segregation and to deny citizens the First Amendment privilege of peaceful assembly and protest.

I hope you are able to see the distinction I am trying to point 20
out. In no sense do I advocate evading or defying the law, as would
the rabid segregationist. That would lead to anarchy. One who
breaks an unjust law must do so openly, lovingly, and with a willingness to accept the penalty. I submit that an individual who breaks
a law that conscience tells him is unjust, and who willingly accepts
the penalty of imprisonment in order to arouse the conscience of the
community over its injustice, is in reality expressing the highest
respect for the law.

Of course, there is nothing new about this kind of civil disobe- 21
dience. It was evidenced sublimely in the refusal of Shadrach,
Meshach, and Abednego to obey the laws of Nebuchadnezzar, on
the ground that a higher moral law was at stake. It was practiced
superbly by the early Christians, who were willing to face hungry
lions and the excruciating pain of chopping blocks rather than submit to certain unjust laws of the Roman Empire. To a degree, academic freedom is a reality today because Socrates practiced civil
disobedience. In our own nation, the Boston Tea Party represented a
massive act of civil disobedience.

We should never forget that everything Adolf Hitler did in 22
Germany was "legal" and everything the Hungarian freedom fighters did in Hungary was "illegal." It was "illegal" to aid and comfort
a Jew in Hitler's Germany. Even so, I am sure that, had I lived in
Germany at the time, I would have aided and comforted my Jewish
brothers. If today I lived in a Communist country where certain
principles dear to the Christian faith are suppressed, I would openly
advocate disobeying that country's anti-religious laws.

I must make two honest confessions to you, my Christian and 23
Jewish brothers. First, I must confess that over the past few years I
have been gravely disappointed with the white moderate. I have
almost reached the regrettable conclusion that the Negro's great
stumbling block in his stride toward freedom is not the White Citizen's Counciler or the Ku Klux Klanner, but the white moderate,
who is more devoted to "order" than to justice; who prefers a negative peace which is the absence of tension to a positive peace which
is the presence of justice; who constantly says, "I agree with you in
the goal you seek, but I cannot agree with your methods of direct
action"; who paternalistically believes he can set the timetable for
another man's freedom; who lives by a mythical concept of time and
who constantly advises the Negro to wait for a "more convenient

season." Shallow understanding from people of good will is more frustrating than absolute misunderstanding from people of ill will. Lukewarm acceptance is much more bewildering than outright rejection.

I had hoped that the white moderate would understand that law and order exist for the purpose of establishing justice and that when they fail in this purpose they become the dangerously structured dams that block the flow of social progress. I had hoped that the white moderate would understand that the present tension in the South is a necessary phase of the transition from an obnoxious negative peace, in which the Negro passively accepted his unjust plight, to a substantive and positive peace, in which all men will respect the dignity and worth of human personality. Actually, we who engage in nonviolent direct action are not the creators of tension. We merely bring to the surface the hidden tension that is already alive. We bring it out in the open, where it can be seen and dealt with. Like a boil that can never be cured so long as it is covered up but must be opened with all its ugliness to the natural medicines of air and light, injustice must be exposed, with all the tension its exposure creates, to the light of human conscience and the air of national opinion, before it can be cured.

In your statement you assert that our actions, even though peaceful, must be condemned because they precipitate violence. But is this a logical assertion? Isn't this like condemning a robbed man because his possession of money precipitated the evil act of robbery? Isn't this like condemning Socrates because his unswerving commitment to truth and his philosophical inquiries precipitated the act by the misguided populace in which they made him drink hemlock? Isn't this like condemning Jesus because his unique God-consciousness and never-ceasing devotion to God's will precipitated the evil act of crucifixion? We must come to see that, as the federal courts have consistently affirmed, it is wrong to urge an individual to cease his efforts to gain his basic constitutional rights because the quest may precipitate violence. Society must protect the robbed and punish the robber.

I had also hoped that the white moderate would reject the myth concerning time in relation to the struggle for freedom. I have just received a letter from a white brother in Texas. He writes: "All Christians know that the colored people will receive equal rights eventually, but it is possible that you are in too great a religious hurry. It

24

25

26

has taken Christianity almost two thousand years to accomplish what it has. The teachings of Christ take time to come to earth." Such an attitude stems from a tragic misconception of time, from the strangely irrational notion that there is something in the very flow of time that will inevitably cure all ills. Actually, time itself is neutral; it can be used either destructively or constructively. More and more I feel that the people of ill will have used time much more effectively than have the people of good will. We will have to repent in this generation not merely for the hateful words and actions of the bad people, but for the appalling silence of the good people. Human progress never rolls in on wheels of inevitability; it comes through the tireless efforts of men willing to be co-workers with God, and without this hard work, time itself becomes an ally of the forces of social stagnation. We must use time creatively, in the knowledge that the time is always ripe to do right. Now is the time to make real the promise of democracy and transform our pending national elegy into a creative psalm of brotherhood. Now is the time to lift our national policy from the quicksand of racial injustice to the solid rock of human dignity.

You speak of our activity in Birmingham as extreme. At first I 27 was rather disappointed that fellow clergymen would see my non-violent efforts as those of an extremist. I began thinking about the fact that I stand in the middle of two opposing forces in the Negro community. One is a force of complacency, made up in part of Negroes who, as a result of long years of oppression, are so drained of self-respect and a sense of "somebodiness" that they have adjusted to segregation; and in part of a few middle-class Negroes who, because of a degree of academic and economic security and because in some ways they profit by segregation, have become insensitive to the problems of the masses. The other force is one of bitterness and hatred, and it comes perilously close to advocating violence. It is expressed in the various black nationalist groups that are springing up across the nation, the largest and best-known being Elijah Muhammad's Muslim movement. Nourished by the Negro's frustration over the continued existence of racial discrimination, this movement is made up of people who have lost faith in America, who have absolutely repudiated Christianity, and who have concluded that the white man is an incorrigible "devil."

I have tried to stand between these two forces, saying that we 28 need emulate neither the "do-nothingism" of the complacent nor the hatred and despair of the black nationalist. For there is the more excellent way of love and nonviolent protest. I am grateful to God that, through the influence of the Negro church, the way of nonviolence became an integral part of our struggle.

If this philosophy had not emerged, by now many streets of the South would, I am convinced, be flowing with blood. And I am further convinced that if our white brothers dismiss as "rabble-rousers" and "outside agitators" those of us who employ nonviolent direct action, and if they refuse to support our nonviolent efforts, millions of Negroes will, out of frustration and despair, seek solace and security in black-nationalist ideologies—a development that would inevitably lead to a frightening racial nightmare. 29

Oppressed people cannot remain oppressed forever. The yearning for freedom eventually manifests itself, and that is what has happened to the American Negro. Something within has reminded him of his birthright of freedom, and something without has reminded him that it can be gained. Consciously or unconsciously, he has been caught up by the *Zeitgeist*, and with his black brothers of Africa and his brown and yellow brothers of Asia, South America, and the Caribbean, the United States Negro is moving with a sense of great urgency toward the promised land of racial justice. If one recognizes this vital urge that has engulfed the Negro community, one should readily understand why public demonstrations are taking place. The Negro has many pent-up resentments and latent frustrations, and he must release them. So let him march; let him make prayer pilgrimages to the city hall; let him go on freedom rides—and try to understand why he must do so. If his repressed emotions are not released in nonviolent ways, they will seek expression through violence; this is not a threat but a fact of history. So I have not said to my people, "Get rid of your discontent." Rather, I have tried to say that this normal and healthy discontent can be channeled into the creative outlet of nonviolent direct action. And now this approach is being termed extremist. 30

But though I was initially disappointed at being categorized as an extremist, as I continued to think about the matter I gradually gained a measure of satisfaction from the label. Was not Jesus an extremist for love: "Love your enemies, bless them that curse you, do good to them that hate you, and pray for them which despitefully use you, and persecute you." Was not Amos an extremist for justice: "Let justice roll down like waters and righteousness like an 31 everflowing stream." Was not Paul an extremist for the Christian gospel: "I bear in my body the marks of the Lord Jesus." Was not Martin Luther an extremist: "Here I stand; I cannot do otherwise, so help me God." And John Bunyan: "I will stay in jail to the end of my days before I make a butchery of my conscience." And Abraham Lincoln: "This nation cannot survive half slave and half free." And Thomas Jefferson: "We hold these truths to be self-evident, that all men are created equal. . . " So the question is not whether we will be extremists, but what kind of extremists we will be. Will we be extremists for hate or for love? Will we be extremists for the preservation of injustice or for the extension of justice? In that dramatic scene on Calvary's hill three men were crucified. We must never forget that all three were crucified for the same crime—the crime of extremism. Two were extremists for immorality, and thus fell below their environment. The other, Jesus Christ, was an extremist for love, truth, and goodness, and thereby rose above his environment. Perhaps the South, the nation, and the world are in dire need of creative extremists.

I had hoped that the white moderate would see this need. Perhaps I was too optimistic; perhaps I expected too much. I suppose I should have realized that few members of the oppressor race can understand the deep groans and passionate yearnings of the oppressed race, and still fewer have the vision to see that injustice must be rooted out by strong, persistent, and determined action. I am thankful, however, that some of our white brothers in the South have grasped the meaning of this social revolution and committed themselves to it. They are still all too few in quantity, but they are big in quality. Some—such as Ralph McGill, Lillian Smith, Harry Golden, James McBride Dabbs, Anne Braden, and Sarah Patton Boyle—have written about our struggle in eloquent and prophetic terms. Others have marched with us down nameless streets of the South. They have languished in filthy, roach-infested jails, suffering the abuse and brutality of policemen who view them as "dirty nigger-lovers." Unlike so many of their moderate brothers and sisters, they have recognized the urgency of the moment and sensed the need for powerful "action" antidotes to combat the disease of segregation.

Let me take note of my other major disappointment. I have been so greatly disappointed with the white church and its leadership. Of course, there are some notable exceptions. I am not unmindful of the fact that each of you has taken some significant stands on this issue. I commend you, Reverend Stallings, for your Christian stand on this past Sunday, in welcoming Negroes to your worship service on a nonsegregated basis. I commend the Catholic leaders of this state for integrating Spring Hill College several years ago.

But despite these notable exceptions, I must honestly reiterate   34 that I have been disappointed with the church. I do not say this as one of those negative critics who can always find something wrong with the church. I say this as a minister of the gospel, who loves the church; who has nurtured in its bosom; who has been sustained by its spiritual blessings and who will remain true to it as long as the cord of life shall lengthen.

When I was suddenly catapulted into the leadership of the bus   35 protest in Montgomery, Alabama, a few years ago, I felt we would be supported by the white church. I felt that the white ministers, priests, and rabbis of the South would be among our strongest allies. Instead, some have been outright opponents, refusing to understand the freedom movement and misrepresenting its leaders; all too many others have been more cautious than courageous and have remained silent behind the anesthetizing security of stained glass windows.

In spite of my shattered dreams, I came to Birmingham with the   36 hope that the white religious leadership of this community would see the justice of our cause and, with deep moral concern, would serve as the channel through which our just grievances could reach the power structure. I had hoped that each of you would understand. But again I have been disappointed.

I have heard numerous southern religious leaders admonish   37 their worshipers to comply with a desegregation decision because it is the law, but I have longed to hear white ministers declare: "Follow this decree because integration is morally right and because the Negro is your brother." In the midst of blatant injustices inflicted upon the Negro, I have watched white churchmen stand on the sideline and mouth pious relevancies and sanctimonious trivialities. In the midst of a mighty struggle to rid our nation of racial and economic injustice I have heard many ministers say: "Those are social issues, with which the gospel has no real concern." And I have watched many churches commit themselves to a completely other-worldly religion which makes a strange, un-Biblical distinction between body and soul, between the sacred and the secular.

I have traveled the length and breadth of Alabama, Mississippi, and all the other southern states. On sweltering summer days and crisp autumn mornings I have looked at the South's beautiful churches with their lofty spires pointing heavenward. I have beheld the impressive outlines of her massive religious-education buildings. Over and over I have found myself asking: "What kind of people worship here? Who is their God? Where were their voices when the lips of Governor Barnett dripped with words of interposition and nullification? Where were they when Governor Wallace gave a clarion call for defiance and hatred? Where were their voices of support when bruised and weary Negro men and women decided to rise from the dark dungeons of complacency to the bright hills of creative protest?"

Yes, these questions are still in my mind. In deep disappointment I have wept over the laxity of the church. But be assured that my tears have been tears of love. There can be no deep disappointment where there is not deep love. Yes, I love the church. How could I do otherwise? I am in the rather unique position of being the son, the grandson, and the great-grandson of preachers. Yes, I see the church as the body of Christ. But, oh! How we have blemished and scarred that body through social neglect and through fear of being nonconformists.

There was a time when the church was very powerful—in the time when the early Christians rejoiced at being deemed worthy to suffer for what they believed. In those days the church was not merely a thermometer that recorded the ideas and principles of popular opinion; it was a thermostat that transformed the mores of society. Whenever the early Christians entered a town, the people in power became disturbed and immediately sought to convict the Christians for being "disturbers of the peace" and "outside agitators." But the Christians pressed on, in the conviction that they were "a colony of heaven," called to obey God rather than man. Small in number, they were big in commitment. They were too God-intoxicated to be "astronomically intimidated." By their effort and example they brought an end to such ancient evils as infanticide and gladiatorial contests.

Things are different now. So often the contemporary church is a weak, ineffectual voice with an uncertain sound. So often it is an archdefender of the status quo. Far from being disturbed by the presence of the church, the power structure of the average community is consoled by the church's silent—and often even vocal—sanction of things as they are.

But the judgment of God is upon the church as never before. If 42 today's church does not recapture the sacrificial spirit of the early church, it will lose its authenticity, forfeit the loyalty of millions, and be dismissed as an irrelevant social club with no meaning for the twentieth century. Every day I meet young people whose disappointment with the church has turned into outright disgust.

Perhaps I have once again been too optimistic. Is organized reli- 43 gion too inextricably bound to the status quo to save our nation and the world? Perhaps I must turn my faith to the inner spiritual church, the church within the church, as the true *ekklesia*[2] and the hope of the world. But again I am thankful to God that some noble souls from the ranks of organized religion have broken loose from the paralyzing chains of conformity and joined us as active partners in the struggle for freedom. They have left their secure congregations and walked the streets of Albany, Georgia, with us. They have gone down the highways of the South on tortuous rides for freedom. Yes, they have gone to jail with us. Some have been dismissed from their churches, have lost the support of their bishops and fellow ministers. But they have acted in the faith that right defeated is stronger than evil triumphant. Their witness has been the spiritual salt that has preserved the true meaning of the gospel in these troubled times. They have carved a tunnel of hope through the dark mountain of disappointment.

I hope the church as a whole will meet the challenge of this deci- 44 sive hour. But even if the church does not come to the aid of justice, I have no despair about the future. I have no fear about the outcome of our struggle in Birmingham, even if our motives are at present misunderstood. We will reach the goal of freedom in Birmingham and all over the nation, because the goal of America is freedom. Abused and scorned though we may be, our destiny is tied up with America's destiny. Before the pilgrims landed at Plymouth, we were here. Before the pen of Jefferson etched the majestic words of the Declaration of Independence across the pages of history, we were here. For more than two centuries, our forebears labored in this country without wages; they made cotton king; they built the homes of their masters while suffering gross injustice and shameful

2. The Greek New Testament word for the early Christian church (Editors' note).

humiliation—and yet out of a bottomless vitality they continued to thrive and develop. If the inexpressible cruelties of slavery could not stop us, the opposition we now face will surely fail. We will win our freedom because the sacred heritage of our nation and the eternal will of God are embodied in our echoing demands.

Before closing I feel impelled to mention one other point in your 45 statement that has troubled me profoundly. You warmly commended the Birmingham police force for keeping "order" and "preventing violence." I doubt that you would have so warmly commended the police force if you had seen its dogs sinking their teeth into unarmed, nonviolent Negroes. I doubt that you would so quickly commend the policemen if you were to observe their ugly and inhumane treatment of Negroes here in the city jail; if you were to watch them push and curse old Negro women and young Negro girls; if you were to see them slap and kick old Negro men and young boys; if you were to observe them, as they did on two occasions, refuse to give us food because we wanted to sing our grace together. I cannot join you in your praise of the Birmingham police department.

It is true that the police have exercised a degree of discipline in 46 handling the demonstrators. In this sense they have conducted themselves rather "nonviolently" in public. But for what purpose? To preserve the evil system of segregation. Over the past few years I have consistently preached that nonviolence demands that the means we use must be as pure as the ends we seek. I have tried to make clear that it is wrong to use immoral means to attain moral ends. But now I must affirm that it is just as wrong, or perhaps even more so, to use moral means to preserve immoral ends. Perhaps Mr. Connor and his policemen have been rather nonviolent in public, as was Chief Pritchett in Albany, Georgia, but they have used the moral means of nonviolence to maintain the immoral end of racial injustice. As T.S. Eliot has said, "The last temptation is the greatest treason: To do the right deed for the wrong reason."

I wish you had commended the Negro sit-inners and demon- 47 strators of Birmingham for their sublime courage, their willingness to suffer, and their amazing discipline in the midst of great provocation. One day the South will recognize its real heroes. They will be the James Merediths, with the noble sense of purpose that enables them to face jeering and hostile mobs, and with the agonizing loneliness that characterizes the life of the pioneer. They will be old, oppressed, battered Negro women, symbolized in a seventy-two-year-old woman in Montgomery, Alabama, who rose up with a sense of dignity and with her people decided not to ride segregated buses, and who responded with ungrammatical profundity to one who inquired about her weariness: "My feets is tired, but my soul is at rest." They will be the young high school and college students, the young ministers of the gospel and a host of their elders, courageously and nonviolently sitting in at lunch counters and willingly going to jail for conscience' sake. One day the South will know that when these disinherited children of God sat down at lunch counters, they were in reality standing up for what is best in the American dream and for the most sacred values in our Judaeo-Christian heritage, thereby bringing our nation back to those great wells of democracy which were dug deep by the founding fathers in their formulation of the Constitution and the Declaration of Independence.

Never before have I written so long a letter. I'm afraid it is much   48
too long to take your precious time. I can assure you that it would have been much shorter if I had been writing from a comfortable desk, but what else can one do when he is alone in a narrow jail cell, other than write long letters, think long thoughts, and pray long prayers?

If I have said anything in this letter that overstates the truth and   49
indicates an unreasonable impatience, I beg you to forgive me. If I have said anything that understates the truth and indicates my having a patience that allows me to settle for anything less than brotherhood, I beg God to forgive me.

I hope this letter finds you strong in the faith. I also hope that   50
circumstances will soon make it possible for me to meet each of you, not as an integrationist or a civil-rights leader but as a fellow clergyman and a Christian brother. Let us all hope that the dark clouds of racial prejudice will soon pass away and the deep fog of misunderstanding will be lifted from our fear-drenched communities, and in some not too distant tomorrow the radiant stars of love and brotherhood will shine over our great nation with all their scintillating beauty.

Yours for the cause of Peace and Brotherhood,
MARTIN LUTHER KING, JR.

Meanings and Values

1a. Does King's purpose in this essay go beyond responding to the criticism of the white clergymen?

b. If so, what is his broader purpose?

2. Reconstruct as many of the arguments in the clergymen's letter as you can by studying King's refutation of their accusations.

3. What arguments are used in the essay to justify the demonstrations?

4. Summarize the distinction King makes between just and unjust laws.

5a. What kind of behavior did King expect from the white moderates?

b. Why was he disappointed?

6. How does King defend himself and his followers against the accusation that their actions lead to violence?

7. What is the thesis of this essay?

8. Like many other argumentative essays, this was written in response to a specific situation; yet it is widely regarded as a classic essay. What qualities give the essay its broad and lasting appeal?

Argumentative Techniques

1. How does King establish his reasonableness and fairness so that his audience will take the arguments in the essay seriously even if they are inclined at the start to reject his point of view?

2. Identify as many of the expository patterns as you can in this essay and explain what each contributes to the argument. (See "Guide to Term": *Unity*.)

3a. What standard techniques of refutation are used in this essay to deal with the accusations made by the clergymen? (Guide: *Refutation*.)

b. Are any other strategies of refutation used in the essay?

4a. State the argument in paragraph 6 as a syllogism. (See the introduction to Section 10, "Reasoning by Use of *Induction* and *Deduction*.")

b. Do the same with the argument in paragraphs 15–22.

5. Identify several examples of inductive argument in this essay.

6. At what points in the argument does King use several examples, where one would do, in order to strengthen the argument through variety in evidence?

Diction and Vocabulary

1. Locate an example of each of the following figures of speech in the
    essay and explain what it contributes to the argument. (Guide: *Figures of Speech.*)

a. Metaphor.

b. Allusion.

c. Simile.

d. Paradox.

2a. Discuss what resources of syntax King uses to construct a 28-line
    sentence in paragraph 14—without confusing the reader. (Guide:
    Syntax.)

b. Choose a paragraph that displays considerable variety in sentence
    length and structure and show how King uses variety in sentence
    style to convey his point. (Guide: *Style/Tone.*)

3. Choose two paragraphs, each with a different tone, and discuss how
    the diction of the passages differs and how the diction in each case
    contributes to the tone. (Guide: *Diction.*)

4. In many passages King uses the resources of diction and syntax to
    add emotional impact to logical argument. Choose such a passage
    and discuss how it mingles logic and emotion.

Suggestions for Writing and Discussion

1. Use some of King's arguments to construct a defense of a more
    recent act of protest or to encourage people to protest a policy you
    consider unjust. Or, if you wish, draw on his arguments to attack a
    recent protest on the grounds that it does not meet the high stan-
    dards he sets.

2. Discuss the practical consequences of King's distinction between just
    and unjust laws.

3. To what extent does the racism against which King was protesting
    still exist in our society? Has it been replaced by other forms of dis-
    crimination?

(NOTE: Suggestions for topics requiring development by use of ARGUMENT follow.)

Writing Suggestions for Section 11
Argument

Choose one of the following topic areas, identify an issue (a conflict or problem) within it, and prepare an essay that tries to convince readers to share your opinion about the issue and to take any appropriate action. Use a variety of evidence in your essay, and choose any pattern of development you consider proper for the topic, for your thesis, and for the intended audience.

1. Gun control.
2. The quality of education in American elementary and secondary schools.
3. Treatment of critically ill newborn babies.
4. Hunting.
5. Euthanasia.
6. Censorship in public schools and libraries.
7. College athletics.
8. The problem of toxic waste or a similar environmental problem.
9. Careers versus family responsibilities.
10. The separation of church and state.
11. Law on the drinking age or on drunk driving.
12. Evolution versus creationism.
13. Medical ethics.
14. Government spending on social programs.
15. The quality of television programming.
16. The impact of divorce.
17. The effects of television viewing on children.
18. Professional sports.
19. Violence in service of an ideal or belief.
20. Scholarship and student loan policies.
21. Low pay for public service and the "helping" professions.
22. Cheating in college courses.
23. Drug and alcohol abuse.
24. Product safety and reliability.
25. Government economic or social policy.

Further Readings

Andrew Holleran is a novelist and essay writer. His articles have appeared in *New York* magazine, *Christopher Street*, *The Advocate* and other publications. He has published two novels: *Dancer from the Dance* (1978) and *Nights in Aruba* (1983). A collection of his essays, *Ground Zero*, was published in 1988. "Bedside Manners" is taken from it. The essay begins with personal events, but quickly moves to consider the relationships between sickness and health and between living and dying that set boundaries on all human lives. Its movement thus resembles the ripples from a stone thrown in the water. In the end, Holleran asks readers to consider not simply the narrower meanings of "the plague" but also the larger challenges it poses.

Bedside Manners

"There is no difference between men so profound," wrote Scott Fitzgerald, "as that between the sick and the well." 1

There are many thoughts that fill someone's head as he walks 2 across town on a warm July afternoon to visit a friend confined to a hospital room—and that is one of them. Another occurs to you as you wait for the light to change and watch the handsome young basketball players playing on the public court behind a chicken wire fence: Health is everywhere. The world has a surreal quality to it when you are on your way to the hospital to visit someone you care for who is seriously ill: Everyone in it, walking down the sidewalk, driving by in cars, rushing about on a basketball court with sweat-stained chests, exhausted faces, and wide eyes, seems to you extremely peculiar. They are peculiar because they are free: walking under their own power, nicely dressed, sometimes beautiful. Beauty does not lose its allure under the spell of grief. The hospital visitor still notices the smooth chests of the athletes in their cotton shorts as they leap to recover the basketball after it bounces off the rim. But everything seems strangely quiet—speechless—as if you were watching a movie on television with the sound turned off, as if everyone else in the world but you is totally unaware of something: that the act of walking across York Avenue under one's own power is essentially miraculous.

Every time he enters a hospital, the visitor enters with two simultaneous thoughts: He hates hospitals, and only people working in them lead serious lives. Everything else is selfish. Entering a hospital he always thinks, *I should work for a year as a nurse, an aide, a volunteer helping people, coming to terms with disease and death.* This feeling will pass the moment he leaves the hospital. In reality the visitor hopes his fear and depression are not evident on his face as he walks down the gleaming, silent hall from the elevator to his friend's room. He is trying hard to stay calm.

The door of the room the receptionist downstairs has told the visitor his friend is in is closed—and on it are taped four signs that are not on any of the other doors and are headlined, WARNING. The visitor stops as much to read them as to allow his heartbeat to subside before going in. He knows—from the accounts of friends who have already visited—he must don a robe, gloves, mask, and even a plastic cap. He is not sure if the door is closed because his friend is asleep inside or because the door to this room is always kept closed. So he pushes it open a crack and peers in. His friend is turned on his side, a white mound of bed linen, apparently sleeping.

The visitor is immensely relieved. He goes down the hall and asks a nurse if he may leave the *Life* magazine he brought for his friend and writes a note to him saying he was here. Then he leaves the hospital and walks west through the summer twilight as if swimming through an enchanted lagoon. The next day—once more crossing town—he is in that surreal mood, under a blue sky decorated with a few photogenic, puffy white clouds, certain that no one else knows . . . knows he or she is absurdly, preposterously, incalculably fortunate to be walking on the street. He feels once again that either the sound has been turned off or some other element (his ego, perhaps with all its anger, ambition, jealousy) has been removed from the world. The basketball players are different youths today but just as much worth pausing to look at. He enters the hospital one block east more calmly this time and requests to see his friend—who is allowed only two visitors at a time, and visits lasting no more than ten minutes. He goes upstairs, peeks around the door, and sees his friend utterly awake. The visitor's heart races as he steps back and puts on the gloves, mask, cap, and robe he has been told his friends all look so comical in. He smiles because he hopes the photograph that made him bring the copy of *Life* to the hospital—Russian women leaning against a wall in Leningrad in bikinis and winter coats, taking the sun on a February day—has amused his friend as much as it tickled him.

"Richard?" the visitor says as he opens the door and peeks in. 6
His friend blinks at him. Two plastic tubes are fixed in his nostrils bringing him oxygen. His face is emaciated and gaunt, his hair longer, softer in appearance, wisps rising above his head. But the one feature the visitor cannot get over are his friend's eyes. His eyes are black, huge, and furious. Perhaps because his face is gaunt or perhaps because they really are larger than usual, they seem the only thing alive in his face; as if his whole being were distilled and concentrated, poured, drained, into his eyes. They are shining, alarmed, and—there is no other word—furious. He looks altogether like an angry baby—or an angry old man—or an angry bald eagle.

And just as the hospital visitor is absorbing the shock of these 7
livid eyes, the sick man says in a furious whisper, "Why did you bring me that dreadful magazine? I hate *Life* magazine! With that stupid picture! I wasn't amused! I wasn't amused at all! You should never have brought that dreck into this room!"

The visitor is momentarily speechless: It is the first time in their 8
friendship of ten years that anything abusive or insulting has ever been said; it is as astonishing as the gaunt face in which two huge black eyes burn and shine. But he sits down and recovers his breath and apologizes. The visitor thinks, *He's angry because I haven't visited him till now. He's angry that he's here at all, that he's sick.* And they begin to talk. They talk of the hospital food (which he hates too), of the impending visit of his mother (whose arrival he dreads), of the drug he is taking (which is experimental), and of the other visitors he has had. The patient asks the visitor to pick up a towel at the base of the bed and give it to him. The visitor complies. The patient places it across his forehead—and the visitor, who, like most people, is unsure what to say in this situation, stifles the question he wants to ask, *Why do you have a towel on your forehead?* The patient finally says, "Don't you think I look like Mother Teresa?" And the visitor realizes his friend has made a joke—as he did years ago in their house on

Fire Island: doing drag with bedspreads, pillow cases, towels, whatever was at hand. The visitor does not smile—he is so unprepared
for a joke in these circumstances—but he realizes, with relief, he is
forgiven. He realizes what people who visit the sick often learn: It is
the patient who puts the visitor at ease. In a few moments his ten
minutes are up. He rises and says, "I don't want to tire you." He
goes to the door and once beyond it he turns and looks back. His
friend says to him, "I'm proud of you for coming."

"Oh—!" the visitor says and shakes his head. "Proud of *me* for   9
coming!" he tells a friend later that evening, after he has stripped off
his gown and mask and gone home, through the unreal city of people in perfect health. "Proud of me! Can you imagine! To say that to
me, to make *me* feel good! When he's the one in bed!" The truth is he
is proud of himself the next time he visits his friend, for he is one of
those people who looks away when a nurse takes a blood test and
finds respirators frightening. He is like almost everyone—everyone
except these extraordinary people who work in hospitals, he thinks,
as he walks into the building. The second visit is easier, partly
because it is the second, and partly because the patient is better—the
drug has worked.

But he cannot forget the sight of those dark, angry eyes and the   10
plastic tubes and emaciated visage—and as he goes home that
evening, he knows there is a place whose existence he was not aware
of before: the foyer of death. It is a place many of us will see at least
once in our lives. Because modern medicine fights for patients who
a century ago would have died without its intervention, it has created an odd place between life and death. One no longer steps into
Charon's boat to be ferried across the River Styx—ill people are now
detained, with one foot in the boat and the other still on shore. It is
a place where mercy looks exactly like cruelty to the average visitor.
It is a place that one leaves, if one is only a visitor, with the conviction that ordinary life is utterly miraculous, so that, going home
from the hospital on the subway, one is filled with things one cannot
express to the crowd that walks up out of the station or throngs the
street of the block where he lives. But if the people caught in the
revolving door between health and death could speak, would they
not say—as Patrick Cowley reportedly did as he watched the men
dancing to his music while he was fatally ill, "Look at those stupid
queens. Don't they *know?*" Guard your health. It is all you have. It is
the thin line that stands between you and hell. It is your miraculous

possession. Do nothing to threaten it. Treat each other with kindness. Comfort your suffering friends. Help one another. Revere life. Do not throw it away for the momentous pleasures of lust, or even the obliteration of loneliness.

Many homosexuals wonder how they will die: where, with whom. Auden went back to Oxford, Santayana to the Blue Nuns in Rome. We are not all so lucky. Some men afflicted with AIDS returned to die in their family's home. Others have died with friends. Some have died bitterly and repudiated the homosexual friends who came to see them; others have counted on these people. Volunteers from the Gay Men's Health Crisis have cooked, cleaned, shopped, visited, taken care of people they did not even know until they decided to help. One thing is sure—we are learning how to help one another. We are discovering the strength and goodness of people we knew only in discotheques or as faces on Fire Island. We are following a great moral precept by visiting the sick. We are once again learning the awful truth Robert Penn Warren wrote years ago: "Only through the suffering of the innocent is the brotherhood of man confirmed." The most profound difference between men may well be that between the sick and the well, but compassionate people try to reach across the chasm and bridge it. The hospital visitor who conquers his own fear of something facing us all takes the first step on a journey that others less fearful than he have already traveled much further on: They are combining eros and agape as they rally round their stricken friends. As for the courage and dignity and sense of humor of those who are sick, these are beyond praise, and one hesitates where words are so flimsy. As for a disease whose latency period is measured in years, not months, there is no telling which side of the line dividing the sick and the well each of us will be on before this affliction is conquered. We may disdain the hysteria of policemen and firemen who call for masks, and people who ask if it is safe to ride the subway, and television crews who will not interview AIDS patients. For they are not at risk—those who are, are fearlessly helping their own. This is the greatest story of the plague.

MARGARET ATWOOD was born in Ottawa, Ontario, in 1939. After attending college in Canada, she went to graduate school at Harvard University. She has had a distinguished career as a novelist, poet, and essayist, and is generally considered to be one of the central figures in contemporary Canadian literature and culture. Atwood's international reputation as a writer rests on her novels, including *The Edible Woman* (1960), *Surfacing* (1972), *Life Before Man* (1979), *Bodily Harm* (1982), *The Handmaid's Tale* (1986), *Cat's Eye* (1989); *The Rotten Bride* (1993) and her short stories, including *Bluebeard's Egg and Other Stories* (1986), though she has written poetry, television plays, and children's books as well. Her essays were collected in the volume *Second Words* (1982) and have continued to appear in magazines such as *Ms., Harper's, The Humanist, The New Republic,* and *Architectural Digest.* As an essayist, Atwood frequently writes about issues in contemporary culture and society, including the nature of Canadian culture and relationships between Canada and the United States.

Pornography

In the following essay, Atwood addresses the question of pornography with a directness and originality that are characteristic of her work. This essay originally appeared in *Chatelaine Magazine,* a mass-circulation women's magazine. As you read the selection, consider how well it addresses both the concerns of its original audience and the concerns about pornography a somewhat wider audience might have.

When I was in Finland a few years ago for an international writers' conference, I had occasion to say a few paragraphs in public on the subject of pornography. The context was a discussion of political 1 repression, and I was suggesting the possibility of a link between the two. The immediate result was that a male journalist took several large bites out of me. Prudery and pornography are two halves of the same coin, said he, and I was clearly a prude. What could you expect from an Anglo-Canadian? Afterward, a couple of pleasant Scandinavian men asked me what I had been so worked up about. All "pornography" means, they said, is graphic depictions of whores, and what was the harm in that?

Not until then did it strike me that the male journalist and I 2 had two entirely different things in mind. By "pornography," he meant naked bodies and sex. I, on the other hand, had recently been doing the research for my novel *Bodily Harm,* and was still in a state of shock from some of the material I had seen, including the Ontario Board of Film Censors' "outtakes." By "pornography," I meant women getting their nipples snipped off with garden shears, having meat hooks stuck into their vaginas, being disemboweled; little girls being raped; men (yes, there are some men) being smashed to a pulp and forcibly sodomized. The cutting edge of pornography, as far as I could see, was no longer simple old copulation, hanging from the chandelier or otherwise: it was death, messy, explicit and highly sadistic. I explained this to the nice Scandinavian men. "Oh, but that's just the United States," they said. "Everyone knows they're sick." In their country, they said, violent "pornography" of that kind was not permitted on television or in movies; indeed, excessive violence of any kind was not permitted. They had drawn a clear line between erotica, which earlier studies had shown did not incite men to more aggressive and brutal behavior toward women, and violence, which later studies indicated did.

Some time after that I was in Saskatchewan, where, because of 3 the scenes in *Bodily Harm,* I found myself on an open-line radio show answering questions about "pornography." Almost no one who phoned in was in favor of it, but again they weren't talking about the same stuff I was, because they hadn't seen it. Some of them were all set to stamp out bathing suits and negligees, and, if possible, any depictions of the female body whatsoever. God, it was implied, did not approve of female bodies, and sex of any kind, including that practised by bumblebees, should be shoved back into the dark, where it belonged. I had more than a suspicion that *Lady Chatterley's Lover,* Margaret Laurence's *The Diviners,* and indeed most books by most serious modern authors would have ended up as confetti if left in the hands of these callers.

For me, these two experiences illustrate the two poles of the emotionally heated debate that is now thundering around this issue. They also underline the desirability and even the necessity of defining the terms. "Pornography" is now one of those catchalls, like "Marxism" and "feminism," that have become so broad they can mean almost anything, ranging from certain verses in the Bible, ads for skin lotion and sex tests for children to the contents of Penthouse, Naughty '90s postcards and films with titles containing the word *Nazi* that show vicious scenes of torture and killing. It's easy to say that sensible people can tell the difference. Unfortunately, opinions on what constitutes a sensible person vary.

But even sensible people tend to lose their cool when they start talking about this subject. They soon stop talking and start yelling, and the name-calling begins. Those in favor of censorship (which may include groups not noticeably in agreement on other issues, such as some feminists and religious fundamentalists) accuse the others of exploiting women through the use of degrading images, contributing to the corruption of children, and adding to the general climate of violence and threat in which both women and children live in this society; or, though they may not give much of a hoot about actual women and children, they invoke moral standards and God's supposed aversion to "filth," "smut" and deviated *perversion*, which may mean ankles.

The camp in favor of total "freedom of expression" often comes out howling as loud as the Romans would have if told they could no longer have innocent fun watching the lions eat up Christians. It too may include segments of the population who are not natural bedfellows: those who proclaim their God-given right to freedom, including the freedom to tote guns, drive when drunk, drool over chicken porn and get off on videotapes of women being raped and beaten, may be waving the same anticensorship banner as responsible liberals who fear the return of Mrs. Grundy, or gay groups for whom sexual emancipation involves the concept of "sexual theatre." *Whatever turns you on* is a handy motto, as is *A man's home is his castle* (and if it includes a dungeon with beautiful maidens strung up in chains and bleeding from every pore, that's his business).

Meanwhile, theoreticians theorize and speculators speculate. Is today's pornography yet another indication of the hatred of the body, the deep mind-body split, which is supposed to pervade Western Christian society? Is it a backlash against the women's movement by men who are threatened by uppity female behavior in real life, so like to fantasize about women done up like outsize parcels, being turned into hamburger, kneeling at their feet in slave-like adoration or sucking off guns? Is it a sign of collective impo-tence, of a generation of men who can't relate to real women at all but have to make do with bits of celluloid and paper? Is the current flood just a result of smart marketing and aggressive promotion by the money men in what has now become a multibillion-dollar indus-try? If they were selling movies about men getting their testicles stuck full of knitting needles by women with swastikas on their sleeves, would they do as well, or is this penchant somehow pecu-liarly male? If so, why? Is pornography a power trip rather than a sex one? Some say that those ropes, chains, muzzles and other restraining devices are an argument for the immense power female sexuality still wields in the male imagination: you don't put these things on dogs unless you're afraid of them. Others, more literary, wonder about the shift from the 19th-century Magic Woman or Femme Fatale image to the lollipop-licker, airhead or turkey-carcass treatment of women in porn today. The proporners don't care much about theory; they merely demand product. The antiporners don't care about it in the final analysis either; there's dirt on the street, and they want it cleaned up, now.

It seems to me that this conversation, with its *You're-a-prude/You're-a-pervert* dialectic, will never get anywhere as long as we continue to think of this material as just "entertainment." Possi-bly we're deluded by the packaging, the format: magazine, book, movie, theatrical presentation. We're used to thinking of these things as part of the "entertainment industry," and we're used to thinking of ourselves as free adult people who ought to be able to see any kind of "entertainment" we want to. That was what the First Choice pay-TV debate was all about. After all, it's only entertain-ment, right? Entertainment means fun, and only a killjoy would be antifun. What's the harm?   8

This is obviously the central question: *What's the harm?* If there isn't any real harm to any real people, then the antiporners can tsk-tsk and/or throw up as much as they like, but they can't rightfully expect more legal controls or sanctions. However, the no-harm posi-tion is far from being proven.   9

(For instance, there's a clear-cut case for banning—as the federal 10
government has proposed—movies, photos and videos that depict
children engaging in sex with adults: real children are used to make
the movies, and hardly anybody thinks this is ethical. The possibilities for coercion are too great.)

To shift the viewpoint, I'd like to suggest three other models for 11
looking at "pornography"—and here I mean the violent kind.

Those who find the idea of regulating pornographic materials 12
repugnant because they think it's Fascist or Communist or otherwise
not in accordance with the principles of an open democratic society
should consider that Canada has made it illegal to disseminate material that may lead to hatred toward any group because of race or religion. I suggest that if pornography of the violent kind depicted these
acts being done predominantly to Chinese, to blacks, to Catholics, it
would be off the market immediately, under the present laws. Why
is hate literature illegal? Because whoever made the law thought
that such material might incite real people to do real awful things to
other real people. The human brain is to a certain extent a computer:
garbage in, garbage out. We only hear about the extreme cases (like
that of American multimurderer Ted Bundy) in which pornography
has contributed to the death and/or mutilation of women and/or
men. Although pornography is not the only factor involved in the
creation of such deviance, it certainly has upped the ante by suggesting both a variety of techniques and the social acceptability of
such actions. Nobody knows yet what effect this stuff is having on
the less psychotic.

Studies have shown that a large part of the market for all kinds 13
of porn, soft and hard, is drawn from the 16-to-21-year-old population of young men. Boys used to learn about sex on the street, or (in
Italy, according to Fellini movies) from friendly whores, or, in more
genteel surroundings, from girls, their parents, or, once upon a time,
in school, more or less. Now porn has been added, and sex education in the schools is rapidly being phased out. The buck has been
passed, and boys are being taught that all women secretly like to be
raped and that real men get high on scooping out women's digestive
tracts.

Boys learn their concept of masculinity from other men: is this 14
what most men want them to be learning? If word gets around that
rapists are "normal" and even admirable men, will boys feel that in
order to be normal, admirable and masculine they will have to be

rapists? Human beings are enormously flexible, and how they turn out depends a lot on how they're educated, by the society in which they're immersed as well as by their teachers. In a society that advertises and glorifies rape or even implicitly condones it, more women get raped. It becomes socially acceptable. And at a time when men and the traditional male role have taken a lot of flak and men are confused and casting around for an acceptable way of being male (and, in some cases, not getting much comfort from women on that score), this must be at times a pleasing thought.

It would be naïve to think of violent pornography as just harmless entertainment. It's also an educational tool and a powerful propaganda device. What happens when boy educated on porn meets girl brought up on Harlequin romances? The clash of expectations can be heard around the block. She wants him to get down on his knees with a ring, he wants her to get down on all fours with a ring in her nose. Can this marriage be saved? 15

Pornography has certain things in common with such addictive substances as alcohol and drugs: for some, though by no means for all, it induces chemical changes in the body, which the user finds exciting and pleasurable. It also appears to attract a "hard core" of habitual users and a penumbra of those who use it occasionally but aren't dependent on it in any way. There are also significant numbers of men who aren't much interested in it, not because they're undersexed but because real life is satisfying their needs, which may not require as many appliances as those of users. 16

For the "hard core," pornography may function as alcohol does for the alcoholic: tolerance develops, and a little is no longer enough. This may account for the short viewing time and fast turnover in porn theatres. Mary Brown, chairwoman of the Ontario Board of Film Censors, estimates that for every one mainstream movie requesting entrance to Ontario, there is one porno flick. Not only the quantity consumed but the quality of explicitness must escalate, which may account for the growing violence: once the big deal was breasts, then it was genitals, then copulation, then that was no longer enough and the hard users had to have more. The ultimate kick is death, and after that, as the Marquis de Sade so boringly demonstrated, multiple death. 17

The existence of alcoholism has not led us to ban social drinking. On the other hand, we do have laws about drinking and 18 driving, excessive drunkenness and other abuses of alcohol that may result in injury or death to others.

This leads us back to the key question: what's the harm? Nobody knows, but this society should find out fast, before the saturation point is reached. The Scandinavian studies that showed a connection between depictions of sexual violence and increased impulse toward it on the part of male viewers would be a starting point, but many more questions remain to be raised as well as answered. What, for instance, is the crucial difference between men who are users and men who are not? Does using affect a man's relationship with actual women, and, if so, adversely? Is there a clear line between erotica and violent pornography, or are they on an escalating continuum? Is this a "men versus women" issue, with all men secretly siding with the proporners and all women secretly siding against? (I think not; there *are* lots of men who don't think that running their true love through the Cuisinart is the best way they can think of to spend a Saturday night, and they're just as nauseated by films of someone else doing it as women are.) Is pornography merely an expression of the sexual confusion of this age or an active contributor to it? 19

Nobody wants to go back to the age of official repression, when even piano legs were referred to as "limbs" and had to wear pantaloons to be decent. Neither do we want to end up in George Orwell's *1984,* in which pornography is turned out by the State to keep the proles in a state of torpor, sex itself is considered dirty and the approved practise it only for reproduction. But Rome under the emperors isn't such a good model either. 20

If all men and women respected each other, if sex were considered joyful and life-enhancing instead of a wallow in germ-filled glop, if everyone were in love all the time, if, in other words, many people's lives were more satisfactory for them than they appear to be now, pornography might just go away on its own. But since this is obviously not happening, we as a society are going to have to make some informed and responsible decisions about how to deal with it. 21

JOHN MCPHEE

Born in 1931 in Princeton, New Jersey, John McPhee studied at Princeton University and Cambridge University in England. McPhee wrote for *Time* magazine and is now a regular contributor to the *New Yorker*. McPhee has written twenty-two books on an astonishingly wide range of topics. His subjects include the history and popularity of oranges, in *Oranges* (1967); the pine barrens of central New Jersey, in *The Pine Barrens* (1968), the headmaster of a prep school, in *The Headmaster* (1966); the Scottish Highlands, in *The Crofter and the Laird* (1969); the Swiss army, in *La Place de la Concorde de las Suisse* (1984); and the geology of North America, in *Basin and Range* (1981), *In Suspect Terrain* (1983), *Rising from the Plains* (1986), *The Control of Nature* (1989), and *Assembling California* (1992). "Earthquake"[1] is a chapter from *Assembling California*. In the piece, McPhee combines a dramatic narrative of a recent earthquake, the 1989 earthquake in the San Francisco Bay area, with a detailed explanation of the earthquake process itself. In this selection, as in most of his writing, McPhee manages to present highly technical information and explanations in a clear, straightforward manner. A careful reading of this piece will reveal, however, the artfulness and sophistication of McPhee's work. His careful selection of detail, his arrangement of the parts of an explanation, his dazzling shifts in focus and clever transitions, and his spare and precise diction are all models of the kind of art that expository writing can achieve. This selection as a whole, as well as individual sentences and paragraphs, are worth not only a careful reading but also one or more re-readings. In re-reading, pay special attention to the way McPhee manages to maintain the drama of the event while at the same time commenting on its scientific, social, and political aspects.

Earthquake

There is a swerve in the San Andreas Fault where it moves through 1
the Santa Cruz Mountains. It bends a little and then straightens
again, like the track of a tire that was turned to avoid an animal.

[1]Editors' title.

Because deviations in transform faults retard the sliding and help strain to build, the most pronounced ones are known as tectonic knots, or great asperities, or prominent restraining bends. The two greatest known earthquakes on the fault occurred at or close to prominent restraining bends. The little jog in the Santa Cruz Mountains is a modest asperity, but enough to tighten the lock. As the strain rises through the years, the scales of geologic time and human time draw ever closer, until they coincide. An earthquake is not felt everywhere at once. It travels in every direction—up, down, and sideways—from its place and moment of beginning. In this example, the precise moment is in the sixteenth second of the fifth minute after five in the afternoon, as the scales touch and the tectonic knot lets go.

The epicenter is in the Forest of Nisene Marks, a few hundred yards from Trout Creek Gulch, five miles north of Monterey Bay. The most conspicuous nearby landmark is the mountain called Loma Prieta. In a curving small road in the gulch are closed gates and speed bumps. PRIVATE PROPERTY. KEEP OUT. This is steep terrain—roughed up, but to a greater extent serene. Under the redwoods are glades of maidenhair. There are fields of pampas grass, stands of tan madrone. A house worth two million dollars is under construction, and construction will continue when this is over. BEWARE OF DOG. 2

Motion occurs fifty-nine thousand eight hundred feet down— the deepest hypocenter ever recorded on the San Andreas Fault. No drill hole made anywhere on earth for any purpose has reached so far. On the San Andreas, no earthquake is ever likely to reach deeper. Below sixty thousand feet, the rock is no longer brittle. 3

The epicenter, the point at the surface directly above the hypocenter, is four miles from the fault trace. Some geologists will wonder if the motion occurred in a blind thrust, but in the San Cruz Mountains the two sides of the San Andreas Fault are not vertical. The Pacific wall leans against the North American wall at about the angle of a ladder. 4

For seven to ten seconds, the deep rockfaces slide. The maximum jump is more than seven feet. Northwest and southeast, the slip propagates an aggregate twenty-five miles. This is not an especially large event. It is nothing like a plate-rupturing earthquake. Its upward motion stops twenty thousand feet below the surface. Even so, the slippage plane—where the two great slanting faces have moved against each other—is an irregular oval of nearly two 5 hundred square miles. The released strain turns into waves, and they develop half a megaton of energy. Which is serious enough. In California argot, this is not a tickler—it's a slammer.

The pressure waves spread upward and outward about three   6
and a half miles a second, expanding, compressing, expanding, compressing the crystal structures in the rock. The shear waves that follow are somewhat slower. Slower still (about two miles a second) are the surface waves: Rayleigh waves, in particle motion like a rolling sea, and Love waves, advancing like snakes. Wherever things shake, the shaking will consist of all these waves. Half a minute will pass before the light towers move at Candlestick Park. Meanwhile, dogs are barking in Trout Creek Gulch. Car alarms and house alarms are screaming. If, somehow, you could hear all such alarms coming on throughout the region, you could hear the spread of the earthquake. The redwoods are swaying. Some snap like asparagus. The restraining bend has forced the rock to rise. Here, west of the fault trace, the terrain has suddenly been elevated a foot and a half— a punch delivered from below. For some reason, it is felt most on the highest ground.

On Summit Road, near the Loma Prieta School, a man goes up   7
in the air like a diver off a board. He lands on his head. Another man is thrown sideways through a picture window. A built-in oven leaves its niche and shoots across a kitchen. A refrigerator walks, bounces off a wall, and returns to its accustomed place. As Pearl Lake's seven-room house goes off its foundation, she stumbles in her kitchen and falls to the wooden floor. In 1906, the same house went off the same foundation. Her parents had moved in the day before. Lake lives alone and raises prunes. Ryan Moore, in bed under the covers, is still under the covers after his house travels a hundred feet and ends up in ruins around him.

People will come to think of this earthquake as an event that   8
happened in San Francisco. But only from Watsonville to Santa Cruz—here in the region of the restraining bend, at least sixty miles south of the city—will the general intensity prove comparable to 1906. In this region are almost no freeway overpasses, major bridges, or exceptionally tall buildings. Along the narrow highland roads, innumerable houses are suddenly stoop-shouldered, atwist, bestrewn with splinters of wood and glass, even new ones "built to code." Because the movement on the fault occurs only at great depth, the surface is an enigma of weird random cracks. Few and

incongruous, they will not contribute to the geologic record. If earthquakes like Loma Prieta are illegible, how many of them took place through the ages before the arrival of seismographs, and what does that do to geologists' frequency calculations?

Driveways are breaking like crushed shells. Through woods and fields, a ripping fissure as big as an arroyo crosses Morrill Road. Along Summit Road, a crack three feet wide, seven feet deep, and seventeen hundred feet long runs among houses and misses them all. Roads burst open as if they were being strafed. Humps rise. Double yellow lines are making left-lateral jumps.

Cracks, fissures, fence posts are jumping left as well. What is going on? The San Andreas is the classic right-lateral fault. Is country going south that should be going north? Is plate tectonics going backward? Geologists will figure out an explanation. With their four-dimensional minds, and in their interdisciplinary ultraverbal way, geologists can wiggle out of almost anything. They will say that while the fault motion far below is absolutely right lateral, blocks of rock overhead are rotating like ball bearings. If you look down on a field of circles that are all turning clockwise, you will see what the geologists mean.

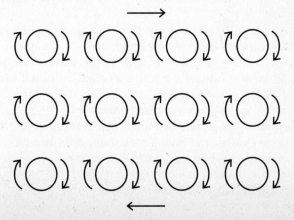

Between one circle and the next, the movement everywhere is left lateral. But the movement of the field as a whole is right lateral. The explanation has legerdemain. Harry Houdini had legerdemain when he got out of his ropes, chains, and handcuffs at the bottom of the Detroit River.

All compression resulting from the bend is highest near the 10 bend, and the compression is called the Santa Cruz Mountains. Loma Prieta, near four thousand feet, is the highest peak. The words mean Hill Dark. This translation will gain in the shaking, and appear in the media as Dark Rolling Mountain.

At the University of California, Santa Cruz, three first-year 11 students from the East Coast sit under redwoods on the forest campus. As the shock waves reach them and the trees whip overhead, the three students leap up and spontaneously dance and shout in a ring. Near the edge of town, a corral disintegrates, horses run onto a highway, a light truck crashes into them and the driver is killed. Bicyclists are falling to the streets and automobiles are bouncing. Santa Cruz has been recovering from severe economic depression, in large part through the success of the Pacific Garden Mall, six blocks of old unreinforced brick buildings lately turned into boutiques. The buildings are contiguous and are of different heights. As the shock waves reach them, the buildings react with differing periods of vibration and knock each other down. Twenty-one buildings collapse. Higher ones fall into lower ones like nesting boxes. Ten people die. The Hotel Metropol, seventy years old, crashes through the ceiling of the department store below it. The Pacific Garden Mall is on very-young-floodplain river silts that amplify the shaking—as the same deposits did in 1906.

Landslides are moving away from the epicenter in synchrony 12 with the car alarms. As if from explosions, brown clouds rise into the air. A hundred and eighty-five acres go in one block slide, dozens of houses included. Hollister's clock tower falls. Coastal bluffs fall. Mountain cliffs and roadcuts fall.

The shock waves move up the peninsula. Reaching Los Gatos, 13 they give a wrenching spin to houses that cost seven hundred and fifty thousand dollars and have no earthquake insurance. A man is at work in a bicycle shop. In words that *Time* will print in twenty-four-point type, he will refer to the earthquake as "my best near-death experience." (For a number of unpublished fragments here, I am indebted to editors at Time Warner, who have shared with me a boxful of their correspondents' files.)

Thirteen seconds north of the epicenter is Los Altos, where Harriet and David Schnur live. They grew up in New York City and have the familiar sense that an I.R.T. train is passing under their home. It is a "million-dollar Cape Cod," and glass is breaking in every room. This is scarcely their first earthquake. 14

David: "Why is it taking so long?" 15

Harriet: "This could be the last one. Thank God we went to *shul* during the holidays." 16

The piano moves. Jars filled with beans shatter. Wine pours from breaking bottles. A grandfather clock, falling—its hands stopping at 5:04—lands on a metronome, which begins to tick. 17

The shock reaches Stanford University, and sixty buildings receive a hundred and sixty million dollars' worth of damage. The university does not have earthquake insurance. 18

The waves move on to San Mateo, where a woman in a sixteenth-floor apartment has poured a cup of coffee and sat down to watch the third game of the World Series. When the shock arrives, the apartment is suddenly like an airplane in a wind shear. The jolt whips her head to one side. A lamp crashes. Books fall. Doors open. Dishes fall. Separately, the coffee and the cup fly across the room. 19

People are dead in Santa Cruz, Watsonville has rubble on the ground, and San Francisco has yet to feel anything. The waves approach the city directly from the hypocenter and indirectly via the Moho. Waves that begin this deep touch the Moho at so slight an angle that they carom upward, a phenomenon known as critical reflection. As the shaking begins in San Francisco, it is twice as strong as would generally be expected for an earthquake of this magnitude at that distance from the epicenter. 20

Two men are on a motor scooter on Sixteenth Street. The driver, glancing over his shoulder, says, "Michael, stop bouncing." A woman walking on Bush Street sees a Cadillac undulating like a water bed. She thinks, What are those people *doing* in there? Then the windows fall out of a nearby café. The sidewalks are moving. Chimneys fall in Haight-Ashbury, landing on cars. In Asbury Heights, a man is watering his patch of grass. He suddenly feels faint, his knees weaken, and his front lawn flutters like water under wind. Inside, his wife is seated at her seven-foot grand. The piano levitates, comes right up off the floor as she plays. She is thinking, 21

I'm good but not this good. A blimp is in the air above. The pilot feels vibration. He feels four distinct bumps.

In Golden Gate Park, high-school girls are practicing field   22
hockey. Their coach sees the playing field move, sees "huge trees . . . bending like windshield wipers." She thinks, This is the end, I'm about to fall into the earth, this is the way to go. Her players freeze in place. They are silent. They just look at one another.

In the zoo, the spider monkeys begin to scream. The birdhouse   23
is full of midair collisions. The snow leopards, lazy in the sun with the ground shaking, are evidently unimpressed. In any case, their muscles don't move. Pachy, the approximately calico cat who lives inside the elephant house, is outside the elephant house. She refused to enter the building all day yesterday and all day today. When someone carried her inside to try to feed her, she ran outside, hungry.

At Chez Panisse, in Berkeley, cupboard doors open and a chef's   24
personal collection of pickles and preserves crashes. The restaurant, renowned and booked solid, will be half full this evening. Those who come will order exceptionally expensive wine. Meanwhile, early patrons at a restaurant in Oakland suddenly feel as if they were in the dining car of a train that has lurched left. When it is over, they will all get up and shake hands.

In the San Francisco Tennis Club, balls are flying without being   25
hit. Players are falling down. The ceilings and the walls seem to be flowing. Nearby, at Sixth and Bluxome, the walls of a warehouse are falling. Bricks crush a car and decapitate the driver. Four others are killed in this avalanche as well.

In the hundred miles of the San Andreas Fault closest to San   26
Francisco, no energy has been released. The accumulated strain is unrelieved. The U.S. Geological Survey will continue to expect within thirty years an earthquake in San Francisco as much as fifty times as powerful. In the Survey's offices in Menlo Park, a seismologist will say, "This was not a big earthquake, but we hope it's the biggest we deal with in our careers." The Pacific Stock Exchange, too vital to suffer as much as a single day off, will trade by candlelight all day tomorrow.

Passengers on a rapid-transit train in a tube under the bay feel   27
as if they had left the rails and were running over rocks. The Interstate 80 tunnel through Yerba Buena Island moves like a slightly writhing hose. Linda Lamb, in a sailboat below the Bay Bridge, feels

as if something had grabbed her keel. Cars on the bridge are sliding. The entire superstructure is moving, first to the west about a foot, and then back east, bending the steel, sending large concentric ripples out from the towers, and shearing through bolts thicker than cucumbers. This is the moment in which a five-hundred-ton road section at one tower comes loose and hinges downward, killing the driver of a car below and breaking open the lower deck, so that space gapes to the bay. Heading toward Oakland on the lower deck, an Alameda County Transit driver thinks that all his tires have blown, fights the careening bus for control, and stops eight feet from a plunge to the water. Smashed cars vibrate on the edge but do not fall. Simultaneously, the Golden Gate Bridge is undulating, fluctuating, oscillating, pendulating. Daniel Mohn—in his car heading north, commuting home—is halfway across. From the first tremor, he knows what is happening, and his response to his situation is the exact opposite of panic. He feels very lucky. He thinks, as he has often thought before, If I had the choice, this is where I would be. Reporters will seek him later, and he will tell them, "We never close down." He is the current chief engineer of the Golden Gate Bridge.

Peggy Iacovini, having crossed the bridge, is a minute ahead of 28 the chief engineer and a few seconds into the Marin Headlands. In her fluent Anglo-Calif she will tell the reporters, "My car jumped over like half a lane. It felt like my tire blew out. Everybody opened their car doors or stuck their heads out their windows to see if it was their tires. There were also a couple of girls holding their chests going oh my God. All the things on the freeway were just blowing up and stuff. It was like when you light dynamite—you know, on the stick—it just goes down and then it blows up. The communication wires were just sparking. I mean my heart was beating. I was like oh my God. But I had no idea of the extent that it had done."

At Candlestick Park, the poles at the ends of the foul lines throb 29 like fishing rods. The overhead lights are swaying. The upper deck is in sickening motion. The crowd stands as one. Some people are screaming. Steel bolts fall. Chunks of concrete fall. A chunk weighing fifty pounds lands in a seat that a fan just left to get a hot dog. Of sixty thousand people amassed for the World Series, not one will die. Candlestick is anchored in radiolarian chert.

The tall buildings downtown rise out of landfill but are deeply 30 founded in bedrock, and, with their shear walls and moment frames and steel-and-rubber isolation bearings, they sway, shiver, sway again, but do not fall. A woman forty-six floors up feels as if she were swinging through space. A woman twenty-nine floors up, in deafening sound, gets under her desk in fetal position and thinks of the running feet of elephants. Cabinets, vases, computers, and law books are flying. Pictures drop. Pipes bend. Nearly five minutes after five. Elevators full of people are banging in their shafts.

On the high floors of the Hyatt, guests sliding on their bellies   31 think of it as surfing.

A quick-thinking clerk in Saks herds a customer into the safety   32 of a doorjamb and has her sign the sales slip there.

Room service has just brought shrimp, oysters, and a bucket of   33 champagne to Cybill Shepherd, on the seventh floor of the Campton Place Hotel. Foot of Nob Hill. Solid Franciscan sandstone. Earthquakes are not unknown to Shepherd. At her home in Los Angeles, pictures are framed under Plexiglas, windowpanes are safety glass, and the water heater is bolted to a wall. Beside every bed are a flashlight, a radio, and a hard hat. Now, on Nob Hill, Shepherd and company decide to eat the oysters and the shrimp before fleeing, but to leave the champagne. There was a phone message earlier, from her astrologer. Please call. Shepherd didn't call. Now she is wondering what the astrologer had in mind.

A stairway collapses between the tenth and eleventh floors of   34 an office building in Oakland. Three people are trapped. When they discover that there is no way to shout for help, one of them will dial her daughter in Fairfax County, Virginia. The daughter will dial 911. Fairfax County Police will teletype the Oakland police, who will climb the building, knock down a wall, and make the rescue.

Meanwhile, at sea off Point Reyes, the U.S. Naval Ship Walter S.   35 Diehl is shaking so violently that the officers think they are running aground. Near Monterey, the Moss Landing Marine Laboratory has been destroyed. A sea cliff has fallen in Big Sur—eighty-one miles south of the epicenter. In another minute, clothes in closets will be swinging on their hangers in Reno. Soon thereafter, water will form confused ripples in San Fernando Valley swimming pools. The skyscrapers of Los Angeles will sway.

After the earthquake on the Hayward Fault in 1868, geologists   36 clearly saw that dangers varied with the geologic map, and they wrote in a State Earthquake Investigation Commission Report, "The portion of the city which suffered most was . . . on made ground." In one minute in 1906, made ground in San Francisco sank as much as three feet. Where landfill touched natural terrain, cable-car rails bent down. Maps printed and distributed well before 1989—stippled and cross-hatched where geologists saw the greatest violence to come—singled out not only the Nimitz Freeway in Oakland but also, in San Francisco, the Marina district, the Embarcadero, and the Laocoönic freeways near Second and Stillman. Generally speaking, shaking declines with distance from the hypocenter, but where landfill lies on loose sediment the shaking can amplify, as if it were an explosion set off from afar with a plunger and a wire. If a lot of water is present in the sediment and the fill, they can be changed in an instant into gray quicksand—the effect known as liquefaction. Compared with what happens on bedrock, the damage can be something like a hundredfold, as it was on the lakefill of Mexico City in 1985, even though the hypocenter was far to the west, under the Pacific shore.

In a plane that has just landed at San Francisco International Airport, passengers standing up to remove luggage from the overhead racks have the luggage removed for them by the earthquake. Ceilings fall in the control tower, and windows break. The airport is on landfill, as is Oakland International, across the bay. Sand boils break out all over both airfields. In downtown San Francisco, big cracks appear in the elevated I-280, the Embarcadero Freeway, and U.S. 101, where they rest on bayfill and on filled-in tidal creek and filled-in riparian bog. They do not collapse. Across the bay, but west of the natural shoreline, the Cypress section of the Nimitz Freeway—the double-decked I-880—is vibrating at the same frequency as the landfill mud it sits on. This coincidence produces a shaking amplification near eight hundred per cent. Concrete support columns begin to fail. Reinforcing rods an inch and a half thick spring out of them like wires. The highway is not of recent construction. At the tops of the columns, where they meet the upper deck, the joints have inadequate shear reinforcement. By a large margin, they would not meet present codes. This is well known to state engineers, who have blue-printed the reinforcements, but the work has not been done, for lack of funds.

The under road is northbound, and so is disaster. One after the last, the slabs of the upper roadway are falling. Each weighs six hundred tons. Reinforcing rods connect them, and seem to be helping to pull the highway down. Some drivers on the under road, seeing or sensing what is happening behind them, stop, set their emergency brakes, leave their cars, run toward daylight, and are killed by other cars. Some drivers apparently decide that the very columns that are about to give way are possible locations of safety, like doorjambs. They pull over, hover by the columns, and are crushed. A bank customer-service representative whose 1968 Mustang has just come out of a repair shop feels the jolting roadway and decides that the shop has done a terrible job, that her power steering is about to fail, and that she had better get off this high-speed road as fast as she can. A ramp presents itself. She swerves onto it and off the freeway. She hears a huge sound. In her rearview mirror she sees the upper roadway crash flat upon the lower.

As the immense slabs fall, people in cars below hold up their   39
hands to try to stop them. A man eating peanuts in his white pickup feels what he thinks are two flat tires. A moment later, his pickup is two feet high. Somehow, he survives. In an airport shuttle, everyone dies. A man in another car guns his engine, keeps his foot to the floor, and races the slabs that are successively falling behind him. His wife is yelling, "Get out of here! Get out of here!" Miraculously, he gets out of here. Many race the slabs, but few escape. Through twenty-two hundred yards the slabs fall. They began falling where the highway leaves natural sediments and goes onto a bed of landfill. They stop where the highway leaves landfill and returns to natural sediments.

Five minutes after five, and San Francisco's Red Cross Volunteer Disaster Services Committee is in the middle of a disaster-preparedness meeting. The Red Cross Building is shivering. The committee has reconvened underneath its table.   40

In yards and parks in the Marina, sand boils are spitting muds   41
from orifices that resemble the bell rims of bugles. In architectural terminology, the Marina at street level is full of soft stories. A soft story has at least one open wall and is not well supported. Numerous ground floors in the Marina are garages. As buildings collapse upon themselves, the soft stories vanish. In a fourth-floor apartment, a woman in her kitchen has been cooking Rice-A-Roni. She has put on long johns and a sweatshirt and turned on the television to watch the World Series. As the building shakes, she moves with experience into a doorway and grips the jamb. Nevertheless, the vibrations are so intense that she is thrown to the floor. When the shaking stops, she will notice a man's legs, standing upright, outside her fourth-story window, as if he were floating in air. She will think that she is hallucinating. But the three floors below her no longer exist, and the

collapsing building has carried her apartment to the sidewalk. Aqueducts are breaking, and water pressure is falling. Flames from broken gas mains will rise two hundred feet. As in 1906, water to fight fires will be scarce. There are numbers of deaths in the Marina, including a man and woman later found hand in hand. A man feels the ground move under his bicycle. When he returns from his ride, he will find his wife severely injured and his infant son dead. An apartment building at Fillmore and Bay has pitched forward onto the street. Beds inside the building are standing on end.

The Marina in 1906 was a salt lagoon. After the Panama Canal   42
opened, in 1914, San Francisco planned its Panama-Pacific International Exposition for the following year, not only to demonstrate that the city had recovered from the great earthquake to end all earthquakes but also to show itself off as a golden destination for shipping. The site chosen for the Exposition was the lagoon. To fill it up, fine sands were hydraulically pumped into it and mixed with miscellaneous debris, creating the hundred and sixty-five dry acres that flourished under the Exposition and are now the Marina. Nearly a minute has passed since the rock slipped at the hypocenter. In San Francisco, the tremors this time will last fifteen seconds. As the ground violently shakes and the sand boils of the Marina discharge material from the liquefying depths, the things they spit up include tarpaper and bits of redwood—the charred remains of houses from the earthquake of 1906.

GLORIA ANZALDUA

GLORIA ANZALDUA is a writer who explores and celebrates her Spanish and Indian heritage in poetry and in prose. She was a co-editor of the collection *This Bridge Called My Back: Writing by Radical Women of Color* (1983). In 1987, she published *Borderlands/La Frontera: The New Mestiza* and in 1990 she edited *Making Face, Making Soul; Hacienda Caras: Creative and Critical Perspectives by Women of Color*. In addition, she is a contributing editor of the journal *Sinister Wisdom*. "Tlili, Tlapalli" is a section of *Borderlands/La Frontera*. The mixture of cultures and beliefs in this selection may make it difficult to follow in places, but most readers will find the journey rewarding. Along the way they will encounter insights into the sources of Anzaldúa's writing that may suggest ways of looking at their own writing and their own experiences. The ways of looking at life, poetry, reality, and magic in a culture different from main-stream American culture can shed light on the ways most Americans view these aspects of life. At the very least, the essay can be a source of disagreement that sharpens the readers' own beliefs. We have chosen not to translate the passages written in Spanish because we believe that the untranslated passages allow students in a class to approach (and understand) the text in different ways depending on their knowledge of Spanish (or their lack of knowledge). These different perceptions may be in themselves instructive and may be the source of fruitful discussions.

Tlili, Tlapalli: The Path of the Red and Black Ink

"Out of poverty, poetry;
out of suffering, song."

—a Mexican saying

1

When I was seven, eight, nine, fifteen, sixteen years old, I would read in bed with a flashlight under the covers, hiding my self-imposed insomnia from my mother. I preferred the world of the

2

imagination to the death of sleep. My sister, Hilda, who slept in the same bed with me, would threaten to tell my mother unless I told her a story.

I was familiar with *cuentos*—my grandmother told stories like   3
the one about her getting on top of the roof while down below rabid coyotes were ravaging the place and wanting to get at her. My father told stories about a phantom giant dog that appeared out of nowhere and sped along the side of the pickup no matter how fast he was driving.

Nudge a Mexican and she or he will break out with a story. So,   4
huddling under the covers, I made up stories for my sister night after night. After a while she wanted two stories per night. I learned to give her installments, building up the suspense with convoluted complications until the story climaxed several nights later. It must have been then that I decided to put stories on paper. It must have been then that working with images and writing became connected to night.

Invoking Art

In the ethno-poetics and performance of the shaman, my people, the   5
Indians, did not split the artistic from the functional, the sacred from the secular, art from everyday life. The religious, social, and aesthetic purposes of art were all intertwined. Before the Conquest, poets gathered to play music, dance, sing, and read poetry in open-air places around the *Xochicuahuitl, el Arbol Florido,* Tree-in-Flower. (The *Coaxihuitl* or morning glory is called the snake plant and its seeds, known as *ololiuhqui,* are hallucinogenic.[1]) The ability of story (prose and poetry) to transform the storyteller and the listener into something or someone else is shamanistic. The writer, as shape-changer, is a *nahual,* a shaman.

In looking over the book from which this essay was taken, I see   6
a mosaic pattern (Aztec-like) emerging, a weaving pattern, thin here, thick there. I see a preoccupation with the deep structure, the underlying structure, with the gesso underpainting that is red earth, black earth. I can see the deep structure, the scaffolding. If I can get the bone structure right, then putting flesh on it proceeds without too many hitches. The problem is that the bones often do not exist prior

[1]R. Gordon Wasson, *The Wondrous Mushroom: Mycolatry in Mesoamerica* (New York, NY: McGraw-Hill Book Company, 1980), 59, 103.

to the flesh, but are shaped after a vague and broad shadow of its form is discerned or uncovered during beginning, middle, and final stages of the writing. Numerous overlays of paint, rough surfaces, smooth surfaces make me realize I am preoccupied with texture as well. Too, I see the barely contained color threatening to spill over the boundaries of the object it represents and into other "objects" and over the borders of the frame. I see a hybridization of metaphor, different species of ideas popping up here, popping up there, full of variations and seeming contradictions, though I believe in an ordered, structured universe where all phenomena are interrelated and imbued with spirit. This book seems an assemblage, a montage, a beaded work with several leitmotifs and with a central core, now appearing, now disappearing in a crazy dance. The whole thing has had a mind of its own, escaping me and insisting on putting together the pieces of its own puzzle with minimal direction from my will. It is a rebellious, willful entity, a precocious girl-child forced to grow up too quickly, rough, unyielding, with pieces of feather sticking out here and there, fur, twigs, clay. My child, but not for much longer. This female being is angry, sad, joyful, is *Coatlicue*, dove, horse, serpent, cactus. Though it is a flawed thing—a clumsy, complex, groping blind thing—for me it is alive, infused with spirit. I talk to it; it talks to me.

I make my offerings of incense and cracked corn, light my candle. In my head I sometimes will say a prayer—an affirmation and a voicing of intent. Then I run water, wash the dishes or my underthings, take a bath, or mop the kitchen floor. This "induction" period sometimes takes a few minutes, sometimes hours. But always I go against a resistance. Something in me does not want to do this writing. Yet once I'm immersed in it, I can go fifteen to seventeen hours in one sitting and I don't want to leave it. 7

My "stories" are acts encapsulated in time, "enacted" every time they are spoken aloud or read silently. I like to think of them as performances and not as inert and "dead" objects (as the aesthetics of Western culture think of art works). Instead, the work has an identity; it is a "who" or a "what" and contains the presences of persons, that is, incarnations of gods or ancestors or natural and cosmic powers. The work manifests the same needs as a person, it needs to be "fed," *la tengo que bañar y vestir*. 8

When invoked in rite, the object/event is "present"; that is, "enacted," it is both a physical thing and the power that infuses it. It 9 is metaphysical in that it "spins its energies between gods and humans" and its task is to move the gods. This type of work dedicates itself to managing the universe and its energies. I'm not sure what it is when it is at rest (not in performance). It may or may not be a "work" then. A mask may only have the power of presence during a ritual dance and the rest of the time it may merely be a "thing." Some works exist forever invoked, always in performance. I'm thinking of totem poles, cave paintings. Invoked art is communal and speaks of everyday life. It is dedicated to the validation of humans; that is, it makes people hopeful, happy, secure, and it can have negative effects as well, which propel one towards a search for validation.[2]

The aesthetic of virtuosity, art typical of Western European cultures, attempts to manage the energies of its own internal system such as conflicts, harmonies, resolutions and balances. It bears the presence of qualities and internal meanings. It is dedicated to the validation of itself. Its task is to move humans by means of achieving mastery in content, technique, feeling. Western art is always whole and always "in power." It is individual (not communal). It is "psychological" in that it spins its energies between itself and its witness.[3]

Western cultures behave differently toward works of art than do tribal cultures. The "sacrifices" Western cultures make are in housing their art works in the best structures designed by the best architects; and in servicing them with insurance, guards to protect them, conservators to maintain them, specialists to mount and display them, and the educated and upper classes to "view" them. Tribal cultures keep art works in honored and sacred places in the home and elsewhere. They attend them by making sacrifices of blood (goat or chicken), libations of wine. They bathe, feed, and clothe them. The works are treated not just as objects, but also as persons. The "witness" is a participant in the enactment of the work in a ritual, and not a member of the privileged classes.[4]

Ethnocentrism is the tyranny of Western aesthetics. An Indian mask in an American museum is transported into an alien aesthetic

[2]Robert Plant Armstrong, *The Powers of Presence: Consciousness, Myth, and Affecting Presence* (Philadelphia, PA: University of Pennsylvania Press, 1981), 11, 20.

[3]Armstrong, 10.

[4]Armstrong, 4.

system where what is missing is the presence of power invoked through performance ritual. It has become a conquered thing, a dead "thing" separated from nature and, therefore, its power.

Modern Western painters have "borrowed," copied, or other- 13 wise extrapolated the art of tribal cultures and called it cubism, surrealism, symbolism. The music, the beat of the drum, the Blacks' jive talk. All taken over. Whites, along with a good number of our own people, have cut themselves off from their spiritual roots, and they take our spiritual art objects in an unconscious attempt to get them back. If they're going to do it, I'd like them to be aware of what they are doing and to go about doing it the right way. Let's all stop importing Greek myths and the Western Cartesian split point of view and root ourselves in the mythological soil and soul of this continent. White America has only attended to the body of the earth in order to exploit it, never to succor it or to be nurtured in it. Instead of surreptitiously ripping off the vital energy of people of color and putting it to commercial use, whites could allow themselves to share and exchange and learn from us in a respectful way. By taking up *curanderismo*, Santeria, shamanism, Taoism, Zen, and otherwise delving into the spiritual life and ceremonies of multi-colored people, Anglos would perhaps lose the white sterility they have in their kitchens, bathrooms, hospitals, mortuaries, and missile bases. Though in the conscious mind, black and dark may be associated with death, evil, and destruction, in the subconscious mind and in our dreams, white is associated with disease, death, and hopelessness. Let us hope that the left hand, that of darkness, of femaleness, of "primitiveness," can divert the indifferent, right-handed, "rational" suicidal drive that, unchecked, could blow us into acid rain in a fraction of a millisecond.

Ni cuicani: I, the Singer

For the ancient Aztecs, *tlilli, tlapalli, la tinta negra y roja de sus códices* 14 (the black and red ink painted on codices) were the colors symbolizing *escritura y sabidurìa* (writing and wisdom).[5] They believed that through metaphor and symbol, by means of poetry and truth, communication with the Divine could be attained, and *topan* (that which

[5]Miguel Leon-Portilla, *Los Ansiguos Mexicanos: A traves de sus cronicas y cantares* (Mexico, D.F.: Fondo de Cultura Economica, 1961), 19, 22.

is above—the gods and spirit world) could be bridged with *mictlán* (that which is below—the underworld and the region of the dead).

> Poet: she pours water from the mouth of the pump, lowers the 15
> handle then lifts it, lowers, lifts. Her hands begin to feel the pull from
> the entrails, the live animal resisting. A sigh/ rises up from the
> depths, the handle becomes a wild thing in her hands, the cold sweet
> water gushes out, splashing her face, the shock of nightlight filling the
> bucket.

An image is a bridge between evoked emotion and conscious 16 knowledge; words are the cables that hold up the bridge. Images are more direct, more immediate than words, and closer to the unconscious. Picture language precedes thinking in words; the metaphorical mind precedes analytical consciousness.

The Shamanic State

When I create stories in my head, that is, allow the voices and scenes 17 to be projected in the inner screen of my mind, I "trance." I used to think I was going crazy or that I was having hallucinations. But now I realize it is my job, my calling, to traffic in images. Some of these film-like narratives I write down; most are lost, forgotten. When I don't write the images down for several days or weeks or months, I get physically ill. Because writing invokes images from my unconscious, and because some of the images are residues of trauma which I then have to reconstruct, I sometimes get sick when I *do* write. I can't stomach it, become nauseous, or burn with fever, worsen. But, in reconstructing the traumas behind the images, I make "sense" of them, and once they have "meaning" they are changed, transformed. It is then that writing heals me, brings me great joy.

To facilitate the "movies" with soundtracks, I need to be alone, 18 or in a sensory-deprived state. I plug up my ears with wax, put on my black cloth eye-shades, lie horizontal and unmoving, in a state between sleeping and waking, mind and body locked into my fantasy. I am held prisoner by it. My body is experiencing events. In the beginning it is like being in a movie theater, as pure spectator. Gradually I become so engrossed with the activities, the conversations, that I become a participant in the drama. I have to struggle to "disengage" or escape from my "animated story," I have to get some sleep so I can write tomorrow. Yet I am gripped by a story which won't let me go. Outside the frame, I am film director, screenwriter, camera operator. Inside the frame, I am the actors—male and female—I am desert sand, mountain, I am dog, mosquito. I can sustain a four- to six-hour "movie." Once I am up, I can sustain several "shorts" of anywhere between five and thirty minutes. Usually these "narratives" are the offspring of stories acted out in my head during periods of sensory deprivation.

My "awakened dreams" are about shifts. Thought shifts, reality   19
shifts, gender shifts: one person metamorphoses into another in a world where people fly through the air, heal from mortal wounds. I am playing with my Self, I am playing with the world's soul, I am the dialogue between my Self and *el espíritu del mundo*. I change myself, I change the world.

Sometimes I put the imagination to a more rare use. I choose   20
words, images, and body sensations and animate them to impress them on my consciousness, thereby making changes in my belief system and reprogramming my consciousness. This involves looking my inner demons in the face, then deciding which I want in my psyche. Those I don't want, I starve; I feed them no words, no images, no feelings. I spend no time with them, share not my home with them. Neglected, they leave. This is harder to do than to merely generate "stories." I can only sustain this activity for a few minutes.

I write the myths in me, the myths I am, the myths I want to   21
become. The word, the image and the feeling have a palatable energy, a kind of power. *Con imagenes, domo mi miedo, cruzo los abismos que tengo por dentro. Con palabras me hago piedra, pájaro, puente de serpientes arrastrando a ras del suelo todo lo que soy, todo lo que algún día seré.*

> *Los que están mirando (leyendo)*   22
> *los que cuentan (o refieran lo que leen)*
> *Los que vuelven ruidosamente las hojas de los códices.*
> *Los que tienen en su poder*
> *la tinta negra y roja (la sabiduría)*
> *y lo pintado,*
> *ellos nos llevan, nos guían,*
> *nos dicen el camino.*[6]

Writing Is a Sensuous Act

> *Tallo mi cuerpo como si estuviera lavando un trapo. Toco las saltadas*   23
> *venas de mis manos, mis chichis adormecidas como pájaras a la anochecer.*

[6]Leon-Portilla, 125.

Estoy encorbada sobre la cama. Las imagenes aleteán alrededor de mi cama como murciélagos, la sábana como que tuviese alas. El ruido de los trenes subterráneos en mi sentido como conchas. Parece que las paredes del cuarto se me arriman cada vez más cerquita.

Picking out images from my soul's eye, fishing for the right   24
words to recreate the images. Words are blades of grass pushing
past the obstacles, sprouting on the page; the spirit of the words
moving in the body is as concrete as flesh and as palpable; the
hunger to create is as substantial as fingers and hand.

I look at my fingers, see plumes growing there. From the fin-   25
gers, my feathers, black and red ink drips across the page. *Escribo con
la tinta de mi sangre.* I write in red. Intimately knowing the smooth
touch of paper, its speechlessness before I spill myself on the insides
of trees. Daily, I battle the silence and the red. Daily, I take my throat
in my hands and squeeze until the cries pour out, my larynx and
soul sore from the constant struggle.

Something to Do with the Dark

"Quien canta, sus males espanta."   26

—un dicho

The toad comes out of its hiding place inside the lobes of my brain.
It's going to happen again. The ghost of the toad that betrayed me—   27
I hold it in my hand. The toad is sipping the strength from my veins,
it is sucking my pale heart. I am a dried serpent skin, wind scuttling
me across the hard ground, pieces of me scattered over the country-
side. And there in the dark I meet the crippled spider crawling in the
gutter, the day-old newspaper fluttering in the dirty rain water.

*Musa bruja, venga. Cubrese con una sábana y espante mis demonios que
a rempujones y a cachetadas me roban la pluma me rompen el sueño. Musa,*   28
¡misericordia!
*Óigame, musa bruja. ¿Porqué huye usté en cara? Su grito me desarrolla
de mi caracola, me sacude el alma. Vieja, quítese de aquí con sus alas de
navaja. Ya no me despedaze mi cara. Vaya con sus pinche uñas que me des-
garran de los ojos hasta los talones. Váyase a la tiznada. Que no me coman,
le digo. Que no me coman sus nueve dedos caníbales.*
*Hija negra de la noche, carnala, ¿Porqué me sacas las tripas, porqué car-
das mis entrañas? Este hilvanando palabras con tripas me está matando. Jija
de la noche ¡vete a la chingada!*

Writing produces anxiety. Looking inside myself and my expe-   29
rience, looking at my conflicts, engenders anxiety in me. Being a

writer feels very much like being a Chicana, or being queer—a lot of squirming, coming up against all sorts of walls. Or its opposite: nothing defined or definite, a boundless, floating state of limbo where I kick my heels, brood, percolate, hibernate, and wait for something to happen.

Living in a state of psychic unrest, in a Borderland, is what   30
makes poets write and artists create. It is like a cactus needle embedded in the flesh. It worries itself deeper and deeper, and I keep aggravating it by poking at it. When it begins to fester I have to do something to put an end to the aggravation and to figure out why I have it. I get deep down into the place where it's rooted in my skin and pluck away at it, playing it like a musical instrument—the fingers pressing, making the pain worse before it can get better. Then out it comes. No more discomfort, no more ambivalence. Until another needle pierces the skin. That's what writing is for me, an endless cycle of making it worse, making it better, but always making meaning out of the experience, whatever it may be.

> *My flowers shall not cease to live;*   31
> *my songs shall never end:*
> *I, a singer, intone them;*
> *they become scattered, they are spread about.*

> —*Cantares mexicanos*

To write, to be a writer, I have to trust and believe in myself as   32
a speaker, as a voice for the images. I have to believe that I can communicate with images and words and that I can do it well. A lack of belief in my creative self is a lack of belief in my total self and vice versa—I cannot separate my writing from any part of my life. It is all one.

When I write it feels like I'm carving bone. It feels like I'm cre-   33
ating my own face, my own heart—a Nahuatl concept. My soul makes itself through the creative act. It is constantly remaking and giving birth to itself through my body. It is the learning to live with *la Coatlicue* that transforms living in the Borderlands from a nightmare into a numinous experience. It is always a path/state to something else.

In *Xóchitl* in *Cuícatl*[7]

[7]In *Xóchitl* in *Cuícatl* is Nahuatl for flower and song, *flor y canto.*

She writes while other people sleep. Something is trying to   34
come out. She fights the words, pushes them down, down, a woman
with morning sickness in the middle of the night. How much easier
it would be to carry a baby for nine months and then expel it per-
manently. These continuous multiple pregnancies are going to kill
her. She is the battlefield for the pitched fight between the inner
image and the words trying to recreate it. *La musa bruja* has no manners. Doesn't she know, nights are for sleeping?

She is getting too close to the mouth of the abyss. She is teeter-   35
ing on the edge, trying to balance while she makes up her mind
whether to jump in or find a safer way down. That's why she makes
herself sick—to postpone having to jump blindfolded into the abyss
of her own being and there in the depths confront her face, the face
underneath the mask.

To be a mouth—the cost is too high—her whole life enslaved to   36
that devouring mouth. *Todo pasaba por esa boca, el viento, el fuego, los
mares y la Tierra.* Her body, a crossroads, a fragile bridge, cannot support the tons of cargo passing through it. She wants to install 'stop'
and 'go' signal lights, instigate a curfew, police Poetry. But something wants to come out.

Blocks (*Coatlicue* states) are related to my cultural identity. The   37
painful periods of confusion that I suffer from are symptomatic of a
larger creative process: cultural shifts. The stress of living with cultural ambiguity both compels me to write and blocks me. It isn't
until I'm almost at the end of the blocked state that I remember and
recognize it for what it is. As soon as this happens, the piercing light
of awareness melts the block and I accept the deep and the darkness
and I hear one of my voices saying, "I am tired of fighting. I surrender. I give up, let go, let the walls fall. On this night of the hearing of faults, *Tlazolteotl, diosa de la cara negra*, let fall the cockroaches
that live in my hair, the rats that nestle in my skull. Gouge out my
lame eyes, rout my demon from its nocturnal cave. Set torch to the
tiger that stalks me. Loosen the dead faces gnawing at my cheekbones. I am tired of resisting. I surrender. I give up, let go, let the
walls fall."

And in descending to the depths I realize that down is up, and   38
I rise up from and into the deep. And once again I recognize that the
internal tension of oppositions can propel (if it doesn't tear apart) the
mestiza writer out of the *metate* where she is being ground with corn
and water, eject her out as *nahual,* an agent of transformation, able to

modify and shape primordial energy and therefore able to change
herself and others into turkey, coyote, tree, or human.

I sit here before my computer, *Amiguita*, my altar on top of the   39
monitor with the *Virgen de Coatlalopeuh* candle and copal incense
burning. My companion, a wooden serpent staff with feathers, is to
my right while I ponder the ways metaphor and symbol concretize
the spirit and etherealize the body. The Writing is my whole life, it
is my obsession. This vampire which is my talent does not suffer
other suitors.[8] Daily I court it, offer my neck to its teeth. This is the
sacrifice that the act of creation requires, a blood sacrifice. For only
through the body, through the pulling of flesh, can the human soul
be transformed. And for images, words, stories to have this trans-
formative power, they must arise from the human body—flesh and
bone—and from the Earth's body—stone, sky, liquid, soil. This
work, these images, piercing tongue or ear lobes with cactus needle,
are my offerings, are my Aztecan blood sacrifices.

[8]Nietzsche, in *The Will to Power*, says that the artist lives under a curse of being
vampirized by his talent.

A Guide to Terms

Abstract *(See Concrete/Abstract.)*
Allusion *(See Figures of Speech.)*
Analogy (See Section 4.)
Argument is writing that uses factual evidence and supporting ideas to convince readers to share the author's opinion on an issue or to take some action the writer considers appropriate or necessary. Like exposition, argument conveys information; however, it does so not to explain but to induce readers to favor one side in a conflict or to choose a particular course of action.

Some arguments appeal primarily to reason, others primarily to emotion. Most, however, mix reason and emotion in whatever way is appropriate for the issue and the audience. (See Section 11.)

Support for an argument can take a number of forms:

1. *Examples*—Real-life examples, or hypothetical examples (used sparingly) can be convincing evidence if they are typical and if the author provides enough of them to illustrate all the major points in the argument or combines them with other kinds of evidence. (See Perry, Jarvis, Keller, Jacobs.) Some examples are *specific*, referring to particular people or events. (See Perry, Keller.) Others are *general*, referring to kinds of events or people, usually corresponding in some way to the reader's experiences. (See Lynn.)

2. *Facts and figures*—Detailed information about a subject, particularly if presented in statistical form, can help convince readers by showing that the author's perspective on an issue is consistent with what is known about the subject. (See Lynn.) But facts whose accuracy is questionable or statistics that are confusing can undermine an argument.

3. *Authority*—Supporting an argument with the ideas or the actual words of someone who is recognized as an expert can be an effective strategy as long as the author can show that the expert is a reliable witness and can combine the expert's opinion with other kinds of evidence that point in the same direction.

4. *Personal experience*—Examples drawn from personal experience or the experience of friends can be more detailed and vivid (and hence more convincing) than other kinds of evidence, but a writer should use this kind of evidence sparingly because readers may sometimes suspect that it represents no more than one person's way of looking at events. When combined with other kinds of evidence, however, examples drawn from personal experience can be an effective technique for persuasion. (See Keller, Jacobs.)

In addition, all the basic expository patterns can be used to support an argument. (See Section 11.)

Cause (See Section 6.)

Central Theme (See *Unity*.)

Classification (See Section 2.)

Clichés are tired expressions, perhaps once fresh and colorful, that have been overused until they have lost most of their effectiveness and become trite or hackneyed. The team is also applied, less commonly, to trite ideas or attitudes.

We may need to use clichés in conversation, of course, where the quick and economical phrase is an important and useful tool of expression—and where no one expects us to be constantly original. We are fortunate, in a way, to have a large accumulation of clichés from which to draw. To describe someone, without straining our originality very much, we can always declare that he is *as innocent as a lamb, as thin as a rail,* or *as fat as a pig;* that she is *as dumb as an ox, as sly as a fox,* or *as wise as an owl;* that he is *financially embarrassed* or *has a fly in the ointment* or *her ship has come in;* or that, *last but not least, in this day and age,* the *Grim Reaper* has taken him to *his eternal reward.* There is indeed *a large stockpile* from which we can draw for ordinary conversation. But the trite expression, written down on paper, is a permanent reminder that the writer is either lazy or not aware of the dullness of stereotypes—or, even more damaging, it is a clue that the ideas themselves may be threadbare, and therefore can be adequately expressed in threadbare language.

Occasionally, of course, a writer can use obvious clichés deliberately (see Lawrence, par. 1; Ehrenreich, "Star"; Stone). But usually to be fully effective, writing must be fresh, and should seem to have been written specifically for the occasion. Clichés, however fresh and appropriate at one time, have lost these qualities.

Closings are almost as much of a problem as introductions, and they are equally important. The function of a closing is simply "to close," of course, but this implies somehow tying the entire writing into a neat package, giving the final sense of unity to the whole endeavor, and thus leaving the reader with a sense of satisfaction instead of an uneasy feeling that there ought to be another page. There is no standard length for closings. A short composition may be effectively completed with one sentence—or even without any real closing at all, if the last point discussed is a strong or climactic one. A longer piece of writing, however, may end more slowly, perhaps through several paragraphs.

A few types of weak endings are so common that warnings are in order here. Careful writers will avoid these faults: (1) giving the effect of suddenly tiring and quitting; (2) ending on a minor detail or an apparent afterthought; (3) bringing up a new point in the closing; (4) using any new qualifying remark in the closing (if writers want their opinions to seem less dogmatic or generalized, they should go back to do their qualifying where the damage was done); (5) ending with an apology of any kind (authors who are not interested enough to become at least minor experts in their subject should not be wasting the reader's time).

Of the several acceptable ways of giving the sense of finality to a paper, the easiest is the *summary*, but it is also the least desirable for most short papers. Readers who have read and understood something only a page or two before robably do not need to have it reviewed for them. Such a review is apt to seem merely repetitious. Longer writings, of course, such as research or term papers, may require thorough summaries.

Several other closing techniques are available to writers. The following, which do not represent all the possibilities, are useful in many situations, and they can frequently be employed in combination:

1. *Using word signals*—e.g., *finally, at last, thus, and so, in conclusion,* as well as more original devices suggested by the subject itself. (See Simpson.)

2. *Changing the tempo*—usually a matter of sentence length or pace. This is a very subtle indication of finality, and it is difficult to achieve. (For examples of modified use, see Simpson, Walker, Cisneros, Mansnerus.)

3. *Restating the central idea of the writing*—sometimes a "statement" so fully developed that it practically becomes a summary itself. (See Catton, Quindlen.)

4. *Using climax*—a natural culmination of preceding points or, in some cases, the last major point itself. This is suitable, however, only if the materials have been so arranged that the last point is outstanding. (See Catton, Lawrence, Walker, Theroux.)

5. *Making suggestions,* perhaps mentioning a possible solution to the problem being discussed—a useful technique for exposition as well as for argument, and a natural signal of the end. (See Coudert, Keller.)

6. *Showing the topic's significance,* its effects, or the universality of its meaning—a commonly used technique that, if carefully handled, is an excellent indication of closing. (See Buckley, Lawrence, Noda, Kean.)

7. *Echoing the introduction*—a technique that has the virtue of improving the effect of unity by bringing the development around full circle, so to speak. The echo may be a reference to a problem posed or a significant expression, quotation, analogy, or symbol used in the introduction or elsewhere early in the composition. (See Buckley; Ehrenreich, "Men"; Kunz.)

8. *Using some rhetorical device*—a sort of catchall category, but a good supply source that includes several very effective techniques; pertinent quotations, anecdotes and brief dialogues, metaphors, allusions, ironic comments, and various kinds of witty or memorable remarks. All, however, run the risk of seeming forced and hence amateurish; but properly handled, they make for an effective closing. (See White, Lopate, Lawrence, Simpson, King.)

Coherence is quality of good writing that results from the presentation of all parts in logical and clear relations.

Coherence and unity are usually studied together and, indeed, are almost inseparable. But whereas unity refers to the relation of parts to the central theme (See *Unity*.), coherence refers to their relations with each other. In a coherent piece of writing, each sentence, each paragraph, each major division seems to grow out of those preceding it.

Several transitional devices (See *Transition*.) help to make these relations clear, but far more fundamental to coherence is the sound organization of materials. From the first moment of visualizing the subject materials in pattern, the writer's goal must be clear and logical development. If it is, coherence is almost ensured.

Colloquial Expressions are characteristic of conversation and informal writing, and they are normally perfectly appropriate in those contexts. However, most writing done for college, business, or professional purposes is considered "formal" writing; and for such usage, colloquialisms are too informal, too *folksy* (itself a word most dictionaries would label "colloq.").

Some of the expressions appropriate only for informal usage are *kid* (for child), *boss* (for employer), *flunk, buddy, snooze, gym, a lot of, phone, skin flicks, porn*. In addition, contractions such as *can't* and *I'd* are usually regarded as colloquialisms and are never permissible in, for instance, a research or term paper.

Slang is defined as a low level of colloquialism, but it is sometimes placed "below" colloquialism in respectability; even standard dictionaries differ as to just what the distinction is. (Some of the examples in the preceding paragraph, if included in dictionaries at all, are identified both ways.) At any rate, slang generally comprises words either coined or given novel meanings in an attempt at colorful or humorous expression. Slang soon becomes limp with overuse, however, losing whatever vigor it first had. In time, slang expressions either disappear completely or graduate to more acceptable colloquial status and thence, possibly, into standard usage. (That is one way in which our language is constantly changing). But until their "graduations," slang and colloquialism have an appropriate place in formal writing only if used sparingly and for special effect. Because dictionaries frequently differ in matters of usage, the student should be sure to use a standard edition approved by the instructor. (For further examples, see Viorst; Wolfe; Simpson, pars. 8, 16, 17; Williams, pars. 8, 11, 12.)

Comparison (See Section 3.)

Conclusions (See *Closings.*)

Concrete and **Abstract** words are both indispensable to the language, but a good rule in most writing is to use the concrete whenever possible. This policy also applies, of course, to sentences that express only abstract ideas, which concrete examples can often make clearer and more effective. Many expository and argumentative paragraphs are constructed with an abstract topic sentence and its concrete support. (See *Unity.*)

A concrete word names something that exists as an entity in itself, something that can be perceived by the human senses. We can see, touch, hear, and smell a horse—hence *horse* is a concrete word. But a horse's *strength* is not. We have no reason to doubt that strength exists, but it does not have an independent existence: something else must *be* strong or there is no strength. Hence *strength* is an abstract word.

Purely abstract reading is difficult for average readers; with no concrete images provided, they are constantly forced to make their own. Concrete writing helps readers to visualize and is therefore easier and faster to read.

(See *Specific/General* for further discussion.)

Connotation and **Denotation** both refer to the meanings of words. Denotation is the direct, literal meaning as it would be found in a dictionary, whereas connotation refers to the response a word *really* arouses in the reader or listener. (See Wolfe, par. 14; Cramer; Jacobs; Lawrence.)

There are two types of connotation: personal and general. Personal connotations vary widely, depending on the experiences and moods that an individual associates with the word. (This corresponds with personal symbolism; See *Symbol.*) *Waterfall* is not apt to have the same meaning for the happy young honeymooners at Yosemite as it has for the grieving mother whose child has just drowned in a waterfall. General connotations are those shared by many people. *Fireside,* far beyond its obvious dictionary definition, generally connotes warmth and security and good companionship. *Mother,* which denotatively means simply "female parent," means much more connotatively.

A word or phrase considered less distasteful or offensive than a more direct expression is called a *euphemism,* and this is also a matter of connotation. (See Mitford, Jacobs.) The various expressions used instead of the more direct "four-letter words" referring to daily bathroom events are examples of euphemisms. (See Wolfe's "mounting.") *Remains* is often used instead of *corpse,* and a few newspapers still have people *passing away* and being *laid to rest,* rather than *dying* and being *buried.*

But a serious respect for the importance of connotations goes far beyond euphemistic practices. Young writers can hardly expect to know all the different meanings of words for all their potential readers, but they can at least be aware that words do *have* different meanings. Of course, this is most important in persuasive writing—in political speeches, in advertising copy-writing, and in any endeavor where some sort of public image is being created. When President Franklin Roosevelt began his series of informal radio talks, he called them "fireside chats," thus putting connotation to work. An advertising copywriter trying to evoke the feeling of love and tenderness associated with motherhood is not seriously tempted to use *female parent* instead of *mother.*

In exposition, where the primary purpose is to explain, the writer ordinarily tries to avoid words that may have emotional overtones, unless these can somehow be used to increase understanding. In argument, however, a writer may on occasion wish to appeal to the emotions.

Contrast (See Section 3.)

Deduction (See Section 10.)

Denotation (See *Connotation/Denotation.*)

Description (See Section 8.)

Diction refers simply to "choice of words," but, not so simply, it involves many problems of usage, some of which are explained under several other headings in this guide, e.g., *Clichés, Colloquial Expressions, Connotation/Denotation, Concrete/Abstract*—anything, in fact, that pertains primarily to word choices. But the characteristics of good diction may be more generally classified as follows:

1. *Accuracy*—the choice of words that mean exactly what the author intends.

2. *Economy*—the choice of the simplest and fewest words that will convey the exact meaning intended.

3. *Emphasis*—the choice of fresh, strong words, avoiding clichés and unnecessarily vague or general terms.

4. *Appropriateness*—the choice of words that suit the subject matter, the prospective reader-audience, and the purpose of the writing.

(For contrasts of diction see Stone, Hills, Welsch, Walker, Eiseley, King, Rodriguez, Cisneros, Anzaldúa.)

Division (See Section 2.)

Effect (See Section 6.)

Emphasis is almost certain to fall *somewhere,* and the author should be the one to decide where. A major point, not some minor detail, should be emphasized.

Following are the most common ways of achieving emphasis. Most of them apply to the sentence, the paragraph, or the overall writing—all of which can be seriously weakened by emphasis in the wrong places.

1. By *position*—the most emphatic position is usually at the end, the second most emphatic at the beginning. (There are a few exceptions, including news stories and certain kinds of scientific reports.) The middle, therefore, should be used for materials that do not deserve special emphasis. (See Buckley, for saving the most significant example unit last; Keller, for a forceful beginning; Catton, par. 16; Raybon, for gradually increasing emphasis; and Hall, for the long-withheld revelation of the real central theme.)

A sentence in which the main point is held until the last is called a *periodic sentence,* e.g., "After a long night of suspense and horror, the cavalry arrived." In a *loose sentence,* the main point is disposed of earlier and followed by dependencies, e.g., "The calvary arrived after a long night of suspense and horror." (See Peterson, first sentence, for an effective periodic sentence that introduces an essay, and for an effective periodic sentence that acts as a transition between sections of an essay.)

2. By *proportion*—Ordinarily, but not necessarily, important elements are given the most attention and thus automatically achieve a certain emphasis.

3. By *repetition*—Words and ideas may sometimes be given emphasis by reuse, usually in a different manner. If not cautiously handled, however, this method can seem merely repetitious, not emphatic. (See Atwood; Cramer, who repeats words to give them varied meanings and highlight their importance; Ehrenreich, "Star," which provides an ironic example of the strategy.)

4. By *flat statement*—Although an obvious way to achieve emphasis is simply to *tell* the reader what is most important, it is often least effective, at least when used as the only method. Readers have a way of ignoring such pointers as "most important" and "especially true." (See Catton, par. 16, Hills, pars. 13, 21.)

5. By *mechanical devices*—Emphasis can be achieved by using italics (underlining), capital letters, or exclamation points. But too often these devices are used, however unintentionally, to cover deficiencies of content or style. Their employment can quickly be overdone and their impact lost. (For a limited and therefore emphatic use of italics and capitalization, see Faraday.)

6. By *distinctiveness of style*—The author can emphasize subtly with fresh and concrete words or figures of speech, crisp or unusual structures, and careful control of paragraph or sentence lengths. (These methods are used in many essays in this book: see Buckley; Twain, who changes style radically for the second half of his essay; Catton; Stone, who uses numerous puns, Wolfe; Rodriguez and Cisneros, who draw on Spanish expressions; Curtin, pars. 7–15.) *Verbal irony* (see *Irony*), including *sarcasm* (see Buckley, Atwood) and the rather specialized form known as *understatement*, if handled judiciously, is another valuable means of achieving distinctiveness of style and increasing emphasis. (See Wolfe, Mitford, Hills, Ehrenreich, "Star.")

Essay refers to a brief prose composition on a single topic, usually, but not always, communicating the author's personal ideas and impressions. Beyond this, because of the wide and loose application of the term, not really satisfactory definition has been universally accepted.

Classifications of essay types have also been widely varied and sometimes not very meaningful. One basic and useful distinction, however, is between *formal* and *informal* essays, although many defy classification even in such broad categories as these. It is best to regard the two types as opposite ends of a continuum, along which most essays may be placed.

The formal essay usually develops an important theme through a logical progression of ideas, with full attention to unity and coherence, and in a serious tone. Although the style is seldom completely impersonal, it is literary rather than colloquial. (For examples of essays that are somewhere near the "formal" end of the continuum, see Buckley, Lynn, Eiseley, Catton, Winn, Helman, Lawrence.)

The informal, or personal, essay is less elaborately organized and more chatty in style. First-person pronouns, contractions, and other colloquial or even slang expressions are often freely used. Informal essays are less serious in apparent purpose than formal essays. Although most do contain a worthwhile message or observation of some kind, an important purpose of many is to entertain. (See Kunz, who mixes humorous examples with serious discussion; Stone; Wolfe; and Hills.)

The more personal and intimate informal essays may be classifiable as *familiar* essays, although, again, there is no well-established boundary. Familiar essays pertain to the author's own experience, ideas, or prejudices, frequently in a light and humorous style. (See Buczynski, Peterson, Viorst, Curtin, White, Greene, Cramer.)

Evaluation of a literary piece, as for any other creative endeavor, is meaningful only when based somehow on the answers to three questions: (1) What was the author's purpose? (2) How successfully was it fulfilled? (3) How worthwhile was it?

An architect could hardly be blamed for designing a poor gymnasium if the commission had been to design a library. Similarly, an author who is trying to explain for us why women are paid less than men cannot be faulted for failing to make the reader laugh. An author whose purpose is simply to amuse (a worthy goal) should not be condemned for teaching little about trichobothria. (Nothing prevents the author from trying to explain pornography through the use of humor, or trying to amuse by comparing two Civil War generals, but in these situations the purpose has changed—and grown almost unbearably harder to achieve.)

An architect who was commissioned to design a gymnasium, and who, in fact, designed one, however, could be justifiably criticized on whether the building is successful and attractive *as a gymnasium.* If an author is examining matters of mental and physical health (as is Mansnerus), the reader has a right to expect sound reasoning and clear expository prose; and varied, detailed support ought to be expected in an essay that looks at the physical basis of human behavior (Perry and Dawson) or at the mental dimensions of medical practice (Helman).

Many things are written and published that succeed very well in carrying out the author's intent—but simply are not worthwhile. Although this is certainly justifiable grounds for unfavorable criticism, readers should first make full allowance for their own limitations and perhaps their narrow range of interests, evaluating the work as nearly as possible from the standpoint of the average reader for whom the writing was intended.

Figures of Speech are short, vivid comparisons, either stated or implied; but they are not literal comparisons (e.g., "Your car is like my car," which is presumably a plain statement of fact). Figures of speech are more imaginative. They imply analogy but, unlike analogy, are used less to inform than to make quick and forceful impressions. All figurative language is a comparison of unlikes, but the unlikes do have some interesting point of likeness, perhaps one never noticed before.

A *metaphor* merely suggests the comparison and is worded as if the two unlikes are the same thing—e.g., "the language of the river" and "was turned to blood" (Twain, par. 1) and "a great chapter in American life" (Catton, par. 1). (For some of the many other examples in this book, see Eiseley, Helman, Cramer, Hamill, King.)

A *simile* (which is sometimes classified as a special kind of metaphor) expresses a similarity directly, usually with the word *like* or *as* (Eiseley, par. 4, Lopate, par. 12).

A *personification*, which is actually a special type of either metaphor or simile, is usually classified as a "figure" in its own right. In personification, inanimate things are treated as if they had the qualities or powers of a person. Some people would also label as personification any characterization of inanimate objects as animals, or of animals as humans.

An *allusion* is literally any casual reference, any alluding, to something, but rhetorically it is limited to a figurative reference to a famous or literary person, event, or quotation, and it should be distinguished from the casual reference that has a literal function in the subject matter. Hence casual mention of Judas Iscariot's betrayal of Jesus is merely a reference, but calling a modern traitor a "Judas" is an allusion. A rooster might be referred to as "the Hitler of the barnyard," or a lover as a "Romeo." Many allusions refer to mythological or biblical persons or places. (See Buckley, par. 11; Wolfe, title and par. 1; Peterson, for numerous allusions to songs and song titles; and Simpson, par. 2, for a discussion of some commonly employed allusions.)

Irony and paradox (both discussed under their own headings) and analogy (see Section 4) are also frequently classed as figures of speech, and there are several other less common types that are really subclassifications of those already discussed.

General (See *Specific/General.*)

Illustration (See Section 1.)

Impressionistic Description (See Section 8.)

Induction (See Section 10.)

Introductions give readers their first impressions, which often turn out to be the lasting ones. In fact, unless an introduction succeeds in somehow attracting a reader's interest, he or she probably will read no further. The importance of the introduction is one reason that writing it is nearly always difficult.

When the writer remains at a loss to know how to begin, it may be a good idea to forget about the introduction for a while and go ahead with the main body of the writing. Later the writer may find that a suitable introduction has suggested itself or even that the way the piece begins is actually introduction enough.

Introductions may vary in length from one sentence in a short composition to several paragraphs or even several pages in longer and more complex expositions and arguments, such as research papers and reports of various kinds.

Good introductions in expository writing have at least three and sometimes four functions.

1. *To identify the subject and set its limitations*, thus building a solid foundation for unity. This function usually includes some indication of the central theme, letting the reader know what point is to be made about the subject. Unlike the other forms of prose, which can often benefit by some degree of mystery, exposition has the primary purpose of explaining, so the reader has a right to know from the beginning just *what* is being explained.

2. *To interest the readers*, and thus ensure their attention. To be sure of doing this, writers must analyze their prospective

readers and the readers' interest in their subject. The account of
a new X-ray technique would need an entirely different kind of
introduction if written for doctors than if written for the campus
newspaper.

3. *To set the tone* of the rest of the writing. (See *Style/Tone*.)
Tone varies greatly in writing, just as the tone of a person's voice
varies with the person's mood. One function of the introduction
is to let the reader know the author's attitude since it may have
a subtle but important bearing on the communication.

4. *Frequently*, but not always, *to indicate the plan of organization*. Although seldom important in short, relatively simple compositions and essay examinations, this function of introductions
can be especially valuable in more complex papers.

These are the necessary functions of an introduction. For
best results, keep these guidelines in mind: (1) Avoid referring
to the title, or even assuming that the reader has seen it. Make
the introduction do all the introducing. (2) Avoid crude and
uninteresting beginnings, such as "This paper is about. . . ." (3)
Avoid going too abruptly into the main body—smooth transition
is at least as important here as anywhere else. (4) Avoid overdoing the introduction, either in length or in extremes of style.

Fortunately, there are many good ways to introduce expository writing (and argumentative writing), and several of the
most useful are illustrated by the selections in this book. Many
writings, of course, combine two or more of the following techniques for interesting introductions.

1. *Stating the central theme*, which is sometimes fully enough
explained in the introduction to become almost a preview-
summary of the exposition or argument to come. (See Tajima,
Noda, Kean, Mansnerus, Viorst.)

2. *Showing the significance of the subject*, or stressing its
importance. (See Catton, Wolfe, Simpson.)

3. *Giving the background of the subject*, usually in brief
form, in order to bring the reader up to date as early as possible
for a better understanding of the matter at hand. (See Stone,
Lynn.)

4. *"Focusing down" to one aspect of the subject*, a technique
similar to that used in some movies, showing first a broad scope
(of subject area, as of landscape) and then progressively
narrowing views until the focus is on one specific thing

(perhaps the name "O'Grady O'Connor" on a mailbox by a gate—or the silent sufferers on Buckley's train). (See also Rooney, Quindlen.)

5. *Using a pertinent rhetorical device* that will attract interest as it leads into the main exposition—e.g., an anecdote, analogy, allusion, quotation, or paradox. (See Goodman, Welsch, Simpson.)

6. *Using a short but vivid comparison or contrast* to emphasize the central idea. (See Murray.)

7. *Posing a challenging question,* the answering of which the reader will assume to be the purpose of the writing. (See Lawrence, Buczynski.)

8. *Referring to the writer's experience with the subject,* perhaps even giving a detailed account of that experience. Some writings are simply continuations of experience so introduced, perhaps with the expository purpose of making the telling entirely evident only at the end or slowly unfolding it as the account progresses. (See White, Jacobs, Keller.)

9. *Presenting a startling statistic or other fact* that will indicate the nature of the subject to be discussed.

10. *Making an unusual statement* that can intrigue as well as introduce. (See Kean, Wolfe, Gansberg, Ehrenreich, "Star.")

11. *Making a commonplace remark* that can draw interest because of its very commonness in sound or meaning.

Irony, in its verbal form sometimes classed as a figure of speech, consists of saying one thing on the surface but meaning exactly (or nearly) the opposite—e.g., "this beautiful neighborhood of ours" may mean that it is a dump. (For other illustrations, see Stone, Wolfe, Mitford, Walker.)

Verbal irony has a wide range of tones, from the gentle, gay, or affectionate to the sharpness of outright *sarcasm* (see Buckley), which is always intended to cut. It may consist of only a word or phrase, it may be a simple *understatement* (see Mitford, Ehrenreich, "Star"), or it may be sustained as one of the major components of satire.

Irony can be an effective tool of exposition if its tone is consistent with the overall tone and if the writer is sure that the audience is bright enough to recognize it. In speech, a person usually indicates by voice or eye-expression that he is not to be taken literally; in writing, the words on the page have to speak for themselves. (See Stone for the use of parentheses to indicate ironic or humorous statements.)

In addition to verbal irony, there is also an *irony of situation*, in which there is a sharp contradiction between what is logically expected to happen and what does happen—e.g., a man sets a trap for an obnoxious neighbor and then gets caught in it himself. Or the ironic situation may simply be some discrepancy that an outsider can see while those involved cannot. (See Lawrence, pars. 11–12.)

Logical Argument (See Section 11.)

Loose Sentences (See *Emphasis*.)

Metaphor (See *Figures of Speech*.)

Narration (See Section 9.)

Objective writing and **Subjective** writing are distinguishable by the extent to which they reflect the author's personal attitudes or emotions. The difference is usually one of degree, as few writing endeavors can be completely objective or subjective.

Objective writing, seldom used in its pure form except in business or scientific reports, is impersonal and concerned almost entirely with straight narration, with logical analysis, or with the description of external appearances. (For somewhat objective writing, see Simpson; Staples, par. 1; McPhee.)

Subjective writing (in description called "impressionistic"— see Section 8) is more personalized, more expressive of the beliefs, ideals, or impressions of the author. Whereas in objective writing the emphasis is on the object being written about, in subjective writing the emphasis is on the way the author sees and interprets the object. (For some of the many examples in this book, see Twain, Lopate, Wolfe, Mitford, Welsch, Lawrence, Staples, after par. 1, Eiseley, Ehrenreich.)

Paradox is a statement or remark that, although seeming to be contradictory or absurd, actually contains some truth. Many paradoxical statements are also ironic.

Paragraph Unity (See *Unity*.)

Parallel Structure refers in principle to the same kind of "parallelism" that is studied in grammar: the principle that coordinate elements should have coordinate presentation, as in a pair or a series of verbs, prepositional phrases, gerunds. It is often as much a matter of "balance" as it is of parallelism.

But the principle of parallel structure, far from being just a negative "don't mix" set of rules, is also a positive rhetorical device. Many writers use it as an effective means of stressing variety of profusion in a group of nouns or modifiers, or of emphasizing parallel ideas in sentence parts, in two or more sentences, or even in two or more paragraphs. At times it can also be useful stylistically, to give a subtle poetic quality to the prose.

(For illustrations of parallel parts within a sentence, see Murray, pars. 21, 26; Wolfe, pars. 1, 4; of parallel sentences themselves, see Goodman, pars. 2, 7; Catton, par. 14; of both parallel parts and parallel sentences, see Twain, Maynard, Viorst; of parallel paragraphs, see).

Periodic Sentence (See *Emphasis.*)

Persona refers to a character created as the speaker in an essay or the narrator of a story. The attitudes and character of a persona often differ from those of the author, and their persona may be created as a way of submitting certain values or perspectives to examination and criticism. The speaker in Ehrenreich's "Star Dreck" is clearly a persona and advocates actions that the author would consider abhorrent if put into practice.

Personification (See *Figures of Speech.*)

Point of View in *argument* means the author's opinion on an issue or the thesis being advanced in an essay. In *exposition*, however, point of view is simply the position of the author in relation to the subject matter. Rhetorical point of view in exposition has little in common with the grammatical sort and differs somewhat from point of view in fiction.

A ranch in a mountain valley is seen differently by the ranch hand working at the corral, by the gardener deciding where to plant the petunias, by the artist or poet viewing the ranch from the mountainside, and by the geographer in a plane above, map-sketching the valley in relation to the entire range. It is the same ranch but the positions and attitudes of the viewers are different.

So it is with expository prose. The position and attitude of the author are the important lens through which the reader sees the subject. Consistency is important, because if the lens is changed without sufficient cause and explanation, the reader will become disconcerted, if not annoyed.

Obviously, since the point of view is partially a matter of attitude, the tone and often the style of writing are closely linked to it. (See *Style/Tone*.)

The expository selections in this book provide examples of numerous points of view. Bradley's and Twain's are those of authority in their own fields of experience; Mitford's is as the debunking prober; Ehrenreich's is that of the angry observer of human behavior. In each of these (and the list could be extended to include all the selections in the book), the subject would seem vastly different if seen from some other point of view.

Process Analysis (See Section 5.)

Purpose that is clearly understood by the author before beginning to write is essential to both unity and coherence. A worthwhile practice, certainly in the training stages, is to write down the controlling purpose before even beginning to outline. Some instructors require both a statement of purpose and a statement of central theme or thesis. (See *Unity, Thesis*.)

The most basic element of a statement of purpose is the commitment to "explain" or, in some assignments, to "convince" (argument). But the statement of purpose, whether written down or only decided upon, goes further—e.g., "to argue that 'dirty words' are logically offensive because of the sources and connotations of the words themselves" (Lawrence).

Qualification is the tempering of broad statements to make them more valid and acceptable, the authors themselves admitting the probability of exceptions. This qualifying can be done inconspicuously, to whatever degree needed, by the use of *possibly, nearly always* or *most often, usually* or *frequently, sometimes* or *occasionally*. Instead of saying, "Chemistry is the most valuable field of study," it would probably be more accurate and defensible to say that it is for *some* people, or that it *can* be the most valuable. (For examples of qualification, see Mansnerus.)

Refutation of opposing arguments is an important element in most argumentative essays, especially where the opposition is strong enough or reasonable enough to provide a real alternative to the author's opinion. A refutation consists of a brief summary of the opposing point of view along with a discussion of its inadequacies, a discussion which often helps support the author's own thesis.

Here are three commonly used strategies for refutation:

1. *Pointing out weaknesses in evidence*—If an opposing argument is based on inaccurate, incomplete, or misleading evidence, or if the argument does not take into account some new evidence that contradicts it, then the refutation should point out these weaknesses.

2. *Pointing out errors in logic*—If an opposing argument is loosely reasoned or contains major flaws in logic, then the refutation should point these problems out to the reader.

3. *Questioning the relevance of an argument*—If an opposing argument does not directly address the issue under consideration, then the refutation should point out that even though the argument may well be correct, it is not worth considering because it is not relevant.

Refutations should always be moderate in tone and accurate in representing opposing arguments; otherwise, readers may feel that the writer has treated the opposition unfairly and as a result judge the author's own argument more harshly.

Rhetorical Questions are posed with no expectation of receiving an answer; they are merely structural devices for launching or furthering a discussion or for achieving emphasis. (See Hall, par. 6; Lawrence; Ehrenreich, "Men," par. 1; Coudert, pars. 5, 6; Jacobs, par. 7; Perry, par. 16.)

Sarcasm (See *Irony*.)

Satire, sometimes called "extended irony," is a literary form that brings wit and humor to the serious task of pointing out frailties or evils of human institutions. It has thrived in Western literature since the time of the ancient Greeks, and English literature of the eighteenth century was particularly noteworthy for the extent and quality of its satire. Broadly, two types are recognized: *Horatian satire,* which is gentle, smiling, and aims to correct by invoking laughter and sympathy, and *Juvenalian satire,* which is sharper and points with anger, contempt, and/or moral indignation to corruption and evil.

Sentimentality, also called *sentimentalism,* is an exaggerated show of emotion, whether intentional or caused by lack of restraint. An author can sentimentalize almost any situation, but the trap is most dangerous when writing of timeworn emotional symbols or scenes—e.g., a broken heart, mother love, a lonely death, the conversion of a sinner. However sincere the author may be, if readers are not fully oriented to the worth and uniqueness of the situation described, they may be either resentful or amused at any attempt to play on their emotions. Sentimentality is, of course, one of the chief characteristics of melodrama. (For examples of writing that, less adeptly handled, could easily have slipped into sentimentality, see Buczynski, Peterson, Twain, Catton, Raybon, Staples, Curtin, Simpson, Gansberg, Cisneros, Greene.)

Simile (See *Figures of Speech.*)

Slang (See *Colloquial Expressions.*)

Specific and **General** terms, and the distinctions between the two, are similar to concrete and abstract terms (as discussed under their own heading), and for our purpose there is no real need to keep the two sets of categories separated. Whether *corporation* is thought of as "abstract" and *Ajax Motor Company* as "concrete," or whether they are assigned to "general" and "specific" categories, the principle is the same: in most writing, *Ajax Motor Company* is better.

But "specific" and "general" are relative terms. For instance, the word *apple* is more specific than *fruit* but less so than *Winesap*. And *fruit*, as general as it certainly is in one respect, is still more specific than *food*. Such relationships are shown more clearly in a series, progressing from general to specific: *food, fruit, apple, Winesap;* or *vehicle, automobile, Ford, Mustang.* Modifiers and verbs can also have degrees of specificity: *bright, red, scarlet;* or *moved, sped, careened.* It is not difficult to see the advantages to the reader—and, of course, to the writer who needs to communicate an idea clearly—in "the scarlet Mustang careened through the pass," instead of "the bright-colored vehicle moved through the pass."

Obviously, however, there are times when the general or the abstract term or statement is essential—e.g., "A balanced diet includes some fruit," or "There was no vehicle in sight." But the use of specific language whenever possible is one of the best ways to improve diction and thus clarity and forcefulness in writing.

(Another important way of strengthening general, abstract writing is, of course, to use examples or other illustrations. See Section 1.)

Style and **Tone** are so closely linked and so often even elements of each other that it is best to consider them together.

But there is a difference. Think of two young men, each with his girlfriend on separate moonlit dates, whispering in nearly identical tender and loving tones of voice. One young man says, "Your eyes, dearest, reflect a thousand sparkling candles of heaven," and the other says, "Them eyes of yours—in this light—they sure do turn me on." Their *tones* were the same; their *styles* considerably different.

The same distinction exists in writing. But, naturally, with more complex subjects than the effect of moonlight on a lover's eyes, there are more complications in separating the two qualities, even for the purpose of study.

The tone is determined by the *attitude* of writers toward their subject and toward their audience. Writers, too, may be tender and loving, but they may be indignant, solemn, playful, enthusiastic, belligerent, contemptuous—the list could be as long as a list of the many "tones of voice." (In fact, wide ranges of tone may be illustrated by essays in this book. Compare, for example, those of the two parts of Twain; Eiseley and Mitford; Viorst and Lynn; Staples and Ehrenreich; Stone and Helman.)

Style, on the other hand, expresses the author's individuality through choices of words (See *Diction.*), sentence patterns (See *Syntax.*), and selection and arrangement of details and basic materials. (All these elements of style are illustrated in the contrasting statements of the moonstruck lads.) These matters of style are partially prescribed, of course, by the adopted tone, but they are still bound to reflect the writer's personality and mood, education and general background.

(Some of the more distinctive styles—partially affected by and affecting tone—represented by selections in this book are those of Viorst, Wolfe, Buckley, White, Noda, Stone, Anzaldúa, Eiseley, Cramer, Quindlen, Staples, Walker, and Rodriguez.)

Subjective Writing (See *Objective/Subjective.*)

Symbol refers to anything that although real itself also suggests something broader or more significant—not just in greater numbers, however, as a person would not symbolize a group or even humankind itself, although a person might be typical or representative in one or more abstract qualities. On the most elementary level, even words are symbols—e.g., *bear* brings to mind the furry beast itself. But more important is that things, persons, or even acts may also be symbolic, it they invoke abstract concepts, values, or qualities apart from themselves or their own kind. Such symbols, in everyday life as well as in literature and the other arts, are generally classifiable according to three types, which, although terminology differs, we may label *natural, personal,* and *conventional.*

In a natural symbol, the symbolic meaning is inherent in the thing itself. The sunrise naturally suggests new beginnings to most people, an island is almost synonymous with isolation, a cannon automatically suggests war; hence these are natural symbols. It does not matter that some things, by their nature, can suggest more than one concept. Although a valley may symbolize security to one person and captivity to another, both meanings, contradictory as they might seem, are inherent, and in both respects the valley is a natural symbol.

The personal symbol, depending as it does on private experience or perception, is meaningless to others unless they are told about it or allowed to see its significance in context (as in literature). Although the color green may symbolize the outdoor life to the farm boy trapped in the gray city (in this respect perhaps a natural symbol), it can also symbolize romance to the young woman proposed to while wearing her green blouse, or dismal poverty to the woman who grew up in a weathered green shanty; neither of these meanings is suggested by something *inherent* in the color green, so they are personal symbols. Anything at all could take on private symbolic meaning, even the odor of marigolds or the sound of a lawnmower. The sunrise itself could mean utter despair, instead of fresh opportunities, to the man who has long despised his daily job and cannot find another.

Conventional symbols usually started as personal symbols, but continued usage in life or art permits them to be generally recognized for their broader meanings, which depend on custom rather than any inherent quality—e.g., the olive branch for peace, the flag for love of country, the cross for Christianity, the raised fist for revolutionary power.

Symbols are used less in expository and argumentative writing than in fiction and poetry, but a few authors represented in this book have either referred to the subtle symbolism of others or made use of it in developing their own ideas. Eiseley says that the old men clung to their seats as if they were symbols.

Syntax is a very broad term—too broad, perhaps, to be very useful—referring to the arrangement of words in a sentence. Good syntax implies the use not only of correct grammar but also of effective patterns. These patterns depend on sentences with good unity, coherence, and emphasis, on the use of subordination and parallel construction as appropriate, on economy, and on a consistent and interesting point of view. A pleasing variety of sentence patterns is also important in achieving effective syntax.

Theme (See *Unity*.)

Thesis In an argumentative essay, the central theme is often referred to as the thesis, and to make sure that readers recognize it, the thesis is often summed up briefly in a *thesis statement*. In a very important sense, the thesis is the center of an argument because the whole essay is designed to make the reader agree with it and, hence, with the author's opinion. (see *Unity*.)

Tone (See *Style/Tone*.)

Transition is the relating of one topic to the next, and smooth transition is an important aid to the coherence of a sentence, a paragraph, or an entire piece of writing. (See *Coherence*.)

The most effective coherence, of course, comes about naturally with sound development of ideas, one growing logically into the next—and that depends on sound organization. But sometimes beneficial even in this situation, particularly in going from one paragraph to the next, is the use of appropriate transitional devices.

Readers are apt to be sensitive creatures, easy to lose. (And, of course, the writers are the real losers since they are the ones who presumably have something they want to communicate.) If the readers get into a new paragraph and the territory seems familiar, chances are that they will continue. But if there are no identifying landmarks, they will often begin to feel uneasy and will either start worrying about their slow comprehension or take a dislike to the author and the subject matter. Either way, a communication block arises, and very likely the author will soon have fewer readers.

A good policy, then, unless the progression of ideas is exceptionally smooth and obvious, is to provide some kind of familiar identification early in the new paragraph, to keep the reader feeling at ease with the different ideas. The effect is subtle but important. These familiar landmarks or transitional devices are sometimes applied deliberately but more often come naturally, especially when the prospective reader is kept constantly in mind at the time of writing.

An equally important reason for using some kinds of transitional devices, however, is a logical one: while functioning as bridges between ideas, they also assist the basic organization by pointing out the *relationship* of the ideas—and thus contributing still further to readability.

Transitional devices useful for bridging paragraph changes (and, some of them, to improve transitional flow within paragraphs) may be roughly classified as follows:

1. *Providing an "echo"* from the preceding paragraph. This may be the repetition of a key phrase or word, or a pronoun referring back to such a word, or a casual reference to an idea. (See Lopate, last two paragraphs; Wolfe, especially from pars. 1 to 2 and 4 to 5; Mitford.) Such an echo cannot be superimposed on new ideas, but must, by careful planning, be made an organic part of them.

2. *Devising a whole sentence or paragraph* to bridge other important paragraphs or major divisions. (See Lynn, pars. 11, 20, and 21; Mansnerus, pars. 6, 41.)

3. *Using parallel structure* in an important sentence of one paragraph and the first sentence of the next. This is a subtle means of making the reader feel at ease in the new surroundings, but it is seldom used because it is much more limited in its potential than the other methods of transition. (See Lawrence, pars. 1 to 2.)

4. *Using standard transitional expressions,* most of which have the additional advantage of indicating relationship of ideas. Only a few of those available are classified below, but nearly all the selections in this book amply illustrate such transitional expressions:

Time—soon, immediately, afterward, later, meanwhile, after a while.

Place—nearby, here, beyond, opposite.

Result—as a result, therefore, thus, consequently, hence.

Comparison—likewise, similarly, in such a manner.

Contrast—however, nevertheless, still, but, yet, on the other hand, after all, otherwise.

Addition—also, too, and, and then, furthermore, moreover, finally, first, second, third.

Miscellaneous—for example, for instance, in fact, indeed, on the whole, in other words.

Trite (See *Clichés*.)

Unity in writing is the same as unity in anything else—in a picture, a musical arrangement, a campus organization—and that is a *one*-ness, in which all parts contribute to an overall effect.

Many elements of good writing contribute in varying degrees to the effect of unity. Some of these are properly designed introductions and closings; consistency of point of view, tone, and style; sometimes the recurring use of analogy or thread of symbolism; occasionally the natural time boundaries of an experience or event, as in the selections of Hall, Mitford, Cramer, Simpson, Gansberg, Orwell, and McPhee.

But in most expository and argumentative writing the only dependable unifying force is the *central theme*, which every sentence, every word, must somehow help to support. (The central theme is also called the *central idea* or the *thesis* when pertaining to the entire writing and is almost always called the *thesis* in argument. In an expository or argumentative paragraph it is the same as the *topic sentence*, which may be implied or, if stated, may be located anywhere in the paragraph, but is usually placed first.) As soon as anything appears that is not related to the central idea, there are *two* units instead of one. Hence unity is basic to all other virtues of good writing, even to coherence and emphasis, the other two organic essentials. (See *Coherence, Emphasis*.)

An example of unity may be found in a single river system (for a practical use of analogy), with all its tributaries, big or little, meandering or straight, flowing into the main stream and making it bigger—or at least flowing into another tributary that finds its way to the main stream. This is *one* river system, an example of unity. Now picture another stream nearby that does not empty into the river but goes off in some other direction. There are now two systems, not one, and there is no longer unity.

It is the same way with writing. The central theme is the main river, flowing along from the first capital letter to the last period. Every drop of information or evidence must find its way into this theme-river, or it is not a part of the system. It matters not even slightly if the water is good, the idea-stream perhaps deeper and finer than any of the others: if it is not a tributary, it has no business pretending to be relevant to *this* theme of writing.

And that is why most students are required to state their central idea or thesis, usually in solid sentence form, before even starting to organize their ideas. If the writer can use only tributaries, it is very important to know from the start just what the river is.